D0211958

THE

MARCUS GARVEY

AND

UNIVERSAL NEGRO
IMPROVEMENT ASSOCIATION

PAPERS

SUPPORTED BY
The National Endowment for the Humanities
The National Historical Publications and Records Commission

SPONSORED BY
The University of California, Los Angeles

EDITORIAL ADVISORY BOARD

Herbert Aptheker

Mary Frances Berry

John W. Blassingame

John Henrik Clarke

Stanley Coben

Edmund David Cronon

Ian Duffield

E. U. Essien-Udom

Imanuel Geiss

Vincent Harding

Richard Hart

Thomas L. Hodgkin†

Arthur S. Link

George A. Shepperson

Michael R. Winston

Marcus Garvey and the UNIA in Convention

THE
MARCUS GARVEY
AND
UNIVERSAL NEGRO
IMPROVEMENT ASSOCIATION
PAPERS

Volume II
27 August 1919–31 August 1920

Robert A. Hill
Editor

Emory J. Tolbert
Senior Editor

Deborah Forczek
Assistant Editor

University of California Press
Berkeley   Los Angeles   London

University of California Press
Berkeley and Los Angeles, California

University of California Press, Ltd.
London, England

This volume has been funded in part by the National Endowment
for the Humanities, an independent federal agency. The volume has
also been supported by the National Historical Publications and
Records Commission and the University of California, Los
Angeles.

Documents in this volume from the Public Record Office are ©
British Crown Copyright 1920 and are published by permission of
the Controller of Her Britannic Majesty's Stationery Office.

Designed by Linda Robertson and set in Galliard type.

Copyright ©1983 by The Regents of the University of California

Library of Congress Cataloging in Publication Data
Main entry under title:

The Marcus Garvey and Universal Negro Improvement Association
   papers.

   1. Garvey, Marcus, 1887–1940. 2. Universal Negro Improvement
Association—History—Sources. 3. Black power—United States—
History—Sources. 4. Afro-Americans—Race identity—History—
Sources. 5. Afro-Americans—Civil rights—History—Sources.
6. Afro-Americans—Correspondence. I. Hill, Robert A.,
1943–   . II. Garvey, Marcus, 1887–1940. II. Universal Negro
Improvement Association.

E185.97.G3M36   1983   305.8'96073   82-13379
ISBN 0-520-05091-6

Printed in the United States of America

1 2 3 4 5 6 7 8 9

853313

LIBRARY
ALMA COLLEGE
ALMA, MICHIGAN

To
St. Clair Drake

CONTENTS

DOCUMENTS

CONTENTS

CONTENTS

xiii

CONTENTS

CONTENTS

ILLUSTRATIONS

Marie Barrier Houston
NW, 17 December 1921

Amy Jacques
NW, 17 March 1923

Adrian Johnson
UNIA Almanac, 1922

D. D. Lewis
UNIA Almanac, 1921

William Matthews
NW, 17 December 1921

George Alexander McGuire
UNIA Almanac, 1921

George Wells Parker
Monitor, 5 October 1918

Henry Vinton Plummer
UNIA Almanac, 1921

Hudson Pryce
UNIA Almanac, 1921

Rudolph E. B. Smith
UNIA Almanac, 1922

Wilford Smith
NW, 17 December 1921

Gabriel Stewart
NW, 17 December 1921

O. M. Thompson
UNIA Almanac, 1922

R. H. Tobitt
UNIA Almanac, 1921

Fred A. Toote
UNIA Almanac, 1921

James B. Yearwood
UNIA Almanac, 1922

Universal Millinery Store
Courtesy of Robert A. Hill

BSL Delegation in Cuba
Courtesy of Edward D. Smith-Green family

BSL Delegation in conference
Courtesy of Edward D. Smith-Green family

Inspection of the S.S. *Yarmouth* by UNIA members
Courtesy of Edward D. Smith-Green family

Joshua Cockburn, E. D. Smith-Green, and two
unidentified UNIA leaders in Cuba
Courtesy of Edward D. Smith-Green family

ACKNOWLEDGMENTS

The preparation of the present volume was greatly assisted by the cooperation of a large number of institutions and individuals. It is a pleasure to
acknowledge our deep gratitude to the various archives, manuscript collections, and governmental agencies that facilitated our research and collection
of the documents here reprinted. We would therefore like to express our
thanks to the staffs of the Office of the Secretary of State, Dover, Delaware;
the New York Bureau of Corporations, Office of the Secretary of State,
Albany; the Federal Bureau of Investigation of the United States Department of Justice; the National Archives and Records Service, Washington,
D.C.; the National Records Center, Suitland, Maryland; the Federal Ar-
chives and Records Center, Bayonne, New Jersey; the Schomburg Center for
Research in Black Culture, New York; the New York Public Library, New
York; the Hall of Records of the New York Supreme Court, New York; the
Butler Library, Columbia University; the New York State Archives, Albany;
the University of Massachusetts Library, Amherst; the Island Record Office,
Spanish Town, Jamaica; and the Public Record Office, Kew Gardens, Surrey,
England.

The following libraries were responsible for supplying information used
in the annotations of the documents: the Enoch Pratt Free Library, Baltimore; the Boston Athenaeum; the Boston Public Library; the Brown University Library, Providence, Rhode Island; the National Library of Canada,
Ottawa; the Carnegie Library of Pittsburgh; the Bicentennial Library, Chat-
tanooga, Tennessee; the Social Sciences and History Division of the Chicago
Public Library; the Joseph Regenstein Library, University of Chicago; the
Cleveland Public Library; the Low Memorial Library, Columbia University;
the Library of Congress, Washington, D.C.; the District of Columbia Public
Library; the Milton S. Eisenhower Library, Johns Hopkins University, Bal-
timore; the Robert W. Woodruff Library for Advanced Studies, Emory
University, Atlanta; the University of Georgia Library, Athens; the George-
town University Library, Washington, D.C.; the Hamilton College Library,
Clinton, New York; the History Faculty Library, Oxford University; the
Illinois State Historical Library, Springfield; the Jersey City Public Library,
Jersey City, New Jersey; the Agriculture and Applied Science Library,

Kansas State University, Manhattan; the Langston Hughes Memorial Library, Lincoln University, Lincoln University, Pennsylvania; the Commonwealth of Massachusetts State Library, Boston; the Memphis/Shelby County Public Library and Information Center, Memphis; the Memphis State University Libraries, Department of Special Collections; the Museum and Library of Maryland History, Baltimore; the National Library of Jamaica (formerly West India Reference Library), Kingston; the Staats- und Universitätsbibliothek, Göttingen; the Norfolk Public Library, Norfolk, Virginia; the Astor, Lenox, and Tilden Foundation of the New York Public Library, New York; the Elmer Holmes Bobst Library, New York University; the Panama Canal Commission Library-Museum, Balboa Heights; the Free Library of Philadelphia; the Seattle Public Library; the Staats- und Universitätsbibliothek, Frankfurt; the University of Tennessee Library, Knoxville; the Tokyo Metropolitan Central Library; the Jesse Ball Dupont Library, University of the South, Sewanee, Tennessee; the Virginia State Library, Richmond; the Virginia Polytechnic Institute and State University Libraries, Special Collections, Blacksburg; the Enid M. Baa Library and Archives, St. Thomas, Virgin Islands; the Florence Williams Public Library, St. Croix, Virgin Islands; the Frederiksted Public Library, St. Croix, Virgin Islands; the Cruz Bay Public Library, St. John, Virgin Islands; and the Carter Woodson Regional Library, Chicago. We are also grateful to the efficient staff of the Reference and Interlibrary Loan departments of the University Research Library, University of California, Los Angeles, who considerably lightened our research burden while cheerfully adding to their own.

Information that supports annotations to the text came from the following archives and historical societies: the Archives and Historical Collections of the Episcopal Church, Austin, Texas; the Atlanta Historical Society; the Chicago Historical Society; the Federal Archives and Records Center, East Point, Georgia; the Federal Archives and Records Center, Bayonne, New Jersey; the Harris County Heritage Society, Houston, Texas; the Harvard University Archives; the Historical Commission of the Southern Baptist Convention, Nashville; the Houston Metropolitan Research Center; the Ferdinand Hamburger, Jr., Archives, Johns Hopkins University; the University of Louisville Archives and Records Center, Louisville, Kentucky; the Maryland Historical Society, Baltimore; the Division of Archives and Manuscripts of the Minnesota Historical Society and the Minnesota Historical Society Research Center, St. Paul; the Rolvaas Memorial Library Archives, Saint Olaf College, Northfield, Minnesota; the Nebraska State Historical Society, Lincoln; the New England Historic Genealogical Society, Boston; the New York Historical Society, New York; the Oberlin College Archives, Oberlin, Ohio; the Ohio Historical Society Archives, Columbus; the Historical Society of Pennsylvania, Philadelphia; the Urban Archives Center, Temple University, Philadelphia; the Tennessee State Library Archives, Nashville; the History of Medicine and Archives, University of

Texas Medical Branch, Galveston; the Ticonderoga Historical Society, Ticonderoga, New York; the Tufts University Archives, Medford, Massachusetts; the Virginia Historical Society, Richmond; and the Western Reserve Historical Society, Cleveland.

Several governmental agencies also cooperated in furnishing valuable data. They include the Office of the Clerk of the Supreme Court of California, San Francisco; the Canal Zone Government, Balboa Heights; the Circuit Court of Cook County, Chicago; the Cook County Department of Corrections, Chicago; the Military Personnel Records Department of the National Personnel Records Center, St. Louis; the Bureau of Records and Statistics of the Department of Health, New York; the Cultural Education Center of the New York State Education Department, Albany; the Office of the Illinois Secretary of State, Springfield; the State Registrar of Vital Records of the Maryland Department of Health and Mental Hygiene, Baltimore; the United States Office of Personnel Management, Washington, D.C.; the United States Military Academy, West Point; the Federal Bureau of Investigation of the United States Department of Justice, Washington, D.C.; the United States Naval Academy, Annapolis; and the Veterans Administration, Washington, D.C. A continuing debt of gratitude is owed to the remarkably industrious and efficient archival research staff of the National Historical Publications and Records Commission, Washington, D.C., for tracking down numerous elusive leads in the National Archives collections which ultimately have borne most welcome fruit.

Important biographical data about many alumni were provided by the offices of alumni affairs at Alabama Agricultural and Mechanical University, Normal; the English High School, Boston; Boston University; the College of the Holy Cross, Worcester, Massachusetts; the University of Chicago; Fisk University, Nashville; Fordham University and Fordham University School of Law, Bronx, New York; the Hampton Institute, Hampton, Virginia; McGill University, Montreal; Meharry Medical College, Nashville; the University of Minnesota, Minneapolis; Morehouse College, Atlanta; the University of Nebraska, Omaha; Phillips Academy, Andover, Massachusetts; the New England Conservatory, Boston; Northwestern University, Evanston, Illinois; Washington and Lee University, Lexington, Virginia; and Waynesburg College, Waynesburg, Pennsylvania.

We are also grateful for assistance provided in the gathering of biographical information to the Association of the Bar of the City of New York; Baker and Hostetler, Counselors at Law, Cleveland; Brunini, Everett, Beanland and Wheeless, Attorneys at Law, Vicksburg, Mississippi; the Diocese of New York of the Protestant Episcopal Church, New York; the New York Genealogical and Biographical Society, New York; the New York State Bar Association, Albany; the Los Angeles County Bar Association, Los Angeles; the South Dakota Bar Association, Pierre; and Van Aken, Bond, Witchers, Asman and Smith, Attorneys at Law, Cleveland.

The project is also greatly indebted for a wide range of research assistance to the following individuals: Neville N. Clarke, Jamaican Consul General, San José, Costa Rica; Robert Neymeyer, Iowa City, Iowa; Herbert J. Seligmann, Addison, Maine; Tom Shick, University of Wisconsin, Madison; W. F. Elkins, London; Brian Willan, London; Mrs. Lois Hercules Kewig (formerly Mrs. F. E. M. Hercules), Chicago; and Frank E. M. Hercules (son of F. E. M. Hercules), New York. A special word of recognition and appreciation must also be expressed to David Langbart, Archivist with the Diplomatic Records Branch of the National Archives and Records Service in Washington, D.C., for uncovering copies of the extremely valuable *Negro World Convention Bulletin* published in August 1920.

The project also wishes to thank the family of Edward David Smith-Green for permission to reprint the rare photographs of the 1920 voyage of the Black Star Line's *Yarmouth* to Cuba. We also thank Her Majesty's Stationery Office for permission to reprint documents from the Public Record Office, and the estate of Mrs. Shirley Graham Du Bois and the University of Massachusetts Press, publishers of *The Correspondence of W. E. B. Du Bois*, for permission to reprint items from the Papers of W. E. B. Du Bois in the University of Massachusetts Library, Amherst. A special word of gratitude is also due to Marcus Garvey, Jr., for his permission to reprint letters by his father.

Once again the members of the Editorial Advisory Board have rendered excellent service on behalf of the project. Their criticisms and comments have been a source of guidance and inspiration. We hereby express our heartfelt appreciation for their continued interest and support in the face of their own pressing commitments.

The project also takes this opportunity to record its continued appreciation for the support of its sponsors: the National Endowment for the Humanities, the National Historical Publications and Records Commission, and the African Studies Center of the University of California, Los Angeles. We would also like to express special appreciation to Dr. Michael Lofchie, Director of the African Studies Center, UCLA, for making our association with the center such a pleasant and rewarding experience.

The editorial and production staff members of the University of California Press are also to be complimented for the high standards of professional attention that they have continued to show to the publication of *The Marcus Garvey and Universal Negro Improvement Association Papers*. It is an honor and a special privilege to be associated with such a staff. We would also like to thank Robin Haller for her expert preparation of the indexes for Volumes I and II.

The major work of the project has been carried on by a truly exemplary staff of coworkers. The editor wishes to acknowledge his profound gratitude for their dedication and resourcefulness. The success of the project continues to be ensured by the contributions of Diane Lisa Hill, Administrative Assistant; Ruth Schofield, Secretary; Michael Furmanovsky and Janice Wilcots, Graduate Student Assistants; Deborah Forczek, Assistant Editor; and

Emory J. Tolbert, Senior Editor. We also extend our appreciation to two former members of the project's staff, Carol Rudisell and Althea Silvera, who contributed to the preliminary work of research and organization for the present volume. The annotations pertaining to African personalities mentioned in the text of the present volume were prepared by Gregory A. Pirio, Assistant Editor for the African series of the edition.

INTRODUCTION

The second volume of *The Marcus Garvey and Universal Negro Improvement Association Papers* covers a period of rapid growth in the Garvey movement: August 1919 through August 1920. The volume begins with the aftermath of Garvey's successful meeting in Carnegie Hall on 25 August 1919 and ends with the UNIA's First International Convention of the Negro Peoples of the World. With ample justification the *Negro World*, official newspaper of the UNIA, pronounced the convention "a unique and glorious achievement" and called Garvey "this now world-famed man."

The convention met exactly two and one-half years after Garvey's February 1918 reorganization of the depleted and splintered New York division of the UNIA. Between the spring of 1918 and the summer of 1919, Garvey and the fledgling UNIA refined their message of African redemption in light of the changing world scene and the troubled state of the black community. During the year before the convention, Garvey introduced his plan for establishing an African republic by calling attention to Liberia's desperate financial state and the unsatisfactory progress of negotiations to secure a loan from the United States. He also linked his plan to a growing sentiment within the UNIA rank and file in favor of a scheme for Liberian colonization that would inaugurate a back-to-Africa program.

Garvey's many projects gained greater credibility when he announced in September 1919 that the Black Star Line, the all-black merchant marine he had planned since early in the year, was about to purchase its first vessel. Before the August 1920 convention the Black Star Line would gain control of three vessels—a cargo ship, an excursion boat, and a converted yacht—and the largest of the three, the *Yarmouth*, would make two voyages to the West Indies.

In spite of this, the Black Star Line acquired a growing cast of critics, who doubted the company's claim to ownership of the *Yarmouth*. Garvey moved swiftly to refute their charges of fraud by mounting a vigorous counterattack in the *Negro World* and subsequently launching a flurry of libel suits. Despite these efforts, an angry investor in the UNIA's Harlem restaurant made an attempt on Garvey's life, an incident that, ironically, increased Garvey's popularity. Within a week of the attack, Garvey made a series of spectacular public appearances before thousands of cheering admirers who seemed to accept the assertion that his critics had plotted his assassination. Moreover, the incident inspired a marked increase in public notice of Garvey, and whereas a recent stock-selling tour of several midwestern cities had been less than successful, the sale of Black Star Line stock now made a significant jump. During October 1919 alone, over eleven thousand shares of Black Star Line stock were purchased.

This volume also documents the broadening federal investigation of the Garvey phenomenon. The United States Department of Justice, alerted that Garvey planned a trip to the Panama Canal Zone, began an intensive search for evidence in Garvey's background that would identify him as an undesirable alien. J. Edgar Hoover, then an assistant to the attorney general, continued his inquiry into grounds for bringing deportation proceedings against Garvey, while Bureau of Investigation special employees, posing as UNIA sympathizers, reported on Garvey's meetings, conducted interviews, and gathered evidence. To the extent that agents and informers rendered accurate accounts of what they heard and observed, their reports offer a valuable portrait of day-to-day operations within UNIA headquarters, as well as the official perception of the still largely anonymous UNIA rank and file. These investigative reports include the results of interviews that constitute an extensive, if biased, collection of oral sources. They also reveal the various strategies that officials contemplated for containing the movement.

Garvey's critics and opponents, however, did little to diminish his personal popularity and the movement's momentum as the August convention approached. With more success than any previous black leader in promoting a convocation, Garvey presented the UNIA convention as a turning point in the history of black-white relations. His propaganda received, moreover, the welcome aid of national and international events. As racial conflicts spread during the "Red Summer" of 1919, Garvey continued an unrelenting assault on white violence in his newspaper editorials and speeches, repeatedly linking race riots in the United States with similar phenomena in England and with strikes and popular disturbances in the West Indies, Central America, and Africa. The result was mounting official opposition in America and Europe to the spread of the Garvey movement, which was seen as a major ideological force in the promotion of radical consciousness among blacks in the United States and in colonized nations.

The UNIA's 1920 convention, therefore, offered far more than the ceremonial pomp and oratory that dominated the formal proceedings. By the time the delegates started assembling, Garvey's vision of racial greatness had already fired the popular imagination of blacks. With the successful launching in November 1919 of the first ship of the Black Star Line, the boldness of Garvey's promise not only seemed to have been vindicated, but his vision came to appear more and more attractive as the answer to the postwar problems blacks faced everywhere. During the period of July 1919 to August

1920, UNIA members and sympathizers bought stock in the Black Star Line with such enthusiasm that sales reached a total of 96,285 shares.

Under these circumstances, the primary task of the 1920 convention was the formal ratification of Garveyism as the guiding doctrine of the movement. How it evolved as an ideology and how it was able to influence the struggle for black rights in 1919 and 1920, while offering a program for African independence and racial autonomy, form an essential part of the subject of this volume. At the same time, Garvey intended that the legislation and elective offices created during the convention would form a veritable government in exile for Africa, marking a fulfillment of his ambition to engage in the practice of statecraft and create the symbols of black nationhood and sovereignty. In this context, the spectacular quality of the August 1920 convention announced a new watershed in black history.

EDITORIAL PRINCIPLES AND PRACTICES

I. Arrangement of Documents

Documents are presented in chronological order according to the date of authorship of the original text. Enclosures and attachments to documents, however, do not appear in strict chronological sequence, but are printed with their original covering documents. Enclosures have been set in italic type in the table of contents for identification.

The publication date of news reports, speeches, and periodical articles is given on the place and date line within square brackets. In the case of news reports, speeches, and periodical articles containing the date of original composition, that date chronologically supersedes the date of eventual publication and is printed within double square brackets on the place and date line of the document.

Bureau of Investigation reports that give both the date of composition and the period covered by the report are arranged according to the date of composition.

Documents that lack dates and thus require editorial assignment of dates are placed in normal chronological sequence. When no day within a month appears on a document, it is placed after the documents specifically dated on the latest date within that month. Documents that carry only the date of a year are placed according to the same principle. Documents that cover substantial periods, such as diaries, journals and accounts, will appear according to the date of their earliest entries.

When two or more documents possess the same date, they are arranged with regard to affinity to the subject of the document that immediately precedes them or that which immediately follows them.

II. Form of Presentation

Each document is presented in the following manner:

A. A caption introduces the document and is printed in a type size larger than the text. Letters between individuals are captioned with the names of the individuals and their titles; captions, however, include a person's office only upon that person's first appearance. The original titles of published materials are retained with the documents; however, the headlines of some news reports are abbreviated or omitted, in which case this is indicated in the descriptive source note to the document.

B. The text of a document follows the caption. The copy text of letters or reports is taken from recipients' copies whenever possible, but in the absence of a recipient's copy, a file copy of the letter or report is used. If the file copy is not available, however, and a retained draft copy of the letter is found, the retained draft copy is used as the basic text.

C. Following the body of the text, an unnumbered descriptive source note describes editorially the physical character of the document by means of appropriate abbreviations. Moreover, a repository symbol gives the provenance of the original manuscript or, if it is rare, printed work. Printed sources are identified in the following manner:

   1. A contemporary pamphlet is identified by its full title, place and date of publication, and the location of the copy used.

   2. A contemporary essay, letter, or other kind of statement that appeared originally in a contemporary publication is preceded by the words "Printed in . . .," followed by the title, date, and, in the case of essays, inclusive page numbers of the source of publication.

   3. A contemporary printed source reprinted at a later date, the original publication of which has not been found, is identified with the words "Reprinted from . . .," followed by the identification of the work from which the text has been reproduced. The same applies to any originally unpublished manuscript printed at a later date.

D. Numbered textual annotations that explicate the document follow the descriptive source note. The following principles of textual annotation have been applied:

   1. Individuals are identified upon their first appearance, with additional information about them sometimes furnished upon their later appearance in a document where such data provide maximum clarification. Pseudonyms are identified, wherever possible, by a textual annotation.

   2. Reasons for the assignment of dates to documents or the correction of dates of documents are explained in those instances where important historical information is involved.

   3. Obscure allusions in the text are annotated whenever such references can be clarified.

   4. Printed works and manuscript materials consulted during the preparation of textual annotations appear in parentheses at the end of each annotation. Frequently used reference works are cited in an abbreviated form, and the complete table may be found in the list of Abbreviations of Published Works.

5. Garvey's appeal case (*Marcus Garvey* v. *United States of America*, no. 8317, Ct. App., 2d Cir., 2 February 1925) contains the complete transcript of his original mail fraud trial (*United States of America* v. *Marcus Garvey et al.*, C31-37 and C33-688, U.S. District Court, Southern District of New York, May 1923). Trial documents reprinted in the volume and references to the trial in annotations to documents are taken from the transcript used in the appeal case.

III. Transcription of Text

Manuscripts and printed material have been transcribed from the original text and printed as documents according to the following principles and procedures:

A. Manuscript Material
   1. The place and date of composition are placed at the head of the document, regardless of their location in the original, but exceptions are made in the cases of certificates of vital registration and documents in which original letterhead stationery is reproduced. If the place or date of a letter (or both) does not appear in the original text, the information is supplied and printed in italics at the head within square brackets. Likewise, if either the place or date is incomplete, the necessary additional information is supplied in italics within square brackets. Superscript letters are brought down to the line of type, and terminal punctuation is deleted.

      In the case of Bureau of Investigation reports that were submitted on printed forms, the place and date are abstracted and placed at the head of each document, while the name of the reporting agent is placed at the end of the document on the signature line. In the case of United States Postal Censorship reports, which were also prepared on printed forms, the narrative section of the report is printed in roman type. The other sections of the censorship reports, containing recorded analytic and filing information, have been treated as printed forms.

      The formal salutation of letters is placed on the line below the place and date line, with the body of the text following the salutation.

      The complimentary close of letters is set continuously with the text in run-in style, regardless of how it was written in the original.

      The signature, which is set in capitals and small capitals, is placed at the right-hand margin on the line beneath the text or complimentary close, with titles, where they appear, set in uppercase and lowercase. Terminal punctuation is deleted.

When a file copy of a document bearing no signature is used to establish the text but the signatory is known, the signature is printed in roman type within square brackets.

The inside address, if significant and not repetitive, is printed immediately below the text.

Endorsements, docketings, and other markings appearing on official correspondence, when intelligible, are reproduced in small type following the address, with appropriate identification. In the case of other types of documents, such as private correspondence, endorsements and dockets are reprinted only when they are significant.

Minutes, enclosures, and attachments are printed in roman type following their covering documents and placed after the annotation material of their covering documents. Whenever minutes, enclosures, or attachments are not printed, this fact is always recorded and explained. Whenever a transmission letter originally accompanying an enclosure or attachment is not printed, the omission is noted and the transmission document identified and recorded in the descriptive source note.

2. Printed letterheads and other official stationery are not reproduced, unless they contain significant information, in which case they are reprinted above the date line. In cases where they are not reprinted, they are sometimes abstracted, and the information is placed in the descriptive source note. Printed addresses are reproduced only upon the first appearance.

3. In general, the spelling of all words, including proper names, is preserved as written in the manuscript and printed sources. Thus, personal and place names that are spelled erratically in the original texts are regularized or corrected only in the index. However, serious distortion in the spelling of a word, to such an extent as to obscure its true meaning, is repaired by printing the correct word in italics within square brackets after the incorrect spelling. Mere "slips of the pen" or typographical errors are corrected within the word and printed in roman type within square brackets; however, some typographical errors that contribute to the overall character of the document are retained.

4. Capitalization is retained as in the original. Words underlined once in a manuscript are printed in italics. Words that are underlined twice or spelled out in large letters or full capitals are printed in small capitals.

5. Punctuation, grammar, and syntax are retained as found in the original texts. In the case of punctuation, corrections that are essential to the accurate reading of the text are provided within square brackets.

If, however, a punctuation mark appears in a document as a result of typographical error, it is corrected in square brackets or, in some instances, silently deleted.

6. All contractions and abbreviations in the text are retained. Abbreviations of titles or organizations are identified in a list of abbreviations that appears at the front of the volume. Persons represented by initials only will have their full names spelled out in square brackets after each initial on their first appearance.

7. Superscript letters in the text are lowered and aligned on the line of print.

8. Omissions, mutilations, and illegible words or letters have been rendered through the use of the following textual devices:

   a) Blank spaces in a manuscript are shown as [   ]. If the blank space is of significance or of substantial length, this fact is elaborated upon in a textual annotation.

   b) When a word or words in the original text must be omitted from the printed document because of mutilation, illegibility, or omission, the omission is shown by the use of ellipses followed by a word or phrase placed in square brackets in italics, such as: . . . [torn], . . . [illegible], . . . [remainder missing].

   c) Missing or illegible letters of words are represented by suspension points within square brackets, the number of points corresponding to the estimated number of letters omitted. The same holds true for missing or illegible digits of numbers.

   d) All attempts have been made to supply conjecturally missing items in the printed document, according to the following rules:

      (1) if there is no question as to the word, the missing letter is supplied silently;

      (2) if the missing letter(s) can only be conjectured, the omission is supplied within square brackets and printed in roman type. Uncertainty of the conjecture, however, is indicated by a question mark within the square brackets in the document.

9. Additions and corrections made by the author in the original text have been rendered as follows:

   a) Additions between the lines are brought onto the line of type and incorporated into the body of the text within diagonal lines / /.

   b) Marginal additions or corrections by the author are also incorporated into the printed document and identified by the words [in the margin] italicized in square brackets. Marginal notes made by someone other than the author are treated as an endorsement and are printed following the text of the document.

   c) Words or groups of words deleted in the original, as in a draft, are restored in the printed document. The canceled word or phrase is indicated by canceled type at the place where the deletion occurs in the original text. If a lengthy deletion is illegible, this is indicated by the words [*deletion illegible*].

B. Printed Material

Contemporary printed material has been treated in the same manner as were original texts and has been transcribed according to the same editorial principles as was manuscript material.

1. In the case of originally published letters, the place and date of composition are uniformly printed on the place and date line of the document, regardless of where they appear in the original, and placed within double square brackets. Those elements that have been editorially supplied are italicized.

2. Newspaper headlines and subheads are printed in small capitals. Headlines are punctuated as they are in the original; however, they are reproduced in the printed document in as few lines as possible. Unless the headline would otherwise become distorted, ornamental lines appearing within the headlines are not retained.

3. Words originally printed in full capitals for emphasis or for other reasons are usually printed in small capitals. Boldfaced type that appears within the text is retained.

4. The signature accompanying a published letter is printed in capitals and small capitals.

5. Obvious typographical errors and errors of punctuation, such as the omission of a single parenthesis or quotation mark, are corrected and printed within square brackets in roman type.

6. In the case of a printed form with spaces to be filled in, the printed words are designated in small capitals, while the handwritten or typewritten insertions are designated in italics with spaces left before and after the small capitals to suggest the blank spaces in the original form.

TEXTUAL DEVICES

[ ]	Blank spaces in the text.
[. . .], [. . . .]	Suspension points indicate approximate number of letters or digits missing in words or numerals (not to exceed four) and not conjecturable.
[[ ]]	Double square brackets are used to give the composition date of a published letter or news report if the publication date differs.
/ /	Incorporation into the text of addition or correction made above or below the line by author.
[roman]	Conjectural reading for missing, mutilated, or illegible matter, with a question mark inside the square bracket when the conjectural reading is doubtful. Also used in editorial correction of typographical errors in original manuscript or printed document. Also used to indicate the publication date of a news report or periodical article.
[*italic*]	Assigned date of any undated document; editorial comment inserted in the text, such as [*endorsement*], [*illegible*], [*remainder missing*], [*sentence unfinished*], [*torn*], [*enclosure*], [*attachment*], [*in the margin*].
~~canceled~~	Textual matter deleted in the original but restored in the text.

SYMBOLS AND ABBREVIATIONS

Repository Symbols

The original locations of documents that appear in the text are described by symbols. The guide used for American repositories has been *Symbols of American Libraries*, eleventh edition, (Washington, D.C.: Library of Congress, 1976). Foreign repositories and collections have been assigned symbols that conform to the institutions' own usage. In some cases, however, it has been necessary to formulate acronyms. Acronyms have been created for private manuscript collections as well.

Repositories

AFRC   Federal Records Center, East Point, Georgia
           RG 163   Records of the Selective Service System

De-SS   Office of the Secretary of State of Delaware, Dover

DJ-FBI   Federal Bureau of Investigation, United States Department of Justice, Washington, D.C.

DNA   National Archives, Washington, D.C.
           RG 26   Records of the United States Coast Guard
           RG 28   Records of the Post Office Department
           RG 32   Records of the United States Shipping Board
           RG 41   Records of the Bureau of Marine Inspection and Navigation
           RG 59   General records of the Department of State
           RG 60   General records of the Department of Justice
           RG 65   Records of the Federal Bureau of Investigation
           RG 84   Records of the Foreign Service posts of the Department of State
           RG 85   Records of the Immigration and Naturalization Service
           RG 165   Records of the War Department, General and Special staffs; Records of the Office of the Chief of Staff

IRO	Island Record Office, Spanish Town, Jamaica
MU	University of Massachusetts Library, Amherst
N	New York State Library, Albany
NFRC	Federal Record Center, Bayonne, New Jersey
N-SS	Office of the Secretary of State of New York, Albany
NN	New York Public Library, New York
NN-Sc	The Schomburg Center for Research in Black Culture, New York Public Library, New York
NNC	Butler Library, Columbia University
NNHR	New York Supreme Court, Hall of Records, New York
PRO	Public Record Office, London

    CAB   Cabinet Office
    CO   Colonial Office
    FO   Foreign Office

SDNY	Southern District Court of New York
WNRC	Washington National Records Center, Suitland, Maryland

    RG 185   Records of the Panama Canal

Manuscript Collection Symbols

AAG	Amy Ashwood Garvey Papers, Lionel Yard Collection, New York
JEB	John E. Bruce Papers, *NN-Sc*
LC	Lusk Committee Papers, *N*
NCF	National Civic Federation Papers, *NN*
W	The *World* Collection, *NNC*
WEBDB	W. E. B. Du Bois Papers, *MU*

Descriptive Symbols

The following symbols are used to describe the character of the original documents:

ADS	Autograph document signed
ALS	Autograph letter signed
AMS	Autograph manuscript
AMSS	Autograph manuscript signed
AN	Autograph note

ANI	Autograph note initialed
D	Document
DS	Document signed
L	Letter
LS	Letter signed
MS	Manuscript
N	Note
TD	Typed document
TDS	Typed document signed
TL	Typed letter
TLI	Typed letter initialed
TLR	Typed letter representation
TLS	Typed letter signed
TMS	Typed manuscript
TN	Typed note
TNI	Typed note initialed
TNS	Typed note signed

Published Works Cited

ATOR	*African Times and Orient Review*
BFQ	*Bartlett's Familiar Quotations*, fifteenth edition
BM	*Black Man*
CBD	*Chambers's Biographical Dictionary*
CD	*Chicago Defender*
DAB	*Dictionary of American Biography*
DG	*Daily Gleaner*
DNB	*Dictionary of National Biography*
EA	*Encyclopedia Americana*
EB	*Encyclopaedia Britannica*
EWH	*Encyclopedia of World History*
JNH	*Journal of Negro History*
NCAB	*National Cyclopedia of American Biography*
NW	*Negro World*
NWCB	*Negro World Convention Bulletin*

NYB	*Negro Year Book*
NYT	*New York Times*
PP	*Parliamentary Papers*
WBD	*Webster's Biographical Dictionary*
WWCA	*Who's Who of Colored America*
WWCR	*Who's Who of the Colored Race*
WWJ	*Who's Who in Jamaica*
WWW	*Who Was Who*
WWWA	*Who Was Who in America*

Other Symbols and Abbreviations

Included are abbreviations that are used generally throughout annotations of the text. Standard abbreviations, such as those for titles and scholastic degrees, are omitted. Abbreviations that are specific to a single annotation appear in parentheses after the initial citation and are used thereafter in the rest of the annotation.

ABB	African Blood Brotherhood
ACL	African Communities' League
AFL	American Federation of Labor
AME	African Methodist Episcopal Church
AMEZ	African Methodist Episcopal Zion Church
ASAPS	Anti-Slavery and Aborigines' Protection Society
BSL	Black Star Line, Incorporated
BWI	British West Indies
CB	Companion of the Order of the Bath
CMG	Companion of the Order of Saint Michael and Saint George
CSO	Colonial Secretary's Office
DSM	Distinguished Service Medal
GPO	Government Printing Office
IWW	Industrial Workers of the World
KB	Knight of the Order of the Bath
KBE	Knight of the British Empire
KCMG	Knight Commander of the Order of Saint Michael and Saint George
MID	Military Intelligence Division

MP	Minute Paper
NAACP	National Association for the Advancement of Colored People
OBE	Order of the British Empire
RG	Record Group
UNIA	Universal Negro Improvement Association

Monetary Symbols

d.	English pence
s.,/-	English shilling
£	English pound

CHRONOLOGY

August 1919–August 1920

1919

25 August	Garvey holds mass meeting at Carnegie Hall in New York to promote sale of BSL stock.
28 August	Three indictments are filed by the grand jury against Garvey, charging him with criminal libel against Edwin P. Kilroe, Edgar Grey, and Richard Warner.
29 August	Garvey is arraigned before Court of General Sessions and committed briefly to the Tombs prison in New York; released from the Tombs after paying a $3,000 bail.
3 September	Garvey pleads not guilty to charge of criminal libel.
ca. 1–5 September	New York District Attorney Swann takes over investigation of BSL's finances from Assistant District Attorney Edwin P. Kilroe.
10 September	British colonial secretary authorizes West Indian governments to introduce legislation to suppress the *Negro World* and other publications considered seditious.
12 September	Governor of British Guiana introduces first reading of seditious publications bill.
14 September	UNIA members and BSL stockholders inspect S.S. *Yarmouth*, docked at 135th Street and the North River in Harlem.
15 September	Bureau of Investigation instructs New York division that it wishes to establish "sufficient evidence against Garvey to warrant the institution of deportation proceedings."

15 September	BSL board of directors authorizes contract for purchase of S.S. *Yarmouth*.
16 September	Garvey appears before New York Assistant District Attorney Kilroe for further questioning regarding BSL's finances.
17 September	BSL signs contract to purchase S.S. *Yarmouth* for $165,000.
19 September	Garvey initiates libel action against the *Chicago Defender*.
20 September	BSL board of directors approves contract for purchase of S.S. *Yarmouth*.
26 September	British Guiana legislature passes second reading of seditious publications bill.
28 September	Garvey arrives in Chicago to address BSL campaign meetings.
29 September	Robert S. Abbott, publisher of the *Chicago Defender*, counters by bringing libel action against Garvey.
30 September	Garvey is arrested in Chicago for violation of the Illinois Blue Sky Law.
1 October	St. Vincent passes ordinance prohibiting importation of *Negro World*.
2 October	Garvey is convicted in Harrison Street Court in Chicago on Blue Sky Law violation and fined $100.
3 October	Garvey leaves Chicago to return to New York.
ca. 4–11 October	Permanent UNIA and BSL offices are opened at 54–56 West 135th Street in Harlem.
14 October	Marcus Garvey shot and wounded in an assassination attempt by George Tyler.
15 October	Suicide of George Tyler while in jail.
19 October	Garvey's first speech in Philadelphia after assassination attempt.
19–21 October	UNIA mass meetings held in Philadelphia.
20 October	Memorandum of agreement signed between North American Steamship Company and BSL for the sale of the S.S. *Yarmouth*.
24–26 October	UNIA mass meetings held in Newport News, Virginia.

28 October	*The National Prohibition Act passes, over Wilson's veto.*
30 October	UNIA mass meeting in Madison Square Garden.
31 October	BSL holds reception for stockholders aboard S.S. *Yarmouth*.
October	Costa Rica prohibits circulation of *Negro World*.
1 November	Garvey appoints Joshua Cockburn commander of S.S. *Yarmouth*.
5 November	Plans to float second BSL ship, the S.S. *Phyllis Wheatley*, announced.
23 November	S.S. *Yarmouth*, to be renamed S.S. *Frederick Douglass*, leaves New York Harbor for maiden BSL voyage to West Indies and Central America.
7 December	S.S. *Yarmouth* departs Cuba for Jamaica.
10 December	E. D. Smith-Green, Secretary of BSL, shot in New York; S.S. *Yarmouth* arrives in Kingston.
14 December	Henrietta V. Davis and Cyril Henry visit Panama on behalf of BSL.
22 December	St. Kitts-Nevis passes ordinance against seditious publications.
25 December	Garvey marries Amy Ashwood in Liberty Hall ceremony.
26 December–8 January	Garvey and Amy Ashwood Garvey spend honeymoon in Toronto and Montreal.

1920

8 January	Samuel Augustus Duncan, West Indies Protective Society, circulates letter to British Colonial Office regarding Garvey's "radicalism"; Garvey returns to New York from Canada.
16 January	*Prohibition goes into effect in the United States.*
17 January	S.S. *Yarmouth* leaves New York for Havana with cargo of whiskey.
19 January	S.S. *Yarmouth* found sinking 101 miles outside New York Harbor; assisted by Coast Guard.
22 January	Military Intelligence Division is warned of the threat of Universal African Legion.

22 January	Rumors of dissension among BSL and UNIA officers printed in *New York News*.
23 January	Negro Factories Corporation files certificate of incorporation.
3 February	U.S. Government Prohibition agents seize S.S. *Yarmouth*'s cargo.
5 February	S.S. *Yarmouth* allowed to sail to Cuba.
9 February	Capital stock of BSL increased.
13 February	Bureau of Investigation decides to investigate claims concerning UNIA's drilling with firearms.
14 February	Fred D. Powell resigns as general secretary of BSL.
22 February	Garvey announces plans to enlarge Liberty Hall.
24 February	Strike by 12,500 West Indian employees of the Panama Canal and the Panama Railway (70 percent of the work force); Garvey cables sympathy to strikers and sends financial assistance.
25 February	*Amsterdam News* retracts statement on BSL.
26 February	Garvey introduced at UNIA meeting as "prospective president of the new republic to be established in Africa."
27 February	Garvey announces that BSL is recapitalizd at $10 million.
February	Antigua and Dominica each pass seditious publications prohibition ordinances.
6 March	Garvey separates from Amy Ashwood Garvey.
13 March	BSL files suit against George W. Harris and New York News Publishing Company for libel.
13 March	Garvey announces removal of Fred D. Powell and B. C. Buck from the UNIA and BSL.
19 March	*U.S. Senate rejects Treaty of Versailles by a vote of 49 to 35.*
25 March	BSL files suit against W. A. Domingo and New Negro Publishing Company for libel.
27 March	The *Emancipator* launches its investigation of Garvey and the BSL.
28 March	Garvey addresses Liberty Hall meeting on "Enemies of His Organization."

3 April	Cyril Briggs, *Crusader*, offers reward to prove BSL claims of ownership of the S.S. *Yarmouth*.
9 April	Marcus Garvey, Sr., dies in Jamaica.
9 April	Trinidad passes seditious ordinance against publications from the United States "apparently having no other object than to excite racial hatred." Grenada passes similar ordinance.
11 April	Liberty Hall meeting features speeches by John E. Bruce, Joseph Douglass, and Arthur Schomburg.
22 April	BSL's S.S. *Shadyside* begins excursions along Hudson River.
29 April	Trinidad passes amendment prohibiting importation of *Negro World*.
1 May	Opening date of the first NFC laundry announced.
3 May	Garvey announces plans for a millinery factory.
5–7 May	Garvey speaks in Cleveland.
7 May	Passport Division of the Department of State investigates plan of J. W. H. Eason and Hubert Harrison to visit Liberia for the UNIA.
7 May	S.S. *Yarmouth* arrives in Philadelphia.
9 May	BSL announces acquisition of third vessel, S.S. *Kanawha*.
ca. 12 May	S.S. *Yarmouth* arrives in Boston.
May	Organization of the first chapter of Black Cross nurses in Philadelphia.
7 June	Opening of *BSL v. Robert S. Abbott Publishing Company*.
10 June	Amy Ashwood Garvey claims Garvey abandoned her.
18 June	J. A. Plummer resigns from *Negro World*.
19 June	Advertisement appears for NFC's Universal Millinery Store.
19 June	BSL wins libel suit against *Chicago Defender*.
ca. 19 June	Regular meeting of BSL Board of Directors.
20 June	"Abyssinian" Riot in Chicago.
21–23 June	Garvey speaks in Philadelphia.

25–26 June	Garvey speaks in Pittsburgh.
28 June	BSL requests to change S.S. *Kanawha* from American to British registry.
28 June	St. Lucia passes seditious publications ordinance.
ca. June	E. D. Smith-Green writes to secretary of state of Delaware protesting management of BSL.
15 July	Garvey brings suit for annulment against Amy Ashwood Garvey.
16 July	Garvey invites Du Bois to allow himself to be nominated for the position of "leader of negro people of America" at UNIA's August convention; Du Bois refuses.
24–25 July	Garvey speaks in Washington, D.C.
26 July	First annual BSL stockholders' meeting held.
26 July	Approval of sale of S.S. *Kanawha* to BSL by United States Shipping Board.
31 July	E. D. Smith-Green and Joshua Cockburn dismissed from BSL.
1 August	Opening of UNIA's First International Convention of Negro Peoples of the World and parade.
2 August	Garvey addresses opening convention session at Madison Square Garden.
8 August	UNIA convention takes up collection for Marcus Garvey Defense Fund.
9 August	UNIA convention begins debate on Declaration of Rights.
10 August	Garvey makes apology and retraction in court of libel against Assistant District Attorney Edwin P. Kilroe.
13 August	Adoption and signing of Declaration of Rights of the Negro Peoples of the World, otherwise known as Declaration of Independence.
17 August	Garvey cables striking policemen in Jamaica conveying sympathy and support of UNIA convention.
18 August	Convention nominates candidates for UNIA offices.
20 August	Convention elects Garvey provisional president of Africa.

21 August	Garvey publishes retraction in *Negro World* concerning Kilroe, Warner, and Grey.
26 August	Convention elects high officers of UNIA.
31 August	UNIA convention closes.
31 August	Official inauguration of elected UNIA officers; 31 August declared as "international holiday" of Negro's independence.
August	Costa Rica confiscates copies of *Negro World* from the mails.

THE PAPERS

VOLUME II
27 August 1919–31 August 1920

Report by Special Agent C-C

New York, N.Y. Aug. 27 [*1919*]

In re: Negro Radical Activities in New York City, N.Y.

Spent the morning [*26 August*] with Prof. W. H. Ferris, literary editor of *The Negro World* at the office discussing the Press story, from Washington, D.C., concerning the unAmerican influences which are at the bottom of the Negro's unrest. Prof. Ferris attributed the unrest to be due to the constant [ag]itation of the Southerner and that the hope of the Negro was in the Socialist Party. He was of the opinion that Marcus Garvey should not have made the statements which he made at the big meeting.[1]

Had a friendly chat with the various officers at the Marcus Garvy[2] headquarters.

Had a talk with Dr. Shaw,[3] of Boston, stopping for a short time at 43 W. 132 St. He was of the opinion that Marcus Garvey was too radical in his talk at the Big Meeting.

Had a talk with I. B. Allen, office cor. 7th. Ave., and 133 W[.] Allen been an associate of Marcus Garvy in his work and soon found that Marcus Garvy was a fake and he, Allen had got in trouble with the Dept. of Justice's men when he would not tell the truth concerning unAmerican remarks which Marcus Garvy had made. Allen thinks that all of the type of Garvy and his W[es]t Indian Friends are doing the Negro race harm by their actions. . . .

Investigation to be continued.

C-C

[*Endorsement*] EmR

DNA, RG 65, file OG 258421. TD. Final sentence and endorsement are handwritten.

1. A reference to the UNIA mass meeting in Carnegie Hall on 25 August 1919.
2. Special Agent C-C consistently misspelled Garvey's name.
3. Rev. Dr. Matthew A. N. Shaw.

The Black Star Line *is going* "Over the Top"

STOCKS WILL BE ON SALE AT THIS BIG MEETING

The Shares in the Black Star Line are sold at $5.00 each and you can buy as many as you want and make money

Hon. MARCUS GARVEY
World Famed Orator who has Travelled the World
President of the Universal Negro Improvement Association and Managing Editor of the "Negro World" will speak

ADMISSION FREE   BOX SEATS, (EACH) 50c.

Box Seats can be had at 56 West 135th Street, New York City
of W......
of The Black Star Line

Grand Re-Union
—OF THE—
Negro Peoples of the World
—OF—
AMERICA, AFRICA, WEST INDIES
CANADA
CENTRAL AND SOUTH AMERICA
At The Famous
CARNEGIE HALL
7th Avenue. Between 56th and 57th Streets   New York

Monday Night, August 25th, 1919
At 8:30 Sharp

A RALLY FOR
The Black Star Line Steamship
CORPORATION

STAGED BY
THE UNIVERSAL NEGRO IMPROVEMENT ASSOCIATION

(Source: DNA, RG 65, file OG 374508).

2

W. E. B. Du Bois to James Burghardt

[*New York*] August 27, 1919

Dear Jim:

Don't under any circumstances invest any money on the Black Star Line.[1] The District Attorney of New York County has pronounced its methods fraudulent.

How are you and how is the family? I am hoping to run up your way in my car this fall. Very sincerely yours,

[W. E. B. Du Bois]

[*Address*] Mr. James Burghardt,
206 Putnam Street, Bennington, VT.

MU, WEBDB, reel 7, frame 687. TL, carbon copy.

1. James Burghardt had written the following to Du Bois on 21 August 1919: "Dear Sir: Do you consider money invested in the Black Star Line Inc. with offices in the Crescent Building 36 & 38 West 135 St. a safe investment? An early answer would relieve the minds of quite a number of people in this vicinity" (MU, WEBDB). Burghardt was the family name of Du Bois's mother, which, according to Du Bois, was the "black side" of his family (W. E. B. Du Bois, *Darkwater: Voices from Within the Veil* [1920; reprint ed., New York: Schocken Books, 1969], pp. 5–9).

Report by Special Agent C-C

New York, N.Y. Aug. 28 [*1919*]

In re: Negro Radical Activities in New York City[,] N.Y.

Called at the office of *The Negro World* and visited the various officers there. I am to assist the Capt. of the Black Star Steamship Co., as a technical advisor., which has the approval of Marcus Garvy. I told Garvy of the expected presence, in the city, of the President elect of Liberia,[1] Africa, at the request of Garvy I am to find where he is stopping so that Garvey can invite him to speak at one of his meetings at Liberty Hall and to have a conference with him.[2]

Had an appointment with Dr. M. A. N. Shaw which he failed to keep.

I met and spent the afternoon [*27 August*] with E. H. Armstrong, 234 W 53 St[.,] here on a vacation from Washington, D.C., where he works as a messenger. He is the president and organizer and founder of the National Association for the Consolidation of the Colored Race. He is a Negro and his parents are from the West Indies or Central America. His organization has for its purpose the combining of the Negro producers, as farmers, mechanics, etc., for commercial ends. The organization has a membership of 3[8?],000 which he claims to be mostly in the South. The secret purpose of the organization is for the demanding of their rights in this country. I knew

him in Washington. I introduced him to Marcus Garvy. He is to speak at the
Salem Church, West 133 Street near the corner of Lenox Ave., at 4 P.M. on
Sunday, August the 31st. He invited me to speak with him at the same
meeting[.] He invited me to 225 West 138 St. to meet Mrs. T. J. Ricks who
had been associated with him in several organizations here when he lived
here. His home is in Brooklyn, N.Y.

Garvy is to hold a Big Meeting in Philadelphia, Aug. 31, and in Boston,
Mass. Sept. 4.

C-C

[*Endorsement*] EmR

DNA, RG 65, file OG 258421. TD. Handwritten endorsement.

    1. Charles Dunbar Burgess King (1877–1961) was born in Monrovia, Liberia, received an
LL.D. degree at Liberia College, and practiced law in Montserrando County, Liberia. In 1906
he was appointed attorney general, and in 1912 he was selected as Liberian secretary of state. He
was nominated for the presidency in January 1919 and was elected in May 1919, while attending
the Paris Peace Conference. He visited the United States in August 1919 to negotiate a U.S.
government loan of $5 million in order to pay off Liberia's debts to European bankers. King's
visit, which ended in failure, was monitored by British intelligence; according to one report,
"When asked what he thought of the agitation among the American Negroes, the coloured
President of Liberia said that that was a matter entirely for the American Negroes; he was a
Liberian and was concerned only with Liberian politics" (PRO, CAB. 24/89, G.T. 8289,
"Unrest among the Negroes," special report no. 10, 7 October 1919, p. 10). King remained
president until 1930, when a League of Nations' exposé of " 'shocking' conditions of slavery in
Liberia" led to his resignation (DNA, RG 59, file 882.51/1259; *NYT*, 5 September 1961; *Philadelphia Tribune*, 13 September 1919; *Philadelphia Tribune*, 20 September 1919; Nancy K. Forderhase, "The Plans That Failed: The United States and Liberia, 1920–1935," [Ph.D. diss., University of Missouri, 1971]; Lloyd N. Beecher, Jr., "The State Department and Liberia, 1908–1941:
A Heterogeneous Record," [Ph.D. diss., University of Georgia, 1971]).
    2. King neither conferred with Garvey nor spoke at any UNIA meetings during his Ameri-
can visit.

The People of the State of New York
v. Marcus Garvey

City Magistrates' Court, Borough of
Manhattan, Second Dist. New York,
August 28, 1919

The Court:

    The Defendant, who is the /managing/ editor of a weekly newspaper
known as the Negro World, was arraigned before me on August 7, 1919,
charged with wilfully and maliciously violating the provisions of Sec. 1340 of
the Penal Law, in that he did cause to be printed and published in this paper
a statement, in which statement the defendant exposed Edwin P. Kilroe, an
Assistant District Attorney of the County of New York, to hatred, contempt,
ridicule or obloquy, it being charged that the same injured said Kilroe in his

business or occupation, under circumstances as follows, viz.: That said Kilroe, on August 2d, 1919, was an Assistant District Attorney of the City and County of New York, and in such capacity he was legally investigating the affairs of an organization known as the "Black Star Line," of which concern the defendant is President, for the reason that complaint had been made that the affairs of the said Company had been conducted in an illegal manner; that under date of August 2d, 1919, in said newspaper, there was printed and published on page 2 thereof, a statement headed "Two Negro Crooks Use Office of Deputy District Attorney Kilroe to Save Themselves from Jail." The said newspaper and said printed statement therein was attached to and made part of the complaint before me. It is further charged in the complaint that said printed statement is false and libellous, and caused to be published by the defendant in order to expose said Kilroe as aforesaid. On his arraignment the defendant pleaded not guilty, and his Counsel, Mr. Vorhaus,[1] stated that there was no dispute about the publication of said article, and defendant admitted that he wrote the article, was responsible for the said newspaper, and for everything that appeared in such newspaper.

The Court inquired if defendant desired to put in any defense or offer any testimony, and defendant's Counsel stated defendant did not at that time; and it was agreed between the parties that the matter should be submitted to the Court upon briefs, and if the Court held as a matter of law that the said article was libellous, that then the question of submitting the testimony might be taken up later on. No briefs have been submitted by either side.

In said article, the following statements appeared: *"Kilroe wants to get Mr. Garvey out of the way*, because he is a thorn in the side of white vagabonds, who have robbed, exploited and murdered the negro. Kilroe has kept the company of Negroes who have robbed the Universal Negro Improvement Association *so as to get them to frame up against Mr. Garvey. Kilroe is endeavoring to get Mr. Garvey out of the way* because he realizes that to strike the shepherd he will scatter the sheep, but he is mistaken, for on Sunday night fully one thousand young men promised to avenge the life or the imprisonment of Marcus Garvey on a frame-up by white men. [W]hen Mr. Garvey returned to New York he started an investigation to have the men arrested and then they sought the aid of Kilroe, *who offered them immunity if they would frame up Mr. Garvey. Kilroe is shielding this man* [*Edgar M. Grey*], who is a disgrace to the Negro race, in that he and Richard E. Warner, during the absence of Mr. Garvey from New York did things that even /the/ devil ought to be ashamed of."

Malice is essential in a criminal libel; but the term "malice" in Sec. 1340 means simply "intentional and wilful." People v. Hebbard, 96 Misc. 617. Roberson v. Rochester, etc. Company, 171 N.Y. 556.

Criminal intent is a necessary element of the crime, and the statute must be construed strictly in favor of the accused. People ex rel. Carvalho v. Warden, 144 App. Div. 24.

It is well settled that words employed in an alleged libel are to be construed by Courts and juries in the plain and popular sense in which other people would naturally understand them. The scope of the entire article is to be considered, and such construction put upon its language as would be naturally given to it. More v. Bennett, 48 N.Y. 475. It was held in the case of People v. Sherlock, 166 N.Y. 187, that while the jury is to be the judge of the law and the fact, questions as to the competency of evidence offered by either party are to be decided by the Court in the same manner as upon other trials. Where no proof is given by the defendant of the truth of the libellous charge, and /he/ has testified fully to his motive and intent in publishing it, his testimony that at the time of the publication he believed the article to be true is properly excluded, since his belief can operate only in mitigation of punishment, and not as a defense, except in the case of excusable libel. Nor is the testimony admissible on the question of good faith in the publication of a privileged communication, where it was not confined to those having an interest in the information, but was published in a newspaper which was for sale and circulated among the public generally.

As to articles being published concerning men holding public office, as in the case at bar, the following publications have been held to be libellous: charging a candidate with corruption (Powers v. DuBois, 17 Wend. 63); charging a Senator with corrupt conduct as Senator is actionable, though his term of office had expired before its publication (Crane v. Riggs, 17 Wend. 209); that a member of Congress was a fawning sycophant, a misrepresentative in Congress, and a grovelling office-seeker, and that he abandoned his post in Congress in pursuit of office (Thomas v. Croswell, 7 Johns, 264).

With these adjudications in mind, the question before me is whether such a charge as is set forth in this publication is calculated to injure the character of Assistant District Attorney Kilroe, or to degrade him in public estimation? If it is, the Court is required to establish, as a matter of law, that the charge is libellous. No extrinsic fact need be stated to give point or meaning to the charge. The language of the alleged libel is to be understood as used in the ordinary and most natural sense. Giving this construction to the language used by the defendant, the charge is obviously calculated to degrade the character of the Complainant (an Assistant District Attorney) in the public estimation; it imputes to him in terms clear and unequivocal, conduct highly dishonorable, /if not/ criminal; such as, to the extent it may be believed, must bring upon him public contempt and indignation. Such a charge does not need the aid of any averment or innuendo to make it libellous.

It appearing to me that the crime mentioned in the information, and set forth in the article annexed thereto has been committed, and that there is sufficient cause to believe the Defendant Marcus Garvey guilty thereof, I order that he be held to answer the same, and that he be admitted to bail in the sum of $3,000, and be committed to the Warden and Keeper of the City

Prison of the City of New York, until he give such bail. Dated, New York, August, 1919

> GEORGE W. SIMPSON
> City Magistrate
> City of New York

People v. *Garvey*, no. 126535, Ct. Spec. Sess., N.Y. County Ct., 9 August 1920. TDS.

1. David Vorhaus (1895–1964) was admitted to the New York bar in 1918 after obtaining his law degree from Harvard. He practiced for forty-six years with the firm of House, Grossman, Vorhaus and Hemley (Association of the Bar of the City of New York, *Memorial Book*, 1964).

British Military Intelligence Report

[*New York*] August 29th, 1919

NEGRO AGITATION

. . . Universal Negro Improvement Association:

The Universal Negro Improvement Association held a regular meeting at Liberty Hall on Sunday night, August 17th, at which the Rev. Jonas introduced the Persian Consul General,[1] who visited the meeting at the request of Rev. Jon[a]s to give out information touching the late visit of the Abyssinian Mission, and that he might "understand the negro better." John Wesley Hill, the Chancellor of Lincoln Memorial University[2] spoke denouncing Bolshevism, and was followed by Dr. M. N. Shaw, the representative of the U.N.I.A. in Massachusetts, defending Bolshevism in the following terms:

> ". . . As far as the Negro is concerned there is no democracy in America, but America is the greatest plutocracy in the world, that it is governed and controlled by a few capitalist grafters, and all the Negro gets for his service for over 300 years is lynching and burning and segregation and jim-crowism. That if the majority means Bolshevism, then the negro has no cause against Bolshevism, because the negro should always be with the majority where he can get his rights—those rights which he is not getting in the United States. . . . some white men speak through ignorance about the negro situation, but it is for every white man in America to know that below the Mason and Dixon line the greatest barbarity is committed. . . . How can negroes be against the majority rule that would mean freedom?"

All during the course of Dr. Shaw's address the people cheered wildly. A big reunion of negroes of "America, Africa, the West Indies, South and Central America and Canada, the biggest ever staged in the United States of America" was widely advertised to be held in Carnegie Hall Monday night, August 25th, /1919/ attracting the attention of Assistant District Attorney Archibald Stephenson, of counsel for the Lusk Committee, who attended with detectives of the Bomb Squad and stenographers who took notes of the speeches. It is expected that action will be taken against Garvey for he had previously promised the District Attorney to sell no more shares in the Black Star Line, and to "tone down" his public utterances. . . .[3]

In a letter published in the "Negro World" of August 23rd, Garvey said:

> "The cry of bleeding Africa at home and Africa abroad has reached the high heavens, and we who have been resurrected from the trenches of France and Flanders and have returned to our native habitats in America, Africa and the West Indies with the new spirit to do and achieve in the cause of suffering humanity have pledged ourselves. . . .There must be freedom. Freedom of will and freedom of action should be the prerogative of every race and every nation, and as the Irish is striking forward with his indominable will, as also the Hindu and the Egyptian, so must the Negro. In the matter of the Black Star Line let me say that we expect every negro in America, the West Indies, South and Central America, Canada and Africa will be a stockholder."

A letter is also published in this issue of the "Negro World" from J. T. Bishop, President of the West Indies Trading Association, Ltd.,[4] Toronto, Canada, containing the following:

> "On reading the "Negro World" edition of August 2nd, my people and I join in conveying to you our heartfelt sympathy at the monstrous treatment meted out to you in your championing the cause of the oppressed. However, be courageous and carry on. We in Canada share with you things in common, in our struggle for right against might. Our rank and file are not immune of such contemptuous rascals—they are found elsewhere also . . . The slogan of our people should be: Organize, Unite, Cooperate. That's the keynote of success, that's the secret of the Anglo-Saxons' dominance."

The same issue contains a complaint from Mr. Sylvest[er] Roberts, 133 Tragarete Road, Trinidad, that the "Negro World" and the "Crisis" had been removed from bundles of papers sent to him. They say that this is the only one of numerous complaints that the "Negro World" is being surreptitiously removed.

Milton J. Marshall, of New York, scheduled to speak in New Orleans for the Black Star Line was prevented from doing so by the authorities in that city. . . .[5]

DNA, RG 165, file 10218-364/3. TD, transcript. Copy supplied by Lt. Col. Norman G. Thwaites, British Provost Marshal's Office, New York; transmitted in Maj. H. A. Strauss to director of the Military Intelligence Division, New York, 5 September 1919 (DNA, RG 165, file 10218-364/4 190X) and also in C. J. Scully to Bureau of Investigation Assistant Director and Chief Frank Burke, 7 September 1919 (DNA, RG 65, file OG 3057).

1. H. H. Topakyan had served as Persian consul general from 12 May 1909 to 1 May 1915 and later served as provisional consul general, from 14 October 1920 to 8 April 1922. On several occasions, Topakyan claimed to represent Abyssinian interests in the United States, though no evidence to substantiate this has been found. He nonetheless acted as an escort to the Abyssinian mission that visited the United States in August 1919 and arranged a dinner for the mission at the National Democratic Club—a dinner that was abruptly canceled when the club discovered the group's racial identity. In August 1922, Topakyan conveyed a message, purportedly from the king and queen of Abyssinia, to the third UNIA convention at Liberty Hall, which called for the immigration of qualified black Americans to Abyssinia. In a dispatch to the Department of State on 8 September 1922, the British consul general in New York drew the department's attention to the fact that Topakyan had recently been dismissed as Persian consul general as a result of complaints made against him; it also alleged that Topakyan had subsequently attempted to secure appointment as consul or consul general of Abyssinia, apparently without success (*NYT*, 4 August, 5 August, and 5 October 1919; DNA, RG 59, file 911I. 25-84a).

2. Rev. Dr. John Wesley Hill (1863–1936) was chancellor of Lincoln Memorial University, Harrogate, Tenn. for two decades (1916–36). Becoming a Methodist preacher after his graduation from Boston Theological Seminary in 1889, Hill won a reputation as a political speaker and fund raiser. In 1911, while serving as minister for the Metropolitan Temple, New York, Hill visited the Far East and established two branches of the International Peace Forum in Japan and China. In 1914 he became the first general secretary of the World Court League in the United States (*WWW*, vol. 1; *NYT*, 4 October 1936).

3. Excerpts of the Carnegie Hall address by Garvey and Shaw followed.

4. J. T. Bishop was president of the West Indies Trading Association Ltd., formed in Toronto in 1916. He was formerly secretary-treasurer of Grant's African Methodist Episcopal Church, Toronto (*NW*, 1 March 1919).

5. The omitted material did not refer to Garvey.

Reports by Special Agent C-C

New York, N.Y. Aug. 30 [*1919*]

In re: Negro Radical Activities in New York, N.Y. Garvy Meeting at Liberty Hall.

I attended a meeting [*24 August*] at Liberty Hall, W 138 St. between 7th. and Lenox Ave. Attend[a]nce about 500 of Negroes from the West Indies Central America, etc. there were few if any American Negroes present[.] The Negro World was sold as well as stock for the St[ea]mship Co. and members received their cards for the benefic[ia]l part of the organization.

Dr. M. A. N. Shaw, of Boston, Mass., spoke and explained the meaning of Bolshevik to be a Russian word which means Majority and means the same as our word democracy or the rule of the majority and that there was nothing bad in it all. He spoke of Socialism to mean that they who produced sh[o]uld have the fruits of their labor and he [who?] did not work should not receive anything[.] He who produced should receive in proportion to the work of production and that the wealth of Wall street belonged /to/ those who produced it. He told them that the debt which was owed the Negro for his toil as a slave should be paid and that was enormous. Advised the New Negro not to give an inch but to insist on his being treated as an American citizen. Commended Marcus for his work.

Prof. W. H. Ferris, the literary editor[1] of *The Negro World* since about Aug. 18, 1919 (spoke before Dr. Shaw). His talk had to do with the history of the Negro.

Marcus Garvey then spoke. He was well pleased with the story in the New York Times of the 24th. inst., which referred to the unrest among the Negroes and refering to *The Negro World*. He denied that the unrest of the Negro was due to or was aided by the Bolshevik, I.W.W. Socialists or any political Party. His organization was a blackman's party. Mentioned the struggle between Capital and Labor and he would combine with that party or side which would give the Negro what the Negro wanted.

Spoke against the young Negro going to France and said that Trotter was doing wrong in encour[a]ging them to go because the French were just as bad as the Southerners. The common people had no prejudice but that they could be changed over night just as they were in England to want to fight when they had no grievance. He deplored the fact that the young N[eg]ro wanted to go to France so he could "go" with the white women advised them to stay here and be content with his own as they could only "go" with the common women of France. He should respect his /own/ women.[2] Spoke of the possibilit[i]es of the Black Star St[ea]mship Co. and the establishment of a Republic in Africa. In announcing the Big Meeting to be held a[t] Carnegie Hall he gave notice that the same would be done in all the large cities of the U.S. to tell the country what the Negro wants in this country. I was asked to speak at a later meeting which I accepted.

Mrs. H. [V]inton-Davis, National Organizer, of the Universal Negro Improvement Association and African Communities Leagues of which Marcus is the founder and holds the position of President-General. Her talk was brief lauded the work of the organization telling of the growth in the West Indies, Central America, etc. from where she had just come.[3] Spoke of how the Negro was treated in this country and that they should be men and get their rights.

Again at 8:30 P.M. the hall was crowded, about 2,000, at which time M. Garvy, Ferris and Davis spoke along the same lines though more extended. Those meetings are held every Sunday and several times a week. Collections are taken at these meetings[.]

The spirit of these meetings is decidedly unAmerican and has for their object among other thing[s] to try and create a feeling against the white people of the World and the Colored Peoples. He /Garvy/ is working with similar organizations of Colored peoples in the various parts of the World as Abys[s]inia, India, Southern Africa, Congo, Central America, South America, but he does not seem to get the ear of the American Negro, those connected with him are after what they can get in money and p[r]ominence.

Investigation to be continued.

C-C

[*Handwritten endorsements*] IWW Negro
act. EmR
[*Stamped endorsement*] FILE BUREAU FILE

DNA, RG 65, file OG 258421. TD.
1. Ferris replaced W. A. Domingo as literary editor.
2. In a speech delivered at the Palace Casino on 27 July 1919, Trotter declared that "when the colored soldiers return with their French wives, they should be received with open arms. They are not 'white women' as we understand that expression over here. They are lovely French women of high character and warm humanity" (DNA, RG 165, file 10218-345-2, 31 July 1919).
3. No information regarding this trip has been found.

New York, N.Y. Aug. 30 [*1919*]

In re: Negro Radical Activities in New York, N.Y.

Spent the morning [*28 August*] at the office of *The Negro World* and assisted in the mailing of the paper which has a large foreign circulation in the West Indies and Central America a number of copies go to Africa. M. Garvy was at the court. . . .

At 9 P.M. I attended a meeting at Liberty Hall, between 7th. Ave., and Lenox on W 138 street, to hear Dr. [M].A.[N]. Shaw who gave a patriotic address to an audience of 2,000 of the followers of M. Garvy. Admission 35 cents. I left at 12:50 at the close of the address, the audience remained until 1:30 A.M. to hear the remain[d]er of the musical program.

Some of the statements made in the address were:

The Caucasian lost in the World war just ended.
The Caucasian does not [t]ell the truth.
I believe the Negro should use all his strength for defense.
Every Negro should have two guns and two ra[z]ors on and
not hidden to be used for defense and not for offense.

The tenor of his talk was that the Negro in this country, and his talk was addressed to the American Negro, was not treated justly in this country and his advi[c]e was for them to take their rights under the law and with-in the law.

The white man is not fair and just and takes advantage of the Negro.

The Negro was encouraged to be proud of the Negr[o]'s achiev[e]ments which [are] superior to that of the whites when it is considered the opportunities which the Negro has had.

He stated that he was a national officer of the National Equal Rights League whose purpose was to teach the Negro how to function in the Democracy of this country.

Investigation to be continued.

C-C

[*Endorsement*] EmR

DNA, RG 65, file OG 258421. TD. Handwritten endorsement.

Editorial in the *Crusader*

[August 1919]

MARCUS GARVEY.

Marcus Garvey, founder and president of the Universal Negro Improvement Association and African Communities League, appears to have come out victor in the first round of the fight made against him by his enemies.

The accusations brought against him are unproven, the case of his enemies being thrown out of the District Attorney's office. Mr. Garvey's only set-back is a warning from that office to cease solicitation of contributions for the propose[d] Black Star Line. And Mr. Garvey's own indiscretion made this necessary. Had he brought the Black Star Line before the public in a thoroughly business-like manner and offered it to the race through the selling of shares, instead of as an opportunity for enthusiastic race members to subscribe to a privately owned line, this warning would not have been necessary.

The Black Star Line is a good business proposition and should have been put before the public as [s]uch from the very start. However, we all make mistakes, but it is never too late to rectify the mistakes we honestly make. And Mr. Garvey has already taken steps to rectify his and is now offering stock of the incorporated Black Star Line to the race at $10 a share.

So far, so good. His friends are satisfied even if his enemies, not naturally, are far from being satisfied. But we wish Mr. Garvey would once and for all recognize the peculiar circumstances and environment affecting this race of ours and operating to create distrust among Negroes of their own race. Because of his splendid work in the past, and the greater promise of the future, we would be extremely sorry to have aught happen that would destroy or in any way affect for the worst the wide influence of Mr. Garvey. Our advice to him, therefore, is to take the race and his associates more into his confidence as befits a democratic era. His mind h[a]s been too imperialistic and arbitrary in the past.

Printed in the *Crusader* 1 (August 1919): 8–9.

Report by Special Agent C-C

New York, N.Y. Sept. 5 [*1919*]

In re: Negro Radical Activities in New York, N.Y.

. . . Visited the Garvy office [*4 September*]; they bank their funds in a bank at the corner of 7 Ave. and 135 St. *The Negro World* circulation has increased 1000[1] this week. Garvy was in Boston attending the Big Meeting at which he is to speak, 5th inst. Met [a] Rev. Jordan, a Baptist Missionary and secy. of the National Baptist Convention[2] [w]ho tried to get Garvy to link up with the American Negro but failed. The attached circular gives the cuts of the officers who frequent the office. . . .[3]

Investigation to be continued.

C-C

[*Endorsements*] LR EmR

DNA, RG 65, file OG 258421. TD, carbon copy. Handwritten endorsements.

1. A previous report from agent C-C (28 August 1919) estimated the circulation of the *Negro World* at fifty thousand (DNA, RG 65, file OG 329359).

2. Lewis Garnett Jordan (1853–1939), a well-known Baptist missionary, was born a slave. A dynamic preacher and a campaigner for temperance, Jordan became corresponding secretary of the Foreign Mission Board of the National Baptist Convention in 1896, a post that he held for twenty-six years. Under his guidance the board sent more than forty missionaries to South America, the West Indies, and Africa, and on several occasions Jordan visited these areas himself. In 1904 he attended the World's Missionary Conference of Edinburgh. In 1919, the year he met Garvey, Jordan entered the business world, forming the African Steamship and Saw Mill Co. in partnership with Bishop W. H. Heard. The UNIA in Philadelphia used his People's Church for meetings. He retired from active service in 1921 and devoted himself to work on a Baptist history (*Crisis* 20, no. 5 [September 1920]: 239; *WWCA*, vol. 2; *JNH* 24 [1939]: 243–44; Lewis Garnett Jordan, *Up the Ladder in Foreign Missions* [Nashville: National Baptist Publishing Board, 1901]; *Pebbles from an African Beach* [Philadelphia, Pa.: The Lisle-Carey Press, 1918]; *Negro Baptist History, U.S.A., 1750–1930* [Nashville: The Sunday School Publishing Board, 1930]).

3. The omitted material did not pertain to Garvey.

Comment in the *Chicago Defender*

[6 September 1919]

WEEKLY COMMENT

Such meetings as that of the Marcus Garvey one Monday night, Aug. 25, in Carnegie Hall are more harmful than helpful to the Race. We say Marcus Garvey because it would appear that he alone is the whole association [as] whose president he is listed. In the first place, the man who got himself misquoted in all the white dailies of Tuesday morning, Aug 26, is not an American citizen. Our Race, it is true, is struggling hard here for justice, but the fiery little man who wants to start a black star line to Africa will find conditions almost as bad in his own country, where he might better center his activities. His organization, too, is composed mainly of foreigners, and certainly does not represent one iota of the American Race man[.] Our people will not be frightened into quitting their fight for equality, but we can well dispense with the help of a man like Garvey.

Printed in the *Chicago Defender*, 6 September 1919.

Reports by Special Agent C-C

New York, N.Y. Sept. 9 [*1919*]

. . . Sp/e/nt the day [*8 September*] at the Headquarters of M[ar]cu/s/ Garvy assisting i[n] the folding of circulars which they take with them when they hold the Big Meeting and which are being made ready for the Pittsburg[h] meeting; I could find none which are being sent in the mails. Certificates were being made out for individuals who came in to get them. These certificates were for shares in the Black Star Steamship Line. I assi[s]ted in the writing of folders for *The Negro World* to be sent to the Domestic Agents. I had a very satisfactory talk with the Capt. Cockburn and his private secretary and he has accepted [m]y offer to be his technical assistant and wants my help which I hope to give him. This room is on the third floor of 56 W 135 St. I saw a clerk assorting a large number of letters he was not able to tell me whether they were for subscriptions [or] not. The office is being reorganized. I was introduced to Chas. J. Taylor, 156 W 131 St who is the book-keeper, a black man about 5ft. 6in. wt. 170lb., about 50yrs. age and smooth round head with a clean face. The private secy. of the Capt. [i]s Miss Whittingham, phone Aud. 6706. In the office I found a helper, a messenger or janitor, who has no confidence in the Ship scheme; he has grouch against the whole ship's crew. I shall cultivate this gentlem[a]n's friendship.

Went to the second floor where I met Marcus Garvy and gave him a clipping for *The Negro World* which he told me to have put in the hands of the literary editor for publication and which I did. After he left I had a chance to see his desk which was covered with papers, letters etc. I saw nothing told to find. A clerk was making out cards with the names of the members of the beneficial part of the organization. Mrs. H. [V]inton-Davis the International Organizer was present at her desk working(?)

At the request of the General Secy. Amy Ashwood I took her fountain pen to 10 Cortland St. to have it repaired and brought it to her when it was finished. This Miss Ashwood seems to be Marcus Garvy's chief assistant[,] a kind of managing boss.

They have two forms of letter heads which they use[;] will report on this later.

C-C

DNA, RG 65, file OG 258421. TD.

New York, N.Y. Sept. 11 [*1919*]

. . . Went [*10 September*] to the Marcus Garvy office where I worked in the third floor office. I learned that a white man had been at the office on the evening of Sept. 9 and had been talking about a steamship which he had for sale, a pencil diagram of the two decks were on a small piece of paper and on the reverse side there were arithmetic calculations and the largest term being 14,000. I learned that a smaller boat was being considered, the first being 2,500 tons. The boat under consideration being 250 feet long and 44 ft. wide, tonnage 1300. The boat is supposed to be in the East River and is not far away. Lillian Whittingham, 201 W 1[36?] St., care of Buchanan, phone Aud. 6706., is the private secy. of the Capt. of the Black Star S[t]eamship Line, Inc.

Marcus Garvy was in the office working at his desk. He is carrying on a big rally at the Liberty Hall to get money for the Black Star Line Inc., and gets as much as $700 to $800 per night.

A Big Meeting is planned for Chicago, Ill. the date is not yet set.

A number of foreign Negro[es] were paying for their shares but I did not see one American Negro the time I was there. . . .

C-C

[*Endorsement*] Noted F.D.W.

DNA, RG 65, file OG 258421. TD. Stamped endorsement.

Meeting of the BSL Board of Directors

New York City, September 11th, 1919

MEETING OF THE BOARD OF DIRECTORS[1] HELD AT 120 W[.]
138TH ST. NEW YORK CITY, SEPTEMBER 11TH, 1919.

The meeting was called to order at 11:30 P.M. by the President who stated that it was with the object of hearing Capt. Cockburn's report on his negotiations with the shipping firm downtown relative to the purchase of the Steamship Yarmouth.[2]

The Captain was then called upon for his report in which he stated that the ship, when examined by himself and the Engineer was in seaworthy condition.

He advised the board to negotiate a charter for the ship on Saturday morning, the 13th of September at which time it is intended to make the first payment of $16,500.00 on the Yarmouth. The cost of the charter will be about $2,000 per month, and he explained if even the Corporation did not make money on her charter, the psychological effect on the people would be so great that the chartering of the ship alone would boost the sales of stock, whereby the finances of the Corporation would be augmented by said sales of stock.

An itemized report of the cost of chartering and possible profits was submitted.

It was resolved by Motion that the Charter be negotiated on Saturday morning at 10:30 and for one month, besides making the first payment of the ship.

The President then served notice on the Directors that there would be a meeting on Friday night [*12 September*]. He stated that it was the intention to have the Black Star Line controlled by U. N. I. A., but having had no money the public had to be appealed to. He proposed to enlarge the directorate of the Black Star Line so as to have the Association protected by not allowing persons who were not members to be on the directorate to control the stock.

It was moved by Mr. Tobias and seconded by Mr. Certain that the meeting be adjourned until Friday night and carried unanimously.

E. D. SMITH-GREEN
Secretary

Reprinted from *Garvey* v. *United States*, no. 8317, Ct. App., 2d Cir., 2 February 1925, government exhibit no. 143.

1. The directors consisted of Marcus Garvey, president; Jeremiah M. Certain, first vice-president; Henrietta Vinton Davis, second vice-president; Edward D. Smith-Green, secretary; Fred D. Powell, assistant secretary and assistant treasurer; and George W. Tobias, treasurer.

2. The holding company, Harriss, Magill & Co., cotton and ship brokers located at 15 William Street, New York, owned the North American Steamship Co., which was the legal proprietor of the S. S. *Yarmouth* (*NYT*, 23 July 1916).

Reports by Special Agent C-C

New York, N.Y. Sept. 1[3] [*1919*]

In re: Negro Radical Activities in New York, N.Y.

. . . Reported at the office [*11 September*] where I did retune [*routine*] work on reports and had a conference with Mr. C. J. Scully.

Visited 2152 5th. Ave. and there saw A. W. Whaley and a H. J. Jones, 323 W 40 street and of the British Colonial Club at 17 Moore St. Jones is the head stewar[d] on the Yarmouth, the steamship which Marcus Garvy is making plans to buy.[1] This boat is at the foot of 135 street and Riverside Drive.

Jones called to See Capt. Cockburn, of the Black Star Line to give him some inf[or]mation concerning certain defects in the boat.[2]

I have been asked to see that Mrs. H. Vinton Davis, the International Organizer of the Ga[r]vy organization has an opportunity to speak before the Baptist Convention at Newark, on the 12th. inst.

I met a Mrs. Young, a waitress in the first Negro Cafe from the N.E. Corner of Lenox Ave. and 135 St. She says that the members of the Garvy organization are to go to see the first steamship of the Black Star Line and the boat is to be named Marcus Garvy. She intimated that there was a secret part to the organization and that Garvy did not intend to stay in this country very long as his work would be done and before the District Attorney could do anything to him. . . .

C-C

[*Handwritten endorsements*] IWW Negro Act NY L. J.
[*Stamped endorsement*] Noted F.D.W.

DNA, RG 65, file OG 258421. TD.

1. Garvey's first payment on the S.S. *Yarmouth*, for $16,500, was made on 15 September 1919. The agreed-upon purchase price of $165,000 was eventually increased to $168,500 as a result of the extensions in the schedule of payments granted by the owners at Garvey's request.

2. Immediate and extensive repairs to the vessel were necessary at the time of its acquisition by the Black Star Line. These were the first of many such costly repairs.

New York, N.Y. Sept. 13 [*1919*]

. . . Worked at the office on reports and had a conference with and received special instructions from Mr. C. J. Scully.

Called at the Garvy office and there met Capt. Coc[k]burn who asked me to go, with him and to aid him in the testing of the boilers of the S. S. which Marcus Garvy expects to buy. I examined the paper giving the details of the boat. We are to go to the boat on S[at]urday about noon.

I learned that Garvy expects to be out of town in a few days but just where I have not learned; his desk was covered with mail, opened, the nature of which I could not learn. The shares are being bought fast. The special ral[ly] which is being held at the Liberty Hall is obtaining a large number of share holders. . . .

The address of Mrs. Henrietta Vinton Davis, the International Organizer of the Garvy organization is 202 W 143 St. and 1219 Linden St. N.E., Washington, D.C.

L[ea]rned that a business meeting was held tonight [*12 September*] at the [L]iberty Hall at which time the cost of the boat and other business matters were discussed. . . .

C-C

[*Endorsement*] Noted F.D.W.

DNA, RG 65, file OG 258421. TD. Stamped endorsement.

New York, N.Y. Sept. 13 [*1919*]

. . . Worked in the o[f]fice of Marcus Garvy and learned that the SS Yarmouth had been bought for $165,000 and that the stockholders would go on it Sunday [*14 September*] to inspect the boat. The boat is to be taken over by the B[la]ck Star Line Co. about the last of October, in the meantime it is to go on another voyage to the West Indies. . . .

Attended a meeting of Garvy's at the Liberty Hall which was crowded every seat being taken. At this meeting Garvy told the peopl[e] about the boat being here etc., and of the future plans to have many more boats as well as to do a large manufact[u]ring business in Harlem. Many persons bought shares of stock in the Black Star Line Co. . . .

C-C

DNA, RG 65, file OG 258421. TD.

Frank Burke to George F. Lamb,[1] Division Superintendent, Bureau of Investigation, New York

[*Washington, D.C.*] September 15, 1919

Dear Sir:

From the report of informant "C-C" for August 24, 1919, I notice that it is stated that MARCUS GARVEY has been speaking at meetings which are decidedly un-American and has a following among the white and colored people. As Marcus Garvey is an alien, it is particularly desirous of establishing sufficient evidence against him to warrant the institution of deportation proceedings. Any advocation by him of opposition to law and order would be ground upon which to base a request for deportation.[2] Therefore, kindly have the informant give particular attention to this phase of the question and to obtain information concerning the same which may arise from time to time. Very truly yours,

[FRANK BURKE]
Assistant Director and Chief

[*Typewritten reference*] JEH-GPO

DNA, RG 65, file OG 329359. TL, carbon copy.

1. George F. Lamb was division superintendent of the Bureau of Investigation's First District (New York, New Jersey, and the New England states) from July 1919 to March 1921 (*NYT*, 26 February 1921).

2. Under the October 1918 amendment to the Immigration Act of 1917, any alien who advocated or belonged to any organization that advocated anarchism, syndicalism, or violent revolution was subject to deportation. Frank Burke's letter was written just prior to the period when the Department of Justice's legal proceedings against radical aliens reached their height. In the period from November 1919 to January 1920, approximately 5,000 arrest warrants were issued, but only 556 were upheld. Ultimately, 591 aliens were deported under the 1918 amendment, including 35 aliens arrested as part of the Buford deportations. None of the alien West Indians who were members of the radical movement, whether white or black, were ever arrested or charged under the amended act (Robert K. Murray, *Red Scare: A Study of National Hysteria, 1919–1920*, rev. ed. [New York: McGraw-Hill, 1964], p. 251).

[*Washington, D.C.*] September 15, 1919

Dear Sir:

From the report of "C-C" for August 25, 1919, relative to a meeting held at CARNEGIE HALL on August 25, 1919, I note that reference is made to certain statements of MARCUS GARVEY and that he made an appeal to have a white man lynched for every negro who was lynched. Will you kindly corroborate these statements made in this report, as I am particularly desirous of requesting the Commissioner-General of Immigration to institute deportation proceedings against this individual. Very truly yours,

[FRANK BURKE]
Assistant Director and Chief

[*Typewritten reference*] JEH-GPO

DNA, RG 65, file OG 329359. TL, carbon copy.

[*Washington, D.C.*] September 15, 1919

Dear Sir:

I note from the report of "C-C" for August 29, 1919, that it is stated that while at lunch with PROF. WHALEY, it was ascertained from a man that MARCUS GARVEY had a well drilled military organization for the purpose of protection and to prevent anyone from disturbing the meetings which he addresses. This information is of particular importance and I desire that further inquiry be made along these lines, substantiating the same. Very truly yours,

[FRANK BURKE]
Assistant Director and Chief

[*Typewritten reference*] JEH-GPO

DNA, RG 65, file OG 329359. TL, carbon copy.

Report by Special Agent C-C

New York, N.Y. Sept. 18 [*1919*]

In re: Negro Radical Activities in New York, N.Y.
. . . Worked at the office [*17 September*] of the Black Star Line Co. Marcus Garvy and the head officers were at the District Attorney's office.
Shares of stock in the boat were being bought by persons, Negro[es].
The private secy. of the Captain of the Black Star Line said that the boat cost from 48,000 to 50,000 dollars, the first payment was $16,500 and the treas. had a certified check which he showed the District Attorney for $5,000. The boat was a tramp steamer and very poor. The company had hoped to buy a better one but failed. The boat was bought from a white man by the name of Harris,[1] who was at the District Attorney's office and show the receipt for the first payment. . . .
Investigation to be continued.

C-C

[*Handwritten endorsements*] IWW Negro Act NY L. J.
[*Stamped endorsement*] Noted F.D.W.

DNA, RG 65, file OG 258421. TD.
1. William L. Harriss of Harriss, Magill & Co.

Robert Adger Bowen to William H. Lamar

New York, N.Y. September 22, 1919
PERSONAL

My dear Judge Lamar:
I send you the issue of *The Negro World* for Sept. 20[1] that you may read the letters pro and con on page 9 by Claude McKay[2] and W. H. Ferris literary editor of the Negro World. You will notice that McKay advocates Bolshe-

vism as a means of freedom for the negro. Very truly yours,

ROBERT A. BOWEN

[*Typewritten reference*] RAB:MR
[*Endorsement*] Horton

DNA, RG 28, file B-500, "Negro World." TLS, recipient's copy. Handwritten endorsement.

1. Not retained.
2. Claude McKay (1889–1948), Jamaican-born poet and novelist and for a number of years a Communist, was a major literary figure in the Harlem Renaissance of the 1920s (*DAB; WWW*; Wayne Cooper, ed., *The Passion of Claude McKay* [New York: Schocken Books, 1973]).

Arthur Bishop to the *Negro World*

[[New York City, Sept. 22, 1919]]

. . . Sir:—

Mr. Claude McKay's defense of Bolshevism and radicalism in general in your last issue is very interesting. Likewise the rejoinder of the distinguished author of the African Abroad.

As the question of political attachment is one of vital importance to the individual and to the race in particular, it is well that you permit its discussion in the columns of The Negro World.

I have come to the conclusion that capitalism is bad, unconscionably, irredeemably bad. Like a hug[e] python, it has wound itself round and round its victim, the working man, who has always been at its mercy. The recent great war, the direct result of capitalistic greed and the intrigue and jealousies of these scheming rascals, furnishes the final and unanswerable argument for the destruction of the system that produced it, etc.

[ARTHUR BISHOP]

Printed in *NW*, 25 October 1919. Original headlines omitted.

A. L. Flint, Chief, Panama Canal Office, to Chief, Bureau of Investigation

Washington, September 22, 1919
Confidential

Sir:

The following confidential cablegram, dated today, has just been received from Colonel Chester Harding,[1] Governor of The Panama Canal, Balboa Heights, Canal Zone:

> "Rumored here that Marcus Garvey negro agitator will arrive here latter part of month from nature of speeches and writings that I have seen believe this man should be excluded from Zone ascertain from Department of Justice if they have information concerning this man and his operations which would corroborate my judgment concerning him rush reply."

Will you kindly furnish bearer whatever information you may have regarding Marcus Garvey, referred to in the above cable, in order that the same may be cabled to Governor Harding on the Isthmus? Very respectfully,

A. L. FLINT[2]
Chief of Office

[*Typewritten reference*] S-JRT
[*Endorsement*] Ack. 9/23/19 G[*eorge*] R[*uch*][3]

DNA, RG 65, file OG 329359. TLS, recipient's copy. Handwritten endorsement.

1. Chester Harding (1866–1936), an army officer born in Mississippi, served for several years as a division engineer of the Panama Canal, later becoming governor of the canal in 1917 as well as president of the Panama Railroad Co. (*Panama Canal Record* 10, no. 30 [14 March 1917]: 380, and 14, no. 27 [16 February 1921]; *Panama Canal Star and Herald*, 12 November 1936).

2. Arthur Lewis Flint (1872–1936) served for several years as general purchasing officer of the Panama Canal Co. In 1915 he was appointed chief of the Washington office, a position he held until his death (*Washington Herald*, 19 May 1936; official personnel file, National Personnel Records Center; WNRC, RG 185, file 2-c-104[1]).

3. George F. Ruch (1898–1938) served as a special agent of the Bureau of Investigation from June 1918 until July 1924. He was appointed assistant director in January 1925, when J. Edgar Hoover was appointed director. Ruch and Hoover were classmates at George Washington University Law School (Official personnel file, National Personnel Records Center).

Report by Special Agent C-C

New York, N.Y. Sept. 23 [*1919*]

In re: Negro Radical Activities in New York, N.Y.

. . . Visited the office of Marcus Garvy and found that he and several officers had gone to Philadelphia. With the party was a new member, Cyril

Henry,[1] a Jam/a/ica /Negro from/, West Indies, and he has been elected a member of the Board of Directors and an assistant treasurer. Two clerks were checking up the receipts for shares of stock for the last week and the largest amount which I heard re[a]d was $50.00. . . .

Investigation to be continued.

C-C

[*Handwritten endorsement*] I W W Negro Act LJ
[*Stamped endorsements*] Noted F.D.W. FILE J. E. H.

DNA, RG 65, file OG 258421. TD.

1. Cyril H. Henry (1885–1946) immigrated to the United States from Jamaica and attended the English High School in Boston. In 1909 Henry wrote several letters to Jamaican news-papers opposing the idea of U.S. annexation of Jamaica and urging readers to develop commerce and industry in the island rather than depend on the United States. He graduated from Ontario Agricultural College, Guelph, in chemistry in 1919. After joining the UNIA, he served as treasurer of the Negro Factories Corp. and as assistant treasurer of the Black Star Line. In December 1920 he accompanied Bishop Matthew S. Clair on a mission to Liberia, where in 1921 he became principal of the White Plains Industrial Mission. He worked as a missionary for the Board of Missions in west Africa from 1921 to 1930 and for the Ganta Mission in west Africa from 1930 to 1938. He was appointed principal of Monrovia's high school in 1938 and died in 1946 in Liberia (DJ-FBI, NY 10068161; *DG*, 12 February 1931; *New York Age*, 25 December 1920; alumni records, University of Guelph).

Bureau of Investigation Report

New York City. Sept. 23, 1919

. . . Under date of September 15th five[1] letters signed by Chief Burke and initialed JEH, were forwarded to this office, all of which were concerning the activities of *Marcus Garvey*.

In one of the letters it treats of a statement made by Garvey at a meeting in Carnegie Hall on August 25th, in which it is alleged he made an appeal to have a white man lynched for every negro who was lynched.

In connection with this, you are advised that a short time ago the speech of Marcus Garvey, as reported by stenographer Smart, was forwarded to Washington and Mr. Ruch informs me that a photostat copy of same was made, therefore, it is respectfully suggested that a search of the files be made regarding same.

Referring to the second letter concerning the un-American speeches of Marcus Garvey, you are advised that informant C-C has been keeping a close watch on the activities of this man and, again, we are receiving information regarding him from another source.[2] All information thus obtained will be immediately forwarded to Washington.

C-C has been instructed to secure further information regarding the Boule Society,[3] Lieut. Chas. E. Lane, Jr.,[4] as well as complete detailed data concerning the alleged military organization said to be recently formed by Garvey. . . .

Mr. Ruch of the Washington Office conferred with this informant and further directed him as to what was desired in connection with his investigations.

C. J. SCULLY

[*Endorsement*] Noted F. D. W.

DNA, RG 65, file BS 198940. TD. Stamped endorsement.

1. Only three of the five letters appear to have survived.
2. A possible reference to Col. Norman G. Thwaites of the British Provost-Marshal's Office, New York.
3. Alpha Boule was the name of a fraternity formed by some black academics at Howard University, derived from the Greek word, *boule*, the name of the legislative body of ancient Greece. Military intelligence agents investigating the group in 1919 incorrectly concluded that it was a secret nationwide conspiratorial organization among the black population, with Washington, D.C., headquarters (DNA, RG 165, file 10218-336, and RG 65, file OG 258421).
4. Lt. Charles E. Lane served in the 367th Infantry during World War I and later became a captain in the Fifteenth Infantry. A Howard University Law School graduate in 1919, Lane later became manager of the Lincoln Theatre in Washington, D.C. (*WWCA*, vol. 1).

Frank Burke to A. L. Flint

Washington. September 23, 1919

Dear Sir:—

Replying to your communication of the 22nd instant requesting information regarding MARCUS GARVEY, the negro agitator, to be transmitted to Colonel Chester Harding, Governor of the Panama Canal.

After reviewing our file on this subject I find that GARVEY is the editor of a negro publication entitled "THE CRISIS."[1] He has played an active part in the formation of various negro organizations. He has been particularly active in the movement to colonize Africa.

The Bureau of Investigation has received numerous complaints regarding GARVEY's radical activities, but to this date nothing definite has been ascertained. Speeches which he has given in New York in the past have been somewhat of a general nature, covering the negro situation in this country as a whole. Notwithstanding the a-foregmentioned numerous complaints, GARVEY, to the knowledge of the Bureau, has been very discreet in his remarks. Very truly yours,

FRANK BURKE
Assistant Director and Chief

[*Printed*] ADDRESS REPLY TO CHIEF,
BUREAU OF INVESTIGATION, AND REFER
TO INITIALS.
[*Handwritten insertion*] G. F. R.

[Typewritten reference] GFR-END
[Endorsement] CONFIDENTIAL

WNRC, RG 185, file 91/209. TLS, recipient's copy. Stamped endorsement.
  1. An erroneous reference to the official journal of the NAACP.

Robert Adger Bowen to William H. Lamar

New York, N.Y. September Twenty-fifth 1919
Personal

My dear Judge Lamar:—
  I send you the September 27th issue of the NEGRO WORLD[1] that you may read the leading editorial on the NEGRO WORLD's attitude toward that element of the race represented by the late Booker T. Washington and his followers. This discrediting of Booker Washington and his influence is frequently to be met in the more radical negro press, and the feeling makes a significant milestone in the viewpoint reached by such publications as the NEGRO WORLD and the various Negro Monthlies. . . . Yours very truly,
ROBERT A. BOWEN

[Typewritten reference] RAB:PVF
[Endorsement] Horton

DNA, RG 28, file B-500, "Negro World." TLS, recipient's copy. Handwritten endorsement.
  1. Not retained.

George F. Lamb to Frank Burke

New York City September 25, 1919

Attention: Mr. G. F. Ruch

Dear Sir:
  Referring to your telephonic conversation with Agent Scully today concerning a report made by Informant C. C., regarding the departure from New York of Marcus Garvey, Agent Scully informs me that after a search of his files he finally located the report made concerning Garvey,[1] in a desk which was used by C. C. during his stay in New York, and which report was never at any time turned over to the Radical Division, therefore, Agent Scully claims that his division had no knowledge whatsoever of the departure of Garvey for Philadelphia.

Regarding the continuance of the services of Dr. Craig in this district, I am advised by Mr. Scully that at the present time there seems to be no immediate need for the return of Dr. Craig to this district, as the negro situation has greatly quieted down during the past two or three weeks and it would appear that the contemplated race riots will not take place, and therefore in view of this I fail to see any reason why Dr. Craig should return to this district.

During the operations of Dr. Craig in New York he secured from this office the sum of thirty dollars advanced him in the absence of his securing his salary check from Washington. It is respectfully requested that this amount be deducted from Dr. Craig's account and that same be forwarded here to New York.

I am attaching hereto the report found by Agent Scully. Respectfully,

G. F. LAMB
Division Superintendent

[*Typewritten reference*] CJS-JWD
[*Endorsements*] Noted F. D. W. FILE G. F. R.

DNA, RG 65, file OG 329359. TLS, recipient's copy. Stamped endorsement.

   1. Report made 23 September 1919, printed above.

Editorial Letter by Marcus Garvey

[[Pittsburgh, Sept. 25, 1919]]

Fellowmen of the Negro Race:

   Greeting.

   . . . The first ship of the Black Star Line was inspected at 135th street and the North River in New York City, Sunday, September 14, by fully four thousand members of the race. This ship that is to be rechristened the Frederick Douglas, will be ready and will sail from New York on the 31st of October as the property of the Negro people of the world, purchased through the stockholders of the Black Star Line Steamship Corporation. This corporation needs $80,000 more to make it possible to clear the ship of all [e]ncumbrances to sail on the 31st of October, and I am here appealing to every member of the race to do his and her duty now; and right now. Every Negro must buy shares in the Black Star Line Steamship Corporation, of 56 West 135th street, New York City.

   Any Negro after the 31st of October not a stockholder in the Black Star Line Steamship Corporation will be worse than a traitor to the cause of struggling Ethiopia, for in this effort to free the race economically, our ancient foes are lined up against us, and for any Negro to stand off and allow the few of the race to fight and win out in this great struggle would be action no less than a crime. The Negro race has served the other races for centuries, and the time is now when we should serve ourselves. The shares in the Black Star Line are sold at $5.00 each, and each person can buy from one to two hundred shares and make money. The capital stock of the corporation will be increased in a very short time, which will mean that the par value of the stock will go up. Buy your shares today and you will make money in the next few months. The Black Star Line Steamship Corporation will own and control steamships to trade to all parts of the world. The corporation will offer employment to thousands of our men and women.

Surely at this crucial time, when the race is on trial, no one will desert the ranks, but all of us will stand together and present to the world a merchant marine fleet owned and controlled by the Negro peoples of the world.

If you have five hundred dollars to invest for profit, then invest it now in the Black Star Line. If you have four hundred, three, two, one or fifty dollars, twenty-five, or ten, call or write to the corporation and send in your application for shares with your money.

A greater and more prosperous day is in store for the Negro, but he himself must so act today, as to assure the good things coming.

Fellowmen, I implore that you be true at this time. Remember, the 31st day of October will be the day of triumph or defeat for the Negro, and every man and woman after that date will either hold her head up in pride or hang it in shame.

The call is for action, now or never.

Feeling sure that you will answer this call. With best wishes, Yours fraternally,

MARCUS GARVEY

Reprinted from *Garvey* v. *United States*, no. 8317, Ct. App., 2d Cir., 2 February 1925, government exhibit no. 25. Original newspaper headlines omitted.

UNIA Meeting in Pittsburgh

[[Pittsburgh, Pa. 26 September *1919*]]

Last night [*25 September*] this city was captured by the Universal Negro Improvement Association of New York after a great Mass Meeting held at the Rodman Street Baptist Church, Sheridan and Collins Avenues. This meeting was held for the purpose of explaining to the people of this city the aims and objects of the great organization known as the Universal Negro Improvement Association.

The principal speakers of the evening were Mr. Marcus Garvey, the President-General, and Miss Henrietta Vinton Davis, the International Organizer. The people who listened to these two foremost representatives of the organization were more than enthused with the new doctrine taught them.

Miss Davis, in opening the meeting, said that she was indeed glad to be with the people of Pittsburgh to be able to tell them about the great uplift movement that was now sweeping the entire world of Negroes. She said just twenty-two months ago a few Negro men and women met together in New York City and organized themselves into the first American Division of the Universal Negro Improvement Association. From the few members the organization has grown so much in strength that today, in New York alone, there are 7,500 members, and branches of the association are established in twenty-five States of the Union and in every Central American and West Indian country, as also on the great Continent of Africa. The association has not failed to impress the New Negro with the message of the day. It was the message of organized determination for the general advancement of each and every one within the race. To her, she said, the time had come for every Negro to link himself and herself up with this greatest of all movements, for united we can break away from the barriers that have been placed in our way for these hundreds of years, and carve a way to a brighter destiny.

At the close of Miss Davis' address, she introduced Mr. Marcus Garvey as the speaker of the evening.

Among other things, Mr. Garvey said that it was to him more than a pleasure to be in Pittsburgh to represent the Universal Negro Improvement Association and to explain the purpose of the Black Star Line Steamship Corporation. He said that we were living in a commercial and industrial age when every race of mankind was endeavoring to strike out independently for their own development. To look at the other peoples of the world one would find them actively engaged in the great calling of commerce and industry. Now that peace has been restored to the world you will find great countries like Japan, Germany, France, England, America and Canada preparing for a commercial rivalry never planned nor experienced before. Each nation will be endeavoring to outdo the other in the great commercial race of life, and for that there will absolutely be no mercy shown to the weaker peoples and nationalities of the world whose products and raw materials will be wanted to swell the financial returns of these great contending nations for supremacy.

When we look at Africa, we find that country to be a mart of robbers and exploiters. The great mineral and agricultural lands of our fathers are to be exploited by all the nations of the world, and we, of the Universal Negro Improvement Association, having studied the situation most carefully, have decided to do our best to prevent the further merciless exploitation of the African, American and West Indian Negroes. We argue that if white men can exploit Negroes, then Negroes ought to be able to not exploit themselves, but to trade with one another legitimately in the interest of the entire race.

The white man has no monop[o]ly of knowledge, for the common education that man receives today through the schools, colleges and universities is as much known to the Negro as to the white man. If it is in the field of science, art or literature, you can find the Negro capable of taking his stand against the white man. In the field of politics and of the military art, the Negro is equal to the white man.

Therefore, all that is necessary on the part of the Negro is the proper application of that knowledge which he possesses, so as to enable him to take advantage of the opportunities of life. There is a great world to conquer, the world of nature. Since the white man has made conquests in all directions and the Asiatic peoples have also made conquests, the time has come for four hundred millions of Negroes to unite themselves together to make an industrial and commercial conquest in the great creation that God has given us, so that in the next generation the race to which we belong may be able to live in peace and contentment and not be subjects of the old time order of things.

As a people we cannot continue to tamely submit to the indignities heaped upon us by other races that call themselves superior. When we scrutinize the attitude of the American, English, French and German white man, we find that all four have the same opinion of the Negro. They all believe that the Negro should be a subject race; that he is not to have self-government; that he is not capable of taking a place in the great governments of the world. In Washington there is no office for the Negro, except that of a lackey and a footman. In London the best position a Negro can get, if they will employ him, is that of a janitor or a messenger. In France there is a camouflage to let Negroes believe that democratic France means so much to the Negro, but beneath the surface there is that deep-seated prejudice in France that will one day burst out even with more detriment to the Negro than there has been in the Southern States of the United States.

The history of German atrocities in Togoland and in East Africa testify to the fact that the German is no better than the Southerner, and the Southerner is no better than the Englishman, and the Englishman is no better than the Frenchman.

Hence, we of the Universal Negro Improvement Association have come to realize that all white men are white men. Therefore, the time should be when all Negroes should be Negroes, whether we are French, British, American or German born. The Negro has suffered four hundred milli[o]n strong. Hence, he ought to organize four hundred million strong. And we have come to you good people of Pittsburgh tonight to ask you to link yourselves up to the millions who are now flocking to the leadership of this Association. When we leave your city, we trust we will be able to say to others in other parts of the world that Pittsburgh did her duty.

At the close of Mr. Garvey's address a large number of persons joined the Association and formed the nucleus of the Pittsburgh Division of the Universal Negro Improvement Association.

Printed in *NW*, 11 October 1919. Original headlines omitted.

British Military Intelligence Report

[*New York*] September 27, 1919

NEGRO AGITATION

. . . Universal Negro Improvement Association

Marcus Garvey and his clerical force of the Universal Negro Improvement Association appeared before District Attorney Kilroe, Tuesday, Sept.
16th, and was thoroughly grilled as to the possibility and earnestness of
himself and his colleagues to launch and operate "The Black Star Line"[.]
Kilroe plainly told Garvey that he expected to put him on trial before the
Grand Jury, convict and deport him to Jamaica. He also told Garvey to be in
readiness on Monday Sept. 21st, to tell the Grand Jury about his personal
income.

Another memorable meeting of the Universal Negro Improvement
Association was held last Sunday night (Sept. 21st) in Liberty Hall. The
interest of the people in the floating of the Black Star Line had not been
decreased one iota by the persecution of Mr. Garvey. Garvey's speech in part
was as follows:

"For over two months we have heralded all over the world
the news that the Negro peoples are about to start a line of
steamships known as the Black Star Line. As other races are
organizing to prevent us carrying out our determination, we are
organizing to carry out our determination. . . . . . The Negro has
begged for fifty years. He is prepared to beg no longer, but to take
400,000,000 strong. If you expect the world to laugh at you, you
make a big mistake. You must be serious with the world. There
can be no life when man has to bow down to other men. The
Negro has bowed down too long. The time has come for us to
make some one else bow."

" . . . Some of the old-time Negroes said: [']You can't get any
ship, dock or captain,' But we got the ship ~~the cargo~~ the dock and
the captain. Then they said: 'You can't get any cargo'. But out of
the West Indies and Central America, South America and Africa
we can get plenty of cargo. They have called special legislative
sessions in Trinidad and British Guiana to pass laws to prevent the
Negro World being circulated there."

"The objective of the Universal Negro Improvement Association is the founding of a great independent African Republic.
Let Japan get into power tomorrow and she would probably be
harder than the Anglo-Saxon. The only security you have is force,
and force within yourselves. That force you can get by organizing.

The impending clash will be between white Europe and brown and yellow Asia. We now ask you to help us."

On the evening of September 22nd, Marcus Garvey opened a series of meetings in Philadelphia, the first of which was held in the People's Church, 15th and Christian Streets.[1] I am giving you below a few excerpts from his speech:

" . . . Verily it can be said that Eth[i]opia is stretching out her hands. To him the hour for united action was now, and that was why the Universal Negro Imp[r]ovement Association was determined to draw into one united body all the Negro peoples of the world. . [.]"

"The white man has conquered, the yellow man is conquering, and now the time has come for the black man to go forth and conquer, not only in the field of war. . . . and that was why the people of the Universal Negro Improvement Association had inaugurated the Black Star Line. We of New York are determined to make our power felt in the great industrial and commercial balance. . . . Outside of God there is no power on earth or in hell to stop the onward march of the New Negro. . . ."

"I care not what others may say, but I feel and believe that the Negro is having his last fling for liberty. . . . " "The masses are going to rule. The few little despots and robbers who used to run the world are now being sent to their graves, and before another ten years roll by all of them will be buried by the hands of the masses."

" . . . Four hundred million Negroes must be united. There is no skylarking about the matter. . . . We want workers, men and women, who are going to build. All of us must be builders[.] We have a whole continent to redeem. We have to redeem it through blood and fire. Africa, Mother Africa, is calling for help and four hundred million of us are getting ready to avenge the wrong done to our own dear mother. You talk about war, you talk about battles, victory and defeat[.] Oh, God, the greatest of battles is still to come, and the children of Eth[i]opia are depending upon Thee to lead them victorious. . . ."

It is reported that at the close of Garvey's address hundreds of persons joined the Philadelphia Division of the Association.

Garvey was also to speak in Philadelphia, September 23rd and 24th, after which he was to leave for Pittsburgh on his way to Chicago to answer the Chicago Defender for statements that paper made in its issue of Sept. 6th and 13th respectively.

Mr. Garvey announced at the meeting held on Sept. 22nd that the Black Star Steamship Corporation had sued the Chicago Defender for $200,000 damages for a libel that appeared in that paper against the corporation under date of September 20.[2] He also stated that he had caused suit to be instituted against the same paper for $100,000 damages for a libelous statement that was published in the same issue against him.[3]

An appeal was sent by Garvey from Pittsburgh, under date of September 25th, addressed to Fellowmen of the Negro Race, urging the negroes to buy stock in the Black Star Steamship Corporation. . . .

While in Chicago, Garvey expects to hold several meetings. He announces a grand re-union and rally of the negro peoples of the world of America, Africa, West Indies, Canada, Central and South America at the Eighth Regiment Armory, Sunday afternoon and night, September 28th and at Friendship Baptist Ch[u]rch, Monday night, Sept. 29th Fulton Ave., M. E. Church, Tuesday night, September 30th Eight[h] Regiment Armory, Wednesday night October 1st, a rally for the Black Star Line Steamship Corporation, staged by the Universal Negro Improvement Association.

"The people of Chicago will now have the opportunity of hearing the greatest living Negro Orator, who will answer 'The Chicago Defender,' the greatest champion of human rights."[4]

The Universal Negro Improvement Association is advertising 10,000 leaders to send into new fields. A six months course of instruction will be necessary for each applicant. . . .

DNA, RG 165, file 10218-364/7. TD, transcript. Transmitted in Maj. H. A. Strauss to the director of the Military Intelligence Division, 17 October 1919 (DNA, RG 165, file 10218-364/8).

1. Garvey's address was delivered at the conference of the Colored Protective Association, a group formed in Philadelphia on 14 August 1918 by black ministers and lay representatives as a response to the Philadelphia race riot of that summer. Under the presidency of Dr. R. R. Wright, Jr., the association sought to become a legal protective organization for the blacks who were arrested and without legal defense. Among its demands were calls for the hiring of black policemen and for an end to racial discrimination. Through its religious network, the membership of the association grew, a fact that contributed to its success in mobilizing the black community (*Philadelphia Tribune*, 17 August 1918).

2. *Black Star Line* v. *Robert S. Abbott Publishing Co.*, no. 20-263, SDNY, 1919.

3. *Garvey* v. *Robert S. Abbott Publishing Co.*, no. 20-365, SDNY, 1919.

4. On 29 September 1919 Robert Abbott, editor of the *Chicago Defender*, filed a $100,000 damage suit against Garvey in Chicago for a statement aimed at black Chicagoans published in a special edition of the *Negro World*. Abbott quoted Garvey's statement in his complaint:

The editor of this paper [*Chicago Defender*] . . . in one breath bursts out his whole soul in love for his race . . . and in another breath reveals the fact that he and his paper are ashamed of being connected with the Negro race in that they advise every black man [,] woman and child to bleach their black skin and straighten their kinky hair through the articles and full-page advertisements published in said paper. . . . He [Abbott] . . . is so ignorant and incapable of fulfilling the position of an editor that his frothy utterances from time to time have caused the entire race to be most seriously embarrassed. The paper [*Chicago Defender*] . . . appeals to the lowest and worst in the race. It has built up a tremendous circulation throughout the country through cheap sensation and through the large circulation of the paper it is able to do more harm than good to the Negro race than any other agency known to us (*Abbott* v. *Garvey*, no. B-56668, Cook County Cir. Ct., April 1921).

In a default judgment, a trial jury awarded damages of $5,000 to Abbott in April 1921.

Col. Chester Harding to A. L. Flint

Balboa Heights, C.Z. September 27, 1919
Confidential

Sir:

Referring to my confidential cable to you of the 22nd instant, and to your reply of the 24th instant,[1] regarding the negro agitator, Marcus Garvey, I inclose clippings from the Panama "Star & Herald" of September 16th and September 27th, in reference to the activities of the so-called "Black Star Line", which is being promoted by Marcus Garvey and his associates. You will note that these dispatches are identical, and were sent from New York on the same date. The "Gleaner", which is a reputable paper published at Kingston, Jamaica, in printing the dispatch, explained that it came from an unknown source, but the "Star & Herald" published the dispatch without any explanation, as a "special cable", thus giving the impression that it was from a known correspondent and was authentic.

All the circumstances indicate that these dispatches were sent by Marcus Garvey himself, or by his associates, and are a part of their propaganda to stimulate the sale among the negroes here and in the West Indies of stock in the "Black Star Line". I do not know what amount of stock is being sold on the Isthmus, but I am quite sure in my own mind that no subscriber will ever see his money again, and it is unfortunate that means cannot be found to put a stop to such a palpable fraud. However, from what I have read of the case in the New York papers, it seems that Garvey has managed, so far, to keep within the law.

As the information herein may be of interest to the Department of Justice, it is requested that you transmit it to them. Respectfully,

CHESTER HARDING
Governor

Incl.—2 clippings.

[*Address*] Chief of Office, The Panama Canal, Washington, D.C.
[*Endorsement*] Send copy to Atty Gnrl with orig clippings

WNRC, RG 185, file 91/212. TLS, recipient's copy. Handwritten endorsements.

1. Flint had passed on Frank Burke's message indicating that the Department of Justice received "numerous complaints regarding Garvey's radical activities" but that "so far as they are aware he has been discreet in his remarks" (A. L. Flint to Chester Harding, 24 September

1919, WNRC, RG 185, file 91/209). However, a Bureau of Investigation report written on 25 September 1919 stated that "this man [Garvey] is reported to have stirred up a great deal of dissatisfaction among the loyal negro element in the Harlem District" (WNRC, RG 185, file 91/210). On 27 September Harding cabled Flint twice. The contents of one cable are printed above; the other cable requested that the State Department's Passport Control Division refuse Garvey permission to depart for the Canal Zone, arguing that his visit "would be detrimental to the interests of our West Indian Employees" (Chester Harding to A. L. Flint, 27 September 1919, WNRC, RG 185, file 91/211). Governor Harding's concern grew out of a series of recent labor strikes in the Canal Zone (2 May 1919, longshoremen; 20 September 1919, deckhands). However, the most serious canal labor struggles of this period would come on 24 February 1920, when members of the United Brotherhood of Maintenance of Way Employees and Railroad Shop Laborers and their sympathizers struck.

Enclosure

[*Balboa Heights, Panama Canal Zone*]
27 September [*1919*]

CLIPPING FROM PANAMA STAR & HERALD, SEPT. 27TH.

"—THE BLACK STAR LINE.—

"The Gleaner of the 16th inst. publishes the following:

"Yesterday the Gleaner received the following special cablegram signed "Exchange, New York" We do not know who sent us the cablegram, but it reads as follows:

"Exchange, New York, Sept. 15.—Yesterday was a red letter day in the history of negroes of the United States, the first ship of the Black Star Line Steamship Corporation of which Marcus Garvey is President, was inspected by thousands of negroes in New York. She will sail on October 31."[1]

WNRC, RG 185, file 91/213. TD, transcript.

1. Although officially launched on 31 October 1919, the S. S. *Yarmouth* did not actually leave New York until 23 November. Its planned sailing of 31 October was prevented by the vessel's owners because the Black Star Line had not arranged to insure the ship.

Address by Rev. J. W. H. Eason

[[Chicago, 30 September 1919]]

. . . Mistress of Ceremony,[1] Ladies and Gentlemen:—I am delighted tonight to greet the representatives of the colored peoples of the city of Chicago. It has been my desire for some time to have the opportunity of seeing more of my people of this section of the country, and of having an opportunity to talk to them heart to heart, and to feel their pulses as it were, and to see if they are thinking in this section of the country as we are thinking in the East, in South and Central America and the islands of the sea and far off Africa, and in all parts of the world where people of African descent reside.

I am sure that you have come to learn more of the Universal Negro Improvement Association for our mutual good. The Negroes of the world have become aroused as never before with the idea of taking something for themselves and of protecting themselves, not because they have a desire to do harm to anybody, but they have organized to protect themselves from the offense of others. And I know their cause is just,

"For right is right since God is God,
    And right the day will win;
To doubt would be disloyalty,
    To falter would be sin."

I bring to you the greetings tonight of thousands of our people in our organization in New York, in Pennsylvania, in South and Central America, in the islands of the sea, and even in the far off Africa. I have dreamed dreams and seen visions, and have come to the conclusion that the Almighty Spirit has made of one blood all nations to dwell upon the face of the earth, and that they themselves are to teach the world the grand and glorious lesson of the fatherhood of God and the brotherhood of man; and that being true, we feel that if we can get this same spirit imbued in the hearts and minds of the four hundred millions of our people of African descent throughout the world, that we can be able to help make the world safe for every human being that trods this mundane sphere.

We believe that all men should have a chan[c]e to get up, and that no man should be constantly kept down. We believe in the infinite development of the mind and the soul of man to such an extent that their minds can be so enlightened as to have patience with the weakness of the weak and the strength of the strong, to the extent that their souls may become so enlarged that they can have love and sympathy for all mankind, be he yellow, be he red, be he brown, be he white, or be he black.

So, therefore, the Universal Negro Improvement Association and African Communities League has come into existence for the express purpose, primarily, of uniting all the black folks throughout the world, that we, in turn, might see to it that all wickedness and all discrimination, and all segregation, and all wrongs be forever banished from the earth. And with all due respect to what all the other peoples have done in times past, it will take the black folks to do this very thing because we have more religion than anybody else. We have taken our religion into business, into commerce, into industry, into all our institutions; in fact, it helps to make us better in this world. And if we can live right in this world the life in the world to come will take care of itself. I hear people very often say that I have a home in heaven, but I have never seen anybody in my life very anxious to go there. They love to stay here on this earth just as long as they can, and it is natural. We are in this world to make the world better because we live in it, and if we fail to play our part the world becomes worse because of our having lived in it, and we do not want that. We want the world to be better, and just here I am reminded that the Universal Negro Improvement Association and African Communities League stands for all those things that I am trying in this broken manner to represent to you.

So, my friends, we are striving to get a part of this world's goods, since we know that a part of it belongs to us as well as to anybody else. The world and all the good things thereof were created and prepared for all mankind, and there is room enough in the world for everybody to live and for everybody to get along without anybody doing harm to anybody else. And we have been praying for a long time for the golden age to come when the lion and the lamb shall lie down together with a little child to lead them on. And now we have started to perfect this idea, and so, with this Universal Negro Improvement Association and African Communities League touching every Negro throughout the world, whether he be under the American flag, whether he be under the English flag, whether he be under the French flag, whether he be under the Belgian flag, or even the German flag, or under his own Liberian or Abyssinian flag of Africa, we have come to the conclusion that we are the descendants of the black man, Ham;[2] and that being true, there is no African Negro, there is no East Indian Negro, there is no French Negro, there is no German Negro, and there is no American Negro; but there is just simply one Negro the world over. If you do not believe it you ought to have been in France the other day on one of those beautiful streets there when an African Negro, an American Negro and a West Indian Negro were standing together, and as they were gathered together a white cracker from the Southern States of America passed by and said: "Get out of the way, nigger." The American Negro said, "He is talking to you." The West Indian Negro said, "He is talking to you." The African Negro said, "He is talking to you." So these three Negroes realized that they were all the same Negroes and immediately formed themselves into a league, called The Black Trio.

We are all Negroes and since we are Negroes, although I was born in America, I am just as good as anybody born in England; although you were born in the West Indies, you are just as good as any Negro born in Africa. And since we are all Negroes, we might just as well get together and teach the world a lesson as to how to treat our brothers; how to treat a human being anywhere and at all times. And after all, the black peoples of the world are the most sympathetic and the easiest to forgive of all the peoples that have ever lived upon the face of the earth; and that being true, it is easier for us to bring into existence the idea of civilization that Sir Thomas More[3] and other poets in times past dreamed, and wrote, and spoke about; and so, as I look down the valley of time as far as human eye can see and observe the wonders of the world and all the wonders that will be, I see the black peoples throughout the world coming together in one solid phalanx, marching forward with their faces towards the sun, having as their motto emblazoned in golden letters upon the banner of liberty wafted by the breezes, "One God, One Aim, One Destiny," the motto of the Universal Negro Improvement Association and African Communities League. And then holding up and supporting and sustaining that banner the world over will be four hundred million black folks marching to the tune, "Onward, Christian Soldiers, marching as to war, with the cross of Jesus going on before."

And do you know, my friends, that the story has spread abroad from time to time that the Negro was a dying race, and that here in America every once in a while the news comes out that the Negroes are dying out? Do you know we live better and longer than anybody? If you put the other folks in the same conditions and the same environments as we are living, you would certainly see a change. Talk about living! Talk about dying! If we lived in the houses on the boulevard with all the comforts and sanitary conditions, with bathrooms on every floor and in some of the private rooms, we would live on and never die. Put the other folks down somewhere in some of those other alleys and little, narrow streets, where some of us live, they would die in fifteen minutes of heart disease.

Every once in a while the cry comes up that we are a dying people and when the census is taken every ten years, here in the United States of America, we are one million more than we were ten years before that time, and if we keep on multiplying as we are multiplying it will not be very many years before we will be almost numerically as strong as anybody else in America. If it were not for the immigration we would be pretty well equal now. Very few Africans come here, and if they do, they come to study and return. A few of our people who have come here from other parts of the world are making good, and in view of the fact that we are all of Negro blood, irrespective of place of birth, we have decided to come together here to do something for our Fatherland over there. And that is where this Universal Negro Improvement Association and African Communities League comes in and plays such a prominent part. We are living, of course, to do the best we can for the American Negro, for the West Indian Negro and for the South and Central American Negro. And in view of the fact that the white man has spoken so well of Africa, we think it is good for us to be there. We are going there to take charge of the industry, the commerce, the government and everything, and we are going to treat the other folks well, because we cannot afford to do otherwise, as we are too righteous to be murderers, to be robbers and plunderers.

And so, friends, when I once said that I had not lost anything in Africa and I heard my other brothers and sisters say the same thing, we were young then and did not have our eyes open, but since these white people have been going to Africa and getting vastly rich in rubber, gold, diamonds, rubies, ivory, and everything else that is imaginably good and great, we have got our eyes open and have decided that we have lost a whole lot out of our home. In fact, we lost our birthright over there, and we are anxious now to get together by buying ships of our own and trading between Africa and the islands of the sea by the Black Star Line which is to be owned and controlled by us so that we can go home when we like and anchor there and take charge of our homeland. The time is coming; it may be far off, but I am a seer of visions and a dreamer of dreams, and I believe in dreams and visions.

I have decided to run for the presidency of the African Republic, but if I fail, I will not care, because I am sure that some black man will be elected and he is just as much a Negro as I am. We intend to establish a government in Africa, and w[e] do not think anybody will try to deny us of our Africa, as they did not deny the Irishman his Ireland, the Japanese his Japan, and we are going to stand together and be able to withstand all opposition that may come against [us] and go forward anyhow.

We believe that if our brain, our brawn and our bodies could help to develop America and make this virgin wilderness bloom and blossom as a race, if you turn us loose for a little time in Africa we will transform that virgin country into a garden of paradise, and Ethiopians will again live, act and talk, and be recognized as kings and queens and as princes in ebony walking upon the face of the globe.

Citizens of Chicago, members of this Negro race, lovers of liberty, and friends, let me appeal to you tonight, as one of you, and as one who believes in progress along all lines, and as a fellow sufferer with you in different sections of the country with injustices heaped upon us, let me plead with you to be just and fear not. Be brave, be courageous, be industrious, treat every man with proper respect, fear God, take courage and go forward, and wherever you may be placed, occupy the position of a man, and let the world know that you stand foursquare to all the breezes that blow.

And again, in conclusion, the Lord made us to be proud of our lineage, to be proud of our color, to be proud of our own people, and especially to be proud of our own women.

During this twentieth century there came a man upon the scene to teach his people race loyalty, to teach them to fear God and know him, to teach them to unite the world over, and for the advancement and for the propagation of the best ideas that the world has ever seen. Black but honorable, a Negro but with motives pure, a man of African descent but with a brain that comprehends the mysteries and the knowledge of the world, a man who traces his ancestry back for thousands of years until it goes back to the mighty black kings who founded the pyramids of Egypt; he is now upon the scene as the president general of the Universal Negro Improvement Association and African Communities League and the president of the great Black Star Line Steamship Corporation. I refer to the honorable Marcus Garvey. He has been chosen by black men to be their leader and to be their spokesman, and we believe that we have reached the place now where we can pull out our own leaders and they will have to do as we say, otherwise we will pull them down. And if the white folks choose a leader for us, that man will have to do as the white folks bid him, otherwise you know what will happen. If the white folks hire DuBois and Moton and men of that sort and they did not do what those white folks told them to do, they would cut off their beard. But we have decided that they have served their day and generation, and we are not satisfied with doing good or well. We want to do better and best, realizing with Browning that success is not, endeavor is all.[4]

And so we are endeavoring to pick out and support and sustain our own leaders that they can lead us to our place in the sun. We are living in a new age, in a new day, and I want these people here tonight to tell their brothers and sisters here and everywhere that there is a great movement in the world now. The New Negro in this age can do things as he has never seen nor done them before, and with race pride dominating their breasts, with love of humanity thrilling their emotions, and with their desire to know more of the affa[i]rs of the world and to do more for the advancement and for the good of humanity at large, the New Negro has caught the vision and he is going forward with a pace and a great rapidity that cannot be impeded. And ere long we will find ourselves on the hilltop of fame and success and with one voice we will soon be forced to exclaim, "Princes again have come out of Egypt and Ethiopia has stretched forth her hands unto God."

May I conclude by stating that every man and woman of African descent is a member of the Universal Negro Improvement Association and African Communities League, because every one wants to improve himself or herself in every respect. And since we are so surrounded and so situated we can form African Communities anyhow. But in order to become an active member, to have a voice in the Association and in the General Convention to be held annually, it becomes necessary to become a member by paying an entrance fee of twenty-five cents and a monthly subscription of like amount thereafter. And our object of being here is to organize the Chicago Division as we have organized throughout this country and throughout the world.

Printed in *NW*, 11 October 1919. Original headlines omitted.

1. A reference to Henrietta Vinton Davis, whose opening speech has been omitted.
2. Ham (or Cham) was the youngest of Noah's three sons. According to the biblical account, his descendants migrated southward after the great flood, eventually becoming the peoples of Africa. The biblical reference to Cush and Sheba as descendants of Ham is sometimes cited to support the contention that Egypt and Ethiopia were populated by Ham's descendants (Gen. 9:20–27; Thomas Gossett, *Race: The History of an Idea in America* [New York: Schocken, 1965], pp. 4–5; Winthrop D. Jordan, *White over Black: American Attitudes Toward the Negro, 1550–1812* [Chapel Hill: University of North Carolina Press, 1968] pp. 17–20).
3. Sir Thomas More (1478–1535) was an English statesman, lawyer, and author whose best-known work was his essay *Utopia*, written in 1516 (*WBD*; Alistair Fox, *Thomas More: History and Providence* [New Haven, Conn.: Yale University Press, 1982]).
4. A paraphrase of a line in Robert Browning's 1873 poem "Red Cotton Night-Cap Country" (*The Complete Poetic and Dramatic Works of Robert Browning*, Cambridge Edition [Boston: Houghton Mifflin, 1895], p. 771).

Withdrawal by W. A. Domingo from the *Negro World*

[September 1919]

Mr. W. A. Domingo takes this opportunity of informing the public that he is no longer connected with The Negro World.[1] He also wishes to disabuse the minds of many of his acquaintances and friends who have unconsciously identified him with the various business projects of the Universal Negro Improvement Association.

It is his intention shortly to publish a weekly newspaper of scientific radicalism and fearless opinion.[2]

Printed in the *Messenger* 2 (September 1919): 32. Original headline omitted.

1. Domingo subsequently described his break with Garvey in detail:
   I edited the paper (*Negro World*) for about eleven months. During that time Mr. Garvey became dissatisfied because I did not boost his ideas, so he used the front page of the paper for a signed article setting forth his personal propaganda. So much at variance were our views on the character of his propaganda that he had me "tried" before the executive committee of the UNIA, for writing editorials not in keeping with the programme he had outlined. I convinced the nine persons who composed the committee that I had not violated the terms of my engagement and they gave me a sustaining verdict. This happened a little after Mr. Garvey had launched his idea of the Black Star Line. Prior to this he had asked me to write editorials and speak on the street corners in support of the project, and I refused because I believed the undertaking unsound economically. A few weeks after my "trial," I sent him my resignation and stated among other reasons that I differed wildly from his methods which were medieval, obscure and dishonest, even characterizing the Black Star Line as "bordering on a huge swindle." That was in the summer of 1919 and I severed my connection with him and the organization. (W.A. Domingo to the editor, "Mr. W. A. Domingo's Connection with the UNIA," *Gleaner*, 15 June 1925).

2. This was the short-lived black socialist weekly the *Emancipator* (13 March–24 April 1920), published by the New Negro Publishing Co., of which Domingo was treasurer and Frank R. Crosswaith secretary. Domingo was editor in chief and Chandler Owen, A. Philip Randolph, Cyril V. Briggs, Richard B. Moore, and Anselmo Jackson were contributing editors. British Military Intelligence took note of this in its report of 27 September 1919, which stated: "The Negro Socialists of New York are waging a campaign for funds with which to publish a Negro Socialist weekly. A company has been formed and Thomas A. E. Potter, an active Socialist party member for the past 17 years, has been elected president. . . . The Negroes have sent out an appeal to all members of the Socialist Party for funds, which are to be sent to Thomas A. E. Potter, 2411 Seventh Ave" (DNA, RG 165, file 10218-364/7).

Bureau of Investigation Report

New York City Oct. 1–[*19*]19

IN RE MARCUS GARVY Negro Radical Leader.

This day [*27 September*] this office ascertained that MARCUS GARVY was scheduled to speak at Chicago tomorrow, and therefore the following telegram was sent to Division Superintendent BRENNAN:

"Marcus Garvy Negro radical leader scheduled to speak meeting Eighth Regiment Armory, thirty fifth and Forest Avenue, Chicago, tomorrow afternoon and evening. Suggest both meetings be covered and in event he leaves your city please wire office covering his destination to cover his movements."[1]

For the benefit of the Chicago Office, MARCUS GARVY, who is an alien, is a well known radical leader among the negroes of this city. His speeches of late have been of an inflammatory nature and he at present is endeavoring to finance an organization known as the "Black Star Steamship Company", a proposed line of steamships owned and operated chiefly by negroes. This organization will probably be the subject of an investigation for the Post Office Department in the near future.

It is the opinion of the New York Office that GARVY, if permitted to talk freely would be the direct cause of race riots.

C. J. SCULLY

[*Endorsements*] H.W.G. [INDEX]ED FILE
J. E. H.

DNA, RG 65, file OG 329359. TD. Stamped endorsements. A copy of this report was furnished to the bureau's Chicago office.

1. On 26 September 1919, Frank Burke, chief of the Bureau of Investigation, had written to the division superintendent in Chicago requesting that a stenographic report of this speech be prepared (Frank Burke to Edward J. Brennan, 26 September 1919, DNA, RG 65, file OG 329359).

Editorial Letter by Marcus Garvey

[[Chicago, Ill., October 1st, 1919]]

Fellowmen of the Negro Race,

Greeting: Once more the white man has outraged American Civilization and dragged the fair name of the Republic before the Court of Civilized Justice.

Another riot has visited the country and Omaha, Nebraska, has placed her name upon the map of mob violence,[1] so it can be seen that the mob spirit is spreading all over, going from South to East, to mid-West and then to the West.

Mobs of white men all over the world will continue to lynch and burn Negroes so long as we remain divided among ourselves. The very moment all the Negroes of this and other countries start to stand together, that very time will see the white man standing in fear of the Negro race even as he stands in fear of the yellow race of Japan today.

The Negro must now organize all over the world, 400,000,000 strong, to administer to our oppressors their Waterloo.

No mercy, no respect, no justice will be shown the Negro until he forces all other men to respect him. There have been many riots in the United States and England[2] recently, and immediately following the war of Democracy, there will be many more as coming from the white man. Therefore, the best thing the Negro of all countries can do is to prepare to match fire with hell fire. No African is going to allow the Caucasian to trample eternally upon his rights. We have allowed it for 500 years and we have now struck.

Fellowmen of the World, I here beg of you to prepare, for a great day is coming—the day of the war of the races, when Asia will lead out to defeat Europe[,] and Europe and the white man will again call upon the Negro to save them as we have often done.

The New Negro has fought the last battle for the white man, and he is now getting ready to fight for the redemption of Africa. With mob laws and lynching bees fresh in our memories, we shall turn a deaf ear to the white man when Asia administers to him his final "licking," and place and keep him where he belongs.

If the white men were wise, they would have treated Negroes differently, but to our astonishment they are playing the part of the dog by biting the hand that feeds. If it were not for the Negro, the white man would have been lost long ago. The black man has saved him and the only thanks we get today is mob law.

Let every Negro all over the world prepare for the new emancipation. The Fatherland, Africa, has been kept by God Almighty for the Negro to redeem, and we, young men and women of the race, have pledged ourselves to plant the flag of freedom and of Empire.

Our forces of industry, commerce, science, art, literature and war must be marshalled when Asia or Europe strikes the blow of a second world war. Black men shall die then and black women shall succor our men, but in the end there shall be a crowning victory for the soldiers of Ethiopia on the African battlefield.

And now let me remind all of you, fellowmen, to do your duty to the Black Star Line Steamship Corporation, of 56 West 135th Street, New York City, United States of America. This corporation is endeavoring to float a line of steamships to handle the Negro trade of the world, to run a line of steamships, between America, Canada, South and Central America, the West Indies and Africa, to link up the Negro peoples of the world in trade and commerce. The shares are now going at $5.00 each, and I now ask you to buy as many shares as you can and make money while the opportunity presents itself. You can buy from one to two hundred shares right now.

Send in today and buy 5, 10, 20, 40, 100 or 200 shares. Write to The Black Star Line Steamship Corporation, 56 West 135th Street, New York, N.Y., U.S.A. With very best wishes, Yours fraternally,

MARCUS GARVEY

Printed in *NW*, 11 October 1919; reprinted in the *Emancipator*, 27 March 1920. Original headlines omitted.

1. The race riot in Omaha broke out on 28 September 1919 and involved several thousand people. The riot occurred at the Omaha courthouse, which was eventually set on fire and destroyed by a white mob in its effort to seize William Brown, who was charged with attacking a white girl. Brown was finally seized, shot, and lynched (Arthur Waskow, *From Race Riot to Sit-in* [Garden City, N.Y.: Doubleday, 1966], pp. 110–20).

2. Race riots, directed principally against West Indians and West Africans, but against other nonwhites as well, broke out in June 1919 in Cardiff, Newport, Barry, and Swansea in South Wales. The riots began on 6 June 1919 in Newport. There were no serious injuries, but considerable damage to property resulted, and twenty-seven blacks and three whites were arrested. The riots in Cardiff from 11 to 16 June were more serious, and at least three men were killed. At one point, five thousand white rioters stormed the home of a black man and then set fire to other buildings where blacks resided. On 14 June 1919 troops were sent into Cardiff, and local newspapers called for the deportaton of "coloureds." Liverpool, whose black population of about five thousand resided primarily in the dock areas, also experienced an outbreak of rioting. Disturbances began in May after Liverpool police fought with a group of blacks who ran a gaming house. At one point, as many as seven hundred blacks—attacked by mobs of up to two thousand whites—were forced to seek shelter with the police. Local white opposition to fraternization between black men and white women, and job competition were cited as causes. After the riot there were several calls for repatriation of blacks. Blacks who were arrested were placed in an internment camp pending repatriation, although very few took the offer of a free passage home (Kenneth Little, *Negroes in Britain* [London: Routledge & Kegan Paul, 1948], pp. 79–82; Roy May and Robin Cohen, "The Interaction Between Race and Colonialism: A Case Study of the Liverpool Race Riots of 1919," *Race and Class* 16 no. 2 [October 1974]:111–26).

Bureau of Investigation Report

Chicago, Ill. Oct. 3, 1919

In re: Marcus Garvey (Negro)[,] President-General Universal Negro Improvement Association[,] President "Black Star Line Steamship Corporation."

. . . Pursuant to orders from Division Superintendent E. J. Brennan, and in compliance with instructions contained in telegram from Assistant Director and Chief Burke, dated September 27, 1919, and telegram of the same date from Acting Division Superintendent Lamb, New York City, Employe in company of Special Employe [*M.*] Wolff proceeded to the Illinois 8th Regiment Armory, 3515 Forest Ave., to cover a meeting to be held by *Marcus Garvey*, Negro agitator from New York, at 2:30 P.M.

On receipt of above mentioned telegram from Assistant Director and Chief Burke on Saturday afternoon, September 27, 1919, which stated that Garvey was reported speaking at Chicago on Sunday the 28th and if possible secure stenographic report of the speeches, Employe immediately got in touch with the Editor of the Chicago Defender by 'phone and information was given that *Garvey* would talk at two meetings at the 8th Regiment Armory. Sept. 28th, 2:30 and 8:30 P.M. respectively.

Practically the only advertising that the meetings were given, was the display of a large sign in front of the Armory reading as follows:—

Mass meeting Extraordinary, 8th Reg. Armory, Sunday
Sept. 28, 1919–2:30 and 8:30 P.M.

Wednesday October 1, 1919 7 to 11 P.M.
Hon. Marcus Garvey, Pres. Black Star Line SS Corporation will
answer the "Chicago Defender."
 Universal Negro Improvement Ass'n of the World Incorp.
2:30 P.M. Session.—

About 250 persons were present. Miss Amy Ashwood opened the meeting and introduced J. M. George,[1] an attorney recently of Canada, and now a
resident of Chicago, as Chairman of the day. By Chairman George: After
delivering a short address regarding the benefits the negro throughout the
world would receive through the organization of the Negro Improvement
Association and Negro Communitist [*Communities?*] League, he asked that
the crowd stand up and sing "My country T'is of Thee.["]

Of the 250 persons present it appeared as if only about ten knew the
song.

Miss Henrietta Davis read a prayer from the Constitution of the
Association.

Chairman George then introduced Miss Davis as the first speaker of the
day.—

By MISS DAVIS: I am pleased to come here as a member of an organization that stands for fair play and which means so much to the Negro peoples
of the world, the time is ripe, the hour has struck when the Negro sho/uld/
arise in his might, he has been docile for so many years, in fact he has been
sleeping these many years, dreaming and seeing visions indeed, and at this
particular time when all nations are adjusting themselves in the readjustment
of the world's affairs the Negro is standing up protesting the wrongs that he
has suffered for so many hundred years, he is now standing up in the full
manhood of his strength and begging and demanding as a citizen of the
world the rights that he might enjoy. He has grown weary and tired of the
political promises that have been made to him, the Negro of Africa shall once
more enjoy [his] own Country, the negro has been forced into the slave
shops [*ships?*] some 250 years ago, having been brought over to this country
and other countries without their consent, families were separated and
scattered throughout the world, these people were of blood of our blood and
bone of our bone. (Miss Davis then spoke of Marcus Garvey, the man of the
hour, and a native of Jamaica, who has studied the negro question, and has
launched the Universal Negro Improvement Ass'n for the betterment of the
negroes throughout the world.) I say that we as Negroes must stand together, unite, and unless we do the mighty hand of the Anglo-Saxon will
crush us. (Miss Davis then pleaded for liberal donations to help defray the
heavy expense of bring[ing] the members from N.Y., which cost in the
neighborhood of $3,000.00).

Miss Davis then introduced Marcus Garvey, stating that he was representing the Negroes['] hopes, their ideas and ideals.

By MARCUS GARVEY: It is indeed a pleasure for me to be here this afternoon, I am sent here by the Universal Negro Improvement Association of New York, representing an organization of four hundred million negroes to answer the Chicago Defender. Before I speak about the Chicago Defender I want to tell you about the Universal Negro Improvement Association, what it stands for, the purpose of which organization is to draw the four hundred million negroes of the world together and unite into this great organization. (Garvey then spoke at length in general of the Association, pertaining [to] the benefits derived, etc.) The time has come for the negro people of the world to unite (great applause)[,] for 22 months we have engineered a campaign in the great city of New York, we started 22 months ago with only 13 members, and now we have an organization of 5,500 members in the District of Harlem, New York, and right now we have 7,500 in greater New York which includes Brooklyn. We are organizing all over, yes, even on the west coast of Africa. I am sent to Chicago not to represent a New York organization but to represent a National organization scattered all over the world. The Universal Negro Improvement Ass'n of New York organized a company by the name of the Black Star Line Steamship Corporation, incorporated in the State of Del[a]ware with a capital of $500.000.00, for what purpose, the purpose is to run a line of steamships between the United States of America to the West Indies, South and Central America and Africa. The time has come for the negro to make good in the commercial and industrial world. We realize that God created the world, gave it to man, but he did not say the white man or the yellow shall rule it, but he said man you are the law of creation. We have been unable to stop them, and now his last attempt is to rob the entire country of Africa, but he shall only do so over the dead bodies of four hundred million negroes. (Great Applause). I am here this evening to represent the new negro and what does the new negr[o] hopes for [.] [F]irst of all he says that if he was good enough for him to die in France for the white man, if he was good enough to save the European and to save the Frenchmen, then he is good enough for him to save himself. This is the age where all men are striking now for their rights—have you heard the cry of the Russians, the cry of the Irishmen, the cry of the Hindoos, can't you hear the cry of the Negroes? We stand upon an independent platform, the white man has absolutely no control[;] this is an organization that the white man cannot use. (applause) If the white man has a million dollars to give we don't want it, because we are afraid of admitting him into our organization. (Garvey spoke at length relative to his trouble with Assistant District Attorney Kilroe of New York, and that up to this time he has been unable to get one indictment against him.) (Garvey also commented at length on the cheap Negro press of New York, and cheap petty negro politician[s] who were endeavoring to stand in the way of the success of the Association[.]) If the white man thinks the new negro will continue to stoop to him he has another thought coming[.] [T]he negro is prepared to give him trouble and if he does not want trouble he better give the negro everything that belongs to him and if he wants to retain the friendship of the negro let the negro have his rights all over the world, because as in wars of the past he will want the negro to save him, the negro has saved him long enough now it's high time that the negro saves himself. It took the negroes to stop the Kaiser, and it was two negroes from New York that taught some of the white men how to fight. —when the clash between the white man and the yellow man comes the first thing the negro will do, getting away from them—let Japan or China get into power tomorrow and they will treat the negro as bad as the white man has for the last 300 years. (Garvey then made inflammatory remarks about the "niggers" of Chicago standing against the association and the Black Star Line S.S[.] Co., particularly those connected with the Chicago Def[e]n[d]er) We are not fighting the District Attorney's Office of New York, or the District Attorney, we are fighting Kilroe that cheap Irishman, and [h]e got the cheap Negro press thinking that he intimidated me, he said he was going to take me before the Grand Jury but he fell down on the job as he did not have a case against me. The question is now before you, what is the negro going to do to save himself. Yes, we are prepared for the next war, but not to fight for the white or yellow man, we shall be ready to go to war to fight for the negro, to free and redee[m] Africa. What are you hoping for, they have told you in Washington we are not wanted, they have told [u]s in Boston, in Chicago the same, —did we bring ourselves here? (With much vehemence and emotional) No, No, and we are going to stay here until we are ready to move and we are not going to move until we feel secured. I will remain in Chicago until Friday night [*3 October*] where a meeting will be held in this hall. (Garvey then advocated the sale of shares of the Black Star Line S.S[.] Co., and instructed his agents to proceed through the audience to solicit membership to the Association.)

The day session adjourned at 5:45 P.M.

Evening Session 8:00 P.M.

About 250 negroes were present, approximately 60 percent of the negroes present at the day session attended this second meeting of the day.

Chairman George again presided, and the meeting proceeded with the same formal[i]ties as the day session, such as songs and recitations.

MISS HENRIETTA DAVIS was introduced as the first speaker, and she practically repeated her discourse of the afternoon session.

Chairman George next introduced Marcus Garvey the man of the hour[.]

BY MARCUS GARVEY: (Garvey practically reiterated his speech of the afternoon session and following are quoted some of the additional remarks which he made and which the Department may be interested to know.) I am going to follow the leadership of a new man, that man who was made out of the hardships out of the battlefronts of France and Flan[d]ers, that Negro brother of mine who is out to fight to preserve, that is who went out to fight in France and Flanders will be my leader today, so I am prepared to say to the other negroes of the world the time has come [for] you to organize and even die for yourself. (Great applause) If sixty million German[s] have kept the world at bay for 4-1/2 years how long will four hundred million negroes keep the world at bay. (applause) But we do not want this[,] we want to live at peace with the world[.] We do not want to start any riots, but we say this before any one moves to get me I am going to get him first, and that is the spirit of New York City, but I trust no more riots visit these United States of America. We are not against the white man, but we are saying we are for the negro—anything that stands in the Negro[']s way the negro will down it. Robert Emm[e]tt gave his life for Irish independence, and the new negro is ready to give his life for the freedom of the negro race.

Chas. Hatfield Dickerson, claiming to be a graduate of Yale, and employed at the Chicago Post Office in the mailing Division, was the next speaker and although not as radical as Garvey, delivered a long speech practically along the same lines.

(Dickerson after the meeting came to Employe and whispered in his ear, that the white men were his best friends, and asked that no offence be taken at what he had said.)

The meeting adjourned at 11:30 P.M.

JAS. O. PEYRONNIN

[*Handwritten endorsement*] E[*dward*]
J B[*rennan*] maw
[*Stamped endorsement*] Noted F. D. W.

DNA, RG 65, file BS 198940. TD. Copies of this report were furnished to the bureau's Washington, D.C., Chicago, and New York offices.

1. John M. George (b. 1890) graduated with an LL.B. degree from Hamilton College of Law in 1918 and became a justice of the peace (*WWCA*).

British Military Intelligence Report

[*New York*] October 3rd, 1919

NEGRO AGITATION
UNIVERSAL NEGRO IMPROVEMENT ASSOCIATION

The Universal Negro Improvement Association held a regular meeting in Liberty Hall last Sunday night (Sept. 28). In the absence of Marcus Garvey in the far West, the meeting was called to order by Prof. William H. Ferris, M.A., Literary Editor of "The Negro World" and Author of "The African Abroad". Below are a few extracts from "The Negro World" report of his speech:

On account of the extensive program Prof. Ferris gave only part of his address. He pictured the crowd that would gather in New

York to see the first steamship of the Black Star Line sail for the West Indies and Central and South America.

He pictured the crowd that would gather in those places to see the boat steam in. He said that the launching of the ship will send a thrill to the Negroes of two hemispheres and will lift the standing of the Negro race throughout the civilized world. Marcus Garvey was an instrument in the hands of Providence for uplifting the Negro peoples of the world.

. . . Never in one single year have so many newspapers and magazines radical in utterance, and ably edited, been issued by Negro editors. Ten years ago, Editor William Monroe Trotter, of the Boston Guardian,[1] and Editor Harry Smith,[2] of the Cleveland Gazette, stood almost alone, but now they have company.

. . . The Bolshevist movement in Russia and Germany and the spread of Socialism in America is one of the outgrowths of the war. The colored thinkers have been caught up in the wave of this socialistic thought. One of the new journals, The Messenger, edited by Messrs. Randolph and Owens, is in reality Socialism seen through colored eyes. The new thought in theology, philosophy, politics and sociology is what we find expressed in the new journals.

. . . What does the present literary activity on the part of colored writers mean? It means that when a world-wide movement has been started to wipe out race distinction caste and prejudice, the black man desires to be included, especially since his sword and purse helped lay low Prussianism. . . .

The same issue of the "Negro World" (Oct. 4) states that Sunday, September 28th was a "red letter day in the history of the colored people of Chicago" for it was the occasion of the visit of President-General Marcus Garvey of the Universal Negro Improvement Association and African Communities' League. Garvey was accompanied by a party of officers of the Association from New York. He spoke in the interest of the organization and the Black Star Line Steamship Corporation. "For the last two weeks thousands and thousands of copies of The Negro World have been seen in every section of the great metropolis" continues the paper.
Among other things, Mr. Garvey said:

"The Universal Negro Improvement Association is a movement among Negroes, the purpose of which is to draw into one united whole the four hundred million Negroes of the world. . . . We believe that the time has come in the history of the Negro . . . when we should be united in one great whole for one common purpose.

. . . Because of our disorganization the white American is lynching and burning us below the Mason and Dixon line, the Frenchman is exploiting us in Africa, as all the white peoples of the world are doing. They have parceled out Africa among themselves and deprived the Negro of his own home. Because of this disorganization all of Africa has been parceled out to all other peoples of the world except to Africans.[3]

We have engineered a great movement in the great city of New York. We have organized every West Indian Island, we have organized the South and Central American countries, and still we have done more, on the West Coast of Africa we are strongly organized. . . .

What has brought us here? Some two months ago the Universal Negro Improvement Association of New York organized a company by the name of the Black Star Line Steamship Corporation, in the State of Delaware, with a capital of $500,000. . . . Our purpose was and is to run a line of steamships between the United States, the West Indies, South and Central America, Canada and Africa, carrying freight and passengers. Our determination was and is that since the white man has made good out of commerce and industry, since the yellow man of Asia is making good out of commerce and industry, the time has come for the Negro to make good out of commerce and industry also.

. . . The black man and the yellow man have allowed the white man to get away with murder for thousands of years. What has the white man done but corrupted the world? His last attempt now is to rob the continent of Africa with its twelve million square miles.

We of the Universal Negro Improvement Association have pledged our lives to protect the four hundred millions Negroes of the world . . . and here I am this afternoon to represent the New Negro and what the New Negro stands for. If we could have fought for the white man in France and Flanders, then we, as Negroes, can fight and die for ourselves today. The same blood that my cousins and brothers gave to save the white man in the recent war, this man standing here is willing to give in Africa, in the South, in the West Indies or anywhere for the rights of the Negro.

Have you not heard the cry of the Hindu? Why can't you hear the cry of the Negro? Four millions of Irishmen and women are struggling for the independence of Ireland. Twelve millions of Jews are clamoring for the restoration of Palestine. The Egyptians are determined to get Egypt as an independent country. Three hundred millions of Indians are determined to have India. Four hundred million Negroes realize that the time has come to restore Africa to the Africans. We are here to say that we have absolutely no compromise to make as far as the race is concerned.

I am representing an organization over which the white man has no control. We are not going to admit him into our ranks to camouflage us any longer, as he has done for over three hundred years. We say we are just going to try our own leadership for fifty years more. And thank God, we have succeeded splendidly in twenty-two months.["]

In referring to the "Chicago Defender", Garvey had the following to say:—

Two months ago, we organized a steamship corporation in the State of Delaware. Our purpose was to run a line of steamships between America, Canada, the West Indies, South and Central America and Africa. . . .

White papers like the New York World and the New York Tribune made all sorts of misrepresentations against the Black Star Line. And we went out with our only paper, the Negro World, and whipped them all, and two Sundays ago we presented the f[ir]st ship of the Black Star Line to the Negro peoples of the world.

The Chicago Defender in its issue of the 13th of this month published an article in which they said that the case of Garvey and Kilroe had become so important that the district attorney had to take the matter out of the hands of his assistant.[4] They made up lying publications to further prejudice the minds of the people against the corporation, when they knew them to be false. But up to now the District Attorney has not interfered. The Assistant District Attorney said to me that next Monday he was going to indict me before the Grand Jury. At 10:30 I was down there to meet the Grand Jury, and all that Kilroe said was, 'I am not ready yet.' He had no case. He is just making a fool of himself. . . .

I have pledged myself to travel throughout the 48 states of the Union and before my tour is ended there will be very little left of the Chicago Defender on State Street. The Black Star Line is going to let them prove the things they have stated.

The people of New York, Philadelphia, Newport News, Panama, and the West Indies have invested their thousands of dollars in the Black Star Line for the purpose of floating the line of steamships, and any man, white or black, who stands in the way of the Black Star Line had better look out, because we are out for business and not for fun. . . .

Our organization is a strong one. The Association has a standing membership of 5,500 in New York. . . .

The "Negro World" went on to say that Garvey was scheduled to speak in Chicago all during the week until Friday [3 October], when he expected to return to New York.

It is reported in the "Chicago Defender" issue of October 4th, that Garvey "instead of sailing on the Atlantic Ocean en route to some foreign port," had anchored at the Harrison Street Police Station Wednesday morning, (Oct. 1). "Garvey was placed under arrest by Detective George Friend (white) of the bureau and spent a portion of Tuesday . . . at the detective bureau, endeavoring to explain the ramifications of the Black Star Line venture, and the purpose of the Negro Improvement Association. The detective disturbed Garvey as he stood on the platform at the Eighth Regiment Armory . . . on the verge of telling a crowd of people the glories of the proposed Black Star Line, when Detective Friend calmly walked to the stage and 'demobilized' the project. The officer was accompanied by Private Detective S. A. Bruseaux,[5] of the Keystone Detective Agency, who collected evidence against Garvey and his concern, and reported his findings to Attorney General Brundage.[6] The Keystone Detective Agency, acting in the interest of the citizens of Chicago, purchased $10 worth of stock from Garvey, who is charged with violating the blue sky law."[7]

The "Defender" continues:

"Monday (Sept. 29) in the life of the Black Star Line was indeed 'blue Monday'. By the way of a beginner, the Chicago Defender as a corporation filed a suit for $100,000 against Garvey, charging him with malicious libel. The papers were served on Garvey at his lodging place (4458 Prairie Ave.) by Deputy Sheriff Springer (white). After this action was taken, Garvey is said to have informed his associates to please 'lay off the Defender.' It appeared that Garvey's utterances were heeded by his followers, for at the meeting Tuesday nothing was said about the Defender."

DNA, RG 165, file 10218-364/5. TD, transcript. Enclosed in a memorandum from H. A. Strauss, Office of Military Intelligence, New York, to the director of the Military Intelligence Division, 29 October 1919 (DNA, RG 165, file 10218-364/9 190X).

1. The *Guardian* was established in Boston in November 1901 by William Monroe Trotter. In its first issue Trotter announced: "We have come to protest forever against being proscribed or shut off in any caste from equal rights with other citizens" (*Guardian*, 9 November 1901). The *Guardian* became the major propaganda vehicle for Trotter's many civil rights efforts, including his National Equal Rights League. By 1920 the *Guardian* had a long-standing reputation as one of the most radical black newspapers in America (Stephen R. Fox, *The Guardian of Boston* [New York: Atheneum, 1970]; Georgetta Merritt Campbell, *Extant Collections of Early Black Newspapers: A Research Guide to the Black Press, 1880–1915, with an Index to the Boston Guardian, 1902–1904* [Troy, N.Y.: The Whitston Publishing Company, 1981]).

2. Harry C. Smith (1863–1941), former member of the Ohio House of Representatives, founded the *Cleveland Gazette* in 1883. Smith was a participant in the Niagara movement, a militant advocate of black civil rights, and a fellow radical journalist and friend of William Monroe Trotter (*WWCR*).

3. Of the former German colonies in Africa, the Paris Peace Conference awarded mandates for South-West Africa (now known as Namibia) to South Africa; for Togoland and the Cameroons (both of them partitioned) to France and Great Britain; for the greater portion of German East Africa (known as Tanganyika) to Great Britain; and for the remaining portion of German East Africa (now known as Urundi-Burundi) to Belgium (William Roger Louis, "The United States and the African Peace Settlement of 1919: The Pilgrimage of George Louis Beer," *Journal of African History* 4 [1963]: 413–33; "The United Kingdom and the Beginning of the Mandates System, 1919–1922," *International Organization* 23 [winter 1969]: 73–96).

4. The offending article in fact appeared in the 6 September 1919 issue of the *Chicago Defender*, printed in Vol. II, p. 14. The issue of the newspaper for 13 September 1919 is missing from the original collection.

5. Sheridan Alexander Brusseaux (1890–1930) received his high school education in Little Rock, Ark., and graduated from the University of Minnesota, Minneapolis, in 1914. He became a Secret Service agent for the U.S. government in Europe (1914–19) and in 1919 founded the first black national detective agency (*WWCA*).

6. Edward Jackson Brundage (1869–1934) was attorney general of Illinois from 1917 to 1925 (*WWWA*, vol. 1; Illinois State Bar Association, *Proceedings* [n.p., 1934], pp. 204–5).

7. For this case, see *People of the State of Illinois* v. *Marcus Garvey*, no. 258703, found in DNA, RG 65, file BS 198940-106.

Capt. John B. Campbell, Acting Military Intelligence Officer, Chicago, to Brig. Gen. Marlborough Churchill

Chicago October 4, 1919

SUBJECT: JOHN GARVY, NEGRO AGITATOR, NEW YORK CITY.
(NO DMI FILE NO.)

1. This office is informed that a Negro agitator from New York City, named John Garvy, has been in Chicago for the last four days delivering inflammatory speeches in the Negro District, also selling stock for a Black Belt Steamship Company, said to have been organized by Negroes, in New York City.

2. He was arrested by City Detectives, on a charge of violating the Illinois Blue Sky Law.

3. Our informant states that subject is an eloquent speaker, and a dangerous agitator. He advocates racial antagonism toward the Whites, and is urging an uprising by all Negroes, claiming they are a superior race.

JOHN B. CAMPBELL
Captain, USA

DVB-P
No encl.

Copy to Major H. A. Strauss, I.O., New York City.
[*Endorsement*] A. C. DUNNE, M.I. #4 10/7/19

DNA, RG 165, file 10218-373/1. TDS, recipient's copy. Stamped endorsement.

Bureau of Investigation Reports

Chicago, Ill. Oct. 5, 1919

In re: MARCUS GARVEY (NEGRO AGITATOR), President-General "Negro Improvement Association," President "Black Star Line S/S Corporation."

. . . As announced by subject, and, also, as advertised in the edition of the "Negro World" of New York City for September 27, 1919, copies of which paper were liberally distributed "free of charge" to all attendants of the previous day's meetings, Employe in company of Special Employe Wolff proceeded to the Friendship Baptist Church, No. 218 North Ada St., Chicago, to cover the third meeting [*29 September*] of the Universal Negro Improvement Association with MARCUS GARVEY, as the principal speaker.

There were about ten negroes present to attend this meeting, and in conversation with some of the members of the "Garvey" party from New

York, it was ascertained that the failure of a crowd to be present was due to the fact that the Minister or Pastor of the Church had failed to make any announcements of the meeting before his congregation. Garvey arrived at the Church hall at 8:30 P.M. in company of Amy Ashwood and Henrietta Davis, leaders of the association, and Garvey was very much exasperated at not being able to hold a meeting. He further remarked that the meeting advertised to be held on September 30, 1919 at the Fulton Church would be cancelled and instead held at the 8th Armory.

The small gathering departed from the Church at 9:50 P.M.

JAS. O. PEYRONNIN

[*Handwritten endorsements*] EJB maw
[*Stamped endorsement*] Noted F.D.W.

DNA, RG 65, file OG 329359. TD. Copies of this report were furnished to the bureau's Washington, D.C., Chicago, and New York offices.

Chicago, Ill. Oct. 5, 1919

. . . Continuing reports for September 28th and 29th relative to the above, Employe in company of Special Employe Wolff proceeded to the Illinois 8th Regiment Armory, 3515 Forest Avenue to cover the fourth meeting of the Universal Negro Improvement Association and Black Star Line Steamship Corporation with "MARCUS GARVEY" as the principal speaker.

[A]t 8:15 P.M. [*30 September*], Employe and Employe Wolff, waiting in an ante-room adjoining the entrance of the hall, noticed Detective S[e]rgeant Geo. E. Friend of the Chicago Detective Bureau sizing the place, and being acquainted with him, Employe, with Employe Wolff, approached him. He immediately stated that he had a warrant of arrest for "Marcus Garvey" a negro from New York who was selling shares or stock of the Black Star Steamship Line without proper license. Dect. Sergt. Friend read the warrant to Employe, and in substance read as follows: "Violation of an act regulating the sale or other disposition of securities, approved and enforced June 10, 1919," sworn out by Attorney-General Brundage of the State of Illinois. Dect. Sergt. Friend stated that he would get his man right away, therefore proceeded to take "Garvey" in custody. He took Garvey in custody as he was preparing to step on the speakers' platform. Desiring to have all the information possible in the case, Employe and Employe Wolff accompanied Dect. Sergt. Friend, and on apprising Garvey of his arrest, Garvey was astounded, and pleaded with Dect. Se[r]gt. Friend to wait until the meeting was over, and that he was ignorant of the laws of Illinois and should be given some consideration. Friend without any ceremonies informed him that he was under arrest and that the "wagon" would be over for him in a minute. Amy Ashwood, Secretary of Garvey, who seemed to be particularly interested in Garvey, asked that he /be/ taken in a taxi, but Friend replied that the wagon would serve the purpose. Garvey was taken out through the rear entrance of the hall on his request so that the assemblage (about 175 negroes) would not know of his arrest. Garvey was taken to the Detective Bureau, and Employe and in Company of Employe Wolff, after the meeting, proceeded to that Bureau to ascertain any information that would be of interest to the Department. Garvey was locked up with the other prisoners at the station, and in the office of the Bureau was Attorney W. E. Mollison[1] (Negro) waiting for a bondsman.[2] At midnight L. Ford of Room 901 City Hall Sq. Bldg. signed Garvey's bond in the sum of $1,000.00. The case will come up for hearing at 9:00 A.M. October 1, 1919 before Judge Howard Hayes[3] of the Harrison St. Court.

Report will continue as to the results of the case.

J. M. George, Chairman of the Sunday meetings was present at the meeting and again acted as Chairman. Henrietta Davis, of New York; Chas. Hatfield Dickerson of Chicago; and Dr. [J]. W. Eason of Philadelphia, Pa., addressed the meeting.

By Henrietta Davis: (After deliberating at length on the Universal Negro Improvement Assoc[ia]tion, she made the follow[*ing*] remarks)[:] The 20th century negro has taken hold of himself, he has made up his mind that he has fully grown to that point of realization that he now demands the same rights that all other men created have, he protests against the injustices done him throughout this land and "Jim Crowism", and in his manhood he is going to fight that thing to the very last ditch.

Dr. Eason of Philadelphia next spoke and he said nothing that would be of interest to the Department.

Chas. H. Dickerson, the last speaker, of Chicago, urged that every negro in Chicago become a member of the Association, and strongly supported the ideas of Garvey.

The usual collection took place, and no announcement was made of the amount taken.

Meeting adjourned at 11:00 P.M.

JAS. O. PEYRONNIN

[*Endorsement*] EJB

DNA, RG 65, file OG 329359. TD. Handwritten endorsement. Copies of this report were furnished to the bureau's Washington, D.C., Chicago, and New York offices.

1. Willis E. Mollison (b. 1859), a prominent Mississippi black lawyer during the post-Reconstruction period, was educated at Fisk University, Nashville, and Oberlin College, Oberlin, Ohio. He served as superintendent of public education in Issaquena County, Mississippi (1881–83), and later as clerk of the local circuit courts (1883–92). In 1892 he represented Mississippi at the Republican National Convention and continued to do so for many years. In 1893 he became the first black district attorney in Mississippi. During this period, Mollison branched out into business, setting up the Lincoln Savings Bank of Vicksburg and becoming its first president. In 1917 he moved to Chicago (*WWCR*; Irwin C. Mollison, "Negro Lawyers in Mississippi," *JNH* 15, no. 1 [1930]: 41).

2. Roger Williams Woodfolk (b. 1890) was a black postal clerk in Chicago. He was also president of the R. W. Woodfolk and Co. Bank located in Chicago (GSA, National Personnel Records Center, personnel file).

3. Howard Wood Hayes (b. 1877) was elected a judge of the municipal court in November 1916 (*The Book of Chicagoans* [n.p., 1917]).

Chicago, Ill. Oct. 5, 1919

. . . Continuing reports for September 28th, 29th and 30th relative to the above subject [*Garvey*], Employe in company of Special Employe Wolff proceeded to the Harrison St. Court, 625 South Clark St., to witness the trial of "Marcus Garvey", scheduled for 9:30 A.M. [*1 October*], who was arrested, as covered in report of September 30, 1919, on the night of September 30, 1919 on the charge of violating what is called the "Illinois Blue Sky Law"—"An Act regulating the sale or other disposition of securities" approved and enforced June 10, 1919. Attorney W. E. Mollison, negro, requested a continuance of the case until Thursday morning October 2, 1919, which was granted by Judge Howard Hayes. Mr. Raymond S. Pruitt,[1] attached to the Attorney-General's office, State of Illinois, appeared in court to prosecute. S. A. Brusseaux, negro, Manager of the Keystone National Detective Agency, Chicago, was in the company of Mr. Pruitt, and on approaching Brusseaux, who was formerly an operative of the American Protective League with a good record, stated as follows: (In confidence). That he was employed under cover by the "Chicago Defender", a negro weekly paper, to report the activities of "Marcus Garvey", and so he ascertained that Garvey was selling shares of the Black Star S/S Line Corporation in Illinois without proper license or authority, he purchased two shares of the stock, on the strength of which he signed complaint against "Garvey" and warrant of arrest was recommended by Attorney General Brundage for the State of Illinois.

Report will follow on the results of the trial.

The Universal Negro Improvement Association and Black Star Line S/S Corp. held their fifth meeting at 8:30 P.M. at the 8th Regiment Armory, and this meeting was attended by approximately 250 negroes, the majority of that number having attended the previous meetings.

The meeting opened with J. M. George as Chairman. My Country T'is of Thee was sung and a prayer recited by Miss Henrietta Davis.

By MISS HENRIETTA DAVIS: (She practically repeated her speech of the previous days, and following are the additional remarks which she made): Ever since 1914 the Negro began to question why it was that he should be called upon to go to France and Flanders to lay down his life so that Democracy may prevail and Liberty should not perish from the earth, and not receive the same privileges and considerations that other men have received. The negro does not differ from any other race of people, the same hopes, the same aspirations, the same diseases, affect him that affect other races of mankind. If there is any difference the difference is stamina, I think the negro has just a little more than any one else. He has evidence to that by being able to live under the worst conditions of slavery that mankind has been called upon to bear. You have got to keep marching steadily on until you reach the very summit of your ambition.

Dr. [J. W.] Eason of Philadelphia, Pa. was the next speaker and his speech consisted of no remarks that would be of interest to the Department.

The gathering manifested their pleasure at the introduction of "Marcus Garvey" by shouting at the top of their voices "three cheers for Garvey".

BY MARCUS GARVEY:

Friends, first of all let me thank you good people of Chicago for attending these meetings—when I leave Chicago at the end of the week, I will take back to New York to the thousands of members of the association, to the thousands and thousands of followers and sympathizers the great message you have sent them. As I traveled throughout the length and brea[d]th of this country I have indeed discovered the new spirit of the new negro and I was skeptical of the new spirit of Chicago but tonight I am skeptical no more. (Applause) I have seen from your demonstrations of tonight that Chicago is as ready as New York in the great spirit of the movement. (Garvey then utilized some time abusing the representatives and owner of the "Chicago Defender" and concluded with remarks, that "if it takes us a million dollars we shall get even with the ["]Chicago Defender" for the injustices they have done the negro race.") We have whipped the white men of New York and the cheap negro press who opposed us to a frazzle and we are going to do the same thing with the ["]Chicago Defender." (Applause) 22 months ago in the city of New York 13 men and women met at a place called "Lafayette home" on 131st St. and 7th Ave., and in that period of time the Universal Negro Improvement Association has grown to 7,500 members in greater N.Y. In Newport News, Va., 7,000 strong. In places like Washington, Pittsburg[h], Philadelphia, Boston, and in 25 States of the Union the association is growing strong. (Garvey then related at length regarding his arrest on the charge of violating the "Illinois Blue Sky Law" and stated that his Attorneys in New York said it was all right to sell the stock of the Black Star Line in Illinois, but it was apparent that he was ignorant of the Blue Sky Law.) Well to get to the point these "niggers" of Chicago are fighting us so you can see what they have done. I did not come here to sell shares but came here to defend the organization against the Chicago Defender. In New York we are fighting the Assistant District Attorney there, on two occasions I went to jail in New York, one time for fifty five minutes and another time for fifty minutes, but last night I was put away for about two hours, it was the longest time that I have ever been in jail, but I want to impress upon you that it was for a good cause. (Applause.) If necessary I will spend 20 years in the same jail for the Universal Negro Improvement Ass'n. When I think of Debs, of Robert Emmett, the sacrifices they have made, there is no sacrifice that I will not make for four hundred million negroes. (Applause) WE ARE NOT AGAINST ANYBODY BUT WE ARE FOR THE NEGRO. THE WHITE MAN HAS BEEN FOR HIMSELF FOR THOUSANDS OF YEARS, THE YELLOW MAN HAS BEEN FOR HIMSELF, and the time has come for the negro to look for himself in every way, and that is why we are determined to launch the first ship OF THE BLACK STAR LINE EVEN IF WE HAVE TO FLOAT IT IN AN OCEAN OF BLOOD. We are not established like the owners of the White Star Line, we are not that rich because the whit[e] man has run us for 250 years. All the wealth the white man has today will not be enough to pay the negro when the negro presents his bill. We are telling the white men of the world that we have fought your last battle. (Applause) (After severely criticising lynchings, etc., stated) when we are organized and when a negro is lynched we will press a button and twenty white men will be put to death in Africa. It is time for us to have pride, God created us all alike, he never said White man nor Black Man nor yellow man you shall be a slave, but we have allowed the white man to get away with murder. The Black Star Line will be supported by every negro throughout the world, and in the next 24 months there will be over 100 ships under the control of the Black Star Line. The negro was called to dig the Panama Canal, and if the negro can link up two oceans and go on the battlefield to save the white man then the negro is able to construct and support the Black Star Line. (Applause) (Garvey then appealed to those present to join the Association) It cost the Negro Improvement Ass'n $2,000.00 to send 8 delegates to Chicago. (Garvey also stated that "Negro World" the association's paper had a circulation of 125,000.[)] Garvey then appealed to every person present to at least donate a dollar to help defray the expenses.

I am aware that the two gentlemen present are from the Government, Department of Justice. The Department of Justice has constantly had men watching me, I know that on one occasion the Government paid as high as $60.00 to take my speeches. I will say that I had no interf[er]ence of the Department of Justice and that so far they have nothing on me.

Meeting adjourned at 11:15 P.M.

JAS. O. PEYRONNIN

[*Handwritten endorsement*] maw
[*Stamped endorsement*] Noted F. D. W.

DNA, RG 65, file OG 329359. TD.

1. Raymond S. Pruitt (1887–1957) was a graduate (1912) of Northwestern University Law School, Chicago, who served as an assistant Illinois attorney general from 1917 until 1920 (*NYT*, 2 September 1957; James C. Fifield, ed., *The American Bar, 1926* [New York: James C. Fifield Co., 1926], p. 221).

Chicago, Ill. October 6, 1919

. . . Continuing reports for September 28, 29, and 30, and Oct. 1, 1919 relative to the above mentioned subject, Employe in company of special Employe Wolff proceeded to the Harrison Street Court to witness the trial of "*Marcus Garvey*," scheduled for 9:30 A.M. [*2 October*], on the charge of violating "Illinois Security Law" commonly known as the Blue Sky Law. The State was represented by Raymond S. Pruitt, assistant to Attorney-General Brundage, and W. E. Mollison, negro, represented "Garvey". Mollison immediately entered a plea of guilty, which was accepted by the Court, and Judge Howard Hayes on endeavoring to ascertain /the penalty/ from the Assistant Attorney-General, Mollison asked that a $25.00 fine be allowed, but

Assistant Attorney General Pruitt recommended the $100.00 fine, which the Judge upheld. Mr. Pruitt requested the Judge to order "Garvey" out of town, but Judge Hayes stated that this was out of his jurisdiction. The fine included costs, which amounted to $108.00[.]

The sixth meeting of the Universal Negro Improvement Association and Black Star Line S/S Corp. was held at 8:30 P.M. at the [8]th Regiment Armory, 3515 Forest Ave. About 250 persons were present and the majority of that number were persons who had previously attended the meetings. Miss Henrietta Davis and Dr. [J.] W. Eason, as well as C. H. Dickerson addressed the gathering, and all of them practically repeated their speeches made at previous meetings.

The crowd rose to their feet and loudly cheered when *Miss Davis* introduced *Marcus Garvey*, the man of the hour.

BY MARCUS GARVEY: (Garvey practically repeated his speeches of September 28th and October 1st, as covered in reports for those dates, and such remarks which might be of interest to the Department are herewith quoted) We leave here after our meeting tomorrow night by the midnight train for New York. When we came here as I stated last night we were skeptical as touching the attitude of the people here, the negro citizens, because in your midst there exists a newspaper called the Chicago Defender that has been trying for over two and a half months to scatter through the length and brea[d]th of this country misrepresentations of the Universal Negro Improvement Ass'n, of which I am acting President-General, and Acting President of the Black Star Line S/S Corp. My people in New York at great expense over $3,000 sent us here, eight of us to lay the cause before you. We will have nothing to tell the 7,000 members of that great city of New York other than that Chicago is ready, even as New York is ready for the great march of the negro. I have had some unpleasant experience during my stay here in that my arch enemy plotted to have me jailed. (Full information regarding the arrest of Garvey is covered in Employe's reports for Sept. 30th and October 1, 1919) This trouble has caused me or rather cost me $500.00 with the return of the stock that we sold since we were here amounting to $95.00. I was fined $108.50, had to pay my attorney $100.00 and $150.00 otherwise, but the money does not matter it is the principle. I was prosecuted by the Attorney General of the State of Illinois. About 400 of you have joined the association since we have been here. It shows that with proper leadership you will be more than 10,000 strong. I have been able to find out that there are good negroes in Chicago and very bad "niggers." The bad nigger is the man that is making trouble for the negro race not so much the white man. I want to say a few words now about the Chicago Defender, that the Black Star Line have $800,000.00 of business with the Chicago Defender until the 31st of December of this year and that business will have to be settled if it takes a million dollars to settle it as to put the Chicago Defender out of business.[1] They told us in New York we could not start a Black Star Line[.] The District Attorney in New York tried his best to prevent us going ahead with the Black Star Line. We have demonstrated to the people of New York of both races that we have been able to put thru a Black Star Line in only six weeks. We have told them that we will have the Black Star Line even if we have to float the ships in an ocean of blood. We are not selling any stock now in Chicago on account of the Law.[2] We have whipped the biggest newspaper in the world, The New York World, and we can easily whip the Chicago Defender. Any one who attempts to rob me of my good name must rob me of my life. The District Attorney of New York came out and opposed me, opposed the Black Star Line as one man, even then the entire press lined up with the District Attorney, but with all that within six weeks we were able to present the first ship of the Black Star Line. The negro has fought for the last time for the white man and the next war will find him fighting absolutely for himself. Expressing ourselves like Patrick Henry, we negroes do not care what others may say but as for us give us liberty or give us death. (Practically every negro in the place stood on their feet and cheered vociferously) What do I care for prison bars if it will mean the liberty of four hundred million negroes. *In just 24 hours every white man in the West Indies will be swept off the face of the globe if anything is done to Marcus Garvey in New York.* (The negroes again stood on their feet at the conclusion of Garvey's speech, and cheered loudly.)

Meeting adjourned at 11:30 P.M.

JAS. O. PEYRONNIN

[*Handwritten endorsements*] EJB maw
[*Stamped endorsement*] Noted F.D.W.

DNA, RG 65, file OG 329359. TD. Copies of this report were furnished to the bureau's Washington, D.C., Chicago, and New York offices.

1. Garvey brought suit for $200,000 damages on 1 October 1919 against Robert S. Abbott in the Illinois Circuit Court of Cook County for defamation of character; however, the suit was ultimately dismissed in January 1922 for want of prosecution.

2. On 10 October 1919, only a few days after Garvey's trial, he and E. D. Smith-Green applied to the Illinois secretary of state to admit the Black Star Line into the state for the purpose of transacting business. They stated then that $52,285 in BSL stock had been subscribed to overall, and that the BSL had $25,000 cash in the bank. They also reported a total of $16,500 paid toward the purchase of a ship (*Yarmouth*). The BSL received legal permission to do business, but in November 1921, their authority to operate in Illinois was revoked because of failure to file an annual report or pay franchise tax. (Archives of the State of Illinois, RS103.112 and RS103.113).

Chicago, Ill. October 8, [19]19

. . . Continuing reports for September 28, 29 and 30, 1919 and October 1, 2, and 3, 1919 relative to the above subject, Employe talked to Mrs. Mary Johnstone of No. 4458 Prairie Ave., at whose home "*Marcus Garvey*" and *Amy Ashwood*, Secretary of Garvey, had rooms, and it was ascertained from her, although she did not know when Garvey departed, that he talked over the 'phone with the Baltimore & Ohio R.R. Ticket Office about 2:30 P.M. of the previous day for information relative to trains for New York. She could not apprise Employe of anything definite. Garvey, however, mentioned at every meeting which he addressed in Chicago that he intended to leave at midnight Friday [*3 October*] for New York in order to be present in that city by Sunday.

The following telegram was sent to Acting Division Superintendent Lamb, New York:—

"Sun[day] September twenty seventh relative Marcus Garvey best information obtainable   subject departed for New York yesterday afternoon or evening probably via Baltimore & Ohio Railway   balance of party departed at eleven forty last night via Pennsylvania [*rail*]road Pittsburg[h] train probable destination New York   understand Garvey to address meeting in New York Sunday."

There are attached herewith two copies of Circular issued by the Black Star Line, Inc., which have the photograph of "*Marcus Garvey*" and other members of the corporation. These circulars were distributed freely at every meeting. Same are submitted to the bureau for information. There are also attached herewith clippings from the "Chicago Defender" of the editions of Sept. 6, 26, and 27th and October 4, 1919[1] (similar clippings will be submitted to New York Office with copy of this report), also clipping from the "Chicago Tribune" October 1, 1919 Edition.[2] For the information of the Bureau, Washington, there are also attached herewith two copies of the newspaper "NEGRO WORLD"[3] published by the Universal Negro Improvement Association and edited by ["]*Marcus Garvey*"

SUMMARY: The majority of the negroes who attended the meetings referred to, were practically all negroes who migrated to Chicago from the South since 1917. Employe talked to probably 50 negroes of the higher type, who were either born or raised in Chicago, and who attended one or two of these meeting, and this class of negroes do not appear to be in sympathy with *Marcus Garvey*. Some of them seem to believe that "Garvey" is a [sh]rewd fak[e]r and is out for the money, while others are absolutely against him on account of endeavoring to separate the negro from the white man, and destroy whatever friendship that now exists between them. Although Garvey said in some of his speeches that Chicago was as ready as New York, it was ascertained, in course of conversation, from negroes who were close to Garvey that he was very much disappointed at the small attendances, small collections, and the small number of applications for membership. Figuring conservatively it is estimated that not more than 2500 negroes attended all the meetings. As stated in previous reports, negroes who took interest in *Garvey* attended all meetings. However, notwithstanding the fact that "*Garvey*" did not successfully carry out his program in Chicago as he had anticipated, there is no question of a doubt that if he is permitted to hold many more of these meetings in Chicago, he will probably be successful in inoculating his radical ideas in some of these negroes['] heads, and which will probably result in creating trouble in a community which has just subsided from race riots. . . .

JAS. O. PEYRONNIN

DNA, RG 65, file OG 329359. TD. Copies of this report were furnished to the bureau's Washington, D.C., Chicago, and New York offices.

1. "District Attorney Swan Now Handling Garvey Case—Takes Black Star Line Investigation away from Assistant," *Chicago Defender*, 6 September 1919; "Attorney Bares N.Y. Editor's Plot—Mark Garvey Found Guilty of Criminal Libel; Recalls Other Schemes," ibid., 20 September 1919; "Law Is Still on Mark Garvey's Trail," ibid., 27 September 1919; "Brundage 'Sinks' Black Star Line—Air Castle Steamship Sails into Illinois Without Blue Sky License Garvey Put under Arrest," ibid., 4 October 1919.

2. "Arrest Checks Voyage of the Black Star Line—Stock Salesman for New Ship Company Seized," *Chicago Daily Tribune*, 1 October 1919.

3. Not retained.

William H. Lamar to Third Assistant Postmaster General, Division of Classification

[*Washington, D.C.*] October 8, 1919

Third Assistant,
Division of Classification.

Replying to your letter of July 11, file 187166, you are informed that the "Negro World," published at New York, New York, issues of June 7, 14, 21 and 28, 1919, are not considered either singly or in relation to each other in violation of the provisions of the Espionage Act.

[WILLIAM H. LAMAR]
Solicitor

DNA, RG 28, file B-500, "Negro World." TL, carbon copy.

A. H. May to W. E. B. Du Bois

San Andres Isle, Republic of Colombia
Oct. 8/[*19*]19

Dear Sirs:

Believing that you are [*in a*] position to know all about the standing of the many Negroes' concerns in America I am asking you to send me, by return mail, all particulars about the Black Star Line as myself & others of this island desire to invest a few dollars in the enterprise if it is founded & backed by the right Negroes.

Thanking you in advance for your kind & prompt attention, I am, Yours very truly

A. H. MAY

MU, WEBDB Papers, reel 7, frame 1088. ALS, recipient's copy.

Melvin J. McKenna, Inspector, Department Intelligence Office, Chicago, to Capt. W. L. Moffat, Jr., Military Intelligence Division

[*Chicago*] October 8, 1919

. . . Subject: John Garvy, Negro Agitator

Growing out of my investigation of the case, I was unable to obtain any data on John Garvy, but however learned considerable concerning one Marcus Garvey, a radical Negro agitator.

Marcus Garvey is Managing editor of "The Negro World", 36–38 West 135th St., N.Y. City, a copy of that newspaper of August 2, 1919 is hereto annexed and made a part of this report.

On the first page of the issue of August 2nd attention is directed to the article "The Negro in the next world War. Black men of the World, Prepare! Prepare!" The article signed Marcus Garvey explains itself.

Interviewed Assistant District Attorney Kilroe New York County, who stated that the August Grand Jury file[d] three indictments against Marcus Garvey charging him with criminal libel for the article prepared and published by him in "The Negro World" of August 2, 1919 on page two thereof bearing the following heading "Two Negro crooks use office of Deputy District Attorney Kilroe to save themselves from jail".

With reference to "The Black Star Line," Inc. Mr. Kilroe stated that the case will be presented to the Grand Jury for indictment. It appears that Garvey as President of the Black Star Line has misappropriated funds of the alleged steamship company and has also fraudulently issued stock applying the proceeds thereof to his own personal gain. Also in violation of the Federal Revenue Stamp Act. Hereto annexed are copies of statements signed by Edgar M. Grey and Richard [E.] Warner[1] which are self explanatory and upon which the Grand Jury will act.

On page 4 of "The Negro World" of August 2, 1919 attention is directed to the advertisement of "The Black Star Line.["] The following are some of the statements:—"A direct line of steamships—to be owned, controlled and manned by Negroes to reach the Negro peoples of the World.["] "The Black Star Line, Inc. is the result of a Herculean effort on the part of Hon. Marcus Garvey, world famed Negro orator, who in May, 1917 formed a society known as the Universal Negro Improvement Association and African Communities League, of which he is now President-General".

Mr. Kilroe stated that the Chicago authorities ought to indict Garvey if he is doing anything out of the way in view of the riots there. Respectfully submitted,

[MELVIN J. McKENNA]

DNA, RG 165, file 10218-373. TL, carbon copy.

1. See DNA, RG 165, files 10218-373/3 and 10218-373/4; printed in Vol. I, pp. 462–65.

Robert Adger Bowen to William H. Lamar

NEW YORK. N.Y. October 9, 1919

PERSONAL

My dear Judge Lamar:

THE NEGRO WORLD for the 11th of October, bears a display headline, Negroes Prepare Yourselves, and in an address by Marcus H. Garvey gives some very radical utterances—very radical, indeed.

I have not held the paper for your decision in that respect, but have notified the Department of Justice both here and in Washington. Your own copies of the paper are being sent you by the Post-Office, and I hope you will give your attention to this article. Very truly yours,

ROBERT A. BOWEN

[*Typewritten reference*] RAB:MR
[*Handwritten endorsement*] Judge Horton

DNA, RG 28, file B-500, "Negro World." TLS, recipient's copy.

George F. Lamb to Frank Burke

New York City, October 11, 1919
Attention: MR. HOOVER.

Frank Burke, Esq.,
Dear Sir:

Enclosed herewith please find copy of the "Negro World" for Saturday, October 11th, which publication is the one edited by Marcus Garvy, the well known radical Negro leader. Your attention is particularly called to the article on the first page under the caption "Blackmen all over the world should prepare to protect themselves."[1] Very truly yours,

G. F. LAMB
Division Superintendent

[*Typewritten reference*] CJS-JWD
[*Stamped endorsement*] NOTED F. D. W.
[*Handwritten endorsement*] HWG

DNA, RG 65, file OG 329359. TLS, recipient's copy. Inside address omitted.

1. See also Robert A. Bowen to William H. Lamar, 9 October 1919, DNA, RG 28, file B-500, "Negro World."

Article in the *Negro World*

[11 October 1919]

GREATEST MEETING IN HISTORY OF UNIVERSAL NEGRO IMPROVEMENT ASS'N HELD IN LIBERTY HALL

Before seven o'clock last Sunday evening [*5 October*] great crowds of people wended their way to Liberty Hall, New York. Before eight o'clock the big hall was filled to overflowing and hundreds of people were congested around the doors and windows. The sidewalk, the doors, the aisles, the room running off from the platform, the steps leading up to the platform and even the platform itself was literally jammed with people. As it was thousands of people were unable to get into the building. Excitement was at fever heat. What was the cause of the agitation that drove over six thousand Negroes to Liberty Hall? Why, don't you know, the Chicago Defender cited in a headline that the Black Star Line had been sunk. The people didn't know whether the boat had been sunk in the Atlantic Ocean or in Lake Michigan. They didn't know whether it had been sunk by a mine or submarine. And they came to find out whether it was at the bottom of the sea or afloat. But most of them believed that it was still above the water and intact. They didn't see how the ship could get from North River up into the waters of Lake Michigan. But the vast majority came out to show Marcus Garvey that they were with him heart and soul and that they appreciated his efforts to lift the Negro race to a higher standard.

The preparatory meeting was held Sunday afternoon, when Mr. Bayne presided. Miss Henrietta Vinton Davis, Mrs. Branch of Liberia,[1] Prof. W. H. Ferris and Hon. Marcus Garvey were the speakers. Mrs. Branch and Miss Waytes gave helpful and uplifting talks the preceding week. Miss Ida Ash had also been helpful during the week by her brilliant solos and recitations.

An interesting f[ea]ture of the Sunday afternoon meeting was the presentation by Miss Love to Miss Henrietta Vinton Davis, the International Organizer, of a beautiful bouquet of roses and chrysanthemums, amid great applause.

Promptly at 8:30 o'clock Mr. John G. Bayne sounded the gavel and called the meeting to order. Seated on the platform were Hon. Marcus Garvey, Miss Henrietta Vinton Davis, Miss Ida Ash, Capt. Justin Cockburn, Mr. Bayne, Mr. D. D. Shirley[2] and W. H. Ferris.

An interesting program was rendered, as follows:

Singing	From Greenland's Icy Mountains
Prayer	Read by Miss Amy Ashwood
Selection	The Black Star Line Band
Recitation	Mr. Sebastion
Solo—"Rose in the Bud"	Miss Ida Ash
Negro Folk Songs	Acme Quartette
Solo	Mrs. Louise Walker
Recitation	Mr. LaMotte[3]
Address	Mr. Ferris
Address	Miss Davis
Address	Mr. Marcus Garvey
Address	Mr. Newhall

PROF. W. H. FERRIS' ADDRESS

Prof. W. H. Ferris, M.A., author of "The African Abroad" and literary editor of The Negro World, was the first speaker called upon. Prof. Ferris stated that in his career he had been identified with many movements whose purpose was the lifting of the Negro race to a higher standard of civilization. He had been connected with the McKinley Club of New Haven, Conn., the State Sum[n]er League of Connecticut, the Afro-American Council,[4] the Boston Suffrage League[5] and the Niagara Movement.[6] But he had never in his experience as a journalist, preacher and lecturer witnessed the crowds and enthusiasm which were generated by the Universal Negro Improvement Association. The other movements aimed to lift the civil and political status of the American Negro. But the Universal Negro Improvement Association was attempting a colossal task. It was attempting to inspire the Negro peoples of the world with the spirit of progress. And it hoped to develop a Republic in Africa which would stand as an eternal testimony to the Negro's capacity for self-government. The Universal Negro Improvement Association also endeavored to help the sick and succor the oppressed. The other radical movements were wise in contending for the ballot. But they presented no constructive program to put bread in the mouths of the black races and to lift the economic status of the Negro in the Western Hemisphere. The nineteenth century saw the overthrow of the doctrine of the divine right of kings. The great problem of the twentieth century is the color line,[7] the rating of a man by his color rather than by his worth as a man. Prestige and standing in the commercial and economic worlds is a potent weapon with which to buck the color line.

MISS DAVIS' ADDRESS.

Miss Henrietta Vinton Davis, the International Organizer said: "I am very proud to see this crowd in Liberty Hall. It shows that you are keen in the present situation. We expected a fight in Chicago and we had ammunition. They had machine guns, but we had bombs. History repeats itself. The Hon. Marcus Garvey is the Solomon of the present day. Solomon was a black man. He had the wisdom of the world in his head. We have the reincarnation of King Solomon in Marcus Garvey. The fields of Africa, South America and the West Indies are being tilled, and the crops are being harvested to load the ships of the Black Star Line. With the help of the Negroes of America, with the help of the Negroes of the West Indies, with the help of the Negroes of Central America, with the help of the Negroes of South America, with the help of the Negroes of Africa, we will launch the Black Star Line.

"We are coming from the forests, we are coming from the plantations[,] we are coming from the high seas, 400,000,000 strong to answer the call of Marcus Garvey."

HON. MARCUS GARVEY'S ADDRESS.

Then Prof. W. H. Ferris introduced the Hon. Marcus Garvey as the race statesman, who had a vision, a goal, an objective and a constructive program. He was the Joshua, who would lead the Negro out of the wilderness of political and economic bondage to the Promised Land of liberty and economic opportunity. He said: "I now introduce the hero of the hour, the man of destiny of the Negro race, the Hon. Marcus Garvey." So great was the applause that it was five minutes before Mr. Garvey could speak. The audience gave him three cheers. It was a regular ovation.

Mr. Garvey said: "Everywhere I went in Chicago groups of people were reading the 'Negro World.' The 'Negro World' paved the way. Despite the heavy rain, great crowds assembled in the Eighth Regiment Armory. Mr. D. D. Shirley, the National Organizer, opened the meeting and introduced Attorney J. M. George, former chairman of the Advisory Board of the Montreal Division of the U.N.I.A., as the chairman of the meeting. He introduced Miss Henrietta Vinton Davis. She spoke three-quarters of an hour and introduced me. I spoke for an hour and answered the misrepresentations of the 'Chicago Defender.' We never discovered how weak the

'Chicago Defender' was in its own town until that Sunday afternoon meeting. It is the most unpopular paper in Chicago. Although the heavy rain dampened the ardor of the A.M.E. members, so that they did not go out to hear the conference appointments read out, it did not prevent the people from coming out in great numbers at night to hear about the Universal Negro Improvement Association.

"They say that everything is fair in love and war. I like to give a man a fair chance to fight. I do not like to strike a man in the back.

"Some of the most prominent men came upon the platform and took up the fight against the 'Chicago Defender' where I left off. The five hundred members in Chicago elected the editor of 'The Whip'[8] to whip the 'Chicago Defender.' We had bankers and publishers on the platform and men of all classes in the audience.

"The Negro people in Chicago are a progressive set. They are progressive in society, business and politics. Ninety per cent. of the business in Chicago is controlled by Negroes. They have three banks. Where the better class Negroes of Chicago reside is better than Riverside Drive, where the white people live. We have worked for the white man for 250 years and we are getting part of our wages back.

"Where killing is concerned, the Negroes never take the initiative. The Negroes did not start the riot in Chicago, but they finished it. The Negroes in Chicago declared State street to be the Hindenburg Line and as they smashed the Hindenburg Line in France they would hold the Hindenburg Line in Chicago. I told them in Chicago that I admired their spirit, the spirit of self-defense. We do not have time to waste with riots in New York. You have Negroes from all parts of the country and all parts of the world in New York. You have here the Mexican Negro, the Central American Negro and the South American Negro. Those Negroes do nothing but fight all the time. You have the Cuban Negro and you know what a guerilla warfare they waged. That is all I have to say.

"You have the West Indian Negro, and he is largely responsible for British holdings in Africa today. He didn't have any better sense than to give the Africans' land to the British. And then you have the Hell Fighters.[9] I advise our white friends, please let us live in peace. We are prepared to live in peace till judgment day.

"You have brought this movement to the stage where your success is next door. All that you have to do is to stick and stay."

Mr. Newhall, the president of the Boston Branch of the Universal Negro Improvement Association, was introduced and made appropriate remarks. The shelling of the Black Star Line by a Western sheet has not even caused the line to rock. The loyal supporters in New York, Philadelphia, Newport News, Central America, South America, the West Indies and Africa see in the launching of the first steamship the dawning of a new day, the ushering in of a new era for the Negro race. Never were the Harlem backers more hopeful and more determined to do their bit and go over the top.

Printed in *NW*, 11 October 1919. Original headlines omitted.

1. John E. Bruce praised Sarah Branch for her fund-raising ability in notes written for his "Bruce Grit" column: "Sister Sarah Branch is a fine type of African womanhood and is a good organizer an indefatigable worker an enthusiastic speaker and can get more money for the association in a drive than almost any other woman speaker on the list of speakers" (NN-Sc, JEB Papers).

2. Darby (or Derby) Disraeli Shirley in 1919 was chairman of the advisory boards of both the UNIA and the BSL. By January 1920 he was commander of the Universal African Legion as well as a partner of S. G. Kpakpa-Quartey, a Ghanaian merchant, in an enterprise called African International Traders (*NW*, 31 July 1920; DNA, RG 165, file 10218; AFRC, RG 163, registration card).

3. Louis La Mothe (b. 1893), born in Port-au-Prince, Haiti, was employed as an elevator operator in New York City in 1917. Because of his experience as a seaman, he was hired as purser on the *Yarmouth* after he joined the UNIA in 1919; he met Garvey through Cyril Henry. La Mothe was aboard the *Yarmouth* during its first two voyages, after which he was reassigned and became passenger traffic manager for the Black Star Line. After a month in charge of passenger ticket sales, he was sent to Cuba as a stock salesman for the BSL. Six months later he resigned and returned to New York (DJ-FBI, Bureau of Investigation's interview with Louis La Mothe, 6 March 1922; AFRC, RG 163, registration card).

4. The Afro-American Council was organized in 1898, after the Afro-American League, founded in 1890 by Timothy Thomas Fortune, had become defunct. Ferris was a recent graduate of Yale University when he attended the 1903 meeting of the council in Louisville, Ky., as part of the Boston delegation, which also included William Monroe Trotter and George W. Forbes. His alliance with the radical Boston contingent ended, however, with his break from Trotter in 1907 (Stephen R. Fox, *The Guardian of Boston*, pp. 46–47, 108–9; Emma Lou Thornborough, *T. Thomas Fortune: Militant Journalist* [Chicago: University of Chicago Press, 1972]).

5. The Boston Suffrage League was organized in 1903 by fifty black opponents of Booker T. Washington under the leadership of William Monroe Trotter. They especially wanted President Theodore Roosevelt to "dispense with" Washington as the primary black political spokesman. The league was formed in the aftermath of the Boston riot, when Trotter and his allies interrupted Washington's speech in Boston in 1903. Trotter and two of his associates were arrested and sentenced to jail terms (Fox, *The Guardian of Boston*, pp. 49–57).

6. The Niagara movement, founded in 1905 by a group of blacks led by W. E. B. Du Bois, first convened at Niagara Falls to demand equal rights for blacks and to oppose the accommodationist strategy of Booker T. Washington. William Ferris was identified with the radical Boston branch of the movement; when Du Bois and his allies moved to exclude the radicals in 1907, however, Ferris broke with the radicals, who were led by Trotter, and joined the mainstream of the movement (Charles Flint Kellogg, *NAACP* [Baltimore: Johns Hopkins University Press, 1967], pp. 23–24; Fox, *The Guardian of Boston*, pp. 108–9; W. E. B. Du Bois, "The Niagara Movement," in *The Autobiography of W. E. B. Du Bois* [New York: International Publishers, 1968], pp. 236–53).

7. Taken from W. E. B. Du Bois, *To the Nations of the World, Address of the Pan-African Conference* (London, 1900), in which he states: "The problem of the twentieth century is the problem of the color-line, the question as to how far differences of race—which show themselves chiefly in the color of the skin and the texture of the hair—will hereafter be made the basis of denying over half the world the right of sharing to their utmost ability the opportunities and privileges of modern civilization." Du Bois later repeated the first part of this statement in *The Souls of Black Folk* (Chicago: A. C. McClurg, 1903).

8. William C. Linton was the southern-born editor of the *Whip*. In June 1919 Linton, educated at Morris Brown College, Atlanta, and Syracuse University, Syracuse, N.Y., joined with Joseph D. Bibb and Arthur C. MacNeal, two lawyers recently graduated from Yale University, to establish the *Whip*. The *Whip* sought an audience among young blacks and

workers, stressing the need for black economic and political unity. Although it continued into the 1930s, the *Whip* was never a major competitor to Chicago's largest black newspaper, the *Defender* (*Whip*, 24 June 1919; Allan H. Spear, *Black Chicago* [Chicago: University of Chicago Press, 1967], p. 186).

9. A reference to the 369th Infantry Regiment, which arrived in France early in 1918 and began fighting in April. Serving with the French army, this black American regiment was the first unit of the Allied armies to reach the Rhine. The name Hell Fighters is thought to have been given to the group by the Germans, who faced them in battle for 191 days (Arthur E. Barbeau and Florette Henri, *The Unknown Soldiers: Black American Troops in World War I* [Philadelphia: Temple University Press, 1974], pp. 116–22).

Negro World Announcement

[11 October 1919]

WARNING!!!

TO OUR AGENTS, REPRESENTATIVES AND BRANCHES ALL OVER THE WORLD

You are hereby warned that several unscrupulous persons operating from New York, United States of America, have been trying to get in touch with you as their representatives and to reach the people of your respective communities for the purpose of exploitation. They realize that the Universal Negro Improvement Association stands out to protect the rights of all the people, hence they have been scattering false reports about the Association and the Black Star Line Steamship Corporation. You are requested to forward to our office any such misleading statements sent to or made to you by these unscrupulous persons, newspapers and periodicals, and we further beg to warn our agents and the people of West Africa to be careful in their dealings with a certain New York enterprise that is playing to the race loyalty of our people to get them to invest in selfish and personal enterprises. Yours truly.

UNIVERSAL NEGRO IMPROVEMENT ASSOCIATION OF THE WORLD
Head Office, 56 West 135th Street,
New York City, U. S. A.

Printed in *NW*, 11 October 1919.

NEGROES SHOULD PREPARE

THE NEGRO WORLD

A Newspaper Devoted to the Interests of the Negro Race Without the Hope of Profit as a Business Investment.

VOL. III. No. 8.   NEW YORK, SATURDAY, OCTOBER 11, 1919.   PRICE: THREE CENTS IN GREATER NEW YORK. FIVE CENTS ELSEWHERE.

BLACKMEN ALL OVER THE WORLD SHOULD PREPARE TO PROTECT THEMSELVES

Negroes Should Match Fire With Hell Fire

So Says Leader of Great Movement

Fellowmen of the Negro Race,

Greeting: Once more the white man has outraged American civilization and dragged the fair name of the Republic before the Court of Civilized Justice.

Another riot has visited the country and Omaha, Nebraska, has placed her name upon the map of mob violence, so it can be seen that the mob spirit is spreading all over, going from South to East, to mid-West and then to the West.

Mobs of white men all over the world will continue to lynch and burn Negroes so long as we remain divided among ourselves. The very moment all the Negroes of this and other countries start to stand together, that very time will see the white man standing in fear of the Negro race even as he stands in fear of the yellow race of Japan today.

The Negro must now organize all over the world, 400,000,000 strong, to administer to our oppressors their Waterloo.

No mercy, no respect, no justice will be shown the Negro until he forces all other men to respect him. There have been many riots in the United States and England recently, and immediately following the war of Democracy, there will be many more all over the world, to run a '

No African is going to allow the Caucasian to trample eternally upon his rights. We have allowed it for 500 years and we have now struck.

Fellowmen of the World, I here beg of you to prepare, for a great day is coming—the day of the war of the races, when Asia will lead out to defeat Europe and Europe and the white man will again call upon the Negro to save them as we have often done.

The New Negro has fought the last battle for the redemption of Africa, and he is now getting ready to fight for the redemption of Africa. With mob laws and lynching bees fresh in our memories, we shall turn a deaf ear to the white man when Asia administers to him his final "licking," and place and keep him where he belongs.

If the white men were wise, they would have treated Negroes differently, but to our astonishment they are playing the part of the dog by biting the hand that feeds. If it were not for the Negro, the white man would have been lost long ago. The black man has saved him and the only thanks we get today is mob law.

Let every Negro all over the world prepare for the new emancipation. The Fatherland, Africa, has been kept by God Almighty for the Negro to redeem, and we, young men and women of the Empire, have pledged ourselves to plant the flag of freedom and of

Our forces of industry, commerce, science, art, literature and war must be marshalled when Asia or Europe strikes the blow of a second world war. Black men shall die then and black women will succor our men, but in the end there shall be a crowning glory for the soldiers of Ethiopia on the African battlefield.

And now let me remind all of you, fellowmen, to do your duty to the Black Star Line Steamship Corporation, of 56 West 135th street, New York City, United States of America. This corporation is endeavoring to float a line of steamships to handle the Negro ships, between America,

The shares are now going at $5.00 each, and I now ask you to buy as many shares as you can and make money while the opportunity presents itself. You can buy from one to two hundred shares right now.

Send in today and buy 5, 10, 20, 40, 100 or 200 shares. Write to The Black Star Line Steamship Corporation, 56 West 135th Street, New York, N. Y., U. S. A.

With very best wishes,

Yours fraternally,
MARCUS GARVEY

Chicago, Ill.,
October 1st, 1919.

THE BLACK STAR STEAMSHIP LINE IS ATTRACTING ATTENTION IN THE WEST INDIES

Barbadian Writer Says It Shows the Value of Organization.

To the Editor,

Sir: Be good enough to allow me a little space in your valuable newspapers to make a few passing remarks to the thinking readers of Barbados.

This desire has been prompted by the reading of a telegram published in one of our daily newspapers concerning the launching of a Black Star steamship. The note states that the 14th of this month was taken as a red letter day in the history of the Negroes of America. What about Barbadian Negroes? Do we here in Barbados welcome the event as a red letter day in the history of our race? This event is sufficient evidence for us here of the value of organization. Organization is a strong wall and a tower not to be broken. The word organization is spelled in the homely adage we use almost every day, namely, united we stand, divided we fall. Think of the organization which such an enterprise as the launching of a steamship entails, my Barbadian Negro brethern, and learn to appreciate unity and organization more, so that we in Barbados may be able to stand by each other for our advancement. Organization is the solution of all our problems.

Thanking you, Mr. Editor,
Blackie, The Weekly Illustrated Paper, Barbados.

WEST INDIAN PAPER PROTESTS AGAINST ATTEMPT TO SUPPRESS THE NEGRO WORLD

We direct attention to an article appearing on page two of this impression with reference to legislation aimed at restricting the liberty of the press. The question which presents itself to one's mind is: What need is there for such drastic action as is contemplated by the governing authorities in British Guiana. We feel positive that the members of the Court of Policy will exercise more judgment than the authors of the iniquitous ordinance and will refuse to give it serious consideration. Are the minds of the Guianese being contaminated and through what source? We have an idea that the legislation is aimed at the "Negro Worl'." newspaper; but, we ask, is it wise to use a sledge hammer to destroy an ant? We do not mean to infer that the individual who set out to kill an ant with a sledge hammer would be regarded as a lunatic, and with respect to the tactics advocated by the wiseacres in Demerara we say they are outrageously absurd. The "Negro World" should be read and reread, and if the penalty for reading that paper were death, martyrs should be found ready and willing to be sacrificed in this good cause. In spite of our boasted civilization the man of today scarcely differs from his predecessor of a thousand years ago. The bigot of ancient days persecuted people for reading the Bible and the modern bigot would revive the inquisition, the star chamber, the pillory. People of British Guiana, members and non-members of the labor union, consult your own tastes and read all the literature which falls into your hands dealing with your race. Do not be dictated to as to what you should read and what you should not read by any Irish extremist. This advice is intended for West Indians also.—The Weekly Illustrated Paper, Barbados, B. W. I.

PROMINENT CITIZEN OF ST. THOMAS COMMENDS UNIVERSAL NEGRO IMPROVEMENT ASSOCIATION

The U. N. I. A. and the Declaration of Independence Champion the Same Principle: Democracy — The "Black Star Line" Is Upheld.

Editor, "Negro World."

Dear Mr. Editor:—We are at the beginning of an age in which it will be insisted that the same standard of conduct and of responsibility for wrong done shall be observed among the nations as by the individuals.

Individual neutrality is no longer desirable where the peace of our race is involved, and the freedom of our people, and the terror to that peace and freedom lies in the existence of what is called "national Sport." It must be a partnership of opinion like that of the Universal Negro Improvement Association.

We are glad now that we see the fact with our eyes in our more tense about them, so that our anxiety to become members of our race could be vanished, and instead of helping to promote its welfare would put in our claim with the 400,000,000 Negroes of the world. I take the opportunity then to recommend to my fellowmen of the race on this side of the continent the Universal Negro Improvement Association, whose principles are made up of "All men are counted equal."

I am a lover of human justice and the principles of the right of mankind, and since .... opened with in our race and the association of which Mr. .... very is president .... to me .... I am ....

No station or individual can do no less but home with the existing circumstances long enough to be careful to our demands. Read the declaration of the American Independence and see the principles laid down. Are they not justified by, and are they better than those .... by the Universal Negro Improvement Association. Should these principles be unhazardly maintained they would put the finishing touch to what America fought for—democracy. A method to uphold these principles is the buying of stocks in the Black Star Line. It will evolve the utmost practicable co-operation in counsel with the Negro communities of the world.

The period during which the patience your race has exercised, a patience never before exercised in the history of the world, is a period of unprecedented endurance. All kinds of societies have been formed, protesting against the many wrongs, but only to be met by newer means of destruction. Our object, then, is to vindicate the principles of our rights as against selfishness, and to set up amongst the 400 trodden-under-feet millions such a concert of purpose, and of action as will henceforth insure the strict observance of the principles given us since the foundation of the world.

Thanking you for space, I am, yours fraternally,
DAVE DAVIDSON,
Vice-President of St. Thomas Branch.
7 King St., St. Thomas, U. S. Virgin Islands.

A BARBADIAN WRITER ENDORSES THE BLACK STAR STEAMSHIP LINE

Organization Can Transform an Idle Dream Into a Reality.

"HURRAH FOR THE BLACK STAR LINE OF STEAMERS!

That this kind of craft could be owned and operated by Negroes some thought impossible. but determination, perseverance and organization have contributed in making a reality of what many considered an idle dream."—By the Strolling Scribbler in the Weekly Illustrated Paper, Barbadoes, B. W. I.

✦✦✦✦✦✦✦✦✦✦✦✦✦✦✦✦✦✦✦✦✦✦✦✦✦✦✦✦✦✦✦✦✦✦✦✦✦

HON. MARCUS GARVEY, World Famed Orator

Who Has Just Returned From a Triumphant Tour of the West, Will Speak for "The Black Star Line" at Huge Convention at

LIBERTY HALL (THE OLD METROPOLITAN BAPTIST CHURCH)

120 WEST 138th STREET, Between 7th and Lenox Avenues, New York

Subject: "The Manhood of the New Negro"   Sunday (Tomorrow), October 12th, at 3:40 and 8:30 Sharp
✦✦✦✦✦✦✦✦✦✦✦✦✦✦✦✦✦✦✦✦✦✦✦✦✦✦✦✦✦✦✦✦✦✦✦✦✦

J. Edgar Hoover to Special Agent Ridgely

WASHINGTON, D.C., October 11, 1919

MEMORANDUM FOR MR. RIDGELY.

I am transmitting herewith a communication which has come to my attention from the Panama Canal, Washington office, relative to the activities of MARCUS GARVEY. Garvey is a West-Indian negro and in addition to his activities in endeavoring to establish the Black Star Line Steamship Corporation he has also been particularly active among the radical elements in New York City in agitating the negro movement. Unfortunately, however, he has not as yet violated any federal law whereby he could be proceeded against on the grounds of being an undesirable alien, from the point of view of deportation. It occurs to me, however, from the attached clipping that there might be some proceeding against him for fraud in connection with his Black Star Line propaganda and for this reason I am transmitting the communication to you for your appropriate attention.

The following is a brief statement of Marcus Garvey and his activities:

Subject a native of the West Indies and one of the most prominent negro agitators in New York;

He is a founder of the Universal Negro Improvement Association and African Communities League;

He is the promulgator of the Black Star Line and is the managing editor of the Negro World;

He is an exceptionally fine orator, creating much excitement among the negroes through his steamship proposition;

In his paper the "Negro World" the Soviet Russian Rule is upheld and there is open advocation of Bolshevism. Respectfully,

J. E. HOOVER

[*Typewritten reference*] JEH-GPO

DNA, RG 60, file 198940. TMS, recipient's copy.

Bureau of Investigation Report

[*New York, ca. 14 October 1919*][1]

Marcus Garvey, n[eg]ro, was born in Jamaica, B[r.] West Indies.

Age 32 years. 5 ft. 7-1/2 in., 170 lbs., very dark complexion, clean shaven, marked round shoulder, small oriental eyes, very quick tempered.

From a boy in Jamaica he was never fond of work, was never known to have held a steady position, but was very fond of spending his time around barber and tailor shops, debating and dreaming big ideas as to how he could get money without working.

He worked for a short period in the Jamaica Government Printing office where he first caught the newspaper fever, and started to organize a negro association for the purpose of creating dissention among the black negroes and light complexioned ones. His bone of contention was that too much favors were shown to them by giving them most of the government positions.

About this time he fell in love with a colored girl, named Amy Ashwood, who helped him in all his get-rich-quick schemes. He rented halls and small country churches in the Island, and pulled off such things as Flower Day, Pledge Day, etc., charging an admittance fee. His headquarters was Kingston, Jamaica, where he started his color campaign in earnest, making capital of the fact that the dark or black negroes were antagonists to the light or mulatto[e]s. Of course, he made a few dollars by uniting the black ones in a small body and named it the Jamaica Improvement Association, where they met and discussed anti-White affairs.

However, on account of Garvey's determination of rule or ruin, autocracy, bulldozing, dictating and frequent outbursts of temper, his then small organization was always changing officers every few weeks. Then he and the girl Ashwood, his sweetheart, were to pull off concerts and entertainments for the benefit of certain charities, the report was that the money was never used for these purposes, which caused a great scandal. The leading daily newspaper, called the "Jamaica Gleaner" turned their guns against him.

Garvey then got in the habit of contracting numerous debts which he refused to pay. This kept him in a fuss all the time with people whom he was quite willing to insult and fight when asked to be paid.

On one occasion in the city of Kingston, Jamaica, he was locked up and fined for riding in a cab, after which he refused to pay the driver, and in addition assaulted the cab driver.

It is reported that on account of his checkered career, Garvey was compelled to quit Jamaica, leaving big scandal behind him. He then sailed for Port Limon, Central America, where he soon started his old tricks of living off his wits by using the color question.

There he started a two sheet weekly newspaper. However, it was not very long before he was arrested on an outbound steamer in Port Limon Harbor for debts he had contracted, and the report was that he had failed to give proper account of money he had collected.

During Garvey's wanderings, his sweetheart, Amy Ashwood, left Jamaica for Panama, where she lived for some time and during the war associated herself with various War Works, but especially anything where it was collecting money from the Public. Once she started a "Red Cross Fund" in Panama for the benefit of the West Indian soldiers, and so as to give it the color of official stamp, went so far as to obtain the permission and secure the presence of the British Consul to one of her functions. There were lots of scandals as regards what Ashwood did with the moneys collected.

Garvey landed in the U.S.A. about 1915,[2] visited New York, where he represented himself as "Marcus Garvey, Jr." of the Jamaica Improvement Association, Kingston, Jamaica, W.I.

He mixed in considerabl[y] among the West Indian negroes and especially those from Jamaica, and also posed as a staunch Catholic.[3] He stated that his object in America was to collect money under the auspices of the so-called Jamaica Association with which to build an industrial school in the Island, somewhat similar to the Booker T. Washington Tuskeg[e]e School. This so-called school was primarily for poor colored girls.

He stated that he intends to make a lecture tour over the country, then return Home.

First, Garvey got the sympathy of his own people, then posing as a Catholic, he introduced himself to Father Plunket,[4] the priest of St. Mark's Hall, 138th Street between Lenox and Fifth Avenue, in the heart of the negro settlement. He obtained the church hall, and started his lectures and begging and collecting funds for his mythical school, using the color question as his basis.

He visited Philadelphia, Boston, Baltimore, Chicago, also the South and West, lecturing to the church folks, telling them how the white men in his Island were ill-treating his women, and left them poverty stricken.

At all these places, of course, the preachers would give Garvey their church and school houses freely, and Garvey would take up a collection at every lecture.

After a few months tour, he returned to New York, hung around here and said nothing more about his school in Jamaica. Of course, when pressed, he would give as an excuse, that owing to the war, it was hard for him to obtain quick passage home, etc.

After a while, Garvey was next found holding a meeting in the Lafayette Hall, 131 St. and Seventh Ave. on Sunday afternoon, charging a 15 cents admittance fee. This was not well attended at first. Then Garvey started his association, calling it the "Negro Improvement Society and African Communities League."

Here he found out that to get a good following in New York among his race, it was necessary to be a Soap-box orator. So, after a while, he took up his stand on Lenox Avenue.

He told his hearers that all negroes must go back to Africa, drive the white people out, build up an empire, including a negro navy and army, etc., appoint Ambassadors, etc., and take away all the gold mines in Africa from the white men.

At first he was not taken seriously, but he kept everlastingly at it and finally succeeded in getting a few followers.

About this time it seems as if Garvey's resources were running low, so he posed as a Catholic, got some classy letter-heads printed, with cable address, etc., and started to send out hundreds of begging letters to Catholic priests, Bishops, and even to the then Arch-Bishop. He was appealing to them for money to help him on the imaginary Jamaica school proposition, turning their moneys to his own account.

He kept this up for nearly one year, then it seems as if Father Plunket got wise and returned to the donors several letters from Garvey in which moneys were enclosed; in fact Father Plunket said that Garvey was not a real Catholic, but was a real imposter, and at present he owes Father Plunket some money. Since this occurrence Garvey pulled off the crucifix he was wearing and in his street corner talks, denounced the Pope himself.

Garvey started to build up an organization. His chief mainstay and strength was preaching anti-white propaganda, denouncing all government as loony, as it was controlled by white people.

His next move was to tell his followers that it was his intention to build a very large school in New York in which he would train young negroes [in?] anti-white ideas, and send them to different parts of the world wherever large negro populations were to be found so as to quickly bring about a real negro empire in Africa. He gave them 'collections' and made all of them pledge to go about the streets and collect the necessary moneys. In short, Garvey got a large sum of money from this, and that's the last was ever heard about this great big school.

As is his custom, Garvey, when not allowed to have him his own way, changed his officers who dared to disagree with him or would get rid of any member who would be unwise enough as to ask some question about finances.

The next move of Garvey was to explain to his followers that to succeed quickly with his movement, it was necessary for him to have a newspaper, so he asked them to loan money to start the very first negro daily newspaper. However, after he had collected large sums, he explained to them that he only got enough money with which to start a weekly paper.

He called this paper "The Negro World" which is made up of clippings from various white dailies of injustices to the negro. Garvey would change the headlines, add inflammatory sentences, insert anti-white sub-headings and, in short, lead the negroes to believe that the white race is entirely against them. Above all, he led them to believe that all the news in "the Negro World" was all truth, and the white paper all lies.

They labored under the impression that Garvey had go[t] representatives all over the world who send him these anti-negro and anti-white news. So far, this paper has done more to put the negro against the white race than any other agency.

Garvey discouraged intelligent business men from becoming members of his organization, as they might question his actions, but he would willingly elect ignorant, illiterate men to offices who he could control. About this time he started to issuing bonds to his members (promissory notes) of $25.00 each, with which he promised to give them a Restaurant. He sold over

$2,000 worth, or in plain words, Garvey borrowed that amount of money from them. He rented 56 West 135th St., started a Restaurant and in less than two months the place was in a bankrupt state. However, Garvey kept it going by securing new loans at every Sunday Meeting.

Just about this time he told his followers that he meant to give them a new business every month in Harlem, and so would like to raise enough money with which to open a large grocery store. He again sold bonds of over $1,000, but the grocery failed to materialize.

A man named Tayler[5] tried to kill Garvey by shooting several days ago. Tayler was one of those members from whom Garvey had borrowed money with which to open this grocery store. Tayler, not seeing the grocery, asked repeatedly for his money. Garvey refused to give up, and after making insulting remarks, and empty promises, he and his other followers insisted on Tayler accepting shares in the "Black Star Line" for his money, but he refused, so after several rows, he shot at Garvey. Tayler was arrested but committed suicide in jail.

Last June, Garvey's restaurant and newspaper were bordering on bankruptcy and to keep them going, he still continued at his Sundays and Thursdays meetings to borrow from his members, who were fanatics and blind with his anti-white propaganda. Debts were piling up, bills were pouring in, collectors were busy and so far as is know[n], within the past few months, Garvey has had seven convictions for non-payment of wages.

Just about this time, Garvey rented a church, called a big mass meeting and there announced that the negro should have their own steamships, and he was going to build a line of steamers to trade between Africa and here, to be known as the "Black Star Line".

He first wanted $5,000,000 for this steamship line and would ask the negroes all over the world to contribute, alloting so much to each country.

This huge sum was to be raised by donations o[r] popular subscription, all moneys coming to Garvey, and when he has collected enough, then he would buy five (5) ships, which should sail October 31, 1919.

He started mass meetings, gave out envelopes for subscription. The first Sunday night he collected nearly $400.00.

Around this time Amy Ashwood arrived from Panama and joined Garvey, her sweetheart, and up until now is his confidential "General Lady Secretary" travelling up and down the country with him.

While Garvey was in the height of raising money for a $5,000,000. steamship by free-will offering, on the complaint of four of his members, named: Rob[i]nson, Mitchell, Johnson and Cox, Assistant District Attorney, Edwin P. Kilroe, summoned Garvey with his books for an investigation.

This investigation by the District Attorney angered both Garvey and his sweetheart who spoke very insolently and disrespectfully, saying Mr. Kilroe had no right to summon them. This first episode ended by Garvey being warned to discontinue collecting money from the Public for this steamship line, or else he would put him in jail. The Sunday night after, Garvey at his meeting, made an attempt to raise a collection, but the District Attorney detectives, also policemen, blocked his game.

So as to spur his followers on to putting up more money, he preached to them at his meetings that the white men were afraid of them, and that's why Mr. Kilroe is worrying him. He urged them to put up more and buy a ship.

During all this time, his paper, "The Negro World" was abusing and criticizing the District Attorney's office. The District Attorney called him to his office again for investigation, and warned him at least three or four times. Garvey, now seeing that he was up against it, incorporated in the state of Delaware for $500,000 at $5.00 per share instead, and left immediately for Newport News and Norfolk, Va.

He sold out nearly a whole stock certificate book, sent back some of the money, to liquidate other debts in New York.

However, Garvey returned to New York with the same lame excuse, that the stock certificate was lost with the names and record of the people who bought stocks in Norfolk and Newport News and up until this, those names have never been found.

In other words, Garvey could not tell who bought the stock in the South, and how much was paid to him.

Again he was called down to the District Attorney's office and told to find the book.

Garvey has not bought a ship as yet [but?] this is what he has done to attract capital. The ship propagan[da] [ha]s been setting his followers wild. He told them that the ship is [to] have negro captain, mate and crew. Cost of freight and passengers [is] to be at least one-third of what the white steam-ship company is ch[arg]ing.

Of course, this has got them crazy, [esp]ecially the West Indians, who are at least three-quarter of his mem[ber]s.

To deceive his following and at the [sam]e time trying to avoid getting into the clutches of the law, on the [31]st of October, when he promised them a ship, Garvey, a few weeks [ag]o, paid a sum of $16,000 on an old 1300-ton ship called the "Yarmo[uth]" from the North American Company, arranging to purchase the ship f[or] $165,000, agreeing to pay $83,000 on or before October 31st, so as [to] get possession of her, then pay about $3,000 per month till end of pa[yme]nt.

Garvey is now waging a vigorous camp[aig]n so as to meet this amount. A few Sundays ago he made arrangements wi[th] the ship owner that, in view of the coming purchase, to allow his foll[owe]rs to inspect the ship between 9 a.m. and 5 p.m. Garvey seized up[on] the opportunity to tell his followers that he had bought the ship al[read]y, and this would be the first ship of the "Black Star Line". Th[ousa]nds went over the North River to view the ship after which Garvey [s]old thousands of dollars worth of stock, as they are still laboring under the false impression that they own one ship already.

Some poor colored people have inv[est]ed their entire life's savings in this Garvey's "Black Star Line" sch[eme.] Some have sold their property, and still others are neglecting their homes to buy stocks with him.

(1)   Two weeks ago Garvey was arrested in Chicago for violating the Blue Sky Law, selling stock [w]itho[ut] a license, fined about $150.00 and made to return the money to the poor fools.

(2)   About a month and a half [ago] he was arrested for criminally libeling the District Attorney.

(3)   Two weeks after he was arrested on a grand jury indictment for criminal libel on three c[o]unt[s].

The following cases are against him:

(1)   Criminal Libel against Dist. Atty.

(2)   Three counts of grand jury criminal libel.

(3)   "The Chicago Defender" agent suing for libel.

(4)   Edgar Gray, his As[st]. ex-Secretary—suit $20,000 Libel.

(5)   R. G. Warren, ex-[Sec]retary—$20,000 Libel.

In addition, for the [pa]st four weeks, the Grand Jury has got all of the Books of "Black Sta[r] Line" which they are investigating, pending indictment. Moreover, a Dist. Atty. told Garvey openly that he [w]ill be sending him to jail for fraud, then deport him. He is to appear again before the Grand Jury some time this week for indictment. Garvey appeals to the rac[ial] feelings of his people, then with the [po]or fools. . . .[6]

DNA, RG 65, file OG 185161. TD.

1. This undated document has been assigned a date of ca. 14 October 1919, since the report was written a few days after the 14 October 1919 assassination attempt on Garvey. From the context of the report, it is clear the author was stationed in New York City.
2. Garvey arrived in the United States on 24 March 1916.
3. Although it is not known exactly when Garvey became a Roman Catholic (he was baptized in the Church of England), he was married in a Catholic ceremony to Amy Ashwood in their public Liberty Hall wedding of 25 December 1919 (Amy Ashwood Garvey, "Portrait of a Liberator," [unpublished MS], chap. 6, p. 19, and chap. 7, p. 2a). Garvey also received the Catholic church's last rites before his death in 1940 (Robert A. Hill, interview with Amy Jacques Garvey, 1973; Amy Jacques Garvey, *Garvey and Garveyism*, p. 261).
4. Rev. Christopher J. Plunkett (1867–1939), born in Dublin, served as pastor of Harlem's first Catholic parish, the Church of St. Mark the Evangelist, on Lenox Avenue and 138th Street. Educated in Ireland and France, where he was ordained in the Holy Ghost Fathers in 1893, Plunkett served as rector of the Church of St. Peter Claver in South Philadelphia from 1894 until his transfer to Harlem in 1912. As pastor of St. Mark's, he reportedly converted four thousand persons to Catholicism. After nineteen years in New York, he undertook missionary work in Arecibo, Puerto Rico, and in 1933 he was appointed provincial for the Holy Ghost Fathers order in the United States (*NYT*, 18 August 1939; Holy Ghost Fathers Archives, 1923).

5. Garvey's assailant was George Tyler (1880?–1919), who was born in Richmond County, Virginia. Tyler moved to New York sometime between 1917 and 1919; during this period he sold copies of the *Negro World* in Harlem. Running from the UNIA's office after shooting Garvey, Tyler was apprehended by the police and detained in the Harlem prison. The following morning, Tyler was taken to the first floor of the prison, shaved, and permitted to prepare for his arraignment hearing in the Washington Heights court on charges of felonious assault. As he returned to his third-floor cell to retrieve his clothing, he abruptly turned, leaped over the railing, and fractured his skull, an injury that proved fatal (*Philadelphia Tribune*, 18 October 1919; *NYT*, 17 October 1919; death certificate, Bureau of Vital Records, Department of Health of the City of New York; AFRC, RG 163, registration card; DNA, RG 65, file OG 329359).

6. Since this report ends rather abruptly, it has been assumed that pages are missing.

R. P. Stewart, Assistant Attorney General, to William B. Wilson, Secretary of Labor

[*Washington, D.C.*] October 15, 1919

Sir:

Referring to your letter of August 16th (54735-36), I have the honor to transmit herewith a copy of a letter, and its original enclosures, received from Mr. A. L. Flint, of Panama, relative to the operations of Marcus Garvey, said to be an alien.

In the event your Department determines that there is no action it can take looking to the deportation to Garvey, it is suggested that you refer all the papers to the Postmaster General in order that an investigation may be conducted for the purpose of determining whether Garvey has been guilty of using the mails in furtherance of a scheme to defraud. Respectfully, For the Attorney General,

(Signed) R. P. STEWART
Assistant Attorney General

Enclosure No. 8163.
[*Typewritten references*] WCH-ECT RPS-

DNA, RG 60, file 198940-4. TL, carbon copy.

Maj. H. A. Strauss to Director, Military Intelligence Division

New York City Oct. 15th, 1919

. . . Subject: Marcus Garvey.

1. In the New York Times of October 15th, 1919, is an article regarding the above subject, who is the Editor of the Negro World. It states that Garvey was shot and seriously wounded while at work in his office on

October 14th, 1919. He was taken to the Harlem Hospital suffering from three bullet wounds. The shooting, according to the police, occurred during a controversy between Garvey and George Tyler of 156 West 131st Street. The police say that Tyler had been affiliated with Garvey in his newspaper work and other projects. Tyler has been arrested on a charge of felonious assault.

H. A. STRAUSS,
Major, U.S.A.
By: W. L. MOFFAT, JR.,
Captain, U.S.A.

WLM:w
Copy to DIO, Chicago.
[*Endorsements*] CAPTAIN SNOW MI-4
A. C. DUNNE

DNA, RG 165, file 10218-373. TLS, recipient's copy. Stamped endorsements.

Bureau of Investigation Report

New York City Oct. 17–[19]19

IN RE *Marcus Garvey* Negro Radical Leader.

Information was received at this office today [*14 October*] to the effect that Marcu/s/ Garvey, editor of the "Negro World", was shot and badly wounded during the afternoon by one George Tyler, a negro clerk, who claims that Garvey owes him considerable money.

Garvey is now in the Harlem Hospital, and his assailant has been held without bail at the West 135th Street Station. It is my intention to have an agent interview Tyler in the course of a few days, inasmuch as it is believed that Tyler is in possession of considerable information regarding the activities of the man he assaulted.

C. J. SCULLY

[*Endorsements*] FILE J. E. H. Noted F. D. W.

DNA, RG 65, file OG 329359. TD. Stamped endorsements.

Memorandum of Agreement

[*New York*] 20th day of October, 1919

MEMORANDUM OF AGREEMENT made and executed this 20th day of October, 1919, by and between North America Steamship Corporation, Ltd., a corporation organized and existing under the laws of the Dominion of

Canada, having an office at Halifax, Nova Scotia (hereinafter called "the Vendor"), and Black Star Line, Inc., a corporation organized and existing under the laws of the State of Delaware, having an office at 56 West 135th Street, New York City (hereinafter called "the Purchaser"),

WITNESSETH: That

WHEREAS, an agreement was entered into between the parties hereto on the 17th day of September, 1919, for the sale by the Vendor and the purchase by the Purchaser, of the Canadian Steamship Yarmouth, registered at Yarmouth, Nova Scotia, owned by North America Steamship Corporation, Ltd. And

WHEREAS, the parties hereto desire to modify the terms of said agreement[1] as hereinafter set forth,

NOW THEREFORE, in consideration of the mutual promises herein contained, and of the sum of One Dollar by each of the parties hereto to the other in hand paid, receipt of which is hereby mutually acknowledged, it is agreed between the parties hereto as follows:

FIRST: The purchase price for said Steamship Yarmouth shall be One hundred and sixty-eight thousand five hundred dollars ($168,500) in United States currency, instead of the sum of One hundred and sixty-five thousand dollars ($165,000), as provided for in said agreement of September 17, 1919, of which said purchase price the purchaser has heretofore paid the sum of Sixteen thousand five hundred dollars ($16,500), and the balance of said purchase price shall be paid by the purchaser to the vendor at the office of Harriss, Magill & Co., Inc., 50 Broad Street, New York City, as follows:

$3,500 in cash on the execution of this agreement receipt whereof is hereby acknowledged.

[$]50,000 cash upon delivery by the vendor to the purchaser at the office of Harriss, Magill & Co., Inc., 50 Broad Street, New York City, of the bill of sale and certificates hereinbefore referred to and delivery of the Steamship Yarmouth as hereinbefore referred to.

The balance of the purchase price, to wit,

$98,500 shall be paid by the purchaser to the vendor in ten (10) equal monthly instalments of $9,850 each, commencing thirty (30) days after the payment of the $50,000 above mentioned. The said instalment payments shall bear interest at the rate of 6% per annum, and the indebtedness therefor shall be evidenced by ten (10) promissory notes each in the sum of $9,850, with interest at 6% from the date of delivery of the bill of sale. The said promissory notes shall be secured by a mortgage on the said Steamship Yarmouth on the usual Custom House form, which shall be executed by the purchaser and delivered to the vendor

concurrently with the delivery by the vendor to the purchaser of the said vessel and its equipment and the said bill
of sale and certificates above referred to. The said notes
shall be executed by the purchaser in favor of Harriss,
Magill & Co., Inc., as payee, and the said mortgage shall
be executed by the purchaser in favor of Harriss, Magill &
Co., Inc., as mortgagee.

It is further understood and agreed that in case of default
by the purchaser in the payment of any of the said notes
and the same remaining unpaid for five days, all of the said
notes remaining unpaid at such time shall immediately
become due and payable with interest.

SECOND: Except as hereinbefore modified all the terms, covenants and
conditions in said agreement of September 17th, 1919, shall continue and be
in full force and effect in the same manner as if the same were herein
specifically and at length set forth, except that the insurance shall be increased
to $100,000.00 from $75,000.00, and that the figures in paragraph[s] Seven
and Eighth shall be changed from $65,000 & $83,500 to $98,500, and $16,500
shall be changed to $20,000, and the figures in paragraph Ninth from
$16,500 shall be changed to $20,000, and in paragraph Tenth the figure shall
be changed from $16,500 to $20,000.

IN WITNESS WHEREOF, the parties hereto have caused this instrument
to be executed by their respective officers thereunto duly authorized in their
behalf, and their respective seals to be hereto affixed, the day and year first
above written.

> NORTH AMERICA STEAMSHIP
> CORPORATION, LIMITED
> By W. L. HARRISS.

Witness:
  LEO H. HEALY.
BLACK STAR LINE, INC.,
(Seal)

> By MARCUS GARVEY,
> President.

Witness:
  E. D. SMITH-GREEN.
(Seal)

Printed in *Garvey* v. *United States*, no. 8317, Ct. App., 2d Cir., 2 February 1925,
government exhibit no. 10.

1. The Black Star Line was allowed to lease the S.S. *Yarmouth* prior to the registration of
the bill of sale and the legal transfer of the ship.

British Military Intelligence Report

[*New York*] October 20, 1919

NEGRO AGITATION

. . . Universal Negro Improvement Association.

The following letter written by Marcus Garvey under date of Oct. 14th, just five minutes before being shot, was published in the "Negro World["] of Oct. 18th:

"I write to you this week to advise that the Universal Negro Improvement Ass'n is depending on each and every one of you to do your best by the Black Star Line S.S. Corporation . . . between this date . . . and the 30th instant."

["]You will remember that this Association has promised to launch the S.S. Frederick Douglas' on the morning of the 31st of Oct[.] for the Black Star Line . . ."

"The declaration of the New Negro has been made. He is determined to pave a way for himself in the great fields of commerce and industry. He has made up his mind to take hold of the political machinery and blast a way to political independence . . . The 31st day of October will settle once for all the manhood of the New Negro. As President General of the Universal Negro Improvement Ass'n, I have to comply with my duty in beseeching every man and woman of the race to be loyal to the colors of the Red, Black and Green. Men and women of scattered Eth[i]opia, let me implore you to do your duty by the Black Star Line by buying your shares today . . ."

"It is but right that the Negro should strike out independently so as to insure his economic future. The Black Star Line affords a grand opportunity to every Negro to insure himself against misfortune. There is a world to be conquered for the Negro . . . The Negro must become a builder. He must become the architect of his own fate and, realizing that, the New Negro needs to be serious in his endeavors."

"To you, fellowmen and women in the City of New York and the State of New Jersey, I hereby beg to inform you that on Thursday night, the 30th inst[an]t, at 8 o'clock, the Universal Negro Improvement Ass'n will stage a gigantic mass meeting in Madison Square Gardens . . in the interest of the Black Star Line. This meeting will be the climax . . . the campaign of two and one-half months in the interest of the Black Star Line S.S. Corporation . . ."

["]Following the meeting on the night of the 30th, on the [m]orning of the 31st, the S.S. "Frederick Douglas["] will be loosed from her mooring and bid adieu in her first voyage across the Atlantic . . ."

At a meeting of the Universal Negro Improvement Association held in Liberty Hall on the evening of October 12th, Mr. J.S. Taylor, president of the Newport News Branch, contributed $10,000 for the Black Star Line from his division.

Mr. Garvey electrified the audience when he said that the climax of the movement would be reached on Oct. 30th, when a mammoth mass meeting would be held in Madison Square Garden:

"Already the people in Jamaica are preparing a cargo for the first ship of the Black Star Line . . . The policy of this Association is that the Negro must have a country and government of his own.["]

This meeting will be a celebration of the launchi[n]g of the S.S. "Frederic/k/ Douglas, the first ship of the Black Star Line Steamship Corporation,["] according to the "Negro World." It is reported that orators of internati/onal/ reputation will speak on this occasion.

In spite of being confined in Harlem Hospital, Marcus Garvey, through the "Negro World" of Oct. 18th, issued a call to the people of Philadelphia for a series of mass [*deletion illegible*] meetings to be held Oct. 19, 20, and 21[;] to the people of Newport News for Oct. 24, 25 and 26, and to the people of Portsmouth, Va. for Oct. 20, all in the interest of the Black Star Line. The "Negro World" stated that it was expected Mr. Garv[e]y would be well enough to address these meetings.

In a previous report reference was made to a letter written by Marcus Garvey from Chicago, under date of Oct. 1st, published in the "Negro World" of Oct. 11th. We now learn that the Japanese Commercial Weekly are sending this letter of Garvey's to the Japanese press, and that Mr. Komuri of this publication is reported to have said that Garvey's statement about the ["]day of the war of the races" was good [a]gitation [*deletion illegible*] for Japan["]. . . .[1]

In this connection, it is interesting to note the attached hand-bill advertising an opening drive for the Black Star Steamship Corporation, Wednesday, Oct. 22nd, bearing the following headline:

["]COME AND HEAR THE JAPANESE REPRESENTATIVE
SPEAK ON THE BLACK STAR LINE."

It is reported that the Japanese are working to sell a 4,000-ton ship to Garvey.

Hubert Harrison and the "New Negro".[2]

. . . Robert [*Hubert*] Har[r]ison spoke at Rush Memorial Church, Sunday afternoon, Oct. 19th on the subject of the Black Star Line. He said, among other things, that nations and people never rose to power without ships; that by means of ships they could carry passengers and men to other countries, that they could be passed th[ro]ugh as working men; that they could get their literature through; that the promotion of the Black Star Line was not for its present value but for its future value;—

Sunday evening (Oct. 19th) he spoke at Lafayette Hotel, on the subject of the "Back to Africa Movement." He said that the negroes should centralize like the Irish and other nations in one place which is practically their fatherland, that Africa was their fatherland. That if they kept together they could create a power in Africa, centralizing their forces with those of Egypt, Abyssinia, Liberia and other countries. . . .[3]

DNA, RG 65, file OG 3057. TD, carbon copy. Enclosure to a letter from George F. Lamb to Frank Burke, 31 October 1919 (DNA, RG 65, file OG 3057). This letter referred to the report as having been furnished "by Colonel Thwaites of British Military Intelligence." Copies of this report are also found in DNA, RG 165, file 10218-364-12. Except otherwise noted, ellipsis marks in the document appear in the original.

1. Two paragraphs of Garvey's editorial letter of 1 October 1919 were quoted.
2. The beginning of this section noted the reappearance of the *New Negro*. Its editors, Hubert Harrison and August Valentine Bernier, proclaimed it "an organ of the international consciousness of the darker races, especially of the negro race." The report also quoted a lengthy section from an article in the October 1919 issue, "Two Negro Radicalisms."
3. The omitted material described the Abyssinian crown prince's mission to the United States.

Speech by Marcus Garvey

[[Philadelphia, Pa. Oct. 20, *1919*]]

Mr. President, Lady President, Officers, Members and Friends of the Universal Negro Improvement Association of Philadelphia, Pa.:

It is indeed a pleasure for me to be out with you here this morning. This is my first public appearance since last Tuesday. (Cheers.) My people in New York did not want me to leave bed, but I really wanted to see the good and faithful members of the Philadelphia Branch of the Universal Negro Improvement Association. (Applause.)

I am not going to make much of a speech this morning, in that I intend to speak to you at some length this afternoon.

I suppose the white newspapers of this city and the Negro newspapers have conveyed to you the old-time impression, the wrong impression of the truth. I was shot in the office of the Association last Tuesday, some time after eleven o'clock. The papers said the man shot me because I owed him $25. Now, I am here in Philadelphia to say to you and to the world that at no time in my life have I ever borrowed ten dollars from any man.

It happened that the man was a member of the Universal Negro Improvement Association in New York. He was one of those bad members that the others had to expel. It would appear that some time early this year the officers of the Association decided to open a restaurant, and bonds were issued in the name of the Association at $25 each. It would appear that some of our enemies got hold of this man and tried to make capital out of him.

You will realize that the paper known as the "Chicago Defender," after having libelled myself and the Black Star Line, is now facing action of $800,000. You will also realize, as in New York City, the Universal Negro Improvement Association is not only the strongest Negro m[o]vement, but it is the strongest movement in the city and State of New York. There is no white or Negro organization in New York as strong as the Universal Negro Improvement Association. We have been able to overthrow the political gangsters in New York City. Recently we had a fight with some white people there so as to make the Black Star Line a [pos]sibility. They told us we could not launch any steamships[,] we told them we will, and despite all they said we demonstrated that the New Negro meant what he said.

There are the "Chicago Defender," a paper that is facing an action of $800,000, the politicians living in our neighborhood whom we have defeated, and the white men who lined up against the Black Star Line, whom we have defeated. So, if you can reason the matter out, you will find out the cause of my having been shot last Tuesday. They knew well I did not borrow any money from that man, but they said that so as to prejudice the minds of the people. That is the impression they try to give you so as to defeat the objects for which we have organized ourselves; but, thank God, I am very much alive (cheers) and the man whom they sent to do the job, he is no more. (Cheers.) I, personally, never touched him because I was at a particular distance from him, but they who employed him know now that he is dead.

So that you will understand the situation, this afternoon I will tell you more of the affair, and I will talk to you about things pertaining to the Universal Negro Improvement Association and the Black Star Line. But let me say, they have sent up the stocks in sales 2,000 per cent., because twenty-four hours after the man shot me cable messages were sent from all parts of the West Indies and from Central America, pledging their further determination to launch the Black Star Line and to stand by the Universal Negro Improvement Association and African Communities' League. (Cheers.) The last two telegrams received—one last night which reached us from the Panama Branch of thirteen thousand Negroes, and the other was from the Toronto, Canada, Branch of the Universal Negro Improvement Association. Thus you will realize that they have not done us one bit of harm. They have caused me to remain in bed when I never expected that, but they have done more for us than I could have done for the movement in four days.

As I have said before, they are welcome to my life at any time if that life can be given to the advancement of this movement. The assassin shot me in the head, but it just grazed by; he shot two in the right leg and one in the left leg. But if the shots caused the organization to advance 2,000 per cent., then I am satisfied to die, because that will be the complete success of our race.

Whilst they were trying to persecute me in Chicago, the people in my own native home town captured that city that day and beat up every white man they saw.[1] They had to close their businesses down and run away. So you will realize that the Universal Negro Improvement Association is sweeping the world. Last night one of our African members in New York, a prominent African, came to me and said he had just got news from Sierra Leone that a few weeks ago the natives cleaned out every white man they found in Sierra Leone.[2] (Cheers.) The "Negro World" has done the job. And I want you to do your job today by buying as many shares as you can afford in the Black Star Line, because the white man is a strategist; he is not asleep. When he sees the action of the Negroes in the West Indies, when he sees the action of the Negroes in Africa, he is going to make an attempt to cut off communication. That will be the time for you to open up communication for yourselves, and the best way of opening up communication will be through the Black Star Line, because four hundred millions of us have declared that we are going to float it even if we have to float it in an ocean of human blood. Because we realize the seriousness of the age in which we live—a very serious age—and I want you to treat it thus. Do your very best during the campaign that we are going to wage which will extend from today . . . [*words mutilated*] shares in the Black Star Line. Remember that you are not losing your money, you are not giving away your money; you will be investing your money to bring returns to you in the future. There can absolutely be no failure in the Black Star Line because the money that the officers take from you and issue you a certificate for, that money goes to purchase the ships of the Black Star Line.

The first ship will be under our control on the 31st of this month. It will cost you $165,000 and it will be insured for $200,000 before it sails. Therefore, if the ship goes down you will be $35,000 to the good. But the ship will not go down because we will be having one of the best maritime captains to steer the good ship along. So that I want you to do your very best. The climax of our campaign, as announced through the "Negro World," will be reached Thursday night, the 30th of this month, when the New York Division of the Association will stage in the Madison Square Garden a monster mass meeting. The Madison Square Garden is the biggest public hall in the world. It seats between fifteen and twenty thousand people at one time. It will be the first time in the history of the Negro of this country that he will meet fifteen thousand strong in such a public hall.

Those are the accomplishments that are worrying the white people of New York. They ask, "How far are these Negroes going?" We have gone from Liberty Hall into their exclusive Carnegie Hall, and now we have left

Carnegie Hall for the biggest public hall in the world. The white man is prejudiced. But how did the black man get there? Because of the black man's money. Therefore, you will realize this one thing: The thing that counts in this world is money, it is material wealth. Today we are determined to get our portion of the material wealth in this world, and when we get it to the extent that we want it, we know there will be no more color line.

The white man has got his portion of the material wealth of the world. He has his millions, but he protects it with his gun. If he is threatened with the loss of his possessions he calls out his army and his navy to protect it. We have to get our portion of the material wealth of this world, but we must also be able to protect it so that we can keep that wealth. That is why the Universal Negro Improvement Association does not stop at the Negro accumulating money, but we realize the necessity of protecting that accumulation, and we can ony protect it when we have behind us a strong government (cheers) so that when the individual, when the race, or when the nation infringes upon the rights of the Negro, the Negro can call upon the strength of his government to protect him.

So in closing this morning I want you to realize that we have still a big job to accomplish. We can only do so through the united effort of each and every one of us. You can do your share today by the Black Star Line by investing as much as you possibly can.

Invest in the Black Star Line Corporation so as to bring returns in material wealth which you so much desire.

Mr. Garvey also spoke last night to thousands in the same church. Fully five thousand people were unable to gain admission to the building. He speaks tonight and tomorrow night, after which he leaves for another section of the country. The meetings will be continued by the International Organizer, Miss Henrietta Vinton Davis, assisted by the other local officers, until the 29th instant.

Printed in *NW*, 25 October 1919.

1. A reference to the riot that occurred 9 October 1919 in Kingston, Jamaica. The riot began when police put down a disturbance involving discharged seamen of the S.S. *Orca*, one of the ships that transported West Indian soldiers and civilians back to the West Indies from Liverpool and Cardiff after race riots had occurred there. During the transatlantic trip between 10 and 23 September, the sailors first registered their protest aboard the vessel. Five sailors were arrested for mutiny, but poor jail facilities on board and continual attempts by black sailors and civilians to release the arrested men created an unrelieved state of crisis throughout the trip. After two weeks of sporadic violence in Kingston, on 9 October the rioters forced the Immigration Office to close while police reinforcements were summoned. In his report to the colonial secretary, the deputy inspector general of police said that the black seamen had "attacked some white seamen and knocked them about badly" and justified his use of large numbers of police. When rioting ended, fifteen persons had been arrested for rioting and fourteen for looting (A. R. Gilbert to H. Bryan, 29 September 1919, and B. Toole to Viscount Milner, 9 October 1919, PRO, CO 318/349).

2. This was a reference to disturbances in Sierra Leone beginning in July 1919, which were caused by postwar economic discontent among government workers, merchants, and laborers. The first incident was a strike called on 14 July by the technical staff and laborers in public works and railroads demanding war bonuses similar to those given to clerical workers. A march was later organized by a group of young mercantile clerks in Freetown, which ended in

widespread rioting beginning on 18 July and continuing for over a month, taking the form of attacks on the shops and homes of Syrian merchants. Indignation over the racial disturbances in Cardiff and Liverpool also affected the racial climate in Sierra Leone, where an increasing race consciousness was manifested among blacks. Anti-Syrian rioting spread beyond Freetown into other areas, continuing for several months, so that between July and October troops from the Gold Coast were sent into Sierra Leone to help control the disturbances. Attacks against English merchants, however, seem to have been uncommon during this period (J. Ayodele Langley, *Pan-Africanism and Nationalism in West Africa, 1900–1945* [London: Oxford University Press, 1973], pp. 205–14).

Bureau of Investigation Report

New York City Oct. 21–[*19*]19

IN RE MARCUS GARVEY Negro Radical Leader.

On October 14th the New York newspapers carried an account of the shooting of Marcus Garvey by George Tyler, the account stating that the shooting had been caused by a debt owed by Garvey to Tyler. Believing, however, that there was something more to the affair, Agent Scully instructed me to interview Tyler to ascertain what information he had regarding Garvey's connections and activities. The following day, however, the newspapers contained an account of Tyler's death in the Harlem Jail, stating that Tyler had leaped from a cell to the ground, being killed instantly. Conclusion.

M. J. DAVIS

[*Endorsement*] Noted F. D. W.

DNA, RG 65, file OG 329359. TD. Stamped endorsement.

Speech by Marcus Garvey

[[Philadelphia, Pa., Oct. 21, 1919]]

HON. MARCUS GARVEY, FOREMOST ORATOR OF THE RACE, DELIVERS BRILLIANT SPEECH IN PHILADELPHIA

BIG SUCCESS FOR UNIVERSAL NEGRO IMPROVEMENT ASSOCIATION

. . . Last night the People's Church, corner of Fifteenth and Christian street, was the scene of wild enthusiasm, when the Honorable Marcus Garvey, president-general of the Universal Negro Improvement Association and president of the Black Star Line Steamship Corporation, appeared to speak. Mr. Garvey opened a campaign here last Sunday which opening was very successful. Thousands jammed the church, and thousands were turned away unable to get admittance.

... MR. GARVEY'S SPEECH.

Mr. President, Lady President, Ladies and Gentlemen: Once more it is my pleasure to be with you. That you have turned out in such large numbers tonight proves beyond the shadow of a doubt that you good people of the race in Philadelphia are very much alive to the principles, to the aims, to the objects of the greatest movement among Negroes in the world today—the Universal Negro Improvement Association and African Communities League. It is the greatest movement in the world, because it is the only movement today that is causing the white man to tremble in his shoes. (Cheers.) The white man has had the policies of our great men or the great leaders of the past. They have had the policies of Booker Washington, they have had the policies of the other great leaders of this country, of the West Indies and of Africa, but out of these policies nothing ever came to the Negro, and the white man was satisfied. They have buried our great leader in America, Booker Washington, and yet we have achieved nothing by way of our own initiative. They have buried the great leaders of the Negro race of other countries, and yet we have achieved nothing, except in the Republic of Haiti, where one Negro repelled them and established an independent republic. I speak of Haiti. They did not like Toussaint L'O[u]verture because he had initiative. They lied to him, they deceived him, and when he had just a little faith still in them they destroyed that faith. They made a prisoner of him, took him to France, and there he died. Thank God, as Toussaint L'Ouverture in his time was able to inspire the other men of his country to carry on the work until Haiti was made a free country, so today we have inspired not one, not two, but hundreds of thousands to carry out the work even if they imprison one or kill one.

It is for me to say to you faithful members and followers of the Universal Negro Improvement Association in Philadelphia that the movement that you are in is a movement that is causing not merely the individual white man, but governments to be living in fear as touching the outcome of the Negro peoples of the world through their determination in the Universal Negro Improvement Association.

THOUSANDS JAMMED HALL.

Last night, after I was through addressing my people in New York, about 5,000 of them jammed themselves into Liberty Hall, overtaxing the capacity of that building, and we had to turn away about 10,000, and there were fully 3,000 around the building, trying to get in last night. The biggest meeting we ever had in Harlem was last night, when we had fully between twenty and thirty thousand Negroes trying to get into Liberty Hall. After I was through addressing the good people there, one of the members brought me a letter he had received from his friend in Panama. They did not know that the Universal Negro Improvement Association has secret service men all over the world now, and the letter said that just two hours before he read a cable which was sent by the Canal Commission in Panama beseeching Washington not to give a passport to Marcus Garvey to visit Panama, because if he landed there, there would be trouble for the white man there.[1] Now, you know who are the people who are controlling the Panama Canal under this administration. They are Southern white men. The chicken is going home to roost. We told those Southern crackers that one day the Negro would get even with them. You see how cowardly they are. Now, I am quite away in New York and they are begging the people here not to let me get out of New York to go there. But to show you how puzzled they are: My District Attorney friend in New York has been trying for many months to get me expelled from the country. Some want me to go and some don't want me to go. What must I do? To my mind, it is a question of being between hell and the powder house. (Laughter.)

ANCIENT FOE PUZZLED.

Now, that is what we can compliment ourselves for today. We have our foe, our ancient foe, puzzled. He does not know what to do with the New Negro; but the New Negro knows what to do with himself. And the thing that we are going to do is to blast a way to complete independence and to that democracy which they denied us even after we left the battlefields of France and Flanders. We, the New Negroes, say there is no turning back for us now. There is nothing else but a going forward, and if they squeal in America or anywhere else we are going forward. Why, we are not organized as four hundred millions yet, and they are so scared. Now, what will happen in the next five years when the entire four hundred millions will have been organized? All the lynching in the South will be a thing of the past. We are determined in this association to bring the white man to his senses. We are not going to fight and kill anybody because he has more than we have. But if there is anybody taking advantage of the Negro, whether he be white, red or blue, we are going to organize to stop him. We believe that white men have as much right to live as yellow men; we believe that yellow men have as much right to live as red men; we believe red men have as much right to live as black men, and we believe that black men have as much right to live as all men. Therefore, if any race of mankind says that the other race must die, it is time for that race that is dying to organize to prevent themselves from dying. And as for me, the sweetest life in the world to me is the life of my race. I cannot change my race overnight. You cannot change your race overnight. We have not been able to change our race for three hundred years. No one can change our race overnight. God created us what we are and we are going to remain what we are until Gabriel blows his horn.

Therefore we are of the Negro race and we are suffering simply because we are of the Negro race, and, since we are four hundr[e]d million strong, it is for us to organize that strong to protect our race. And I want you young men, you middle aged men and you old men of the race and women also to realize that this is the age of action—action on the part of each and every individual of every race. If there is a white man who does not love the white race, to his race he is an outcast; if there is a yellow man that does not love his race, to the yellow race he is an outcast: if there is a Negro who does not love the black race, to his race such a Negro is an outcast and should be trampled to death.

FARCE OF BROTHERHOOD.

We have lived upon the farce of brotherhood for hundreds of years, and if there is anybody who has suffered from that farce it is the Negro. The white man goes forth with the Bible and tells us that we are all brothers, but it is against the world to believe, against all humanity to believe, that really there is but one brotherhood. And if there are six brothers in any family, at least those six brothers from natural tie ought to be honest in their dealings with each other to the extent of not seeing any of the six starve. If one has not a job, naturally the others would see to it that the one that is out of a job gets something to eat and a place to sleep so as to prevent him from starving and dying. This is brotherhood. Now there is one brother with all the wealth; he has more than he wants, and there is the other brother. What is he doing to the other brother? He is murdering the other brother. He is lynching the other brother, and still they are brothers. Now, if I have any brother in my family who has no better love for me than to starve me, to whip me and to burn me, I say, brother, I do not want your relationship at all. To hell with it.

No, sir, I strike against the idea of brotherhood as coming from that man. I believe in the brotherhood of man. I believe in the fatherhood of God, but as man sinned and lost his purpose ever since the fall of Adam and Eve, I also realize that man has lost his closest connection, his closest tie, with his God. And since man is human, since man has lost his instinct divine, I am not going to trust man. From the attitude of man, from the action of man today, I can see that every one is looking out for himself where the question of race comes in. The white race is looking out for the white race; the yellow race is looking out for the yellow race or Asiatic race. The time has come when the Negro should look out for himself and let the others look out for themselves. This is the new doctrine today. It is the doctrine of Europe. Europe is looking out for the white man. It is the doctrine of Asia. Asia is looking out for the yellow man. So should Africa look out for the black man, the Negro. And since they (the whites) have divided up Africa, having a part in America, a part in Canada, a part in the West Indies, a part in Central America, a part in South America and a part remaining in Africa, we are saying that the time has come that there should be a united Africa. And before a united Africa comes, Ethiopia, as scattered as she is, must stretch forth her hands unto God.

TIME TO HELP SELF.

Tonight the Universal Negro Improvement Association is endeavoring to teach Negroes that the time has come for them to help themselves. We have helped the white man in this Western Hemisphere for over three hundred years until he has become so almighty that he respects not even God himself. The white man believes that there is only one God, and that is the white man. We have a different idea about God. We believe that there is but one God, and he is in a place called heaven. There is a heaven, we believe, and a God presides over that heaven, and as far as the Negro is concerned that God is the only being in the world whom we respect. We believe with Theodore Roosevelt, "FEAR GOD AND KNOW NO OTHER FEAR."[2] And if every Negro in Philadelphia could just get that one thought into his or her mind, to fear God and him alone and let the world take care of itself, the better it would be for each and every one.

WHITE MAN'S IMPERIAL MAJESTY.

The white man comes before you in his imperial and majestic pomp and tries to impress upon you the idea that he is your superior. Who made him your superior? You stick his face with a pin and blood runs out. You stick the black man's face with a pin and blood runs out. Starve the white man and he dies. Starve the black man and he dies. What difference is there, therefore, in black and white. If you stick the white man, blood come[s] out. If you starve the white man he dies. The same applies to the black man. They said the white man was the superior being and the black man was the inferior being. That is the old time notion, but today the world knows that all men were created equal. We were created equal and were put into this world to possess equal rights and equal privileges, and the time has come for the black man to get his share. The white man has got his share and more than his share for thousands of years, and we are calling upon him now to give up that which is not his, so that we can have ours. Some of them will be wise enough and sensible enough to give up what is not theirs to save confusion. You know when a man takes what is not his, the one from whom he took that thing is going to take him to court so as to recover his loss. Now, the Negro is going to take somebody to a court of law one day. This court is not going to be presided over by the white man. It is the court to be presided over and decided by the sword. Yes; the sword will decide to whom belongs the right.

AFRICA TO CALL FOR A JUDGMENT.

And I want you men of Africa, you men of the Negro race, to prepare for the day when Africa will call for a judgment. Africa is preparing to call for a judgment, and that judgment we must have, and it will be a judgment in favor of four hundred million oppressed people. And the marshal who will carry out the authority of the court will be the new Toussaint L'Ouverture with the sword and the banner of the new African Republic. You black men of Philadelphia sit here tonight as jurors in the case where judgment is to be given in favor of the Negro, and I am now asking you jurymen: Gentlemen of the jury, what is your verdict? Cries of: "Africa must be free!" Now, if Africa is to be free, it means, therefore, that Philadelphia has given her verdict as we have in New York. It is now for the judge to give his finding. The judge will give his finding after all the jurors of the Negro race, four hundred million, will have given their verdict. And then after the judge gives his finding he will have to find a marshal to serve the writ, who will require the New Negro to help him to serve this writ, because the man to whom this writ is to be served is of a desperate character, because he prefers to shed blood and take lives before he will give up what is not his. You have to spill blood in Africa before you get what is belonging to you.

A NEGRO GOVERNMENT.

Therefore, you will realize that the Universal Negro Improvement Association is no joke. It is a serious movement. It is as serious a movement as the movement of the Irish today to have a free Ireland; as the determination of the Jew to recover Palestine. The Negro peoples of the world should be so determined to reclaim Africa and found a government there, so that if any black man in any part of the world is abused we can call the mighty power of Africa to come to our aid. Men, a Negro government we had once, and a Negro government we must have again. Tell me that I must live everlastingly under the domination of a white man, that I must bequeath to my children white overlordship, then I say, let me die now, Almighty God. If there is no better future in the world for me than to be the slave of a white man, I say, take the life you gave me. I do not want it. You would not be my God if you created me to be a slave to other men; but you are my God and will continue to be my God if you created me an equal of all men.

LIFE GIVEN FOR A PURPOSE.

Men, I want you to realize that the life you live was given you for a purpose; not for the purpose of being a slave, not for the purpose of being a serf, but for the purpose of being a man, and for that purpose you must live, or it is better you die.

THE NEGRO WILL DIE ECONOMICALLY.

Now I want to come to the practical, common sense side of this question. We have started an agitation all over the world. It is the agitation of self-reliance wherein the Negro must do for himself. I want you to understand that if you do not get behind this agitation and back it up morally and financially you are only flirting with your own downfall, because the world in which we live is today more serious than ever it was. White and yellow men have become more selfish today than they were before causing the terrible war, the terrible conflict, of 1914 to 1918. They destroyed all that they spent years and years to build and all the time and energy they gave us counted for nought because of the destruction. They have, therefore, lost their sympathies for other men. They have lost their sympathies for other races and have settled down to see nothing else but their own interest until they will have succeeded in rebuilding themselves. During this selfish, soulless age it falls to the province of the Negro to take the initiative and do for himself; otherwise he is going to die. He is going to d[ie,] as I stand on this platform tonight[,] economically in America; he is going to die economically under the yoke of Britain, of France and of Germany. He is going to die in the next one hundred years if he does not start out now to do for himself.

DEAR AMERICA FOR WHITE MEN.

I want you to realize that this dear America, the greatest democracy in the world for white men, the greatest republic in the world for white men, that this America is becoming more prejudiced every day against the Negro. Month by month they are lynching more Negroes than they ever did before;[3] month by month more riots are going on in the industrial sections of this country than ever before. This is an indication of the spirit of the people that are living today. It is the spirit that will be bequeathed to their children and to the unborn posterity of the white race. If you think that the white man is going to be more liberal to Negroes than they are at present, you are making a big mistake. Every succeeding generation of the white race is getting more prejudiced against the Negro. It is time, therefore, for the Negro to look out for the future for himself.

FOUR HUNDRED MILLION WHITES.

We have in America ninety million white fellow citizens, and they are lynching us by the dozen every day. In the next one hundred years you are going to have four hundred million people (white) in America. Now, if they are lynching twelve a day with their ninety millions, how many are they going to lynch when they are four hundred millions. I want you to figure this out for yourselves. And it is because our old time leaders failed to see this that we of the Universal Negro Improvement Association say that the old time leadership must go.

NEGROES FLIRTING WITH THEIR GRAVES.

Again I want you to understand that economically we are flirting with our graves if we do not start out to make ourselves economically independent. This war brought about new conditions in America and all over the world. America sent hundreds of thousands of colored soldiers to fight the white man's battles, during which time she opened the doors of industry to millions of white American men and women and created a new problem in the industrial market. And now the war is over and those millions who took the places of the soldiers who have returned home say: "We are not going to give up our jobs. We are going to remain in the industrial life of the world.["] This makes it difficult for returned soldiers to get work now. There will be sufficient jobs now for returned soldiers and for white men, because abnormal conditions are still in existence, but in the next two years these abnormal conditions will pass away and the industries will not be opened up for so long.[4] It means that millions are going to starve. Do you think the white industrial captains are going to allow the white men and the white women to starve and give you bread? To the white man blood is thicker than water.

Therefore, in the next two years there is going to be an industrial boomerang in this country, and if the Negroes do not organize now to open up economic and industrial opportunities for themselves there will be starvation among all Negroes. It is because we want to save the situation when this good time shall have passed by and the white man calls you, "My dear John, I haven't any job for you today," and you can leave the white man's job as a porter and go into the Negro factory as a clerk, you can leave the white man's kitchen and go into your home as the wife of a big Negro banker or a corporation manager.

THE BLACK STAR LINE.

That is why we want the Black Star Line so as to launch out to the Negro peoples of the world, and today the richest people of the world are the Negro people of Africa. Their minerals, their diamonds, their gold and their silver and their iron have built up the great English, French, German and Belgian Empires. Men, how long are we going to allow those parasites to suck the blood out of our children? How long? I answer for those who are active members of the Universal Negro Improvement Association and African Communities League, "Not one day longer." No parasite shall continue to feed off my body, because I want to have a healthy body. I have not sufficient blood to give to any parasite, because when I get sick I will need every drop of my blood to sustain me until I am well, so while I am well I will have to take off that parasite and throw it away. The time has come for the Negro to exert his energy to the utmost to do. Men and women of Philadelphia, the question is now for you to decide. Are you ready tonight or are you going to wait for two years more to be ready. The answer is, "You must be ready now[.]" Thank God, there are millions of us who are ready already, and when the Black Star Line sails out, by the demonstration of the Black Star Line spontaneously and simultaneously, millions will become [wealthy?].

Some Bad Negroes.

Some bad Negroes, and I understand some are in Philadelphia, say there will be no Black Star Line. I am only sorry that I have not the time to waste or the strength or energy to give away that when I come against those bad Negroes to just get a big stick and give them a good walloping, because such Negroes are not entitled to courteous treatment. I want you active members not to waste time with such Negroes, but to put them down. Mark them well, because those are the same guys who, after you have achieved through your sacrifice, will go around and say: "We did it; we did it." The so-called big Negroes are the ones who have kept back the race. Some of them are doctors and lawyers and other professionals. They feel they are not belonging to the other class of Negroes. Those are the people who have done nothing to help the race because they sell out the race. This Black Star Line we are putting forward is an industrial proposition, and we are putting this proposition forward not by the big Negroes, but by the small Negroes. The first ship of the Black Star Line that we are to float on the 31st of this month will be owned not by the big Negroes, but by the small Negroes, and on that day we are going to say to the big Negroes, "Now, who are the big Negroes?" We who have made the Black Star Line possible are the big Negroes. In New York we have discarded that kind of big Negroes. If they want to be big, they have to come right in line with other Negroes and show how big they are. We are not going to take it for granted that you are big. You have to show how big you are, not by the amount of money that you have, not by the automobile that you can afford to run, but by your sacrifice for your race. The sacrifice that you are prepared to make, that is how we are going to make men big. The so-called big Negro tells you that he is an aristocratic Negro; he is a gentleman. I want to know where the Negro aristocrat came from. A little more than fifty years ago Abraham Lincoln took up the pen and liberated four million Negroes. He did not say to any particular one, "You are a big Negro," or "You are an artistocrat," or "You are inferior." Victoria, eighty-two or eighty-three years ago, took up the pen and liberated a few million Negroes in the West Indies, but she did not classify them. All of us got our emancipation on equal terms, and it is for those who have the noblest blood, feeling and sentiment towards humanity to come out and do service so as to distinguish ourselves from the rest. Have they done it? Outside of Booker Washington and Frederick Douglass, there is not another aristocratic Negro in America. Douglass and Washington are the only two Negroes in this country who went out and did service so as to make themselves singular among the Negroes of America. It was not a matter of money that made these two men big Negroes. It was nobility of soul, of spirit, to do service to suffering humanity, and that made them different from the rest of the people. That made them aristocrats among their own. But these fat headed, big belly politicians who have robbed the people in their votes at the polls for a few dollars go among the people and say: "We are the aristocrats; we are the big

Negroes." Indeed, I refuse to respect any such big Negroes. Show me the Negro of Booker Washington's stamp, show me the Negro of Frederick Douglass' stamp, and I will say, "There go the aristocratic Negroes of the race!"

NOBILITY THROUGH SERVICE.

Men become noble through service. Therefore, if any Negro wants to call himself an aristocrat, a nobleman, before he will get that respect from me he will have to do some service to the Negro race. So you lawyers, you doctors and you politicians who think you are big Negroes we want to tell you that you are nothing for us, of the Universal Negro Improvement Association and African Communities League. You have to do service, and the time will come when we will give you a chance, when we will give you the opportunity to do service, because we are going to want hundreds of you professional men to lead the Negro forces on to VICTORY.

So tonight I want you men and women to understand that there is a chance for every one of you tonight to do service to your race, to humanity, before I leave this building for New York, and that is to help to launch on the 31st of this month the first ship of the Black Star Line. I want you all to buy as many shares as you can. If you can buy twenty, buy them; if you can buy fifteen, buy them; if you can buy ten, buy them. Buy as many as you possibly can, so as to render service to yourselves, service to your race, service to humanity.

Printed in *NW*, 1 November 1919. Original headlines abbreviated.

1. A possible reference to the cablegram from Chester Harding, governor of the Panama Canal Zone, which A. L. Flint forwarded to the chief of the Bureau of Investigation, 22 September 1919, printed above.

2. There is no evidence that Theodore Roosevelt originated this saying, although he may have used it in speeches. It is attributed to William Smyth (1765–1849), a religious leader (*Encyclopedia of Religious Quotations* [Westwood, N.J.: Fleming H. Revell Co., 1965], p. 329).

3. According to the *Negro Year Book*, 76 blacks were lynched in 1919, the largest number since 1908, when 89 were lynched. The highest number of lynchings of blacks for a year in which records were kept was 162 lynchings, in 1892 (*NYB*, 1947, p. 307).

4. Garvey's speech was made during the postwar boom, which lasted from April 1919 to January 1920. After a mild recession immediately following the war, an economic boom swept much of the industrialized world, with the United States, Britain, and Japan enjoying the greatest upsurge in economic activity. Rapidly rising prices fueled the economic upturn, caused by an increase in demand during a period in which factories had not fully converted from war production. Soon inflation reached its apex, and a precipitous drop in the economy followed (Derek H. Aldcroft, *From Versailles to Wall Street, 1919–1929* [Berkeley, Los Angeles, London: University of California Press, 1977], pp. 55–77).

Editorial Letter by Marcus Garvey

[[Philadelphia, Pa., October 22, 1919]]

MARCUS GARVEY, WORLD-FAMED ORATOR AND LEADER OF UNIVERSAL MOVEMENT, SENDS GREAT MESSAGE

Fellowmen of the Negro Race, Greeting:

Once more it is my privilege to write to you, bidding you be of good cheer in the noble cause we are espousing for the new emancipation of our oppressed race.

Last Tuesday [*14 October*] I had the first experience of being shot with the intention to kill, for the purpose of defeating the great movement of the Universal Negro Improvement Association. The would-be assassin, who from all appearances was "set-up" to do the "job," did not succeed as he intended because Providence was not ready for me to yield my life.

The coward attacked me while I was unprepared, and at the time when there was no one in the immediate surroundings of my private office but the two lady secretaries of the Association, in that all the other officers at the time were at another part of the building. He succeeded in shooting me four times, but by the help of the Almighty, I am still alive and he is dead. The unfortunate creature who acted, I believe, not on his own will, but by the desire of others, has thrown away his life, and the tale that would have been told to the world is lost to the ear of justice.

The enemies of our cause are many and they have plotted all kinds of outrages, but in the end they are only courting their own defeat. The Universal Negro Improvement Association is too strong to be destroyed by any human agency. We have our part to play on the stage of life, and regardless of all consequences we mean to go forward "fearing God and knowing no other fear."

It is time that the world understood that the New Negro has no apology to make for his present attitude. As a race we have been abused and disadvantaged long enough to strike now against a perpetuation of same.

The New Negro of the world wants his liberty, and not even the powers of hell will stop him in his determination. Men may shoot at or kill our leaders, one by one, but every time that is done, one hundred more spring up to carry on the cause.

Newspapers may lie about us as they desire to, yet truth and justice are sure to win out at the end, even as the Universal Negro Improvement Association is winning out today. The enemies of the press tried to make capital out of a lie that the shooting was caused over the dispute of money so as to prejudice the minds of the public. I personally have never had any financial transaction with the man other than that the man was once a member of the Universal Negro Improvement Association of New York, and was expelled from active membership because of his bad behavior at all times. The enemies of our cause got hold of the man, had him make up a story that would involve me and then "do the job." The man is dead and I am still alive to continue the work of the Universal Negro Improvement Association, and that is enough satisfaction for me.

I have to return my thanks and appreciation to the thousands of members who called to see me during my illness, and who sent telegrams and letters of regret. I have also to express my thanks to the foreign branches for the many cables they have sent expressing their sympathy.

And now I have to remind everybody about the great mass meeting that is to be staged by the Universal Negro Improvement Association at the Madison Square Garden, 26th street and Madison avenue, on Thursday night, the 30th of October, at 8 o'clock, in the interest of the Black Star Line Steamship Corporation. People will [be] coming from all parts of the country to attend this meeting. It will be a night of jubilee for twenty thousand Negroes. Every progressive Negro shall report at Madison Square Garden, the biggest public hall in the world so as to have it [known] that the New Negro is very much alive to his economic future.

Please do your best between now and the 31st to buy as many shares as you can in the Black Star Line Steamship Corporation of 56 West 135th street, New York.

Feeling sure that you will do your duty, and with best wishes for your success, Yours fraternally,

MARCUS GARVEY

Printed in *NW*, 25 October 1919. Original headlines abbreviated.

Report of UNIA Meeting

[*Negro World*, 25 October 1919]

TEN THOUSAND NEGROES TRY TO GET INTO LIBERTY HALL

The news that Hon. Marcus Garvey, the president-general of the Universal Negro Improvement Association, had been shot by an assassin (who later committed suicide), but was sufficiently recovered to speak in Liberty Hall on last Sunday night [*19 October*], drew the largest crowd of Negroes, who ever assembled in a hall in New York city. Nearly three thousand persons were wedged and jammed in Liberty Hall. The hall-ways, aisles, side rooms, steps and platform, and every nook and corner were packed with people. And the crowd outside the hall was still larger.

Thousands crowded the sidewalks and street adjoining the building. Around every window and door, hundreds were clustered, and hundreds left after trying in vain to get near the windows and doors.

Shortly before nine o'clock, amid deafening cheers and applause, Mr. Marcus Garvey alighted from his carriage and supported by his cane and friends, entered the hall and ascended the platform.

Miss Henrietta Vinton Davis, the International Organizer, presided over the meeting with her usual grace and dignity. An interesting program was rendered as follows:

Singing .... From Greenland's Icy Mountains
Prayer .... Read by Miss Davis
Selection .... Black Star Line Band
Violin Solo .... Master Patrick
Baritone Solo (horn) .... Mr. Jones
Solo, "I'm Always Chasing Rainbows" .... Miss Ida Ash
Address .... Prof. W. H. Ferris
Original Poem, "A Call to the [Ne]gro" .... Mr. La Mott
Address .... Dr. J. W. H. Eason
Selection .... Black Star Line Band
Songs .... Acme Quartette
Address .... Marcus Garvey
Solo .... Madame Houston[1]

The entire program gave great satisfaction. And the solos of Madame Marie Barrier Houston and Miss Ida Ash were the musical hits of the evening.

MISS DAVIS' SPEECH.

Miss Henrietta Vinton Davis, the International Organizer, said:

"This is a red letter night for the Universal Negro Improvement Association. We have with us our champion, the champion of the Negro peoples of the world, in the person of Hon. Marcus Garvey. Many have wondered what the Universal Negro Improvement Association stands for. It stands for the intellectual, moral, political, industrial and commercial uplifting of the Negro peoples of the world. It aims to lift the Negro race to the same plane of civilization on which other races live."

PROF. W. H. FERRIS' SPEECH.

Prof. Ferris said that as he surveyed the immense crowd he felt like Abraham Lincoln did at the anniversary of the Battle of Gettysburg.[2] The occasion was so vast and fraught with such momentous consequences that human words were unable to express the sentiments of the hour. There were times in the history of Rome, England, France and America when there was need for a strong man to take the reins of authority in his hands, direct the course of events and bring order out of chaos. Such men were Julius Caesar, Oliver Cromwell, Napoleon Bonaparte, George Washington and Abraham Lincoln. They have been called "Men of the Hour" and "Men of Destiny." They have been called "Men of the Hour" because they successfully met a crisis, and they have been called "Men of Destiny" because they have shaped human history. And in the Hon. Marcus Garvey the Negro peoples of the world have a "Man of the Hour" and a "Man of Destiny." (Cheers and applause.)

Though the South was conquered in war when General Robert Lee surrendered his sword to U. S. Grant at the Appomattox Court House,[3] she was not conquered in spirit. At first the South shot down the Negroes at the polls and stuffed ballot boxes. Then it started the barrage fire for disfranchisement and jim crowism[.] In 1889 Mr. Henry Grady,[4] the silver-tongued orator of Atlanta, Ga., came to Boston and told the Bostonians how much he loved the Neg[r]o. He spoke feelingly of his black Mammy. That gave the South its cue and for twenty-four years it played on that harp. In the spring of 1913 it sounded another note when it started the segregation propaganda.[5] And in the spring of 1918, when black soldiers began to go to France in great numbers, the South unmasked, threw away all camouflage and announced its purpose to disseminate his color prejudice throughout the civilized world.

And what is the dominant note in that color propaganda? It is that no matter how scholarly, cultured, refined and noble a man of color may become, no matter how much wealth he acquires, no matter how brave he shows himself in battle, "he, the black man, is a Nigger just the same." And against that propaganda Marcus Garvey has launched the idea that the Negro was created in the divine image and that his brain, his soul and his nerve, his character and his heart, rather than his color, should determine his ultimate rating. And he has shown that the Negro's successful entry into the commercial world will help to give him prestige and achieve standing. By its deeds and achievements, a race will be finally judged.

DR. J. W. H. EASON'S SPEECH.

Rev. Dr. J. W. [H.] Eason, pastor of the People's Metropolitan Church of Philadelphia, delivered a very eloquent and thoughtful address, which was interspersed with wit and humor. Dr. Eason said in part:

"I have heard many preachers and leaders say, 'Ask and it shall be given; seek and ye shall find.'[6] And they have been asking and seeking for a long time and have received little in return. Nearly all that the Negro has found is a hard time in this world and a promissory note in the next world. But I hear few preachers say, 'Knock and the door shall be opened.'

"For our part we are going to unite, 400,000,000 people, and we will ask, seek and knock at the same time. My subject tonight is 'The Strike Is On.' Instead of organizing for a strike, we have been getting together and breaking up a strike that other men have made. When your enemies insult you and trample you under foot, strike with all your powers and your enemies shall make love to you. I have been through the mill and know what it is to face opposition within and without. The strike is on against the self-appointed, white-man-picked leader. The strike is on against the opposition that comes from the other race. The strike is on against all proscriptions, discriminations and injustices. We believe that what is good for other men is good for us. If the others have succeeded through commerce and indu[s]try, so can we. It sometimes becomes necessary to answer back in order to let the world know the truth. This organization means to tell you the truth and set you free. Some people say, "The white man won't give me what I ought to have." But you don't give yourself what you ought to have. The strike is on for better things. The way to help God to answer your prayers is to ask God to teach you to help yourself. There is just as much religion in making positions for our boys and girls and in buying stock for steamships, which will bring interest for years to come, as there is in being on our knees asking God to do for us what we ought to do for ourselves. If you knock and strike long enough, all opposition will get out of your way. Because one man, Marcus Garvey, broke the way for liberty, millions of black persons will pass through the pearly gates of an earthly paradise."

HON. MARCUS GARVEY'S SPEECH

When Miss Henrietta Vinton Davis, in her inimitable way, introduced the Hon. Marcus Garvey as our incomparable leader, pandemonium reigned. It was nearly five minutes before the cheers and applause subsided. Mr. Garvey spoke, leaning on his cane, and held the audience spellbound. Mr. Garvey said:

"You heard of the accident of Tuesday, but the wrong report was sent out and the wrong impression prevails. Nearly all the white newspapers of the city and nearly all the Negro newspapers have made it their point to lie every time the Universal Negro Improvement Association, the Black Star Line and myself are mentioned. The New York World and the New York News said that Marcus Garvey was shot by George Tyler because he had borrowed $25 from said Tyler. That is a lie. I have never borrowed a dollar from any man in my life.

"It would appear that six or seven months ago the executives of the Universal Negro Improvement Association decided to issue promissory notes of $25 each to sixty members to launch a restaurant, etc., which notes would be redeemed in January, 1920. Tyler fell into the hands of enemies of the Universal Negro Improvement Association because I had caused some politicians to lose their jobs. They doped him and sent him to me. At the time he called, I was extremely busy with the affairs of the U.N.I.A. and the Black Star Line. I told him I was very busy and to call again. He could have seen other members, but he came to get me. Tyler shot me four times, one bullet glanced my forehead, another scraped the knee and two entered the right leg below the knee."

TRIBUTE TO MRS. MAY CLARKE ROACH.

"That I am here tonight is due to the indomitable determination of Mrs. May Clarke Roach, who stood between me and Tyler, after I fell from the shooting, and prevented him firing into my body again. Miss Amy Ashwood was behind me."

Continuing amid deafening applause Mr. Garvey said:

"What they have done to me has only made me more determined to carry on the work of the Universal Negro Improvement Association. I am more satisfied than ever that the Universal Negro Improvement Association has entered world affairs to stay in until judgment day.

"We have to make good because the whole world is watching New York to see if the New York Negro will make good. There is not one portion of the civilized world that does not know that the Negroes are endeavoring to launch the first ship of the Black Star Line on October 31st."

A feature of the evening was the number of prominent citizens who occupied seats on the platform; Captain Justin Cockburn and wife, Mr. John E. Bruce and wife, Mr. George Young[7] of Young's Book Exchange and Mr. Roberts of Panama were among the numbers. So keen was the interest that crowds remained in Liberty Hall a half hour after the meeting had adjourned.

Printed in *NW*, 25 October 1919.

1. Marie Barrier Houston was the leader of the Salem Methodist Episcopal Church Choral Society (*New York Age*, 18 January 1919).

2. The Battle of Gettysburg, between Union and Confederate troops, took place 1–4 July 1863. On 19 November 1863, when the Pennsylvania battlefield was designated as a cemetery in honor of the soldiers who died there, Abraham Lincoln (1809–1865) delivered the Gettysburg Address.

3. The Confederate forces, led by Robert E. Lee (1807–1870), surrendered to Ulysses S. Grant (1822–1885) and the Union army on 9 April 1865 (*WBD*).

4. Henry Woodfin Grady (1850–1889), Georgia-born orator and journalist, was known as the spokesman of the "New South." The speech referred to was "The Race Problem in the South," delivered in Boston in December 1889. In it, Grady reiterated the determination of the South to maintain white supremacy but claimed that since the Civil War, blacks had been given considerable economic rights. As the editor of several papers, including the *Atlanta Constitution*, Grady devoted his editorials to his ideas for a North-South reconciliation based on the industrialization of the South and on a paternalistic alliance of white landowners and industrialists with black farmers (Arthur S. Link et al., *The American People* [Arlington Heights, Ill.: AHM Press, 1981], p. 515; *WBD*).

5. Probably a reference to the resurgence of segregationist policies when Woodrow Wilson took office in March 1913 and large numbers of Southern politicians came to Washington. The first Congress of the Wilson administration received the largest number of bills advocating discrimination against blacks in the nation's history. Although most of these bills were defeated, Wilson nevertheless issued an executive order providing segregated eating and rest-room facilities for federal employees. The secretary of the treasury and the postmaster general, both of whom headed departments that employed large numbers of blacks, segregated the offices in which blacks worked. In addition, local Internal Revenue agents and postmasters were allowed to reduce the rank of black civil servants or to dismiss them. Applications that

required photographs were also used to bar blacks from civil service (Rayford Logan, *The Betrayal of the Negro*, enlarged ed. [London: Collier-Macmillan, 1965], pp. 359–70; Henry Blumenthal, "Woodrow Wilson and the Race Question," *JNH* 48 [January 1963]: 1–21).

6. A paraphrase of Matt. 7:7.

7. George Young (1870–1935) was a self-taught bibliophile and bookseller. He was born near South Boston, Halifax County, Va., the son of former slaves. While working as a Pullman porter and as a Post Office employee for a number of years, he amassed a collection of rare books and pamphlets by and about blacks. He established a bookstore in Harlem in 1915 and joined with other bibliophiles, among them Arthur A. Schomburg and Richard B. Moore, to form study and discussion groups. He eventually sold many of his books to the New York Public Library (*DAB*).

Editorial in the *Negro World*

[*Negro World*, 25 October 1919]

THE "STAR"[1] OF NEWPORT NEWS UNDER AN ECLIPSE.

It has not been the custom of The Negro World to enter into any controversy with other newspapers, even when they take issue with the position of our editorials. We present our views as clearly and as forcibly as we can, and if our brother journalists dissent from our views we are not disposed to quarrel with them. If an editor looks at things from a different angle and observation point than we do, we are not disposed to quarrel with him. It is his divine right and prerogative to express the truth as he sees it. For this reason, when the "Star" of Newport News, Va., took issue with an editorial in The Negro World on the possible trend of affairs in Howard University, we took no offence. When it challenged, in the next issue, a statement of a reader of The Negro World regarding the late Booker T. Washington, we took no offence.

But in the issue of Friday, October 17, the "Star" of Newport News, Va., in one editorial, attacked the Universal Negro Improvement Association and in another editorial the Black Star Line. It made four [distortions?] of facts which were not true, and for this reason we answer [*line mutilated*] [those?] editorials.

[*Paragraph mutilated*.]

["][*Two lines mutilated*] communities (Imperial [........]) organization embracing the millions of men, women and children of Negro blood and of African descent of all countries of the world, striving for the Freedom, Manhood and Nationalism of the Negro, and to hand down to posterity a Flag of Empire—to restore to the world an Ethiopian Nation one and indivisible out of which shall come our princes and rulers—to bequeath to our children and our Grand Old Race the heritage of an Ancestry worthy of their time and thoughtful of the future. Resting on the strength and mercy of Almighty God, and on the effort and faith of our people all over the world, we, the undersigned, as officers of the New York Division," etc.

In a word, the Universal Negro Improvement Association is striving for freedom and manhood. All the rest of the world is striving for the same things. The U.N.I.A. is also desirous of building up a republic in their fatherland; the Jews and Poles are desirous of doing the same, and we rest the case for the U.N.I.A. here.

Then the "Star" goes on in an editorial, under the caption "Guard Our Earnings" to say: "It will take many a $90,000 to make it (the Black Star Line Corporation) do enough business to ever pay the investors one cent of dividend, let alone make the money they put into it secure." Demosthenes said in one of his orations: "I appeal from Philip drunk to Philip sober." And we appeal from a man who does not know to a man who knows. Mr. John E. Bruce, known to the newspaper world as Bruce Grit, is president of the Negro Society for Historical Research. He and his friend, Mr. A. A. Schomburg,[2] who has a magnificent Negro library, correspond with scholarly Negroes of both hemispheres. And this is what Mr. Bruce says in an article published in the current issue of The Negro World: "My correspondents in Africa along the west coast seem to regard it as a blessing and hail it as the harbinger of a new day for our oppressed people here and there. When this ship is launched and makes one trip to Africa, she will bring back a cargo that will almost if not quite pay for it. A dozen trips will make its promoters independently rich, for the products of Africa, the West Indies, Central and South America, will find a ready sale here, especially raw products, and there are hundreds of well-to-do merchants and traders along these African coasts who will gladly avail themselves of the opportunity to ship their goods on the good ships Frederick Douglass and Robert Small[s][3] and Martin R. Delaney,[4] the General Budhoe,[5] and To[us]saint L'Ouverture, when these latter shall be put in commission and sally forth on the proud bosom of the mighty Atlantic with their messages of hope to the Negroes of the world."

If we had space we could tell of Americans and Englishmen who made fortunes out of the West Indies, Central and South America. It was a Harvard professor of world-wide fame who visited these countries and called our attention to their possibilities for men of African descent. We could tell of Englishmen and Germans who went to the west coast of Africa on borrowed capital and made millions. Every week we receive letters from the West Indies, from Central America and South America, and from Africa, written by gentlemen of education and experience, speaking of the possibilities of black men sailing to and trading with these countries. And we would like to ask the editor of the "Star" of Newport News, who speaks with so much authority, "What do you know directly from travels about the British West Indies, Central America, South America and Africa?" The letters we receive from these places confirm the statements of officials of the Black Star Line Steamship Company, who have traveled or lived in these countries.

Then again the "Star" of Newport News asks: "The most important question to consider is when and where have the men who are launching this stupendous scheme learned their lessons of navigation and control of ships?"

We can easily answer this question. Both the captain and the navigator are men of ripe experience.

Capt. Joshua Cockburn, the captain of the S.S. Frederick Douglass of the Black Star Line, was born in the Bahama Islands. He has been going to sea from 1894 to 1918 on sail boats and steamships and has cruised all over the world. He was in command of sailing vessels under the British flag just after the Spanish-American War. He also sailed out of England to various parts of the world as chief officer of steamships and has been in command from 1908 till 1918.

He carries with him this credential:

This is to certify that Joshua Cockburn, master of the flotilla storeship "Trojan," Nigerian Marine, has been awarded a mention in the London Gazette of the 6th September, 1916, by order of Their Lords' Commissioners of the Admiralty, for good services in action rendered by him during the operations in the Cameroons.

ADMIRALTY,
6th September, 1916.

Captain Cockburn also carries with him this credential:

GOVERNMENT OF NIGERIA CERTIFICATE OF SERVICE.
    Name of Officer—Joshua Cockburn.
    Position Held and Department—Captain S.S. "Trojan," Marine Department.
    Period of Service—From 4th September 1908 to 25th March, 1917.
    Efficiency—A good seaman and a keen, hardworking officer.
    General Conduct—Satisfactory. He was at all times found to be strictly sober and attentive to his duties.

J. PERCIVAL (Director of Marine)
Head of Department.
Date, August 20th, 1918

Captain Cockburn also carries with him this credential:

ST. JOHN AMBULANCE ASSOCIATION CERTIFICATE.

Certificate of Examination.

"This is to certify that Joshua Cockburn has been examined by me in Liverpool on the 6th day of December, 1910, and is qualified to render first aid to the injured."

Signed, LEWELLYN MORGAN,
Surgeon Examiner.

Captain Cockburn also carries with him this credential:

PILOTAGE BOARD CERTIFICATE $\frac{39}{817}$ RENEWAL.

"This is to certify that Joshua Cockburn has been examined by the Board and has satisfied the Board that he is a fit and proper person to hold a licence as a pilot for the port of Lagos (Africa). The 11th day of April, 1917.

A. B. CROSSE,
Harbor Master (Acting)

Last, but not least, Captain Cockburn carries with him this credential[:]

BY THE LORDS OF THE COMMITTEE OF PRIVY COUNCIL FOR TRADE—CERTIFICATE OF COMPETENCY AS MASTER OF FOREIGN-GOING SHIP.

To Joshua Cockburn:
Whereas it has been reported to us that you have been found duly qualified to fulfill the duties of Master of a Foreign-going Ship in the Merchant Service, we do hereby, in pursuance of the Merchant Shipping Act, 1894, grant you this certificate of Competency.
By Order of the Board of Trade this 5th day of June, 1915.
ERNEST G. MOGGRIDGE, one of the Assistant Secretaries to the Board of Trade
C. JONES, Registrar General
Registered at the Office of the Registrar General of Shipping[.]

We ask the learned and [*erudite*?] editor of the Star of Newport News, Va., after reading these testimonials from the officials of the British Government, does he think that Captain Cockburn has not "learned his lessons of navigation and control of ships?" It would have been wisdom on the part of the editor of The Star, before he insinuated that no man in the Negro race had the intelligence, training and experience to command a boat, to have written to the officials of the Black Star Line and inquired who their captain was, what was his experience, and what credentials did he bear.

Well has the poet said: "Fools rush in where angels fear to tread."

The editorial in The Star concludes, "How, then, can the Negro Improvement Society, without money and without experience, do what others with both are unable to do to any great degree of satisfaction?" This question represents the superlative degree of asininity. The editor is making generalizations about something of which he knows absolutely nothing. He knew nothing whatever about the financial standing of some of the gentlemen of color in New York, Philadelphia, Newport News, Colon, Panama and Africa, who are interested in this enterprise. He does not know how many of the promoters of this enterprise have lived in the British West Indies and Latin America and have traveled considerably in Africa and know trade conditions in those countries at first hand.

The editorial also says: "A ship has to be manned by a sufficient crew." It would surprise the editor of The Star to know how many engineers, mechanics, seamen, stewards, and stewardesses of training and experience and with recommendations have already appl[i]ed for positions. That editorial in The Newport News on "Guard Our Earnings" was not written from actual knowledge of conditions in the British West Indies, Latin America and Africa, and from actual knowledge of the personnel of the officers of the Black Star Line Steamship Company and of the S.S. Frederick Douglass, but it was conjured up in the imagination of the well-meaning but mistaken editor. It was a pipe dream. We suggest that in the future, before the editor of The Star launches out in hasty generalizations and rash statements, he first acquaint himself with the facts in the case. He had the wisdom of the ostrich. The ostrich imagines because it cannot see the pursuer, therefore the pursuer cannot see it. And the editor of The Star imagines because he doesn't know a Negro who can navigate a ship, therefore none exists. He imagines that because he knows nothing at first-hand about the British West Indies, Latin America and Africa, therefore no other black man knows about them. We do not impugn the motives of the editor. He means well, but he is trying to write in a learned and scholarly manner about things he knows nothing whatever about. And when a man does that, he becomes a blundering upstart, or to be more polite, a Parvenue.

The editor of The Star says[,] "Several people have asked us what we thought of the Negro Improvement Society and the Black Star Line." Why didn't he say, "I know nothing whatever about trade conditions in the West Indies, Latin America and Africa. I know nothing about the personnel of the management." Instead of writing learnedly like a dilettante, attempting to instruct the people about something he knows nothing whatever about, and masquerading like "the ass in the lion's skin" in Aesop's Fables.

Printed in *NW*, 25 October 1919.

1. The *Star* was edited by M. N. Lewis (*NYB*, 1919).

2. Arthur Alonzo Schomburg (1874–1938), scholar and bibliophile, was a member of the Puerto Rico Revolutionary party and secretary of the Las Dos Antillas Cuban Revolutionary party in the late 1890s. Born in Puerto Rico and educated at St. Thomas College, Virgin Islands, Schomburg immigrated to the United States in 1891. He worked as a law clerk and teacher, using his earnings to build up an extensive collection of books that would later become the basis for the Schomburg Collection, purchased by the National Urban League and donated to the New York Public Library in 1926. A president of the American Negro Academy and a cofounder of the Negro Society for Historical Research, Schomburg devoted his life to the collection and preservation of all literature pertaining to the African and black contribution to world culture and history (*JNH* 23 [July 1938]: 403–4; *WWCR*, p. 237).

3. Robert Smalls (1839–1915), a black shipmaster and major general in the South Carolina State Militia. Smalls later became a South Carolina state legislator and a United States

congressman (Okon Edet Uya, *From Slavery to Public Service: Robert Smalls, 1839–1915* [New York: Oxford University Press, 1971]).

4. Martin Delaney (1812–1885), social reformer, editor, and soldier, was a leading proponent of pan-Africanism in the nineteenth century (*WBD*).

5. It has not been possible to identify any historical figure by this name.

Article by John E. Banton

[*Negro World*, 25 October 1919]

MARCUS GARVEY, THE DANIEL OF THE RACE

A LOYAL SON OF AFRICA PLEADS THAT THE AMERICAN NEGRO AND THE WEST INDIAN NEGRO UNITE.

Void of intellectual learning, I must admit my incapability in finding words sufficiently appropriate for discussing the subject that I choose to write you about. But aided by common knowledge and the learning of experience, I am convinced that on your shoulders you wear a head burdened with thoughts and ideas that lead even to success.

When you first launched the ideas of your organization, I had the misfortune of butting up with men of your own race and from your own land criticizing you to the detriment of your character, and even expressing their opinions in regards to the soundness of your mental facilities, but in the shortness of time they have confounded themselves, and, like the dog, they have returned to their vomit, eating their own words and today they are acclaiming you the Daniel of the race.

In attending your meetings, one would imagine that the people came to hear "Great Caesar" speak, in the person of Marcus Garvey, and the controlling influence that you are able to exercise over your hearers shows the greatness that is in you, also the infinite confidence of your hearers. With your far-reaching ideas, you have awakened the consciousness of the race, wa[king] them to realize the mental possibilities of the Negro if they would but bestir themselves, if they would unite in one spirit to emancipate themselves from the obligations of the white man. You recall their attention to the tide which flows in the affairs of men, which when taken at the flood leads on to fortune.[1] Like a good fraternal brother, you have drawn them out into the light of a new age, pointing them to success, showing them their praise of life and how they can attain it by mobilizing their intellectual forces for the building up of the Negro's independence on the basis of commerce and industry. But until the American Negro rids himself of his foolish conception in believing that he is superior to the West Indian Negro, until he ceases to criticize and despise his West Indian brother, the downfall of the Negro must be accepted as the natural ignorance of the Negro himself.

You must be distinguished from among the other leaders of the race, bending their energies and spending their intellect and subordinating their ambition for the benefit of their race, for in your emotion of outburst you have created a sentiment that is absorbing the questionable minds of the Caucasian. Some leaders of the race have exhausted their emotional outburst on the avenues of New York, and yet the people perish for they are without a vision. For where there is no vision the people perish.

You have organized the intelligence of the people so that the affairs of their lives may mingle with the commercial avenues of the seas, bearing on their own ships the products of industry to all the people of the land.

JOHN E. BANTON
145 W. 143d street, New York City.

Printed in *NW*, 25 October 1919.

1. A paraphrase of a line from Shakespeare's play *Julius Caesar* (act 4, sc. 3, line 127).

Article by J. Arthur Davis

[*Negro World*, 25 October 1919]

HON. MARCUS GARVEY AND OUR FOSSILIZED MISSIONARIES

The great vision of Hon. Marcus Garvey, founder of the Universal Negro Improvement Association, for the union of blacks everywhere and his dream of the Black Star Steamship Line to link them together in travel and commerce, is a practical proposition that is finding, it seems, ready response in the new Negro.

It is not only practicable, but it has always been a necessity. It has needed an international leader. Heretofore, the homelike inclination of the race has narrowed its horizon and our leadership has been local and scarcely national; appointed and not produced. Every great crisis both makes and unmakes great men. This leader, 32 years of age, from the West Indies, has been produced by the new race self-consciousness born of the great war, which has made black men everywhere discover each other and feel like brothers, both those of the United States, Central and South America, the West Indies and Africa.

In the realization of this dream, he has already organized large numbers in the above named countries and the proposed company has purchased a ship. Like Bishop Turner, he dreams of a Negro flag in Africa.[1] Like our missionaries, he claims that if Africa is to be saved, it must be saved by black men. But he would save it by wholesale, while our missionaries have been trying to save it by the retail. For fifty years they have been raising money to that end. We do not criticise their good intentions, but their stupid methods. To send one missionary with a Bible in one hand and a hoe in the other to

III

Christianize and industrialize three hundred million natives is an absurd procedure. They could just as easily have established a steamship line and carried a substantial civilization.

The most concrete example of missionary stupidity is now under way. On the eighth of this month a couple, who have been educated in this country, the husband as a doctor and the wife as a sick nurse, will sail for Liberia with three children. Rev. Jordan has raised among the Baptists six thousand dollars to defray their expenses. This sum is to pay transportation for them and himself, to buy $500 worth of medicine for the natives, condensed milk for the children, Bibles and song books, clothes, etc., and an ox yoke for himself to use to instruct the natives in driving oxen. With fifty times this much money which the two and one-half million Baptists could raise in one week as an investment in a steamship line to Liberia, we could carry missionaries, commerce and develop a real and substantial civilization.

If we are to be free like other people, we must develop world travel and commerce. We cannot live unto ourselves. A free and aggressive spirit knows neither opposition nor boundaries.

We wish for Hon. Marcus Garvey success in organizing Chicago this week and can earnestly encourage with him the elimination of all fossilized leadership.

Printed in *NW*, 25 October 1919. Original headlines abbreviated.

1. Bishop Henry McNeal Turner (1831–1915) was the leading black advocate of Afro-American immigration to Africa after the Civil War. As an AME bishop from 1880 to 1915, Turner succeeded in establishing the AME church in South Africa and West Africa. In 1876 Turner declared that "the time is near when the American people of color will seek that general clime [Africa] as the European has this Western world, and there erect the UNITED STATES OF AFRICA," (*African Repository* 52, no. 3 [July 1876]: 86; Edwin S. Redkey, ed., *Respect Black: The Writings and Speeches of Henry McNeal Turner* [New York: Arno Press and the New York Times Publishing Co., 1971]; Edwin S. Redkey, *Black Exodus* [New Haven, Conn.: Yale University Press, 1969]).

Report of UNIA Meeting

[[Newport News, Va., Oct. 25, 1919]]

STIRRING SPEECH DELIVERED BY HON. MARCUS GARVEY IN THE SOUTH

. . . Last night the First Baptist Church of this city was the scene of wildest enthusiasm when the Hon. Marcus Garvey and party entered the building for the purpose of starting a campaign for sales of stocks in the Black Star Line Steamship Corporation of which Mr. Garvey is President. The party consisted of Mrs. Estelle Matthews, President of the Ladies' Division of the Philadelphia branch of the Universal Negro Improvement

Association; Miss Amy Ashwood, General Secretary of the Ladies' Division of the New York branch of the Universal Negro Improvement Association; Mr. Elie Garcia, General Secretary of Philadelphia Division of the Universal Negro Improvement Association,[1] and Mr. Robert Cross, official stenographer of the Black Star Line Steamship Corporation and reporter of The Negro World.

Seated on the platform were Hon. Marcus Garvey, Mr. R. H. Taylor, President of the local division of the Universal Negro Improvement Association; Mrs. Estelle Matthews, Rev. Dr. Taylor and others. Mr. R. H. Taylor presided, and at the close of his opening remarks he introduced Dr. Taylor, the Treasurer of the local division of the Universal Negro Improvement Association, who gave a stirring address, in which he said that this organization is going to stand as long as God lives. In the last great war, he said, the white men told the colored ministers of the Gospel to teach their people patriotism for America so that all our men may go to France and fight and die for the white man's democracy, and the colored parsons were very active in so doing. He said that our colored men were deceived by the colored parsons, for they told us that we also were going to enjoy that democracy and liberty after we returned from the war. But now that we have returned, instead of getting the liberty and democracy for which we fought and died in France and Flanders, he said, we are being lynched and burned more than ever. Mr. Taylor said that if the preachers cannot lead him temporally they cannot lead him spiritually. He said that many of our colored organizations have broken down because they had the wrong leaders, leaders who were chosen by [the] white man. But he was glad to say that tonight we have a leader that a white man did not put before us. We have a leader, he said, that God sent to us. He exhorted us to stand by this leader, the Hon. Marcus Garvey, and hold up his arms and victory shall be ours.

MRS. MATTHEWS' ADDRESS.

Most Honorable President-General, Ladies and Gentlemen—I assure you it affords me great pleasure at this most opportune time to come to you this evening with a message. I come to you from the City of Brotherly Love and from the Philadelphia Division of the Universal Negro Improvement Association. But as I come to you in these serious times, when right is on the scaffold and wrong is on the throne, when we can almost smell the smoke of our lynched brothers and sisters, when we can hear the cries of our brothers and sisters for mercy in Georgia and other states, up to now we have not been able to do anything but pity them. We can even hear the cries of millions of our unborn children for mercy, and up until this present time we have not made the way clear for them. Friends, we are living in a serious age, and the thought comes to me tonight that the hour has struck for Negro manhood and womanhood for action.

Three Million Gallons of Whiskey in Africa.

For five hundred years the Anglo-Saxon, the white man, the worst enemy that the Negro ever had, has been acting for us. He has acted for our brothers and sisters in Africa. One writer says in the course of four short years the white men of England and America sent three million gallons of whiskey to help civilize our black brothers when they acted for them, and that is why we are divided today. We have allowed the white man, the white woman, to act for us, and they have acted along every line and we are dismembered, disorganized, confused and puzzled until we do not know where to go or what to do. We do not know whom to follow. They have acted for us and told us we could not organize; we could not think for ourselves; we could not fight for ourselves.

We have proven him a liar in that line. (Cheers.) We have proven that we can fight for him when he runs, and we are now going to fight for ourselves. (Cheers.)

We have allowed him to act for us in making us pay more taxes for our back alley houses and unsanitary conditions of our streets in our large cities. We have allowed the white man to act for us, and there we have sent our boys and girls to build up those disreputable places, while the white was out in the suburbs in mansions and did not come near us. We have allowed him to act for us in doing everything.

Negroes Told Not to Organize.

The white man has told you not to organize because you cannot get any leader and that your leaders have betrayed you, and we have allowed them to lead us, and they have been leading us right back into slavery. They have led us so much that the majority of Negroes like white men and they mistrust their own. All the deviltry we have had among ourselves was caused by the drops of white blood we had in us.

I beg you men and women of my race, tonight, if I can do any good, I want to make you think. No race can rise except they begin to think. We must think for ourselves and stop letting the white man think for us. How can we think for ourselves? The cause is here, the man is here, the problem is before you. We have heard him talk time and again. Some of us are sta[u]nch members; others are not. But as the great leader, the Hon. Marcus Garvey, talks tonight, I want you to sink every word into your hearts.

Mr. Garvey's Address.

Mr. President, Officers and Members of the Newport News Division of the Universal Negro Improvement Association—Indeed, it is a pleasure to be with you. From the first time I visited your city I became impressed with your earnestness. Ever since I came here and went away an impression, an indelible impression, was made on me relative to your earnestness in the great onward and upward movement engineered under the leadership of the Universal Negro Improvement Association.

Since I visited you last the Universal Negro Improvement Association has grown financially and otherwise, numerically, to the extent that tonight, this very hour the Universal Negro Improvement Association is regarded as the strongest Negro movement in the world. (Cheers.) We have been able to force entry into every civilized country where Negroes live, and tonight the colors that you and I are wearing in Newport News are being worn by Negroes all over the world.

U.N.I.A. SERIOUS MOVEMENT.

As I have told you in many addresses before, the Universal Negro Improvement Association is a very serious movement. We are out for serious business. We are out for the capturing of liberty and democracy. (Cheers.) Liberty is not yet captured, therefore we are still fighting. We are in a very great war, a great conflict, and we will never get liberty, we will never capture democracy, until we, like all the other peoples who have won liberty and democracy, shed our sacred blood. This liberty, this democracy, for which we Negroes of the world are hoping, is a thing that has caused blood as a sacrifice by every people who possess it today.

THE DEFEAT OF GERMANY.

The white man of America who possesses his liberty and his democracy won it through the sacrifice of those thousands of soldiers who fought and fell under the leadership of George Washington. The French people, who are enjoying their liberty and their democracy today, are enjoying it because thousands of Frenchmen fought, bled and died to make France safe. That America, England and France have had peace with the world and with themselves is simply through the fact that they have defeated Germany and won for themselves liberty and democracy.

LIBERTY AND DEMOCRACY EXPENSIVE.

Therefore, you will realize that liberty and democracy are very expensive things, and you have to give life for it. And if we Negroes think we can get all these things without the shedding of blood for them we are making a dreadful mistake. You are not going to get anything unless you organize to fight for it. There are some things you can fight for constitutionally, such as your political rights, your civic rights, but to get liberty you have to shed some blood for it. And that is what the Universal Negro Improvement Association is preparing your minds for—to shed some blood so as to make your race a free and independent race. That blood we are not going to shed in Newport News, that blood we are not going to shed in America, because America will not be big enough to hold the Negro when the Negro gets ready. But that blood we are preparing to shed one day on the African battlefield, because it is the determination of the New Negro to re-possess himself of that country that God gave his forefathers. Africa is the richest continent in the world; it is the country that has given civilization to mankind and has made the white man what he is.

WHAT THE WHITE MAN OWES THE NEGRO.

After the white man is through abusing the Negro, when he gets back his sober senses, he will realize that he owes all he possesses today to the Negro. The Negro gave him science and art and literature and everything that is dear to him today, and the white man has kept them for thousands of years, and he has taken advantage of the world. He has even gone out of his way to reduce the African that gave him his civilization and kept him as a slave for two hundred and fifty years. But we feel that the time has come when we must take hold of that civilization that we once held. The hour has struck for the Negro to be once more a power in the world, and not all the white men in the world will be able to hold the Negro from becoming a power in the next century. Not even the powers of hell will be able to stop the Negro in his onward and upward movement. With Jesus as our standard bearer the Negro will march to victory.

THE NEGRO RULES.

There will be no democracy in the world until the Negro rules. We have given the white man a chance for thousands of years to show his feeling towards his fellowmen. And what has he done up to this twentieth century? He has murdered man; he has massacred man; he has deprived man of his rights even as God gave to man. The white man has shown himself an unfit subject to rule. Therefore he has to step off the stage of action.

I believe it is Shakespeare who said:

> "The Quality of mercy is not strained,
> It droppeth like the gentle rain from heaven
> Upon the place beneath;
> It is twice blessed;
> It blesseth him that gives and him that takes."[2]

Has the white man any mercy? Not before the black man returns to power will there be any mercy in the world. The Negro has been the savior of all that has been good for mankind.

But the future portends great things. It portends a leadership of Negroes that will draw man nearer to his God, because in the Negroes' rule there will be mercy, love and charity to all.

Man Created for a Purpose.

I want you colored men and women in Newport News to realize that you form a great part in this creation, for God has created you for a purpose; that purpose you have to keep in view; that purpose you must live. God said through the Psalmist that Ethiopia shall stretch forth her hands unto him and that princes shall come out of Ethiopia. I believe fervently that the hour has come for Ethiopia to stretch forth her hands unto God, and as we are stretching forth our hands unto God in New York, in Pennslyvania, in the West Indies, in Central America and in Africa and throughout the world I trust that you in Newport News are stretching forth your hands unto God.

Endless Chain of Negroes.

There is an endless chain of Negroes all over the world, and wherever Negroes are to be found this day they are suffering from the brutality of the white man, and because Negroes are suffering all over the world we feel that the time has come for the four hundred millions of us scattered all over the world to link up our sentiment for one common purpose—to obtain liberty and democracy.

Africa Must Be Restored.

I want you to understand that you have an association that is one of the greatest movements in the world. The New Negro, backed by the Universal Negro Improvement Association, is determined to restore Africa to the world, and you scattered children of Africa in Newport News, you children of Ethiopia, I want you to understand that the call is now made to you. What are you going to do? Are you going to remain to yourselves in Newport News and die? Or are you going to link up your strength, morally and financially, with the other Negroes of the world and let us all fight one battle unto victory? If you are prepared to do the latter, the battle is nearly won, because we of the Universal Negro Improvement Association intend within the next twelve months to roll up a sentiment in the United States of America that will be backed up by fifteen million black folks, so that when in the future you touch one Negro in Newport News you shall have touched fifteen million Negroes of the country. And within the next twenty-four months we intend to roll up an organization of nearly four hundred million people, so that when you touch any Negro in Newport News you touch four hundred million of Negroes all over the world at the same time.

Liberty or Death.

It falls to the province of every black man and every black woman to be a member of the Universal Negro Improvement Association, because there is but one purpose before us, which is the purpose of liberty—that liberty that

Patrick Henry spoke about in the legislature of Virginia over one hundred and forty years ago. We new Negroes of America declare that we desire liberty or we will take death. (Cheers.) They called us out but a few months ago to fight three thousand miles away in Europe to save civilization, to give liberty and democracy to the other peoples of the world. And we fought so splendidly, and after we died, after we gave up our blood, and some of us survived and returned to our respective countries, in America, in the West Indies, in Central America and in Africa, they told us, as they told us in the past, that this country is the white man's country. What is it but menial opportunities for you where you live in contact with white men? Because they have told us that in America, because they have told us that in France, because they have told us under the government of Great Britain that our opportunities are limited when we come in contact with white men, we say the war is not over yet. The war must go on; only that the war is not going on in France and Flanders, but the war will go on in the African plains, there to decide once and for all in the very near future whether black men are to be serfs and slaves or black men are to be free men.

BLACK MEN ARE GOING TO BE FREE.

We have decreed that black men are going to be free as white men are free or as yellow men are free. We have declared that if there is to be a British Empire, if there is to be a German Empire, if there is to be a Japanese Empire, if there is to be a French Republic and if there is to be an American Republic, then there must be a black republic of Africa. (Cheers.)

THE WHITE MAN HID THE BOOK FROM THE NEGRO.

The New Negro has given up the idea of white leadership. The white man cannot lead the Negro any longer any more. He was able through our ignorance to lead us for over three hundred years since he took us from Africa, but the New Negro has learned enough now. When the white man took the black man from Africa he took him under a camouflage. He said to the Queen of England that he was taking the black man from Africa for the purpose of civilizing and Christianizing him. But that was not his purpose. The white man's purpose for taking the Negro from his native land was to make a slave of him, to have free labor. Some of us were brought to the Southern States of this country, some of our brothers and sisters were taken to Central America and others were taken to the West Indian Islands, and we labored under the bonds of slavery for 250 years. The white man never schooled us for the 250 years. He hid the book from us, even the very Bible, and never taught the Negro anything.

THE NEGRO MADE A RUSH FOR THE BOOK.

But God moves in a mysterious way,[3] and he brought about Lincoln and Victoria, and he said, "You must let those people free," and they did let us free. As soon as we were freed we made a rush to get the book, and we did get the book. We got the Bible first, and we began to sing songs and give praise to God, and that is why the Negro shouts so much in church. But after he was through with the first he got hold of the school book and went from his A B C to Z, and what has happened in fifty years? There is not a white man so educated that you cannot find a Negro to equal him. None in France, none in England, none in America to beat the Negro educationally, and because we stand equal with him we say no longer shall the white man lead us, but we shall lead ourselves.

THE NEGRO AND THE GUN AND POWDER.

If we had not a complete training in knowledge before 1914 in that we only knew the book and were only able to read and write, they of themselves gave us training and placed two million of us in the army and gave us gun and powder and taught us how to use them. That completed the education of the Negro. Therefore, tonight the Negro stands complete in education. He knows how to read his book, he knows how to figure out, and he knows how to use the sword and the gun. And because he can do these things so splendidly, he is determined that he shall carve the way for himself to true liberty and democracy which the white man denied him after he was called out to shed his blood on the battlefields of France and Flanders.

THE BLACK STAR LINE STEAMSHIP CORPORATION.

I did not come down to Newport News to talk to you merely from a sentimental standpoint. I have come to talk to you from a sentimental and business standpoint. We cannot live on sentiment. We have to live on the material production of the world. I am here representing the Black Star Line Steamship Corporation of the world. The purpose of the Black Star Line Steamship Corporation is to float a line of steamships to run between America, Canada, the West Indies, South and Central America and Africa, carrying freight and passengers, thus linking up the sentiment and wealth of the four hundred million Negroes of the world. Every day I spend away from New York means a financial loss of $5,000 a day; but I have sacrificed all that to come and speak to you in Newport News, because you in Newport News have a history in connection with the Black Star Line.

FIRST STOCK SOLD.

I want to say to you that on the 31st of this month the S.S. Frederick Douglas will sail out of New York harbor, the property of the Black Star Line—the property of the Negro peoples of the world. I also want you to understand that the first stock that was sold in the Black Star Line was sold in the Dixie Theatre in Newport News. (Cheers.) The first five hundred dollars that we sold was sold in Newport News. Therefore, you gave the real start to the Black Star Line, and as you started the Black Star Line we want you to finish the Black Star Line.

So that is why I took the chance of leaving New York to speak to you in Newport News. I telegraphed your President a few days ago and asked him up to a conference to let him see what New York is doing to come back and tell you. The Negroes are alive in New York and they are alive in Philadelphia also. New York is supplying its quota to the Black Star Line and so is Philadelphia. I have taken the chance to come to Newport News to find out if you are going to supply your quota towards the Black Star Line. I want you to understand that opportunity is now knocking at your door. You know that opportunity knocks but once at every man's door. The Black Star Line is the biggest industrial and commercial undertaking of the Negro of the Twentieth Century. The Black Star Line opens up the industrial and commercial avenues that were heretofore closed to Negroes.

THE NEGRO MUST PROTECT HIMSELF.

Every ship, every house, every store the white man builds, he has his gun and powder to protect them. The white man has surrounded himself with all the protection necessary to protect his property. The Japanese Government protects the yellow man, and the English, German, French and American Governments protect the white man, and the Negro has absolutely no protection. And that is why they lynch and burn us with impunity all over the world, and they will continue to do so until the Negro starts out to protect himself. The Negro cannot protect himself by living alone—he must organize. When you offend one white man in America, you offend ninety millions of white men. When you offend one Negro, the other Negroes are unconcerned because we are not organized. Not until you can offer protection to your race as the white man offers protection to his race, will you be a free and independent people in the world.

Printed in *NW*, 1 November 1919. Original headlines abbreviated.

1. Elie Garcia was born in Haiti and educated in Haiti and France. He visited the United States for the first time in 1916 and returned to New York the next year. After residing there for several months, he went to West Virginia, where he was employed in a United States government laboratory in Nitro, W. Va., during the war and where UNIA member Eliézer Cadet also worked. When the laboratory closed at the war's end, Garcia went to Philadelphia and engaged in various business activities, including sales of stock for the Black Star Line. As secretary of the Philadelphia UNIA division and a successful stock salesman, Garcia was soon promoted to the position of Black Star Line representative for Philadelphia; Garvey later invited him to head a UNIA commission to visit Liberia in 1920. From Liberia Garcia sent a confidential report to Garvey outlining the favorable prospects for UNIA investment but excoriating the Americo-Liberians because of their domination of the indigenous population. Garcia's visit to Liberia stretched into mid-August 1920, when the UNIA convention in New York was in session. In July 1920, a Black Star Line stockholders' meeting made him a director. A few weeks later he was made assistant secretary of the BSL, and in October 1920 he became secretary, a position he held until he was indicted, along with Garvey and others, for mail fraud in early 1922 (*Marcus Garvey* v. *United States*, no. 8317, Ct. App., 2d Cir., 2 February 1925, pp. 2022–122; *NW*, 27 January 1923).

2. *The Merchant of Venice*, act 4, sc. 1, line 184.
3. An allusion to hymn no. 35, the Olney Hymns (1799) of William Cowper (1731–1800) (*BFQ*).

Editorial Letter by Marcus Garvey

[[Newport News, October 29, 1919]]

Fellowmen of the Negro Race, Greeting:

"Away down" in Virginia I have been for a few days testing out the sentiment of our people as touching their outlook on things temporal, and I have discovered that the Negro of the South is a new and different man to what he was prior to the war.

The bloody war has left a new spirit in the world—it has created for all mankind a new idea of liberty and democracy, and the Southern Negro now feels that he too has a part to play in the affairs of the world. A new light is burning for our brothers at this end. They are determined that they too shall enjoy a portion of that democracy for which many of their sons and brothers fought for and died for in France.

The New Negro manhood movement is not confined to the North alone, it has found its way far down South and there are millions of black folks here who mean to have all that is coming to them or they are going to die in the attempt of getting same.

I cannot but encourage the spirit of my brothers all over the world who are struggling for manhood and freedom rights.

This is the age of helpful action, and it falls to the province of every Negro to help his brother to a fuller realization of the opportunities of life. Now is the time for all of us, fellowmen, to join in and help in the spreading of the doctrines of the Universal Negro Improvement Association. We have to utilize every energy we possess to redeem the scattered millions of our race. There is no time to waste about East, West, North or South. The question of the Negro should be the only question for us. We have remained divided long enough to realize that our weakness as a race is caused through disunity. We can no longer allow the enemy to penetrate our ranks. We must "close ranks" and make up our minds all over the world either to have full liberty and democracy or to die in the attempt to get it.

The salvation of our race depends upon the action of the present generation of our young men. We fellows who could have died by the millions in battle fighting for the white men, must now realize that we have but one life to give and since that life could have been given in France and Flanders for the salvation of an alien race, we ought to be sensible enough to see and realize that if there is to be another sacrifice of life, we shall first give that life to our own cause.

Africa, bleeding Africa, is calling for the service of every black man and woman to redeem her from the enslavement of the white man. All the sacrifice that must be made, therefore, shall be of the Negro, for the Negro and no one else.

Whether we are of America, Canada, the West Indies, South or Central America or Africa the call for action is ours. The scattered children of Africa know no country but their own dear Father and Motherland. We may make progress in America, the West Indies and other foreign countries, but there will never be any real lasting progress until the Negro makes of Africa a strong and powerful Republic to lend protection to the success we make in foreign lands.

Let us therefore unite our forces and make one desperate rush for the goal of success.

And now that we have started to make good by uniting ourselves, let us spare no effort to go forward. The Black Star Line that we are giving to the world calls for the support of every Negro, and it is pleasing for me to say that our people in Virginia are doing most splendidly their part to help this Corporation fly the colors of the Negro on the high sea.

Buy all the shares you can now in the Black Star Line and make money while the opportunity presents itself. You may buy your shares today at $5.00; in the very near future you will have to pay more. Write or call on the Black Star Line 56 West 135th Street, New York, and purchase all the shares you want. With very best wishes for your success. Yours fraternally,

MARCUS GARVEY

Printed in *NW*, 1 November 1919. Original headlines omitted.

Richard W. Flournoy, Jr. to A. L. Flint

WASHINGTON October 29, 1919

Sir:

The Department has received your letter of October 11, 1919,[1] /2d after 213/ in which you refer to your letter of September 29, concerning Marcus Garvey, a negro agitator, whose departure for the Panama Canal Zone you wish to prevent.

On October 16, the Department wrote /letters/ to the Collectors of Customs at the ports of New York, New Orleans, Baltimore, Boston and Norfolk, in which they were requested not to issue a seaman's card to enable Garvey to depart from the United States. This Department has, of course, taken appropriate action to prevent his obtaining an American passport for the purpose.

I am, Sir, Your obedient servant,

R. W. FLOURNOY, JR.
Chief, Division of Passport Control

COPY to Governor, in duplicate.
[*Endorsements*] Mr. F— Will send copies
to Isth. Dodge Handle. [F.?]

WNRC, RG 185, file 91/215. TLS, recipient's copy. Corrections and endorsements are handwritten.

1. Not found.

Report by John F. Daly,[1] Certified Shorthand Reporter

Madison Square Garden,
New York, N. Y.,
October 30, 1919

JUBILEE OF UNIVERSAL NEGRO IMPROVEMENT ASSOCIATION.
PROFESSOR BUCK AND MARCUS GARVEY.

PROFESSOR BUCK.

Honorable President General, Officers, and Members of the Universal Negro Improvement Association, African Communities League, and the Black Star Line:

My subject tonight is entitled, "The Demand of the Hour". Were you to ask every man, every woman, and perhaps some of the little ones, they would say to you, as you mentioned the Black Star Line, as you mentioned the Universal Negro Improvement Association, that it is nothing strange; that it is nothing new, or, "We thought of that fifty years ago". But there is an old saying in the good book, and if you will read it, it tells you that, "God moves in a mysterious way his wonders to perform; he dashes in the sea and rides upon the storm".[2] There is also another statement there which reads, "A thousand years is but a day with God".[3] There has never been a great movement or any great cause on earth but that there was a man prepared to handle that situation. But before him in every case you have a lot of little fellows and a number of big fellows, but they will fail before they reach the point they are trying to make, and they go on year after year but the work is never done until the man whom God has ordained steps on earth before mankind (applause).

And as you look upon things around you and read carefully you will find this condition existing at all times; that in every century and during all time there is always a man fit for the time in which we live. I must try to prove that to you.

John Brown died because he attempted to free the black people of America.[4] They were not made free then, but it is the purpose of Almighty God that all great things in the human history must receive their birth when it concerns the liberty of man through human blood (applause). Therefore John Brown's blood had to be spilled, but that blood went into Mother Earth and in language of fire a few years after that spoke to an entire nation, and the world knew that millions of black people would be forced to be set free.[5] But it was not the intention of the white man to let the negro go free, but God said he had to do it and he was forced to do it (applause). And that same God is saying to you, the white peoples of the world, "I am going to show you that I have heard the call of Ethiopia, and four hundred million strong they are coming out and they are going to march under the leadership of the one man I have selected in the person of Marcus Garvey (great applause). And remember this: I gave you centuries in which to prove yourselves not autocrats, not conceited monkeys, but men fearing me and worshipping me; you have failed, and the people that you're trying to crush, they are going to stand up before you and all the world will know that I am The Lord, Thy God". (applause)

I know tonight under the sound of my voice there are men representing other races who when they hear such a speech laugh, smile and call us "fool negroes" because we believe in God. But, my friends, they smiled at old Daniel; they smiled at the three Hebrew children; they smiled and crucified the Son of God; but Christianity did not die; Christianity will not die, for God has ordained it that if other races fail, four hundred million black folks are going to carry Christianity on to its great end.

I am not here, my friends, to preach a sermon, but I want to show you before I touch this great work which we are doing that we are going forward with no fear but that of God, and we intend to go forward no matter how we go—we are willing and ready to go, if we have to go, to the height of our ambition not only through fire but over mountains of dead bodies and (voice drowned by applause).

We are not preaching anarchy. No. We have too much sense for that. We are not preaching the overthrowing of any nation or government. No. We have never tried that and we are not trying it now. But we are getting together, man for man, and we are trying—and we know we are going to succeed—to bring all the people of black skin in this world together. I know for hundreds of years there has been but one great fear in the hearts of the white man. He has learned this lesson; that a divided family cannot stand,

and when he instituted that worthless law—a worthless thing called slavery—he realized that there was only one way to protect his o[wn] dirty self,
and that was to keep the black people one from another; and so long as he
can keep them that way he realized he would be safe.

Tonight we are telling him not only in words, but we are showing it to
him in action—and in that action we want him to realize that we are not
playing; we mean business (applause); and he will find we mean business to
such an extent that if our men are not enough, by the living God, our women
are ready to[o]—(applause)—and if you never had a fight with a woman,
you ask the Italians what the Abyssinian King did to him with women,[6] and
they will tell you how black women can fight when their honor is at stake
(applause).

I said, my friends, that we are going through it all. You have succeeded
for years—the enemy, the white man—through the instrument of treacher-
ous black men; but you know that you can't find traitors among us, and I am
going to tell you, Mr. Paleface, that one year from now when a black man
proves himself a traitor to his race because you advise him to, that black man
will find that Hell is safer than this earth (applause). And I say to you that a
man who would make himself a black traitor for a few filthy dollars—as one
traitor, Judas, was told in the good book—"It would be better that you had a
millstone around your neck and at the bottom of the ocean"[7] than to try to
stop this movement (applause).

For years, I said, you kept us apart, and even now there are some of us
who think that because the negro was born in Africa and one in the E[ast]
Indies and the other in South America, that there is a difference between us,
but, my friends, heed not to that kind of teaching. All of us came from one
place. You and I in this generation might not be able to say we were born in
Africa, but I for one would to God that I had the honor of saying that
tonight (applause). For when I look back to that continent—and I spent
eighteen months of my boyhood days there—when I look at it and realize
every time I see a wealthy woman, paleface, walking the streets dressed in her
diamonds and looking a[t] me with scorn, my very blood rushes to my head
and I say, "My God, how long shall she scorn me or her make [*mate*?] scorn
me when they are wearing the jewels that came from my country?" (great
applause)—for which they did not pay one single cent and in most cases
killed our black people to get the diamond. Then I look at their automobile
rushing on their rubber tires and see them seated there in their stolen luxury,
I go back in my mind's eye to the Congo River[8] and see them getting the
rubber in its raw state from my people and giving them nothing for it, and I
ask, "How long is that going to be?"

But, my friends, you can go for centuries and succeed in your meanest,
but up there is a man who weighs every man for what he is doing and what he
is worth, and every day he writes something either for you or against you,
and he watches the people that you in your false pride think you are superior

to and he says, "Never mind. In my own time I am going to bring out that very object you despise to such a grandeur and such strength that alongside of them you would look like pigmies" (applause).

That time is here. We have the beginning in our leader, and there is one thing I want to say to you. All though the history of the prejudice paleface nation, when a black man did anything, anything great, the first thing they would ask was "What is his color?" Somebody said, "Why, he is a light colored man". The white man will say, "It is the white blood in him that acted". (laughter) But, thank God, tonight look at him and he is black all over (applause)—(pointing to Marcus Garvey)—and what is greater than all things, unlike the old ante-bellum negro, he is not ashamed of that color (applause).

We are here and we are here to let them know that the battle is on; the battle is on, my friends. My people are not leaving him to face the dangers alone, but they are standing behind him, and as our great speaker, Rev. Eason said, and I am going to make it stronger—I am going to try to make that speech of his stronger right there, for being a preacher he would not tell it—but the people who are standing behind this black man tonight, I want to tell you, four hundred million strong, in a few days you will realize that they are ready to go through Hell for it (applause). And those of you who stood alongside of the blackman on the fields of Flanders know that when he gets ready he can go through Hell for some months (applause). When you get started you have got to make Hell a little hotter than it was over there.

Now, my friends, you are here tonight not to hear speeches alone, but as we are talking remember the Black Star Line must not go over the top with but one ship. Though you have paid for that ship, we want you to understand that one ship will never touch the white man's civilization or will never touch his great strength commercially. You must be able to stand to him ship to ship as well as man for man (applause). Buy your stocks in the Black Star Line. It is the great chain that will connect all the black peoples of the world together, and he knows it better than you, and he is afraid of it. So make your vaunting good and buy stocks in the Black Star Line. The United States Government told you to buy Liberty bonds till it hurt. Buy Black Star Line shares till it pains (applause). Buy, and buy again.

Now, my friends, another thing; another great thought. Remember that we accept nothing from the other side, not one dollar, not one penny (applause). Therefore all our expenses must be born[e] by our people and you can dig down in your pockets and put up any kind of building you please for a church edifice. You can also dig down in your pocket and put moneys together in the Marcus Garvey defense fund. Why? Because they are after him, for they are afraid of him, and we intend to protect him to a man (applause), and we must get our dollars together to do it and I am going to call for a collection now. The ushers are going around among you to collect that collection, and I am going to stand here and see you begin to do it right. Don't put your little penny in if you can afford a dollar. Don't put your five-cent pieces if you can afford a half dollar. Don't put a dime if you can afford twenty-five cents, but put all you can afford, for remember we have sworn, come will or woe. We have started out to success and we are going to do it no matter what it costs, and to begin with you must prepare yourselves to defend him—not only his life, for you know they are all going to be careful how they try to take that the next time—for we are surrounding him to such an extent somebody, if they never smelt the fires of Hell, will smell it when they start again; and we are not challenging you, but we say this: "Don't get foolish now and think it is vain boast or you will see what Hell is". But realize this, that though we can throw our bodies before him in defense of his life, we need money to defend him in the law (applause).

Now, ladies and gentlemen, my time is up, for I am disobeying orders now by being five minutes overtime. I want to see you begin that collection. Now, put your money there; don't forget; this is the Marcus Garvey defense fund you're collecting, and this vast audience, this great throng here tonight, should not give less then $700.00 in that defense. Now, will the band kindly give us a tune?

MARCUS GARVEY

Miss Chairman, ladies and gentlemen: Once more it is my pleasure to address you. I am here tonight to represent the interests of the Universal Negro Improvement Association and the Black Star Line Steamship Corporation. About twenty-four months ago thirteen negro men and women organized in this city of New York the New York Division of the Universal Negro Improvement Association. When we organized it was suggested by some of our friends that we were attempting to do the impossible. Yet we were determined to carry through the work we dedicated ourselves to.

It is for me to tell you tonight that from the thirteen of us members who founded the New York Division of the Universal Negro Improvement Association we have grown into an organization of over two million active members of the same association all over the United States (applause). We have been able to establish branches of our association in twenty-five states of the union. We have been able to plant branches of our association in every West Indian island (applause).

Therefore I am here tonight representing not a New York organization, not an organization that is confined to the Western hemisphere alone, but I am representing an organization of four hundred million black men and women all over the world (applause). And I am here tonight to tell you that the Universal Negro Improvement Association breathes the spirit of the new negro, and the new negro has this declaration to make: that we new negroes out of the sacrifice of our blood mean to blaze our way to complete independence and make the negro free for everlasting.

The new negroes realize that we have fought in many a battle for the white man. Tonight we men who represent the four hundred million negroes say that the next fight will be fought to make the negro a free and independent race (applause), and all the other races of the world to take care of themselves. We of the Universal Negro Improvement Association have absolutely no apology to make neither to yellow men nor to white men. We realize that four hundred millions of us have suffered long enough now to think about our own business (applause). The new negro realizes that he has but one life, and he reasons this way: If I can give my life for the white man, I can give that life for myself.

The message I have to deliver to the world for the new negro is that there is no longer any cowardice in the negro. We have eliminated cowardice. And if the white man or the yellow man expects to find cowardice in the negro, he is only making a mistake. The boys of the New York Fifteenth were not cowards in France. The boys of the Illinois Eighth were not cowards in France. The boys they took from the West Indies were not cowards in France. The boys from all the different states of Africa were not cowards in France. We men who represent the American negro, the West Indian negro and African negro from the battlefields of France and Mesopotamia, we have one declaration to make to the world. We went out to fight for the sacred principles of democracy; we went out to save mankind, and up to now the negro has not received democracy. Therefore we intend to carry on the war until we receive democracy (great applause). The war for that will keep on. The war we intend to carry on is not a war in Europe, will not be a war in America, but it will be a bloody war between black and white on the African battle plains (applause).

We were misinformed about Africa for three hundred years. But in 1919 the new negro is not misinformed about Africa. He is well informed about Africa, and he knows that Africa is the richest continent in the world (applause). He knows that Africa is the bone of contention between white men and yellow men (applause). He knows that the fight between Great Britain and Germany was a fight for African aggrandisement.[9] Up to now the Kaiser would have been giving them trouble if it were not for the negro. It took the boys of the New York Fifteenth and the boys of the Illinois Eighth to bring the Kaiser to his knees (applause). We brought the Kaiser to his knees because we believed we were fighting a sacred cause. We fought under the light of democracy. Hence we say we have defeated the Kaiser and have given victory to the Allies, England, France and Italy, but we are not through with the war because we intend to take Africa for the four hundred million black folks of the world.

From Madison Square Garden tonight I give a challenge to the white race of the world. You have used the black man in this war to help you. But the black man has started to fight for himself. It will be a terrible day when black men draw the sword to fight for their liberty (applause), and that day is coming. And we can see Japan preparing for that day. We can see Europe preparing for that day, the day of the war of the races. That will be a bloody day. That will be a bloody day. Japan has been engaged for about twenty years in preparation for that day. The sword of Europe is already sharpened. The four hundred million black men have just started to sharpen their sword (applause). The last shall be the first and the first shall be the last.[10]

I speak this way not because I hate the white man, not because I hate any of God's children. No; I hate no man, because it is not in the good book to hate any one. It is because the negro has been so charitable. It is because the negro has been so merciful—while the white man has dominated over the negro for over five hundred years. They went to the west coast of Africa and took fourteen million of us and transplanted us across the seas to this western hemisphere—the Georgias of America, and several millions of us in the West Indian islands, the Jamaicas, the Barbadoes, and Trinidad. I think I can see the day—oh, the picture is before me in Madison Square garden tonight. The spirit of my forefathers calls out to me for revenge (applause)[.]

How did they bring us into slavery? They went to Queen Elizabeth and said, "We want to help your colonies in America and the West Indies. We therefore want a command from you which will empower us to take the blacks from Africa and take them to the colonies". She asked, "What compensation will you give those blacks of America", and they said, "We will civilize them and we will care for them". On those pretenses the Queen signed the charter which empowered those enlightened men to take the other forty millions of us black folks from Africa to these shores. For two hundred and fifty years they never taught us any lessons except that of the white man's. They hid the very Christian bible and religion from us except that which told us that black men were created to be hewers of wood and drawers of water.[11] For two hundred and fifty years they used us for slavery and serfdom, but there is a day of reckoning and there is a God Almighty.

They set free thousands of West Indian negroes eighty-three years ago. They hid the book from us for two hundred and fifty years, but what has happened? Fifty years, fifty-five years, sixty years after Abraham Lincoln let loose the negro in America; eighty three years after Victoria let loose the Negro in the West Indies, what has happened? If you can find a white man in the world, you can find a black man who can take his place. If you can find a white man who is a great scientist, you can find a negro who is also a great scientist. If you can find a white man who is a political economist, you can also find a negro who is a political economist. If white men have passed through Harvard and through Yale and through Cornell and Columbia, if white men have passed through Oxford, Cambridge; if white men have passed through the University of Paris and Berlin, you can find negroes who have passed through the same universities (applause). If white men are able to lead black men, black men are able to lead black men (applause). Therefore negroes repudiate the leadership of a white man, even as the yellow man repudiates the leadership of a white man, and in the name of God, the new negro pledges his life, pledges his blood, to revenge the blood of his forefathers.

As Patrick Henry said in the Virginia legislature over one hundred and forty years ago, "I care not what others may say, but as for me, give me liberty or give me death." I am calling upon you four hundred million blacks to make up your minds to give your blood to make a free and independent African republic.

Three hundred years ago there were no black men, women and children in the United States of America. Forty millions of black men and women have built up the great American republic. The American republic is reared upon the blood of millions of black men and women. The great British empire is built upon the blood and sacrifice of a million of black men. From the time of Cicero[12] England has been living as a parasite on the great continent of Africa, but today every black man intends to pick on the parasite, intends to pick on the parasite and throw the parasite away (applause). We say if Africa is good enough to build up England, if Africa is good enough to build up France, if Africa is good enough to build up Italy and to build up Belgium (laughter), the Belgium of Leopold of the Congo, then Africa ought to be good enough for finding a home and a place in the sun[13] for the black Ethiopians scattered all over the world.

Therefore if the white American say[s] America is for the white man; if the Englishman is saying, "England is for the Englishman["]; if the Frenchman is saying, "France is for the Frenchman", then the black man ought to say, "Africa is for the black man". We say this: that if it is right for the white man to rule; if it is right for the yellow man to rule, then it is also right for the black man to rule (applause). The white man has ruled for thousands of years with injustice. When the negro starts to rule, he will rule with mercy, because he believes in the sentiment of Shakespeare: "The quality of mercy is not strained; it droppeth as the gentle rain from heaven upon the place beneath; it is twice blessed. It blesseth him that gives and him that takes". We believe in such sentiments, and for that therefore the white man may take bread with the negro if he treats the negro right, but he may take death from the negro if he continues to brutalize the negro.

The black man loves the white man's civilization and why? Because we gave that civilization to him. We love the white man's civilization today because we gave that civilization to the white man.

Look how he is ruling down South. He lynches and he burns black men every day. No record in history can show where the negro ever committed such outrages when he was in power. But we would like our fellow citizens in this western hemisphere of the white race to understand that the new negro has enough sense to understand that he has the balance of power in the world (applause), and the war of races that I spoke of a while ago will be a bloody conflict between yellow Asia and white Europe. Those two races will start the conflict in the war of the races, and the black man is going to take up a position looking on (applause). Then if we can remember that the white man has treated us fairly when he is threatened with defeat, we will go to his rescue, but if we can remember that he never treated us fairly we will allow the Jap to give him what he is looking for (applause)[.]

We are ready now to fight the battles of the white man if the white man will give us what we are looking for—liberty and democracy. Give us our share of democracy and we promise you that the yellow peril[14] that threatens you, when it is about to subdue you, we will come, four hundred millions strong, to your rescue. But if you continue to stifle, if you continue to suppress us all over the world, when the time comes instead of helping you, we shall take up our swords and—(voice drowned by applause).

And before I go further I want every man and every woman in this great hall tonight to become a member of the Universal Negro Improvement Association, the organization that stands for the rights of the negro. You can become a member of the Universal Negro Improvement Association by giving in your name to the ushers with your fee of twenty-five cents. The secretary takes your name and writes to you notifying you of the first general meeting of the association, at which you are presented with a certificate of membership by the committee. When you get your certificate you are called upon to pay regular monthly dues of twenty-five cents. Twenty cents go into the general fund of the association for the carrying out of the object, and the rest goes into the sick and death benefit fund. We want you to understand that what you may be unable to do for yourselves you can have your own race do for you through the Universal Negro Improvement Association. So while the ushers are canvassing for shares of the Black Star Line, I want you also to join the association. I will devote the next ten minutes of my address to the Black Star Line Corporation.

We organized the Black Star Steamship Corporation three months ago, incorporating under the laws of the State of Delaware for $500,000. We have exhausted nearly half of the capital obtained by the selling of stock. We are about to float tomorrow the first ship of the Black Star Line, the S.S. "Frederick Douglas" (applause). At twelve o'clock tomorrow noon all the stockholders of the Black Star Line and the Universal Negro Improvement Association will have the privilege of seeing the launching of the ship at 125th Street and the North River. You will see the colors here of the Black Star Line from the mast-top. We want you to understand that the launching of the "Frederick Douglas" is only a start in the great enterprise we are under-taking because it is the intention of the Black Star Line Steamship Corpora-tion within the next twenty-four months to build fifty more ships. The next ship we intend to launch in January will be named the S. S. "———", and the other ship we will launch we will call the "[B]ooker T. Washington".[15] So I want you all to buy up your shares tonight in the Black Star Line. In the next thirty days we will reach $10,000,000. It will be a capitalized corporation of ten million dollars. Therefore we are offering you now the last chance to buy your shares at $5.00 each, and I want you men and you women tonight to buy as many shares as you possibly can as the ushers wait upon you. At the close you can come to the front and buy your shares—those who do not buy from the ushers. I have to thank you ever so much for the splendid response you have given to the many appeals, and I trust you will be on hand tomorrow at Liberty Hall, 128 West 136th Street. I thank you.

✱✱✱✱✱

(Note—Parts of this speech were unreportable due to the capacity of the hall and the fact that the reporter was some distance away from the speaker, and these elements were aggravated to a great extent by the occasional indistinctness of Garvey and his tendency to turn around and address the people in the gallery in back of him. These slight omissions have been indicated by the use of the asterisk.)

DNA, RG 65, file OG 185161. TD.

1. John F. Daly (d. 1948) was born in Brooklyn; he worked as a stenographer in the Supreme Court of New York County for over twenty-five years (*NYT*, 28 February 1948).

2. The correct quotation from William Cowper's hymn is: "He plants his footsteps in the sea / And rides upon the storm" (*BFQ*).

3. A possible paraphrase of Ps. 90:4 ("For a thousand years in thy sight are but as yesterday when it is past").

4. John Brown (1800–1859) was a militant opponent of slavery. In 1856 Brown led several sorties against slaveholders and their supporters in Kansas. In 1859 he led the abortive attack on the federal arsenal in Harpers Ferry, W. Va., in the hope that it would stir the slaves into forming a paramilitary unit to overthrow slavery. Brown was captured at Harpers Ferry, tried, and executed (*WBD*).

5. According to the 1860 census, there were 3,953,760 slaves in the United States. The passage of the Thirteenth Amendment to the Constitution in 1865 officially ended slavery in the United States and emancipated over 4,000,000 blacks.

6. A posssible reference to the resounding defeat of the Italian colonial forces by King Menelik II at Adowa in 1896. Menelik's army "did not consist of fighting men only; there were women, grandfathers, lame people, babies, priests, lepers: every kind of individual." An Italian army officer remarked, "It is not an army . . . it is an invasion—the transplanting of a whole people" (George Fitz-Hardinge Berkeley, *The Campaign of Adowa and the Rise of Menelik* [London: Constable, 1935], pp. 10–11).

7. This quotation from Luke 17:2 does not refer to Judas but to the general prospects of the nonbeliever.

8. The Congolese were forced to produce India rubber for the large export market controlled by the Belgians. The treatment of Congolese workers by the authorities of King Leopold II (1835–1909) became a cause for international protest, with reports of starvation, torture, murder, and dismemberment. Since taxes were paid in rubber, Congolese workers were often forced to collect it without compensation. Some reforms were brought about through international pressure and by the death of Leopold in 1909 (S. J. S. Cookey, *Britain and the Congo Question, 1885–1913* [New York: Humanities Press, 1968], pp. 129–30; W. R. Louis, ed., *E. D. Morel's History of the Congo Reform Association* [Oxford: Clarendon Press, 1968]; Stanley Shaloff, *Reform in Leopold's Congo* [Richmond: John Knox Press, 1970]).

9. Garvey's view of Africa as the prize over which World War I was fought was also held by other black leaders, although his belief that the battle over Africa was between "white men and yellow men" was less widely held. At the outset of the war, W. E. B. Du Bois contended that the conflict had "African roots," stating in a number of speeches that Britain, France, Germany, and Italy had engaged in struggles over African land for several decades, and that the war was a natural outgrowth of such European imperialist conflicts. In Du Bois's view, Europe had created a "labor aristocracy" that had ended the most extreme forms of exploitation of European labor, forcing capitalists to turn to Africa and other nonwhite territories to continue their exploitation of labor and resources (W. E. B. Du Bois, "The African Roots of War," *Atlantic Monthly* 115 [May 1915]: 707–14).

10. A paraphrase of Luke 13:30.

11. A paraphrase of Jos. 9:21.

12. Garvey's reference to Cicero (106–43 B.C.) is misleading. The first English forays into West Africa occurred in the 1550s (Winthrop D. Jordan, *White over Black*, paperback ed. [Baltimore: Penguin Books, 1969], p. 3).

13. The phrase "a place in the sun" gained currency after Bernard von Bulow's speech, "A Promise for Germany," given on 6 December 1897 before the Reichstag (*BFQ*).

14. Garvey was not alone in his belief that a clash between Asians and Europeans was imminent, nor was his prediction of a racial conflict unique. The term *yellow peril* originated with Kaiser Wilhelm II, who interpreted the Russo-Japanese conflict (1904–5) as a racial confrontation in which Russia represented the white race. In 1906, with the Panama Canal under construction and Japanese expansion in the Pacific under way, a clash between the United States and Japan was widely predicted. The kaiser, anxious to foment such a conflict, circulated a story to the effect that the Japanese had entered into a secret alliance with Mexico for the purpose of attacking the Panama Canal. The *New York Evening Sun* soon carried the story to the American public, claiming that the American ambassador to Mexico had been handed a copy of the secret treaty and had presented it to the president. This false story heightened fears of a yellow peril among Americans and increased the continuing suspicion of Japanese intrigues (Barbara Tuchman, *The Zimmerman Telegram* [London: Constable & Co., 1958], pp. 25–38; *Spectator*, 11 December 1897; George Sylvester Viereck, *The Kaiser on Trial* [New York: Greystone Press, 1937]).

15. The S.S. *Booker T. Washington* was the name given to the S.S. *Goethals* when it was purchased and rechristened by the Black Star Line in 1924. Garvey acquired the seized former German ship for $100,000 and spent an additional $25,000 to recondition it. In April 1926, however, the vessel fell under the auction hammer for a mere $25,000 (Robert A. Hill, "Marcus Garvey and the Federal Prosecution Efforts, 1918–1927" [unpublished MS]).

Intelligence Report of Meeting at Madison Square Garden

[*New York*] October 30, 1919

Thursday night, October 30th, the Negroes held a mass meeting at Madison Square Garden to celebrate the purchasing of the first vessel of the Black Star Line. About 6000 colored people were present and most of the group wore the colors of the new colored flag—red, green and black.

There were several singers—The first woman had a voice like a canary bird and sang about "Twittering birds in a gilded cage". The second singer was someone of prominence in the Colored World, and had a wonderful voice. In the middle of her encore "Annie Laurie", the crew of the new Black Star Liner came in and the howling and yowling of the mad mob drowned all the music. The quartette of "The Crew" then sang some songs of what they were going to do and the place went wild. It made one think of a foot-ball crew.

The Hon. Marcus Garvey, D.S.O.E. made a powerful speech quoting from the Bible "The first shall be last and the last shall be first" and since the negro had just started to awaken and move they would be the first. Th[i]s present war would seem insignificant when the race war took place. They had no intentions of fighting in Europe or the U.S. but expect to combine all the negroes and take Africa[.] "Africa", he said, "is the richest country in the world and we are going to go back there where Democracy has never been corrupted although the different tribes have had kings." Garvey also said that ["]we negroes are now wetting up the swords to fight for freedom and if the white people treat us right we will combine, otherwise the negroes will join Japan and the East.["] Garvey then gave the final warning that the colored people were going to be free even if it proved necessary to do it by violence. The crowd again went wild and some cried "Amen".

A minister from Philadelphia[,] /Rev. J. W. H. Eason/[,] then said that the reason the world had become so upset was because religion had been set aside. He also preached retribution for all the lynchings and mal-treatments of the negro. The crowd then cried "We'll get them yet" and howled like a lot of mad dogs. A collection was then taken to see if they could not buy 50 boats for the Black Star Line and subscriptions for shares at $5 each were taken over and over again from the crowd, stating always that "the palefaces, white people" were not wanted.

The U.S. flag was pointed to and questions asked: "Has the Black Man ever put a stain on it? Answer, "No, but the U.S. government has soiled it—and were ashamed[.]"

"Did the Negro soldiers in France fail in the fight for Democracy?" "No, but the Peace Conference has." There were several more pointed remarks made and after each a howl of anger from the mob and much stamping and whistling to show the contempt of the government.

The last speaker was the Abyssinian Prince. He was arrayed in all his glory like a Solomon—high-jew[e]led crown on his head and royal robes of brilliant hues and jewels. His voice was so weak that one could not hear a word. He spread his arms and blessed the people and the crowd dispersed.

One white woman offered to subscribe to the Cause and an usher looked the "Pale Face" over and said, "I'll confer with the others, but we don[']t want your money." The colored woman disappeared but failed to return.

DORIS HENRY

N, LC, part one, box 4, investigative file 1. TD.

ALL THOUGHTFUL NEGROES

WHO DESIRE TO PREPARE

Against the Future, and Who Seek Comfort and Happiness Will

INVEST IN

THE
BLACK STAR
LINE, Inc.

BUY YOUR SHARES TODAY!

The First Ships of the Corporation Will Float Between the 31st of October and 31st of December, 1919

Send in for Your Stocks Now

THE NEGRO IN THE REALM OF COMMERCE

Every Negro Should Buy Stocks
in the

BLACK STAR LINE STEAMSHIP CORPORATION

Capitalized at $500,000, Under the Laws of the State of Delaware, United States of America

A LINE OF STEAMSHIPS TO RUN BETWEEN AMERICA, AFRICA, THE WEST INDIES, CANADA, SOUTH AND CENTRAL AMERICA, CARRYING FREIGHT AND PASSENGERS

THE BLACK STAR LINE Will Open Up Untold Possibilities for the Race. Stocks Sold Only to Negros.

You Can Buy From One to Two Hundred Shares at $5.00 Each

Buy Now! Call or Write the Main Office

Black Star Line, Inc.

56 WEST 135th STREET

New York City, New York, U. S. A.

NEGROES AWAKE!

The hour has come to save your Race from the burning stake.

INVEST IN

THE BLACK STAR LINE

(*Source*: N, LC).

Robert Adger Bowen to William H. Lamar

NEW YORK. N.Y. October 31, 1919

PERSONAL

My dear Judge Lamar:

The Negro World for Nov. 1st is well worth your attention as being throughout devoted to the inflamatory utterances of Marcus Garvey. I have no spare copy to mark for you, but I understand that you get the Negro World in your office, and I refer you especially to the first paragraphs of column 1, page 1, the editorial—Socialism and the Negro (not objectionable in itself), the last paragraph of p. 3 and top of p. 4, and the whole of page 6 and column 1 of page 7.[1] Very truly yours,

ROBERT A. BOWEN

[*Typewritten reference*] RAB:MR

DNA, RG 28, file B-500, "Negro World." TLS, recipient's copy.

1. Copy was not retained in the files.

Report of UNIA Meeting

[*Negro World*, 1 November 1919]

That Liberty Hall has become the Mecca of the Negroes of Greater New York was indicated by the fact that over six thousand persons flocked there last Sunday night [*26 October*]. Nearly three thousand persons were wedged and jammed in the hall. Nearly as many were clustered around the building on every side and hundreds were turned away.

Hon. Marcus Garvey has made the meeting of the Universal Negro Improvement Association a permanent feature in the life of the Negroes of Harlem.

The Hall began to fill before seven o'clock. At 7.45 P.M., Mr. F. G. Malbra sounded the gavel and called the meeting to order and acted as master of ceremonies until Prof. W. H. Ferris came in at 8.30 o'clock.

Seated on the platform were Rev. and Mrs. J. W. H. Eason, Mr. Bayne, Mr. D. D. Shirley, Mr. Malbra, Mr. Moore and the entertainers. The following programme was rendered:

Singing .... "From Greenland's Icy Mountains"
Prayer .... [   ]
Selection .... Black Star Line Band
Solo .... Miss Richards

Violin Solo .... Master Wilkinson
Piano Solo .... Miss Wilkinson
Recitation—"Over the Top" .... Mr. Sebastion
Recitation—"Brandywine" .... Master Lambert Tobias
Soprano Solo .... Madame Louise Brown
Address .... Mr. Shirley
Baritone Solo .... Mr. Vanpatton
Piano Solo .... Miss Irene Callender
Address .... W. H. Ferris
Selection .... Band
Songs .... Acme Quartette
Address .... Rev. Dr. J. W. H. Eason
Solo .... Madame Houston

The programme gave great satisfaction. The solos of Madame Marie Barrier Houston and the singing of the Acme Quartette made a decided hit. The singing of Mrs. J. W. H. Eason and Miss Idah Ash during the week gave satisfaction. Mrs. Eason has a rich, full mezzo-soprano voice.

Mr. D. D. Shirley's Address.

Mr. D. D. Shirley, the National Organizer, spoke hopefully regarding the Negro's entrance into the commercial and business worlds.

The Negro's salvation rested in himself. He must become economically self-sustaining.

Prof. W. H. Ferris' Address.

Prof. W. H. Ferris, A.M., the author of "The African Abroad" and the Literary Editor of the Negro World, first read extracts from a letter from Hon. Marcus Garvey. Then he read the government notice published by the St. Vincent Government Gazette, where Gov. G. B. Haddon-Smith, Governor and Commander-in-Chief of the Windward Islands, promised to punish by fine or imprisonment anyone found circulating the Negro World.[1] Prof. Ferris said: "What shall we say of it? You have all heard of Charles Darwin, who popularized the theory of evolution. He championed the theory of natural selection and held that the ape was a remote ancestor of man. But one aspect of the Darwinian evolution fell down, because the missing link between man and the lower animals had never been found. The advocates of slavery believed at one time that the Negro was the missing link. But his achievements in the intellectual, musical and artistic worlds, his progress in accumulating a billion dollars' worth of property in America and in accumulating a bank account, which runs up into the hundreds of millions, has eternally lifted him out of the category of "Missing Links" between man and the ape. But there is one aspect of Darwin's theory that is true. Darwin speaks of the struggle for existence and the law of the survival of the fittest,[2] which holds sway throughout the universe. In every form of life, from the lowest to the highest, from the battling organisms in the ground up to the politicians striving for the presidential nomination, this struggle goes on. Every time disease germs invade the system there is a battle royal between the disease germs and the white blood corpuscles. As to whether you throw off the disease or the disease takes root in your system depends upon which one of the combatants wins out.

["]And according to the principle of the struggle for existence and the law of the survival of the fittest, if the Negro is physically, intellectually, morally and spiritually fit, if he can face obstacles and difficulties and still press forward, if he can face disfranchisement, Jim Crowism, limited educational privileges and restricted economic opportunity and still struggle on under the eternal and immutable laws which were ordained by the Almighty God, he will come into his own. The Negro has been caught up in the world's movement for freedom. And Gov. Smith is bucking against the Zeit Ge[i]st. Marcus Garvey is the Christopher Columbus of the Negro race. (Cheers.) Christopher Columbus discovered a new continent in seeking a new sea route to India, and Marcus Garvey discovered a new career for the Negroes of the Western Hemisphere, the career of commercial activity and enterprise.["]

DR. J. W. H. EASON'S ADDRESS.

Dr. J. W. H. Eason, pastor of the People's Church, Philadelphia, spoke on "The Rise of an Old People." Dr. Eason said:

This convention tonight surpasses anything I have seen at any place anywhere. Negroes are gathered here from all quarters of the globe. It is a source of consolation to find our people getting together. They have heard the clarion call of Marcus Garvey, and they are crying out: 'Father Garvey, we are coming 400,000,000 strong."

Before the law of St. Vincent was passed the Negroes caught the spirit. They may stop the Negro World for a while, but they cannot stop the Negro spirit. They may stop the Negro World because it expresses the plain, blunt truth. But truth crushed to earth will rise again, the eternal ears of God just heard.[3]

The ancient Ethiopian[s] and the ancient Egyptians who occupied Egypt were the descendants of Ham and the propagators of ancient civilization. Herod[o]tus and Homer testify to this. We taught the world the alphabet, we taught the world science, we taught astronomy, we taught the world philosophy, and, of course, we taught the world how to tell fortunes.

The engineering skill of all the nations cannot tell how those blocks of stones weighing tons were erected in their places in the vast Pyramids.

Julius Caesar said that these people living in Brit[ai]n were too dull to make good slaves. And yet the descendants of these people have the audacity to want to rule the world and not ask the other people how they want to be ruled.

We have been fighting the white man's battle and now we will fight our own battles. And I thank God for the Kaiser and Marcus Garvey. The Kaiser did us a lot of good through his own devilment. The nations of Europe found it a hard job to whip the Kaiser. France marshalled her black soldiers, England [*marshalled*] her black soldiers and America marshalled her black soldiers.

I have read ancient mediaeval and modern history. Do you know that I find that no nation ever got any of the goods of life without fighting for them? We are now fighting for our place in the sun of the commercial world. Nearly all of Africa is more civilized than Georgia, Alabama, Mississippi, Louisiana, Texas and Arkansas.

The ancient people have been represented in modern times by Frederick Douglas, J. C. Price,[4] Toussa[i]nt l'Ouverture and Marcus Garvey. Marcus Garvey possesses the eloquence of Frederick Douglas, the race pride of J. C. Price and the fighting spirit of Toussa[i]nt l'Ouverture.

The rise of an old people is seen in the Negro's idea of his God, his angels and heaven. We have learned that black is beautiful, black is noble and that black is the standard for the time. Negroes are now beginning to paint their angels with black faces, woolly hair and rosy cheeks.

Then in a dramatic manner Dr. Eason placed little Master Lambert Tobias on a chair and said, pointing to him:

The Anglo-Saxon says to this little colored boy: "You need not hope, you need not aspire, thus far shalt thou go and no farther."

The Universal Negro Improvement Association says to the colored youth: "Rise, shine, for the light is coming.[5] You can be anything under God's heaven you want to be."

The audience went away happy. They had been entertained by inspiring music, had been electrified by soul stirring eloquence and had seen the scrolls of ancient and modern history unrolled before their eyes.

Printed in *NW*, 1 November 1919. Original headlines omitted.

1. The notice read:
   1. Any person who knowingly brings into the Colony, or who procures the introduction into the Colony of, or who has in his possession or circulates any copy of a New York paper called "The Negro World", shall be guilty of an offence against this Regulation.
   2. Any person alleged to be guilty of an offence against the above Regulation may be tried by a Court of summary jurisdiction, and on conviction for such an offence, shall be liable to imprisonment with or without hard labour for a term not exceeding six months or to a fine not exceeding one hundred pounds or to both such imprisonment and fine.
   3. The Colonial Postmaster or any person appointed by him for the purpose, may, without reference to the Administrator, detain and destroy any copies of "The Negro World." (*Saint Vincent Government Gazette* 52, no. 56 [1 October 1919]; W. F. Elkins, "Marcus Garvey, the *Negro World*, and the British West Indies: 1919–1920," *Science and*

Society 36 [spring 1972]: 63–77; Governor Haddon-Smith, "Importation of Seditious Paper 'Negro World,' " 7 October 1919, PRO, CO 321/306, 63570).

2. Although both these phrases were popularly attributed to Charles R. Darwin (1809–1882), Darwin himself gave credit to English sociologist Herbert Spencer (1820–1903) for their origin (*BFQ*).

3. This quotation is from William Cullen Bryant's poem "The Battlefield" (1839). Marcus Garvey would later use the poem's ninth stanza on his dedication page of vol. 2 of *Philosophy and Opinions* (*BFQ*).

4. Joseph C. Price (1854–1893) was an AME Zion minister and a renowned orator. He was born in Elizabeth City, N.C., and educated at Lincoln University, Lincoln University, Pa. He served as president of Livingstone College, Salisbury, N.C., from 1882 until his death (J. W. Hood, *One Hundred Years of the African Methodist Episcopal Zion Church* [New York: AME Zion Book Concern, 1895], pp. 458–59; Garland I. Penn, *The Afro-American Press and Its Editors* [Springfield, Mass.: Wiley and Co., 1891], pp. 124–26).

5. A paraphrase of Isa. 57:19.

Bureau of Investigation Report

New York City Nov. 1st, 1919

IN RE: NEGRO ACTIVITIES Mass meeting of Negroes to celebrate the floating of first steamship of the Black Star Line.

Tonight [*30 October*], in company with Reporter John Daly, I attended a Mass meeting at Madison Square Garden, New York, held under the auspices of the Universal Negro Improvement Society and African Communities League.

The occasion was the celebration of the flo[a]ting of the first ship of the "Black Star Line," inaugurated by Marcus Garvey in New York and now organized, per his statements, in 27 states.

About 7,000 negroes attended. The chairman was Miss Henrietta Vinton Davis[.] Before any of the speeches were delivered, two large silk green flags were unfurled. These flags contained red silk stripes running from tip to tip and crossing each other, with a large black star covering the point where the stripes intersect. This, I presume is the flag or flags to be carried on the ship. Capt. Cockburn and his negro crew, all in uniform, were also presented to the audience and it was announced the ship would be launched from 135th St. & N.R. at 12.30 p.m. on Oct. 31st. It is named the "Frederick Douglass".

It was announced that $500,000.00 had so far been collected in stock subscriptions for this steamship line, and that the corporation would be recapitalized so as to bring the total allowable up to $10,000,000 in order to purchase additional ships.

The first speaker was the Rev. Dr. Eason, from Philadelphia, who announced himself as "a new minister of the new century of the new negro". A large part of his talk was taken up imploring the persons present to subscribe to stock for, as he said "if the blacks are set free commercially they are set free every other way."

At one point in his speech he quoted Patrick Henry in the following manner:

"The blacks are saying to the world:
Give me liberty or I will give you death!"

This was greeted with tremendous applause and cries of "Tell them again". He added that since the ending of the war the blacks had come to the conclusion that they could fight their own battles politically, commercially and every other way.

Following him was Professor Buck, also of Philadelphia, who made an extremely bad speech, from the point of inciting race hatred. He expressed his hatred of the white race in no unreserved terms, at several points making statements which to the writer were as close to advocating riot and revolution as have ever been heard. Some of his remarks were:

["]We will get to our goal if we have to go over mountains of dead bodies and thru a sea of blood!"

"We are standing behind this man (Garvey) tonight, four hundred million strong, and in a few days you will realize that they are ready to go thru Hell for him and those of you who fought alongside of the black man in Flanders know that when he gets ready he can go thru Hell for something.["]

"We must be able to stand against the white man ship for ship and man for man."

Professor Buck, I believe for the benefit of the few white reporters present, tried to impress them that the Negroes are good Christians and God-fearing citizens who are not advocating Anarchy or bomb-throwing, yet he, in a very sincere and excited manner, shouted to the audience that it was their duty as God-fearing persons to rise in their might and wrest from the Whites that which they have deprived the Negro race for centuries; to give up their lives, if need be, for the revenge that is due them for the injustices suffered. In very dramatic style he told the audience of the difficulty he has restraining himself from jumping at the throat of the prosperous whites, "who sneer at me while they are wearing diamonds that come from *my* country; whose automobiles are cushioned with tires made from the rubber that comes from *my* country." The approval of the audience was demonstrated all thr[ough]out his speech by applause and shouts of approval.

Garvey then took the stand. While Buck's speech was bad, Garvey's made it seem very conservative. He stated that he now carried a body-guard so that the next person who is "hired" to kill him will receive like punishment. He became so excited and spoke so quickly at times that it was impossible to make out some of his remarks. Some which were recorded by the writer, however, are:

"The next war in which the negro fights will be a fight to make a free negro race."

"We fought for democracy and we have not up to now received it. Therefore, we intend to carry on the war until we receive democracy.["]

"Ah, it will be a bloody day when Black meets White on the African battlefields."

"Africa is the bone of contention between the whites and blacks; the fight between England and Germany was for African aggrandisement, and the Kaiser would still be on his throne if it were not for the negro."

"We are not thru with the fight, for we intend to take Africa for the 400,000,000 black folks of the world."

"It will be a terrible day when black men draw the sword to fight for their liberty.["]

"We can see Japan preparing for the day. We can see Europe preparing for the day—the day of the war of the races. Oh, that will be a bloody day! Japan has been sharpening the sword of the East for about 50 years in preparation for the day. Four hundred million black men have just started to sharpen their swords.["]

"The spir[it] of my forefathers calls out to me here tonight for *Revenge!*"

"The new negro pledges his blood and his life to revenge for his forefathers. I am calling upon you 400,000,000 blacks to give up blood to make a free African republic."

Garvey criticized the visit of the Belgian crown heads to this country,[1] which was approved of by hisses and bo[o]s from the audience.

It is very apparent that Garvey has been preached about so much that the negroes here have beg[u]n to look upon him as some sort of a Savior or divine spirit. His appeals for funds was answered by a shower of five, ten, twenty and even one hundred dollar bills, which were pledged for stock in the new steamship line. Agent sat in back of the collector, and observed a leather bag of large size filled to the top with these subscriptions.

Garvey is without doubt one of the worst inciters in the United States today among the negroes, who, I believe, would do almost anything for him. If there should be any race trouble in New York at any time there is no doubt that Garvey is sowing the seeds now for it.

M. J. DAVIS

[*Handwritten endorsement*] W.S.R.
[*Stamped endorsements*] Noted F.D.W. FILE J.E.H.

DNA, RG 65, file OG 185161. TD, recipient's copy.

1. King Albert I, Queen Elizabeth, and Prince Leopold (Leopold III) of Belgium visited the United States from 3 October until 1 November 1919. Their American cross-country tour was widely reported in the press (*NYT*, 2 October, 3 October, 28 October, and 1 November 1919).

Marcus Garvey to Capt. Joshua Cockburn

[New York, 1 November 1919]

Sir,

You have been appointed Commander of the S.S. Yarmouth at a Salary of Four Hundred Dollars ($400.00) per month, to date from Nov. 1st, 1919, and half monthly salary two hundred dollars ($200.00) per month from Sept. 19th, 1919 to Oct. 31st, 1919.

Signed MARCUS GARVEY,
President
M.G.

As per shipping rate.
[*Address*] 201 West 128th St.,
New York City.

Printed in *Garvey* v. *United States*, no. 8317, Ct. App., 2d Cir., 2 February 1925, government exhibit no. 31.

Newspaper Report

[*New York World*, 1 November 1919]

NEGRO STOCKHOLDERS VISIT BLACK STAR SHIP

INSPECT VESSEL, WHICH PROVES TO BE THE SMALL YARMOUTH BUILT 32 YEARS AGO

At noon yesterday, at 135th Street and the Hudson River, a reception was held by the officials of the Black Star Line, organized in the interest of negro trade, for the stockholders in the new steamship company.

The many subscribers had been invited to inspect the first ship of the line and they went in style. Automobiles of every description were lined up and the pier was thronged.

It had been announced at a mass meeting of negroes in Madison Square Garden Thursday night, where Marcus Garvey[,] President of the Universal Negro Improvement Association, spoke, that the first ship was the Frederick Douglass. The vessel turned out to be the small Yarmouth, which was built thirty-two years ago and ran for years between Yarmouth, N. S., and Boston. The name Yarmouth is still painted on her bows and she is under British registry. While the Black Star Line flag flew from her mainmast, Harriss, Magill & Co. still own her. They have chartered her only to the Black Star Line.

Capt. Joshua Cockburn, a colored master with a British license, commands her. He was busy showing the shockholders about the ship yesterday, but another officer in a bright new uniform said he did not know when the ship would sail or where. "Maybe we will go to Newport News or maybe somewhere else," he said.

He denied the vessel would carry passengers. Asked if she had any cargo he said he did not know what was below deck.

Printed in the *New York World*, 1 November 1919.

Marcus Garvey to Isaac D. White, *New York World*[1]

NEW YORK, U.S.A. November 1 1919

Dear Sir:—

You will find herein enclosed the statement of correction made by me which we ask that you publish in your issue of tomorrow as a correction of the mis[s]statement made in your paper of today's date on the second column of the seventeenth page re Negro Stockholders Visit Black Star Line Steamship. Yours truly,

> BLACK STAR LINE CORPORATION.
> MARCUS GARVEY
> President

NNC, *W.* TLS, recipient's copy.

1. Isaac Deforest White (1864–1943), was a member of the staff of the *New York World* from 1886 until the paper's demise in 1931. In 1910 he was placed in charge of the newspaper's legal department and became an expert in libel law. Joseph Pulitzer (1885–1955), the paper's publisher, named White in 1913 to head a new department, the Bureau of Accuracy and Fair Play, formed to answer complaints of inaccuracies in news presentations. Garvey addressed White in this capacity (*NYT*, 25 September 1943).

Cable Address: "Slib," New York   Telephone: Harlem 2877

BLACK STAR LINE, Inc.

(Line of Steamships to run between America, Canada, South and Central America, the West Indies and Africa, carrying freight and passengers.)

MARCUS GARVEY
President

JEREMIAH M. CERTAIN
First Vice President

HENRIETTA VINTON DAVIS
Second Vice President

ED. D. SMITH-GREEN
Secretary

FRED D. POWELL
Assistant Secretary

GEORGE TOBIAS
Treasurer

UNIVERSAL BUILDING, 56 WEST 135TH STREET

NEW YORK, U.S.A. _____ November 1 19 19

Mr. I. B. White,

Morning Editorial Room,

New York World.

Dear Sir:-

You will find herein enclosed the statement of correction made by me which we ask that you publish in your issue of tomorrow as a correction of the mistatement made in your paper of today's date on the second column of the seventeenth page re Negro Stockholders Visit Black Star Line Steamship.

Yours truly,

Black Star Line Corporation.

Marcus Garvey

President.

Enclosure

Correction

Yesterday we published a news article in which we stated that ~~the~~ Harris McGill & Co. were still owners of the steamship "Yarmouth" which is advertised by the Black Star Line Steamship Corporation as their first ship, and that the ship was only chartered to the Black Star Line Steamship Corporation.

The statement as made was incorrect and the fact is that the Black Star Line Steamship Corporation have bought on contract the S.S. Yarmouth which they will re-christen the S.S. Frederick Douglas, for $168[,]ooo.oo

This correction is made so as not to place the Black Star Line in a wrong light before the public. We regret the publication.

NNC, *W*. TD, recipient's copy. Heading and corrections are handwritten by Garvey.

Statement by Ida E. Ash

[*Negro World*, 1 November 1919]

"BE YE ASHAMED TO CALL THYSELF A NEGRO, IF YE BE CONTENTED WITH CONDITIONS THAT EXIST"

All ye brainless mortals who try to influence people of this glorious race to stand by and not demand may desire to take our liberty for which our men fought so bravely—beware. If you like to be a footstool for the Anglo-Saxon, go to them, but by the gods of Egypt, when this race comes into its own, ask us for naught, for ye shall not even receive the crumbs from the table of those who have won.

Can you show us proof of what you have attained by this contented attitude? No, a thousand times no.

Can we get our rights by pleading to the Anglo-Saxon for mercy? Cover your face in shame when you mock our people for their call to the better nature of man, which came from God, but which has not been used for the betterment of our race.

The principles of the Universal Negro Improvement Association challenge you. We can at least show you the Black Star Line, which we hope every able-bodied person will support. Our president-general, Hon. Marcus Garvey, has proved without a doubt that "In unity there is strength." So, Negroes of the world, arm yourselves with ambition and perseverance and no one can keep you from gaining the knowledge which shall make you victors over your enemies within and without.

> IDA ESTINA ASH,
> 3rd Lady Vice-President,
> New York Division

Printed in *NW*, 1 November 1919

Post Wheeler, United States Legation, to Robert Lansing, Secretary of State

Stockholm, November 3, 1919

The Stockholm TIDNINGEN publishes a sen/s/ational despat[c]h from its London correspondent stating that the tension between whites and negroes in the United States is becoming constantly greater, that the negroes have established an American African steamship line called the Black Star Line and that the near departure from New York of its first steamer will be signalized by festivities of a character hostile to the whites. It alleges that "the leader of America's greatest colored organization declares that colored men are no[w] beginning to prepare for a war between the races and boasts that the next time they begin fighting it will be for the enfranchisement of the negroes and that the war will be the bloodiest the world has ever seen." Copy to London.

[POST] WHEELER[1]

DUL
Telegram 4204

DNA, RG 59, file 811.4016/28. TL (telegram), recipient's copy.

1. Post Wheeler (1869–1956) had been a career employee of the State Department since 1906. He assumed his duties as counselor of the U.S. legation at Stockholm in January 1919 (U.S. Department of State, *Register*, 1924 [Washington, D.C.: GPO, 1924], p. 203).

Isaac D. White to Marcus Garvey

[*New York*] November 4th, 1919

Dear Sir:—

I am enclosing herewith clipping from the Morning World of November 2nd, containing the publication suggested by you.

We regret that there was any misunderstanding as to the ownership of your vessel, and are indebted to you for bringing the matter to our attention. Truly yours,

[ISAAC D. WHITE]

1 encl
IDW/r

NNC, *W*. TL, carbon copy.

Enclosure

[*New York World*, 2 November 1919]

BLACK STAR BUYS STEAMER.

PAYS $168,500 FOR YARMOUTH, TO BE RENAMED FREDERICK DOUGLASS.

Leo H. Healy,[1] general counsel for Harriss, Magill & Co., steamship agents and brokers, announced yesterday that the Black Star Line had bought and paid for the steamship Yarmouth, which is to be renamed the Frederick Douglass. The price was $168,500, and payment was made by certified check.

"The statement published today that the vessel was under charter to the Black Star Line," said Attorney Healy, "is technically correct, but this is only a temporary arrangement. She is to be transferred to American registry, and the bill of sale will be delivered to the Black Star Line as soon as this can be done. It may take two or three weeks. The charter will remain in force in the meantime, so that the new owners can send her on any trip they see fit without delay."

Printed in the *New York World*, 2 November 1919.

1. Leo H. Healy (1893–1962), lawyer, was a native of Worcester, Mass., where he graduated from the College of the Holy Cross in 1915. Healy obtained a law degree from Fordham University, Bronx, N.Y., and in 1916 he began his law practice in New York City. After working for Harriss, Magill & Co., he was appointed district attorney of King's County, New York, in 1919 and held this post for five years. In 1927 Mayor James Walker selected Healy to become a city magistrate (*NYT*, 16 November 1927; College of the Holy Cross Archives, 1912 scrapbook).

Editorial Letter by Marcus Garvey

[[New York, Nov. 5, 1919]]

The S.S. Frederick Douglas, Flagship of the Black Star Line, Sails

Second Ship Will Be Named the Phyllis Wheatley[1]

Fellowmen of the Negro Race.

Greetings:—Today I write to you with a heart full of gladness, because we have achieved something for which every Negro should feel glad. We have launched the first ship of the Black Star Line, the S.S. Frederick Douglass. We have done it through an opposition that has no parallel in race achievements[.] When we incorporated the Black Star Line Steamship Corporation we were told by a few white men, supported by a large number of Negro traitors, that we could not do it; that we could not float a ship. First they said that we hadn't the ability to float a ship; next they said that the people would have no confidence in us to buy shares in our Corporation to make it possible for us to buy a ship. So as to back up their declarations they organized themselves into groups to oppose us, but with the grim determination of death, we made up our minds that there would be a Black Star Line, even if we had to float it in an ocean of human blood. Today we are glad because we have floated the S.S. Frederick Douglass, the flagship of our Merchant Marine, but there has been no shedding of blood, so as to make the launching a possibility. On the contrary, some of our bitterest opponents have confessed to their defeat, which confession is good for their souls, because it will, no doubt, make them better men.

On Thursday night, the 30th of October, 15,000 of us assembled in the Madison Square Garden, and there we demonstrated by our actions that we were ready and willing to back up this great commercial enterprise with our money and with our very lives. The meeting we held on that night was the largest ever staged by Negroes in any part of the world. We were able to convince the white race that we were in earnest, and apparently for the very first time they took us at our word. The big white dailies have paid us glowing compliments in this, our achievement, for which we thank them. We have entered the field of commerce, not to take advantage of any race or people, but to gather our share of the wealth there is in the world, that wealth which should be equally distributed among mankind. The first step, the S. S. Frederick Douglass is now afloat, and it is the determination of the directors to float a ship every two months, and we have decided to float the second ship, which will be named the S. S. Phyllis Wheatley, on the first of January, 1920, and I am now asking the hearty co-operation of every Negro, in every part of the world, to do his and her best to make the Phyllis Wheatley as great a success as the S. S. Frederick Douglass. The Phyllis Wheatley will be put on the African route and sail between America, Liberia and Sierra Leone, West Africa. If every member of the race will buy from two to two hundred shares it means that within the next twelve months the Black Star Line will be able to have under its control at least fifty ships flying the Red, the Black and the Green, the colors of the New Negro (copy obliterated).[2]

Let us beseech of every one to (copy obliterated.) time so that the entry we have made into the fields of commerce and industry will be productive of great benefit to those who are most interested by way of investment.

There is a world before us to conquer, and to carry out what we have started let us continue until we have crowned ourselves with victory.

Write or call now at the office of the Black Star Line Corporation, 56 West 135th Street, New York, and buy your shares. With best wishes, Yours fraternally,

MARCUS GARVEY

Printed in *Garvey* v. *United States*, no. 8317, Ct. App., 2d Cir., 2 February 1925, government exhibit no. 27. Original headlines abbreviated.

1. The black poet Phillis Wheatley (1753?–1784) wrote poems on some of the major political events of the American revolutionary era (Arthur P. David and Saunders Redding, *Cavalcade: Negro American Writing from 1760 to the Present* [Boston: Houghton Mifflin Co., 1971], pp. 8–16).

2. The words "copy obliterated" appear in the original document.

Frederick A. Emery to Post Wheeler

Washington, November 7, 1919

Amlegation
    Stockholm

Your 4204, November 3, 2 p.m. There is no crisis between white and negro races in United States. /The conditions are the same as for the past 20 years./ Several sporadic disturbances occurred involving men of both races but the incidents were local in character although they occurred in several cities. Trouble in each case grew out of ordinary quarrels, disturbances in Chicago being caused for instance by dispute regarding bathing beach priv[i]leges and in Washington by attacks on white women. Absurd stories of racial crisis attributable to radical propaganda[.] You may give above facts to press but not as coming from Department or Legation.

F[REDERICK] A. E[MERY][1]

DNA, RG 59, file 811.4016/28. TL (telegram), carbon copy.

1. Frederick A. Emery served as a deputy in the State Department's Office of Foreign Intelligence, which was charged with disseminating news information to consular and diplomatic offices abroad (U.S. Department of State, *Register*, 1918 [Washington, D.C.: GPO, 1918], pp. 30, 107).

W. E. B. Du Bois to A. H. May

[*New York*] November 8, 1919

My dear Sir:

Answering your letter of October 8th, I regret to say that I do not know anything about the Black Star Line. The District Attorney of New York at one time refused to let Mr. Garvey collect any more money for this line. On the other hand the newspapers say that one vessel has been chartered.

I can't advise you to invest money in this enterprise unless you have better sources of information than I command. Very sincerely yours,

[W. E. B. Du Bois]

MU, WEBDB Papers, reel 7, frame 1088. TL, carbon copy.

Report by the British Cabinet Office[1]

[*London*] 10 Nov. 1919

U.S.A.:

Reports from a reliable source indicate that the Negro agitation is beginning to assume international proportions. Large quantities of propaganda literature, calculated to incite racial ill-feeling, have been shipped from the U.S. to Africa and the West Indies. Marcus Garvey's 'Negro World', which is published in New York, already has a wide circulation among the Negroes in the West Indies and Africa, and its teaching has already caused trouble in the Zone of the Panama Canal. Garvey, who is President of the U.N.I.A., informed a large gathering of Negroes, whom he addressed in Madison Square Garden on 30th of October, that "400,000 million black men are beginning to sharpen their swords for the war of races".

PRO, Cab 24/92. TD.

1. Excerpt from "A Monthly Review of the Progress of Revolutionary Movement Abroad" (Home Office, Directorate of Intelligence, report no. 13, 10 November 1919).

Bureau of Investigation Report

Los Angeles Nov. 24, 1919

Re:—"NEGRO WORLD", Marcus Garvey (N.Y.) and W. RAVENWORTH Radical Activities

Under authority of a search warrant, the following letter was removed from the Post Office for examination:

> Envelope addressed: Mr. W. Ravenworth, 508 Maple Ave. Los Angeles, Cal. (crossed out)[.] (Marked in pencil by P.O.) B[ox] c/o Nishida[.] Postmarked: New York. N.Y. College Sta. Nov. 15, 1919, 7 P.M.

"ONE GOD! ONE AIM! ONE DESTINY!
NEW YORK DIVISION
UNIVERSAL NEGRO IMPROVEMENT ASSOCIATION
AND
AFRICAN COMMUNITIES LEAGUE

Marcus Garvey, President
Henrietta Vinton Davis[,] International Organizer
Jeremiah Certain, 1st Vice President
Fred D. Powell,[1] General Secretary
Walter Farrell, Associate Secretary
Ed. D. Smith-Green, Executive Secretary
H. Bain, Chairman Trustee Board
D. D. Shirley, Chairman A[d]visory Board
Granzaline Marshall, Secretary
Janie Jenkins, Pres. for Ladies' Division
Irene W. Wingfield, 1st Vice President
Hannah Nicholas, 2nd Vice President
Ida Ash, 3rd Vice President
Amy Ashwood, General Secretary
May Clarke, Associate Secretary
George Tobias, Treasurer

UNIVERSAL BUILDING 56 West 135th Street
NEW YORK, U.S.A.
October 30th, 1919

Mr. W. Ravenworth,
508 Maple Ave. Los Angeles, Cal.
Dear Sir:

We were very glad to appoint you as an agent for the Negro World papers, and we beg to submit to you the terms if we have not already done so.

We sell you these papers at three cents per copy and you sell there for five cents, two cents going to you for commission and the remaining three cents you will remit to us every two weeks by postal money order.

Do your best to build up a circulation for the paper and be sure to make prompt payments every two weeks.

With best wishes for your success, Yours faithfully,

NEGRO WORLD,
(SGD) MARCUS GARVEY
Manager
Pr. S.A."

ooo-

After being copied this letter was returned to the mails for delivery.

S. A. CONNELL

[*Endorsement*] Noted F.D.W.

DNA, RG 65, file OG 185161. TD. Stamped endorsement.

1. Fred D. Powell, a notary public and law student, served as president of the Philadelphia UNIA division before moving to New York in 1919. On 2 August 1919 the BSL Board of Directors elected him as assistant secretary and made him a director as well. On 8 August 1919 he replaced Janie Jenkins as the assistant treasurer of the BSL, a position he held until 20 September 1919 (*NW*, 13 March 1920; BSL Board of Directors meetings, minutes, from Thomas P. Merrilees, "Summary Report of Investigation of Books and Records of the Black Star Line," 26 October 1922, DJ-FBI).

Editorial Letter by Marcus Garvey

[[New York, November 29, 1919]]

NEGROES, ACQUIT YOURSELVES LIKE MEN

THERE IS A WORLD TO CONQUER

GLORY MUST BE ACHIEVED FOR SCATTERED ETHIOPIA

Fellowmen of the Negro Race,
Greeting:
Last Sunday [*23 November*] at 5 o'clock p.m., the S. S. Frederick Douglass steamed out of New York Harbor on her maiden trip as a Black Star Liner, to the West Indies and Central America. Fully 15,000 Negroes and 1,000 whites saw her off. From early Sunday morning to 5 o'clock there was a constant stream of humanity wending their way to the pier at 135th street and North River, New York, to take a glimpse of the first ship of our Merchant Marine.

In the sailing of the Frederick Douglass the Negro has made his bid for world conquest. It is well that all of us understand that we must now make up our minds to do or die. This age of commercial activity calls for the best of energy in the individual, race and nation. No people can allow themselves to be found wanting in activity in a time so fr[a]ught with trials and troubles for the weak and unprotected of mankind.

The world respects, pays attention to, and helps those of the human race who help themselves, and I now implore every man and woman of our race to strike out with the purpose of achieving for the glory of scattered Ethiopia.

Let our steamship sail the high seas, not one, not two, but hundreds of them. The stronger we become upon land and sea, the more will be the respect shown to us and the greater will be the glory. If I could but get every Negro to see the value of unity then, just in another 12 months, the Negro race would be among the most powerful people on earth. Success and greatness come not only by praying for it but by working for it. The white man has prayed, but the white man has also worked to take himself to the heights he has reached. If Negroes think that races grow great by being satisfied as slaves and peons then they misinterpret the purpose of the Almighty and they hope not to live and die like men.

The great Almighty created man for a supreme purpose, and the black man, according to the will of Providence, is called to live that purpose in equal right to all men. My advice, therefore, to the Negro peoples of the world is to live your purpose. Create, manufacture and make for yourselves. Make up your minds to drive your wedge into the plank of life. Go forth and conquer the forces of nature and reduce them to your will. There is a world of opportunities awaiting us, and it is for us, through unity of will and of purpose, to say we shall and we will play our part upon the great human stage of activity.

We shall start steamship lines, factories and banks. We shall restore Ethiopia to the world. We shall cause men to regard us as equals in achievements, in industry, in commerce, in politics[,] in science, art and education. We shall make of Ethiopia a mighty nation and we of this generation shall cause our children to call us blessed.

If you men and women of the race desire, therefore, to be partners in the great cause of a remodeled world wherein the Negro shall merit respect and esteem, then I say unto you: "Acquit yourselves like men." Help the Universal Negro Improvement Association to become a power in the world, and help the Black Star Line Steamship Corporation to float a new ship every two months.

The second ship of the Black Star Line will be launched between January and February, 1920, for the African trade, and it is now incumbent upon every man and woman of the race to do his and her bit by buying shares in the great corporation (copy missing)[1] shares as you can now, 5, 10, 20, 30, 40, 50, 100 or 200 at $5.00 each, and thereby register your name on the (copy missing)[.] Your shares will mean so much more money to you in the near future. I say invest now, invest quick in the Black Star Line Steamship

Corporation, 56 West 135th Street, New York, U.S.A. With very best wishes for your success, Yours fraternally

MARCUS GARVEY

Printed in *Garvey v. United States* no. 8317, Ct. App., 2d Cir., 2 February 1925, government exhibit no. 28.

1. The phrase appears in the original document.

African Blood Brotherhood Announcement

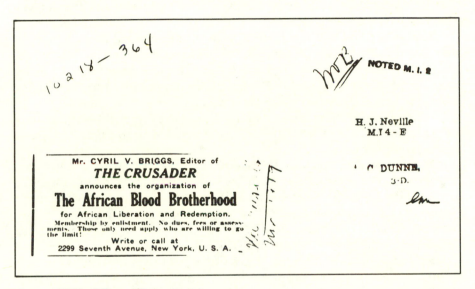

(*Source*: DNA, RG 165, file 10218–364).

Capt. Joshua Cockburn to Marcus Garvey

Sagua, La Grande [*Cuba*] Dec. 2nd 1919

Dear Sir,

I arrived at Sagua at 3.30 p.m. Tuesday Dec. 2nd, 1919 after quite an adventurous trip from New York.

I did not care to disturb your feelings before sailing, and it is for that reason that I did not tell you of the $5000, trick that we had to pay, or to be attached, this came from the arrangements of the Chief Engineer[1] with the North River repairing Company to try and get all they can out of us; I hope you have not paid any such bill or no bills at all without my signature.

Sir we left New York that night because I felt that there was some trick or Scheme on foot to prevent my sailing, but I did not for one moment thoug[h]t that I would have had such nasty plotters with me. The firemen could not raise more than 65—sixty five pounds of steam; and we could not steam more than seven knots per hour.

Going through the Straits of Florida the steam was so low that the ship became uncontrollable, it was just good luck that we were not run into by some other ship; however we managed to work out of the strongest of the current until we came to the Sombrero Cay, from there I took a fresh dep[arture?] for Sagua passing to South of Elbow Cay Light, at 4.45 a.m. Tuesday Dec.2n[d] I gave up the watch to Chief Officer Milne;[2] showing him that I had passed light and as everything was all clear he should keep a good lookout for Cuban Coast. To my very great surprise the man had altered the course and steered back for the light, and was not satisfied until he had the ship aground on the Cay Sal bank, got all hands excited; send out S.O.S. and the Chief Engineer gave instructions to draw fires for abandonment of the vessel, an[d] every thing before I got a chance to give one order, but thanks to God and the great assistance of the third Engineer ([M]r. Francisco)[3] who volunteered to give me sufficient steam, and to the surprise of the "WOULD BE WRECKERS" I got the ship afl[o]at and preceeded on to Sagua, as if there was nothing happened.

She was on the bank for one hour and bumped heavily on the sand, so I may have to Dry Dock her in Jamaica, Kingston; if the Board of inquiries direc[t] it to be done; there is no visible damage done and please dont be uneasy for I took her out of NEW York against wishes and foul work and by the help of God I will bring her back to you in New York. I cannot write all the dirty work that they have tried to do and I am praying daily to keep my temper and patience until I can be rid of them. Gammon[4] who was at /the helm/ the time of grounding will tell you, how the chief mate deliberately altered the course after I went to take a little rest and put the ship ashore thinking perhaps, that would have been the end of it.

He appears to be very sore because one of the crew said, that in a few [y]ears hence, there will be only the Japanese and Black Star Line steamers run[ni]ng the oceans so I suppose he made up his mi[n]d to kill things at once.

I may not get away from here until Saturd[ay] as I will have to be fumigated before going alongside to discharge[.]

The passengers are behaving splendidly, and also the crew and officers; with the exception of a few firemen whom I had to disrate[.]

Please convey greetings to Liberty Hall from steamer "FREDERICK DOUGLASS[."] Yours truly

JOSHUA COCKBURN

NFRC, Marcus Garvey case file of exhibits, C-33-688, FRC 539-440. TLS, recipient's copy.

1. Philip Mayler (b. 1879) was the English-born chief engineer of the *Yarmouth* (DNA, RG 85, file T-715).
2. Frank Milne (Ibid.).
3. Legar Francisco (b. 1885) was listed as the *Yarmouth*'s third assistant engineer (Ibid.).
4. Sailor Jacob Gammon (Ibid.).

Editorial Letter by Marcus Garvey

[[New York, December 3, 1919]]

NEGROES OF THE WORLD, THE ETERNAL HAS HAPPENED

THE NEW NEGRO HAS MADE HISTORY FOR HIMSELF AND ETHIOPIA SHALL BE REDEEMED

Fellowmen of the Negro Race,

Greeting:—

The Eternal has happened. For centuries the black man has been taught by his ancient overlords that he was "nothing," is "nothing" and never shall be "anything."

We black folks believe so much in the omnipotence of the white man that we actually gave in all hope and resigned ourselves to the positions of slaves and serfs for nearly five hundred years. But, thank God, a new day has dawned and all black men of the twentieth century see themselves the equal of all men.

Five years ago the Negro Universal was sleeping upon his bale of cotton in the South of America; he was steeped in mud in the banana fields of the West Indies and Central America, seeing no possible way of extricating himself from the environments; he smarted under the lash of the new taskmaster in Africa; but alas! today he is the new man who has proclaimed to the world that the despised and rejected shall rise, not only from his serfdom and slavery, but to rule and to teach man how to live. The New Negro has risen in the might of his manhood and he has now determined within himself to hold fast to the material glories of life and play his part as a man. There is no going back today in the progress of mankind. The white man has been going forward for thousands of years; the yellow man within the last century made a sprint for commercial, industrial, political and scientific glory and he is now regarded as the equal of his white brother on all lines. The Negro who slept and wallowed in the mire for centuries has just begun to turn and he has now placed his hope in God and himself and he is going forward to achieve.

On the 31st of October the Negro people of the world, acting through six thousand of their representatives in New York, United States of America, purchased a steamship which they are re-christening the S.S. Frederick

Douglass; and they said: "We are doing this because we desire to get our share of the world's goods, so long as creation lasts." The object was to run a line of steamships between the United States, Africa, Canada, the West Indies and Central America. Thousands of black men and white men said that it could not be done. They said that the Negro had no initiative; that he was not a business man, but a laborer; that he had not the brain to engineer a corporation, to own and run ships; that he had no knowledge of navigation, therefore the proposition was impossible.

"Oh! ye of little faith."[1] The Eternal has happened. The Negro incorporated a steamship enterprise by the name of "The Black Star Line;" he placed $500,000 of common stock on the market at $5 a share, and in ten weeks he sold so many shares to his own people that he was able on the 31st of October to take over the first steamship ever owned by the race in modern times. On the 23rd of November the ship sailed out of New York harbor with a Negro captain and Negro crew—a sight that was witnessed by nearly 15,000 people and at the time of writing she is now discharging a load of cement at Sagua, Cuba, in the West Indies.

Verily the Negro has arisen and today he has entered the race of life. He means to play his part and play it well. No more lack of faith, no more lack of confidence, no more belief in the omnipotence of others. The Negro is now a full-grown and wide-awake MAN.

Sons and daughters of Ethiopia, I say unto you, arise! The hour has struck, and Ethiopia is now calling you to achievements and to glory. Let no other sound attract your notice. Heed not the call of any other "voice," for Ethiopia has caught a new vision, and Ethiopia now says, "On to glory."

I beseech you, men and women of the race, to steel your hearts, your minds and your souls for the coming conflict of ideals. The whole world is in turmoil and a revolution threatens. Asia and Europe are preparing for this revolution. It will mean the survival of the fittest, and I now declare that Africa must also prepare; for in the triumph of the forces of white, yellow or black men in this coming revolution will hang the destiny of the world.

Sons and daughters of Africa, scattered though you may be, I implore of you to prepare. Prepare in all ways to strengthen the hands of Mother Africa. Our mother has been bleeding for centuries from the injuries inflicted upon her by a merciless foe. The call is for a physician to heal the wounds, and there can be no other physician than the dark hued son of the mother, and there can be no other nurse as tender and kind as the daughter of this afflicted mother.

Let us not turn back in this determination of ours. Africa must be redeemed, but before her redemption we have to prove to the world that we are fit. The chance to make ourselves fit is now presented to every son and daughter of Africa. We must now achieve in commerce, science, education, art, industry and politics. The Black Star Line Steamship Corporation of 56 West 135th street, New York, is leading the way for the success of the race in commerce and industry. This corporation desires the assistance of every black man, woman and child. The hope of this corporation is to have the ships of the Negro float on every sea. Our commerce shall extend to every nook and corner of the world, through the Black Star Line; it is therefore up to each and every one of the race to do his and her duty by buying shares in this corporation to make it a powerful agency for good. You may buy your shares today and help to found the empire of greatness for the race. Send in or call right now for your shares. Buy 5, 10, 20, 30, 40, 50, 100 or 200. Get busy, every man, for the Eternal has happened.

The biggest thing for the Negro today is the Black Star Line Steamship Corporation, 56 West 135th street, New York, United States of America. With very best wishes for your success, your fraternally,

MARCUS GARVEY

Printed in *NW*, 6 December 1919. This editorial was marked "Exhibit #6" as part of a file of exhibits attached to a letter of 11 May 1921 from J. Edgar Hoover to William L. Hurley (DNA, RG 59, file 000-612).

1. A paraphrase of Matt. 8:26.

Capt. Joshua Cockburn to Marcus Garvey

[*Sagua, La Grande, Cuba*] Dec 5th 1919

Dear Sir;

I received your Telegram on arrival here, and hoping by this time that you will have received my report concerning the accid[ent] of Grounding.

I expect leaving here tomorrow (Saturday) for Kingston, Ja.; none of the crew or passengers were allowed on shore, but I could not prevent having communication with the shore people because the Stevadores had to come on boa[rd] to discharge the cargo and the ship had to be placed alongside the wharf.

People here are just crazy about the organization and had all kinds of entertainments ready for the crew and passengers if they were allowed ashore.

The stevadore's gang containing just a handful of men bought up two hundred and fifty dollars' worth of shares just in a twinkle; we were compell[ed] to say a few words to them from the ship since they were so willing to respond. The Chief Officer and Chief Engineer means nothing but trouble and [I] have all that I want to do in preventing my crew from beating them up; I have to keep begging the men to leave them to me that they should be dealt wi[th] in the proper way; there was a big drunken spree last night with the Chief Mate & Engineer I had to order them to their rooms with a threat, because of the scene he was creating amongst the passengers and shore officials; Miss Davis will probably tell you more about it, I have quite a handful with these two palefaces, but have as much rope as will hang themselves. The people at Havana are mustering in thousands to see the ship and I have no doubt that it would be the means of collecting a Hundred Thousand of Dollars in quick time f[ro]m them because wherever you go it seems to be the same cry for freedom as in New York. From what I see of Sagua I know we would get 100% more in Hava[na] than Jamaica; because the people here has the cash to spare and the people the West Indies are too poor to afford much, so by all means the vessel ought to touch Havana before returning to New York. The Chief Engineer is just returning from ashore against my orders and is intoxicated at the same time he is endeavouring to delay my sailing from here tomorrow, so do not be surprised at anything that may happen; but rest assured that I will do my best under all circumstances to carry this voyage through successfully. I see by the Havana Post that the American Gov[.] is not allowing coal to any Foreign vessels after Dec. 5th. I do not know how well it will work, so you must follow the [o]ther shipping Companies as near as possible, find out how they obtain their bunkers so that we cannot be stung. My cargo is nearly all discharged and with the exceptions of the barrels that these hoodlums broke in New York there is no damage whatever. To clear myself against any accusations of the Chief Engineer I am holding a survey here at Sagua, Cuba; tomorrow to get a Certificate in order that I can proceed to Jamaica where I will demand an Inquiry into the Grounding off Cay Sal, where evidences will be produced. I am afraid I may have to leave the Engineer behind here in Sagua, and if I do you will know long before thi[s] letter reaches you, because I will Cable; I am learning daily all the plans that were laid against us as he has spoken out to the mate and the mate to me[.] I hope you are trying to get an Engineer from Cardiff[1] and also trying to Incorporate in Liberia so tha[t] we can go ahead in the right way. Best wishes to the people at Liberty Hall and with regards to yourself and Staff I remain Yours Faithfully

COCKBURN

Master . . . S.S. Frederick Douglass

NFRC, Marcus Garvey case file of exhibits, C-33-688, FRC 539 440. TLS, recipient's copy.

1. Cardiff, Wales, had a substantial black population living in the city's Adamsdown and South wards. Many black seamen chose Cardiff as their home port because it was a major center of the "tramp trade," which appealed to ships making long voyages. Cardiff, therefore, provided more opportunities for jobs on ships likely to visit ports in the West Indies (Kenneth Little, *Negroes in Britain* [London and Boston: Routledge & Kegan Paul, 1948], p. 57).

The Universal Negro Creed.

I Believe in a Universal Improvement of the Negro Race.

I believe that the Negro race is equal to any other race on this Planet.

I believe that the race was taught to dislike each other through false doctrines.

I believe in having schools to teach Negro History, so that our children may learn more about the great men of their race and be proud of their black skins.

I believe that senses more than sentiment is the best force to apply in order to secure advancement.

I believe that self-respect and dignity demand that I take up life's battles, and fight it out for myself, side by side with those of my own race instead of helplessly begging some other race to help us.

I believe that God created of one blood all nations or men to dwell on the face of this earth.

I believe that co-operation, unity and love, governs success and as a race we have to accept this doctrine or be doomed to failure in the race of life.

I believe that personal ambition, personal efforts and competition is the great need of this race of ours.

I believe in a colourless God.

And I the undersigned from henceforth do resolve and pledge myself to assist in the uplift of my race, and to establish a feeling of solidarity among all my people: believing in the fatherhood of God, and the brotherhood of man, in order that we may restore the ancient glories of Ethiopia.

SIGNED...

PLACE AND DATE..................................

(*Source*: JA, CSO).

British Military Intelligence Report

New York Dec. 10, 1919

NEGRO AGITATION

Universal Negro Improvement Ass'n.

At a regular meeting of the Universal Negro Improvement Association, held at Liberty Hall, on the evening of November 9th, Mr. Hilary R. W. Johnson,[1] of Liberia, was among the speakers. In closing his remarks he expressed the hope that all might have an opportunity of coming to Liberia. Mr. Garvey replied:

> "It is enough for me to say to Mr. Johnson, we are coming to Liberia. Next August we will have a convention in Liberty Hall. And then the headquarters of the Universal Negro Improvement Association will be in Liberia."

Miss Henrietta Vinton Davis, the international organizer, who has been appointed representative of the Association in the West Indies and in Panama and Costa Rica, and who sailed on the S.S. "Frederick Douglass" on its initial trip, leaving New York on November 23rd, had the following to say:

> "I am proud to say that my mission was successful in Washington in obtaining a passport, as a citizen of this country, to go to the West Indies, South and Central America. I had to be patient and hold my temper and had to be persistent and made up my mind that I had to have that passport or know the reason why.

> "I had some very influential friends in Washington who aided me, and backed up by what was behind me in New York, I succeeded in getting the passport.["]

Mr. Garvey said that all those who desired to book their passage to Cuba, Jamaica and Panama, could book the same the following week at the office 56 West 135th street.

> "We secured today the passenger's license from the Canadian government. The S.S. 'Frederick Douglass' will carry fifty first-class passengers. It will be $60 to Cuba, $65 to Jamaica and $80 to Colon. The war tax is $5. We will take you twenty-five per cent cheaper than you can go on any other line.
> While the Peace Conference was in session in France, we sent Mr. Elija Cadet to represent the U.N.I.A. in Paris. He will soon

return to tell us what he learned about the Peace Conference and the world aspects of the race question in Paris. The Negro is now beginning to play a part in world affairs."

Among other things Dr. W. H. Eason, of Philadelphia, said:

"Do you know that we Negroes have gotten to be somebody? Oh yes. In 1920 we will put our candidate in the field. He may not be elected president of the U.S. but he will be president of the Negroes of the world."

The following letter from Marcus Garvey, dated Chicago, November 14th, was published in the "Negro World" of November 15th:

" . . . When I survey the world of political activity, I see Africa as the envied goal of all races. Africa, by the plan of the other races, is to be the mart of exploitation, it is to be the 'No Man's Land' of the races whilst Europe remains in the hands of the white man and Asia the domain of the yellow man. Unconsciously the Negro slept for five hundred years and thereby gave the impression to an envious and avaricious world that all were welcomed to Africa, but today the Negro is fully awake and he is saying to all comers: [']Thus far in Africa and no further.[']"

"Africa supplied forty millions of slaves to the Western world.[2] Africa bled that others might live, but today Africa, through wounds inflicted, has recovered from her affliction and in the full strength of her manhood and womanhood is hurling her defiance to a mad world. Sons and daughters of Africa, arise. . . . The time has come for us to pool our resources and make of ourselves a mighty race and nation. . . ."

An African merchant, S. G. Krakpa-Quartey,[3] of Accra, Gold Coast Colony, W.A., visited the office of the "Negro World" on November 14th and addressed a gathering of the Universal Negro Improvement Association at Liberty Hall the same evening. Mr. Krakpa-Quartey is an importer of provisions, cotton goods, etc., and a exporter of mahogany.

In a letter dated New York, November 22nd, Garvey tells every Negro to think of the revolution that will one day sweep the continent of Africa; that they should dream and plan for that day; that through the Black Star Line black men the world over will be able to say in the future: "We came, we saw, we conquered."

S.S. "FREDERICK DOUGLASS"

Garvey's ship, the "Frederick Douglass," sailed from New York on the afternoon of November 23rd, but was held up in midstream owing to a technical point raised by the American Insurance company. The boat was later insured in a London company, and a wireless was received at Garvey's headquarters later that the boat was safely off the coast of Cape May. At a meeting held the same evening to celebrate the sailing of the steamship, Garvey told of the delay and eulogized the British government for giving them the insurance although the British government did not consider them their friends. He further said:

> "We have created a revolution and it is well that all of us understand it. . . ."
>
> "As George Washington used America to establish the freedom and independence of the white man, so the Negro will use America to establish his freedom and independence. I do not feel that we could have done today in any part of the white world what we have done in America. The American used the brawn of the Negro to be what he is today. The Negro will use America today to be what he wants to be tomorrow. . . . "

We are informed that Garvey got his boat through under peculiar opposition. The District Attorney used all power to have the sale cancelled, but Harriss, Magill & Co., S.S. Agents, would not listen to any proposition made. Mr. Magill, it is stated, is now in Europe. He is said to be an Irish sympathizer and is selling boats to Irish syndicates. From the fact that he is selling boats to Irish syndicates and to negroes, and that they got Trotter to the Peace Conference,[4] it would appear that there is something doing. . . .[5]

A special meeting of the stockholders of the Black Star Line is announced to be held on Dec. 22nd at the office of the company at Liberty Hall, 120 West 138th Street, for the purpose of voting on a proposition to increase its capital stock from $500,000 to $10,000,000.

It is reported that Marcus Garvey will wed Miss Amy Ashwood, General Lady Secretary of the New York Division of the Universal Negro Imp. Ass'n and a Director of the Black Star Line, some time this month. Miss Ashwood helped Mr. Garvey to organize the association and stuck to it when all others failed to give their support.

The Black Star Line, we are informed, recently bought the dwelling houses at #54 West 135th Street. This plot, it is said, together with No. 52 and 56 West 135th Street, now owned by the company, will be improved with a modern five-story office building. . . .

DNA, RG 165, file 10218-364-16. TD, recipient's copy. Originally it appeared as an enclosure to a letter from Maj. H. A. Strauss to the director of the Military Intelligence Division, 20 December 1919 (DNA, RG 165, file 10218-364-17-34x). This report was given to MID by British authorities.

1. Hilary Richard Wright Johnson, Liberian architect and builder, received his college education in the United States. He was the grandson of the Liberian president of the same name, who served from 1884 to 1891, and the son of Gabriel Johnson, the potentate of the

UNIA elected in August 1920. He later served as secretary-general of the Monrovia division of the UNIA after its incorporation at the beginning of 1921, and during the same year he worked as a clerk in the UNIA commissariat in Monrovia, established by the first technical team Garvey sent to Liberia. During 1921, with the assistance of G. O. Marke, the supreme deputy potentate, Johnson also founded and edited a weekly newspaper, the *Liberian Patriot*. He later served as secretary of the YMCA in Monrovia (C. Aboyomi Cassell, *Liberia: History of the First African Republic* [New York: Fountainhead Publishers, 1970]).

2. Estimates of the number of slaves brought to the Western hemisphere during the transatlantic slave trade vary. Philip Curtin's figure of 11 million is often cited as a minimum estimate (Philip Curtin, *The Atlantic Slave Trade: A Census* [Madison: University of Wisconsin Press, 1969], chap. 1; Paul E. Lovejoy, "The Volume of the African Slave Trade: A Synthesis," *Journal of African History*, 2 [1982], pp. 473–501).

3. Sam G. Kpakpa-Quartey, a Muslim merchant from Accra, Gold Coast (now known as Ghana), arrived in New York via Great Britain on 14 November 1919. His mission was to expand commercial and industrial relations between the Gold Coast natives, Europe, and the United States. Four days after his arrival in New York, Kpakpa-Quartey addressed a UNIA gathering at Liberty Hall, where he called for the formation of commercial and industrial corporations capable of employing Africa's resources for the benefit of the black race. By this time he had already established an import-export firm, African International Traders, Inc., in partnership with Shirley and Foreman, Inc.; D. D. Shirley was a member of the advisory board of the BSL and served as commander of the Universal African Legion. Kpakpa-Quartey also incorporated a second firm, S. G. Kpakpa-Quartey Co., Inc., in order to trade in tropical products. He was disillusioned with his American associates, whom he believed had "played upon, fleeced and taken advantage of" him. What became of Kpakpa-Quartey after 1920 is uncertain. A letter appeared in the *Negro World* of 22 October 1921 deploring the lot of unemployed Somali seamen in England, signed by a certain Prof. Karim Abdul Kpakpa-Quartey of the African Association, London (PRO, FO 371/4567; *NW*, 31 July 1920, 22 October 1921; *New York News*, 1 April 1920; Kpakpa-Quartey to Prince Kaba Rega, ca. 7 July 1920).

4. Trotter faced great difficulty securing passage to Europe, as did all of the delegates chosen to attend the Paris Peace Conference at the 1918 meeting of the National Race Congress. None of the delegates were granted passports by the State Department, a fact that forced Trotter to seek another means of reaching France. Trotter eventually secured a job as a cook on the S.S. *Yarmouth*, then a freighter owned by the North American Steamship Corp. of Canada. Upon reaching Le Havre in May 1919, Trotter smuggled himself off the ship and made his way to Paris, where he sought official recognition as a delegate from the National Race Congress. He also mailed a petition from his organization, the National Equal Rights League, to the principal negotiators at Versailles and hounded President Wilson's aides to arrange a meeting for him. Although he was never able to get an official hearing, Trotter seized the opportunity to educate the French public on the status of black Americans by producing and distributing leaflets on the subject (Stephen R. Fox, *The Guardian of Boston*, pp. 223–30).

5. The omitted material did not pertain to Garvey.

Newspaper Report

[[New York, December 11. 1919]]

SEC. BLACK STAR LINE IS SHOT.

EDMUND SMITH GREEN, RECEIVES BULLET WOUND, BUT IT ISN'T SERIOUS

. . . Edmund Smith Green, Secretary of the Black Star Line was shot here yesterday, but the wound was not of a severe description, and his condition is in no way serious. It is not yet known what prompted his assailant to make the attempt upon his life. Like the President of the Line, Mr. Green is a British West Indian, a native [of] British Guiana. His wife died a few days ago and was tendered a public funeral by the citizens of New York.

The capital stock of the Black Star Line has been increased to ten million dollars, and the second ship, according to a statement made by the President, Mr. Marcus Garvey, will be launched in February.

Printed in the *Gleaner*, 13 December 1919. Some of the original headlines have been omitted.

Marcus Garvey to the New York Postmaster

[*New York*] 12/12/19

STANDING ORDER

Sir:

Until otherwise ordered you will deliver registered letters and parcels addrest to Marcus Garvey or Black Star Line, etc to any of the following-named persons: Amy Jacques[1] who are hereby specially authorized to receive and receipt for registered matter as agent.

All previous orders are hereby revoked.

MARCUS GARVEY,
Signature of Addressee
A. E. JACQUES,
Signature of Agent

Printed in *Garvey* v. *United States*, no. 8317, Ct. App., 2d Cir., 2 February 1925, government exhibit no. 150.

1. Amy Euphemia Jacques (1896–1973) became Garvey's confidential secretary and eventually his second wife and the mother of his two sons, Marcus Mosiah Garvey, Jr., and Julius Winston Garvey. She wrote that during one of her first conversations with Garvey, he showed her stacks of mail stored in a large cabinet and complained: "These accumulated while I was on a speaking trip. I haven't the time to help and teach someone to open, sort and put notations on them, before handing the monies enclosed to the treasurer. You see the awful predicament I am in for lack of qualified, honest people" (Amy Jacques Garvey, *Garvey and Garveyism*, p. 40).

Amy Jacques's sparse autobiographical statements indicate that she was born in Jamaica and was the eldest child of Mr. and Mrs. George Samuel Jacques. Her father had spent parts of his childhood in Cuba and had also lived at one time in Baltimore. Her education included high school courses in shorthand and typing. When her father died, Amy Jacques went to work for the family lawyer, but after four years there she grew restless. When the outbreak of World War I interrupted her plans to go to England, she went instead to the United States in 1917. Her first meeting with Garvey and her subsequent mandate to reorganize his office soon led to special status as his confidential secretary. In addition, Amy Jacques and her brother, Cleveland, became Garvey's frequent traveling companions. Amy Jacques assumed her unique role in Garvey's organization shortly before Garvey married his longtime friend and aide, Amy Ashwood. In 1920 Amy Jacques became secretary of the Negro Factories Corp., and her expanded role as Garvey's office manager made her a controversial figure at UNIA headquarters, especially among those who objected to her uncompromising attitude toward efficiency.

Garvey's marriage to Ashwood had clearly failed when they separated after three months. Over two years later, after an initial attempt at annulment, Garvey finally obtained a divorce. On 27 July 1922, under the pressures of Garvey's impending trial and a possible jail term, Amy Jacques, according to her account, agreed to marry him and to become his personal representative. She immediately became his principal aide and a major pro-Garvey propagandist. She edited two volumes of Garvey's most salient statements, *Philosophy and Opinions of Marcus Garvey*, (vol. 1, 1923, and vol. 2, 1925) in an effort to answer his critics. Later, with Garvey incarcerated in Atlanta, she claimed sole authority to speak for him as his most trusted representative.

Amy Jacques Garvey continued to influence Garveyism long after her husband's death in 1940. She became a contributing editor to the *African*, a black nationalist journal published in Harlem in the early 1940s. While residing in Jamaica in the late 1940s, she reorganized the African Study Circle of the World, claiming her place as the rightful successor to its founder, Marcus Garvey. Her correspondence with scholars facilitated the burgeoning research on Garvey beginning in the 1950s, and in 1963 her book, *Garvey and Garveyism* offered her personal account of the UNIA and its leader. When she died in 1973, she had achieved recognition as one of the most important sources for the study and propagation of Garveyism (Amy Jacques Garvey, *Garvey and Garveyism* 1; *DG*, 26 July 1973; *Jamaica Daily News*, 29 July 1973; Amy Jacques Garvey Papers, Fisk University).

Report by Special Agent WW

Nashville, Tenn. Dec. 21, 1919

RACE TROUBLE

As an American, an employee and a negro, I beg to submit the following:

On last Friday in Nashville, Tenn., I went into the barber shop connected with the colored "[Y]" to get a copy of the Chicago Defender and was given along with the Defender a copy of "THE NEGRO WORLD" published in New York and edited by one MARCUS GARVEY. After carefully reading said newspaper, I turned same over to Agent in Charge for his attention.

After considerable experience with negro newspapers as editor[,] circulat[o]r and solicitor and being fully conversant with the hopes, aspirations, loves, fears and hates of negroes generally, as found in the arts, sciences, trades and professions as well as in the lower strata of negro life via pool halls, dance halls, gambling dens, joints etc., it is my opinion that "THE NEGRO WORLD" is—

1. A radical paper of the worst type; because it seeks to stir up strife and dissatisfaction among negroes; because it seeks to, and does, engender hatred in the hearts of black men; because it urges the negroes to fight in violation of the laws of the country; because seemingly it recognizes no law except that propounded by its editor.

2. A menace: because its author seeks to write the darker peoples for so called protection when as a careful reading of the paper will show that the

editor and those in league with him have a dream of world dominion based on selfishness; because its doctrine will cause riots, revolutions, rebellions and finally chaos.

3.   Deserves use of immediate drastic measures to suppress because its editor and leader seeks to organize and form units called branches everywhere and wants ten thousand more agents to spread its doctrine, after six months training; because if unchecked, within a short time, its teachings and doctrines together with the league of which it seems to be a part, will offer a greater menace than that of the Russians, for it will be a growing black peril.

Activities of an International character have been and still are being carried on by this organization (I know Henryetta V. Davis[,] who is connected with this movement, as a clever, educated woman of more than average ability) by at least one or more clever people. Any action against this organization should be as secret as possible.

It is respectfully suggested

1.   That list of Agents of U.N.I.A. and location of branches be furnished[.]

2.   That the black belt be organised against radical doctrine etc. by utilizing negro school heads etc. that they in time be checked up by the Department.

3.   That States of black belt issue counter propaganda from one source.

4.   That this report be given serious consideration.

Investigation continued.

WW[1]

[*Handwritten endorsements*] Ruch Negro Act
[*Stamped endorsements*] Noted F.D.W.
NOTED W.W.G. NOTED G.F.R.

DNA, RG 65, file OG 267600. TD.

1. WW was the code name of a Bureau of Investigation special confidential employee who submitted reports on the Garvey movement beginning in December 1919. The only information found on his identity to date comes from a report sent in February 1920 to Frank Burke, assistant director of the Bureau of Investigation by the bureau's agent in charge at Nashville, Tenn. According to the report, "WW" was William A. Bailey, a black special employee who had worked for the bureau in Birmingham, Ala. He had requested a transfer because his identity had been discovered, and he was subsequently assigned to Nashville. Later, the bureau sent him to New York, where he reported on the Garvey movement and the African Blood Brotherhood (J. M. Fowler to Frank Burke, 20 February 1920, DNA, RG 65, file OG 267600).

Black Star Line to the Canadian and United States Border Authorities

New York, U. S. A. December 26th, 1919

This is To Certify that the holder of this letter whose signature appears below is Marcus Garvey President General of the Black Star Line incorporated under the State Laws of Delaware of the United States of America, domiciled in the City of New York 56 West 135th Street, and that he is sent by the Directors of this Corporation to represent their business interest in the Cities of Toronto, Ottawa, and Montreal. He will remain in Canada for two weeks returning to New York. We ask that all privileges be extended to Mr. Garvey.

> BLACK STAR LINE, INC.
> J. M. CERTAIN,
> Vice President
> E. D. SMITH-GREEN,
> Secretary
> MARCUS GARVEY

Printed in *Garvey* v. *United States*, no. 8317, Ct. App., 2d Cir., 2 February 1925, defendant's exhibit R.

Memorandum for J. Edgar Hoover

[*Washington, D.C.?*] December 29, 1919.

IN RE: UNIVERSAL NEGRO IMPROVEMENT ASSOCIATION

The attached appears to be a discussion of the negro situation throughout the United States and the attempt to organise the negroes into one huge political party through the activities of the Universal Negro Improvement Association. I have carefully read the attached and have been unable to find any anarchistic utterances in same.

Marcus Garvey appears to be one of the principal agitators among the negroes and is the principal financial backer of the Black Star Line, a steamship company organized for the purpose of trading between the United States and Liberia and also south American countries. . . .[1]

I would suggest that the activities of the societies enumerated in the attached report be carefully watched for any violations of Federal Statutes, but at the present time I am of the opinion that our Deportation Laws do not cover the leaders of the Negro Movement as all of them apparently are American citizens. Respectfully[2]

DNA, RG 65, file OG 185161. TD, carbon copy.
  1. The deleted material did not pertain to Marcus Garvey.
  2. Efforts to identify the author of this bureau memorandum have been unsuccessful.

G. C. Wharton to the Third Assistant Postmaster General, Washington, D.C.

Tower Hill, Va 1/5/20

Dear Sir.

I am sending you under separate cover 2 Papers of Dec 27th [19]19[,] one the *Chicago Defender* published in Chicago, the other The Negro World published in New York[.][1] These are being sent through the mails, to the Negroes of this section & are bound to cause trouble sooner or later[.] They refuse now to work for white people, and it seems as if they are only published to add to our already great troubles we have in our country.

The department may be aware of this, but as an American citizen, I thought it my duty to forward same for your investigation[.] Yours Very truly,

G. C. WHARTON

[*Endorsement*] Solicitor

DNA, RG 28, file B-398. ALS, recipient's copy. Handwritten endorsement.
  1. Enclosures not found.

Passengers on the S.S. *Yarmouth* Arriving from Havana[1]

New York, January 7th, 1920

Name in Full		Age.		Calling or Occupation.	Nation- ality.	Race.	Last Permanent Residence.		Place of Birth.	
Family name.	Given name.	Yrs.	Mos.						Country.	City or town.
Headley	Agatha	32		Seam./stress/	Br.	African	Pan.	Colon	Barbados	St. Thomas
Headley	Ena	12		———	Br.	African	Pan.	Colon	Barbados	St. Thomas
Headley	Oscar	9		———	Br.	African	Pan.	Colon	Barbados	St. Thomas
Headley	Rutherford	4	6	———	Br.	African	Pan.	Colon	Barbados	St. Thomas
Headley	Beatrice	2	6		Br.	African	Pan.	Colon	Barbados	St. Thomas
Bynoe	Clara	30		Dom.	Br.	African	Pan.	Colon	Barbados	Christchur[c]h
Bynoe	Ralph	8		———	Br.	African	Pan.	Colon	Barbados	Christchur[c]h
Bynoe	Ida	5		———	Br.	African	Pan.	Colon	Barbados	Christchur[c]h
Bynoe	Ivan		15		Br.	African	Pan.	Colon	Barbados	Christchur[c]h
Williams	Rebecca	29		Laund;/ress/	Br.	African	Pan.	Colon	Jamaica	St[.] Catherine
Jones	Rosenetta	1	6	———	Pan.	African	Pan.	Colon	Panama	Panama
Boyer	Helena	38		Dom./estic/	French	French	Pan.	Colon	Martinique	Fort de France
Martin	Susan	29		Dom./estic/	Br.	African	Pan.	Colon	Jamaica	Manchester
Martin	Mavis	5		———	Br.	African	Pan.	Colon	Jamaica	Manchester

Passengers on the S.S. *Yarmouth* Arriving from Havana[1] (Continued)

New York, January 7th, 1920

NAME IN FULL		AGE.	CALLING OR OCCUPATION.	NATION-ALITY.	RACE.	LAST PERMANENT RESIDENCE.		PLACE OF BIRTH.	
Family name.	Given name.	Yrs. Mos.						Country.	City or town.
Martin	Herbert	2	——	Br.	African	Colon	Pan.	Jamaica	Manchester
Critchlow	Elfrida	29	Dom./estic/	Br.	African	Colon	Pan.	Barbados	St[.] Michael
Allen	/Theresa/	28	Seam;/stress/	Br.	African	Colon	Pan.	St[.] Lucia	Castries
Nelson	Nelcina	56	Cook	Br.	African	Colon	Pan.	St[.] Lucia	Castries
Jordan	Blanche	22	Dom./estic/	Br.	African	Canal Zone	Pan.	Barbados	St. Andrews
Lindsay	Urselina	49	Dom./estic/	D.W.I.	African	Panama	Panama	D.W.I.	St[.] Croix
Flores	Justes	33	A.B. /Cook/	Hond.	African	Colon	Panama	Hon/duras/	Balfetta
Clayton	[Melv]ille	21	Chauf./fer/	Br.	African	Colon	Panama	Jamaica	Kingston
James	Herbert	16	——	Br.	African	Colon	Panama	Jamaica	[Kingston]
Glasse	Granville	17	Sten. /ographer/	Br.	African	Colon	Panama	Jamaica	Kingston

DNA, RG 85, file T-715. Printed form with typewritten and handwritten insertions. The various passenger manifests of S.S. *Yarmouth* have been treated in an excerpted fashion. Certain columns of information were omitted from transcription and rendered as part of the document's annotations, as appropriate.

1. The *Yarmouth* sailed from Havana on 1 January 1920.

Passengers on the S.S. *Yarmouth* Arriving from Jamaica[1]

New York, JAN. 7th 1920

NAME IN FULL		AGE.	CALLING OR OCCUPATION	NATION-ALITY	RACE	LAST PERMANENT RESIDENCE		PLACE OF BIRTH.	
Family name.	Given name.	Yrs. Mos.						Country.	City or town.
Whylie	Maud	23	Milliner	British	West India[n]	Jamaica	Kingston	Jamaica	Westmoreland
Davis	May	18	Milliner	British	West India[n]	Jamaica	Kingston	Jamaica	Kingston
Glegg	Enid	16	Minor	British	West India[n]	Jamaica	/Spanish Town/	Jamaica	St[.] Catherine
Black	Sarah	60	Labourer	British	West India[n]	Jamaica	/Lucea/	Jamaica	Hanover
Spraggs	Eva	31	Maid	British	West India[n]	Jamaica	/Port Royal/	Jamaica	Port Royal
Francis	Robert	27	Chauffe[u]r	British	West India[n]	Jamaica	/St. Thomas/	Kingston	Kingston
Bailey	Headley	28	Engineer	British	West India[n]	Jamaica	Hanover	Kingston	Kingston
Riley	George	35	Mariner	British	West India[n]	Jamaica	Trelawny	Kingston	Kingston
Morrison	Atheil	43	Printer	British	West India[n]	Jamaica	Kingston	Kingston	Kingston

DNA, RG 85, file T-715. Printed form with typewritten and handwritten insertions.

1. The *Yarmouth* sailed from Jamaica on 28 December 1919.

BSL Daily Transaction Report[1]

[*New York*] Jan. 7, 1920

The following is a sample of the daily lists prepared of the names and addresses of persons writing to the BSL and the sums of money that they enclosed in their letters. The letters were handled by a BSL clerk, who wrote out a separate list for each day. The list, along with the actual money received, was handed over to the secretary of the BSL, who issued a signed receipt, and turned the money over to the treasurer to be banked. The reports were kept in files inside Garvey's office.

THE LIST

George S. Taylor, Brooklyn, N. Y	20.00
Simeon McLein, Sagua la Grande, Cuba	15.00
George Allen, Camaguey, Cuba	25.00
Tomas Ruiz, Havana, Cuba	5.00
Oscar Mc. Canna, [C]ristobal, Canal Zone	5.00
G. Edwards	2.41
William Allen, Norfolk, Va.	5.00
Abraham Goddard, Cambridge, Mass.	2.00
Dean Dayrell, Camaguey, Cuba	10.00
Peter Gabrial, Camaguey, Cuba	25.00
Roxan Green, Montclair, N. J.	5.40
Edith Kerr, Cristobal, Canal Zone	5.00
Charles E. Might, Cristobal, Canal Zone	20.00
Fitz Holder, Ancon, Canal Zone	15.00
Ernest Evans, Brooklyn, N. Y.	5.00
Joseph Millings, Moron, Cuba	15.00
Leonard McLean, Oriente, Cuba	125.00
J. E. Smith, Freetown, West Africa	15.00
Adrian Conegan, Cristobal, Canal Zone	10.00
Maude Knight, Ancon, Canal Zone	1.00
Mattie Byrd, Chicago, Ill.	15.00
Percival Allman, C[*anal*] Zone	85.00
Ernest Daniels, Cristobal, Canal Zone	5.00
William Babb, Pariso, Canal Zone	100.00
J. A. Arnall, San Pedro, de Mac[or]is	15.00
Thomas Sterling, Camaguey, Cuba	40.00
William Chrishlow, Balboa, Canal Zone	40.00

$630.81

Recd. by FRED D. POWELL

Asst. Sec.

Marcus Garvey v. *United States*, no. 8317, Ct. App., 2d Cir., 2 February 1925. Defendant exhibit M, p. 2674. The actual exhibit consisted of fifty-three lists, but only one was printed in the trial transcript.

1. The report was prepared by Carrie Leadett, stenographer for the BSL, and submitted to E. D. Smith-Green, BSL secretary. For biographical information on Carrie Leadett, see Vol. 1, p. 228.

British Military Intelligence Report

[*New York*] January 7, 1920

NEGRO AGITATION

Universal Negro Improvement Association

Marcus Garvey in writing from Atlantic City under date of Dec. 9th urged all negroes of the world to make up their minds to redeem Eth[i]opia, that they should pull all together:

> "It becomes incumbent upon us to make up our minds and hearts
> to fight, if needs be, and die, for the principle of a free Africa. . . .
> I therefore advise all Negroes to prepare, so that when the hour
> comes and the blow is to be struck we may all rise, four hundred
> million, to claim our ancestral rights."

For the present, he advised them to start out to build and own factories, banks and steamships, so that they might become more independent. He said that they now had the steamship line, "The Black Star Line," and that as soon as they had placed a sufficient number of ships on the seas, the Universal Negro Improvement Association would open the largest bank in the world and would start to build factories.

At a meeting held in Liberty Hall on Dec. 14th, Marcus Garvey commented on an editorial which appeared in the "African Telegraph" of London—a reprint from the "Daily Sketch", which dealt with the meeting that was held by the association in Madison Square Garden, New York, late October. He expressed his satisfaction that for once the white man realized that the Negro is a fighter and a better one than the Hun; he is a super devil. That was enough to convince the modern white man that he had better be careful how he treats the present-day Negro. Garvey said that he would answer this English paper some time in February on the eve of the launching of the "Phyllis Wheatley[":]

> "We will tell them that we know they have their tanks, we know
> they have their aeroplanes, but we will not tell them what we have
> until we meet them in Africa.

"Men and women of America, the West Indies and Africa, let me
say that your association, the Universal Negro Improvement
Association, is sweeping the world and that you are as strong as
any government today. . . .[1] Let us keep up the will and the
purpose of the U.N.I.A.—the will and purpose to be free.

"The New Negro says there can be no compromise until Africa is
free. Therefore when the next world war comes, the 400,000,000
Negroes will be on a strike, looking for the opportunity to make
Africa free.

"Modern Germany fell and England is about to fall, as she must
fall (prolonged cheers), and after the fall of Europe a new power
shall rise up. Tonight I say unto scattered Eth[i]opia: Acquit
yourselves like men and women and prepare for that day.["]

He said it was rumored in maritime and commercial circles that on the arrival
of the "Frederick Douglass" in Caribbean waters the British Government
would seize the vessel. On hearing this, he said, he laughed because he knew
that the British Government was not looking for trouble, that even if they
had the intention, he was sure they did not want to start another war,
because all Jamaica and all the West Indies where Negroes live are their
powder houses. The Britisher, as well as every white man, knows what it is to
start anything in countries where Negroes outnumber the whites in large
numbers, he said. "If you lynch and burn us here because we are weaker, in
Africa, where we are twenty-eight black men to ten white men, we are going
to play the trick on you there."

In speaking of Liberia, he said that by borrowing $5,000,000 from
America, she had placed herself entirely as a child under the protection of
America,[2] that they all knew that the politics of America is the politics that
will support England and France at any time to crush any rising colored race.

"Therefore we of the U.N.I.A. at this moment have a solemn duty
to perform and that is to free Liberia of any debt that she owes to
any white government.["] (Great applause).

He then told how after the convention to be held next August the headquarters of the association must be transferred to Monrovia, Liberia and that
it would then fall upon them to subscribe that $5,000,000 to free Liberia.

"And if after that convention I have to travel into the re-
motest parts of the world to get contributions to that $5,000,000,
I will make it my duty to travel until it is paid off, because we must
have a free and unfettered government of our own, and the most
promising government at the present time is that of Liberia.

"We are happy to realize that Liberia is going to play a great and important part in the future destiny of the Negro—the Negro of this country, of the West Indies and Africa.

". . They talk about their aeroplanes in this article and about their machine guns. You just wait awhile! In the next two years we are going to show them that out of Africa the newest implements of war will come and all their tanks and machine guns and aeroplanes will be like Santa Claus' toys to what we mean to put out. ."[3]

S. G. Kpakpa-Quartey, a merchant of Accra, Gold Coast Colony (see previous reports) also spoke at the above meeting. Following are a few excerpts from his speech:

"Above all, let us form without delay commercial and industrial corporations and utilize Africa's rich resources for the race, for then, and not before shall the selfish aliens pack up their bags and baggage and sail away for their respective homes and leave Africa for the Africans at home and Africans abroad; and then shall all scattered sons of Eth[i]opia come together for life, liberty and happiness and ultimately for freedom and independence."

"Away with religious fanaticisms for the spirit of commerce and industry is the key to the salvation of our struggling race. Since my arrival in New York City, I have been able by mutual agreements, to consolidate my West African partnership company with Messrs. Shirley & Foreman, Inc. under the laws of the State of New York. The cash capital of this consolidated corporation is $110,000.00 and besides that, the corporation has other valuable properties in Africa."

He said that he would be with them in New York up till next August, before leaving for West Africa, and that between this time and that he hoped to tell them all about their ancient Africa, their homeland.

At a meeting held in Liberty Hall on Sunday night, December 21st, Marcus Garvey announced that the national anthem of the African Republic would be sung for the first time that evening. The words of the anthem were composed and written by members of the Black Star Line. The audience remained standing during the rendering of the anthem by Mme. Houston, soloist of the U.N.I.A.

Garvey next called attention to information which he had received from an educated Negro concerning an invention by a colored man, which, if true, would make the Negro race the rulers of the world. He promised to give it a thorough investigation and report on it at a later date.

He then spoke of the whole-hearted welcome accorded Miss Henrietta Vinton Davis, international organizer, Mr. Cyril Henry, Assistant Treasurer, Capt. Cockburn and the other members of the crew on their arrival at the island of Jamaica.[4]

The marriage of Marcus Garvey and Miss Amy Ashwood took place in Liberty Hall, New York, on Christmas night. All members of the U.N.I.A. were requested to wear their buttons to prove their membership. Garvey and his bride left the city the next day for Canada. The following New Year's greeting was sent by Garvey from Toronto, Canada, Dec. 30th:

> "I take this opportunity of wishing you a Happy and Prosperous New Year. May you the world over so unite in 1920 as to make a redeemed Africa a possibility in the very near future. To insure the success of the race commercially I ask that each and every one buy shares in the Black Star Line."

According to an article in a recent issue of the "Negro World," the Governor of St. Vincent has stirred up a hornet's nest when he insulted the intelligence of a loyal people by prohibiting the entry of the "Negro World" in St. Vincent. "The result of the prohibition in St. Vincent is that there are not sufficient copies of the 'Negro World' to go round in Grenada."

George Tobias, treasurer, of the Black Star Line, in commenting on the suppression of the "Negro World" in a recent issue, says:

> ". . Let the pale-faced British governors suppress the Negro World.[5] The time will come when they will have to run for their very lives with shoes in their hands to find refuge in the Caribbean Sea."

In the "Negro World" of Nov. 29th, Fenton Johnson,[6] editor of the "Favorite Magazine," published in Chicago, says:

> ". . . There is only one thing that our people in Africa can and must do.[7] They must rise up against their oppressors; they must make Africa free for Africans or the black race is lost. They must drive these white upstarts into the sea and set the flag of Eth[i]opia aloft in the sky of liberty."

The following is quoted from the "Negro World" issue of January 3:

> "The Universal African Legion, Mr. D.D. Shirley, commander, meets in Liberty Hall, New York, every Sunday from 12 to 1 p.m. Those desiring information may write Mr. Shirley at 409 Lenox Avenue."

Mr. D.D. Shirley, is a member of the advisory board of the Black Star Line and is also a partner of S.G. Kpakpa-Quartey, a merchant recently arrived from Accra, Gold Coast Colony. The first we had seen of this Universal African Legion was in a letter in the "Negro World" of Nov. 22nd from Ida Estina Ash, Third Vice-president, Ladies' Division, U.N.I.A., from which the following is quoted:

> "We must not forget that we pledged that the old flag of the Black Star Line must never touch the ground, but must wave from the heights of Liberia, our native land, forever, as a symbol of the black man's capacity for self-government. So men, prepare by joining the Universal African Legion, which is now being organized by Mr. D.D. Shirley. . . ."

New Publication—"Weekly Review"

The "Weekly Review" is a new Negro journal devoted to commerce, politics, news, industry and economics. Mr. McDonald McLean is the managing editor, Eric D. Waldron,[8] W.H. Lesesue Howard, U.I. Danton and W.S. McKinney, Jr. are the associate editors, and Miss Myrtle Anderson, Prof. W.H. Ferris and Rev. J.W.H. Eason are contributing editors. W. Leon Chappan is the Brooklyn representative. Mr. McLean edited a paper in Panama and is a loyal supporter of the Universal Negro Improvement Association. Mr. Waldron was reporter of the Star and Herald of Panama. The contributing editors, with the exception of Miss Myrtle Anderson, are connected with Garvey's movement, Prof. Ferris being the literary editor of the "Negro World," Rev. Eason, chaplain general, and Prof. Buck, secretary general of the Universal Negro Improvement Association. The following is an excerpt from an article "England's Economic Position," by Arthur King, in the first issue of the paper (Dec. 13):

> ". . . When we come to that part of the program that aims at intensifying production everywhere within the British Empire we must do our best to arrest production or keep it at a minimum, because we must make it unprofitable for England to hold her colonies.[9] At the same time we must embarrass her by political agitation and propaganda in foreign countries.
>
> ["]In our upward struggle we cannot afford to let any nation or race stand in our paths, and no nation stands so much in our path today as England. Therefore, we must do all in our power to discredit her, disrupt her empire and attain our ends at all costs. And it is not so difficult of attainment as some think . . .[10]
>
> ["]If we do not take advantage of the changes that the war has brought and allow ourselves to be the means of bolstering up

the attenuated existence of England, we will have every reason to regret it. The *fall of imperial England is necessary to our future*.["]

DNA, RG 165, file 10218-364-18-190X. TD, recipient's copy. Enclosure in Maj. H. A. Strauss to the director of the Military Intelligence Division, 13 January 1920 (DNA, RG 165, file 10218-364-190X).

1. Ellipsis marks in the original.

2. In September 1918 the United States Treasury approved a credit of $5 million to Liberia under the provisions of the Second Liberty Loan Act. Heavily in debt to European and American bankers, the Liberian government would reform its finances as part of the agreement. Early in 1920 President Wilson approved the loan, but the Liberian legislature rejected it because of its harsh conditions. According to the loan proposal, the president of the United States would appoint a general receiver, three assistants, and an auditor to control all Liberian customs collections as well as internal revenue. In addition, the general receiver would have the power to approve the Liberian budget and to determine what portion of revenue from customs would be granted to the Liberian government for expenses. The proposal also authorized the president to appoint a commissioner general of the interior and three or more military officers to reorganize the Liberian military along the frontier. Although they rejected the proposal, the Liberian legislature voted to send a commission to the United States to discuss the possibility of another loan arrangement (Nancy Kaye Kirkham Forderhase, "The Plans That Failed: The United States and Liberia, 1920–1935" [Ph.D. diss. University of Missouri, 1971], pp. 15–21).

3. Ellipsis marks in the original.

4. The *Yarmouth* arrived at Kingston on 10 December 1919. According to the *Gleaner*, "thousands of people who had assembled on the waterfront sent up a rousing cheer as the good ship headed to her berth. . . ." Henrietta Vinton Davis, UNIA international organizer, and Cyril Henry, BSL secretary, spoke at the welcoming ceremonies on the pier and later addressed a large UNIA meeting in Kingston (*Gleaner*, 11 December 1919).

5. Ellipsis marks in the original.

6. Fenton Johnson (1888–1958), Chicago-born poet and newspaper editor, published two volumes of poetry before beginning his own publication, *Favorite Magazine*. Monitored by Bureau of Investigation agents, the magazine was on one occasion labeled "very radical in some of its statements." Johnson later worked as the drama editor for the *New York News* (*WWCR*; DNA, RG 65, file OG 3057).

7. Ellipsis marks in the original.

8. Eric Walrond (1898–1966), essayist and short story writer, was born in Georgetown, British Guiana (now known as Guyana), and educated in Colón, Panama. He worked as a reporter on the *Panama Star and Herald*, 1916–18, and he also aided his uncle, H. N. Walrond, in publishing the *Workman* in 1919, before immigrating to New York. Walrond was employed briefly as associate editor of the *Brooklyn and Long Island Informer*, 1919–20, while studying at the City College of New York. He gravitated toward the Garvey movement, and from 1920 until 1922 he served as associate editor of the *Negro World*. A prolific writer during the Harlem Renaissance, Walrond's best-known work was *Tropic Death* (1926). He left the United States on a Guggenheim Fellowship in 1928 and traveled in the Caribbean and Europe, eventually settling in London in 1932. In London Walrond reestablished contact with Garvey, who published several of his essays in the *Black Man* (Robert Bone, *Down Home: History of the Afro-American Renaissance* [New York: G. P. Putnam's Sons, 1975], pp. 171–203; Kenneth Ramchand, *The West Indian Novel and Its Background* [London: Faber and Faber, 1970], pp. 240–41).

9. Ellipsis marks in the original.

10. Ellipsis marks in the original.

List of Aliens Employed as Crew Members on the S.S. *Yarmouth*[1]

New York, Jan. 8th 1920

	Name in Full		Position in Ship's Company	Shipped or Engaged		Age	Race	Nationality
	Family name	*Given name*		*When*	*Where*			
	Cockburn	Joshua	Master					
	Milne	Frank	Chief Officer	17/11/19	New York	40	Scotch	British
	Tucker	Henry	3rd Officer	10/11/19	New York	29	African	British
	Hercules	James	Boatswain	10/11/19	New York	33	African	British
	Gammon	Jacob	Sailor	10/11/19	New York	27	African	British
	Buxton	Joseph	Sailor	10/11/19	New York	31	African	British
/N[o] C[ards]/	DePatters	Charles	Sailor	10/11/19	New York	32	African	D. Guiana
/NC/	Tenryk	Eddie	Sailor	10/11/19	New York	33	African	D. Guiana
	Nahr	Ishmael	Sailor	10/11/19	New York	23	African	Portug[u]ese
/NC/	Lindsay	Andrew	Sailor	10/11/19	New York	21	African	British
	Rollins	Reuben	Deck-boy	18/11/19	New York	22	African	British
	Mayler	Philip	Chief-Engineer	21/11/19	New York	41	English	British
/NC/	Govin	Dillon	1Asst Engineer	7/11/19	New York	38	African	British
	Francisco	Legar	2nd Asst Engineer	7/11/19	New York	35	African	Panamanian
	Birch	Arthur	3rd Asst Engineer	10/11/19	New York	23	African	British

List of Aliens Employed as Crew Members on the S.S. *Yarmouth*[1] (Continued)

	Name in Full		Position in Ship's Company	Shipped or Engaged		Age	Race	Nationality
	Family name	*Given name*		*When*	*Where*			
/NC/	Parris	Joshua	Oiler	10/11/19	New York	35	African	British
	Beucher	Alfred	Oiler	10/11/19	New York	33	African	British
/NC/	Graves	Charles	Oiler	10/11/19	New York	28	African	British
	Fraser	Adolphus	Fireman	10/11/19	New York	36	African	British
	Warren	Harrold	Fireman	10/11/19	New York	27	African	Panamanian
/NC/	Devenish	Charles	Fireman	10/11/19	New York	34	African	Panama[n]ian
	Morris	Gustaves	Fireman	10/11/19	New York	34	African	British
	Licruise	James	Fireman	10/11/19	New York	36	African	British
	Laviscount	John	Fireman	10/11/19	New York	33	African	British
	Hellar	Gladstone	Coal-passer	10/11/19	New York	21	African	British
/NC/	Adams	James	Coal-passer	10/11/19	New York	32	African	British
/NC/	Fitzgerald	Arthur	Fireman	12/19/19	Colon	31	African	British
/NC/	Clarke	Herbert	Fireman	12/19/19	Colon	31	African	British
	Goodhall	Stephen	Ch. Stewar[d]	10/11/19	New York	35	African	British
	Gibson	James	2nd Stewar[d]	10/11/19	New York	50	African	British
	Weston	Charles	Ch[ie]f Cook	10/11/19	New York	37	African	British

	Surname	Given	Position	Date	Port	Age		Nationality
	Burger	Septimus	2nd Cook	10/11/19	New York	40	African	British
/NC/	Lucas	John	Messman	22/11/19	New York	38	African	British
	Wallace	Herman	/Steward/	19/11/19	New York	32	African	British
	Williams	Henry	Pantryman	10/11/19	New York	33	African	British
	Workman	Alfonso	Carpenter	10/11/19	New York	21	African	British
/NC/	Ringwood	Homer	C. Wireless Op.	15/11/19	New York	26	African	British
	LaMothe	Louis	Purser	10/11/19	New York	51	African	British
	Digsby	Chas	Asst. Purser	27/12/19	Jamaica	29	African	British
	Edwards	James	Ship's Surgeon	27/12/19	Jamaica	19	African	British
/NC/	Middleton	Ernest	Messman	27/12/19	Jamaica		African	Costa-Rican
	Joseph	Edgar	Mess-boy					
	Kila[2]	Joseph	2nd Officer	10/11/19	New York	27	Honolulu	American
	Van Der Zee	Perry	Wireless Op	18/11/19	New York	37	African	American
	[MacCloy?]	Henry	Sculleryman	10/11/19	New York	33	African	American

DNA, RG 85, file T-715. Printed form with typewritten and handwritten insertions.

1. The *Yarmouth* sailed from Havana 1 January 1920.
2. The last three entries were handwritten.

Editorial Letter by Marcus Garvey

Montreal, Canada, January 8, 1920

ALL NEGROES SHOULD PULL TOGETHER FOR A STRONG AND UNITED RACE

THE BLOODIEST OF WARS IS YET TO COME, AND NEGROES WORLD OVER SHOULD PREPARE THEMSELVES

Fellowmen of the Negro Race:

Greeting:

It is a pleasure for me to write to you at this time of the New Year, hoping that you have already made up your minds as touching the future of our race. Now is the time for us to redouble our efforts to forge ahead and plant the flag of Victory over the hill top of African Statehood.

The year 1920 must produce to the world the ablest statesmen of the race, for on the first of August will assemble the great convention of The Universal Negro Improvement Association in New York. At this convention the future government of four hundred million black men, women and children will be discussed. This convention, to us, will be greater in importance that the late "Peace Conference at Paris." Neither Wilson, Lloyd-George, nor Clemenceau will be at this convention, but the biggest minds of the Negro Race will be there to discuss and lay down the policy that will govern for all times the great African Republic of the future. The time has really come for the Negro to take himself seriously. The hour is here for us to unite universally and declare for those rights that have been denied us for centuries.

In this New Year we must realize that unity of purpose is paramount to the cause of freedom, and since we desire so much by way of our rights it is for us to make every effort to unite our scattered forces.

After close study of world affairs at the present time, I have discovered that there is a skillfully engineered propaganda among the other races to cause the active-minded Negro to believe that a real effort is being made to better his condition, therefore it is not n[e]cessary for him to have any exclusive organization of his own. It is for me, fellowmen, to advise you that our great danger as a race lies in yielding to any subterfuge put up through the trickery of the other races. It is time that the Negro played his own part in the world affairs and allow the other forces that control to go to Hades, and look after themselves. We have been camouflaged for five hundred years and now the New Negro in this New Year will admit of no interference in his determination to blast a way to independence and true democracy.

Our convention of August will inspire us with the new cry of "Liberty or Death." We may as well prepare ourselves from now on for the bloodiest of all conflicts in that the handwriting on the wall of international discord warns us of the fact that the greatest of wars is now in the making, and before another thirty years roll by the peace of mankind will be disturbed by the roar of the white man's cannon, and men from the four corners of the world will be called again to battle for the preservation of civilization. As a race we have decided already that we have fought the last battle of the white man's; we have died the last time for him, because after fighting his battle for hundreds of years we find ourselves today rejected and despised by him. We shall now prepare to answer the call of Mother Africa when she demands of us our wealth, our strength and genius to deliver her from the grasp of the oppressor.

The unsettled state of the world points to future discords that will end in a bloody warfare, hence it is up to four millions of us to prepare ourselves for that eventful day that is ahead of the human race.

During these times of peace let us lay the foundation for commercial and industrial prosperity. There are golden opportunities ahead of us and all that is necessary is for us to make up our minds to grab them. Let no white, yellow or red man detract you in the one concentrated object we have in view. Let us all pull together and see and hear nothing else but a free Africa and a great and powerful Negro Race. Let other men pray and preach equality of man and the brotherhood. We have heard equality and brother-hood for five hundred years and up to now we have not yet experienced it, whilst all other races are enjoying it. We say "there ain't going to be any equality until the Negro, like the white man, establishes a great government of his own."

Negroes should refuse to listen to any other voice than that of liberty and true democracy. Liberty and true Democracy means that if one man can be the President, King, Premier or Chancellor of a country then the other fellow can be the same also. Give us that liberty and democracy first and then we will listen to you after, but so long as white men are going to rule and brutalize black men just so long must we continue to prepare for the greatest war in the history of the human race.

Go forth therefore, men of the race, and plant your standards during this New Year in the domains of commerce, industry and politics. Fall back on your manhood and let us make one great pull four hundred million strong.

In the matter of the Black Star Line[,] I am now asking each and every one of you to start out now, and right now, to buy shares. If you have bought already, buy some more and help this great Corporation to float the "S. S. Phyllis Wheatley" on the 15th day of February or the 15th day of March. Buy your shares and thereby write your names across the pages of history for all titles, 5, 10, 20, 30, 40, 50, 60, 70, 80, 90, 100 or 200 shares bought by each and every progressive Negro will mean a Black Star Line Fleet of Two hundred ships in twelve months. I say to you men do it now. Write or call the office of "The Black Star Line, Inc.," 56 West 135th street, New York City, United States of America, and thus become a shareholder in the biggest Negro enterprise of the ages.

Again wishing you a bright and prosperous New Year[.] Yours fraternally,

MARCUS GARVEY

Printed in *Garvey v. United States*, no. 8317, Ct. App., 2d Cir., 2 February 1925, government exhibit no. 149.

Samuel Augustus Duncan, Secretary, West Indian Protective Society, to Earl Curzon of Kedleston, Secretary of State for the Colonies

NEW YORK, N.Y. January 8th, 1920

Sir: —

As the Executive Secretary of the West Indian Protective Society of America,[1] I beg to call your attention to the activities of an organization in this country known as the Universal Negro Improvement Association, and African Communities League, at the head of which is a Negro named Marcus Garvey, a native of Jamaica. This Organization is rabidly anti-white and anti-British. Its avowed policy is to stir up trouble between the White and Colored races particularly within the limits of the British Empire. It is needless to say that if the pernicious propaganda of this trouble-making Organization is not effectively checked by proper official action, unnecessary strife will result between White and Colored people in the British Empire, a thing highly to be deplored.

This Organization employs as a medium through which it makes its sordid appeal to the passion of the Colored people; a weekly paper known as the Negro World and published in this City. In several of the West Indian Islands this publication has been banned but it is smuggled in nevertheless by Colored employees on ships plying between the United States and the West Indies and other Agents of this Organization. In this way its propaganda work is carried on in spite of official action taken to keep it out of the Islands. It was on account of the inciting and inflammable and purposely Colored news and Editorial articles in this paper that moved the legislature of British Guiana to enact recently the drastic Newspaper Ordinance.[2]

Another means for carrying on the destructive propaganda of this Universal Negro Improvement Association and African Communities League is the Black Star Line, a Steamship Corporation dominated by the members of this Organization and which owns at the present time the Steamer "Yarmouth" (soon to be known as the Frederick Douglas). [O]f greater importance to Garvey and those associated with him in pushing this world-wide Pro-negro, and Anti-White and Anti-British propaganda than the making of money through freight and passengers, is the effect and impression that the presence of this ship of the Black Star Line is expected to exert upon the Colored people of the Islands when this ship calls at their Ports.

Yet another, and perhaps the most effective way of carrying on this propaganda, is through the members of the aforesaid Universal Negro Improvement Association and African Communities League and the Stock Holders of the Black Star Line who leave this country for the West Indies and who are expected to stealthily work among the natives and stir up strife and discontent among them. These members and stock holders of the above named Organizations faithfully perform the work that the suppressed Negro World cannot do, and thus sow the seeds of discontent among the natives of the Islands to which they go. The recent bloody strikes in Trinidad when several persons were killed and wounded and much injury caused to shipping and other industries can be traced to the subtle agitation and under hand propaganda work of the agencies above referred to.[3] Those of us who are endeavoring by every lawful and legitimate means to bring the two races closer together, and aid in the industrial and educational development of the islands, cannot but view with greatest alarm the unfortunate and destructive activities of this Organization and its medium the Negro World together with the secret activities of its members who go from this country to British Possessions.

In the interest of peace and harmony between the White and Colored people of the Islands, I am calling the attention of the several governors to the foregoing to the end that they will take energetic action to suppress this pernicious foreign agitation. Also I am calling the attention /of the/ several Consuls in the United States to the foregoing to the end that they might scrutinize all Colored persons applying to them for passports to the British Possession—with view of finding out if they are members or stock holders, readers or subscribers to the foregoing Organizations and the Negro World. I have the honor to remain, Very truly yours,

AUGUSTUS DUNCAN
Executive Secretary

PRO, CO 318/360. TLS, recipient's copy, on West Indian Protective Society letter-head. Handwritten corrections.

1. The West Indian Protective Society of America consisted of West Indian blacks residing in the New York City area. Founded in 1916 by Samuel Augustus Duncan, the society was originally set up to aid newly arrived West Indians. A letter written on 25 February 1920 by R. C. Lindsay of the British Embassy in Washington, D.C., to Sir Leslie Probyn, the governor of Jamaica, stated that a representative of the British consul general had attended some meetings of Duncan's society "without . . . being very much impressed by the value of the organization." Lindsay stated that "the members themselves appear to be quite harmless," but he warned that "their Executive Secretary, Mr. Augustus Duncan . . . appears to be something of an agitator" (PRO, FO 115/2619).

2. In October 1919 the Seditious Publications Ordinance went into effect in British Guiana. Under this statute it became a criminal offense to "inflame the minds of the people, and incite them to acts of violence, riot and disorder; to seduce any naval or military man from his allegiance or duty; to bring His Majesty, or the established Government . . . into hatred, contempt or ridicule; and to encourage or incite interference with the administration of law

and order." Conviction meant a $5,000 fine, two years in prison, or both (*Gleaner*, 1 November 1919).

3. The Trinidad Working Men's Association (TWMA) called a strike of stevedores, lightermen, and warehousemen at Port of Spain on 15 November 1919. Garveyites played a prominent role in the strike, especially John Sydney de Bourg, a founder of the TWMA and a leader of its radical faction. The *Negro World* had been unofficially banned in Trinidad. However, after the strike when the ban was made official, speakers at TWMA meetings continued to read "verbatim quotations from the 'Negro World' and the writings of Marcus Garvey . . . " (J. R. Chancellor [governor of Trinidad] to Milner, 30 November 1920, PRO, CO 318/356). The workers struck for higher wages and a shorter workday. Since government opposition to the TWMA had blocked official recognition, local shipping interests showed no disposition to negotiate, and workers from the countryside of Trinidad and from Venezuela were brought in to replace the strikers. Rioting began on 1 December, when strikers and their supporters entered the shipping warehouses that employed strikebreakers, forcing them to close down; afterward, they marched through the city's business district, closing shops and disrupting public transportation. Thousands of people who were not involved in the original strike participated in the three days of disturbances, which became a popular manifestation of discontent with colonial rule. Fearing a general uprising, Gov. John Chancellor created a conciliation board consisting of TWMA representatives, the shipping agents, and the government. The authorities were also concerned during the rioting with the loyalty of the local police, who were mostly black and who "appeared to have looked on and laughed" unless they were given direct orders to act by white officers (Henry D. Baker [American consul], "Rioting in Trinidad," DNA, RG 59, file 844 G. 5045-3). The report of the official commission of inquiry, however, generally commended the police for their loyalty. On 3 December, the shipping agents and the representatives of the Working Men's Association agreed to a 25 percent wage increase. Although the crisis had subsided, rioting continued to spread through rural Trinidad ("Disturbances in Port of Spain: Reports by the Commissioners Appointed to Enquire into the Conduct of the Constabulary," PRO, CO 318; William F. Elkins, "The Trinidad Longshoremen's Strike of 1919," *Science and Society* 33 [Winter 1969]: 71–75; Tony Martin, "Revolutionary Upheaval in Trinidad, 1919: Views from British and American Sources," *JNH* 58, no. 3 [July 1973]: 313–26).

MAGAZINE OF THE DARKER PEOPLES OF THE WORLD

Policy and Purpose, to make an International Platform thru which door the Oppressed Darker People can be protected from Exploitation

R. D. JONAS, Sec'y, 232 W. 136th Street, New York City.

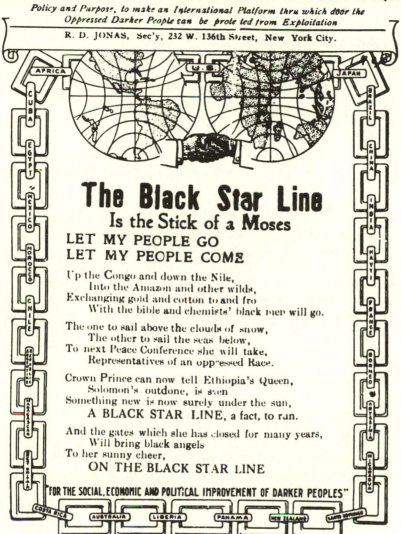

The Black Star Line
Is the Stick of a Moses

LET MY PEOPLE GO
LET MY PEOPLE COME

Up the Congo and down the Nile,
    Into the Amazon and other wilds,
Exchanging gold and cotton to and fro
    With the bible and chemists' black men will go.

The one to sail above the clouds of snow,
    The other to sail the seas below,
To next Peace Conference she will take,
    Representatives of an oppressed Race.

Crown Prince can now tell Ethiopia's Queen,
    Solomon's outdone, is seen
Something new is now surely under the sun,
    A BLACK STAR LINE, a fact, to run.

And the gates which she has closed for many years,
    Will bring black angels
To her sunny cheer,
    ON THE BLACK STAR LINE

"FOR THE SOCIAL, ECONOMIC AND POLITICAL IMPROVEMENT OF DARKER PEOPLES"

(*Source*: DNA, RG 165, file 10218–388).

Bureau of Investigation Report

BOSTON, MASS. JAN. 27, 1920

THE BLACK STAR LINE—HON. MARCUS GARVEY D.S.O.E.[1]

. . . Pursuant to instructions of Division Superintendent Kelleher based upon telephone communication from United Fruit Co.,[2] Boston, Mass., Agent interviewed Mr. Reeves connected with the investigation of above Company and received the following information:

The Black Star Line Inc.—Hon. Marcus Garvey D.S.O.E., President-General Universal Negro Improvement Association of the World and President of the Black Star Line Steamship Corporation, headquarters 56 West 135 St., New York City. The above is known by the Colored Race as the D[i]vine Savior of Ethiopian's.

This Company has chartered the Steamship Yarmouth which made one trip from New York to Colon (Canal Zone) successfully. On the second trip the above steamer had a two million dollar cargo of liquor and as quoted in The GUARDIAN, a newspaper published in Boston, Mass., Saturday January 24, 1920 which stated that the Steamship Yarmouth was bound for Cuba and was caught in a heavy northeastern thirty-five miles off the coast of Cape [M]ay, New Jersey, and was towed into the Delaware Breakwater.

The Steamship Yarmouth is to [be] christened the Frederick Douglas on its return trip in honor of the famou[s] leader who was a shipbuilder by trade.[3] The Black Star Line plans to add a ship every three months. The personnel of the Steamship Yarmouth is as follows:

Captain—colored; first Mate—white; chief Engineer—white; and the rest of the crew colored.

A circular has been distributed among the colored people of Boston headed GREAT MASS MEETING[.]

A call to all the colored people of Boston, Mass to hear the great living negro orator and champion of Negro Rights—Hon. Marcus Garvey D.S.O.E., President-General Universal Negro Improvement Association of the World and President of The Black Star Line Steamship Corporation.

Meeting[s] have been scheduled in different parts [of the] Black Belt of Boston on different dates in January. The circular ends with the following[:] Marcus Garvey is the only man of the race who has compe[l]led the world to recognize that the new Negro is to be reckoned with as an International Power.

COME PREPARED TO BUY STOCK IN THE BLACK STAR LINE
STEAMSHIP CORPORATION AT $5 PER SHARE AND YOU MAY BUY
FROM 5 TO 200 SHARES AND MAKE MONEY.
BE EARLY TO GET SEATS   ALL SEATS FREE.

The above Company is mailing circulars asking for contributions and soliciting for shares to help float the "PHYLLIS WHEATLEY" on 28th, February 1920, which steamer contemplates sailing for Africa.

Another circular entitled "THE NEGRO IN THE REA[LM] OF COMMERCE" which states that The Black Star Steamship Corporation is capitalized at $500,000 under the Laws of the State of Delaware, United States of America. A line of steamships to run between America, Africa, the West Indies, Canada, South and Central America, Carrying Freight and Passengers. Stocks sold only to Negroes.

Miss Henrietta Vinton Davis, Second Vice-President of the above Company is now in Colon. American, 49 years old, residence 1219 Linden St. N.W. Washington, D.C. Received passport between Nov. 1st and Nov. 15th to go to West Indies, South and Central America and try [to] Float Stock of the Black Star Line.

The above possibly made false statements to secure passport.

The officers and directors of the above Company are Hon. Marcus Garvey, President; J. M. Certain, First Vice-President; Miss Henrietta Vinton Davis, Second Vice President; George Tobias, Treasurer; Ed. D. Smith-Green, Secretary; Fred D. Powell, Asst. Sec. and Treas. and Hon. Janie Jenkins. Main office, 56 West 135 St., New York City.

Advices from the Department are requested relative to previous activities of Garvey and his Associates in order that this Bureau may determine whether it will be necessary to cover any activities of these parties in this district.

M. ROBERT VALKENBURGH

[*Endorsement*] Noted F.D.W.

DNA, RG 65, file OG 374508. TD. Stamped endorsement. Copies of this report were furnished to the bureau's Washington, D.C., New York, and Boston offices.

1. Distinguished Service Order of Ethiopia.
2. United Fruit Co., an American-owned company founded in 1899, became a major symbol of American economic imperialism, with company officers enjoying considerable political power in Caribbean and Latin American nations. Company officials were especially concerned about UNIA organizing efforts among laborers on plantations associated with or owned by United Fruit (Henry P. McCann, *An American Company* [New York: Crown Publishers, 1976]).
3. While a slave in Baltimore, Douglass worked as a corker in a local shipyard.

HAVE YOU BOUGHT YOUR SHARES
—— IN ——

THE BLACK STAR LINE?

IF NOT, PLEASE DO SO TO-DAY

The S. S. "FREDERICK DOUGLASS"

Is afloat and has made a successful trip to Central America
and the West Indies

Help Float The "PHYLLIS WHEATLEY"
On 28th February, 1920

She will sail for Africa

BUY YOUR SHARES AT

BLACK STAR LINE, Inc.

56 W. 135th St.   **New York City**

AKINBAMI AGBEBI, General Agent, 32 Moloney Street, Lagos, Nigeria

The Hunt Printing Co. 34 W. 136th St. New York City   Tel. Harlem 9695

(*Source:* Senegalese Archives).

A. L. Flint to Richard W. Flournoy, Jr.

[*Washington, D.C.*] January 29, 1920

Sir:

This office is just in receipt of a special confidential cablegram, /Incl. 229/ dated the 29th instant, from the Governor of The Panama Canal, Balboa Heights, Canal Zone, reading as follows:

> "Local paper publishes alleged cable from Marcus Garvey to an individual here stating he will sail from New York on Steamer FREDERICK DOUGLAS in five days. Please take up with Department of State Division of Passport Control referring to their letter of October 29th and request appropriate action."

A copy of your letter /Incl. 215/ of October 29th, 1919, referred to in the above quoted cablegram, is inclosed herewith for ready reference. As the correspondence will show, Marcus Garvey is a negro agitator whose presence in the Canal Zone is undesirable. Will you please telegraph the Collector of Customs at New York regarding the matter, issuing such instructions as may be necessary to prevent Garvey's sailing for the Canal Zone? Kindly advise at your earliest convenience as to the action you take in this matter. Very respectfully

A. L. FLINT
Chief of Office

Incls: copy ltr. from Div. of Passport Control, Oct. 29, 1919. dup. this ltr.
CC to Governor, in duplicate.

[*Endorsements*] Sent 1/29/20 in double env.
JRT
Sent by Contee 4:10 pm Jan. 29th. JRT.
Call up 2/2 G

WNRC, RG 185, file 91/229. TL, carbon copy. Handwritten endorsements.

GREETINGS

To The NEGRO PEOPLE OF AMERICA

from the

UNIVERSAL NEGRO IMPROVEMENT ASS'N
of the World

and from

THE BLACK STAR LINE, Inc.

56 West 135th Street, New York City, U. S. A.

BIG CONVENTION

OF THE

Negroes of the World

NEW YORK
AUGUST 1 to 31, 1920

WRITE TO HEAD OFFICE

The Hunt Printing Company, 31 W. 138th Street, New York City. Tel Harlem 3686.

(*Source*: DNA, RG 28, file B-500).

Gilbert Grindle, Under Secretary of State, Colonial Office, to the Under Secretary of State, Foreign Office

[*London*] 5 February, 1920

Sir,

I am directed to transmit to you, for any observations which Earl Curzon of Kedleston may wish to make, the accompanying copy[1] of a letter from the West Indian Protective Society of America, calling attention to the activities in the United States and the British West Indies of an organisation known as the Universal Negro Improvement Association and African Communities League.

2. It appears to the Secretary of State doubtful whether it would be possible or advisable to ask the Government of the United States to take any steps for the control of this organisation or of the newspaper "The Negro World" beyond such as it may take in its own interests but he would be glad if His Majesty's Ambassador at Washington could be instructed to keep a watch upon the activities of the Association and to report any information that he may receive which would be of interest to the Colonies concerned, besides communicating it direct to the Governors concerned in cases of urgency.

3. A copy of this correspondence is being sent to the Governors of all the West Indian Colonies. I am, Sir, Your most obedient servant,

G[ILBERT] GRINDLE

[*Typewritten reference*] 3351/1920 8th Jan. 1920 [*Handwritten endorsement*] 2 copies

PRO, FO 371/4567. TLS, recipient's copy.
  1. Printed above, 8 January 1920.

Report by Special Agent WW

New York February 6th, 1920

RE: NEGRO RADICAL ACTIVITIES

. . . For January 27th, 1920.

Spent most of the morning seeking information concerning the activity of Garvey relative to the maiden trip of the Black Star Line Steamship "FREDERICK DOUGLAS" (known also as the "YARMOUTH"). I was fortunate in getting an interview with a man named Edward Timmy, who lives at #485 Carlton Avenue, Brooklyn, who shipped on the steamship as an able seaman.

He related to me the experiences of himself and comrades on the trip. He is a member of the organization headed by Garvey and it was partly thru his interest in same that he consented to make this trip on the vessel. He claims that the crew was wholly incompetent, the fir[e]men consisting of men who had really never been to sea and knew very little about furnaces of any description. He claims that the first assistant engineer was not only unlicensed but also inexperienced. This man is a member of the Longshoreman's Union, as were two or three others of the crew. When about five days out at sea the "firemen" became seasick and wholly unable to resume their responsibility of keeping up enough steam to keep the vessel going and the captain attempted to force them back to their work. This they refused to do and Captain Cockburn then offered them overtime if they went back to work. To this proposition they complied and carried the ship to port. Upon reaching Kingston, Jamaica, the men asked permission to go ashore. The captain refused this permission and the men then asked that they be given some money with which to purchase a few things that they were really in need of. This request was also denied. Thereupon the men took it upon themselves to refuse to do any work unless they were advanced some money. The captain went ashore and returned with a number of the police force of Kingston (white) who told the men that unless they complied with the orders of the captain they would be imprisoned. The men stated they were perfectly willing to return to work but not until their demand for an advance of some money had been complied with. The captain then made a promise that he would pay for anything that the men ordered or purchased on shore, providing the bills were sent to him.

Upon returning to her deck at New York, the men of the vessel were paid off and the men who had been promised overtime pay were not given same. These men took up this matter with the local British consul, and the latter interceded in their behalf with the captain. The captain agreed that the men were entitled to some consideration, but denied having promised them overtime pay. Two of these men who were members of the Longshoremen's U[n]ion went to Garvey and demanded their money. The other men did likewise but were sent back to their captain and were refused an opportunity to state their case to him. The majority of the crew were members of the Garvey organization and that is the reason the matter did not reach the public press and why it was not taken up legally, inasmuch as they do not wish anything detrimental to the interests of the Black Star Line to become public as their savings are invested in it. I believe this man may be useful as a source of information concerning the operations of the Line and I will further cultivate his friendship.

. . . For January 29th, 1920.

Spent the greater portion of the day visiting various barber shops in Brooklyn, which are a general headquarters in the negro settlements for gossip of all sorts. Learned nothing of importance insofar as the radical element is concerned.

During the day I had a very interesting chat with Rev. Spencer Carpentier of the Bridge Street (near Myrtle Avenue) AME Church of this city, who is just recovering from an assault. My visit was sympathetic and I was accorded an hour or so of his time. This man, the radical—or rather liberal—declares himself a thorough American and has repeatedly preached the doctrine to his congregation that "if this country is not good enough for those who come here from other countries to better their condition, they should go back from whence they came and not endeavor to spread their dissention among the people who are loyal Americans." He opposes such men as Garvey and W. A. Domingo and asserts that it is such men as these that hurt the progress of the loyal American Negro. He full[y] agreed with me that such papers as the Messenger should be put out of existence and states that in a September issue of this paper he read an article which openly advocated Bolshevism.

This man is a considerable faster [*factor?*] among the negro element in Brooklyn and beyond doubt will eventually draw the fire of such men as Garvey and Domingo and I feel that the retention of his acquaintance will aid me considerably.

. . . For January 31st, 1920.

Have taken up most of the day with a young man of the name of Leon Munce, who resides at the Y.M.C.A. at Carlton Avenue, Brooklyn. This man is not a very close friend of mine, merely an acquaintance, as I have not known him over three months and have not seen him over four times in the little time I have known him. He has taken an apparent liking to me and is taking me into his confidence. He is a very close friend of the wireless operator of the Black Star Steamship Liner "YARMOUTH" [*deletion illegible*]. When I first met Munce several months ago he was driving a car but for the last two months he has not been working and seems always to have an abundant supply of money. I learned from him today that his father was in the liquor business in Philadelphia (so he said) and he receives an allowance from the father. He took me to his room in the Y.M.C.A. and showed me a wireless outfit that he had rigged up; also showed me how he could pick up messages from the Brooklyn Navy Yard and other nearby and distant stations. To prove to me his close friendship with the operator of the Black Star Line steamship above mentioned, he showed me the chart made up by his friend on the maiden trip of the vessel. I did not allow my curiosity to get the best of me, so I really reserved a lot of things that I would like to have asked, for a future date. I really believe this man possesses a great deal of information concerning the Black Star Line and I shall be careful to handle him properly.

For February 1, 1920

I was today in company with Munce, and spent some time in his room at the Y.M.C.A, where he showed me the photos of his family and told me his personal history. He asked me if I was "interested in the Black Star Line." I told him I was that I hoped in the near future to become a member. He told me this was "O.K. and when you get ready to join I'll give you a little advice." I made discreet inquiries concerning Munce of the Secretary of the Y.M.C.A. and found that Munce is not highly esteemed at this place and, in fact, has been asked to vacate his rooms there. This may be due, however, to the fact that Munce is known to possess a considerable quantity of the Green River Whiskey which is part of the cargo on board the "Yarmouth."

I am /confident/ that this man is not receiving money from his father, as he says, but have not succeeded in confirming my suspicions and will report further on this matter when I secure information definite enough to warrant details.

WW

[*Stamped endorsement*] Noted F.D.W.
[*Handwritten endorsement*] Noted WWG

DNA, RG 65, file OG 258421. TD.

A. L. Flint to Chester Harding

Washington February 7, 1920

Sir:

Referring to previous correspondence in reference to Marcus Garvey, I inclose herewith for your information a clipping from the "Evening Star," of this City, dated the 5th instant, which contains a reference to Garvey. [Re]spectfully,

A. L. FLINT
Chief of Office

In duplicate.
Inclosure

WNRC, RG 185, file 91/233. TLS, recipient's copy.

Enclosure

[[*New York*, February 5, 1920]]

The steamer Yarmouth, with its $4,800,000 cargo of whisky, which was seized by Supervising Prohibition Inspector Shevlin, will be released and allowed to sail for Havana, it was announced, following a long telephone conversation between Mr. Shevlin and the Attorney General's office in Washington. A guard of fifteen prohibition agents will be kept on board, however, until the vessel departs.

While this conversation with Washington was in progress the federal grand jury began investigating the shortage in the Yarmouth's cargo, which developed between her sailing from and returning to New York, Judge Knox ordered Marcus Garvey, the colored president of the Black Star Line, owner of the vessel, to produce all books, papers and manifests hearing on the whisky cargo. Earlier in the day he had refused to produce them on the ground that surrender of the records might tend to incriminate him.

The Yarmouth sailed for Cuba with a heavy list to starboard resulting from hurried efforts to load the ship before midnight January 16, when constitutional prohibition went into effect. Off the New Jersey coast she ran into rough weather and was forced to return to New York for repairs. The captain explained that 500 cases of liquor were thrown overboard before she turned back.

Shortly after her arrival here again workmen were discovered trying to steal away from the Yarmouth with fifty-six bottles of whisky in a small boat. A guard was placed aboard and later the cargo was formally seized.

Printed in the *Washington Evening Star*, 5 February 1920. Original headlines omitted.

Report by Special Agent Jones

NORFOLK, VA. FEB. 9, 1920

UNIVERSAL NEGRO IMPROVEMENT ASSOCIATION (Marcus Garvey) at Newport News, Va.

. . . This investigation [*18–24 January 1920*] in reality centers around the activities of one Marcus Garvey. Agent has been informed that the Bureau has a file covering to a considerable extent the activities of this man GARVEY. Attached hereto will be found GARVEY's history.[1] This was secured by Mr. Reynolds of the Newport News Shipbuilding and Dry Dock Company from some source in New York City.

On January 18th Agent attended two meetings of the above mentioned organization at the Lincoln Theatre Newport News, Va. Agent was introduced to R. H. TAYLOR, President of the Association by Maj. JOSEPH KING,

630 22nd Street, Newport News, Va. who is the head of the military branch of the association. I talked to Majo[r] King who outlined the purpose of the organization as follows: MARCUS GARVEY, President General of this association with headquarters at New York is collecting enough money to pay off the indebtedness of Liberia to this country, and after this has been done the headquarters of this association will be transferred to Monrovia Liberia. In order to be prepared for this movement in Liberia he is going to organize a military branch in this country. I was allowed to read a letter that he had received from Marcus Garvey designating him as Major and instructing him to proceed with the organizing of companies of 64 men each with the proper non-commission officers, officers to be appointed later. Companies to be formed on strictly U.S. Army basis.

King at present has the names of about 200 men who have joined the military branch of the association and who drill every Thursday night at the Elk's Hall, 23rd Street, Newport News, Va. At present I am assisting King in the training of these men, also KING, HENRY PLUMBER[2] and myself are rewriting the U.S. Army Drill Regulations to suit this organization.[3] The part of the General Orders that read: "to take charge of this post and all government property in view" will be changed to read: "to take charge of this post and all Black Star Line property in view." The oath of allegiance that every U.S. soldier takes will be changed so as to read: "To the Hon. Marcus Garvey", instead of "To the President of the United States", and other changes to suit this organization.

The financial end of this organization is in very bad shape and last night a meeting was called to go over the books. I have been appointed a member of the committee to go over the books. TAYLOR seems to be losing hold on these people because of his loose way in handling the finance.

Marcus Garvey is to be here on the 1st of February when he will start his drive for another boat of the Black Star Line of which he has one by name "Yarmouth" to be rechristened the "Frederick Douglas".

I will attend both meetings of the association on the 25th.
Continued.

J. W. JONES[4]

[*Endorsements*] Noted w.w.g Noted f.d.w.

DNA, RG 65, file OG 185161. TD. Stamped endorsements. Copies of this report were furnished to the bureau's Norfolk office.

1. Not found.
2. Henry Vinton Plummer, Jr. (b. 1876), was a real estate operator in Washington, D.C., and Maryland, the head of the Black Star Line Bureau of Publicity and Propaganda, and the chief of Garvey's secret service staff. He was the son of Henry Vinton Plummer, Sr., the first black chaplain to serve in the United States Army after the Civil War. The junior Plummer was born in Maryland and attended public schools in Wyoming and in Omaha. He also attended Omaha Medical College but later chose a law career. After an unsuccessful campaign as a Republican candidate for the Nebraska state legislature, Plummer moved to Washington, D.C. In 1912, he served as assistant sergeant at arms at the Progressive National Convention (*WWCR*; DNA, RG 65, files BS 198940 and BS 202600-68).

3. Jones, along with King and Plummer, compiled "The Official Drill Regulations of the African Legion of the Military Branch of the U.N.I. Association and A.C. League" (DNA, RG 65, file OG 389225).

4. James Wormley Jones (d. 1958) was a Bureau of Investigation confidential informant who infiltrated the UNIA. Adopting the code number 800 for his later reports, Jones used his access to UNIA correspondence and his position in the African Legion to gather data. Born in Virginia, Jones was made a captain in the Ninety-second Division of the United States Army during World War I. In March 1920 when Jones addressed an audience in Liberty Hall, his very light complexion led the audience to assume that he was white. According to the *Negro World*, "he took the opportunity . . . at the beginning of his speech to allay the anxious fears and suspicions of the audience by revealing the fact that he was a Negro" (*NW*, 13 March 1920). Jones was soon placed in charge of registering all incoming mail at UNIA headquarters, and by June 1920 he was adjutant general, or chief administrative officer, of the African Legion (*NW*, 26 June 1920). Jones also infiltrated the African Blood Brotherhood in August 1921 (DJ-FBI, 61–826).

Newport News Division
of the
Universal Negro Improvement Association and African Community League
INCORPORATED

Headquarters: 517 23rd Street, Newport News, Va.

CHARTER No. 6

B. M. TAYLOR President	C. C. JONES Chairman Trustees	MRS. JENNIE CHAPPELL President Ladies' Division
I. C. SHIVERS First Vice-President	HOWARD W POOL Chairman Building Committee	MRS. DAISY WARD First Vice-President
LEVI C WHITING General Secretary	J. R. RINGO Secretary	MRS. ROSA CALDWELL Second Vice-President
J. J. BRYANT Executive Secretary	E. A. EATON Treasurer	MRS. VIOLA WIGGINS Secretary
P. B. SMALL Chairman Advisory Board	J. B. TAYLOR General Treasurer	H. B. JONES Architect

_____ 192_

We, the **UNIVERSAL NEGRO IMPROVEMENT ASSOCIATION AND AFRICAN COMMUNITY LEAGUE, Inc.**, hereby promise to pay to

Mr. _____

the sum of _____   Dollars ($_____)

sixty (60) days after date, for Cash received as loan to the Association, bearing interest at four (4) per cent annually, interest collectible every three months on presentation of this note by _____ , or his or her accredited agent.

**UNIVERSAL NEGRO IMPROVEMENT ASSOCIATION
AND AFRICAN COMMUNITY LEAGUE, Inc.**

_____ President

_____ Ex. Secretary

(*Source*: DNA, RG 65, file OG 185161).

British Military Intelligence Report

[*New York*] February 10, 1920

NEGRO AGITATION

Universal Negro Improvement Association

As previously reported Marcus Garvey spent his honeymoon in Canada. He had expected some recreation while there, but according to the "Negro World" from the moment he landed in Toronto until he returned to New York City, he had been working for the Universal Negro Improvement Association. Three mass meetings were held in Toronto, under the auspices of the Toronto Branch of the U.N.I.A. at Occidental Hall, on the evenings of Jan. 5th, 6th and 7th. Two meetings were held in Montreal. It is reported that Garvey brought back $8,000 from Canada.

At the meeting held in Toronto on the night of Jan. 5th, Garvey was welcomed by Mr. J. T. Bishop, President of the West Indian Trading Association, Ltd. Among other things Mr. Bishop said:

> ". . Britain dominates the world by ships. So we to succeed as a people, to make our voices felt and heard, to occupy a seat among nations, must possess ships, must engage in commerce and industry . ." [1]

> ". . Our associations at this moment are stronger than ever, developing and expending daily. The West Indies Trading Ass'n, Ltd. has a strong following in Sierra Leone, Panama, Cuba, Jamaica, British Guiana, Barbadoes, Dominica, Bermuda and prominent cities of the U.S., thanks to the nobleness of heart and co-operation of Hon. Marcus Garvey . ."

Garvey in a letter dated Montreal, Canada, Jan. 8th, said that now was the time to redouble their efforts to forge ahead and plant the flag of Victory over the hilltop of African Statehood.

> "Our convention of August 1920 will inspire us with the new cry of 'Liberty or Death.' We may as well prepare ourselves from now on for the bloodiest of all conflicts in that the handwriting on the wall of international discord warns us that the greatest of wars is now in the making . . . . We shall now prepare to answer the call of Mother Africa when she demands of us our wealth, our strength and genius to deliver her from the grasp of the oppres-

sor.["] ". . Let us all pull together and see and hear nothing also
but a free Africa and a great and powerful Negro Race . .["]

Dr. James. J. Edwards, of the Oliver Sanitarium, Spanishtown, Kingston, Jamaica, B.W.I. was introduced by Garvey at a meeting held in Liberty
Hall on January 10th.

Among other things Dr. Edwards said that he had devoted his whole
time and attention to training nurses, and when the time came he would
perhaps have 200 nurses to give them, for they would need them if they were
going to fight.

"We of Jamaica will be with you when the time comes for the
great march and the advance is called."

Garvey said in part:

". . . I want you to realize that this is the p[sy]chological moment
for the organization. . It was organization that made the Germans
the power they were in Europe for over 40 years. . . .

["]It was the dream of William the Second for Germany to
rule the world from Potsdam or from Berlin. In his dream he saw
a great Central Empire . . But, as God Almighty would have it,
William declared war several years too soon. He had not yet
gained the strength that was really necessary to make him the
conqueror of the world. And as William of Germany declared
war, so did he lose the war; and in losing the war he lost the vision
of a great Central Africa.[2] But as he lost the vision of a great
Central Africa, in his defeat of 1918, the renewed Negro has caught
the vision of not only a great Central Africa for the Africans, but a
United Africa for the Africans of the world.["]

According to the New York News of Jan. 22nd, an official break in
Germany's [*Garvey's?*] staff of the U.N.I.A. and Black Star Line Corporation
was made apparent at Saturday and Sunday nights' meetings. It is observed
that the break or dissatisfaction is due to the present management. In
Garvey's speech Sunday night he announced that a certain "half drunken
ambitious individual" who is an "officer of the U.N.I.A. and B.S.L. Corporation" had made statements from the platform on the previous night which
were detrimental to the Association and was trying to make trouble among
the members.

The S.S. "Yarmouth," soon to be rechristened the "Frederick Douglass," completed her maiden trip, bringing back 38 passengers in addition to
her cargo and was reported in good seaworthy condition. The trip was
completed on Tuesday night, January 13th.

With much pomp and ceremony the "Yarmouth" cleared this port on Jan. 17th for Havana, with a cargo of liquor valued at $2,000,000. A rough sea came up when the ship reached Cape May and the cargo hastily loaded to get away the day before Prohibition Amendment went into effect,[3] shifted, and it was feared the "Yarmouth" would founder. Coast Guard cutters towed her back to port, however, and after undergoing slight repairs, it was expected she would sail for Havana the latter part of the week. According to press reports, three libel suits were filed against the "Yarmouth", one for $11,791 by the Irvine Engineering Co., for $575 by the Olsen Water & Towing Co., and the third for $365 filed by the Hudson Towboat Co.[4]

At a meeting held in Liberty Hall on the night of January 25th, Garvey said that the past week had been somewhat of a trying week for those who were at the head of the Black Star Corporation:

> "They told you that we had no money in the bank; they told you that our ship was libeled so many times; but yet our bank account stands as strong as ever. The ship 'Frederick Douglass' is still the property of the Black Star Line . .["] "The past week has been a week of brain against brain and out of it the Black Star Line was survived . .

> "In the last week I have had a very hard time, and that is why even though I did not go to Boston, I was not at Liberty Hall all through the week, because I had to plan a way to fight men from two directions—men within the ranks and men without the ranks—white men on the outside and black men on the inside . .

> ". . With all the lies they have told about the Yarmouth it is for me to tell you that your corporation is strong enough to take care of itself even in spite of all that they have done to bring us down. Before we started they were organized to crush us, and they have not stopped yet.

> "Unconsciously on the part of those who are helping me, work was given out to some of the very people who were plotting to overthrow us. Because of lack of real business training of some of our leaders, even though they had the best intentions, they gave out work and never asked how much the work would cost before the work was performed and thus played into the hands of the men who were laying a trap for us. Hence a jo[b] that was not worth more than $1,000, just a few hours before the "Frederick Douglass" was scheduled to sail, they presented a bill charging and demanding . .$11,000 for the work . . They thought that having such a big balance against the Black Star Line they would

make a public announcement of it and all of our creditors would pounce down upon us at the same time, and they would tear the Black Star Line to shreds.["]

On the afternoon of Feb. 3rd, the cargo of the "Yarmouth" was formally seized by the U.S. Government.[5] This action was taken on the ground that quantities of the cargo which were mentioned in the ship's manifests were no longer to be found aboard her. Capt. Joshua Cockburn had a long [*deletion illegible*] talk with Mr. Shevlin, Supervising Federal Prohibition Agent, at his office in the Custom House, and denied all knowledge that any of the cargo of the "Yarmouth" had been placed in a boat alongside to be sold for beverage purposes in Brooklyn. Several stockholders appeared at Mr. Shevlin's office. Among them were Edward L. Smith-Green, secretary; George W. Johnson, traffic manager; Louis D. Lamothe, purser of the vessel, and Marcus Garvey, president of the line. After much burning of long distance wires and a conference in the U.S. Attorney's office, the officials of the Black Star Line were informed that the whiskey ship was free to leave this port as soon as she was pleased. No evidence of the sale of liquor had been forthcoming since the "Yarmouth" returned here although some of her cargo had disappeared. Meanwhile, a prohibition guard will be kept aboard her till she weighs anchor.

The Rev. Dr. R. D. Jonas, Secretary of the League of Darker Peoples, who arrived here from Norfolk, Va. on Feb. 3rd, brought a curious story about the "Yarmouth" which he said he intended to lay before the authorities in the interests of the negro owners of the vessel. These, Dr. Jonas asserted, were being made the victims of much undeserved criticisms on account of the happenings to the ship when they were really deserving of sympathy, because her misfortunes were none of their making.

According to Dr. Jonas, the "Yarmouth" and her colored owners were really the victims of a plot to steal the $2,000,000 liquor cargo she carried, a plot which the bravery of her negro skipper, Captain Cockburn, frustrated. The "Yarmouth" Dr. Jonas said, left port with a slight list to port. She was closely followed by another vessel, and when she was some distance outward in a heavy sea it was discovered that she had mysteriously sprung a leak. A white engineer aboard, who had been taken on at the last minute, rushed up to the bridge and informed the skipper that the boat was sinking and there was nothing to do but take to the boats. "You go back to your job and set the pumps going," Captain Cockburn ordered, according to Dr. Jonas, and the skipper drew a revolver to emphasize the order. The engineer went and the Captain after sending out an S.O.S. as a precaution, accompanied him to investigate the "leak[.]" He had a shrewd suspicion, as a result of his examination, that a seacock had been opened. Anyway, the "Yarmouth" made port under her own steam and with her crew aboard, so that there was no opportunity to salvage the biggest liquor prize that has left this port in many a day, according to the N.Y. Times.[6]

At a meeting held in Liberty Hall on Sunday evening, Feb. 1st, Garvey said that if it had not been for the mishap to the ["]Frederick Douglass," instead of launching the "Phyllis Wheatley" on the 29th of February, as promised, they would have had it now, because two hours before he received the news of the mishap to the "Frederick Douglass" he had just come from inspecting the ship to be known as the "Phyllis Wheatley." He further stated that he had planned a campaign which would have taken him from New York to Pennsylvania, Maryland, Washington, Chicago, and back to New York, winding up at Madison Square Garden, but because of the mishap he had to postpone his campaign.

> ". . But I want you stockholders to realize that your Black Star Line is as strong as it ever was. I want you to understand that if the Black Star Line were put in need of money we could raise $1,000,000 in a month—So I want you to dispel from your mind any fear as instilled into you by the enemy." [". . With all that is said and done, we got incorporated three days ago a Negro Factories Corporation at $1,000,000.[7] This corporation will build factories in Harlem and Brooklyn and will employ thousands of our men and women.["]

> ". . We are engaged in a great warfare. It is a fight that must be fought to the finish; it is a fight that will take the last drop of blood of some of us, but we are prepared to give it . . So, in conclusion, I adjure you to be courageous I ask that you continue the fight. Cease not until victory comes.["]

Negro World:

Hubert H[.] Harrison, former editor of the Clarion and New Negro (defunct) is now associate Editor of the Negro World. Harrison is in charge of the West India[n] News section of the paper.

Agents are wanted for the Negro World in all of the following States, according to a recent issue of the paper: Idaho, Iowa, Kentucky, Maine, Minnesota, Missouri, Montana, Nebraska, Nevada, North Dakota, Oregon, Rhode Island[,] Utah, Vermont, Wisconsin.

According to a letter in the "Negro World" from T[.] H. Fowler,[8] Pt. Limon, C[osta] R[ica,] 5,000 copies of the Negro World were held by order of the Governor,[9] 300 copies being used in the United Fruit Company's store for wrapping parcels, and that the Post Office staff sold papers to stall owners at 40¢ per pound.

Universal African Legion:

Appended is a copy of an anonymous letter with reference to the Universal African Legion, one of Garvey's organizations.[10] According to this letter they have regular drills given by ex-soldiers to hundreds of colored men, and it is their plan to smuggle these men with arms into Africa and the West Indies on the Black Star Line as passengers. Mr. D.D'. Shirley, a member of the Advisory Board of the Black Star Line and a partner of S.G. Kpakpa-Quartey, a merchant recently arrived from Accra, Gold Coast Colony, is the commander of the Legion. This is the second anonymous letter we have received with reference to Garvey and his organizations. Under date of Oct. 3rd, copy of a letter was sent you suggesting that Garvey's various accounts be audited, also that by getting in touch with R.E. Warner and Edgar M. Gray, 2296 7th Avenue, they would have sufficient evidence to convict the man (These men were formerly connected with Garvey and his association[.]) It is barely possible that both of these anonymous letters emanated from the same source, and I would suggest that either Warner or Gray may have written them. Garvey at a meeting held in Liberty Hall on Feb. 1st stated that "There is one fellow who believes he is smart, who was once expelled from the association because of his crooked dealings . . . . Therefore he is endeavoring to do us all the harm he possibly can, not knowing that we know how far he has gone."

AFRICAN SOCIETIES

Mr. F.E.M. Hercules,[11] former editor of the London "African Telegraph,"[12] is visiting in New York for a few weeks, according to press reports. He is investigating the economic[,] social and political conditions under which the Negro is living in the West Indies, in Africa and in America. He has just completed an extended tour through Jamaica, Demerara, Trinidad[,] Barbadoes, Grenada, etc. and two weeks ago he was introduced to the Universal Negro Improvement Association in Liberty Hall. On Sunday Feb. 8th he spoke at Rush Memorial Church on "The Right of the Negro Race to Self-Determination". Hercules is said to represent the African League[13] as organizer and managing director. . . .[14]

South African Delegation:

Appended are several clippings with reference to the recent visit of the South African Delegation to England, of which Sol T. Plaatje[15] was leader.

In a letter addressed to John E. Bruce, an extreme radical, and published in the "Negro World," Plaatje said that he had started a brotherhood in Kimberley, that the first world Brotherhood[16] met last September in London and that he represented South Africa as a President of the Native Brotherhood[17] founded by himself. He further stated that the next one would meet at Washington D.C. next May and that he hoped to attend this too with some Afro-American friends.

DNA, RG 165, file 10218-364-22-190X. TD, recipient's copy. It originally appeared as an enclosure to a letter from Maj. H. A. Strauss, Military Intelligence Division, to the director of MID, 24 February 1920. The report was referred to as having been "received from the British."

1. Unless otherwise stated, ellipsis marks are found in the original document.

2. During 1917 and 1918, Germany's colonial ambitions in central Africa were restated. The German army high command sought to create an African colonial empire stretching from coast to coast, establishing naval bases on the coasts of the Atlantic Ocean and the Indian Ocean. Interest in central Africa was sparked primarily by the rich mineral resources located in Katanga (now known as Shaba). This future central African colonial empire was also to include trading posts and coaling stations. Indeed, as early as the spring of 1918, various German government ministries began discussions to decide where they would be located. The proposed German empire in Africa was eventually to include northern Rhodesia, northern Mozambique, Kenya, Uganda, Congo, Angola, Nyasaland, German East Africa, and German South-West Africa (Fritz Fischer, *Germany's Aims in the First World War* [New York: Norton & Co., 1967], pp. 586–91).

3. The Eighteenth Amendment to the U.S. Constitution, which prohibited the manufacture, sale, and use of alcohol, passed Congress on 28 October 1919 and went into effect on 16 January 1920.

4. According to the court testimony given by Leo H. Healy [of Harriss, Magill & Co.] in 1923: "The boat was ready to sail and I received word that several libels had been placed on it, and I . . . took control of the ship until the libels were taken off" (*Garvey* v. *United States*, no. 8317, Ct. App., 2d Cir., 2 February 1925, pp. 196, 219, 291). After arriving in New York at the end of its first voyage, the *Yarmouth* required substantial repairs before the cargo of whiskey could be taken on board. On 15 January 1920, as the *Yarmouth* was to depart on its second voyage, the Irvine Engineering Co. presented the Black Star Line with a bill for $11,791.74, demanding an immediate payment of $5,000 and threatening to file suit and bring about the seizure of the ship. Garvey was under considerable pressure to have the ship sail with its cargo and therefore paid the amount demanded. However, the Black Star Line immediately brought action against the company to recover half of the $5,000, which Garvey claimed was in excess of what the BSL legitimately owed, as well as to exact other damages totaling $8,700 (NFRC, docket L21-190, *Black Star Line* v. *Irvine Engineering Co.*, 21 January 1920). The case was dismissed on 13 February 1920 because the Supreme Court of the County of New York lacked jurisdiction.

5. Shortly after the *Yarmouth* was towed back to New York Harbor for repairs, workmen were discovered trying to abscond with fifty-six bottles of whiskey in a small boat. The ship was seized and a federal grand jury soon began investigating the shortage in the *Yarmouth*'s cargo, which developed during her brief excursion away from the port of New York. Garvey was ordered to produce all papers, books, and manifests bearing on the whiskey cargo. Earlier that day, Garvey had refused to produce them on the grounds that surrendering the records might incriminate him, but this time he complied. Although the *Yarmouth* was eventually allowed to sail, the problem of pilferage persisted throughout the voyage, according to its captain, Joshua Cockburn. At Garvey's mail fraud trial in 1923, Cockburn recalled: "The crew had stolen several cases of whiskey, and stored them in several parts of the vessel. . . . not knowing that this liquor was on board that the crew had stolen, I proceeded to Jamaica. . . . I therefore reported same to the agent, and asked him to ask the custom house authorities to allow me to amend my manifest on entrance certificate, so that the vessel should not be seized. We did it, and I was allowed to put it ashore in the custom house. The same thing occurred with all of the ports that I entered, such as Colon, Bocas del Toro, Port Limon, Cuba, Norfolk, Virginia . . ." (*Garvey* v. *United States*, no. 8317, Ct. App., 2d Cir., 2 February 1925, pp. 408–9).

6. *NYT*, 5 February 1920.

7. On 23 January 1920 Garvey, William Ferris, and John G. Bayne filed a certificate of incorporation for the Negro Factories Corp. with a notary public in New York City. On 30 January the NFC was incorporated under the laws of the state of Delaware (N-SS, Bureau of Corporations).

8. Teofilo Horace Fowler (d. 1938) was the *Negro World* agent in Port Limón, Costa Rica (Neville N. Clarke [Jamaican consul, Costa Rica] to Robert A. Hill, 18 April 1981).

9. The American consul in Port Limón informed the secretary of state that the *Negro World* was ". . . intended largely for export, and hundreds of thousands of copies are being sent monthly to foreign countries having large Negro populations" (Stewart E. McMillin to Robert Lansing, 21 December 1919, DNA, RG 59, 811.918/1420). Teofilo Fowler had been instructed to recruit and organize a UNIA division in Costa Rica. The Costa Rican government, however, confiscated the UNIA constitution and the charter for the new division when they arrived in the mails from UNIA headquarters in New York on 20 August 1919. Also seized

were "several hundred copies of the Negro World," according to the American vice-consul. He added that the "Governor of the Province is reported to have told Fowler that the publication was purely Bolshevik, and of a nature to cause revolution or race riots in Costa Rica" (E. B. Montgomery to Robert Lansing, 24 August 1919, DNA, RG 59, file 818.4016). The attorney for the United Fruit Co. in Washington later wrote to the secretary of state complaining about the circulation of the *Negro World* in Costa Rica (Walter S. Penfield to Robert Lansing, 25 September 1919, DNA, RG 59, file 811.918/134). His complaint was also sent to the postmaster general and the attorney general (William Phillips [for Robert Lansing] to A. Mitchell Palmer, 27 October 1919, DNA, RG 59, file 811.918/134).

10. The enclosed letter follows this report.

11. Felix Eugene Michael Hercules (1888–1943) was born in Venezuela but grew up in Trinidad, where his father was a civil servant. He graduated from Queen's Royal College, served in the Trinidad civil service, and eventually took a teaching position at Maparima College. Shortly after the outbreak of World War I, Hercules went to England, where he completed an intermediate B.A. degree at London University. During his stay in London, Hercules became acquainted with John Eldred Taylor, the chairman of the Society of Peoples of African Origin (SPAO) and the publisher of the *African Telegraph*. Late in 1918 Hercules became the paper's editor; he also soon became general secretary of the SPAO as well as associate secretary of a similar London-based group, the African Progress Union. When he left London to tour the West Indies on behalf of the SPAO in late June 1919, a racial crisis was mounting in England, resulting from race riots in the spring of 1919 in Liverpool and Cardiff. Hercules' speeches in Jamaica in early July created concern among colonial officials, who believed that the speeches were causing sporadic outbreaks of violence against white sailors. From Jamaica, Hercules traveled to Trinidad and British Guiana. When he attempted to return to Trinidad, local officials, fearful of the labor disturbances that were already spreading throughout the island, refused him permission to disembark.

After a brief stop in Grenada, Hercules set out for the United States, where he was detained briefly but admitted after assuring officials that he did not agree with Marcus Garvey's approach to the race problem and declaring that his only purpose was to promote black economic cooperation. In New York Hercules organized the short-lived African League. He later became a Baptist minister and pastored in Illinois, Arkansas, and Tennessee. Throughout his career, Hercules maintained a reputation as a persuasive orator and an intellectual of considerable talents; he remained in the United States until his death in Chicago in 1943 (William F. Elkins, "Hercules and the Society of Peoples of African Origin," *Caribbean Studies* 11, no. 4 [1971]: 47–59; F.E.M. Hercules to secretary of state for the colonies, 12 June 1919, PRO, CO 318/353 and CO 323/818; DNA, RG 59, file 811.108/913, and RG 65, file OG 378703).

12. The *African Telegraph* was founded in London in November 1914 by John Eldred Taylor, a Sierra Leonean businessman and journalist. Although Taylor muted his criticism of Britain's African policy during the war, the *African Telegraph* emerged as a harsh critic at its conclusion, highlighting a series of floggings in Nigeria in the December 1918 issue. Taylor's report caused a furor in London that led to a widely publicized lawsuit, which he lost. The sensational trial, however, featured many witnesses who testified to the prevalent use of flogging as a punishment in northern Nigeria. Although he was unable to continue his publication, much of the British and West African press considered Taylor the victor, because of his success in bringing the floggings to public attention (Ian Duffield, "John Eldred Taylor and the West African Opposition to Indirect Rule in Nigeria," *African Affairs* 70, no. 280 [July 1971]: 252–68).

13. When he arrived in New York City, Hercules formed the African League in order to provide a new affiliation for himself after the libel suit ended the *African Telegraph*. The league proposed to buy a fifteen-hundred-acre farm in British Guiana and to market produce grown there. A newspaper for publicizing the league's views was also planned, as well as a chain of hostels in Europe for black students. The African League did not advocate setting up a black nation, as Garvey envisaged, but it sought to achieve a "good understanding" among blacks so as to create a "great racial chain" for the promotion of black economic and political advancement (*Emancipator*, 20 March 1920). At meetings in New York City before the UNIA's August 1920 convention, Hercules emphasized his disagreement with Garvey's autocratic methods and promised democracy to the members of the African League.

14. A paragraph on the Ogboni Society has been omitted.

15. Solomon Tshekisho Plaatje (1876–1932) was one of the founders, in 1912, of the South African Native National Congress, the predecessor of the African National Congress. He was elected its general corresponding secretary and two years later was a member of its delegation

to England to protest the South African Native Land Act of 1913, which banned the purchase of land by Africans in white areas and forced black sharecroppers into the position of landless tenant laborers. During his stay in England, Plaatje also published *Native Life in South Africa, before and since the European War and the Boer Rebellion* (London: P. S. King and Son, 1916), a book that argued against the Native Land Act.

Plaatje headed a second delegation to England in June 1919, which succeeded in presenting the case for South African blacks to Prime Minister Lloyd George. With financial support from the Brotherhood movement, an interdenominational Christian group, Plaatje continued on to Canada and the United States in October 1920. He became associated with the Toronto division of the UNIA, and during his tour of the United States, he also met with Marcus Garvey. He delivered two addresses in Liberty Hall in February 1921 on the conditions of black South Africans and on the need for black unity. At the same time, Plaatje developed contacts with other black American organizations and leaders, especially with the NAACP and W. E. B. Du Bois, who invited Plaatje to participate in the Second Pan-African Congress in Europe in 1921. His paper was read for him before the congress, however, since he was unable to attend because of lack of funds.

After spending another year in England, Plaatje returned to South Africa at the end of 1923 and joined the African Peoples Organization, led by Dr. A. Abdurahman. He later represented the African National Congress in 1927 at a government-sponsored conference convened in Pretoria to discuss South Africa's Native Administration Act. He later investigated working conditions among blacks in the Congo (Brian Willan, " 'In Aid of the Most Oppressed Negroes of the World': Sol T. Plaatje's Visit to North America, 1920–1922" [unpublished MS]; *NW*, 27 November 1920, 5 February, 12 February, 19 February, and 26 February 1921; *Guide to the Silas T. Molema and Solomon T. Plaatje Papers: Historical and Literary Papers* [Johannesburg, South Africa: Library of the University of Witwatersrand, n.d.]; W. J. de Koch, *Dictionary of South African Biography*, vol. 1 [Cape Town: Nasionale Boekhandel, 1968]; Mark Lipschutz and R. Kent Rasmussen, *Dictionary of African Historical Biography* [Chicago: Aldine Publishing Co., 1978]).

16. The Brotherhood movement was founded in England in the 1870s as an interdenominational organization to apply the Christian gospel to social problems. Plaatje first encountered the movement in London in 1914. With a membership of over a million, the Brotherhood movement was one of few English organizations opposing the Native Land Act in South Africa, providing Plaatje with the opportunity to speak against it in London and elsewhere (Brian Willan, " 'In Aid of the Most Oppressed Negroes of the World' ").

17. When Plaatje returned to South Africa in 1917 after a stay in London, he sought to establish the Brotherhood movement in Kimberley, his hometown. Disappointed by the failure of Christian churches in South Africa to practice what he perceived as genuine brotherhood, Plaatje secured headquarters for his new organization and gathered a small membership before leaving for England, the United States, and Canada in 1919. Although he impressed audiences wherever he spoke, he was unable to raise sufficient funds for his Brotherhood movement and returned to Kimberley in 1923 heavily in debt. His attempt to expand the movement throughout South Africa met with little success. Finally, the religious and social work Plaatje envisioned for his Brotherhood was left to white missionaries, who never supported Plaatje's efforts and were never comfortable with his nondenominational approach (Brian Willan, " 'In Aid of the Most Oppressed Negroes of the World' ").

Enclosure

New York City [*ca. 22 January 1920*]

Gentlemen:

Believing that it is fraught with incalculable harm to the Negro race in the British Empire, I beg to draw your attention to the activities of the Universal Negro Improvement Association and its organ the Negro World in a stirring up disaffection in British Africa and the West Indies.

Do you know that every Sunday between 12 and 2 p.m. they have regular drills given by ex-soldiers to hundreds of foolish colored men?

Do you know that it is planned to smuggle these men with arms into Africa and the West Indies on the Black Star Line as passengers?

The writer suggests that you send a trusted agent on some pretext to Liberty Hall, 138th Street, any Sunday between 12 and 2 and you will verify his statement. For the sake of peace I suggest that steps be taken to suppress this Universal African Legion that has been organized by Marcus Garvey, as it will surely lead to bloodshed.

> (Signed) A Negro who dislikes the British but who has sense enough to foresee disaster

DNA, RG 165, file 10218-364-20-190x. TL, recipient's copy. This enclosure was summarized in a letter from H. A. Strauss to the director of the Military Intelligence Division on 22 January 1920 (DNA, RG 165, file 10218-364-20-190x).

George F. Lamb to Frank Burke

New York City, February 13, 1920

Attention Mr. Hoover.

Dear Sir:

IN RE: NEGRO ACTIVITIES.

This day Agent Jones of the Norfolk office of Bureau called at this office advising that he is at present engaged in investigating the affairs of the Universal Negro Improvement Association and African Communities League, which organizations are operated by Marcus Garvey, a radical negro of this city.

Mr. Jones was supplied with whatever information this office possessed concerning the aforementioned, and you are hereby advised that Special Employee "W.W." has been directed to join the Universal Negro Improvement Association, for the purpose of ascertaining whether or not said association is drilling with firearms, as reported. Very truly yours,

G. F. LAMB
Division Superintendent

[*Endorsement*] FILE G.F.R.

DNA, RG 65, file OG 185161. TLS, recipient's copy. Stamped endorsement.

News Report in the *Baltimore Afro-American*

[[*New York*, Feb. 25, 1920]]

"AMSTERDAM NEWS" MAKES AMENDS

NEWSPAPER RETRACTS STATEMENT ABOUT BLACK STAR LINE.

. . . Marcus Garvey, president of the Black Star Line and editor of the Negro World, was "all het up" when he read in the Amsterdam News and several other race journals a demand that the steamship company explain its financial operations. In speaking at a public meeting he threatened to sue the Amsterdam News and Chicago Defender each for $20,000 damages if they did not make a retraction. He said he would give the Amsterdam News until Wednesday of last week to chew up their words or face the law.

The Amsterdam News "chewed up its words" by making the following statement in its last issue:

"Several persons have been to us, not all enemies of the Black Star Steamship Corporation and the Universal Improvement Association and its president, Marcus Garvey, to have us publish statements about the corporations and the gentleman. Knowingly, we have always refused publication, but the article which appeared on February slipped through before a thorough investigation was made of the facts.

"Now that we have made investigation we retract the statements without reservation, and trust that our readers will not in any way prejudice their minds against the Black Star Corporation and the Universal Improvement Association, nor the president, Marcus Garvey, because of what was published. We wish the corporation and the president every success."

Printed in the *Baltimore Afro-American*, 27 February 1920; reprinted in *NW*, 13 March 1920.

Edward J. Brennan to Frank Burke

Chicago, Illinois February 26, 1920

Dear Sir:—

ATTENTION: MJD-GFM.

Your letter of the 17th in re MARCUS GARVEY received.

The delay in answering this letter was caused by the fact that the States Attorney's office, Cook County, was closed Monday, Washington's Birthday, and Tuesday being an election day in this City.

A call was made on MR. HETH,[1] Assistant States Attorney in charge of prosecution of I. W. W. cases. He advises that the MARCUS GARVEY indicted,[2] is the New York negro agitator referred to in your letter. They have no tangible evidence on GARVEY other than alleged talks made by GARVEY in the City of Chicago. These talks were overheard and reported by undercover operatives.

MR. HETH advises me that he has not as yet gone over the matter with undercover operatives and at this time is unable to furnish us with any information as to the contents of these talks. Very truly yours,

EDWARD J. BRENNAN
Division Superintendent

TJH
IRF

[*Endorsement*] FILE J.E.H.

DNA, RG 65, file OG 329359. TLS, recipient's copy. Stamped endorsement.

1. Lloyd D. Heth (1886–1959) served as assistant state's attorney from 1919 to 1922 and special assistant state's attorney from 1923 to 1926 (*Chicago Bar Record* 41, no. 3 [December 1959]: 161–62).

2. There was a Marcus Garvey listed among the thirty-two members of the Industrial Workers of the World arrested in Illinois for conspiracy on 30 January 1920. This was either a person with the same name as the UNIA leader or, more likely, a person trying to conceal his real identity by assuming Garvey's name. The assistant state's attorney was convinced, however, that the Garvey under arrest in Illinois was the same man who had been indicted under the Illinois Blue Sky Law the previous October. This mistaken information was passed on to the Bureau of Investigation, whence the New York division superintendent learned that "Marcus Garvey, the negro agitator, has been indicted by the Illinois authorities under the Criminal Syndicalist statute" (Frank Burke to George F. Lamb, 1 March 1919, DNA, RG 65, OG 329359). Based on this misinformation, the United States district attorney for the Southern District of New York opened a special case file on Garvey, placing him under investigation for inciting treason (Robert A. Hill, "Marcus Garvey and the Federal Prosecution Efforts, 1918–1927" [unpublished MS], pp. 30–31).

Reports by Special Agent WW

New York Office [*26 February 1920*]

IN RE: NEGRO RADICAL ACTIVITIES

. . . *February 10th, 1920:*

. . . During my work I made efforts to secure a consensus of opinion regarding the Black Star Line and I learn[ed] that the entire element [*the black people in Brooklyn*] is morally in favor of the project, but that only the minority is financially interested in the scheme.

. . . *February 15th, 1920:*

Today I made a discreet investigation of Mr. Munce, formerly reported upon as being a personal friend of the wireless operator of the Black Star

Line Steamship Yarmouth. I visited a young lady named Ruth Slaughter at Far Rockaway, L. I. and was shown a photograph of this man Munce when he was employed by a Mr. Holly Barton of 351 East 16th Street, Brooklyn. Munce told this young lady that he had been employed by this family for nearly eleven years. Upon inquiry I learned that he had been with this family only about six months and had established a reputation as an inveterate liar. The young lady at Far Rockaway granted him the same reputation. I made this investigation mainly to secure some details of Munce's history and some information as to his veracity, in case I should come in contact with him again during my investigations.

February 16th, 1920:

I called at the Y. M. C. A. in 135th Street, New York City, pursuant to instructions, and learned that meetings were being held at Liberty Hall every evening by the Universal Negro Improvement Association and African Communities League, which is one organization. Marcus Garvey is the chief factor in this organization and the activities of the Black Star Line and a campaign for the establishment of a headquarters of this association in Liberia, for which they are asking a subscription of $2,000,000, are all in progress in this same building. I then visited the residence of one D. D. Shirley, at 409 Lenox Avenue, New York City, pursuant to instructions of Special Agent Faulhaber, to secure his confidence and thereby ascertain the facts in connection with a report concerning the drilling of negroes with arms in Liberty Hall.

February 17th, 1920:

I spent the greater part of the day "soliciting" in the neighborhood of 409 Lenox Avenue, New York City, to establish a subterfuge to call on D. D. Shirley at the above address and secure information concerning the reported drilling of negroes in Liberty Hall and Shirley's /reported/ connection with the movement.

In the evening I attended the meeting of the Universal Negro Improvement Association and African Communities League which was largely attended by the colored people of New York, Brooklyn and many neighboring towns.

The meeting opened with a selection by the Black Star Line's band.

The first speaker of the evening was a Rev. Dr. Gilliard of some Baptist Church in this city. He spoke on "Fundamental Obligations" and dwelt upon the three fundamentals which he termed "Life, Love and Growth" and he applied these fundamentals in a childish manner to the Black Star Line, the Universal Negro Improvement Association and African Communities League and to the establishment of a republic in Africa.

The second speaker was a Rev. Mittens[1] of Waterbury, Conn. who spoke on the possibilities of the race coming into "possession of their own" and the possibilities of uniting with all the members of the race from all over the world and obtaining possession of Africa.

The third speaker was William H. Ferris, an associate editor of the Negro World, who denounced white people thoroughly, saying that he hated them and had no personal or business contact with them. He is supposedly a minister by profession. He pleaded for financial support to the organizations and particularly to the fund for an independent negro republic in Liberia.

He was followed by Hubert H. Harris [*Harrison*], another hater of the white race by assertion, and Harris spoke on the conditions in Liberia, stating that it "is up to our people of this and other countries of color to help these people to adjust their conditions."

February 18th, 1920:

Spent most of the day in the vicinity of 135th Street visiting Liberty Hall in the evening. There the Rev. Mittens made a preliminary address on "THE PROBLEM OF THE NEGRO" followed by Marcus Garvey, who in the remarks of the evening, warned the "colored people to prepare for the Great War that is to come, the War of the Races." He stirred his audience with his enthusia[sm] and stated that they were preparing (meaning the Universal Negro Improvement Association and African Communities League) "for a great convention which is to be held in August of this year, at which representatives from all over the world are to be present". He explained that these representatives would represent the colored element of every nation on the face of the earth. He stated that the "white steamships" would refuse to carry these representatives to and from this country but that the Black Star Line Steamships would do the work. His speech was received with tumultuous cheers and enthusiastic applause, from the fairly large audience attending.

For Feb. 19, 1920:

I noticed that the headquarters of the Universal Negro Improvement Association received many visitors today after last night's enthusiastic meeting. I believe that many of the visitors were subscribers and investors in the Black Star Line and the Association. I spoke to several of the callers and asked them whether or not it is a good investment and that I intended investing in same. They all took great pains to show me that it was the only investment that meant anything at all to a member of the Negro Race. They are firmly convinced that they are going to cause the "acquiring of possession of Africa" and have the most implicit faith in the immediate establishment of a Negro Republic in Liberia. The purpose of the convention in August, I learned, is to bring representatives from the other countries of color all over the world to New York to decide by what means they can go about their work of obtaining Africa.

A musical entert[a]inment was given in Liberty Hall this evening, jokes and songs of the evening referring exclusively to the interests of the Black Star Line. The meeting was well attended but nothing of interest to this office occurred during the evening, the program being entirely composed of entertaining features.

February 20th, 1920:

The day around the Universal Negro Improvement Association and African Communities League's headquarters was very quiet. Very few people visited the place today and some of those who came wore an expression of anxiety. Two men left the headquarters during the afternoon swearing and apparently very much upset over some unpleasing incident. Altho I attempted to secure the details I met with nothing but profane abuse, and did not succeed during the remainder of the afternoon in securing the details of the trouble. I went to Liberty Hall during the evening but nothing of interest occurred.

For February 21, 1920:

I learned today that Garvey is making every effort to get the two millions dollars that he claims to be in need of for the establishing of the headquarters of his association in Africa. Little girls with boxes are soliciting throughout the negro section all day today.

I had a conversation with the Rev. Gilliard at the headquarters of Liberty Hall in the evening in which I expressed my interest in their association and its wonderful work and asked to be given an opportunity to take an active part in this campaign. I was assured by Rev. Gilliard that I would be given an opportunity and am expecting to be formally introduced to Garvey as "one of his lambs" in the near future. I spoke to Rev. Gilliard of the possibilities of the Negro in this country getting justice without going to Africa and cited the instance of the soldiers recently protecting a negro from mob violence.[2] He warned me that I "am doing the race harm by mentioning anything that showed that the white people are doing anything to see that we receive justice" as these things were only done "for grandstand play for the politicians", according to Mr. Gilliard.

February 22nd, 1920:

Spent the day in Harlem and the further my investigation of the negro element in this section proceeds the more am I convinced that the radical element consists almost entirely of the foreign element amongst the colored race.

In the evening a large attendance was present at a meeting at Liberty Hall, where Marcus Garvey was the principal speaker of the evening. Mr. William H. Ferris, self-asserted "hater of the white people" was the first speaker and spoke on "The Wisdom of Solomon". He stated that by "strength only could the negro races overcome the resisting forces that were tending to pull us downward." He claims that the "colored man is to receive his reward in the promised land (Africa) or die in the effort to come into his own."

Dr. Mickens (formerly reported as Dr. Mittens) was the next speaker of the evening. He spoke of the dawning of a new day for the Black man. He claimed that the Constitution of the United States did not in any way include the colored people as it was made by the white people for the white people and in its preparation had no thought of the colored people. He stated that we needed a new Constitution, a new Bible also, as our Bible taught us of white angels and a white God "as we should have a colored God and Angels as well."

Garvey spoke last and stated that he intended building a hall on the plot behind Liberty Hall and would start work upon the hall in about thirty days.[3] His plan is to enlarge Liberty Hall before the August convention previous[ly] reported and make it large enough to afford the space required for the large attendance expected. They are expecting about twenty thousand people to attend this convention.

Garvey claimed that he had been forced to postpone [t]he launching of the s/s "PHYLLIS WHEATLEY" for three or four weeks due to the mishap on the s/s "FREDERICK DOUGLASS" which prevented him from continuing his speaking tour around the country. He also promises in about two weeks to have a ship enroute for Barbados, Trinidad and British Guiana. He begged for the support of the Black Star Line and also for the NEGRO FACTORIES CORPORATION, which is "building factories all over the world for the purpose of manufacturing clothing and shoes." He claimed that his representative sold two thousand dollars worth of shares which were contained in two books and wrote back for twelve more books. He claims that the people of Havana are far ahead of the people of this city and that is his reason for the transfer of the headquarters "from New York to Havana," which I assume referred to the transfer of the home port of the Black Star Steamship Lines. He told the people to wake up and not let the people of Havana get ahead of them, which they assured him vocally they would not. He stated that the Negro had to do more than talk to make himself free and independent. He referred to the history of England and France and also America and stated that the Democracy realized in their struggles was only realized by their spirit to gain their end at any cost, even to the extent of death if necessary. He denounced England and said that he expected no protection from that country or this country or any other country other than Africa. (This last statement receiving tremendous applause.) He claimed that the Negroes all over the world were ready and awaiting "something" but he gave no details in explanation of that "something."

February 23rd, 1920:

Spent the day in Harlem in the vicinity of the Universal Negro Improvement Association. I noticed W. A. Domingo (of the Messenger) enter the headquarters and leave in about ten minutes. This is the first time I have seen Domingo in several weeks. He did not see me.

Visited Liberty Hall in the evening and li[s]tened to some grandiloquent references by Gilliard and Mickens to themselves as the general "solicitors from God's chosen people to inspire the race to flee from *the* country of misery and suffering to the promised lands of Africa."

February 24th, 1920:

Spent the day in Brooklyn; visited the Y. M. C. A. and found quite some interest displayed in the Monster Mass Meeting which is to take place at the Academy of Music on St. Felix Street and Lafayette Avenue, Brooklyn, on Thursday evening, February 26. The American people assume only a certain curiosity and many of them to whom I have spoke concerning this meeting stating that they are attending simply to hear this "wonderful Marcus Garvey" of whom they "have heard so much talk."

I wish to emphasize the fact here that at the meetings I have attended at Liberty Hall I have seen not more than one or two American negroes. I am personally regarded with curious appraisal (being an American Negro) and am treated with a certain amount of reticen[c]e. I can tell a foreign negro practically at sight and a few words of conversation confirms my belief and I can report definitely that these expressing radical sympathies are, with the few exceptions mentioned, all foreign negroes, mostly of West Indian Birth. . . . [4]

WW

DNA, RG 65, file OG 258421. TD.

1. Actually, H. M. Mickens, an AME minister in Waterbury, Conn., and secretary-general of the UNIA. J. D. Brooks, Micken's successor as secretary-general, remarked in June 1920: "I was converted [to the UNIA] on the preaching of Dr. Mickens at New Haven." In June 1921 Mickens had left his post in Connecticut and was pastor of an AME church in Huntington, W.Va. (*NW*, 20 June 1920, 25 June 1921; *Clarion*, 29 April 1920).

2. It has not been possible to find the particular incident of white soldiers protecting blacks from mob violence to which this report refers.

3. On 14 April 1920 the UNIA purchased a large lot next to Liberty Hall for $23,000. The UNIA was to pay for the property in $1,000 installments, paid semiannually until 14 April 1925, when the remainder of the purchase price would be due (New York County Hall of Records, serial no. M 6725).

4. Omitted material pertained to black radical publications.

New York February 26th, 1920

RE: NEGRO RADICAL ACTIVITIES

February 26th, 1920:

Last night I attended the Monster Mass meeting of the Universal Negro Improvement Association and African Communities League at the Academy of Music, Brooklyn, New York, and remained at the work of writing the following report until four a.m. today[.]

The mass meeting was very largely attended.

The entertainment of the evening open[e]d by the Black Star Line Bands rendition of the "National Anthem of Africa."

The first speaker of the evening was a Rev. Dr. Eason, who spoke on the Black Star Line and its progress. He urged the people to support their own enterprises and to stop allowing the white man to invest their money for them. I experienced such great difficulty in hearing him distinctly that I purchased a reserved seat in order to be further up front and to hear plainly.

The next speaker of the evening was a Mr. Davis, who appears to be the main factor in the Brooklyn branch of the Universal Negro Improvement Association, and who delivered a complimentary address to the Hon. Marcus Garvey. He urged the people of Brooklyn to support this institution in its struggle to aid them in regaining possession of their own.

Next was a thrilling address by the Rev. George Frazier Miller of the St. Augustine P. E. Church of Brooklyn. Rev. Miller opposed such men as Booker T. Washington and the Rev. Moton,[1] claiming that they have no initiative and had to wholly report to advise and aid of his white associates whose sole interests are to keep the Negro in a subjective capacity. He stated that at one time he had had his doubts about the materialization of the visions offered by "Honorable" Marcus Garvey to the people of his race, but now that Garvey has proven himself of "supernatural" qualities and has made practical that "which had seemed impossible or preposterous," he (Miller) has been forced to recognize him as the greatest man the race had ever produced. During his address, he referred to the late war and stated that the Department of Justice had held him under observation as an unpatriotic American.[2] He also stated that he remarked during the war, and does now remark, that "the war was not fought for the purpose of making the world safe for Democracy, but for the purpose of making Wall Street safe for foreign loans." (Which latter statement met with overwhelming applause.)

Next came a vocal selection rendered by Madame Houston.

Last, but far from least, was a sensational address by "THE HONORABLE" MARCUS GARVEY, who was introduced as President-General of the African Communities League and the Universal Negro Improvement Association; also President of the Negro Factories Corporation, and Director General of the Black Star Line and "prospective President of the new Republic to be established in Africa."

Garvey outlined the plans of these various institutions and gave the people an illustrative example of how the white man was using their money, realizing 400% on the same and giving the negro about 4% as his share. He stated that there is no reason why the colored people cannot invest their own money in their own enterprises for their own profit and to their own advantage. He outlined the policies of the white race in taking their money, building factories, launching steamships, building homes, and doing everything for the interest of the white race and giving the negro nothing in return for his contribution to the finance required for such work. He claimed that he had not only anticipation of launching a great commercial fleet, but expected that in the near future he could launch a "naval fleet and a fleet of aeroplanes and submarines" and could also "feel assured that he would have the moral and physical support of 4,000,000 people for the purpose of invading Africa and taking possession of it." He showed the people that he is not begging them to support these enterprises, but that it is merely their duty to themselves and to the other colored people of the world to support these enterprises both morally and financially.

He strenuously proclaimed the doctrines of Patrick Henry in his quotation of "GIVE ME LIBERTY, OR GIVE ME DEATH". Garvey said that if it is impossible for the negroes to get a leader to invade Africa he would take up the "sword himself" and "fight for the redemption of his race and nation under the Black, Red and Green" (which is the flag of the new republic). (This met with enthusiastic and tumultuous applause.) Meeting closed about 11:30 p.m.

Feb. 27th, 1920:

. . . Attended meeting of the Universal Negro Improvement Association at Liberty Hall in the evening and a very small crowd was present. Rev. Eason told the people how the natives of Brooklyn had rallied to the support of the Universal Negro Improvement Association and told them that in the end they would have the respect of all nations of the world. He emphasized the fact that no cause has ever been successful without "sacrifice" and stated that "our sacrifice might even mean human life."

Rev. Ea[s]on reported "favorable returns" (without further details) from the West Indies and South Africa.

Feb. 28th, 1920:

. . . The meeting under the auspices of the Universal Negro Improvement Association and African Communities League at Liberty Hall was devoted exclusively to a drive for funds for the extension of Liberty Hall to accommodate the August convention.

February 29, 1920:

Called at the office of the Crusader and tried to secure some information from Mrs. Briggs as to just what the AFRICAN BLOOD BROTHERHOOD constitutes. She informed me that she knew little of this organization and that Mr. /Cyril/ Briggs would be better able to outline the principles of the organization.

She also chatted with me on local gossip and informed me that [a] young lady who resides with her now had formerly been in the employ of Marcus Garvey and that his former employee had "little faith in Garvey in the beginning" and now that Mrs. Briggs has heard this young lady's tale, she (Mrs. Briggs) has less faith than ever in Garvey.

I chatted so long that I reached Liberty Hall rather late and learned that the crowd had filled the hall as early as 5:30 and the place was packed to capacity. I tried to edge my way in and succeeded to some extent, to learn only that an entertainment was in progress which concluded with an appeal for funds for the extension of Liberty Hall and the usual appeal for moral and financial support to the combined negro radical organizations.

March 1st, 1920.

. . . While in the office I was introduced to a young man of the name of Moore,[3] who is with Mr. Domingo on the new publication "THE EMANCI-PATOR" which is expected from the press tomorrow. Moore made a remark to Briggs that "the article in reference to the Department of Justice will not come out in this week['s] publication but will be in the next edition."

No activity at Liberty Hall this day by the Universal Negro Improvement Association and African Communities League.

WW

[*Endorsement*] Noted F.D.W.

DNA, RG 65, file OG 185161. TD. Stamped endorsement.

1. Probably a reference to Robert Russa Moton, principal of Tuskegee Institute.
2. Reports of the Bureau of Investigation's surveillance of George Frazier Miller can be found in DNA, RG 65, files OG 13332-A, 59501, 91928, 254446 and 256421 and files BS 202600-1628 and 202600-1981.
3. Richard Benjamin Moore (1893–1975) joined W. A. Domingo in March 1920 to establish the *Emancipator*. Moore was born in Hasting, Barbados, and educated in the private school of one of the island's best-known tutors, J. J. Lynch. His father was a builder and a businessman who died while Moore was a child. The economic hardship that followed his father's death led Moore and his stepmother to immigrate to New York City in 1909. While continuing his education in New York, Moore began a career of political organizing. He founded the Harlem Pioneer Cooperative Society in 1915, a short-lived business venture, and also was involved in a company that introduced the first Multigraph and Linotype machines to Harlem. By 1917 Moore had undergone a political transformation that found him in association with Harlem's circle of black socialist journalists and organizers. When he became a citizen in 1924, he was a bookseller and had already formed friendships with bibliophiles Arthur Schomburg and George Young. In addition, Moore served as educational director of the African Blood Brotherhood (ABB) in 1921.
Moore's association with the ABB indicated an affinity for socialist thought which eventually led him to join the Communist party in 1926. In 1927 he became the eastern organizer for the American Negro Labor Congress (ANLC) as well as one of its official representatives at the Congress of Oppressed Nations, held in Brussels. Upon his return to the United States, Moore became the ANLC's general secretary and its principal recruiter. After a speaking tour on behalf of the ANLC, Moore returned to New York City, where he organized the Tenants' League (1928) and ran for New York City's Twenty-first Congressional District's seat on the

Communist party ticket. During this time he also edited the *Negro Champion*, the official organ of the ANLC. Moore's political career under the Communist party aegis resumed in 1930, when he ran for state attorney general of New York. One year later he was a candidate for the New York State Assembly, Nineteenth District.

Moore's affiliation with the Communist party ended in 1939, when a power struggle between the older black Communist leadership, among whom Moore was prominent, and the youthful James Ford, the chairman of the party's National Negro Commission, led to Moore's expulsion. Cyril Briggs was also expelled, because of his continuing support, like Moore's, for Negro nationalism. Once outside the party's official circle, Moore devoted his time to organizing the West Indian community in New York City for the support of self-determination and independence for Caribbean nations. Moore remained active in this cause until his death (W. Burghardt Turner, "The Richard B. Moore Collection and its Collector," *Caribbean Studies* 15 [April 1975]: 135–45; DNA, RG 65, file BS 100-25426, and RG 85, Bureau of Naturalization, file no. 2270, C-1949264; J. Cameron Tudor, "Richard Benjamin Moore: An Appreciation," *Caribbean Studies* 19 [April–July 1979]: 169–74).

Marcus Garvey to the BSL Stockholders

NEW YORK, U.S.A. FEBRUARY 27TH 1920

MY DEAR FRIEND AND COMRADE:

I write to you as a fellow stockholder in the Black Star Line Steamship Corporation to let you know that our Corporation is now capitalized at Ten Million Dollars ($10,000,000). We are endeavoring to have this Ten Million Dollars ($10,000,000) fully subscribed so as to build up one of the most powerful merchant marines of modern times. It is our intention to build ships on the most modern plans for traffic between the United States of America, the West Indies, South and Central America and Africa. We want an exceptionally good passenger service so that in the event of any economic set back in this Western Hemisphere, we will be able through our own ships of the Black Star Line, to transport our people in the United States of America, the West Indies, and anywhere else to new industrial fields and thereby enable them to make a satisfactory livelihood. We have to prepare against the hard times of the future, and the best way we can do that is by strengthening our present economic position. The Black Star Line bids fair to open up untold opportunities to every stockholder and every member of the race, therefore I am asking you to make an effort to take out as many more shares as you possibly can at the present time, so as to enable us to have the Ten Million Dollars ($10,000,000) fully subscribed. With this amount of money the Corporation will be able to place the race on such an economic base as to force respect, not only from the opposite race, but from mankind at large. Please call at the office of the Corporation, 56 W. 135th Street, New York, U.S.A. and buy more shares. If you cannot call between 9 A.M. and 8 P.M., you may call at Liberty Hall, 120 W. 138th Street, between the hours of 8.30 P.M. and 11 P.M. If you are out of town, you may send and buy more shares by mail, making your remittances by postal money order or by Bank Draft. All checks and money orders must be made payable to the Black Star

Line, Inc. Trusting to hear from you[.] With very best wishes. Yours faithfully

BLACK STAR LINE, INC.
MARCUS GARVEY
President

P.S. You will find herein enclosed prospectus of the Negro Factories Corporation, organized by the Universal Negro Improvement Association for the purpose of building factories all over the United States of America, the West Indies, South and Central America and Africa, to manufacture all kinds of marketable goods and commodities in the interest of the Negro Race. We ask that you support the Negro Factories Corporation by buying shares therein. You may buy from one to two hundred shares at Five Dollars ($5.00) each.

M. G.

All communications must be addressed to the
Corporation, and not to individuals

DJ-FBI. Printed letter, recipient's copy.

Marcus Garvey to the Governor of British Guiana

NEW YORK, U.S.A. Mar. 2nd, 1920

To His Excellency, The Governor of British Guiana,[1]
Georgetown, Demerara, British Guiana, S.A.
May It Please Your Excellency:—
    I am instructed by the membership of the Universal Negro Improvement Association to draw to your Excellency's attention the following matter:—
    Information has reached us that one Samuel Duncan, who claims to be the Executive Secretary of the West Indian Protective Association, domiciled at New York City, with office at 178 West 135th Street, who is a naturalized American Citizen, but for reasons of his own tries to create the impression that he is a British Subject, has written to you and to several of the other Governors of the Colonies in the West Indies, stating that the Universal Negro Improvement Ass'n., Marcus Garvey, its President, and the Steamship Corporation known as the Black Star Line, Inc. are organizations formed for the purpose of creating disturbance in the various British West Indian Islands. The communication herein referred to, of which Samuel Duncan is author, has also /been/ sent to you with the purpose of causing you to become suspicious and hostile to the said Universal Negro Improvement Association, Marcus Garvey, and the Black Star Line, Inc., and to have you

BIG TIME FOR
THE PEOPLE

OF BOSTON

HEAR

HON. MARCUS GARVEY

The World's Greatest Negro Orator, President-General of the
Universal Negro Improvement Association and President of
the Black Star Line Steamship Corporation

He Will Speak at

THE PEOPLE'S BAPTIST CHURCH

Tremont and Camden Streets

MONDAY and TUESDAY NIGHTS, MARCH 1 and 2

at 8 o'clock sharp

Ebenezer Baptist Church	Zion M. E. Church
West Springfield Street	Northampton St. & Columbus Ave
Wednesday and Thursday Nights, March 3 and 4	**Friday Night, March 5**
at 8 o'clock sharp	at 8 o'clock sharp

Hear This Great Man in One of His Wonderful Speeches on

"THE LIBERATION OF OUR RACE"

THE BLACK STAR LINE

Has Startled the World and He Will Tell You All About It
Many Other Prominent Speakers   Big Musical Program
Come Prepared to BUY Your SHARES in

*"The Black Star Line Steamship Corporation" and the "Negro
Factories Corporation"*

You May Buy From 1 to 200 Shares at $5.00 Each

Be Early to Get Seats and Avoid the Rush   All Seats Free

SIGNED, UNIVERSAL NEGRO IMPROVEMENT ASSOCIATION

(*Source*: NW, 13 March 1920).

and your Government hamper the success of these two Corporations which are legitimate business concerns. It is the intention of our Association to acquaint you of the fact that we have absolutely no purpose or intention, other than the peaceful development of the people of our race and that this man, Duncan, has written to you and the other governors of the Colonies through jealousy of the success of the Organization and individuals connected thereto, and the only reason that can be attributed to the writing to the Governors of the various Colonies is to use their offices as Government Officials to interfere with the success of a legitimate business concern, fostered by his rivals.

I trust that your Excellency will take no notice of the communications sent to you by this man, as in so doing, it will cause our Association to take steps in laying the case before the British Parliament, the Government at large, and the people of the British Empire in General, as the majority of the Members of this Association are British Subjects who have been loyal to their Government in all crises.

Should your Excellency desire, we can therefore supply you with information about this man, Duncan, so as to have you realize the true character of the individual, being a naturalized American Citizen, who for convenience at times claims himself to be a Britisher.

I beg to remain Your Excellency's obedient Servant,

(Sgd) MARCUS GARVEY
Pres. Universal Negro Improvement Ass'n.

PRO, CO 111/630. TLS, transcript, recipient's copy.

1. On 3 March 1920 Garvey sent an identical letter to the governor of St. Vincent (GHStV, secret 21/1919).

Report by Special Agent 800

[*New York*] March 5–12, 1920

Submitting m[y] report for seven days beginning March 5th, I will report the following:

March 5th, 1920

Left Wash. via Penn. R. R. 1;00 P.M. arrived N.Y. 6;30 P.M.

March 6th, 1920

Conference with D. D. Shirley, Chairman Advisory Board Universal Negro Improvement Association. Marcus Garvey was not present as he was in Boston, Mass.

March 7th, 1920

Addressed meeting of the U.N.I.A. in Liberty Hall, am sending my speech as published in the Negro World, the paper of the organization.[1]

March 8th, 1920

Conference with Marcus Garvey learned he [h]as sent to Panama $500. (Five Hundred Dollars) to assist the members of the U.N.I.A of Panama in their strike.

March 9th, 1920

Attended meeting of the U.N.I.A. at Liberty Hall, speeches were made by several members of the association.

March 10th, 1920

Attended meeting of U.N.I.A. and while there Rev. Jonas and his wife came in, Garvey was not present. Wm. H. Ferris Editor of the Negro World was presiding. Jonas spoke in behalf of the association and said during his remarks that he has just come from down south where the Klu Kluck Klan[2] got after him in Virginia and he had to leave. I had a talk with Jonas after the meeting and he said he would be leaving the city in a few days for Charleston, S.C. No one seems to know where Jonas stops while in the city.

March 11th, 1920

Conferences with Marcus Garvey, during my talk with Garvey he asked me if I attended the meeting at Liberty Hall March 10—I told him I had, and he asked me what went on and who was there. I went on to tell him who was there and when I mentioned Jonas he said "that fellow always takes advantages of my absence and comes to the hall". I learned afterwards from Wm. H. Ferris that Garvey knew that, Jonas was to be there.

I am to see Garvey on Monday at his office in regards to a position with him.

March 12th, 1920

Am to attend meeting of U.N.I.A. at Liberty Hall at 6:00 P.M.

I hope this report has covered all details. I have been partly promised a position by Garvey in his office. Will let you know just as soon as I go to work. Respectfully

800[3]

[Stamped endorsements] NOTED J.E.H. Noted F.D.W.
[Handwritten endorsement] Noted WWG

DNA, RG 65, file OG 185161. TD.

1. This speech was published in *NW*, 13 March 1920; printed on pp. 245–246.

2. The Ku Klux Klan was revived in 1915 by William J. Simmons, the son óf a leader in the original Ku Klux Klan, which was founded in 1868 in Pulaski, Tenn., for the purpose of terrorizing recently emancipated blacks in the American South. Although the revived Klan had its headquarters in Atlanta, it grew slowly in the South until 1920, when a vigorous recruitment campaign made it a nationwide phenomenon with strong political influence in Oregon, Texas, Indiana, Wisconsin, and many other states. While emphasizing its opposition to the large flow of immigrants into the United States from southern and eastern Europe after the First World War and maintaining its traditional stand against nonwhites, the revived Klan also increased its popularity among rural and small-town white Protestants by supporting fundamentalist religion and Prohibition and opposing Catholicism. The Klan would later mount a major effort to influence the Democratic party presidential nomination in 1924, though it failed when the candidate it supported, William G. McAdoo, lost the party's nomination. However, scandals involving sexual and financial improprieties among Klan leadership, which came to light as early as 1921, along with the growing political influence of immigrants and Catholics in the urban North, eventually blunted the Klan's drive toward political power (Kenneth Jackson, *The Ku Klux Klan in the City* [New York: Oxford University Press, 1967]; Charles C. Alexander, *The Ku Klux Klan in the Southwest* [Lexington: University of Kentucky Press, 1965]).

3. 800 was the code name used by James Wormley Jones.

Report of UNIA Meeting

[*Negro World*, 6 March 1920]

SACRIFICE AND SUCCESS THE THEME AT LIBERTY HALL

On Sunday night [*29 February*] Liberty Hall was packed to the very doors with an eager and enthusiastic crowd which had come to hear the last words of Mr. Garvey before his departure for Boston, where he will spend a full week lecturing on behalf of the association and the Phyllis Wheatley, the next ship of the Black Star Line. Although the meeting was not called to order before 8.30, hundreds of people had been in their seats from 5:30 for fear of losing an opportunity to get in later. The air was tense with expectation, because it was known that certain mischief-makers had been circulating innuendos which they were too cowardly to put into specific form.

The program which preceded the speaking was of the very highest. The Black Star Line Band and the choir of Liberty Hall rendered selections that were so excellent as to bring out again and again thunders of applause. The hit of the evening was made by Razz and Rosen ("Razz" being the stage name of Mr. Andrea Razafkeriefo,[1] whose poems have been recently appearing in the columns of The Negro World). Razz rendered two songs, entitled "Garvey! Hats Off to Garvey!" and "U.N.I.A.," which raised the roof. The words were skillfully put together and the music was inspiring. Mr. Rosen, who presided at the piano, worked wonders in syncopation on that instrument, so that even the old musicians of the band opened their eyes in astonishment. The two expert entertainers were applauded to the echo and had to come back on the stage to satisfy their admirers.

PROF. FERRIS SPEAKS.

Prof. William H. Ferris was the first speaker of the evening. In the course of a splendid address, he said:

"As I survey the achievements of our great men, and see what they have accomplished in literature, art and music, I see that Marcus Garvey and the U.N.I.A. have achieved as great a measure of success as any. Marcus Garvey has been a pioneer. He has shown the world that the black men and women can be organized outside the church and that they can be organized for purely racial and commercial purposes and motives. And since he has built up his organization here, there are others who have come to New York, and some have gone from New York to other places, trying to do the same thing.

["]It was doubted and believed impossible for a black man to get the Negroes together without the kindly nod and patronage of the white man before this U.N.I.A. was organized. We had been held in leading strings by our white friends so long that we doubted the permanent success of any movement which was not financed and backed and [e]ndorsed and recommended by them. And the very fact that in spite of opposition, in spite of precaution, without asking any of our white friends for permission or assistance, we have gone forward and put a boat upon the high seas and have marshalled and corralled our forces all over the world, is a powerful lesson of what the New Negro is capable of and of what it is possible for him to achieve.

["]The New Negro is getting tired of the doubting Thomases and the pessimists. Men like our Savior, like Morrison,[2] like Alexander Cromwell,[3] who held up the beacon light of hope before us, who inspired us with high motives and lofty idealism—these were real saviors and benefactors. And yet they were criticised. Any movement, any new movement, will be criticised. It has always been so. Any man—Jesus Christ—was criticised in his day. And so was Socrates, George Washington, Abraham Lincoln. Any man with individuality, any movement with individuality, is bound to be criticised. And there is always a testing time and a testing place for different theories of action, for different theories of conduct. This testing will prove the success or failure of any principle of propaganda. All organizations, every business concern, must have competition and must face the struggle for existence. Those that adapt themselves to their environment and those that have vitality, survive; and those that lack it, go down. The U.N.I.A. has shown endurance. It has shown the ability to stand up against opposition. It shows that it has stamina—that quality which is called character. Now the question remains: Can it realize the wonderful opportunities and possibilities which open before it?

["]With millions of Negroes all over the world desiring to improve their economic and civil, and their political condition, it is a just inference that if ten per cent of them could be organized and mobilized and corralled into pooling their interests and massing their forces, they would produce results which would startle and dazzle the world.

["]Whenever I have preached in a colored church or addressed a Southern school and seen the masses of bright, eager faces before me, I have more than once reflected and thought of the undreamt possibilities of the Negro. I have thought that slumbering in these black boys and girls are intellectual powers, moral powers, financial capacities and resources, which only needed a little encouragement and the spur of the opportunity to flame into a bright and shining career. And I believe that one reason why the U.N.I.A. has made a dent upon Negro history has been because it has incarnated the spirit of the New Negro striving for liberty and freedom, and has focussed it towards definite and tangible results.

["]The first conflict which our race will face in the near future is the economic conflict—the struggle for bread, the struggle for existence. And if we can successfully run steamship lines, if we can successfully operate factories, if we can build up concerns, develop plantations, to employ our boys and girls, we will have gained the victory over the economic struggle. And then, when we have our hands upon the arteries of finance and commerce we will be in shape to do wonders for, and work wonders in, Africa.

["]I have never been a pessimist although my words are not always rosy. I have always looked on the bright side of things, and yet I have been thinking and planning the problems and difficulties which will be met in the future, just as a mariner is confident when he meets today's storms without worrying about the storms which he will have to face several months afterwards. With a firm faith in God, and in our leader, and in our own possibilities, let us marshal our forces so that by our deeds and achievements we can show that the new Negro can make good. And when we have turned our race from its state of dependency upon the Anglo-Saxon, and have made it independent socially, independent economically; when we have succeeded as well in the commercial and business world as we have in the musical, literary and artistic world, it will only be a question of time when we will compel recognition.

["]I never did belong to that school of ethnology which believed that God Almighty classified the races according to color, the white man first and superior to all, the yellow man next, the copper-colored man next, the brown man next, and the black man last. I never did belong to that school of ethnology who believed that the dark color was a part of the curse of Canaan.[4] I always believed that color was only skin deep. I was always interested in what was in a man, what was inside of him, how much gray matter he had in his brains, how much surplus energy he had, and the resources he had developed and had at his disposal. That is the way I look at a human. There is not a race that has been persecuted and oppressed and kept down as much as the Negro, and yet he still has that undying hope of optimism. The trials which the Negro has passed through for three hundred years in America—two hundred years of slavery and then forty years of disfranchisement in the name of democracy, would have crushed completely the hope and spirit of almost any other race. And the fact that the Negro has been able to shake this aside, just as the sturdy swimmer has forced his way against the currents of the tide, shows that this race has vitality. And when a race has vitality it has behind it that driving force which will force its way through opposition and struggle on, struggle on, until it reaches the summit.["] (Cheers.)

HON. MARCUS GARVEY SPEAKS
THE YARMOUTH IN HAVANA.

Mr. Garvey said: "I am booked to speak tonight on the subject, "The Dawn of a New Day." Before I do so, however, I desire to acquaint the stockholders of the Black Star Line and the members of the U.N.I.A. of the fact that our ship, the S.S. Yarmouth, was royally welcomed in Havana, Cuba. A great reception was extended to the captain and crew by the civil population of Havana. Mr. Smith-Green, the secretary of the Black Star Line, was sent down to see to the unloading of the cargo, and on his arrival there he found the Havana branch of the association well organized to receive him. As I said a few nights ago, we gave him two stock books of the Black Star Line to take to Havana and the very night that he arrived in Havana he sold out every stock certificate that those two books contained. Yesterday he sent me a cable saying that our movement was so highly thought of and the Black Star Line was so well regarded by the population of Cuba that he was invited by the President of Cuba[5] to explain (in the palace of the President) all about the Black Star Line, (loud cheers) and that the President of Cuba sends greetings to you in Liberty Hall (renewed cheers).

["]There are the things that are causing other fellows to get jealous about the Universal Negro Improvement Association. But they have started too late to do any harm to the U.N.I.A., because we are all over the world now, they will have to become as big as the world to do any harm to the U.N.I.A. and those of you who know Prof. Buck know that he is no bigger than himself. I have no desire to speak about individuals or to enter into personalities, but I understand that this gentleman (Mr. Buck) made use of certain remarks at his meeting today of the African League to which I would like to reply."

MR. BUCK'S BACK-FIRE.

Referring to Mr. Buck's allegation that he was born in the same country as he, Mr. Garvey continued:

"I pay very little attention to where men were born. Nationality as far as the present day Negro is concerned has no attraction for me except he is a real native African. My only regret is that I was not born an African. That I was born in Jamaica was only a matter of accident. I may have been born in Tennessee, or in Georgia, or in Alabama, or anywhere in this Western Hemisphere, but it was not a matter of choice. It is a fact that forty millions of our foreparents were brought to this Western Hemisphere as slaves and we were scattered over the West Indies and America without any choice of our own. Fortunately or unfortunately, I was born in Jamaica, and fortunately for Mr. Buck he was born there, too, he says. He had the audacity to attack my reputation and my standing. I am sorry Mr. Buck did that after he left Liberty Hall in that it would have been a splendid opportunity for me to ask Mr. Buck to show his credentials from Jamaica and in that I would have been ready then as well as now to compare credentials with him. In Jamaica I am known throughout the length and breadth of the country by every man of importance in that country and I have yet to know that I have done anything discreditable to myself or to my country, with the exception that I have started the U.N.I.A. to the displeasure of the government that controls that country. I can return there at any time as I do intend to in the near future in my travels to the West Indies and Central America when the Frederick Douglass arrives here on her return trip, and I feel sure the moment I touch the soil of my country that I will not have to have it announced more than two or three hours before my arrival there, when I will be able to gather four or five thousand of my country men to hear what I have to say."

GARVEY'S REPUTATION IN JAMAICA.

["]When I came to this country I came with credentials from the mayor of the city in which I lived for six years. The past and present mayor of that city knew me as a man and a gentleman and to that extent, when Mrs. Henrietta Vinton Davis landed in Jamaica on the first trip of the Yarmouth and the local branch of the U.N.I.A. I organized there, called a meeting, the man that presided over that meeting was the mayor of the City of Kingston. And I may add that at nearly all of my meetings held in the City of Kingston, he was also chairman of those meetings. Therefore, when I appear before you in New York I do not appear as a man who is not known in his country. I am as much known in Jamaica as I am known in New York City. I am as well known by the Governor of the country as by the humble people of the country, and not only in Jamaica am I known in governmental circles, but also in Great Britain. I have several friends in the House of Commons and when I traveled in England several years ago I met some of the biggest men there. In my country I started my career as a newspaper man, and in that way I became known in public life and mixed in public life for years and years, and wherever the name of Marcus Garvey is mentioned they know who he is. So that at any time when Mr. Buck desires to compare credentials I will be very much obliged for the opportunity, because I feel sure that we have never heard of Mr. Buck in Jamaica.["]

THE CAUSE ABOVE MONEY.

["]I am not in the U.N.I.A. for what it can pay me or give me, because long [ago] I sacrificed my time to the U.N.I.A. in the country wherein I was born[.] I held positions in the country that were envied by some of the best men in that country. Therefore, it was not a matter of necessity as far as money was concerned that impelled me to start the U.N.I.A., for if there is one man that has absolutely no regard for money, that man is Marcus Garvey. Money is no object to me. My object is to see some one help to lift up this down-trodden race with which I am identified, or that race will forever remain a down-trodden one. (Cheers.) Money has absolutely no attractions for me where this great movement is concerned. I[f] it were a matter of money then you would not have had any Liberty Hall and you would not be members of the U.N.I.A., because at the very start I would have started to exact from you that which others have exacted from us and got. When I started the movement there was nobody to give me anything. I made sacrifices in my country and I earned the displeasure of my friends and those who were related to me by blood ties because I gave myself up to the U.N.I.A. I stuck by my race when my race had nothing to give. I labored for five years and traveled in Jamaica, and in this country I traveled for 18 months throughout 25 States without receiving one penny from any one as subsidy. To pr[opa]gate this movement I traveled through this country on my own savings of years so as to study the economic, social and political conditions of my race. I went from New York to Louisiana, from Boston to Chicago and all around through 25 States before I uttered one word about organizing a branch of the U.N.I.A. in New York.

["]When I come to New York two and a half years ago I found a disorganized State among my race here. I found the Americans were against the West Indians and the West Indians were against the Americans—that one side was saying "I am better than you," and the other side was saying the same thing. Knowing my race as I do, I knew that neither American or West Indian occupied a better position than the other. I knew that in the West Indies economic conditions forced the Negro to be a serf and a slave to the white man, and as I traveled through this country I saw a duplication of the same condition. I saw in the West Indies that for 230 years millions of Negroes suffered under the slave system of Great Britain and in this country I saw that for 250 years we suffered under the same brutal system. Therefore, from my knowledge of the history of the Negro in the Western Hemisphere, I saw that the American Negro was no better than the West Indian Negro nor the West Indian Negro any better than the American Negro—we were all fighting and struggling toward one common destiny.

["]Because I saw that, I took the opportunity to organize a branch of the Association in New York. For months and months I spoke to you from the corners of Lenox avenue. Near me on another corner there were other speakers talking about political, domestic and other matters, and when I started to talk about the larger matters of the race they said I was a crazy man. They called me all kinds of names. Nobody paid me and I did not collect any money from white men to subsidize the movement. I [m]ade up my mind to see the matter through because just at that time other races were engaged in seeing their cause through—the Jews through the Zionist movement and the

Irish through their Irish movement—and I decided that, cost what it might, I would make this a favorable time to see the Negro's interest through. And thank God, after two years of campaigning and agitation, we are three million strong tonight.["] (Cheers.)

SACRIFICE AND SUCCESS.

["]But before we became three million strong sacrifices had to be made. Buck and his class did not make any sacrifice. They want to start an African League. I wish them well, that to do so, they have to pass through the same trials and tribulations I passed. If they are prepared for it, I wish them well. But I know the men better than that, and I give their league just two months to last. When men who were getting $30 a week leave a big movement like the U.N.I.A. because we could not afford to pay them more at that time to go into something new because because they want more money, I can predict for that new movement a short life, because with a hundred members how can five or six of them get $50 apiece? If they get theirs, there will be nothing left for the people. If they are determined to make the sacrifice I made when I started the U.N.I.A. I feel sure that in the next few years they will be as strong as the U.N.I.A., and I wish them luck, because we have four hundred millions to organize, and if they can do it as conscientiously and organize another portion of the world as we have done, it means well for Africa. I have no time to waste in trifling with anybody or any organization; I believe in the survival of the fittest; I believe in a righteous cause. If your cause is righteous it is bound to live, and if their cause is righteous let it live. And I feel convinced that our cause is righteous and that is why God has blessed it. (Cheers)

["]There is a great deal of work to do and it calls for sacrifice and determination on the part of those who are leading, and if men believe that money should be the only consideration for leadership, then there can be no successful achievement[.]

["]They have tried to create suspicion about the U.N.I.A., but the answer I have to give them is this: Nine months ago the U.N.I.A. did not have one nickel: today the U.N.I.A. is the richest Negro organization in the United States of America (Cheers.). Five months ago we had no place of our own even to hold a committee meeting. Tonight we own Liberty Hall and the plot of land behind it; we own two buildings at [5]4–56 West 135th street. And if anybody wants to know about the financial standing of the U.N.I.A. let them go to the Chelsea Bank at Seventh avenue and 135th street and ask the manager how our bank account stands. No check of the U.N.I.A. has ever been dishonored and if you desire to know the kind of offices we maintain, at any time you are at leisure, make a visit to our offices at 54–56 West 135th street, and you will find there offices as good as you can find them in the comme[rcial] section downtown.["]

Mr. Garvey then disposed of certa[in] aspersions cast on the U.N.I.A. and the Black Star Line by Mr. Powell, who was formerly connected with the movement and is now identified with the new movement—the African League. Continuing, he said: "I want to say to you members of the U.N.I.A. and stockholders of the Black Star Line that at any time you feel that I am not serving you honestly it is in your power to ask me to resign from the presidency, and I am ready now or at any time a majority of you ask me to resign to step down. I am not in this movement for what you can pay me, because if tomorrow the U.N.I.A. did not have one nickel, I will continue to stick to my work and give my services so long as I can find bread and water to exist on. If at any time you believe that I am acting contrary to your interests I am willing to resign from my position. (Unanimous cries of, "Stay there!")

["]At the coming convention you will have an opportunity to say who your leader shall be, and when that time comes I will refuse to stand for nomination if you do not think I have served your interests faithfully. (Cries of "No, no; stay there!") If any of you who are interested want to know about the finances of the U.N.I.A. or the Black Star Line, you are privileged to ask the treasurer or investigate for yourselves. The enemies of this movement have gone to the District Attorney to ask an investigation of the finances of the Black Star Line and the U.N.I.A., but the District Attorney had already investigated and found the affairs in such splendid condition that he said he was tired of investigating them.

["]So that I hope and trust that you members will not be persuaded to believe that there is anything wrong with the association at the present time. I have tried to do my best to make the movement succeed, and it is succeeding splendidly.

["]I understand also that one of our enemies (Mr. Powell) made the statement that we did not own the Frederick Douglass. If we do not own the Frederick Douglass let somebody who owns it come and take the Frederick Douglass. That is the best answer I can give. Enough has happened to the Frederick Douglass in New York Harbor to prove who is the owner.

["]I am about to leave New York this week because of my promise to the stockholders of the Black Star Line to realize more capital so as to buy more ships. I am booked to speak in Boston under the auspices of the Boston Division of the Association for six days, starting from tomorrow night. Boston promises to subscribe $50,000 to the Phyllis Wheatley, and I am going there to get as much of that $50,000 as I can in six days for the Black Star Line. In leaving New York I am going to leave Liberty Hall in charge of you members. Each member of the U.N.I.A. is to take care of Liberty Hall and take care of his or her own interest, so that no one can come here and try to disrupt your movement. I ask that you give your support to those whom I will leave behind to carry on the work. Continue to buy shares in the Black Star Line and Negro Factories Corporation and carry on the work of the association.["] (Cheers.)

Printed in *NW*, 6 March 1920.

1. Andrea Razafkeriefo (1895–1973) was born Andreamenentania Paul Razafinkeriefo in Madagascar. His father was a Malagasy nobleman, and his mother was a black American and

the daughter of John Waller, once a U.S. consul to Madagascar. He shortened his name to Razaf when he began his career as a poet and lyricist. He was a member of the *Crusader* staff in 1919, and by 1920 he was a frequent contributor to the *Negro World* and an effective street-corner speaker on issues affecting blacks. He achieved his greatest fame, however, in the late 1920s and 1930s, when he wrote songs with his cousin, Fats Waller, the celebrated black jazz composer, and teamed with pianist-composer Eubie Blake and others to write lyrics for such popular black Broadway shows as *Keep Shufflin'*, *Hot Chocolates*, and *Blackbirds of 1930*. During his long career, "Andy Razz" wrote lyrics to over two thousand popular songs, including "Ain't Misbehavin'," "Memories of You," and "Stompin' at the Savoy" (*Ebony* 28, no. 3 [January 1973]: 122; Robert Kerlin, *Negro Poets and Their Poems* [Washington, D.C.: Associated Publishers, 1923], pp. 198–200; Robert Kimball and William Bolcom, *Reminiscing with Sissle and Blake* [New York: Viking Press, 1973], pp. 211–14, 244; *WWCR*; *Crusader* 1, no. 8 [April 1919]: 1; Randall Bennett Woods, *A Black Odyssey: John Lewis Waller and the Promise of American Life, 1878–1900* [Lawrence: The Regents Press of Kansas, 1981]).

2. It has been impossible to identify the Morrison to whom Ferris refers.

3. Probably a reference to Alexander Crummell (1819–1898), one of the leading black intellectuals and orators of the nineteenth century and the freeborn grandson of a west African king. He received a rudimentary education at Mulberry Street School in New York, and among his classmates were Henry Highland Garnet, Samuel R. Ward, and George T. Downing. Crummell also attended the Oneida Institute in New York. After a series of setbacks, he was ordained a priest in 1844. He traveled to England in 1847 hoping to raise funds to establish his own church in New York, and he later entered Queens College, Cambridge, obtaining a B.A. degree in 1853. Crummell then moved to Africa, spending the next twenty years as head of an Episcopalian church in Monrovia, Liberia. Returning to Washington, D.C., in 1873, Crummell founded St. Luke's Protestant Episcopal Church, and he served as its pastor for twenty years. During this period he became involved in the struggle for racial advancement, championed the cause of Liberia, and wrote a number of essays and volumes on racial and theological questions. In 1897 Crummell founded the American Negro Academy in Washington, D.C. For details see Lorraine A. Williams, ed., *Africa and the Afro-American Experience: Eight Essays* (Washington, D.C.: Howard University Press, 1977); Benjamin Brawley, *Early Negro American Writers* (New York: Dover Publications, 1970), pp. 299–305; Benjamin Brawley, *The Negro Genius* (New York: Dodd, Mead & Co., 1939), pp. 100–105; and Alfred A. Moss, *American Negro Academy* (Baton Rouge: Louisiana State University Press, 1981), pp. 19–20; Wilson Jeremiah Moses, *The Golden Age of Black Nationalism, 1850–1925* (Hamden, Conn.: Archon Books, 1978), pp. 59–82.

4. Ham, the youngest of Noah's three sons, viewed the naked body of his drunken father and incurred Noah's anger for the deed. As a result, Noah cursed Ham's son Canaan and declared that Canaan would be the servant of Shem and Japheth, Ham's older brothers. Although the biblical account makes no indication regarding color, accounts of the incident in rabbinical literature, written more than a thousand years after the original text, added dark skin to the penalties of the curse. In the intervening years, slavery in the Near East came to include increasing numbers of black Africans, prompting the wider acceptance of racial stereotypes and giving the curse of Canaan a new application in Jewish lore (Gen. 9; William McKee Evans, "From the Land of Canaan to the Land of Guinea: The Strange Odyssey of the 'Sons of Ham,'" *American Historical Review* 85, no. 1 [February 1980]: 15–43).

5. Mario Garcia Menocal (1866–1941) was the conservative president of Cuba from 1913 to 1921.

Maurice Peterson, British Embassy, to Frederick Watson, British Consul General

Washington D C March 10th, 1920

Dear Watson:[1]

With reference to your letter to Campbell of March 10th, 1919 regarding the West Indian Protective Society of America, this Society has sent in a long complaint to the Colonial Office concerning the activities of a rival organization known as the Universal Negro Improvement Association and African Communities League, which apparently issues a publication called "The Negro World" published in New York.

I propose to let the Foreign Office know that it is a case of the pot and the kettle as between the two Societies, but I should be glad first if you could let me know anything about the Universal Negro Improvement Association and if you could comply with the Colonial Office's request by notifying us from time to time of any of its doings which seem of sufficient importance. Yours sincerely,

M[AURICE] P[ETERSON][2]

PRO, FO 115/2619. TLI, recipient's copy.

1. Frederick Watson (1880–1947) served as the British consul in New York as of 6 March 1919. He was consul general in Great Britain's Philadelphia office from 1923 to 1940 (*WWW*, 1941–1950).

2. Sir Maurice Drummond Peterson (1889–1952) entered the foreign service in 1913 and served in a variety of diplomatic posts, including private secretary to Lord Balfour during the Washington Disarmament Conference (1921–22) and ambassador to the Soviet Union, 1946–49 (*WWW*, 1951–1960).

Article by Fred D. Powell

[*New York News*, 11 March 1920]

BLACK STAR LINE NEEDS BIG CHANGE STATES POWELL

"For the benefit of the pleasing public and to conform with the announcement which I made on the date of the publication of my formal resignation from the Board of Directors of the Black Star Line, dated Feb. 18, of the Amsterdam News (publication), I wish to state just at this time (with all responsibility) that my reason for resigning the Board was (1) due to the fact of the large waste of corporate stock funds of the said corporation, accruing only by the improper manner and methods of the conduct of business; (2) by the most ignorant and unprofitable deal of the famous "Green River whiskey cargo" contract;[1] (3) that outrageous and indecent records of the stock sales in the said corporation; (4) the internal disorder of the office force or a lack of systematical management; (5) that the president of said corporation (Marcus Garvey) persisted in the managing of the corporation 'in this, his own way' regardless of the officers or directors of the said corporation who saw these increasing wrongs and who offered some assistance to rectify matters (the Board, however, failed to council together and attend to their duty as managers of the corporation in the face of this 'bubble' management by the president); (6) that the Board of Directors failed to rectify these matters of mistakes, in that no meeting was held since the 23d day of November, 1919, to the date of my resignation, February 14, 1920; (7) that by such total conduct in the business management of the corporation I calculated an unshakable conviction that it was pure mismanagement.

"And to day I want to say that my conviction is still firm, and unless a change for better is taken, a result will register itself in the pages of Negro history that will reflect shame and discredit to the Negro business man years and years to come. Yea the whole Race. Just at this point I would like to add, as I feel sure I am voicing the sentiment of every thoughtful American Negro and that it can be said without being branded as a Race traitor or disloyal and untrue, that if the Black Star Line wants the real strength of the financial support of the American Negro, then the said corporation must be placed on the best possible business footing, and when operated, operated for profits to the stockholders. The American Negro realizes that the best systematized operation of the business management in said corporation is an experiment to and by the Race[.]

"Before closing this article, I wish to state as for a matter of clearance to the public, that the president of this corporation is publishing in the paper of the 'Negro World' that I am an enemy of the corporation. Well, I want to say that I am not, but, however, if in the judgement of this corporation he should keep before your minds that I was or am, then I will have to remain so, for as a member of the Board of Directors at the time it was my solemn duty as well as legal to protect the interest of the stockholders.

"I wish to say, also, this same president of the Black Star Line Corporation, who is also president of the African League Corporation, the Negro Factories Corporation, the Universal Negro Improvement Association and the New York branch of the U.N.I.A., published in the "Negro World" of the issue of February 21, that I was dismissed from the U.N.I.A. I want to inform the public that I resigned formally as General Secretary of the New York branch of the U.N.I.A. on the 14th day of February, 1920, the same time as that of the Black Star Line.

"So, to the public I will say: be not alarmed at anything Marcus Garvey may say in the "Negro World" in the respect of enemies to the corporation, for he is "boss" in the above-named corporations and associations, and expects the public to hum, do and believe as he requires every one around him in the corporations.

"Again I want the public to understand that I am responsible for the wording and complete structure of this article, and not the editor,[2] who was kind enough to permit me space enough to make good my promise to you, which I made on the 18th of February.

"So I hope that Mr. Marcus Garvey will be not mislead about this publication and censure the News wrongfully, but see me, as I have not yet stated the reserve.["]

(Signed) FRED D. POWELL

Printed in the *New York News*, 11 March 1920.

1. On 1 December 1919 the Pan Union Co. contracted with the Black Star Line to ship a cargo of Green River whiskey on the *Yarmouth*. The cargo was valued at $3 million and was to be delivered to a consignee in Cuba for $9.50 per ton, or a total price of $5,985.00. When an extreme discrepancy between the contractual price agreed to by the BSL and the actual cost of the trip became apparent, the BSL refused to load the *Yarmouth* or to allow it to leave port until the Pan Union Co. paid an additional $13,163.50. Although the company paid under protest, it later sued to recover the additional payment and damages from nondelivery of a portion of the cargo, eventually winning damages of over $8,500.00 (*Garvey* v. *United States*, no. 8317, Ct. App., 2d Cir., 2 February 1925).

2. George Wesley Harris (1884–1948) was editor and publisher of the *New York News* and a leader in Harlem Republican politics. Born in Topeka, Kans., he was educated at Tufts College, Medford, Mass., and Harvard University, where he attended the law school. During his career he was also associate editor of the *New York Age* (1909), part owner of the *Amsterdam News* (1909), New York Republican alderman for Harlem (1920–24), and delegate to the Republican National Convention of 1924 (*NYT*, 28 March 1948; *WWCA*; *Harvard Class of 1907* [Cambridge: Harvard University Printing Office, 1952], pp. 181–82).

Report of UNIA Meeting

[*Negro World*, 13 March 1920]

LIBERTY HALL, NEW YORK CROWDED TO DOORS: GREET MARCUS GARVEY ON RETURN FROM BOSTON

CAPTURED CITY OF "THE 400" FOR UNIVERSAL NEGRO IMPROVEMENT ASSOCIATION AND THE BLACK STAR LINE

It is always a record-breaking crowd that fills Liberty Hall on Sunday nights but it was a super-record-breaking crowd that filled Liberty Hall last Sunday night [*7 March*]. Seats were at a premium, and so was standing room, long before the hour set for the beginning of the program, and vast numbers had to be turned away. A great ovation greeted the Honorable Marcus Garvey on his arrival, following an absence of about a week in Boston in the interests of the U.N.I.A. and the Black Star Line. That was a great message he brought back from Boston. We hope that none will fail to read it.

Preliminary to the speaking, an excellent and diversified program of instrumental and vocal music and literary recitations was rendered. The choir, under the incomparable leadership of Madame Houston, vocal soloist of national fame and of charming personality, performed prodigies. The same was equally true of the band under the indefatigable leadership of Mr. William Isles. Miss Pauline Lee delivered a dramatic recitation on "Vision" that was cheered to the echo. No other woman has ever been heard to recite in quite the way Miss Lee does, and no other one else can. Hers is an inimitable style. Her long drawn out intonations, deep, guttural and . . . [*words mutilated*] peculiar repertoire, but it was nevertheless effective and perfect. It was superb. Other parts of the program were:

Solo—Mr. Offley Waith.
Recital—Mr. Donaldson.
Solo—Mr. Bradley.
Solo—Mr. Howard.

Prof. Ferris Speaks

Prof. William H. Ferris, literary editor of The Negro World, was the first speaker of the evening, and spoke as follows:

I have been reflecting a great deal about the significance of this movement. Dr. Mickens said when he came in tonight: "This is a great crowd." For seven months I have seen this hall packed night after night, and I have seen it crowded most of the nights during the week. It is something else besides the mere getting of dividends on the $50 or $100 or $200 or $500 you have invested that is drawing you out night after night. It is something besides the financial aspect of the business enterprise. I believe the people come to Liberty Hall because they find their souls here.

"What Shall It Profit a Man?"

You know it has been said here more than once that Christ said: "What shall it profit a man if he gains the whole world and lose his own soul?"[1] Preachers have harped upon that doctrine so much that many have lost the psychological aspect of it, and the Psalmist David asks, "In what respect is a man greater than a sheep?"[2] All the sheep needs is to be fed properly, and to have water and a good bed to sleep in, and its wants are satisfied. But man has in him the hunger for the eternal. He has in him that instinct for truth by which he is not satisifed when he satisfies the need of the body, but by which he is satisfied when he unravels the mysteries of space and counts the stars and determines their magnitude, and his mind goes back in history and traces the history of the world from the rocks and reads in ancient monuments man's past record—the instinct to understand the mystery of the universe and to enter into communion with the maker. And in proportion as a man has ideals and an impulse which transcends the demands of the appetite and the physical needs, in that proportion does man ascend from the animal and approach the divine. And I believe that a man has missed his true life unless he has realized and developed his human personality and individuality. Men, when they come to die, who have made fortunes and acquired fame, but who lacked the secret of life—and that is, the development of character and becoming one with the power behind the universe, have felt that there is something lacking in their lives; and that is why all men—black, yellow, brown, copper-colored and white—have the longing for freedom and liberty, because the instinct to expand and develop, the instinct for self-expression, is one of the deepest needs of the human heart. And the reason why we have found fault with some of our Caucasian friends who have financed social and industrial enterprises among us was because they wanted to crush, to repress, to restrain, our soul cultivation; and that is why down in the Sunny South in all the State colleges except Georgia they cut out the classics, philosophy, psychology and sociology, because they knew very well that when a Negro boy began to dip in psychology and commune with the great intellects that are past, he would not be satisfied with jim-crowism and disfranchisement.

NEGROES SPEND MONEY.

Now I was much interested in a remark made by T. Thomas Fortune[3] last evening, when he said that for the last fifty years the Negro has spent too much money building churches and saloons. I believe that the church has been a moral influence in the world and it has had a psychological effect upon men, and I believe that the schoolhouse has implanted ideals in the youth of a race or a nation which have determined their future lives and their future careers; but while you soar in your ethereal dreams and soar in your aeroplanes all men must at least have two square meals a day, and some three; and when hunger is gnawing at a man's vitals, when he does not know where his next meal is coming from he cannot develop his soul culture. The only time that a man can be morally independent is when his material needs are provided for. That is why this country has not produced as many great writers and statesmen as England. The men first had to conquer nature here. They had to reclaim the wilderness, build cities and develop industrial enterprises, and then, when they had leisure, they could cultivate the intellect.

EDITORS FALL BACK ON POLITICIANS.

Our fault at first was that we produced more educated men than we had a professional class to support them. New colored editors had to fall back on politicians to run their papers because there were few colored men in business and hence there were few color[e]d men advertising in their papers. And that is why so many of our editors would have to come out and cuss the white man and then for a short period praise that same man, who was indifferent to the Negro but who would come across with a $500 contribution. Now this seesawing and straddling will always prevail unless we get in a position of economic independence.

Now the reason why I was first interested in this proposition when I came through here last year was I was always interested in intellectual problems—in moral, civil and political problems. But I saw there was a bread and butter proposition connected with this; that this had an objective of putting the Negro in a place where he could earn his own living and would not have to go Monday mornings with his hat in hand and beg for a job. It was because I saw that this would ultimately enable a man to throw back his head and expand his chest and brace up and say: "Good morning, So-and-So[,]" that I saw something connected with it that was an advantage to the race. And it was not what it had already accomplished, but what it was possible to accomplish by disseminating the idea of thrift, self-reliance, self-help, economic self-sufficiency, so that it would give the Negro a standing and a platform whereby he could compel the world to recognize him. (Cheers.)

RECLAIMING AFRICA.

Now there has been a good deal of talk about reclaiming Africa and redeeming Africa and driving the Caucasian out of Africa. Well it can't be done by going out and squaring off and knocking that one and the other. It will be done by our getting machine guns, tanks, aeroplanes, battleships—the machinery which helped to make this war the terrible war it was. But it takes money to do that. It takes that little quality which is called "the root of all evil." Dr. Mickens says brains and money combined are what will give the Negro the platform whereby he could build up an independent civilization in Africa.

Now you know a great many times I have told you about Alexander the Great. It is said that he was the only one who could ride his horse Bucephalus. The horse would get frightened and boisterous at the sight of its own shadow and throw him off. Alexander was a keen observer, and he saw that that horse was afraid of his own shadow, so he took the horse's head and turned it away, and then he mounted the horse and rode off. So many times we have seen our shadow—the shadow of disfranchisement, jim-crowism, restricted opportunity. The colored boy grows up in an environment where he is told: "You must go here because you are colored," and that self-consciousness is borne in upon him, until ultimately, when he looks up to the white man, he sees something more akin to the Almighty than himself. And when that self-consciousness becomes a part of him, that energy and that reserve force, that initiative, that audacity and that spirit of venture that was once a part of him passes away from him, and when it passes away from him he is at the mercy of the race which has hypnotized him.

THE NICKNAME OF THE NEGRO.

But if through racial history[,] if through a memory of what our race has already acquired, and if through a study of the laws of nature we find out that there is only one law which nature recognizes—and that is force; and that if we acquire force all handicaps will give way before us, the Negro race will acquire that audacity, that spirit of venture, that initiative, that courage to plunge into the unknown and blaze unknown paths which will cause every difficulty to recede and fade away. And in the years to come colored boys and girls will not be ashamed to call themselves Negroes. Negro was given to us as a nickname, just as Christianity was a nickname to the Christians; just as Protestant was a nickname; just as Methodist was a nickname given in derision; just as Yankee was a nickname g[iven] in derision. Negro was applied in derision to the black slave fr[om] [A]frica. We want, by our deeds and achievements, to make that a name glorious and illustrious. If we come before the white man with a begging proposition we will be at his mercy and at his will and at his pleasure. But it is only when we have in our hands the money to carry us through our ventures, the brains to plan and scheme for ourselves; it is only when [w]e have in our own will power the energy to carry forward our enterprises, that we can become such an independent force that the other nations and races of the world will recognize us. (Cheers.)

EX-CAPTAIN JONES, U. S. A., SPEAKS.

The next speaker introduced was Mr. Jones, an ex-captain of the U. S. Army and a member of the Newport News division of the U.N.I.A. Mr. Jones, who is very light-complexioned, was mistaken by the audience for a white man, and he took opportunity therefore at the beginning of his speech to allay the anxious fears and suspicions of the audience by revealing the fact that he was a Negro, by virtue of the saying that "one drop of Negro blood made a man a Negro." "I have no more privileges," he said, "than the blackest man in the eyes of the white man. He considers me a Negro just as any Negro. What we have got to learn is to get rid of all this distinction that we have among our own people, because the greatest enemy to the Negro race is the Negro himself[.] (Cheers.) The greatest thing we have got to eliminate is this class distinction among our race. We are a Negro race, and the sooner we get out of our hearts and minds that the class distinction that we are light people or dark people the sooner will we get along." Continuing, he said that behind the Black Star Line and the Negro Factories Corporation there was a gigantic movement, and he described Mr. Garvey as the Moses of the Negro race. The hardest job, he said, Mr. Garvey had before him was to get the masses of colored people together; when that was done wonders could be accomplished. What was Japan but a little insignificant race before she whipped Russia. Nobody knew of her. Germany was a nation of just a few people compared with the Allies whom she fought, and yet she almost whipped them. If the Japanese could do what they did to the Russians, and if the Germans could do what they did, what could four hundred millions of Negroes do, Mr. Jones asked[,] if they became a united race? We have got to learn, he said, that no race of people in the world ever accomplished anything without fighting for it. So if we expect to do anything we have got to shed some blood. (Cheers.) Everybody got something out of the war but the Negro, and if the Negro does not get his now he will never get it as long as he is on this earth. Now is the time for the Negro to get his "while the getting was good."

THE GREAT CONVENTION AND MONEY

In urging allegiance to the U.N.I.[A.] and its a[l]lied movements, Mr. Jones said: "If you are going to be a member be a member; don't be an outsider and a knocker. Come in and join the crowd. It takes money to get things. You can sit up and talk about the great convention and about getting back to Africa, but you cannot have those things without money; you cannot build buildings and start factories and steamship lines on talk; you have got to have money. And another thing we have got to do is to trust our fellowmen. We go out and dump our money into some white corporation and we do not ask who is at the head of it and we don't care; but as soon as we are asked to put money into anything where a colored man is concerned, we hesitate." In conclusion he made a strong appeal for support of the movements.

DR. MICKENS SPEAKS

Mr. President, Ladies and Gentlemen:—I am much concerned about whither we are going. I am not much concerned about where we are now. I believe that the greatest instrument that this race of ours has is Prejudice. The great war, as Captain Jones has said, has done more for everybody else than it has done for us; but I think the one thing that has done more for us than anything else is prejudice—P-R-E-J-U-D-I-C-E! That sounds to my ears like the boy who was asked to spell united and he would always say: U-n-t-i-e-d. However, prejudice is the greatest instrument in the cementing of our racial groups—I mean the groups among us, our racial forces.

THE VALUE OF PREJUDICE

I will give you a story. The late Dr. Kealing[4]—I regard him as one of the philosophers of our day—he said he was sitting down one winter day popping some corn for his little girls, and of course he did not have the modern oven popper of today and he improvised one. And as the corn was popping, it hopped out, and soon almost all the corn would have poppe[d] and then hopped out of the pan. The professor—he was a doctor of philosophy, a man who could easily see things—got a lid and put it on the pan and then the corn began to pop and tried to hop, but it stayed in the pan. Now

Professor Kealing said that the story illustrated race prejudice: That if prejudice had not come into play, the Negro race, in so far as America is concerned, would be no more than a bunch of monkeys, because all the wealth, the fine [loo]king specimens, the educated, would have been in the other races, and out beyond, upon the hills, would have been the refuse. And so prejudice, when a man went to college and got a university education and became wealthy—why, prejudice said: "You are educated, but you are a Negro." And so prejudice in America and all over the World has kept us somehow together.

But now there is a new expression in my mind for prejudice. I believe that Mr. Garvey has put into prejudice, not impotence, weakness, supineness, but he has put into prejudice power—the power of cohesion, the power of alliance. Now you think about it.

GOING TO AFRICA

Somebody said this afternoon we are going to Africa, but I also said this afternoon, that is not Mr. Garvey's first object. That is the ultimation [*ultimatum*], that is the objective goal. But the first object is to get the Negroes who are not in Africa, who in the islands of the sea, in America and everywhere else, have education, civilization, Christianity and the like, to discover themselves: To know and to feel that they are just as much as anybody else. And now the way to do that is just the way he is doing.

NEGRO AND BLACK MAN

He is succeeding where others have failed, because the others legislated and deliberated and wrote and talked. He is succeeding like a good woman who wants to handle a man. She cooks good food; and say, if she ever feeds you, my friend, she has you. (Laughter) Mr. Garvey senses the pulse, the feeling, the psychology of the black man and just as thoroughly understands the white man. Now why do I say that? Because the other men, as I said to Prof. Ferris, arrayed the Negroes against them, and on the other hand they arrayed the white folks against them. Mr. Garvey has been successful in making the white man respect you and he has caused the words Negro and black man to be worth more to the black man tha[n] ever before.

It is a truth that black men do possess a peculiar ignorance—that a man's a fine man because he looks like Captain Jones, and if he happens to look like Dr. Gaillard, there is not much to him. (Captain Jones is typically Anglo-Saxon in features and complexion, whereas Dr. Gaillard is just extremely opposite.) Sure! Now that is born of sheer ignorance. I want to try to straighten my hair. It is all right for a woman, but a man has not got time. The money that I pay the barber to straighten my hair, I will buy books and magazines, and the time it takes him to do it, I will be studying and cultivating thought.

Here is a man (referring to Professor Ferris). His hair is nappy like mine: a Yale and Harvard graduate. (Applause.) A historian recognized by the scholars of the world. A genius—born genius—and leader of men, whose name is soon to become a household word the world over. He is not straightening his hair. (Applause.)

Dr. J. C. Price, America's greatest prohibition orator—I do not drink, of course I do not now; as a matter of fact, I never did—but Professor Price, the world-famed temperance orator. Queen Victoria put her hand upon his head and said his hair was beautiful and asked him how it happened that way.

The one thing that Mr. Garvey is teaching us is this, among other things, that to be a black man is a credit, but it means to be a man, not a thing. Stature does not make a fellow a man—just to weigh so many pounds. Pope, the great writer, looked like an interrogation point.[5] The Apostle Paul had fits at times, but he was a man.[6] And so I say that the strongest word we have is prejudice. I like it.

I like the thing that God has given this leader here. It is hypnotizing, tantalizing, it is mesmerizing. "Do you know," I said to Professor Ferris, "that this house is the greatest clearing house that I know anything about, where you can see anything that is seeable, and that the man who does not get inspiration here must be inanimate?"

When I went to school they told me we learned to do by doing. And so Mr. Garvey is holding, and will hold, the forces of the race. This thing will gather momentum. In the short space of two years 3,000,000 men and women have enrolled under this banner. What will that mean if one person can reach ten persons? Three millions multiplied by ten. You see what a force we will have in a short time!

The remark was made a few days ago: "Well, now, I want to remind you that the high-class folks are not in this movement." Well, this was my answer. I said: "No. God, in choosing men, did not go into the skies to get men; he found them on the earth. He did not go into kings' palaces." I have not the record in history where any great, great man was made from the king's palace. I know some who were held up on pedestals and called great. But all the really great men were obscure. We are going to make this thing go, and we will make the world recognize us, and we will do it by making the Black Star Line a success. (Applause) And by making the Factories Corporation a success. (Applause) You think of the power we will have when Mr. Garvey launches this great Universal Bank. Now think of the folks in this building tonight! If the people put in $10 a week, what would you be worth in fifty weeks? If all of the money every Saturday night we carry to the white folks' bank, that makes him stronger and stronger—if you had that money utilized in building factories and doing other great things that you cannot do now, think of what you could accomplish. It is untied and not united that is holding us back.

And then another thing is going to happen. Think of the clothes being washed. Who is getting the money for it? (Cries of the white folks.) Why can't we have it? That is in Mr. Garvey's scheme.

Think of the insurance money that is spent every week! I was courting a young lady once and the insurance collector came around. We were sitting out on the lawn, and she got up from beside me and went into the house and called in the collector and paid the premium, and she laughed and chatted with him with as much levity and ease as she chatted with me and I got my hat. Now, of course, it was very harsh, but I said: "You have plenty of sense, but have not any soul. Good-by!" Now these jobs ought to be in the hands of colored men. You think of Harlem, with all these men, and yet the majority of the insurance agents are white men. It ought not to be. But it will be so until we take the thing in our own hands. Mr. Garvey aims to do that. We ought to have a number of great things.

I will conclude by saying: Friends, remember that the U.N.I.A. and A.C.L. put power in prejudice. It makes a black man look like any other man that is a man. It makes a black woman just as good as any other woman that is a woman. It makes the black enterprise just as substantial and far-reaching as any other enterprise. It makes the mind of a black man just as great as any other mind.

There are some people who believe that black men do not know anything at all. I have had them to ask me questions and then ask the white man if that is so. I was in a community once where they had a doctor and they did not believe that a colored man could prescribe. I have been in Kansas, where they did not believe a colored man could teach in a school. And, of course, I was in New England, and they told me that to have a colored man teaching— why, what does he know? That is the teaching that has come from the other fellow. The white man has so poisoned our minds, and we have not learned enough to think for ourselves. We do second thinking. We have second thought. We think after he has thought. We only think what he says, and he says this and means that. I sat this morning in Bethel Church and I saw a picture of Christ, and as the minister preached: "They that wait upon the Lord shall renew their strength. They shall mount up with wings as eagles. They shall walk and not be weary: they shall run and not faint." And just above me was this beautiful picture of Christ. A lady beside me said: "That picture attracts me. It does not look like Christ." And I looked at that picture and I said, "That is the truth."

One thing the white folks fail to see: They fail to see the picture of Christ from the black man's viewpoint. We have got that thing to learn, to put into the minds and hearts of our children that the black man can think, and the best way to do it is to build factories, to float ships, to organize and run banks. Yes! let them "bust," and build again. Let the ship sink and then buy more ships. Lose your money and get some more money. Listen to the poet Robert Burns:

"For a' that and a' that,
It's coming yet for a' that,

That man to man the world o'er
Shall brothers be for a' that."[7]

—and I believe it.

I believe that the white man is going to respect us only if we have convinced him this: That I know my rights. Then I must convince him that I know that he knows my rights. And I know that I know that he knows that I know my rights. And that until I know that he knows that I know that I will fight for my rights, and that I will have my rights if I have to fight for my rights, I will have my rights if I must die for my rights.

Listen! Before you die, remember the hot blood in the heart must be guided by the gray matter in the head. Know what you are fighting for. Know what you are going to die for. Know that your cause is right and then go to it. Don't stop to pick flaws by the way. No time to complain. No time to dissemble. No time to fight one another. No time to knock. Now is the time to boost. As the young man sang the other night: "Rally around Garvey!" like the nation rallied around Wilson, the French around Foch, the British around Lloyd George and Haig. Rally! And when America has been thoroughly educated and Garveyized, then shall we march and I can see the picture, I can see in my mind's eye now twelve million black citizens of America, with those of the islands of the sea and from Central and South America, from all over the world, educated, uplifted, discovered, proud, prideful, loyal and royal—and I can see the flag of the green and the black and the red floating to the breeze upon the seven seas, and I can see upon yonder hill the beautiful flag waving in the land of Africa, the home of the gods,[8] the place where liberty first sprang for the black men of the earth. (Applause.) In the words of that great poet:

Marcus Garvey, "Sound to the World in clarion tones
Come along with me.
The best of the world is yet to be."[9]

HON. MARCUS GARVEY SPEAKS.

Mr. Garvey: My subject for tonight is "The New Inspiration." Before I speak on the subject, however, I desire to give you an outline of my trip to Boston. First of all, let me say that Boston is called or known among Negroes as the city of the "four hundred."[10] There is an exclusive class of Negroes who condemn everything that comes to Boston that they are not head of, and that is why there is no great Negro movement in Boston except in name— movements like the Equal Rights League exist as far as Boston is concerned in name only; in that the "four hundred" arrogate to themselves the right to condemn anything that comes to Boston that has not got their approval, which approval is first subject to the approval of "the good white people of Boston." But I want to say that Dr. Eason and myself went to Boston, and we have captured the city of Boston. (Cheers.) We have destroyed the usefulness of the "four hundred" and there "ain't no more four hundred," because we have made six hundred new members for the Boston Division of the U.N.I.A. We had a splendid reception in Boston, and it was said that our meetings were the only meetings ever held by Negroes in Boston that the colored citizens followed from Monday to Friday night; and the crowds grew larger and larger every night. When I arrived there on Monday night at the People's Church at Tremont and Camden streets there were hundreds of people inside and hundreds were turned away, and the crowds multiplied every night right down to Friday night. I was asked to speak on Saturday night, but a terrible blizzard came along and held up railroad trains, so that I had to leave early Saturday in order to be here in Liberty Hall tonight.

BOSTON NEGROES CONSERVATIVE.

It is said that the Negroes in Boston are conservative—that they will not invest in any Negro movement because they are the exclusive "four hundred" but we got from Boston not only moral support, but we got real financial support. They did not buy shares in lots of one or two or five; they bought from ten to fifteen and twenty right up. Therefore, it is for me to tell you that one of the strongest branches of the U.N.I.A. is now located in the city of Boston, the city of the "four hundred." The 2,000 people who assembled in the Columbus Avenue A.M.E. Church on Friday night to hear me asked me to admonish the "four hundred of Boston," and I did that for them, and Saturday the whole talk of the town was that there was no more any "four hundred" in Boston; all that was in Boston that was worth while was the U.N.I.A. and its new doctrine. (Cheers.) I understand that there are some of the "four hundred" in Harlem, and by the way, I want to explain what is meant by the "four hundred."

There are 400 people in Boston who call themselves the aristocracy of the Negro race, in other words, they call themselves "The Dickties." "We are the dickties,"[11] they say, and "we are [far] removed from the mass of the Negro race." They call the white people of Boston "our good white friends" and they try to live near to these good white people and believe themselves so much better and so much more advanced and so much higher up in the social scale than the 12,000 and more of the race who live in Boston. I understand that there are a few of the "four hundred"—I believe they call them the "forty-eight" in New York.

Before I proceed with my subject, I will give you a message to the "forty-eight" of New York even as I gave a message to the "400" of Boston. And let me tell you this about Boston. Night after night as I addressed the throng that assembled to hear me, I saw men and women give an expression of the fullest enthusiasm for these new movements of our[s]. I saw young men, middle-aged men and old men make resolutions they never made before—gained a consciousness they never had before—get a vision that

251

they never had before; and as I walked out of the meetings I found hundreds of men and women determined to reach where we were determined to reach. They had made up their minds that they would see this new movement through to the bitter end, and if you talk about dying for anything in Liberty Hall, let me tell you we have left 600 men and women in Boston who will die before you, if you do not get busy, because they have got the spirit of this new movement and they have got the determination that there must be a free and redeemed Africa—(cheers)—the thing that we are agitating for and stand for in Liberty Hall and our three million members scattered all over the world. The people in Boston realize that life is worth living; that life has [been] given to them by Almighty God for a purpose. They never realized it before, but they realized it all through last week, from Monday night to Friday night, and they have made a resolve that whatsoever is given in this world for any other race is also given for the black race of which they are members in Boston to the extent of 12,000.

We have reached a stage in civilization where we dare not turn back. We have reached the stage that we must go forward, and the question is now, how far are you prepared to go? And we of the U.N.I.A. say we are prepared to go to the limit. (Applause) Whatsoever is possible for man, the black man will make it a possibility for himself. That is the resolution we have; that is the [res]olution that we must carry through this world.

Some of us, because of our environments, lose ho[pe?] sometimes. We get to argue with ourselves that we are unable to accomplish anything. There is a thing called the human will. The will is the thing that rules men; the will is the thing that rules the world. The human will is that force, is that power that the white races have used to make themselves the giants that they are in this world today; and because we fail to use that human will, that accounts for our being pigmies as a race. The time has come when the New Negro has made up in his mind that he will use and exercise his will to the limit, and we say that from our human will whatsoever the other races of the world have achieved we are going to achieve it also. (Cheers) Men, I want you to realize that God Almighty has given us a creation: God Almighty has given us a world; He has given us a province we are to conquer, and the call for our taking advantage of all the privileges that God Almighty has given to us is now. We want you to go out and do. We want you to go out and achieve, even as other men of other races have achieved. There is a great world yet to be conquered; and if you men are to live as men, you have to play your part as men. When 32 years ago I was born into the world, 32 years ago some white boy was born into this world. I was sent to an elementary school; I was sent to a high school; I was sent to a college, and I went to a university. The white boy was sent to a similar school, to a college and to a university. He graduated from his university and was sent out into the world to conquer, to achieve. He made the world his province. What has he achieved in 32 years of time? He has added to fresh laurels to his country, fresh laurels to his nation, fresh laurels to his empire, fresh laurels to his race; his name is a by-word among the millions of his race. His name is honored by the nation that gave him birth. His name is to be written everlastingly across the pages of the history of his empire. I, who was born at the same time as himself, where am I to be found? I am to be found on the street corners blacking some one's shoes, brushing some one's coat; a porter for some one—probably the same fellow who was born into the world at the same time I was born. Can you tell me the reason why such a difference? Because the one man was born to the full conscious[ness]—of himself, of his possibilities. The other fellow had no consciousness of self and naturally he remained always at the foot of the great human ladder. But if for every white child that is born into this world there is also a black child, whatsoever be the aspiration of the white child you will find a similar aspiration in that black child. And if that child as a white child has ambition to rise to the highest heights within the nation—within the empire—if he is to be president of the nation, premier of the empire, the black child is born with the hope of being president of his country and the premier of his empire one day. (Enthusiastic cheers.) And the empire is now in the making, and whilst we are laying the foundation for his great empire, what is happening? Some of our men try to discourage us, try to show us how impossible it is for humble negroes.

We are believing that we are still too humble to soar to the heights of independence and freedom and liberty. They try to circumvent us and show us how powerful the white man is—trying to show that with our meagre strength, materially and otherwise, we will be unable to combat him.

Now, men, I am here at Liberty Hall tonight to answer such men. Let me tell you this, that no race of people in the world have ever won their liberty or their freedom by begging that liberty or begging that freedom. All races, all nations of mankind who have become powerful became so because they had first to fight for that freedom. And in this universal movement of ours those of us who expect to lead must be made up with the determination to sacrifice—that sacrifice that means "If I am to achieve glory I must make up my mind to die in the attempt to get that glory." (Cheers.)

When your leaders feel that way there cannot be any fear of the white man's strength, because the white man's strength is maintained by the sacrifice he is prepared to make. And if you are prepared to make a similar sacrifice, then it will mean "the survival of the fittest." (Cheers.) The white man's strength at the present time is maintained by brute force—that force that Woodrow Wilson tells us about in his great speech in Baltimore three years ago, when he said that force was the only thing that the nation could organize to fight the Germans. And the force that America organized and won the day for the allies is the force that 400,000,000 [*Negroes*] must marshal to make Africa a free and independent republic in the world. (Cheers.)

As I told the men of Boston, I tell you. I want you to leave this room tonight with the same impression that I made on the people of Boston. You must have this one consolation—if you could have died in France and

Flanders for the white man you must make up your minds to die anywhere in your own defense and for your own liberty. (Cheers.)

They tell us the white man will not allow us to get here or to get there. Those of us who are leading this movement are not doing it as children. We are doing it as men—men with developed brains. We know the white man for what he is worth. We know that he is the super-savage of the age; that he kills to satisfy himself and to maintain his power. We know that if we are to get what he has for us we have to make up our minds to die. All of us are not going to die, but some of us will have to die; and those who should be prepared to die first are those who are at least endeavoring to organize you for the objective we have in view. And in my service to my race—in my effort to organize you—I do not care if I die now or fifty years hence.

If you aspire to leadership; if you aspire to liberty, you must make up your minds to die at any time for that liberty, for that freedom that you value so much. (Cheers.) That is the answer I have to give those who are fearful about the white m[a]n. He has but one life to give for mine, and anytime he is willing to give his I am ready to give mine.

To look at me—one out of slavery, the slavery of 250 years in America, the slavery of 230 years in the West Indies—and tell me that I must be fearful of the man who kept me a slave for all that time! My one regret now in Liberty Hall is that I was not born in slavery days. I wish I were born in slavery days. I would have taught some one a lesson then. If I were born eighty-four years ago in the West Indies, in the island of Jamaica, where, fortunately or unfortunately, I was born, tonight Jamaica would not have been a province of England. Jamaica would be a free and independent republic in the Caribbean Islands. But since I was not born then and I am born now, and they own that land out there, and since I am born at a time when Africa is not free, then my life, my blood will be given to Africa's redemption, Africa's freedom and Africa's liberty.

Tell me that I must live everlastingly without a place in the sun. I ask the reason why when God gave everybody the sun. The Kaiser wanted a larger place in the sun, even though he had a place; England wants a bigger and larger place in the sun, even though she has such a large place. Now we also want a place in the sun. (Cheers) It has been winter too long; we want a place in the sun. (Laughter.) How do men get a place in the international and political sun? The Kaiser taught us the way, and we are not going to forget it. The Kaiser taught that sixty million of white people made up with one purpose could keep the world at war for five years. We have enlarged the thought and we say that if sixty million could have kept the world at bay for five years four hundred million ought to be able to do it a little longer. (Cheers.) This African idea, this African proposition is one that you must understand thoroughly. We of the U.N.I.A. are not endeavoring to repatriate at the present moment—immediately—twelve million Negroes of America, or twelve or fifteen million from the West Indies. We are first trying to organize these twelve and fifteen million together with the twenty-five millions in South and Central America, with the one object of a free and redeemed Africa, and we are saying all the millions organized in this Western Hemisphere can be organized until we are ready; until Africa finds a Napoleon, and that Napoleon sends out the bugle call, and then we will march from this Western Hemisphere sixty million strong to meet him in Africa 250 million strong.

It means, therefore, that we have years before us. It might be five years; it might be ten years; it might be twenty years; it might be fifty years; it might be a hundred years. But whensoever the time comes we want to be ready here, sixty million strong. Because we have fought in the last war for the white man, and the next war will be a war for————.

I am here, therefore, preaching preparedness during this time of peace as Roosevelt preached preparedness throughout the nation during the time of peace when the world was at war and America was looking on, and when the time came for the nation to marshal her forces all the men of the nation were ready because of the preparedness propaganda of Roosevelt.

So I do hope in the next five or ten or fifteen or hundred years that every Negro man and woman in this Western Hemisphere will be ready for the call for Africa. Let me tell you that call is coming sooner tha[n] we expect, because we have heard the rumblings in Southeast Africa; we have heard the rumblings in Southwest Africa; we have heard the rumblings in West Africa, and we heard the rumblings in the West Indies and all over this country, and we are looking out for that star—the star of destiny. (Cheers.)

I believe with Josephus Daniels that the next world war will be a war of races, and I believe it will be a bloody conflict—a Titanic struggle between Europe and Asia, with the ninety million yellow and brown peoples of Asia under the leadership of Japan, who shall pit their physical force against the forces of Europe, led either by England or France. Methinks I hear that clash, and methinks I hear the white man call: "Brother Sambo, come over and help us." (Laughter[)]. Methinks I hear Sambo answering in the language of Dr. Eason: "Call me Sambo no more. I am the new Toussa[i]nt L'Ouverture of the Negro race, and I am coming 400 million strong to carve an African imperialism and an African nationalism." While the forces shall contend among themselves we shall make a pathway and an avenue through from this Western Hemisphere on to Africa. Prepare yourselves, men and women.

And now I come to the question of aristocracy—now I come to the question of the "four hundred" of Boston and the "forty-eight" of New York. I challenge any Negro in any part of this Western Hemisphere to be better born than I was born. I challenge any Negro in this Western Hemisphere to have sprung from better parentage than I was sprung from. The parentage of Negroes of this Western Hemisphere sprung from or was the parentage of a slavery of 250 years in America and 230 years in the West Indies. When Abraham Lincoln liberated us in America, when Victoria the good liberated us in the West Indies they never said, "Here, 'forty eight,' you are the aristocrats of the Negro race."

They never said: "Here, '4[oo],' you are the aristocrats of the Negro race." Lincoln said: "Here, 400,000,000, you have your freedom. Go and make the best use you can of it in America." To the millions in the West Indies, Victoria said: "This day you are free. Make the best of your liberty." We were here as slaves for 250 years in this Western hemisphere. When John Hawkins started to trade with Negroes from Africa to this Western hemisphere he told Queen Elizabeth of England that he was taking the slaves or blacks from Africa to transplant to her colonies in the Western hemisphere for the purpose of working them to develop her colonies, and she asked him: "What consideration will you give them to work as slaves?" and he said: "We will civilize and Christianize them, because in their own country they are savages, they are pagans and barbarians." The queen, under this pretense, signed the charter that enpowered Hawkins to take 40,000,000 of us and transplant us to the Western hemisphere—all over the Carolinas and the Jamaicas and the Barbados of the West Indian islands. Now after 300 years, what has happened? Compare the race with any other race. Compare our race with the white race that is now ruling us in this country and in Great Britain—that race that has lynched us below the Mason-Dixon line.

You will remember that in 55 B.C. the English or British were the slaves of the Romans. He was sold in the slave market at Rome—the ancient Briton, the present Anglo-Saxon even as our foreparents were sold in the slave markets of Georgia. When the ancient Britons got their liberty through the overthrow of the Roman Empire they made up in their minds that they would never be slaves again. And these ancient Britons started out to build a civilization of their own—to build a nation of their own; and in the numbers of years what has happened? If you will read English history you will read what daring achievements the Englishman and the ancient Briton and the other white races that came from the other parts of Europe did to help them in their civilization and in the development of their government. You will read in English history of great statesmen like William Earl of Chatham, William Pitt, and statesmen like Disraeli[12] and Gladstone, and going down the line you will read of men like Lord Rosebery, the Balfours,[13] the Asquiths and the Lloyd Georges. What have they done for their race, for their nation, for their empire?

Every succeeding generation of Englishmen have built up a stronger nation, a stronger race, a stronger empire; and as an individual Englishman went out and conquered new territory for the empire, as a single Anglo-Saxon went out and conquered in the domain of science and of art and literature, what did the head of the nation do? The head of the nation took that pioneering Englishman who did so much for his empire and raised him from the common people to the nobility of his time and of his race. Hence we read of William Pitt. Because of the service he did to his empire he was raised to the peerage and was called a noble of Great Britain and he was called the Earl of Chatham. Because of his service to the nation and to his race he was elevated from the common people and placed among the aristo-crats of this country and he became one of the "48" or the "400." That is aristocracy—aristocracy of service and devotion to one's race, to one's coun-try, to one's nation. That is the difference between the common people and the nobles of any country.

As of England, so of Germany. You must have remembered a few years ago of a great German character. His name was Von Bismarck. When there was a disarmed Prussia, he had a vision of a great German empire and he said to his people and to himself, "First I will go out and unite these scattered, suppressed cities and make a great German empire of them and build our-selves a great commercial and industrial nation." After 40 years rolled by he succeeded in uniting the scattered cities of Prussia and succeeded in building up in Germany a great commercial and industrial prestige all over the world[,] and because of what he did for Germany the German Kaiser made him Prince Von Bismarck and numbered him among the "48" and the "400" of Germany.

As of Germany, so of France, so of Italy, so of Russia; so of all the well established and recognized governments; so of Japan, and that is why we have read today of Count Ishii, one-time Ambassador of Japan in this country.[14]

Now let us trace the aristocracy of the "48" and the "400" of the Negro race. In Boston 60 years ago a Negro was born under the same circumstances as another Negro. He went to school and got a little learning; he came out of school and was ready to work and some big white boss said "Come here, John, do you want a job as porter?["] He said "Yes, boss." The boss said, "I want a good boy to work with me; if you are a good boy I will take care of you." He said "Yes boss." He started out to take care of that boy; he pays him $15 a week; the boy realized that he is working for a master—a superior being—and he works his soul out from morning to morn-out; and he sticks to the boss's job for 25 years and the boss said "He is a good nigger," and tells everybody he is a good nigger, and raises his salary from $15 to $25 or 30. He takes care of his good nigger, and [a]fter 20 or 30 years this Negro saves a few thousand dollars and buys a home. In Boston when he gets to that stage he buys a dress suit and tries to imitate the white man out there with his automobile and his thousands and millions of dollars in the bank. He looks at his people and sees a multitude of poor Negroes striving to get somewhere and can get nowhere because of the heavy pressure of the white man. And because he finds himself with $10,000 and a little home he arrogates to himself the right to be one of the "400" of Boston and calls himself a "dickty," an aristocrat, a noble.

Now compare the nobility. You will see the nobility of the white man was nobility gained by service. When Arthur Wellesley was made Duke of Wellington, why was it? Because there was a Waterloo . . . [*line deleted*] it on the battle plains of Belgium and met the tyrant of all Europe, known as

Napoleon at the battle of Waterloo. Arthur Wellesley gave Napoleon the defeat of his life; because of that the British Government raised him to a Dukedom and made him Arthur, Duke of Wellington.

Now let me say to the "400" of Boston and the "48" of New York, if you want to be nobles, if you want to be aristocrats, you will have to go out on the battle plains of Africa and after you will have given a Waterloo to an alien race we will make you the "400" of the Negro race. (Cheers, mingled with laughter.)

And there is a chance for every Negro man in this audience tonight not to be an Arthur, Duke of Wellington, but an Arthur, Duke of the Nigerias; not to be an Earl of Westminster, but to be an Earl of Lagos, or any of the provinces of West Africa.

And through your service to the Africans, in recognition of those services, when we award you a nobility the woman alongside you will also go to the nobility and you will be able to look her in the face and say, "I came, I saw, I conquered." (Cheers.)

Now for a closing word of inspiration. We have seen it is for us to go out and conquer and I am prepared to go forward and conquer or die in the attempt to conquer. Let that be your inspiration as you leave Liberty Hall tonight. Believe that there is a purpose for you in this life; that God Almighty created you to be a man and you must live and die as a man. They have taught us for 300 years that we were to be hewers of wood and drawers of water. That we were to be servants and others masters. I question the right of any God to create me to be a hewer of wood and drawer of water. If there was such a God he is not my God. But I know there is no such a God. God Almighty never created any part of humanity to be hewers of wood and drawers of water. It is a lie and a damnable lie. As the white man has lied us into the tradition, so he has lied to us through Bible and secular history and he wrote that bit of lie in the Bible so as to be able to deceive the world for all time. But in his own words, "You may fool half of the people half of the time, but you cannot fool all of the people all of the time."[15] And though they have fooled us for 300 years into believing that we were destined to be hewers of wood and drawers of water, we now—four hundred millions—believe that we are destined to achieve anything other men can achieve. (Loud and prolonged applause.)

Printed in *NW*, 13 March 1920.

1. A paraphrase of Mark 8:7.
2. Actually a paraphrase of Matt. 12:12.
3. Timothy Thomas Fortune (1853–1928) was editor of the *Negro World* from 1923 until his death. However, Fortune never joined the UNIA nor did he endorse black separatism. He is generally recognized as one of the most influential black journalists of the late nineteenth to early twentieth century. Born in Marianna, Fla., Fortune was the son of a Reconstruction politician. In 1875 and 1876, he attended Howard University, but he apparently never completed either his law courses or his education courses. In 1880 he began his career as a journalist in New York City when he collaborated with two partners to establish the *Rumor*, which later became the *New York Globe*. After four years, the venture ended, but he immediately replaced the defunct paper with a new publication, the *New York Freeman*. In 1885 the *Freeman* became

the *New York Age*, a journal that was soon the nation's leading black newspaper. During this time Fortune developed a close friendship with Booker T. Washington and was his speech writer on several occasions. Fortune's bouts with alcoholism and his general ill health led him to sell his interest in the *Age* in 1907 and to work part-time for several newspapers, including the *Age*, the *Amsterdam News*, and the *Norfolk Journal and Guide*. Fortune's interest in Garvey first appeared when he wrote editorials defending Garvey and supporting his business schemes in the *Journal and Guide*. Fortune, however, was the subject of a highly critical editorial in the 28 June 1919 *Negro World*. Referring to him as "the Afro-American Rip Van Winkle" and alluding repeatedly to his drinking problem and his advanced age, the editorial apparently responded to a critical article by Fortune. When he died in 1928, the *Negro World* then judged Fortune's contribution to blacks as "quite as much as Frederick Douglass, perhaps a little more than Booker T. Washington and less than only Marcus Garvey" (*NW*, 9 June 1928). In a letter to Fortune's son, Garvey referred to the late journalist as "a very good friend and one who did his best to help in the work in which I am engaged" (Marcus Garvey to Dr. Frederick Fortune, 25 July 1928; Emma Lou Thornbrough, *T. Thomas Fortune: Militant Journalist* [Chicago: University of Chicago Press, 1972]; D. W. Culp, *Twentieth-Century Negro Literature* [Atlanta: J. L. Nichols and Co., 1902]).

4. Hightower T. Kealing (1859–1918) was born in Austin, Tex., of slave parents. Kealing later attended Straight University, New Orleans, and Tabor College in Iowa. He organized the Austin high school for black children and was later elected supervisor of schools for blacks in the city. Kealing was president of Paul Quinn College, Waco, Tex., from 1892 to 1896. For the next sixteen years he was editor of the *AME Review*, and for the last eight years of his life he was president of Western University in Quindaro, Kans. (*Kansas City Advocate*, 1 March 1918; *WWCR*).

5. Alexander Pope (1688–1744), English poet, satirist, and polemicist whose most widely read works were the poem "The Rape of the Lock" (1712) and the *Essay on Man* (1733). Pope's deformity resulted from a childhood disease (*WBD*).

6. The Apostle Paul's statement that he was given "a thorn in the flesh" (2 Cor. 12:7) is sometimes considered to be a reference to a physical ailment. However, "fits" are not generally considered a part of his malady.

7. Robert Burns (1759–1796), Scottish poet, was known for his satirical verses and other poems that conveyed the vitality of Scottish folk life and tradition. The poem "For a' That and a' That" was written in 1794 (*CBD*).

8. Edward Wilmot Blyden, in *Christianity, Islam, and the Negro Race* (1887; reprint ed., Edinburgh: University of Edinburgh Press, 1969), cited eulogies to Ethiopia written by Homer and Herodotus. Blyden wrote, "Every year, the poet [Homer] says, the whole celestial circle left the summits of the Olympus and betook themselves, for their holidays, to Ethiopia, where, in the enjoyment of Ethiopian hospitality, they sojourned twelve days" (p. 116).

9. It has not been possible to find any information on this poem.

10. The use of *four hundred* as a reference to an exclusive social set began with social gatherings in the home of Mrs. William Astor, the New York white millionairess whose grand ballroom reportedly would accommodate four hundred guests.

11. *Dickty* was a pejorative term used by blacks to describe those who claimed more sophistication than their peers.

12. Benjamin Disraeli (1804–1881), knighted first earl of Beaconsfield, served in the British Parliament as a Conservative, becoming prime minister in 1874 (*WBD*).

13. The two most prominent Balfours were Arthur James (1848–1930) and his brother Gerald (1853–1945), who succeeded to the earldom in 1930 (*CBD*).

14. Viscount Kikujaro Ishii (1866–1945), Japanese diplomat, was a special envoy to the United States in 1919 (*WBD*).

15. Abraham Lincoln made this statement to a White House visitor: "If you once forfeit the confidence of your fellow citizens, you can never regain their respect and esteem. It is true that you may fool all of the people some of the time; you can even fool some of the people all the time; but you can't fool all of the people all the time" (*BFQ*).

Negro World Editorial Cartoon

"HIS MASTER'S VOICE"

(*Source*: NW, 13 March 1920).

UNIA Notice

[*Negro World*, 13 March 1920]

IMPORTANT NOTICE

All members of the Universal Negro Improvement Association and stockholders of the Black Star Line all over the World are hereby notified that

B. C. BUCK AND FRED D. POWELL

are no longer connected with the above named corporations. Please do not send any money or remittances intended for these corporations to them.

(Signed) MARCUS GARVEY
President

Printed in *NW*, 13 March 1920.

BSL Notice to Stockholders

[*Negro World*, 13 March 1920]

There are more than 15,000 shareholders of the Black Star Line in the district of which New York is the center. We earnestly request them to advise the office whenever they change their addresses.

This step is necessary in order that a correct record be kept regarding each shareholder. As things are now, our stock ledgers show addresses for hundreds of stockholders who have long since moved to new quarters. This fact was strikingly brought to our attention recently when a very large number of circulars [was] returned to us because the addresse[e]s were no longer at the addresses indicated.

WARNING!

Since success has come to the Universal Negro Improvement Association and the Black Star Line many business and other organizations have found it profitable to spring up under names that are somewhat similar. This often causes persons who are friendly to us to believe that these organizations are in some way affiliated with us. We, therefore, find it necessary to warn our friends that the Universal Negro Improvement Association, the Black Star Line Corporation and the Negro Factories Corporations are the only organizations with which our movement is associated. Please govern yourself accordingly.

THE UNIVERSAL NEGRO IMPROVEMENT ASSOCIATION
AND AFRICAN COMMUNITIES LEAGUE,
THE BLACK STAR LINE CORPORATION,
THE NEGRO FACTORIES CORPORATION.
54 and 56 West 135th Street
New York City

Printed in *NW*, 13 March 1920.

Bureau of Investigation Reports

Seattle, Wash. Mar. 16, 1920

BLACK STAR LINE INC. . . . NEGRO ACTIVITIES

As explained by JAMES A. HASSEL, Seattle representative of Black Star Line Incorporated, this organization is now incorporated under the laws of Delaware for a quarter million dollars and plans to establish a line of steamships manned entirely by negroes. The outline as presented by HASSEL was extremely rosy and he represented MARCUS GARVEY, president, as being an extremely wellknown Jamaican negro, editor of a negro paper called "The Negro World". He further explained that Mr. GARVEY could practically control the exports and imports to the West Indies as regards the portion supplied by the negroes.

The Seattle meeting [*14 March*] was opened by prayer by a local negro minister named SIMONS, followed by an exhortation by a negro doctor named ARTHUR WILLIAMS[1] and negro doctor named DAVID T. CARDWELL, urging negroes to put every available cent into stock to further the corporations indicated. The Negro Factories Corporation is affiliated with and under the same management. (see report same date on "Negro Factories Corporation["]).

ROY A. DARLING[2]

DNA, RG 65, file OG 388440. TD. Copies of this report were furnished to the bureau's New York office.

1. Arthur Williams (b. 1881) was born in Magnolia, Miss., and educated at the Columbia Institute of Chiropodists, New York. He moved to Seattle in 1908 (*Who's Who in Religious, Fraternal, Social, Civic, and Commercial Life on the Pacific Coast, 1926–1927* [Seattle: Searchlight Publishing Co., 1927], p. 211).

2. Roy A. Darling (b. 1889) served as a Bureau of Investigation department supervisor in both New York and Chicago. In 1927 he was appointed chief of the undercover Prohibition investigation and enforcement branch in New York (*NYT*, 30 March 1927).

Seattle, Wash. Mar. 16, 1920

NEGRO FACTORIES CORPORATION . . . Negro Activities

As set forth in an address by JAMES A. HASSEL, negro representative of this corporation in Seattle, the object of the organization is to build factories in the United States, Canada, West Indies, South/&/Central America and Africa. The prospectus claims the corporation to be capitalized at one million dollars under the state laws of Delaware and shares were sold at $5.00 each, the statement being made that one could buy as many shares as desired and a rosy picture was presented of the profits to be accumulated at the end of the financial year.

The officials of the "Black Star Line Inc." as well as the "Negro Factories Corporation" are as follows:

MARCUS GARVEY, President
JEREMI[A]H M. CERTAIN, First Vice President
HENRIETTA VINTON DAVIS, Second Vice President
[E]D. D. SMITH-GREEN, Secretary
GEORGE TOBIAS, Treasurer
CYRIL HENRY, Assistant Treasurer

Throughout the lecture made by JAMES A. HASSEL continued reference and comparison was made between the Japanese and the American negro, similarity being drawn between the condition of the Japanese 49 years ago (at which time HASSEL claimed they started to develop their merchant marines as well as naval[)] and the present condition of the American negro. He set forth that the possession and operation of steamships by the colored race would mean their assuming an equal position in the world with various other races.

ROY A. DARLING

DNA, RG 65, file OG 185161. TD. Copies of this report were furnished to the bureau's New York office.

Seattle, Wash. Mar. 17, 1920

UNIVERSAL NEGRO IMPROVEMENT ASSOCIATION (Seattle forum) . . . Negro Activities

Agent attended meeting of Seattle negroes held in Washington Hall under date of Sunday, March 14th, which was advertised in "The Searchlight", a negro newspaper, as the "Grand Forum", at which meeting would be presented "The cause of Unrest in Panama" and "The Progress of the Negro Factories Corporation boom".

From information gained at the lecture, the Universal Negro Improvement Association was incorporated by MARCUS GARVEY, president, address, Universal Building, 56 West 135th Street, New York, and the aim is to unite the negroes throughout the United States into a unit organization for the improvement of their race. The speaker at the local meeting, a negro named JAMES A. HASSEL, 1027 Washington Street, Seattle, Washington, presented the outline of the organization and after the preliminaries explained the "Negro Factories Corporation movement" and the "Black Star Line Incorporated movement" in detail, which resolved itself into a stock selling proposition at $5.00 per share. (See report same date on "Black Star Line Incorporated" and the "Negro Factories Corporation"[)]. Approximately 150 negroes were present, 30 of whom were women.

ROY A. DARLING

[*Endorsement*] Noted F.D.W.

DNA, RG 65, file OG 185161. TD. Stamped endorsement. Copies of this report were furnished to the bureau's New York office.

Frederick Watson to Maurice Peterson

NEW YORK March 18 1920

Dear Peterson,—

With reference to your letter about the West Indian Protective Society of America, and the Universal Negro Improvement Association and African Communities League, there has been a good deal of correspondence about these organizations recently. The former appears to have circularized the different Governors in the British West Indies pointing out the iniquities of the latter, and we have been asked our opinion. They have both written at length to this office endeavoring to obtain some expression of support.[1] As they would use any such letter very widely, we have been extremely cautious in the form of our replies, which have amounted to little more than acknowledgments.

I think that both Societies are probably doing good work of a kind, but they are both run by men who desire to get as much notoriety as possible from the fact that they are in charge. I think it would be injudicious to recognize either one or the other.

I am getting hold of a copy of "The Negro World" which I hope to send you in due course, and shall endeavor to keep in touch with the situation generally, but I think that it is a case for a policy of laissez-faire. Yours sincerely,

FREDERICK WATSON

[*Typewritten references*] NO. 315 FW:KK
8052/20/194

PRO, FO 115/2619. TLS, recipient's copy.

1. This correspondence has not been found.

R. C. Lindsay, British Embassy, to Earl Curzon of Kedleston

Washington, March 19, 1920

My Lord:

With reference to your despatch [No. 194] of February 20th (A472/443/45), I have the honour to state that, so far as can be ascertained through enquiries made by His Majesty's Consulate General at New York, there is little to choose between the two societies referred to in the Colonial Office letter of February 5th, which are at present extensively engaged in defaming each other by circular letters to British authorities of all kinds. Both are probably doing good work of a kind, but are being run by men who are either agitators or at the least self-advertisers.

In this connection I enclose copy of a despatch which I recently addressed to the Governor of Jamaica on the subject of the West Indian Protective Society.[1]

I agree with the Colonial Office view that no useful purpose would be served by representation to the United States Government in respect of one or other of these societies at the present time. But I have asked His Majesty's Consul General at New York to report any of their activities which may seem in any way noteworthy. I have the honour to be with the highest respect, My Lord, Your Lordship's most obedient, humble servant,

R. C. LINDSAY

[*Typewritten reference*] No. 429
[*Stamped endorsement*] A 1849 Mar 31 1920

PRO, FO 371/4567. TLS, recipient's copy.

1. This document, along with the circular letters referred to, will appear in the Caribbean Series of the edition.

Report by Special Agent WW

New York March 20, 1920

In re: *Negro Activities*

March 8, 1920

. . . Still rallying for money for the purpose of enlarging Liberty Hall, at Liberty Hall; with anticipation of the coming convention in the month of August. Nothing of interest to report of this date.

March 9, 1920

. . . Activities at Liberty Hall very quiet. Rev. Eason being the only stir[r]ing feature on the program. He encouraged quite a few subscriptions to the building fund for the purpose of enlarging Liberty Hall. Also claimed that the people of South and Central America were strongly supporting the Black Star Line and the Universal Negro Improvement Assn.

March 13, 1920

. . . Only a small crowd at Liberty Hall, Rev. Mickens and Prof. Ferris taking the active work in hand and appealing to the people to support the enterprises carried on by these organizations operated in Liberty Hall.

March 14, 1920

A very large crowd at Liberty Hall in the eveni[ng]. Prof. Ferris the first speaker of the evening spoke on the Mobilization of Industrial Forces. In the course of his remarks he stated: That the success of the Negro was to be received by his power, which dominated of Might. That it was only through his medium and by fear that the White Man would respect the Negro and give him [d]ue recognition.

Mr. Rudolph Smith[1] spoke on the Negro and His Lack of will power. Mickens spoke on the possibilities of happiness in Africa. Traffic agent Johnson of the Black Star Line, spoke on Africa, and stated that he was willing to give his life for the liberation of this country. (Africa) Capt. Jones of Newport News also made the statement that he was willing to lay down his life to give for his country. (Africa) Garvey the final speaker of the evening ended the show by knocking the Chicago Defender and the New York News, and stated that he intended to make them both tell a Justice just what they knew about the Black Star Line and its activities.

WW

[*Endorsements*] Noted F.D.W. NOTED W.W.G.

DNA, RG 65, file OG 258421. TD. Stamped endorsement.

1. Rudolph E. B. Smith was later elected leader of the American Negroes at the UNIA's third general convention in 1922.

G. Montgomery to William H. Lamar

Reidsville, N.C., March 20, 1920
Second CLASS

Sir:

I am enclosing herewith a part of a mutilated copy of The Negro World dated March 13, 1920, and published at New York, NY.[1]

I have marked on the editorial page the editorial written a part of which has been torn off, which in my judgement contains matter that is questionable as to its admittance to the mails. Will also call your attention to a poem which I have marked in red pencil on page eight, and would respectfully ask your ruling on same. Respectfully,

G. MONTGOMERY
Postmaster

[*Endorsement*] Solicitor Received MAR 22 1920
Post Office Dept.

DNA, RG 28, file B-500, "Negro World." TLS, recipient's copy. Stamped endorsement.

   1. This copy has not survived.

Bliss Morton to Frank Burke

[*Cleveland, ca. 20 March 1920*]

Five stop Garvey Marcus negro agitator of New York arrived Cleveland this Morning and will be kept under surveil[la]nce as much as possible and full reports made.

MORTON

DNA, RG 65, file OG 329359. TL (telegram), recipient's copy.

Article in the *New York News*

25 March 1920

BRITISH OFFICIALS DECLARE YARMOUTH IS NOT OWNED BY BLACK STAR COMPANY

The Emancipator, a local weekly publication, carries in its current issue a cut of the correspondence between Cyril V. Briggs and the Register of British Shipping, which shows that until March 15, 1920 the Black Star Line did not own the "Yarmouth."

The Emancipator continues as follows:

Ever since the S. S. Yarmouth, of the Black Star Line sailed proudly up North River and anchored at the foot of West 135th street four or five months ago, there have been conflicting reports as to the actual ownership of the 32-year-old former coastwise vessel. As a consequence of the uncertainty of ownership, considerable apprehension was felt by investors in the Black Star Line, while many prospective investors decided to investigate the matter.

Because of the wide advertisement given to the project, and its far reaching scope, colored newspapers and magazines published in New York were besieged by inquiries from readers in every State in the Union as well as from Canada, Panama, Africa, Central America and the West Indies.

So as to set speculation at rest and to serve the investigating public to the best of their ability[,] The Emancipator co-operating with Mr. Cyril V. Briggs of the Crusader, contributing editor of this paper, and a leader in the New York Negro Movement as is shown by his editorials in his magazine, decided to get the facts, and herewith present them for the benefit of the public [at] large and the good reputation of Negroes, particularly those of West Indian birth or parentage.

For some time the promoters [of] the Black Star Line inserted a full page ad. in its propaganda organ, The Negro World, with reference to a line of ships "to be owned," etc. As soon as the Yarmouth was taken over the wording of the advertisement was changed from "to be owned" to "owned," carrying the clear implication of ownership. At the same time it was announced that the name of the ship was to be changed to "Frederick Douglass."

At the time of the much advertised mass meeting at Madison Square Garden, the New York World stated that the Yarmouth was chartered. The New York Age, a conservative Negro weekly, then asked if the Black Star Line actually owned the Yarmouth why was the re-christening so long delayed. Intelligent people echoed that question. Responsible officials of the Black Star Line made no explanation and continued openly to state that the Yarmouth was owned by the Corporation.

On the other hand, Prof. Buck and Fred D. Powell, who claimed to know the facts of the matter were bitterly denounced and finally dismissed from any connection with any of the enterprises of the U.N.I.A.

A little before that, mysteriously worded warnings against an un-named bank and certain business enterprises were inserted in the Negro World.

Just then the inquiries from abroad began to pour in upon Mr. Briggs and he was forced to act. As a result of the investigation conducted by Mr. Briggs, who is responsible for first arousing interest in Africa, The Emancipator definitely states with appreciation of all that is involved that the registered owner of The S. S. Yarmouth up to th[e] 15th of March was not the Black Star Line, but the North American Shipping Corporation, 35 Bedford Row, Halifax, N.S.[1] To verify this a[s]tounding discovery a representative of The Emancipator visited the office of the British Consulate at

Whitehall street, and was shown the latest official record as to the present ownership of the S. S. Yarmouth. As the ship sails under the British flag it must have its clearance papers vised by the British Consul, who keeps a complete and up-to-date record of the facts pertaining to ownership of all vessels flying under that flag. The records showed the North American Shipping Corporation, Ltd., as the owner of the Yarmouth. To make assurance doubly sure, the Marine Registry was next examined and the records there confirmed the fact that the Black Star Liner Yarmouth is not owned by the corporation as advertised.

Printed in the *New York News*, 25 March 1920.

1. The North American Shipping Corp. was a Canadian subsidiary of Harriss, Magill & Co. To facilitate purchase of the *Yarmouth*, Garvey formed the Black Star Line of Canada, Ltd., capitalized at $1 million. However, the Canadian Department of Marine refused to register the bill of sale to the *Yarmouth* when the BSL of Canada could not satisfy the department as to its financial condition. The BSL of Canada, therefore, operated the *Yarmouth* under a charter agreement with the North American Steamship Line.

Report by Special Agent WW

New York March 26, 1920

In re: Negro Activities

March 16, 1920

. . . Nothing of interest at Liberty Hall. I was introduced to Rev. Eason, by his brother who was a member of the 367th Infantry of the 92nd Division; who I met in France. Rev. Eason is one of Garvey[']s best m[e]n and is extremely radical and also is known as an acknowledged hater of White People.

March 17, 1920

. . . The colored people of Upper B'klyn., are trying to obtain a charter from the Universal Negro Improvement association for the purpose of starting an or[g]anization in this section of B'klyn. I understand that my name has been suggested as one of the principals in the formation of this branch. I wrote the letter for the secretary, to Marcus Garvey for a charter for the organization. . . .

March 20, 1920

. . . Preparing for a big night at Liberty Hall tomorrow night as Marcus Garvey is to speak on an important topic.

WW

[*Handwritten endorsement*] IWW
[*Stamped endorsements*] NOTED W.W.G. Noted F.D.W.

DNA, RG 65, file OG 258421. TD.

(*Source*: DLC, Miscellaneous Collection of Radical Newspapers and Periodicals).

Analysis of the Black Star Line by Anselmo R. Jackson

[The *Emancipator*, 27 March 1920]

Human beings, as a general rule, are always fascinated by extraordinary projects and unusual performances. Perhaps, this fact serves to explain and justify the intense interest and questioning curiosity which are almost universally manifested in the undertaking of the Black Star Line Steamship Co., Inc. This organization, which is composed entirely of Negroes, was originally capitalized at $500,000 and since raised to ten million dollars, for plans to establish a line of steamships to be owned, managed and controlled as well as manned and offered [*officered*?] by Negroes. The ships, the first of which to be acquired is the Yarmouth which is to be rechristened the Frederick Douglass in honor of the illustrious Negro orator and statesman, are intended to be carriers of Negro merchandise and Negro passengers to and from Africa, the West Indies and North and South America.

The Yarmouth, a 1300 ton boat made its first trip, flying the black, green and red flag of the Black Star Line Company, on Sunday, November 23rd, at 4:10 P.M., bound for Cuba, under the Captaincy of a British-licensed Negro Master Mariner, Captain Joshua Cockburn.

The Black Star Line movement is, in fact, an outgrowth of the Universal Negro Improvement Association and African Communities League. This twin organization was formed several years ago in Jamaica British West Indies by Marcus Garvey who has been its President and General Organizer at various times since its formation. There Garvey, it has been declared by Jamaicans, received considerable assistance from the very element of Jamaicans he would have been forced to oppose had he attempted to ameliorate the social, political and economic conditions of the most unfortunate of the natives. He was then in every sense of the wo[rd] a loyalist. He cautiously refrained from overtly saying or doing anything which could have been calculated as opposition to the dominant whites and the British Government in Jamaica. Garvey was presumably mindful of the repressive methods of England in dealing with anti-government agitators in India and Ireland and of the experiences of a Negro barrister, S. A. Gilbert Cox, a contemporary nationalistic political agitator who had incurred the wrath and antagonism of the British officials in Jamaica by advocating Jamaica for the Jamaicans.

Garvey's organization in Jamaica, however, did not meet with any notable success. It appears that he could not say or do the things, which would have then more greatly vitalized his organization unless he precipitated his own self-destruction. The only policy he could have safely pursued was one of a conservative nature. And this he did.

About three years ago the Hon. Marcus Garvey (as he styles himself) arrived in New York from Jamaica the land of his nativity. He circularized the Negro Section of Harlem to the effect that "Professor" Garvey, "The World-Famed Orator" would make his first public appearance in New York City at St. Mark's Hall, 55 West 138th Street. At this lecture, Garvey completely lost his nerve and was obviously self-cons[c]ious. So serious was his attack of stage-fright, that he fell off the stage, much to the amazement of the audience. The poor showing of the Jamaican agitator did not greatly handicap him as on his second public appearance in New York City, a year later after he had toured the country seeking funds for a proposed Tuskegee Institute in [J]amaica, he made a very favorable impression.

It cannot be denied that the arrival of the now President of the Black Star Line was timely. Outdoors and indoors, Hubert Harrison was preaching an advanced type of radicalism with a view to impressing race-consciousness and effecting racial solidarity among Negroes. The followers of Harrison, responding to his demand that a New Negro Manhood movement among Negroes be organized, formed the Liberty League to [of?] Negro-Americans, a short while prior to Garvey's arrival. The very atmosphe[re] was charged with Harrison's propaganda; men and women of color thruout the United States and the West Indies donated their dollars and pledged their support to Harrison as they became members of the Liberty League.

Garvey publicly eulogized Harrison, joined the Liberty League and took a keen interest in its affairs. Harrison blundered fatally. His errors were so evident that his followers could not but observe them, so costly that interest in the Liberty League waned and Harrison's deserters soon became enthusiastic admirers of Garvey, and accordingly joined the New York branch of the Universal Negro Improvement Association and African Communities League which Garvey, in the meantime, had formed. His failure and the dissatisfaction of his followers notwithstanding[,] Harrison rendered memorable educational and constructive community service to the Negroes of Harlem. It may be truly said that he was the forerunner of Garvey and contributed largely to the success of the latter by preparing the minds of Negroes through his lectures, thereby moulding and developing a new temper among Negroes which undoubtedly made the task of the Jamaican much easier than it otherwise would have been. In justice to both and with equal truth, it may be declared that the success of Garvey was built on the ruins of Harrison's failure. The popularity of the former increased immeasurably, so much so that proportionately as he became a potent factor, his predecessor became a negligible unit.

[The *Emancipator*, 3 April 1920]

As Garvey's organization became more and more prominent, Negroes stopped regarding him as an object of curiosity and began admiring, complimenting and idolizing him. He made powerful and passionate appeals in [*to*?] the race pride and race consciousness of Negroes and received responses in the nature of assurances of allegiance and assistance from Africa, the West Indies, South America and almost every important city in the United States.

It was quite natural that not only men and women with a creditable record of achievement and unimpeachable integrity would be attracted to Garvey's movement, but that professional politicians and all kinds of unprincipled opportunists in quest of easy berths and financially advantageous positions would also join his organization. The latter aroused Garvey's anger and earned his vigorous and repressive antagonism. This element unintentionally gave him a pretext for becoming despotic since his arbitrary attitude could have easily been excused as being absolutely essential to protect the association from members with selfish and sinister purposes.

So far as Negroes are concerned Garvey's projects are as ambitious as his propaganda is all-embracing. His aims may be briefly summarized as follows:

1. To bring about a better understanding and a more sincere spirit of effective co-operation among the peoples of African origin by impressing their community of interests and establishing closer contact among them.

2. To make Negroes more self-respecting, more self-reliant and economically independent.

3. To voice the yearnings of the Africans for liberty and to arrive with inexorable determination until the great dream of "Africa for the Africans" shall have been made a living reality.

Prior to the Black Star Line, Garvey started the publication of the Negro World, the official organ of the Universal Negro Improvement Association and African Communities League. This periodical is a weekly and has been published more than a year. During that period it has been edited by Mr. W. A. Domingo from its first issue until eleven months thereafter when he was succeeded by the Rev. W. H. Ferris, its present editor. Garvey next announced his intention of establishing a chain of restaurants, dry goods and grocery stores to be owned by his organization and to be operated by its members on the membership-co-operative mutual profit-sharing basis. Through the issuance of bonds, some of which he has since redeemed, he collected a considerable sum of money but later learned that he could not execute his plans as formulated on a loose cooperative system and was forced to have both of his organizations legally incorporated. So far, only one restaurant, located at 56 West 135th Street, has been started under a business cooperation [*corporation?*]. The project of the Black Star Line has seemingly delayed the execution of his plans for the operation of cooperate stores. Despite this fact he has organized a $1,000,000 corporation known as the Negro Factories Corp., Inc.

Garvey who has at times unquestionably been "The man of the hour" among Negroes, like all human beings, has many peculiarities. Probably one may gain a fair idea of the man and his methods by taking into account the fact that his head has the shape of the German type and that his temperament and his racial philosophy are not, [*words mutilated*] unlike the temperam[ent] [*or the?*] racial philosophy of Germans. He has neither patience with, nor pity for, failures. He is always feverishly interested in results and is totally disinterested in methods. So over-anxious is he over ultimate results, that he frequently interferes prematurely and unnecessarily assists in the performance of duties allot[t]ed to others. The timeliness of his obtrusion, he justifies by alluding to the alleged disappointing failure of subordinate officials whom he has not directly supervised.

About the beginning of the Fall of 1918, Captain Joshua Cockburn arrived in the city. He was then employed by the Elder Dempster S. S. Co., a Liverpool–West Africa Line, and was on a three months vacation. Captain Cockburn took advantage of the leave granted him and stopped in New York on his way to Nassau, Bahamas, to visit his parents whom he had not seen in 23 years. He then announced that he had brought a message of hope from Africa, referred to that continent as the economic salvation of Negroes everywhere and was reported as having said that he had been commissioned by some wealthy Africans to purchase schooners for trading purposes. It was his appointment under the British crown as master of the S. S. Trojan and S. S. Baman in Nigeria, West Africa and his numerous sailings to the different ports of Africa that probably gave him the opportunity to meet and form the friendship of Africans of good financial standings. He and Mrs Cockburn left for overseas quite hurriedly and did not return to New York until late in the Spring of last year.

Despite his reported authorization to purchase ships for trading purposes, which was published in a Negro Magazine on November 1[5]th, 1918, and Garvey's plan to launch the Black Star Line, announced nearly six months later, it has been declared that it was not before his return to New York from visiting his parents that Captain Cockburn and Garvey were introduced.

The sign of interrogation and the mark of exclamation were alternately visible on the face of nearly every one of Garvey's followers when their leader announced the Black Star Line project. They cheered outwardly, perhaps from sheer force of habit, but during the intervals of speechmaking, and after the meeting was over, they openly indulged in debates as they conceived the magnitude of the task which was proposed. Those Garveyites whose eyes were befogged or who were not sufficiently farsighted to catch a faint glimpse of Garvey's vision, nevertheless, attended the meetings with accustomed regularity, cheered just as lustily, applauded thunderously and otherwise gave unmistakable signs of consistent and continued allegience.

[The *Emancipator*, 10 April 1920]

Most of the Negroes who were not followers of Garvey on first hearing about the Black Star Line announcement, openly sneered, boldly predicted the failure of the movement and early began speculating as to the damaging extent of what they, then, believed to be the certain consequent psychological and financial depression of the predicted failure of the Bla[ck] Star Line.

This outside element, which would have nothing to do with Garvey or his movement, declared him to be an impractical idealist. They contended that Negroes have very little confidence in each other, and that even that little confidence Garvey would surely remove by the failure of his movement. Still there were others who were plainly, but silently indifferent. Indeed, some of those who were unduly talkative were so fervid and persistent as to create the impression that they had some investment scheme to present to the public and that Garvey by the Black Star Line project had forever deprived them of the opportunity to convince the gullible.

Friends and foes as well as those who were plainly indifferentists when the agitation of Garvey began to produce promising results enquired how adequate money to obtain the ships would be secured; where capable officers and experienced men would be found; how Negro merchants in the United States, the West Indies and Africa, who for years have been importing and exporting merchandi[s]e which has been carried by the ships of other steamship companies, now plying between certain ports in the United States, Africa and the West Indies, would be induced to use the Black Star Line ships as carriers. These and other more difficult questions were addressed to the Garvey enthusiasts. They had their expected effect on a proportionately small number, however, as the great majority of friendly skeptics elected to indulge in watchful waiting rather than desert their beloved leader.

It has never been ascertained whether or not Garvey had a long prearranged plan of well-timed appearance for Captain Cockburn, or if Garvey sent out an S.O.S. which reached the Captain and he responded and hastened to Garvey's rescue; but it is certain that when the movement was, perhaps, in its most critical stage, apparently due to the dubious minority within and nothing, save Garvey's emotional oratory, to inspire the members of the organization, Captain Cockburn, resplendent in his gold-braided English Captain's uniform, appeared and addressed the organization and assured the members that he would furnish the officers and the men for the ships and vouched for the cooperative attitude of some of his wealthy and influential African friends.

The very presence of the master mariner imparted a spirit of buoyancy which was naturally intensified by his heartening words of assurance. He gave the members fresh courage and greater determination to work for the success of the Black Star Line. Even those members whose minds' eyes could not look beyond the mist of uncertainty which enshrouded this most significant undertaking of Negroes, on seeing and hearing Captain Cockburn, seemed to be endowed with a strange power of sight. As a result the entire organization functioned as one individual. Each member acted as though he or she realized that success is merely a matter of enthusiasm and efficient effort and believed that the success of the Black Star Line was solely dependent upon him or her.

Negroes everywhere seemed to be fired with the imagination of what the realization of Garvey's dreams would mean. They accordingly rallied to the

West Indian leader and gave positive and eloquent evidence of sincere interest. This spirit, through the signed front page articles of Garvey and the reports of the Sunday night meetings published in the Negro World, quickly spread to other Negro sections, notably Panama and Virginia. Even now, although the Frederick Douglass has been acquired, the sentiment of the different groups of Negroes regarding the object of Garvey and his followers may b[e] [ac]urately summarized as (1) Enthusiastic (2) Apathetic and (3) Pessimistic. The first represents the Garveyites. The second classifies those who are neither exponents nor opponents of the movement, those who claim that they have not had reliable information to enable them to form an intel[l]igent and impartial opinion and who, in the absence of light, refuse to substitute fervor for facts and quite reasonably refrain from wasting their energies generating heat in disputes over the success or failure of the Black Star Line. The third division consists of those who believe that the undertaking is bound to fail; those who are anti-Garveyites, those who hate the man, hate everything he attempts to do and, therefore, are too prejudiced to judge and determine the value of his efforts with any degree of impartiality or intelligence.

Should the affairs of the Black Star Line ever reach the stage where its promoters find themselves in desperate need of operating expenses, and the Garveyites' determined attitude of self sacrificing devotion is not modified, certain pawn-brokers and second-hand furniture dealers will be kept exceedingly busy as there will surely be an incalculable number of wrecked homes among Negroes in Harlem and other Negro communities where the adherents of Garvey reside.

[The *Emancipator*, 17 April 1920]

Their faith in Garvey and the Black Star Line is somewhat similar to one's faith in religious doctrines in that it has been acquired and maintained by unreasoning belief rather than by enlightened examination of facts and subsequent logical deductions. The followers of Garvey believe that to be loyal to Garvey is to be loyal to their race. What they call race loyalty, other Negroes call folly, fanaticism and race frenzy. As to which viewpoint is proper can only be justly determined by the outcome of Garvey's efforts.

It is surprisingly strange that in spite of the blatancy of Garvey's critics and the movement's calamity-howlers that only one of these dared to challenge him to a public debate. The result of this dispute, which was a street corner affair, makes it impossible to state, with any degree of certainty, whether the challenger was actuated by commendable courage or extraordinary foolhardiness. His other critics, knowing the temper of the followers of his organization and realizing that there are no limits to which they would not go for Garvey, are more judicious as to when, where and how they express their criticisms. Then, too, there is that element which is deterred from expressing its antagonism by the economic urge. Even the glib-tongued, catch-penny notoriety-seekers, noted for their recklessness, have been unusually cautious, probably fearing that their attacks on Garvey and the Black Star Line would be more personally costly than beneficial. One of the related pregnant features about this venture is the change of heart of some of its supposedly irreconcilable opponents. Many of these condemned the Black Star Line movement in its earlier stages pitilessly, and prematurely and now that they believe the chances of its failure have been considerably minimized, they have joined the movement, hoping to share its success, rather than to be outside the organization disappointed and disgruntled if it does succeed.

Intelligent well wishers of Garvey have been frankly disappointed with his evasive silence regarding certain pertinent phases of the affairs of the Black Star Line. They believe that if he would be candidly outspoken as to his plans for the operation of the ships and the means whereby the hopes to overcome the inevitable obstacles which will arise in the cour[se] of the fulfilment of his programme that the movement would secure the active and pecuniary support of friendly critics and sympathetic would-be investors.

Negroes with good memories and old note books, as well as those who base their judgment on intelligent premises and are accustomed to weigh facts dispassionately and calculate figures accurately, have long been asking how Garvey intends to s[u]ccessfully compete with well-established, largely capitalized steamship companies whose ships ply between the same ports and are of the identical character as the Black Star Line ships. They concede that if the Black Star Line Co. should alter its published policy to do business on the large scale on which first-class steamship companies operate and should confine its operations to tramp-service that it will indisputably exist. But they declare, citing precedents, fundamentals and authorities in support of their argument, that the very moment the Negro undertaking offers considerable competition to existing companies, that very moment there will be a con-certed attempt to drive it off the seas. They point to the expressed and implied intent to rival which is contained in Garvey's announcement that his passenger service rates will be 25 per cent cheaper than the rates of other companies, and assert that the movement is, in reality—if Garvey's schedule has not been changed—the beginning of a back to Africa movement, and that England, France and the other smaller nations interested in Africa will look upon it with disquiet and disfavor. Knowing the truth about England's history and being convinced that it is just as impossible for England to change her temper as it is for the leopard to change its spots, they insistently argue that England particularly, alone or aided, will bring the pressure of power to bear as soon as the back to Africa movement, which is now in its embryonic stage, assumes threatening proportions. In addition, they say that it is an easy matter for the colonial officials of England or any British . . . [*words mutilated*] any pretext or another, to deny clearance papers to a Black Star Line ship. With veiled sarcasm, they further declare that the fact Marcus Garvey prior to his coming to New York at the outbreak of the world war cabled an avowal of his loyalty to the British throne, as a patriotic British Subject, will make little difference as governments have a double standard of valuation and, at [m]ost, their gratitude is short-lived.

This element, constituting those Negroes who sternly and stubbornly refuse to permit their hearts to govern their heads in deliberations on the Black Star Line because it is a racial venture, reminds those who debate with it that the United Fruit Co., will be one of the chief competitors of the Black Star Line Co., and that the former has a reputation for wrecking its rivals and driving them out of business. As though they believe that a bald statement will not suffice, they specify Cuneo Fruit Co.[,] The Jamaica Northside Fruit Growers' Association, Goffe Bros., Lanassa and Goffe and the Camors Mc-Connell Co., as five of the companies which the United Fruit Co., which is controlled by the Rockefeller interests, has crippled. The Atlantic Fruit Co., they aver, could only survive subsequently, despite the great banking interests back of it, by establishing a working agreement with the United Fruit Co., which is capitalized at $75,000,000 and has enormous and extensive holdings embracing aggregately more than one and a quarter million acres of land, railroads, telephone systems, hotels and factories in Jamaica, Cuba, Costa Rica, Guatemala, Bocas del Toro, Republic de Panama, and other places in the West Indies and Central America in which, they insist, it also exerts powerful political influence to promote its welfare. Moreover, they affirm that the United Fruit Co., controls Elders and Fyffe Steamship Co. and has other subsidiary shipping lines which will most assuredly make its competition keener and more difficult to overcome.

[The *Emancipator*, 24 April 1920]

The Garveyites meet all arguments of cold economics with manifestations of consistent emotion; all statements of facts they match with expressions of super-heated sentiments. They are so sure of the success of the Black Star Line and the redemption of Africa that they refuse to reason as to the possible failure of either effort. To them the achievement of both objects is merely a matter of time, it is inevitable.

On account of their unreasoning and unreasonable attitude of assumption, it is just as easy to debate with the Garveyites as it would be to debate with lunatics who were obsessed with contrary notions and incredible illusions. Most assuredly neither the latter nor the former could be convinced against their will. The Garveyites' manifestations of the blind loyalty are merely expressions of the peculiar psychology which their idol has undeniably developed among them. Garvey's responsibility for the unreasoning and intensely racial state of his followers' minds may be attested by the fact that the former has answered those critics, who have predicted that the competition of the United Fruit Co. will destroy the Black Star Line by passionately narrating how hundreds of black employees of the United Fruit Co. contracted malaria in the swamps of Guatemala and died of that disease subsequently through their faithfulness in contributing by their labor as well as their lives to a successful growth and development of the Rockefeller-controlled company. Drawing the racially-inspiring inference that if Negroes everywhere would serve and sacrifice for the Black Star Line as Negroes of the British West Indies who were imported to Guatemala as laborers served and sacrificed for the United Fruit Co., that the former would become as signal a success as the latter, the Jamaica agitator, with characteristic emotion thus replied to one element of his critics. It is certainly clear that the thousands of Negroes who have heard the speeches or read the writings of President Garvey of the Black Star Line have caught his spirit and are, in truth, reflecting mirrors of his mind. And this, perhaps, accounts for their queer obsessions and their curious monstrosities.

Garvey who is 32 years of age has had a very interesting career. While he has not been what may be properly termed a globe-trotter, he has nevertheless been considerably nomadic as he has travelled to London and nearly every one of the prominent cities of Central America and the United States.

Some years ago, there was a great printers' strike in Jamaica in which Garvey, who is a printer by trade, played a very prominent role. Although the striking printers lost, Garvey emerged from the strike as a leader and was recognized as such by the native folk of Jamaica, where he afterwards, published a weekly newspaper called The Watchman, the publication of which was discontinued after its third issue.

(To be continued)[1]

Printed in the *Emancipator*, 27 March, 3 April, 10 April, 17 April, and 24 April 1920.

1. No additional issues of the *Emancipator* have survived.

George Wells Parker to John E. Bruce

Omaha, Nebraska March 30, 1920

. . . Your letters came to me in good time and were like those of old times, and I read them with a great deal of pleasure. I thank you a thousand times for the information concerning Mr. Garvey. I try to be of an open mind, but the conflicting stories reaching here through the Monitor, the Emancipator, and the Defender, as well as through the Crusader, make a man wonder what is the matter.

The evidence you give me of what Mr. Garvey has done, however, is sufficient answer as to his honesty and earnestness, and that is what I wanted to do. I am satisfied with what you have given me, and I will hereafter be a Garvey booster. He is a man who does things, and is the kind of man the Negro race needs at this time.

GEORGE WELLS PARKER[1]
Author—The Children of the Sun

NN-Sc, JEB. TL (transcript).

1. George Wells Parker (1882–1931) was a medical student from Omaha, Neb., who was one of the cofounders (the others were John E. Bruce and Rev. John Albert Williams) of the Hamitic League of the World.

Report by Special Agent WW

New York April 3, 1920

In re: *Negro Activities.*

March 24, 1920

. . . Visited a concert at Liberty Hall in the evening. Nothing of interest to report, other than Rev. Eason stated that they were going to make an example of the newspapers opposing the Association.

March 26, 1920

Took up most of the day going over the subscription list of the Crusader, arranging many new subscribers in alphabetical order on the list.[1] Briggs claims that Garvey is the hir[e]ling of som[e] white men and that he is not over scrupulous as to what means he uses to obtain money from the members of his race. He admitted that he had formerly had a great respect for Garvey, but he has lost a great deal of his appreciation of his qualities as he does not think that he is dealing fair with his people. He would not follow up these remarks, but left me bubbling over with curiosity[.] He left the office with a smile of appreciation at my appearance of curiosity and anxiety to hear more. Briggs appears to be a man of m[y]stery.

March 27, 1920

Spent most of the day reading over the Negro newspapers and noted with interest the attack upon the Black Star Line Steamship Co. The New York News and the Emancipator stren[u]ously denounces this company and declare that the steamship Yarmouth, which is supposed to be owned by this company is owned by a company known as The North American Steamship Corporation which is a white concern. I can readily understand why Briggs has lost faith in Mr. Garvey as he is the one responsible for the exposure, as it appeared in the Emancipator.

Attended the meeting at Liberty Hall in the evening, which was largely attended. Mr. Johnson of the B[la]ck Star Line assured the people that Mr.

Garvey would explain everything to their satisfaction tomorrow evening [a]t the meeting at Liberty Hall.

He merely stated that the attack upon Mr. Garvey was made through jealousy and for the purpose of testing the strength of faith in the New Negro toward their brother and leader. Mr. Garvey requested him to thank them, as they had stood the test and had proved that the New Negro was a sticker to the end. That not a single Negro had visited the Universal Negro [I]mprovement Association Hdqrs., which view of verifying this slanderous publication brought before the public by the Emancipator. (Cheers)

March 28, 1920

Attended the meeting of the Universal Negro Improvement Association and African Communities League at Libert[y] Hall in the evening. The hall was crowded to its utter capacity. To be exact I have never seen the attendance at Liberty Hall that was there last evening.

The Hon. Marcus Garvey entered the Hall about 8:15 PM, and was greeted by applause by the audience altho a few of these present hissed. The hissing was minoritive.

After a selection by the band, a couple of recitations, a selection by the choir, and a flute solo; Mr. Rudolph Smith was introduced to the audience and spoke ten minutes on the integrity of Mr. Garvey and the confidence of the success of the Black Star Line and its associative organizations.

The next speaker was a Mr. Johnson, an agent of the Black Star Line Steamship Corporation. He spoke about the attack of the Socialists upon the Association. He stated that the editor of the Emancipator was a man of intelligence and was only attacking Mr. Garvey through the spirit of jealousy. He stated th[at] he had been confronted by a person of intelligence and prominence in that community and had been warned that the editor of the Emancipator and its staff was made up of men of unquestionable intelligence and could do much to harm the progress of the Universal Negro Improvement Ass[n]., and its associative enterprises. He told them that the Universal Negro Improvement Assn., had two of the most reno[w]ned orators, in the world in the persons of Mr. Garvey and Rev. Eason.

He also stated that they had a man who knew every principle of Socialism in the person of Mr. Harris[on] of the Negro World.[2] He also stated that the people had absolute confidence in the integrity of Mr. Garvey and that nothing that could be said could change their attitude of confidence and appreciation of his wonderful work.

Mr. Ferris of the Negro World was the next speaker, who spoke the [*ten?*] minutes on the necessity of establishing commercial enterprises of our own so that we would be able to prevent insults and discrimination.

Rev. Eason was the next speaker of the evening, who spoke upon the coming convention. He encouraged the people to rally stronger to the support of the Association now that it was the object of attack by the destructive element of the Negroes and by the White People who were being robbed of their opportunity of swindling the Negroes of their hard earned wages by various crooked schemes. He emphasized the fact that the Negroes did not have confidence enough in themselves and it was through this lack of confidence they refused to invest their money in enterprises controled by members of their race. He ended by saying that if the Negro expected to accomplish anything, he should not wait for the white man to lead him, but should get ou[t] and pave his own way.

The last speaker of the evening was the Hon. Marcus Garvey President General of the Universal Negro Improvement Assn., Black Star Line, Negroes Factories Corporation etc.

He began his remarks by stating that he was not goin[g] to speak upon the subject scheduled for the evening, but was going to speak about the Enemies of his organizations. He said that in the very beginning he felt that no progressive institution was ever organized without a certain amount of sacrifice and this sacrifice was ofttimes made by bloodshed. He stated that he had been surprised that it had not come before now; but he felt that the hour for supreme sacrifi[ce] had arrived and that he was willing to give his life, for the cause of his race and people in their struggle to get their just cons[i]deration and for the redemption of Africa. He claimed tha[t] as things were really at a crucial pitch at this present time that it was the duty of every member of the race to stand by ready to sacrifice all for the preservation of their institutions and for the destruction of their enemies. He advised the people to get together and boycott the Emancipator and drive the publication to the wall.

Mr. Garvey explained to the people that the Yarmouth [w]as owned by the North American Steamship Co., which was owned by the Black Star Line Steamship Co.[3] He stated that through his inability to obtain a crew from captain to stoker of American Negroes[,] he had to obtain a crew of men who were subjects of Great Britain thus making it necessary to launch their boat under the English Flag.[4] As a ship bearing the English Flag and carrying an English crew could not sustain a corporation, established under the name of the North American Steamship Company, [t]he name of the Black Star Line was used in its stead.

Mr. Garvey concluded by saying that in the next three months blood was going to be spilt and that some of those who were present would be dead; as he was confident that these people were determined to destroy every obstacle that in any way was detrimental to their progress.

March 29, 1920

. . . Marcus Garvey held a monster concert and meeting at Liberty Hall in the evening. Other than a splendid musical entertainment and singing by Madame H[ou]ston, there was very little speaking. Marcus Garvey told the people of the atte[mpted] denounce[ment] by their enemies in reference to the ownership of the Yarmouth. He claimed that the editor of the Emancipator was formerly connected with the Black Star Line Corporation and through some obstinate opposition had been released from their employment. He claimed that the attack upon the Black Star Line was brought about by jealousy and for the purpose of trying to destroy the confidence of the race in one another. He told the people that the Black Star Line not only owned the Yarmouth, but was also going to launch an excursion boat,[5] which would sail up the Hudson River and would dock at 135th St., also in a few weeks the Phyliss Wheatley would also be in the waters flying the red, black and green. (the colors of the Line).

March 30, 1920

Briggs is offering the sum of $500.00 for the proof that the Yarmouth is owned by the Black Star Line Steamship Co. He claims that the North American Steamship Corporation, which ow[n]s the steamship Yarmouth, has a capitalization of $100,000,000.

Garvey has threatened to put the Emancipator and the Crusader out of existence but Briggs says that before many weeks have elapsed Garvey will be the one who will be absent.

Very few at Liberty Hall in the evening. Dr. Mickens advised the people to promote their own enterprises and pointed out how the white people did not want us to visit their places of social recreation and stated that the colored people should have the pride to establish their own business and social enterprises.

March 31, 1920

. . . Briggs is having some circulars made for the purpose of advertising the $500. reward for the proof that the Steamship Yarmouth is owned by the Black Star Line.

WW

[*Endorsement*] Noted F.D.W.

DNA, RG 65, file OG 258421. TD. Stamped endorsement.

1. Agent WW, as well as others, infiltrated the *Crusader*'s operations as part of the Bureau of Investigation's surveillance of black radical organizations. WW generally performed clerical duties and aided in distributing the *Crusader*. In 1923 another Bureau of Investigation agent, Earl E. Titus, wrote for the Crusader News Service (DJ-FBI, 61-1122-10).
2. Hubert Harrison was a well-known socialist, although he officially left the party in 1913.
3. Either a garbled report of Garvey's statement or a misleading statement on Garvey's part.
4. At least thirty-one members of the *Yarmouth*'s crew were British subjects (DNA, RG 85, file T-715).
5. The Black Star Line paid $35,000 for the S. S. *Shadyside*, a vessel of 444 gross tons which had been built in 1873. The down payment was $10,000, with the remainder to be paid in monthly installments of $2,000. The *Shadyside* was intended to serve as an excursion boat for trips along the Hudson River, but after a summer of service in 1920, the *Shadyside* proved unprofitable. Finally, after incurring $11,000 in operating losses, the *Shadyside* was retired by the Black Star Line and docked at Fort Lee, N.J. The vessel sank that winter during an ice storm (E. David Cronon, *Black Moses*, p. 85).

Article in the *Emancipator*

[3 April 1920]

Basing his complaint upon the article entitled "Black Star Line Exposed," and "Investo[r]s Demand Statement," Mr. Marcus Garvey, D[.] S. O. E., (Distinguished Service Order of Ethiopia), editor of the Negro World, official of the Negro F[ac]tories Corporation, acting presid[ent] [gene]ral of the U.N.I.A. . . . [*words mutilated*] Communities League, which [*controls the?*] restaurant and publishes the [Neg]ro World, representing the steamship corporation of which he is president, has sued the editor of The Emancipator, W. A. Domingo, and the New Negro Publishing Co. for the modest sum of $400,000.[1]

The lawyer representing the Black Star Line which asserts in the 4th paragraph of the complaint that "practically all of its stockholders and customers are Negroes and the business conducted by it is, and is contemplated to be principally with Negroes[,]" is Mr. Gerald Rosenheim of 42 Broadway.

Printed in the *Emancipator*, 3 April 1920. Original headline omitted.

1. Gerald Rosenheim, as attorney for the BSL, filed a damage suit in the New York County Supreme Court on 25 March 1920, on behalf of the Black Star Line, against the New Negro Publishing Co. and "William" A. Domingo. The suit requested $200,000 in damages from the New Negro Publishing Co. and an equal amount from Domingo (NNHR, case no. 8242).

Death Certificate of Marcus Garvey, Sr. [1]

Saint Ann's Bay Ninth April 1920

Death in the District of *Saint Ann's Bay*. Parish of *Saint Ann*

Date and Place of Death.	Name and Surname.	Sex.	Condition.	Age last Birthday.	Rank, Profession or Occupation.	Certified cause of Death and duration of Illness.	Signature, Qualification and Residence of Informant.	When Registered.
Ninth April 1920. Musgrave Street Saint Ann's Bay Saint Ann	*Marcus Garvey*	*Male*	*Widower.*	*Eighty three years*	*Mason*	*Senile Debility*	*Adassa Harvey Grand-daughter Present at the Death Main Street Saint Ann's Bay Saint Ann*	*Twenty ninth April 1920*

Signed by the said *Adassa Harvey* in presence of *Lula E Hay* Registrar of Births and Deaths *Saint Ann's Bay* District, Parish of *Saint Ann*.

IRO. Printed form with handwritten insertions.

1. Garvey's relationship with his father was strained from his youth until his father's death. Amy Ashwood Garvey recalled an incident from Garvey's youth in Jamaica:

> The police brought the Garvey gang before the Juvenile Court. The charge of wilful destruction was brought against them. They were found guilty and fined £1 or threatened with imprisonment. Naturally the call fell upon his father to pay the fine. He had already been angered by his son's unruly behavior in the past. . . . In his wrath he wiped his hands of his son and urged the Bench to send his son to a reformatory, but the magistrate would not agree. . . . [Garvey's mother] came forward and promised to pay the fine out of savings she could ill afford. (Amy Ashwood Garvey, *Portrait of a Liberator* [unpublished MS], chap. 3)

Garvey's father was an inmate of the St. Ann's Bay Almshouse until 8 December 1919, when a friend and supporter of Garvey removed him. When the senior Garvey died in April 1920, Marcus Garvey apparently defrayed the funeral expenses. Yet when the inspector of the poor in St. Ann's Bay took out a summons against Garvey to pay for his father's periodic stays in the almshouse between 1916 and 1919, Garvey refused, reportedly claiming that "his father had done nothing for him" (PRO, CO 137/747).

Article by Cyril V. Briggs

[The *Emancipator*, 10 April 1920]

YARMOUTH GRANTED CHANGE OF REGISTRY SINCE OCT. 2, 1919

OFFICIAL DOCUMENT REFUTES CHILDISH AND CLUMSY EXPLANATION OF MARCUS GARVEY

After a fortnight of frothy abuse in an attempt to camouflage the real issue behind a smoke screen of legal suits[1] and "literary" mud-slinging, the issue raised by The Emancipator in its edition of March 27, 1920, stands unchanged and unchallenged.[2] Nor have there been any 'takers' for the $500 offer of The Crusader Magazine.

The President of the Black Star Line and his satellites have seen fit to meet facts with vituperation and abuse. This is a course they will have to follow alone. It is a course perhaps dictated by the weakness of their case and by the advantage which Truth ever holds over Error an advantage none the less overwhelming because of the frantic efforts of prostituted literati[3] to defend their newly-won and so soon-endangered meal ticket. The Emancipator has too many facts in its hands to feel any need for descending to the level and example set by the demoralized Garveyites. And after all the puny bolts of pigmy thunder have been launched at us the facts will shine forth in scintil[l]ant light until "from Greenland's icy mountains to Africa's golden sands" stern-visaged Truth shall stand forth triumphant and undenied by even the most misguided fanatic.

Therefore, leaving to the other side the 'pleasure' of the descent to mud, we will now proceed to the exposition of yet other facts in the case. These facts we will present in "deadly parallel" to the statements and claims of Mr.

Marcus Garvey at Liberty Hall Sunday, March 28. Said Mr. Garvey then (according to the Negro World):

"There is one answer I have to give to The Emancipator or any other paper or company of men who write attacks against the Black Star Line[:] whilst you are writing lies, the Black Star Line is doing things in the interest of the people. Whilst they ask the question, Who owns the Yarmouth? we will next Sunday at 10 o'clock give them another question. We will have them ask who owns the "Shadyside" which will be the first pleasure boat of the Black Star Line (vociferous cheers), which will anchor at 135th Street and North River at 10 o'clock next Sunday, and those of you who desire to go for a trip up the Hudson may book your passage with Mr. Johnson during the week and we will take 500 of you on the first pleasure boat of the Black Star Line. (Cheers[)]"

In this statement, Mr. Garvey brands as a lie the documentary evidence this paper presented as to the true ownership of the S. S. Yarmouth, yet fails to take the obviously necessary and according to him, extremely easy step of proving the Black Star Line ownership of the Yarmouth. He challenges us to find out who owns the "Shadyside" in a speech that carries more than an intimation that that boat is owned by the Black Star Line. Well, we accepted the challenge, and here are the facts as to the true ownership up to April 5, 1920, of the "Shadyside": N. Y. Cat. No. 2058.
Department of Commerce.

Certificate of Ownership
of Vessel.
Collector's Office, Customhouse,

New York, N. Y.,
April 5th, 1920.

I hereby certify that, according to the records of this office, the Steam Paddle called the SHADY SIDE of New York, official number 115180, tonnage 444, gross 329 net, built at Bulls Ferry, N. J., in 1873, was last documented in the office July 28, 1913, and in that document, namely a Permanent Enrollment No. 40, the following were cited as her only owners, viz:* THE NORTH AND EAST RIVER STEAM BOAT COMPANY: and that the following sale of said vessel has since been made:

The North and East River Steam Boat Company to Leon R. Swift, consideration One Dollar, dated March 13, 1918, and recorded March 13, 1918, in Book 137-A, Page 30.

*After names, addresses, and shares of owners are cited add "and that the following sales of said vessel have since been made."

Given under my hand and the seal of this office, this 5th day of April, 1920. Hour and minute, 1.30 p.m. Fee 14, 20c 11-5301. 639366.

> JOHN FARRELL,
> Acting Deputy
> Collector.

Directly under the statement of Mr. Garvey last quoted, Mr. Garvey vouchsafed the following information as to why the Yarmouth was not now under American registry and the Black Star Line in full possession of the ship:

". . . Before we can take over completely the Yarmouth, the owners of the Yarmouth will have to get the consent of the Canadian Government, in that the ship was under Canadian registry and flew the Canadian flag to allow the transfer and sale to an American Corporation."

And what are the facts here? Was the transfer of the S. S. Yarmouth delayed because, as Mr. Garvey intimates, the Canadian Government had not yet given its consent to the transfer? Or were there other reasons? Here are the facts. The following letter from the Canadian Department of Marine tells us that that consent was given as long ago as October 2, 1919:

DEPARTMENT OF MARINE
OTTAWA.

30th March, 1920

Cyril V. Briggs, Esq.,
Editor, "Crusader,"
2299 Seventh Avenue,
New York City, U.S.A.

Sir:—

In reply to your letter of the 25th inst., I have to inform you that by M. & F. Order No. 154 in 1919, dated the 2nd October, 1919, permission was granted the owners of the steamer "Yarmouth" to transfer her registry to the United States Flag and to close her registry at the Port of Yarmouth, N. S. on account thereof.

I am, sir, Your obedient Servant,

> E. HAWKEN,[4]
> For Deputy Minister.

Printed in the *Emancipator*, 10 April 1920. Original headlines omitted.

1. *BSL* v. *New Negro Publishing Co.*, NNHR, case no. 8242, 25 March 1920.

2. In this article the *Emancipator* published a letter written on 8 March 1920 on *Crusader* stationery, signed by Cyril Briggs, and addressed to the registrar of British shipping in Nova Scotia. Briggs requested information on the ownership of the *Yarmouth*. At the bottom of the letter was a handwritten note, allegedly signed by the registrar, stating that the *Yarmouth* was owned by the North American Shipping Corp. The editors of the *Emancipator* invited readers

to address inquiries to the registrar so that they might obtain their own proof. The editors also advised readers to take special note of the date stamped on the letter by the Canadian customs office: 15 March 1920 (*Emancipator*, 27 March 1920).

3. An allusion to Hubert H. Harrison.

4. Harold Edwin Anderson Hawken (1879–1936), assistant deputy minister of marine; in 1935 he became chairman of the National Harbours Commission of Canada (*NYT*, 4 August 1936).

Report by Special Agent WW

New York April [2]2, 1920
April 1, 1920

. . . Attended an entertainment at Liberty Hall in the evening which was largely attended. Prof. Ferris encouraged the Negroes to stick to their own race and not to allow Negroes who were tools of the White People to destroy their faith in one another. His motto was, "Be persistent, with the spirit of [']Never Say Die[']".

. . . April 2, 1920

Made out the mailing list of subscribers of the Crusader during the day. Briggs had several boys on the Avenue, distributing circulars advertising the reward of $500 to anyone that could prove that the steamship Yarmouth belonged to the Black Star Line.

April 3, 1920

. . . Briggs tol[d] me today that he believed that there was a military organization somewhere in Harlem that was preparing to train men, so that when the time came for the Colored man to invade Africa he would be prepared. Altho he says that he does not know who these men are, but that he believes that they are a part of /Marcus/ Garvey[']s bunch. I shall look into this [*matter?*] and give a more favorable report at a later date.

. . . April 9, 1920

. . . Prof. Ferris makes an enthusiastic appeal to the members of the Universal Negro Improvement Association to help the fund for the purpose of enlarging Liberty Hall. He claims that the coming convention means the redemption of the Negro [of] the world. Mr. R. Johnson of the Black Star Line told the people to exert every e[ff]ort to help the corporation in its endeavor to launch the other boats that they are expecting to launch in the near future, as they would need as many [b]oats as they can possibly get, for the purpose of bringing their representatives from the other parts of the world to this city for the greatest convention that the world has ever known.

The people are enthusiastically supporting all the activities of this association despite the fact that there is considerable criti[cis]m. They seem to have gone so far that they dare not go back.

April 10, 1920

Distributed a large number of copies to agents of the Emancipator, in Harlem. The circulation of this publication is exceedingly large, altho it is practically a new publication. The exposure of Mr. Garvey by this newspaper seems to have aided its circulation rather than to have proven detrimental to its progress.

April 11, 1920

Liberty Hall was crowded to its utmost capacity last eveni[ng] Sunday; the feature character of the evening was, Mr. Joseph Douglass,[1] great grandson of the deceased Frederick Douglass. Mr. Douglass was introduced to the people by Rev. Ferris, who spoke in length of the wonderful achievements of the late Frederick Douglass. Mr. Douglass said that he thought that the Universal Negro Improvement Association was the most wonderful and the most progressive organization of Colored People in the world. He claimed that there was no power that could destroy their work. He told the people that they could defy the world to oppose their project and that he was filled with pleasure to note that the people were beginning to have more confidence in one another and we[r]e not led by their envious enemies to lose that confidence that had been so firmly established. He promised every support that was in his power to the association and its associate organizations. The next speaker was a man by the name of Mr. Arthur Schomberg who commended the association upon its wonderful work and stated that he was glad to offer all he possessed even his life if necessary for the success of this undertaking and for the progress of his race. He stated that he was connected with the Cuban Revolutionary Party and was proud to have been associated with the movement that had brought Cuba its independence. He next spoke about the wealth of Africa and showed how the slaves had brought many seeds and other materials from Africa to this and other lands and had transplanted the same which had brought wealth to the respective land in which they were planted. He stated that the Africans would be glad to have the people of their race take up the work of utilizing their products and establishing trade for them with the other countries of the world. He like the others claimed that he was willing to give all for the liberation of Africa and for the cause of the Universal Negro Improvement Association. The next speaker Mr. John Bruce spoke of his great respect and admiration for the Hon. Marcus Garvey and for the institutions organized under his direction. He claimed that he would support Mr. Garvey to be a man of character and wonderful ability. He claimed that Mr. Garvey was the most prominent man that the Race has ever had.

WW

DNA, RG 65, file OG 258421. TD.

1. Joseph Henry Douglass (1871–1935), the grandson of the famed black abolitionist and a nationally known concert violinist, toured the United States annually following several years as an instructor at Howard University (*WWCA*).

Article by Cyril V. Briggs

[The *Emancipator*, 24 April 1920]

Now for the Dirty Work

The Emancipator has interfered with the orderly carrying out of certain schemes in Harlem. One iridescent bubble, in particular, has been pricked before the hour set by his Infinitesimalness. The long-impending crash has been brought nearer by The Emancipator's exposure of the tissue of fluent lies and soft-soap from which the bubble was blown.

The plan was to remove headquarters from America—headquarters include the office, safe and contents, of course—beyond the reach of i[r]ate stock-holders and American District Attorneys who might be interested in investigation and punishment. But the crash impends and the way of escape is blocked. The Grand Villain and his dummy directors, forced to stay and face the music, are resigned to taking their chances with the law—the law often miscarries and a clever lawyer can do wonders. They are, however, in deadly fear of that double-edged weapon of their own creation: fanaticism! In desperation they seek once more to direct it from themselves and to their purpose by openly and secretly ad[v]ocating the assassination of those who are directing upon their questionable transactions the X-Ray of Truth.

In desperation they raise the cry of persecution. To escape the logical consequences of their own crass mismanagement and criminal negligence in handling the funds entrusted to their care they seek to shift the blame for the impending disaster to the shoulders of those who have dared to expose the falsity of their claims and weakness of position. The burglar blaming the robbery on the policeman who makes the arrest! The murderer blaming his crime on the State Prosecutor! Certainly they must have a low opinion of Negro intelligence to conceive that Negroes would fall for this latest strategy of their nimble wits. Of what could exposures have been born had there been nothing to expose? Were their acts above board and in the interests of their stock-holders and the race in general, what would it have mattered that the X-Ray of Truth was turned in their direction? That their transactions were exposed to the light of day?

Printed in the *Emancipator*, 24 April 1920.

Report of Meeting at Liberty Hall

[*New York, 25 April 1920*]

Thousands of men and women representing the New Negro type flocked to Liberty Hall Sunday night, April 25, to listen to the messages of hope, of faith, of inspiration and of courage that were delivered by the various speakers. The feature of the evening was the appearance on the platform of Dr. Jordan, the foreign secretary of the National Baptist denomination,[1] and Mrs. Walters,[2] wife of the late Bishop Walters, both of whom expressed astonishment and gratification over the splendid progress attending the efforts of the Hon. Marcus Garvey through the Universal Negro Improvement Association. Mrs. Walters said that she had "been hearing faint rumors of a certain organization that had its great and its large membership in the islands of the seas, that was being recruited there and which was sweeping up this way like a great tidal wave," and so she had come to see and learn for herself. She, indeed, caught the vision of Negro unity—of Negroes in the harness working for Negro uplift and Negro self-determination—of Negroes serious, determined and unafraid; and, therefore, she could exclaim in heartfelt tribute to the man, his work and the organization: "I came, I saw, I am smitten."

Dr. Jordan, who is by virtue of his position in the great Baptist denom[ination] . . . [*words mutilated*] on Negro and African questions and who has just [re]turned from that great continent where he visited the Nigerias, Sierra Leone and Liberia, brought back a message from the little black republic which he declared, 'is the hope of Africa.' And that message is the words of President King who said, when Dr. Jordan intimated to him that "Mr Garvey and his people say they are going to put their headquarters in Liberia after August."—"Well, let them come!"

HON. MARCUS GARVEY SPEAKS.

Preliminary to the introduction of the various speakers, the President General said:

"We are pleased to welcome you once more to Liberty Hall. Tonight we have a brilliant array of speakers—some you have heard before; others you have not yet heard from the platform of Liberty Hall. But, as you are well aware, the objects of the U.N.I.A. are so broad and far-reaching that there are but very few Negroes of any intelligence who are not with the Universal. Our objects seem to reach out to each and every one of average intelligence within the race—our work has become so big, it is spreading itself so far—that we can hardly believe it ourselves.

8,000 MEMBERS IN BELIZE.

["]I have just received a cable from Belize, British Honduras. You will remember that British Honduras was the first British Colony that moved, through its legislative assembly, to place a ban on the Negro World, to suppress it and prevent its circulation in that country. At that time, we had but a circulation of 200 copies weekly in British Honduras, and a branch of the association was not yet organized there. It is six months now since they suppressed the Negro World in British Honduras, and I have just received a cable from the President of the Belize branch of the association, saying that his branch is now 8003 members strong. (Cheers.) That does not mean to say that that is the number of people who are members of the association in British Honduras. He is only speaking for Belize. I know Belize. I have visited Belize twice, and the Negro population of Belize, I believe, is not more than twelve thousand;[3] and if we can have eight thousand in the U.N.I.A. you might see that we own Belize. (Cheers.)

["]What is true of Belize, British Honduras, is also true of the other British colonies in the West Indies; and I think the British Government made a great mistake when they suppressed the Negro World, because they only opened the eyes of those sleeping West Indian Negroes to a realization that the government was trying to keep something from them, to keep them in darkness about the great progress of Negroes of the outer world. And now they have noted trouble for themselves; and we feel sure that erelong they are going to regret the step they took in suppressing the Negro World in the British Colonies."

MR. GILLIARD SPEAKS.

The Rev. Gilliard, Assistant Treasurer of the Negro Factories Corporation was next introduced and said in part:[4]

["] . . . We are entering upon a manufacturing enterprise that has back of it the good will, the support and the finances of 400,000,000 people. Therefore it is a new thing. It is a new beginning in the field of manufacturing: a new beginning in the field of steamship enterprise.

"And lastly, ladies and gentlemen, we are entering upon a new endeavor to gain our territorial greatness in Africa. We are entering upon a new beginning for the purpose of bringing Africa under our control, for our benefit and the development of its resources and its powers and all that it holds within its bosom. We are entering upon a beginning to bring the twelve million square miles of territory in Africa under our control. And this beginning upon which we are entering holds in it great possibilities if we will only grasp the full significance of them."

DR. JORDAN SPEAKS.

The Rev. Dr. Jordan, secretary of the National Baptist Convention, who has just returned from Africa, was next introduced and spoke in part as follows:

"Mr. President, Ladies and Gentlemen: I do not know that I can make much of a hit. I am glad to see you. I have been away for more than six months. More than two months of that time was spent on the continent of Africa, and a part of the time was also spent trying to get there and another part trying to get back. It is not easy to get to Africa. You have got to go to Europe, you have got to go three thousand miles to Liverpool and as far again to get to West Africa. You have got to go six thousand miles in that way, and that is one reason why I am so much in favor of a ship between here and Africa.

"That little country Liberia is the hope of Africa. If you make Liberia what she ought to be it would be like the ef[fervesc]ing of soda in a glass of water. Whatever goes out from there would spread all over Africa, and all Africa would be blessed if you strike Liberia. Now that is the truth, for the reason that there is no other part of all Africa where the white man welcomes you.

"I want to say to you that the Negroes all over the world are awakening, and yet I must say it is not an easy job that you have got. But when I read your paper this week I said Mr. Garvey and some of those with him have go[t] the situation in hand.

"In Liberia I had a chance to have dinner with President King, I said to him: 'Mr. Garvey and his people say they are going to put their headquarters here after August,['] and he said: 'Well let them come.' (Cheers.) I was trying to see if he had been tainted with the attacks that have been made against him. I find that Liberia stands ready to welcome you."

MRS. WALTERS SPEAKS.

Mrs. Walters, the widow of the late Bishop Walters, was next introduced by Mr. John E. Bruce as "President of the Society for African Redemption, a lady who is greatly interested in the welfare and uplift of Africa," and spoke briefly as follows:

["]My Dear Friends: It was quite a surprise to be called on to address this meeting here tonight. I think I was present at Mr. Garvey's first meeting at Palace Casino several years ago when he made his argument to our people concerning this Universal Negro Improvement Association. I listened to it with profound interest, but said to myself, knowing my people as I do, 'While it seems to be a very good scheme, I doubt very sincerely that it will be feasible or that it can work,' and went away with that conviction. But during the intervening years I have been hearing rumors—faint rumors—of a certain organization that had its great and its large membership in the islands of the seas, that was being recruited there and sweeping this way like a great tidal wave.

"And now that I am in the Bureau of Immigration, it was my good fortune to make out the manifest for your ship Yarmouth. Having heard these faint rumors, I began to watch intensely the course of your organization and of your ships that would come in, because it had been said that the Yarmouth would go out, but she would never return. Not being a member of the organization, but being a member of the race, I was intensely interested in the return of that Yarmouth. I searched the archives and found to my great interest that she had returned.

"When I made out the manifest I found that the captain was one Mr. Cockburn, and so then I began inquiring around through the city of your organization. And I can say tonight, briefly, as has been said in classical times: [']I came, I saw, I am smitten.[']" (Cheers.)

REV. EASON SPEAKS

The Rev. Dr. Eason, chaplain general of the U.N.I.A., was the next speaker introduced and said in part:

"We build the ladder by which we climb. Let us bear that in mind. We are working out our own salvation, materially, morally, intellectually and spiritually. We are building from the ground up, and we are building solidly. We are building securely. We are building both for time and for eternity. Following the lead of our matchless leader we are determined to succeed.

"I see no reason why we should not succeed. We know how many rungs it takes in this ladder. We know the material it takes. We have our own builders and our own men to produce the material. We have money to buy the material. Therefore, we are bound to climb.

"As I look upon this vast assembly tonight, feeling your heart throbs and studying the impressions coming from your very souls, I see that the Negro at last has become a serious human being and it is dangerous for any people, or any individual, to tamper with his aspirations (applause).

"The U.N.I.A. and A.C.L., the Black Star Line and the Negro Factories Corporation and its allied organizations are doing the things for the Negro that he has been waiting for hundreds of years. When Columbus started out to discover America, his own people said [it] [co]uld not be done. When Galileo turned his telescope to the heavens and said the earth was round and revolved on its axis, people said he was crazy. They said that Martin Luther, the leader of the great Reformation, should be killed. And though our intrepid leader, Marcus Garvey, is the head of just ordinary Negroes, we are glad that 3,000,000 have already heard the call and enlisted in the cause and 397,000,000 more are saying, 'Give me the news, and I will fall in line.'" (Cheers[.])

MR. G. S. JOHNSON SPEAKS

Mr. G. S. Johnson, passenger agent of the Black Star Line, was next introduced and said in part:

"A few evenings ago it was my very great pleasure to stand here and make a statement that was very bold. I said that the U.N.I.A. was equal to any organized government. I still hold that opinion. For that reason, we have as our ideal the freedom of Africa; and to achieve that ideal, we have decided among ourselves that we will send certain men abroad to look after the interests of our people. We therefore decided to send certain delegates to Africa. Prior to that, knowing that we had entered into the commercial lists, we decided to send a man of sterling qualities and attainments to another part of the world to fight there the commercial and industrial battles of the race. And it is my great pleasure at this time to say (and in saying it I am perfectly sure I am voicing the sentiments of all the members of this association) that our ambassador to Cuba—Mr. Edward Smith-Green—has won in Cuba new laurels for the U.N.I.A." (Cheers[.])

MR. EDWARD SMITH-GREEN SPEAKS

Mr. Edward Smith-Green, secretary of the Black Star Line and executive secretary of the New York Division of the U.N.I.[A]., was the last speaker introduced, and said, in part:

"Mr. Chairman, Fellow Members of the U.N.I.A.[:] I feel exceedingly pleased—and as a matter of fact, can scarcely express my delight—in being with you in Liberty Hall again. It has been exactly two months since I last made my appearance within this famous building—and indeed it is famous; for the name of Liberty Hall is today not only a by-word in the United States, but, so to speak, throughout the civilized world wherever you may go. I am speaking for those parts which I have touched. I have found men and women whispering the name of Liberty Hall almost with reverence, because of the fact that they are looking forward to this spot and thinking of it as holy ground. Here is where their inspiration focuses. Here is where their hopes are buried; and they are breathing its name, not only with respect, but with solemnity. It is therefore up to us to make good the promise that we made; that we will labor in behalf of freedom's call until the chains of bondage are loosened and every man is free.

"I have always taken advantage of my absence from New York to explain as much as possible the great possibilities of the U.N.I.A., especially where black men are concerned; and I have been able to bring back to you messages of love and hope from our brethren across the seas. And as I have just mentioned, because of the fact that we have promised so much; because of the fact that they are looking forward to the accomplishment of so much by us—it is our duty and obligation to make good, not only by words but by deeds. For upon the things we have promised hinges the redemption of the race all over the civilized world."

Printed in *NW*, 8 May 1920. Original headlines omitted.

1. Rev. Lewis Garnett Jordan.

2. Mrs. Lelia Coleman Walters was the second wife and widow of AME Zion bishop Alexander Walters (1858–1917), pastor of the historic Mother Zion Church in New York City and president of the Pan-African Conference held in London July 1900. She was born in Bardston, Ky. AME Zion historian William Walls commented that she "promoted the work of missions" throughout her husband's district until his death (William J. Walls, *The African Methodist Episcopal Zion Church* [Charlotte, N.C.: AME Zion Publishing House, 1974], p. 406; *DAB*).

3. Belize's total population was approximately sixteen thousand in 1920 (Peter Ashdown, "Marcus Garvey, the UNIA, and the Black Cause in British Honduras, 1914–1949" [unpublished MS]).

4. Because of severe mutilations in the original document, the final portions of Gilliard's speech have been omitted.

Editorial Letter by Marcus Garvey

[[New York, April 27, 1920]]

THIRD SHIP OF THE BLACK STAR LINE TO BE LAUNCHED IN A FEW DAYS

GREAT SUCCESS ATTENDING BIGGEST NEGRO ENTERPRISE—NEGROES WILL SOON OWN FLEET OF THEIR OWN—ALL SHOULD HELP BY BUYING SHARES.

Fellowmen of the Negro Race, Greeting:

To you this day I write, hoping that that noble and chivalrous spirit you have exhibited in the past for the upbuilding of the Universal Negro Improvement Association and its allied corporations, the Black Star Line Steamship Corporation and the Negro Factories Corporation, is still being manifest in the cause that has become so dear to us—the cause of the redemption of Africa. It is for me to say to you that the Universal Negro Improvement Association has become a world power. From the four corners of the world there comes a haughty response of race loyalty, race love and race pride. Negroes everywhere are stretching forth their hands in answer to the call of our association and are . . . [*words mutilated*] that the day is drawing near when Ethiopia will once more take her place among the nations of the world. Why[,] the achievement of the Universal Negro Improvement Association seems a miracle. It is marvelous to contemplate when it is to be remembered that two years ago this association was but a struggling, despised movement, and today it numbers three million active members; that it has branches in every country in the world where Negroes live; that it owns property to the extent of millions at home and abroad; that it has been able to give birth to the first Negro steamship corporation in the world—the Black Star Line Steamship Corporation—that now owns two ships and is about to purchase the third which is to be launched on the 9th of May, when it is to be considered that this very organization has also given birth to the Negro Factories Corporation that is about to open on the 1st of May its first factory in New York, and to operate one of the best equipped and up-to-date laundries operated by any race. All these things to the ordinary optimist would seem a miracle, but all these things have been accomplished through the determination of the men and women who banded themselves together as members of the movement. Wherever there is a will there is a way, and the will of the new Negro is to do or die.

Let us take consolation in the fact that other races, other nations have achieved success by their willingness so to do, and whatsoever others have done we also can do and must do. Looking back upon the days past we see the Negro, a despised, lowly slave; we see him environed by ignorance and superstition after his emancipation, but today we behold him a new man with a new soul, with a new view of the things of life. He has caught a new inspiration, the inspiration that teaches him to go forward, upward and onward, and stopping not, but climbing and climbing until he reaches the pinnacle of human achievement and human glory. May I not, man who has lost courage, inspire you to go forward; may I not, woman who has lost the hope of a brighter future, inspire you also to go forward; may I not say to your children, there is a destiny for each and every one, and that destiny is shaped by your own lives. Let your life be such in the fullness of its action as to rise to the highest pinnacle, and there in all your achievement and in all your glory give a lesson to others, so that they likewise may follow in your footsteps. Now we may repeat the sober, thoughtful and inspiring words of Longfellow:

"Lives of great men all remind us,
    We can make our lives sublime,
And departing, leave behind us
    Footprints in the sands of time.
Footprints, that perhaps another,
    Sailing o'er life's solemn main,
A forlorn and shipwrecked brother
    Seeing, might take heart again."[1]

May we not so live, so work and so achieve as to leave [our] footprints on the sands of time, so that succeeding generations of Negroes may take inspiration and courage from the achievement of their forefathers. Men and women of the Negro race, I say to you, go forward and conquer, go forward and achieve. Unite your racial forces so that the Universal Negro Improvement Association in the next two years may number in [its] ranks twenty millions of black warriors—men and w[omen] ready to die if need be for the redemption of A[frica] ... [*words mutilated*] that calls us, that ... [*words mutilated*][.]

The convention of the Universal Negro Improvement Association is now drawing near. Thousands of delegates from all parts of the world will assemble at Liberty Hall, New York, from the 1st to the 31st of August, there to discuss the great problems that confront the race and to legislate for the race's future government. May I not ask you, scattered members of the association and scattered members of the race, to do your very best now in supporting this great movement so as to make the convention a success? May

I not ask you to send in your donations now to help raise the two million dollars asked for? May I not ask you to help float more ships in the Black Star Line Steamship Corporation so that the red, black and green with the black star in the center will fly over the seven seas? May I not ask you to buy shares in the Negro Factories Corporation and put up more factories in the great industrial centers of the world where our people live and move and long for their own in industry and commerce? I feel sure that every man and woman of the race who reads this message will send in immediately and donate to the convention fund or buy shares in these two corporations. Remember, the Black Star Line Steamship Corporation is not a private company. The ships that are owned by this corporation are the property of the Negro race. The Black Star Line Steamship Corporation stands ready at the beck and call of the Universal Negro Improvement Association. The Universal Negro Improvement Association stands for the economic, industrial, commercial, social and political liberation of the Negro peoples of the world. It stands for a free and redeemed Africa. So as to make the realization of these objects possible, we must control steamships, we must control factories, we must control great plants that will work and operate to the will and dictates of the race and not to be controlled by private enterprises. Hence it is up to every Negro, whether he be American, West Indian or African, to support the Black Star Line Steamship Corporation as a race movement and not as a private enterprise.

Be not misled. Let no man, let no company of men swerve you from performing your duty to this great movement. Now the drive for the third ship of the Black Star Line is started. This ship must be launched on the 9th of May and I am asking that each and everyone who reads my message this week send in and buy more shares in the corporation. Buy five, ten, twenty, thirty, forty, fifty, one hundred or two hundred shares. You can buy them at five dollars each. Write or call at the office of the Black Star Line Steamship Corporation, 54–56 West 135th street, New York, U.S.A. With very best wishes for your success. Yours fraternally,

MARCUS GARVEY

Printed in *NW*, 1 May 1920.

1. The quoted passage is the seventh stanza of Henry Wadsworth Longfellow's poem "A Psalm of Life" (*WBD; BFQ*).

Report of UNIA Meeting

[[Philadelphia, April 29, 1920]]

The Philadelphia Division of the U.N.I.A. assembled fully 6,000 persons in a monster mass meeting and concert at the Academy of Music, Broad and Locust streets, on Monday evening April 26 in a drive for funds with which to launch the third ship of the Black Star Line on May 9th. In the words of President Toote, of the local division, "Philadelphia is slow but sure and will some day overtake New York.["] This gigantic crowd that filled the Academy to its utmost capacity assembled despite two adverse conditions:— First, the inclement weather; and, second, the opposing forces at work to destroy and undermine the movement.

. . . HON. MARCUS GARVEY SPEAKS

Mr. Garvey's appearance was greeted with tumultuous applause which lasted for several minutes. He said:—

"Mr. President and Members of the Philadelphia Division. Ladies and Gentlemen:—I am very sorry that I have to make an apology to you tonight for not having the Yarmouth in port.[1] We in New York were also disappointed a few days ago when we held a great meeting in the Manhattan Casino which was organized as a welcome to Henrietta Vinton Davis, Cyril Henry and Captain Cockburn and his crew. Unfortunately the Yarmouth was delayed in Jamaica for three days, and through that she is running three days late. I received a radio message this morning coming to us through the wireless at Fisherman's Point, saying that the Frederick Douglass was making way for Philadelphia. (Cheers.) She being so far away, could not reach Philadelphia before Wednesday evening or Thursday morning. Having also booked Henrietta Vinton Davis and Captain Cockburn of the Yarmouth to be in Boston for the benefit of the Boston Division of the U.N.I.A., on Friday of this week and having been myself scheduled to speak in Tremont Temple, Boston, in order to have the ship there on Friday morning and make it possible for the Negro citizens of Boston to inspect their own ship as you will do in Philadelphia, I sent another radio to the ship this morning telling her to change her course from Philadelphia to Boston, since they would not reach here before Wednesday or Thursday morning—to Boston so as to reach there by Friday. She will leave Boston on Friday night for Philadelphia, to be here on Monday morning. (Cheers.) The good ship therefore will be in Philadelphia next Monday and she will leave next Monday night for New York to discharge her cargo and her passengers. (Cheers.)

HONDURAS NEGROES ANSWER TO TYRANNY.

"I am indeed pleased to be once more with you in the Academy of Music, I am pleased always to be in Philadelphia, but I do not want you to become too bigoted over your strength because there are dozens of branches of the U.N.I.A. that are twice as strong numerically as you are. I have also a cable in my hand which came to me last night while I was presiding over the meeting at Liberty Hall, from one of the Central American countries— British Honduras. Those of you who have been reading the Negro World will remember that about six months ago the government of British Honduras, through its legislature, voted to suppress the Negro World to prevent it from entering into British Honduras, where it had a circulation of 500 copies weekly.[2] We had not yet organized a branch of the U.N.I.A., but the moment that the government closed down on the Negro World the Negro people in British Honduras—in the city of Belize—organized a branch of the U.N.I.A. (Cheers.)[3]

THE HAND OF DESTINY.

"The time is coming—and it is near—when the world will realize that the slavery that the American Negro and the slavery that the West Indian Negro suffered for over 250 years on the one hand and 230 years on the other hand was not a slavery that was borne for nothing; it was borne for something. That something is going to make itself manifest in this 20th century—so help Almighty God. (Loud cheers.)

"Do you think that my forbears were brought into this Western Hemisphere to suffer and bleed and die for nearly 250 years that I might get the civilization that I have now and the Christianity that I have now—for naught? Somebody is making a mistake today, because I am alive today and you are alive also; and because we are alive—not as savages—not as pagans—not as barbarians, but as civilized Christian men, we say what is good in this present age for other civilized Christian men is also good for us. (Cheers.)

["]If independence of government—if freedom of action and all other things are good for white men and yellow men, they are also good for the black man. If the yellow man has to strike out in the interest of Japan—if the white Briton has to strike out in the interest of things white and things English—if the white French are to strike out in the interest of things French and white, then the hour has struck for black men to strike out in the interest of things black and in the interest of Africa. (Cheers.)

"There is a greater hope for me; there is a greater hope for each and every Negro yet unborn. If we cannot see the entire African race freemen, our children yet unborn will see them.

["]It is incumbent upon us to so work to-day as to create a future for ourselves and for our children. We think of the greatness of America—her power—the great influence she wields in the world to-day. And we go back down the ages to the time when America was inhabited by the Indians; when there were no Philadelphias, no Bostons, no New Yorks, no Chicagos. The Pilgrim Fathers came and worked and laid the foundation for the greatness that we see now—the inspirations that we have now. They laid the foundation of American independence, freedom and greatness. As they have done it for their race, so the Negro of to-day should, as the Pilgrim Fathers, lay the foundation for African freedom and Ethiopian greatness in the future. I am glad that there is a Liberia; I am glad that there is an Abyssinia still free and independent in Africa. The God that we worship and fear has never been asleep, and because He has never been asleep, He has ever been watching over the Negro, and He has brought him out of his trials and tribulations to see the light of a new day—the light of liberty for all people—the light of liberty when Ireland cries out for freedom—when Egypt cries out for freedom—when India cries out for freedom—when the Jew cries out to go back and to be restored to Palestine. We have lived to see the day when Ethiopia is stretching forth her hands unto God. (Cheers.)

["]No power on earth can stop the great onward rush of the U.N.I.A. Two years ago we started in New York with 13 men and women; to-day we are 3,000,000 strong. Two years ago no policeman would pay attention to the U.N.I.A. After two years we are causing the crowned heads to say "Where are these Negroes going?" (Cheers). You the members of the U.N.I.A. are so important to-day that you have some of the greatest white statesmen of the world puzzled now. (Applause). But we do not want to puzzle them; and if they do not want to be puzzled, let them hand down to us the things that are ours; if they do not, then they will remain troubled for sometime.

AN INTERNATIONAL CONGRESS OF NEGROES.

["]And here I want to tell you to bear in mind the great convention of Negroes called to assemble on the first day of August. The great Convention will be opened in New York; delegates will be sent from the far corners of the world to New York to represent our race; they will be coming from Africa, from Central and South America, from the West Indian Islands and from the 48 States of the Union. For the first time in the history of the American Negro he will elect a leader for himself. (Cheers). Since we cannot elect a President we will elect a Negro man, a native born American to lead 15,000,000 Negroes. And on the same day we elect a Negro for the American Negroes, we shall elect a leader for all the Negro peoples of the world; so that when England desires to speak to the Negro, or France or Germany desires to speak to the Negro, they will have to address their diplomatic note to the leader of the Negro peoples of the world, and we will debate the question and give them suitable reply.

["]The black men of the world have fought the last war for others. We are now preparing when the clash of arms is again heard—when the war of the races takes place—as Josephus Daniels told us in New York about 15 months ago—we four hundred million blacks are preparing when that great day arrives, when Europe and Asia will be so engaged, that day will be the day of victory for African liberty and African independence.["] . . .[4]

Printed in *NW*, 8 May 1920. Original headlines omitted.

1. The *Yarmouth* was returning from its second voyage for the Black Star Line. A cargo of whiskey had been taken from New York in February 1920 and delivered to Havana. After repairs were made on the *Yarmouth* in Havana, Garvey ordered Joshua Cockburn to display the ship at several ports in Jamaica, Colon, Panama, and Costa Rica before heading for New York in early May. A coal shortage forced the ship to make a stop in Norfolk, Va. Meanwhile, Garvey had scheduled speeches in Philadelphia and Boston, promising local stockholders and UNIA members that they, too, could inspect the *Yarmouth*. Consequently, the *Yarmouth*,

which was carrying a perishable cargo of coconuts, stopped in Philadelphia, and Cockburn made a speech before the local division. When Garvey asked him to continue to Boston, Cockburn objected. As a government witness in Garvey's mail fraud trial in 1923, Cockburn stated:

> Garvey said to me, "Can you take the ship to Boston?" I said, "No, I am bound for New York, my clearance is for New York, and the cargo for New York." He said, "But why, there is going to be a big meeting in Boston, and you will have to take the ship there; can't you arrange it?" I said, "It is rather difficult because I would be passing New York to go to Boston." Well, he says, "Do the best you can because those people there want to see the ship, and the arrangements are made for your coming, and I want you also to speak at the meeting there." I promised that I would do the best I could, that if it was possible to go up to Boston from Philadelphia, passing New York, I would do so; and I did it. (*Garvey* v. *United States*, no. 8317, Ct. App., 2d Cir., 2 February 1925)

The *Yarmouth* arrived in Boston about 12 May, remained for a day, and left for New York to deliver its cargo.

2. The *Negro World* was withheld from distribution in Belize beginning in January 1919 under the Defence of the Colony Regulation. In February 1919 Herbert Hill Cain, editor of the *Belize Independent* and a local black-consciousness leader, went before Acting Governor Walter to demand that the ban be lifted, but he refused. Racial tensions in Belize heightened until 22 July 1919, when a race riot, led initially by dissatisfied black soldiers recently returned from overseas, resulted in assaults on a number of prominent whites during several days of disorder. Even the local police opposed the acting governor, creating the need for a shipment of marines to restore British authority. The commission of inquiry later cited Walter's failure to remove the ban on the *Negro World* as one of the riot's main causes. When Eyre Hutson, the new governor, took office, he conceded that the *Negro World* was smuggled into Belize through Mexico and Guatemala "in larger numbers than before the ban was placed on it." Although he was convinced that the *Negro World* was seditious, he ended the ban but informed the local UNIA that he would "watch closely its [*Negro World*] writings and the policy of its advocate" (Gov. Eyre Hutson to the secretary of state for the colonies, 10 May 1920, PRO, CO 371/4567, 5851; Peter D. Ashdown, "Marcus Garvey, the UNIA, and the Black Cause in British Honduras, 1914–1949" [unpublished MS].

3. The UNIA received increased support after the race riots in Belize (located in the former colony of British Honduras), which occurred July 1919. In April 1920 the charter of the Belize branch of the UNIA was unveiled before an assembled membership of 832. Belize had a total population of about 16,000 in 1920. There were also small UNIA groups in North River, Stann Creek, and Manatee, British Honduras (*Clarion*, 29 April 1920).

4. The last paragraph of Garvey's speech has been omitted, since it was very mutilated on the original document.

Exchange between Marcus Garvey and Cyril V. Briggs

[The *Crusader*, April 1920]

The following letter from Mr. Marcus Garvey, President-General of the Universal Negro Improvement Association and African Communities League, is in response to the article, "A Paramount Chief for the Negro Race," which appeared in last month's CRUSADER:

March 9, 1920

Mr. Cyril V. Briggs, Editor of THE CRUSADER, 2299 Seventh Avenue, New York, N. Y.

Dear Mr. Briggs: A copy of your March number of THE CRUSADER has just reached my hands.

The article under the caption of "A PARAMOUNT CHIEF FOR THE NEGRO RACE" has struck me forcibly. It is the most intelligent explanation of the real purpose of our Convention that I have read from the pen of a contemporary journalist who is not himself a member of the Executive Body.

I have to thank you for this public explanation, and I trust you will be numbered among those who attend our Convention.

We intend sending you an invitation in the very near future. Again I thank you with very best wishes. Yours faithfully,

(Signed) UN. NEGRO IMP. ASSN.
Marcus Garvey, President-General.

We thank Mr. Garvey for this letter of appreciation and take it, too, as an indication of recognition on his part of our attitude as one of friendly and constructive criticism rather than the destructive and malicious criticism which his projects have met with from many quarters. However, to be frank, Mr. Garvey's letter misses the most important point in the article to which he refers, viz: the necessity of extending to all Negro bodies throughout the world the invitation to attend and take part in the proposed Convention for the purpose of electing "His Supreme Highness, the Potentate, His Highness, the Supreme Deputy, and other high officials, who will preside over the destiny of the Negro peoples of the world until an African Empire is founded."

In our opinion this proposal to elect a Potentate or Paramount Chief is fraught with danger to the unity of the race. We do not mean to pretend that no necessity exists for the election of such an official. The need is supreme, but the task for such an election calls for immense and careful preparation and the choice of a point more convenient to the center of the Negro population of the world than is New York City, otherwise we do not see how it would be possible to get together a set of delegates having mandates from all the Negro communities of Africa and the New World, or at least from the majority of these communities; since even under the most favorable conditions and with choice of a more convenient center than New York, it would take months of preparation and much more extensive propaganda than has so far been given the matter to arouse and enlist the support and co-operation of the majority of Negro communities in Africa and the New World. And unless this support and co-operation is secured, the project of electing a paramount chief for the Negro race is doomed to end in failure of the most farcical kind and in all probability will engender enmity and division in place of the unity that Mr. Garvey, along with all other Negro patriots, desire.

While thanking Mr. Garvey for the invitation he extends to us personally, we would prefer to see a public invitation extended to ALL Negro bodies and communities throughout the world, with other assurances that the Convention is really to be in the interests of the Negro Race.

Printed in the *Crusader*, April 1920.

Report of UNIA Meeting

[*Negro World*, 1 May 1920]

BLACK STAR LINE STEAMSHIP CORPORATION STAGES GIGANTIC MEETING AT MANHATTAN CASINO, NEW YORK

Fully 6,000 persons assembled at the Manhattan Casino on Wednesday night, April 21, to give a rousing welcome to Mr. Edward Smith-Green, Secretary of the Black Star Line, on the occasion of his return from the Republic de Cuba, whither he had gone to take charge of the unloading of the famous whiskey cargo of the S.S. Frederick Douglass.

There was disappointment over the fact that the ship was running three days late, thus making unavoidable the absence of Miss Henrietta Vinton Davis, Mr. Cyril Henry, Captain Joshua Cockburn and crew, who it was planned to honor in this public reception along with Mr. Smith-Green; but disappointment immediately gave place to joyful anticipation when it was announced that a special reception would be provided for them on their arrival either at Carnegie Hall or the Madison Square Garden.

Mr. Smith-Green gave an interesting . . . [*four lines mutilated*] traducers of the Black Star Line, white and black, who attempted to make a case of bad faith against it by alleging that the cargo was consigned to no one. In thus easily disposing of this one lie, the way is paved for the easier disposal of the more recent lies and slanders of the subsidized Harlem representatives of the white soviets downtown, choking with rage and bucolic with frenzy because Negroes all over the world show their preference and good taste for racialism as opposed to Socialism, by supporting in the most unmistakable fashion the Hon. Marcus Garvey. There was thunderous applause of several minutes duration when, in the course of his closing remarks, the president general announced: "We have now two boats belonging to the Black Star Line, and in the next five days we will have the third ship. This is the kind of answer we give to our critics." What, indeed, will these howling d[e]rvishes, these calamit[y] howlers, who lack vision, enterprise and courage and who "carry their wishbone where their backbone ought to be," what, indeed, will they say now that they realize that "a black hen lays a white egg, but a yellow heart can have no golden thoughts?"

. . .PROF. FERRIS SPEAKS

Prof. William H. Ferris, M. A., literary editor of the Negro "World," acting as master of ceremonies, said:

Last week I met one of the most distinguished men of our race, and he said, "Even if the 'Yarmouth' had gone down in that storm last January, the Black Star Line would have been a success; because it would have demonstrated the ability of the Negro to get together." And last Monday night I met on my way to Greenwich, Conn., a distinguished representative of the Anglo-Saxon race, two of whose uncles sat in Congress, and he said to me that there was only one Negro enterprise that he wanted to ask anything about, and that was the Black Star Line. He knew that the National Association for the Advancement of Colored People, Hampton, Tuskegee, Atlanta University and Fisk University, represented what the white man could do for the Negro, but the Black Star Line represented what the Negro could do for himself. (Cheers.)

MUST BUILD OWN ENTERPRISES.

What does the U.N.I.A. stand for? What does it mean? It means that the Negro has entered upon an era of achievement. From 1865 to 1895 represented a period of our political power.[1] In 1895 began the era of disfranchisement and for twenty years we have been begging white men to give us jobs in their factories, on their plantations, on their farms and in their mills. But the U.N.I.A. has taken a farther step when it said that the Negro must build his own banks, his own department stores, his own mills and factories and steamship lines. And when the Negro does this, he will get on an economic foundation which will give him real independence.

Great men write their names upon the pages of the world's history because of their deeds and achievements. Alexander of Macedon has had his name ringing down the ages for over 2,700 years. They called him Alexander the Great because he had conquered the then known world. Julius Caesar has had his name singing down the ages of time; and we have produced three black men who have caused their names to ring in the ears of men. One of them was Toussaint L'Ouverture, who was born a slave and never saw a soldier until he was 59 years of age; yet he forged an army which was a thunderbolt, drove out the English, the French and the Spanish and made Haiti a free Nation. (Cheers.) The second man was Frederick Douglass, (Cheers), who was born a slave, yet taught hims[elf] to read and write by using planks for a blackboard and crayon for a pencil, escaped from slavery, faced the mob, and made himself known and respected to the world over as a diplomat, a statesman, an orator and leader of his race. The third great hero which this race has [produced] is the Hon. Marcus Garvey, (Cheers.) I am not [s]aying it for camouflage, nor for soft [so]ap nor pal[aver]. I have been a newspaper man since I was a boy sixteen years of age. I have traveled from

Canada to Florida and from New York to Kansas City, Mo. I have been attending Baptist Conventions, Methodist Conferences and the great Afro-American C[ouncil]; but I have never seen an organization permeated with the spirit of the U.N.I.A. I have been connected with other organizations which have assembled and made eloquent speeches, passed resolutions and made their appeal to Congress, the President of the United States and the American people. But the U.N.I.A. is making an appeal directly to the Negro. It tells that color is only skin-deep; that God Almighty has endowed him with a brain and with a will power, with a nerve force and a muscle force; that he can achieve all that any other man has achieved in the past. (Cheers.)

This is no idle dream. No stream can rise higher than its source. And what was the source of the Negro race? Go back to Homer, go back to Herodotus, go back to Strabo[2] and go back to Lucian:[3] and what do [you] find? You find that the men who by the waters of the Nile and on the plateaus of Ethiopia laid the foundation of the world's civilization were black men. Not only that. Over by the waters of the Euphrates, at Susa in Babylon, there are monuments showing representations of Negro soldiers—showing that black men [fought in the armies] by which Babylon was able to conquer the world.[4]

Coming down to modern times, we find that one of Napoleon Bonaparte's great generals was Alexander Dumas.[5] He was the strongest man in Napoleon Bonaparte's army and commanded a division in the Nile campaign.

Why do I tell you these things? There seems to be a spirit of pessimism taking possession of some Negroes, by which they do not think that other Negroes can do and dare and achieve big things like the Caucasian. Fifteen years of age, I saw Frederick Douglass speaking in New Haven, Connecticut in the greatest opera house of that city, and holding an audience spell-bound—showing what it was possible for the Negro to accomplish and achieve. And it is in the same spirit of daring and venture that I believe the greatness of the Hon. Marcus Garvey lies.

We have produced a great sociologist in Dubois;[6] a great mathematician in Kelly Miller;[7] a great painter in Tanner;[8] a great musician in Coleridge-Taylor;[9] a great physician in Dr. Daniel Williams;[10] a great dentist in Bentley,[11] and great scholars like Blyden and Alexander Crummel and Professor Scarborough.[12] But Marcus Garvey is the Hercules and the Samson of the Negro race. (Cheers) They shut Samson up in the t[ow]n of Gaza, but he bent down and lifted the gates of Gaza upon his back and walked off with them.[13] The Black Star Line and the U.N.I.A. are our gates of Gaza.

We are told, "By your fruits, ye shall know them."[14] The "Yarmouth," Liberty Hall, the "Shadyside," two buildings on West 135th street—all bought within six months—are the fruits of what the Black Star Line and the U.N.I.A. have accomplished and by which they are known. And with these, we can go before the world.

We are now in a new age. We are now in a new era. There was a time when the white man looked on us with pity and sympathy. There was a time when he looked upon us with contempt. But now his curiosity is aroused to see if the New Negro can make good. And if we in America and in Africa can build up republics, can build up [mi]lls, can build up factories, can build up steamboat lines, we will give the lie to those Crackers of the south who said that the Negro can follow white leaders but not leaders of his own. We want to demonstrate in the twentieth century that under the guidance a[n]d leadership of black men, following the plans of black men, the plans of Negro brains, working with Negro hands, we can do all in the commercial world that other men and races can do. (Cheers.)

When you can build yourselves up commercially in New York you won't have to worry about having a Negro representative in Congress. When you make yourselves factors in the commercial life of Philadelphia and in Chicago, you won't have to worry about having a Negro representative in Congress. The world esteems a man or a race by the estimation which it puts upon its own self. You must not only say, as Terrance, that black poet, said in the Coliseum of Rome:—"I am a man, and nothing that is common to humanity is foreign to me,"[15] but you must prove it by your deeds and achievements. And it is because, through Marcus Garvey, two great movements have been launched which shows that the Negro is entering an era of achievement, that we will write a new page upon the world's history. And instead of begging other nations and races for a chance, we will have them coming to us, because we will have something to offer. (Cheers.)

THE REV. ELLEGOR SPEAKS.

The Rev. Wilcolm Ellegor,[16] ex-Professor of Liberia College, at Monrovia, Liberia, was the next speaker introduced, and said:—

Mr. President, Ladies and Gentlemen:—I always have the misfortune to come behind so great an orator as Dr. Ferris. However, I am here tonight to speak briefly to you on the one word:—"Opportunity." We have been hearing for a very long time that we lacked opportunity, that the world lacked opportunity. We have heard from the lips of the Anglo-Saxon—we have heard from the writings of his pen—that the black races, the darker races, are the backward races. But that sentiment is directed more especially to the black men of our race because of the lack of aggression. They think that we lack aggression, and if I am candid and straightforward, I must admit right here that we do lack aggression.

Opportunity now, however, is knocking at our door, bidding us to do, to dare, to win, to achieve, to break down the obstacles of life, the great barriers that hamper our progress. We heard until a few short years ago of the great Ethiopian movement,[17] how it set out to do great things, and how that great movement was tumbled by the iron hand of British imperialism. It was simply because unity was lacking in our people.

There is now a great contention on. And what is that contention? A man had a vision—who that man is, where he was born, has nothing to do with it—and that vision [h]e gave out; and when that vision went to the people who heard it, they came forward and connected themselves with that man. Then there came up other people, trying to crush that man [be]cause of jealousy. Now jealousy will always exist in the world, but we are to take our stand, we are to take that determined place in life, that will break down the barriers of jealousy. There is no power on earth that will ever be able . . . [*words mutilated*] like the cork that always find its way on top the water.

BELIEVES IN FAIR CRITICISM.

I am not one who thinks that we should not be criticized. I believe in fair criticism. I believe in criticism because it is good. It makes men more careful. It makes men at the head of affairs more careful and thorough and particular about their business. Now we have this great organization and I do not feel that this organization has any need whatever to go down, because we have in it the great opportunity of demonstrating to the world that we do not lack the sinew and the muscle and the acumen and the thought of the Anglo-Saxon.

There will always be different groups of people in the world. Among races we have groups. We have some aiming at political eminence, some aiming at industr[i]al eminence, and so forth, but the greatest need is to form an inter-relation of three great groups. What a wonderful opportunity it would be if those groups who interest themselves in intellectual outputs or in political outputs or in commercial outputs would all come together and work for the good of the race!

Now we have got this opportunity; and I do sincerely hope that we will let all petty barriers and differences sink for the sake of the great cause of Negro advancement in this new era now opening to us. The door of opport[unit]y is wide and we should try to open it wider, that we may prove to the Anglo-Saxon that we are like himself, only we have lacked the chance that has come to him through his great numbers and the great might with which he worked to accumulate what he has. I think you will all agree with me that we have the force and we have the power, and that what is needed above all else i[s] an inter-relation between the different groups that divide themselves and fight each other. (Cheers.)

THE REV. DR. EASON SPEAKS

The Rev. Dr. Eason, Chaplain General of the U.N.I.A., was the next speaker introduced and said: Mr. Chairman, officers and members of the U.N.I.A., Black Star Line, Negro Factories Corporation, ladies and gentlemen: I have just gotten in from the city of Brotherly Love after having been there attending to some matters in connection with the Philadelphia Division, and I am glad to be in the City of New York—the city of Sisterly Love

(laughter)—and to be with you on this auspicious occasion is indeed inspiring to me. And when I realize how the members of this organization and
the lovers of our race have stood by the movement in times that were not so
propitious as they are now, and when I remember the sacrifices made by its
founder and his associates during the early days, even during the recent
weeks, I am reminded very much of the old brother who was determined to
stand by his Master. He had been accustomed to swear a little before he
joined the church, and that was the hardest thing to get over and he concluded that he could never do it anymore. He was giving his testimony one
night and he said: "Me forsake my church? Me forsake my Jesus? Me? No,
no! Never! My Jesus took my feet out of the miry clay and placed them on
the rock to stay. Me forsake my Jesus? Me forsake Him after all He has done
for me and the preacher has done for me? Me forsake my leader and my
Jesus? Why—hell—no." (Laughter and applause.)

Ladies and gentlemen: In times past we have stood by this movement
upholding the hands of our President and his associates when the way was
dark and gloomy. But now the sun is shining everywhere, and thousands all
over the world are to-day cheering and hurr[ah]ing. I say, Never now will we
go back! (Cheers.)

But we are here to-night for the express purpose of welcoming our hero
who has been in the Southern countries doing yeoman service for the cause,
and I am sure everybody here rejoices with us as we welcome back to our fold
those who have been out to do and work for the cause and race and for
humanity in general. And as I look into your anxious faces, and observe those
sitting upon the rostrum here, I see written upon their foreheads and in their
very expressions the sweetest word known to mother, to home and heaven—
the word Welcome. (Cheers.)

THE HON. MARCUS GARVEY SPEAKS

The Hon. Marcus Garvey, the President-General of the U.N.I.A., was
next introduced and said:—

Mr. Chairman, Members of the U.N.I.A., Ladies and Gentlemen:—We
are assembled here tonight for the purpose of extending a welcome to the
representative of the U.N.I.A. and the Black Star Line whom we sent abroad
two or three months ago. Doubtless the majority of you will remember the
S. S. "Yarmouth" through the great publicity that was given to the cargo she
removed from New York to Havana when the prohibition law c[a]me into
effect in the United States of America. The S. S. "Yarmouth" of the Black
Star Line was the last ship to sail out of an American port with a cargo of
liquor after the law went into effect. The cargo aboard the "Yarmouth" was
valued at $5,000,000, and because of the great value of the cargo great
interest was manifested in the ship's movements. So as to have the cargo
properly landed in Havana, in that it was so valuable, we had to send our
Secretary—the Secretary of the Black Star Line—to see to the unloading of

the cargo, as also to represent the interests of the U.N.I.A. in the great Republic of Cuba. Mr. Smith-Green is well known to the members of the New York local of the U.N.I.A., in that he is its Executive Secretary. He is also well known to all the stockholders of the Black Star Line in New York . . . [*line mutilated*]. He has been to Cuba. He has travelled throughout the length and breadth of that great Negro Republic. He crossed from Cuba to the island of Jamaica; and we cabled him, as also Captain Cockburn and Miss Davis, to report in New York yesterday.

Mr. Smith-Green reported two days ago, coming back from Jamaica through Cuba. Unfortunately, the "Frederick Douglass," because of a double trip she had to make between Santiago de Cuba and Kingston, is running three days late, and because of this the other delegates will not appear here tonight. But they are due to appear in Philadelphia next Monday, where the Philadelphia branch of the association in the Academy of Music will welcome them. And from Philadelphia the ship will go to Boston to meet the members and stockholders of the Boston Division of the U.N.I.A. in the Tremont Temple, and from there they will come to New York and we will arrange a bigger meeting for them in the Carnegie Hall or the Madison Square Garden. (Great applause.)

Those of you who know Henrietta Vinton Davis know that she is the greatest woman of the Negro race today. (Cheers.) Truly we can say that Henrietta Vinton Davis is the jewel of the Negro race. (Renewed cheers.) Therefore, you will readily understand why Captain Cockburn, Henrietta Vinton Davis and Cyril Henry and the crew of the "Yarmouth" are not here tonight. But you will see them within a couple of days.

It gives me great pleasure, therefore, at this time to present to you one of the returned ambassadors—Mr. Edward Smith-Green, Secretary of the Black Star Line and Executive Secretary of the New York local of the U.N.I.A. (Cheers.)

MR. EDWARD SMITH-GREEN SPEAKS

Mr. Edward Smith-Green, Secretary of the Black Star Line and Secretary of the New York Local of the U.N.I.A., said:—

Mr. President, Fellow-Members and Officers:—It affords me great pleasure to be back with you after an absence of two months. First of all allow me to apologize for not being able to throw my voice any further because of the fact that I contracted a cold on my way from Key West, Florida, to New York.

As it has been said, because of the fact that there was some publicity attached to the S. S. "Yarmouth" on account of the cargo which she carried, the President saw fit to send me abroad to supervise the landing of the whiskey and also to represent the U.N.I.A. and the Black Star Line. When I left here on the 15th of February I regretted very much that I could not have come to Liberty Hall on the previous evening to bid you good-bye. I had my reasons, which I shall explain later on. I can assure you that I feel myself a highly honored man here tonight because I have had the opportunity of being sent abroad as your servant—I will not say ambassador—to represent you. I have done so to the best of my abili[ty] and I return here tonight to assu[re] you that I have brought laurels [for] the U.N.I.A. (Cheers.)

DISCUSSES HIS VOYAGE.

And now, if you will permi[t] me, I will describe my voyage. I [l]eft the Pennsylvania Station at 6:20 [sh]arp on the evening of the 15th of February. I traveled by express train. It took forty-eight hours to reach Ke[y] West from New York. And I want to tell you just a little incident which happened on the trip between New York and Key West. Apparently Southern white men are not accustomed to see a Negro travelling on a Pullman train. While on the train between Miami and Key West, I was in the smoki[ng] room when one of those gentlemen from the South came in while I was [i]n conversation with some Northern white men. The Southerner stepped up to me and said: "Hey! where is [nu]mber 13?" I told him: "I do not kno[w]; ask the porter." He replied: "Ain't you the porter?" I said "No." He then looked me full in the face and said[:] "Hey! where do you come from?" [I] sai[d:] "New York" and he added: "Wh[er]e are you going?" and I repli[ed] "To Havana." He then said: "Loo[k] fellow! you are getting into ba[d] country now." I inquired what he me[a]nt and he answered: "I mean that in t[h]is part of the world, we white folks [a]re not accustomed to ride in a trai[n] with niggers." I said: "You have [m]ade a mistake fellow, you happen no[t] to be talking to a "nigger" this time [but] to a Negro gentleman["]. He got re[d] [in] the face, and I believe if he had [had] the opportunity, he would have [stru]ck me. But as he made a lurch toward me, I very deftly placed my hand in [m]y hip pocket and asked him if he wa[nt]ed to start something. He then coolly walked out while the other men jeered at him.

I arrived at Key West an[d] seven hours after I boarded the [st]eamer leaving for Havana. During [m]y absence from this country, I [re]ceived news that there was a good [d]eal of grumbling about the hold up of the Yarmouth in Havana. Some [p]ersons in New York have seen fit to [say] a lot of caluminous things about t[he] Yarmouth. But the real cause of [the] holdup was that when the Yarmo[ut]h arrived in Havana, the longsh[o]remen were on strike.[18] There were [d]ozens of ships tied up in the harbor. [W]e arrived there just about the tim[e] that the strike was about to be bro[ke]n or we would have been held up th[er]e for a longer period. When I arr[iv]ed in Havana I found that the branc[h] of the U.N.I.A. was well organized, [an]d the members of that branch mad[e] representations that unless the ca[rgo] was immediately discharged they [t]hemselves would go on board and [g]et the cargo off. (Cheers.) Because th[ey] were so determined, the Yarmouth w[as] given a berth within ten days after sh[e] was in Havana, although she cam[e] [in?] fully one month after the oth[er] . . .

[*words mutilated*]. Her whiskey . . . [*words mutilated*] cargo; and although in New [York] [it] was said she was consigned to . . . [*words mutilated*] yet there were representatives [of] consignees in Havana, who came and presented their bills of lading and c[l]aimed their cargo. I want to emphatically say here that the Yarmouth was not held up by the government at all and that we had no hitch where the discharge of the cargo was concerned; that the only thing which pr[e]vented her from leaving Havana earlier was because of the strike condition[s].

HAVANA BRANCH GOING STRONG.

I was in Havana not twenty-four hours when I was in touch with members of the U.N.I.A. down there; and I can assure you that they are going strong. (Loud cheers.) As soon as it became known that I was in Havana, newspaper reporters began pouring in on me at my hotel eagerly asking for reports of exactly what we were doing in New York; but I did not, for perhaps four days, give out the information that I intended to give because there was too much rivalry between the newspapers; and moreover I learned that the biggest newspaper had not yet sent its reporter. I played a waiting game and eventually came a reporter from the paper which has the biggest circulation in Havana. This paper is called "El Mundo," (a white newspaper) and through it the Black Star Line and the U.N.I.A. was given the widest publicity it has ever had in any part of the world. Because of that, and because I was able to express myself in the meetings of the U.N.I.A. one morning there was a knock at the door of my room and on opening a man in the uniform of the Cuban Republic approached me and asked if I was Mr. Smith-Green[.] I said "Yes"[;] he thereupon handed me a letter which he said required an immediate reply. The letter read:

INVITED TO VISIT PRESIDENT.

"Dear Sir: I have been instructed by the President of this republic to ask you to visit him at his palace two days from today, accompanied by the captain of the Yarmouth and his officers." (Cheers.) I can assure you that inasmuch as I was prepared for no such invitation that was the greatest shock of my life. I did not realize that we were so keenly watched; I did not realize that the propaganda was taken even to the palace of the President of the republic. In spite of the shock I made up my mind since the opportunity presented itself that I would appear and present in the strongest language I could the aims and objects of 400,000,000 black men. (Cheers.)

On the morning mentioned the captain in his uniform and officers and men of the Yarmouth got into some automobiles sent for us by the captain of the port. When we reached there we found the harbor police drawn up. As we approached they came to salute. We were there for about five minutes when the captain himself with some other gentlemen and important citizens—representatives of the Cuban Republic—escorted us to the palace of the President. When we arrived there we found a guard of honor drawn up at the gate and as we alighted from the automobiles they came to a salute and we saluted. We entered the elevator and were taken up a few flights. After waiting in the ante-chamber for a few minutes a man appeared dressed in uniform and announced in Spanish that the President required our presence immediately. We marched in, I heading the procession. I found the President, the Colonel of the Camp and other Cabinet officers in the Cabinet chamber, seated around a table. As we approached they rose and the President came forward and asked who I was. I told him and then I introduced him to the captain and other officers. The President then addressed us. I am not able to tell you what he said, but he welcomed us to Cuba. My reply was as follows:—

LAUDS CUBAN REPUBLIC.

"Mr. President:—I feel myself extremely honored to be in your presence here, and I can assure you that I have brought a message from the greatest Negro this world has ever produced to the President of the Greatest Republic in the World—great not because her resources are great; great not because of the martyrs she has produced; great not because of her history; but because of the fact that having us here in your presence you have at least established and shown to the world that the brotherhood of man does exist." (Cheers.)

He was extremely satisfied and gratified and he had his photograph taken with us. This photograph I have brought with me and I will give it to the Negro World for publication. When I was leaving the palace the President told me:—

"As long as you are in Cuba, and whenever you go away and return— you or any representative of the U.N.I.A., or Black Star Line—you are welcome here, and as long as I am President of this Republic, see me for anything you want." (Loud cheers.)

This message I have brought from the President of the great Republic of Cuba. Before we left the palace we were also invited to visit the soldiers' camp, which we did a week later. When we reached Camp Colombo there was another great surprise awaiting us. The Colonel took us in charge and not only showed us around the camp, but we found a part of the army on parade. The band was in attendance and as we approached and after the formalities had been gone through, the National Anthem was struck up and my friends, I can assure you that those men were in earnest—because the major part of the Cuban army consists of Negroes. And when they saw Negroes with the uniform of a steamship line, they thought they would go wild with enthusiasm.

We were royally entertained in that camp, and I also made a speech in the Officers' Club, which you have probably read in the Negro World. We were given the best time of our lives in that camp and we were asked to return to attend the field sports, but we could not. We left and went back down to the boat and there we had the opportunity—as some of the camp officers came down with us—to show them what Negro efficiency stood for. They were entertained on board and the waiters were able to treat them just as nicely as they treated us. They found the Yarmouth in splendid condition; because by the time she arrived in Havana the chief officers had her looking like a yacht. I have no doubt since she has been under the tropical sun, when she arrives in New York you will be exceedingly pleased, for she has been repainted beautifully. Because of that, when those officers came on board and inspected her they felt satisfied that Negro efficiency stood for something since they could produce that which they saw on board.

When I explained to them and showed the photographs of Hon. Marcus Garvey and Frederick Douglass, and told them what they had achieved for our race, they were extremely proud because they realized t[h]at we were in dead earnest—that we did not intend any longer to be dominated by alien races. (Cheers.)

The Cuban Negro has at last got the vision. It strikes me that he has been waiting all these years for something like this to be taken to him, because although he is in the majority like all over the world he has been kept in the same state of slavery. When through the newspapers and in public gatherings I was able to expound the principles of the U.N.I.A. and the Black Star Line they threw their lot in and there was no time I spoke or appeared in public that the hall or building was not crammed to its full capacity, and they had sworn, as it were, that as long as the Negroes in New York representing the U.N.I.A. and the Black Star Line will lead the way for them they intend to follow until such time—if it is necessary—to die for the cause. (Cheers.)

CARVES U.N.I.A. IN TREE

Because of some business in Cuba I could not go on the Yarmouth when she left for Jamaica. But leaving Havana I went to Santiago de Cuba. While there I took the opportunity to visit San Juan Hill—that place made famous in American history because of the valor and bravery of Negroes.[19] As a Negro I thought it would have been a sin not to visit the spot where members of my race had made such a glorious past. I therefore went to the summit of San Juan Hill, and there by the guide I was shown the spot where Roosevelt and his Rough Riders were engaged in the heaviest fighting, and there I saw the "Peace Tree," under which the Spanish and American treaty was signed. I took the opportunity to carve in the tree beside the "Peace Tree" the letters U.N.I.A., for I wanted it to be known in the future that the cause for which we stand had at one time sent a representative down there and that he had pluck enough to leave imprinted on that tree right beside the "Peace Tree" the letters of the greatest movement in the world today.

Going over to Jamaica, I visited the office of the Black Star Line and the U.N.I.A. Over there they are going strong also. They have also sent a message to you that "we on this end are determined to carry on the work and to back you to the limit[.]"

And now, in conclusion, I want to assure you that today the U.N.I.A. and the Black Star Line have been [firm]ly planted in Cuba, and all we must do now is to carry on the work and give the [lie] to those who believe that we are not in earnest, so that those abroad shall not be made to feel ashamed. In Havana there is a very great statue of a Negro—his name is Antonio Maceo—a man who shed his blood so that Negroes should be liberated. It [was] said of Hannibal that when he drew the sword the very world oscillated upon its point. But it has been said of Antonio Maceo that when he drew the sword the very stars stopped in their space. It might be a myth; but the Cuban will tell you that Antonio Maceo was the greatest man in Cuba. In that huge statue he is represented sitting astride a horse [ramp]ant, the reins held in his left hand and a drawn sword in his right hand; his head to the sun and his eyes beaming with fire. Although he died before victory was proclaimed because of his valor his name is memorialized in Cuban history and his statue has been erected as a memento to give an inspiration to those who came after him.

On my way from Jamaica I had the opportunity of stopping off in Hayti for a few hours and there I remembered that that land had produced a great Negro in the person of Toussaint L'Ouverture. And as I looked on the flagstaff and saw the flag of Hayti I doffed my hat in reverence, because having been sent by you I had the opportunity of seeing with my own eyes the people of Hayti and of treading the soil which produced Toussaint L'Ouverture. But my friends, although I felt great abroad I feel greater now. I have mentioned great men, but in this modern age the greatest man the Negro race has produced is our own president—the darling of our race—Marcus Garvey.

PREPARED TO FOLLOW THE SIGN.

After having gone abroad and having all those honors heaped upon me, this is what I want to tell you: That with this sign I have conquered. With this sign of the red, black and green, I was admitted to the presidential palace; with this sign I was admitted to a camp and given military honors; with this sign I was recognized all over the world; and because of that fact I am prepared to follow this sign as long as life lasts; and I call upon you men and women of this race to vow that as long as breath remains in us—as long as we remain upon this earth—we shall do everything to uphold the sign which we have created in the red, black and green—no matter what others may say. Since other races have established empires; since they have produced republics; since they have flags, we are determined that this shall be our sign and because of that let us love it as we love our lives.

I am calling upon the young men of our race particularly to nerve yourselves, because the day is not far distant I believe when we will be called on, and we must be prepared to die for the honor of our race and the honor of our women. And I hope when the time comes that we will go forward manfully. That we will have with us some Toussaint L'Ouvertures and Hannibals, and I know we will have Marcus Garvey. And when that day comes let us not falter but go forward unerringly and unfalteringly wearing the sign of the red, black and green. I believe that one day upon the shores of Africa we will drive the enemy from the soil of our forefathers. On that day perhaps we shall see the great African eagle soaring to the mountain top of Ethiopia and there planting for eternity the flag which the Negro has been able to produce and maintain even at the cost of his blood. (Cheers)

Mr. Hubert Harrison Speaks.

Mr. Hubert Harrison, associate editor of the Negro World, was next introduced and said: It is unfortunate friends that I have to address you. I regret the necessity as much as you do, but the thing has to be gone through with. I did intend to make an address on "The Call to Africa," but cannot do it because it is the call of the audience now. We must adjust ourselves to it nevertheless.

I might stand here as a way-side representative of the African spirit to point out that the biggest thing in this entire organization is that response to the call of Africa. I do not think it means anything to most of you, but to me for a very long time it has meant a great deal. It has meant to me that we who are here, in the West Indies and South Africa, in the United States, are Africans of the dispersion, just like the Jews who were carried away into captivity and were asked to sing the songs of their country. "How can we sing the Lord's songs in a strange land?"[20] they replied. And when we are told what Africa was, when we are told what Africa is today, it does not strike quite the responsive chord that it should.

I have been told that a certain lady was talking about me the other day, and was told by a friend of mine that I had gone away—well, diplomatically speaking, let me say downtown.[21] And she said, "Why, how can he go there? He will feel strange. He will miss a whole lot." "Well," said my friend, "what will he miss?" [S]aid she, "How can he eat raw meat and eat human flesh with those people down there?" And this was from a Negro lady!

She thought that her own people were eaters of human flesh and that they could not do anything else. I am not going to make a speech. I just touch on this point here to show how necessary it is that we get in proper touch with Africa and the Africans—our own Africans. (Cheers.) How are we going to do it? By way of the convention—the great convention of the Negroes of the world that will be different from anything that they have ever had—to meet in Liberty Hall, in a hall owned by Negroes to be built by Negroes, in which Negro delegates, Negro commissioners, Negro representatives, will be able to put the problems of Negroes all over the world, to meet in such a hall, under such auspices, to bring the race together; not like the assembly that met at the University of London in 1911 with Mr. Gustav Spiller and men of that sort.[22] White men drew black men, drew red men and yellow men together. What for? Our own Professor Dubois happened to be there,[23] but he never learned what for, I will tell you what for. Because the white men of the world wanted to get colored men in council to study them, to learn what ached them, so that they could take proper steps by yielding so much to avoid a catastrophe, or by using the strong hand where they were sure the strong hand would go—to rivet the fetters of their own racial damnation [*domination?*], and our great professor could not see it.

But this will be our own convention. It is a thing worthy of the soberest, the gravest, the deepest thought on our part. But thought never will solve any human problems. You have got to dig down in your jeans and throw up "plunks" to make it go. We have got to raise $2,000,000 and more for that convention, and for the college to educate the New Negro free from the domination of the white man's thought. (Loud cheers.) We have got to raise money to establish the headquarters of the Negroes of the world. We have got to make sure that our connections with our mother country—our motherland—will b[e] firm, stable and secure.

We want to make sure, don't we? Well, one way is to talk about it—no[t] with words only, for speech is silver: but something else goes further tha[n] that. The Spaniards say in Port[o] Rico that talk is cheap, but it take[s] money to buy land; and I am here to-night at the tail end of this stream o[f] talk to get money from you. I am askin[g] those who are willing to make the lighter sacrifice—not the sacrifice o[f] your life; not the sacrifice of sickness; but the sacrifice of that whic[h] you can go out and earn over an[d] again (cheers).

CLOSING REMARKS BY HON. MARCUS GARVEY.

In closing the meeting, Mr. Garvey announced that the following day the "Shadyside" of the Black Star Line was prepared to take 500 passengers on excursion up the Hudson River, starting from the foot of 125th street at 12 o'clock. On Sunday she will again make two excursion trips, one at 12 o'clock and another at 3:30. "We have now two boats," he said, "and in the next five days we will have a third ship (cheers). That is the kind of answer we are giving to our critics."

Printed in *NW*, 1 May 1920. Original headlines abbreviated.

  1. This period begins with the close of the Civil War and ends with the year of Booker T. Washington's famous "Atlanta Compromise" speech. Although the congressional Reconstruction (1867–1877) featured some major political reforms in the South on behalf of recently freed blacks, the years after 1877 witnessed a decline in public interest in black rights. Historian C. Vann Woodward has pointed out, however, that blacks continued to hold minor political posts in many parts of the South, especially as Bourbon politicians sought black political support to buttress their power. The failure of the Populist party to sustain a coalition of black

and white voters in the 1890s and its subsequent surrender to racism assisted a broad and largely successful movement in the South to remove blacks completely from the political process (Rayford W. Logan, *The Betrayal of the Negro* [London: Collier-Macmillan, 1954]; C. Vann Woodward, *The Strange Career of Jim Crow* [New York: Oxford University Press, 1957]).

2. Strabo (60 B.C.?–21 A.D.), Greek historian and geographer whose extant work consists of seventeen volumes of *Geographica* (*CBD; WBD*).

3. Lucian, second-century A.D. Greek satirist (*WBD*).

4. The blacks depicted in the monuments at Susa, the capital of Elam, were captives of the Assyrian leader Ashurbanipal, who drove the Ethiopians out of Memphis, Egypt, in 667 B.C., ending a period of Ethiopian rule. Excavations at other sites in Elam, however, have revealed representations of black kings in the palace at Susa (Frank M. Snowden, *Blacks in Antiquity* [Cambridge: Harvard University Press, 1970], p. 114).

5. Alexandre Dumas (1762–1806), father of the noted novelist of the same name, was born Alexandre Davy de la Pailleterie in Santo Domingo. His father was a French colonist and his mother was of African descent. Dumas became a French officer and fought in France's revolutionary and Napoleonic wars, distinguishing himself for military valor during Napoleon's Egyptian expedition of 1798 (*WBD*).

6. Sociology had only recently emerged as a discipline when Du Bois wrote his pioneering work *The Philadelphia Negro* (1899). He had chosen sociology as one of his fields of study while at Harvard, and during his graduate student years, he traveled to Germany, where he studied with Gustav von Schmoller, the renowned sociologist at the University of Berlin (Elliott Rudwick, "W. E. B. Du Bois as Sociologist," in *Black Sociologists*, James E. Blackwell and Morris Janowitz, eds., [Chicago: University of Chicago Press, 1974], pp. 25–55).

7. Kelly Miller was a professor of mathematics and sociology at Howard University. He received his training at Johns Hopkins University, Baltimore (*DAB*).

8. Henry Ossawa Tanner (1859–1937), world-renowned black painter, was born in Pittsburgh. He studied under Thomas Eakins at the Pennsylvania Academy of Fine Arts and under Paul Laurens and Benjamin Constant at the Académie Julian in Paris. In France, Tanner turned away from black subjects to religious themes; his painting *The Raising of Lazarus from the Dead* was purchased by the French government in 1897 (Benjamin Brawley, *The Negro Genius* [New York: Dodd, Mead & Co., 1939]; Wilhelmene Robinson, *Historical Negro Biographies* [New York: Association for the Study of Negro Life and History, 1961], pp. 128–29).

9. Samuel Coleridge-Taylor (1875–1912) was one of Britain's leading musicians and composers. Coleridge-Taylor, whose father was Sierra Leonean, mainly composed choral works; his most famous piece was *Hiawatha's Wedding Feast* (1898). A political activist, Coleridge-Taylor attended the Pan-African Conference in 1900 and served on the executive committee of the Pan-African Association (Averill Coleridge-Taylor, *The Heritage of Samuel Coleridge-Taylor* [London: n.p., 1979]; W. C. Berwick Sayers, *Samuel Coleridge-Taylor, Musician: His Life and Letters* [London: n.p., 1915]).

10. Daniel Hale Williams (1856–1931) graduated from the medical school of Northwestern University, Evanston, Ill., in 1883. He made medical history in 1893 when he performed what has been considered the first successful heart surgery, for which he received wide acclaim. The following year Williams received a presidential appointment as surgeon in charge at Freedman Hospital, Howard University. In 1898 he returned to Chicago and for some time was the only black American on the staff of St. Luke's Hospital; he was also the only black charter member of the American College of Surgeons, organized in 1913. Williams was also an activist in the NAACP (Wilhelmene Robinson, *Historical Negro Biographies*, p. 262; *Negro Almanac*, p. 796).

11. Charles E. Bentley (b. 1859) was educated at Cincinnati High School and received his D.D.S. degree from the Chicago College of Dental Surgery in 1887. He was a professor of oral surgery at the Harvey Medical College and president of the Odontographic Society of Chicago (*WWCA*).

12. William Saunders Scarborough (1852–1926), classical scholar, was born into slavery in Macon, Ga. After obtaining his B.A. (1875) and M.A. (1878) degrees at Oberlin College, Oberlin, Ohio, he embarked on a career as a teacher of Greek at Wilberforce University, Wilberforce, Ohio, in 1887. He taught there until 1891, when he accepted a position as professor of Hellenistic Greek at Payne Theological Seminary. He returned to Wilberforce University in 1895 to serve as professor of Greek and chairman of the classical department and in 1897 became the university's vice-president. He succeeded to the presidency in 1908, a position he held until

1920. A prolific writer, Scarborough published many scholarly works on classical literature. As a vice-president of the American Negro Academy, Scarborough provided an oft-cited example for blacks seeking to dispel prevalent racist notions about analytical ability among members of the race. Scarborough served as a delegate from Wilberforce University to the Universal Races Congress in London in 1911, and after the entry of the U.S. into World War I, he was appointed a member of the Food Commission of Ohio and of the National Council of Defense. In 1921 President Harding appointed him assistant in farm studies in the U.S. Department of Agriculture (*WWCR; JNH* 11 [October 1926]: 689–92; Wilberforce University Archives, *Alumni Necrology, 1925–1930* [n.p., n.d.]).

13. Judg. 16:21–28.

14. Matt. 7:20.

15. These lines came from "*Heauton Timoroumenos*" ("The Self-tormentor") written by Terence (Publius Terentius Afer), the Carthage-born Latin poet and dramatist (190?–159 B.C.).

16. Francis Wilcom Ellegor (1877–1928) was born in Demerara, British Guiana, and educated at Crockett's High School and Durham University, Durham, England. In 1908 he was ordained a deacon in the Protestant Episcopal church in Liberia and became a priest in the same denomination in 1910. He immigrated to New York City in 1916, and he served as the UNIA's high commissioner in 1921. (*NW*, 26 February 1921). At the end of the 1922 UNIA Convention, Ellegor announced his retirement.

17. A possible reference to the African movement of Chief Alfred C. Sam, whose steamship company was popularly known as Ethiopian.

18. Although no organized longshoremen's strike appears to have occurred, there was a continuing crisis over the congested condition of Havana Harbor after the war. Conditions apparently grew worse, since between July and September 1920, there were a number of formal protests by Havana merchants.

19. San Juan Hill was the site of the famous battle of the Spanish-American War, in which the all-black Tenth Cavalry played an important part (Robert Greene, *Black Defenders*, pp. 125 ff.).

20. Ps. 137:4.

21. A possible reference to the location of New York City's passport office, where both Harrison and J. W. H. Eason endeavored to obtain passports to Liberia on behalf of the UNIA during April and May 1920. The Bureau of Investigation instructed the Passport Division of the State Department to deny Harrison and Eason passports because of the radical nature of the UNIA (DNA, RG 65, file OG 185161, 7 May 1920).

22. Gustave Spiller (b. 1864) was the Rumanian-born organizer of the First International Moral Education Congress in 1908 in London and the First Universal Races Congress, held at the University of London 26–29 July 1911. He was also the author of numerous books and articles.

23. W.E. B. Du Bois and Felix Adler, the German-born educator and ethical reformer, were secretaries of the American section of the Universal Races Congress in 1911. At the congress Du Bois delivered an address on blacks in the United States, concluding that "whether at last the Negro will gain full recognition as a man, or be utterly crushed by prejudice and superior numbers, is the present Negro problem in America" (Gustave Spiller, ed., *Papers on Inter-racial Problems Communicated to the First Universal Races Congress Held at the University of London, July 26–29, 1911* [London: P. S. King, 1911], p. 364; Michael D. Biddiss, "The Universal Races Congress of 1911," *Race* 13, no. 3 [July 1971]: 37–46; W. E. B. Du Bois, *The Autobiography of W. E. B. Du Bois* [New York: International Publishers, 1968], pp. 262–63).

BSL Notice

[*Negro World*, 1 May 1920]

WARNING!
WARNING!

It has come to our knowledge that several unscrupulous persons have been scattering false reports and rumors about the Black Star Line for the purpose of selling their private corporation stocks to the supporters of the Black Star Line. Be it known, that the Black Star Line is not a private concern, nor a concern seeking to exploit ou[r] poor race, but that it is a purely race enterprise started for the good of the race, and owned by the race. Beware of private corporations that seek to exploit for personal purposes.

The Black Star Line will appreciate all interested parties sending into its office the names of such unscrupulous persons who try to scatter false reports about the corporation.

(Signed) BLACK STAR LINE, Inc.
MARCUS GARVEY, President

Printed in *NW*, 1 May 1920.

Report of Boston Meeting

[[Boston, Mass., May 1, 1920]]

Yesterday was a gala day not only for Boston but for all New England as well. There was not very much done where colored people were concerned. Everybody took a half holiday off. The excitement was the expected arrival of the S. S. "Frederick Douglass" at the famous Commonwealth Pier, where all famous ships are docked when they come to Boston. Thousands of persons, black and white, thronged the piers for the purpose of witnessing this first post-war concrete evidence of the purpose and determination of the New Negro to strike out for himself. But there was disappointment due to uncontrollable circumstances and the good ship of the line did not arrive on schedule. The good sense and temper of the people kept sweet, however, for they realized that hope was only deferred which maketh the heart gladder when fulfilled.[1] The "Yarmouth" adds another page of historic importance to the long line of historic incidents that make Boston the most historic city in the world, both for the Negro and for the white race.[2] Before her purchase by the Black Star Line Corporation it was here the "Yarmouth" used to sail from. It is the very ship on which William Monroe Trotter made his famous trip in the Peace Conference as a waiter and cook when he could not obtain passports to travel otherwise. From New Bedford to Portland, Me., they came to see the "Frederick Douglass." By the time these lines are published the ship will probably have arrived and 25,000 Negroes in Boston will have enrolled as full-fledged, active members of the U.N.I.A. and A.C.L. Present at the meeting held at the People's Church one of the largest white churches in the city of Boston especially rented for the purpose, from New York were the Hon. Marcus Garvey, president-general of the U.N.I.A.[;] Mr. Edward Smith-Green, secretary of the Black Star Line[;] Rev. Dr. J.W.H. Eason, chaplain-general; Miss Jacques, confidential secretary to the president-general; Mr. Jacques,[3] secretary of the Negro Factories Corporation; Madam Barrier Houston, soloist of the Black Star Line; Miss Revella Hughes[4] and Miss Marianna Johnson, of the New York Conservatory of Music, pianists and accompanists; Mr. Cyril A. Crichlow,[5] official reporter[;] Mr. William Isles and his famous band of the Black Star Line, and officers from the S.S. "Shadyside."

ATTORNEY MATTHEWS SPEAKS.

Attorney W. C. Matthews,[6] a prominent member of the Boston Bar, and also a member of the Boston Division of the U.N.I.A. was Master of Ceremonies, and made the following introductory remarks:

"Our meeting here tonight is in the line with the meetings that we had some weeks ago, when the Hon. Marcus Garvey was in the city and spoke at the various churches here. Some of you who did not hear him then, and who are attending for the first time [a] meeting of this organization will probably be interested and curious to know just what the purposes and the objects of the organization are: and in as few words as possible, I shall try to outline to you just what the organization stands for. The greater and broader purposes will be explained to you by the Hon. Marcus Garvey and the other speakers.

"The U.N.I.A. stands for what its name indicates—universal meaning, including the universe, wherever Negroes live; and it is the object of this organization to stretch forth its hands and to interest the Negro in himself, and to raise and to build itself up within itself and by itself. Wherever there are Negroes I think I am warranted in saying there are branches of this organization. In less time than I should say—two years—there has been many millions added to this organization. Almost every country is represented and a deep and wide interest is manifested in the tenets of the organization. Wherever there is a community of Negroes the U.N.I.A. has been heard of. There has been also heard the Black Star Line. The Black Star Line is, of course[,] of the members of the U.N.I.A. and it adds a connecting or joining link. Wherever the ships of this organization, or of the Black Star Line touches[,] it touches among the friends and members of this organization.

"Many of you probably were disappointed to-day in not seeing the Black Star Liner at Commonwealth Pier. All arrangements had been made. The President General and its officers were in anticipation of having the Captain and other members of the crew here. But matters happened over which we had no control—nothing, of course, disastrous. The ship had to stop to be coaled, and of course, is late in getting here. The ship will get here shortly, however, and you will all have an opportunity to go aboard and see her.

"It was very gratifying to note the [g]reat and widespread interest which was taken by members of the race, and also by members of the white race in the arrival of this ship, which used to run out from this port. As I said, you will have an opportunity later to see this boat when [s]he comes. I dare say she will be here, probably some time early next week.[7]

"This branch of the organization here in Boston started some time in November with about five or seven members in the office of its President, Dr. Gibson.[8] After two or three meetings there the organization outgrew Dr. Gibson's office. We then took the room of the Colored Citizens' Civic League at 830 Tremont street, and in five meetings we outgrew that hall. We are now [q]uartered in the Masonic Building up on Tremont street, and I might say that for the last four Sundays we have overcrowded that hall, and we are now seeking larger quarters if not for a hall of our own. (Applause.)

"I might say that we have increased from a membership of seven to a membership of about [1,]300. (Applause.) And when you have an organization of 1,300 active, energetic, working people in Boston you have performed some feat. We are trying to keep alive and keep high the ideals of the organization. We are trying amongst ourselves to build up race industries and race pride, and we can only do that by deciding to go out and not be employes, but employers. The Negro Factories Corporation and the Black Star Line afford the opportunities for us to make places for those people of our race who have not the opportunity to do those things in the other race. Our ship, manned by a crew of black people from captain to stoker, is an example of what we intend to do with the industries that we shall form within the organization. I might say here tonight that opportunity will be given for every person who is not a member to join the U.N.I.A. and also to take out shares for the Black Star Line and the Factories Corporation. It does not need to be told to you that the opportunity to take out shares of stock in a transportation organization like the Black Star Line is a wonderful opportunity. Thus if you have one or two ships you are bound to make profit out of it. Never was there a time in the history of the world when shipping was in such great demand and when shipping facilities were so scarce.[9] Therefore in offering to you the opportunity exclusively to own a part of a shipping organization of our own is a chance that comes to man but once in a lifetime.

"The Black Star liner 'Yarmouth' has made several trips with very important cargo. I do not suppose any cargo has gone out from the ports of America any more valuable than the cargo that went some few months ago in Cuba and Jamaica. Without doubt there has been turned in to the coffers of the Black Star Line an untold amount of money from this ship.[10] And there is in preparation now a ship many times larger than the "Yarmouth," which in a few weeks will be sailing the seas under the flag of the Black Star Line. (Cheers.)

["]I shall not take up much more of your time with any remarks of my own because I am not as familiar with the subject of the Black Star Line and the Factories Corporation as representative here amongst us, and I shall be very glad to ask Mr. Smith-Green to address you after the orchestra has played a number." (Applause.)

Mr. Edward Smith-Green[,] secretary of the Black Star Line, was next introduced by the chaplain general, Dr. Eason and said:

MR. SMITH GREEN SPEAKS.

Mr. Master of Ceremonies, Honorable President General, Members of the U.N.I.A. of the Boston Branch, Stockholders of the Black Star Line, Fellow Members of the Race: It indeed gives me very great pleasure to be amongst you this evening; and if in the course of my remarks I may seem somewhat provincial, I want you to realize that perhaps it is because I may have come from the metropolis of New York. But I have come also to the great historical city of Boston; and as I stand upon this rostrum and gaze upon the faces of all the men and women in this house, I cannot help but think of the greatness attached to this assembly, especially when it is remembered that you are but the descendents of those men and women which this great city produced, who have made history go down immortalized with great achievements. As I have been introduced by the master of ceremonies as the ambassador of the U.N.I.A. and the Black Star Line, I won't attempt to take to myself that name, as I very much prefer to introduce myself to you as your very humble servant who has had the honor to be sent abroad in the interests of this association and in the interests, for that matter, of millions of black folk of the world—to represent them and you in the sign and in the name of the red, black and green. (Cheers.) I want you to realize that the things that I am to tell you this evening have been made possible only through your co-operation. They have been made possible only through the fact that those people to whom I went realized that I went there not as an individual but rather as a representative of 400,000,000; and as such their doors were open to me—not to me the individual but as a representative of the U.N.I.A. and A.C.L.[,] the Black Star Line Steamship Corporation and the Negro Factories Corporation. (Cheers.) And I would like you also to realize that this is but the stepping stone—and assuredly an object lesson of what co-operation can do. Had I gone as an individual I would not have been the first man of the Negro race to happen to go to a friendly country in the interests of any business. There are hundreds of other men who have gone to other countries in the interests of some business concern: but they have gone as individuals. They have gone, perhaps, representing small groups. But when I went over there, I went representing you; and when I say you, I mean my race. Therefore, understand, that I have returned to the United States of America as the servant of my people, and I am pleased that the opportunity was granted me to represent you. (Cheers.)

Relative to my absence abroad, our president general and the Board of Directors, at the time the "Yarmouth" was about leaving these shores for Havana, because of the publicity which was given to her through the valuable cargo she had on board and because of other business interests we had abroad, decided that some one should go down there in the interests of the corporation and the association as the representative of the corporation, and I happened to be the lucky one to be chosen. Because of business pressure, I could not myself leave on the "Yarmouth." There were other things to be settled in New York. Before my departure the "Yarmouth" had left, and I left about four days after by way of Key West. I left the Pennsylvania station on the train and 48 hours after I departed I was in Key West, Fla. I crossed by the boat and in seven hours I was in Havana. Four hours after I arrived there the "Yarmouth" also arrived; and because of the great publicity which was given to our boat and our corporation, I went over there to find the people, so to speak, in an excited and excitable condition. They were all on edge awaiting the arrival of the boat which would bring to them not only the good message of fellowship, but which in itself represented the novelty of a steamship corporation owned and controlled exclusively and entirely by Negroes and commanded from the commander down to the cabin boy by Negroes. (Cheers.)

When the ship arrived in the harbor she could not drop her anchor fast enough in the stream for launches and all kinds of craft to go out to her, and there was a complete exodus of the people of Havana from their houses into the bay to inspect our ship. And I am perfectly sure, as it was told to me, that when they looked aloft, inasmuch as they saw her strewn with flags, that which held them most [enr]aptured was the flag which black men had at last taken to a foreign country—a flag designed and made by black men, a black star in the center with the red and green surrounding. . . .[11]

HON. MARCUS GARVEY SPEAKS.

The Hon. Marcus Garvey, president general of the U.N.I.A., was next introduced by the Rev. Dr. Eason, chaplain general, and said:

["]Mr. President—I speak of the president of the Boston Division of the U.N.I.A.—Members and Friends: I am as much disappointed tonight as you are not seeing the S.S. "Yarmouth" in port. I as president of the corporation several days ago sent cable messages to the commander of the "Yarmouth" in Bo[cas] del Toro to report in Philadelphia on the 26th and to report in Boston today. Through certain complications as I understand, he has been delayed. Yet he sent me a cable five days ago after he left Jamaica saying that he was making for Philadelphia so as to be there between the 26th and 27th, and then to leave Philadelphia to report today in Boston. We made sure that the good ship would have reached Philadelphia and subsequently come on to Boston on time. To my surprise, expecting to find her near port this morning, I received a cable when I arrived here, in that I left New York at 8 o'clock this morning, saying that the ship was off Jupiter, Florida where she had to put in for coal, and so through the shortage of coal she was unable to make port. I am very much disappointed. If I had the slightest belief that the "Yarmouth" would not have come in here today I would have . . . [*line deleted*] you would have seen at least one of the ships of the Black Star Line. (Cheers.) But I made sure that the "Yarmouth" would have been here, and I wanted the "Yarmouth" because she is the flag ship of the Black Star Line, and more than that, she is the celebrated ship next known to Noah's Ark in that she was the ship that created consternation the other day when she took away a $5,000,000 cargo of whiskey—the last to have been shipped out of the United States. (Cheers.) And I know that the good folks of Boston, like the good folks from the city where Dr. Eason comes (Philadelphia), if they cannot get the whiskey they would at least like to see the ship that took it away. (Laughter.) So for that and several other reasons I wanted "Yarmouth" here.

I did not come here to make a speech to-night. I came to hear for the first time in four months Henrietta Vinton Davis. I came to hear the Ambassadors we sent to the West Indies and Central America speak for the first time after four months and to my sad disappointment I am here to-night not listening to them, but addressing you. I promise to remain in Boston until the ship gets here, if she can get here within the next three days. I have again cabled her this afternoon to report here under all circumstances between now and Sunday or Monday morning; and if I receive word from the Captain to-morrow that he can make port between now and Monday morning I will remain over until Monday night, so that I may be able to appear with Henrietta Vinton Davis to explain the strength and power and force of the Black Star Line Steamship Corporation. (Applause.)

I have to compliment Dr. Gibson, the President, and you, the good members of the branch, for the splendid work you are doing among the good folks of Boston. You are struggling along splendidly. Although you cannot yet be numbered among the stronger branches of the association, yet for the short time you have done splendidly.

As Dr. Eason said, I have been speaking all last week and all this week at Liberty Hall and in Brooklyn and in Philadelphia. Last Monday night I had the pleasure of speaking to nearly ten thousand of the citizens of Philadelphia in the Academy of Music. It was a rainy, stormy night; and when for an ordinary occasion ten or twenty or one hundred people would not have turned out, they turned out there ten thousand strong under the auspices of the Philadelphia Division of the U.N.I.A. to hear what we had to say. Along the Eastern States, along the Atlantic Seaboard, the Universal has absolutely no difficulty in getting every night eight or ten thousand people to hear what we have to say when we announce that we have something to say. And in New York, in the space of six hours, we can always bring five or ten thousand people to hear our message; and so in Philadelphia, and so I want it to be in Boston. (Cheers.) We folks in New York are doing things. New York you

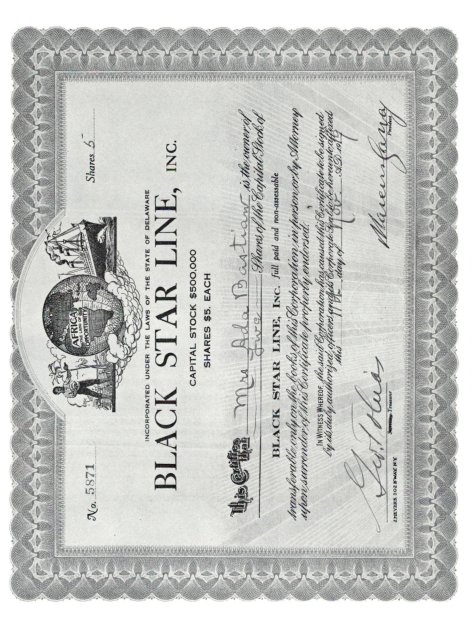

Black Star Line stock certificate

Garvey's sister, Indiana Peart and
his niece, Ruth Peart Prescott

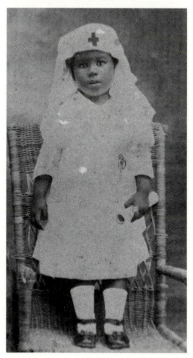

Ruth Peart Prescott in Black Cross nurse uniform

Robert S. Abbott

I. Newton Brathwaite

J. D. Brooks

Cyril A. Crichlow

John Sydney de Bourg

F. W. Ellegor

Arnold J. Ford

E. L. Gaines

Elie Garcia

J. D. Gordon

Cyril Henry

Marie Barrier Houston

Amy Jacques

Adrian Johnson

D. D. Lewis

William Matthews

George Alexander McGuire

George Wells Parker

Henry Vinton Plummer

Hudson Pryce

Rudolph E. B. Smith

Wilford Smith

Gabriel Stewart

O. M. Thompson

R. H. Tobitt

Fred A. Toote

James B. Yearwood

Universal Millinery Store

BSL Delegation in Cuba

BSL Delegation in conference

Inspection of the S.S. *Yarmouth* by UNIA members

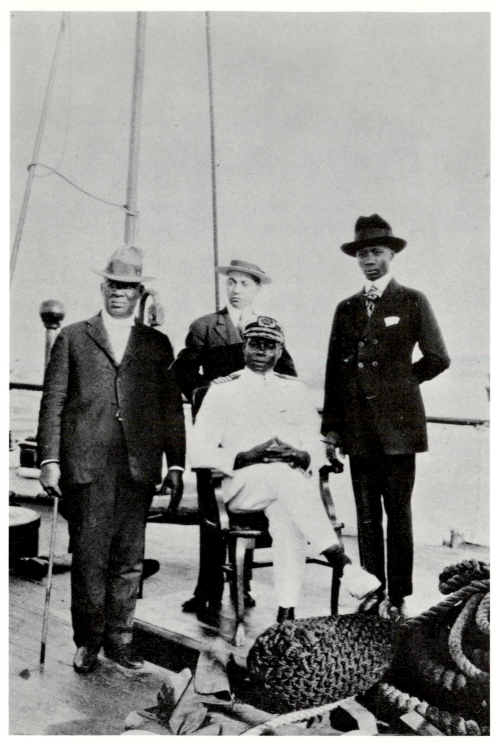

Joshua Cockburn, (seated) E. D. Smith-Green, (right) and two unidentiled UNIA leaders in Cuba

Crew of the S.S. *Yarmouth*

S.S. *Kanawha*

Gabriel M. Johnson

S.S. *Shadyside*

George Osborn Marke

Opening parade of the 1920 UNIA Convention

Universal African Legion in parade

know, is a very hard and difficult state to organize, because so many things go on there. So many things happen in New York; but the U.N.[I].A. has become so powerful that the Negroes will stop anything they are doing when we announce that we have something to tell them. They will even postpone a marriage to hear what the Universal has to say. In many instances people have postponed their arrangements and engagements so as to be present at the meeting of the U.N.I.A. (laughter and applause.)

Now all over the world we are preparing for the greatest meeting to be ever held by us or the race. We are preparing for our great convention which is to assemble in Liberty Hall from the 1st to the 31st of August of the present year. The convention will be held for the purpose of bringing together the delegates of the 400,000,000 Negroes scattered all over the world. At that convention we are to elect the permanent leaders of our movement and association, and for the first time in the history of 15,000,000 American Negroes they will have an opportunity of electing a leader for themselves who will preside over the destinies of the race in this country. We realize that as black folks we will be able to elect a president to sit over us as the nation elects a President to sit in the White House. We are going to elect a leader from the 15,000,000 here, and that leader will have as much voice and power even as the President has among his own people. So that we want you to take interest in this great convention. At the same time, we are to elect the leaders who will govern the destiny of all the Negro peoples of the world. We are remodeling and rebuilding Liberty Hall—the present one in New York—to seat between ten and fifteen thousand people for that convention. They will come from Africa, from South and Central America, from the West Indies, from the forty-eight states of the Union, and I want you to rally around Dr. Gibson in Boston so as to send some delegates from here so that your city and state can be well led after the convention.

Now I promise to speak to you tomorrow night at the Ebenezer Baptist Church, and Sunday afternoon and Sunday night I will tell you as much as I know about the U.N.I.A. and the Black Star Line. Because of the great deal I had to do within the last two weeks I am somewhat tired to-night, I am unable to make a speech, in that I came to hear Miss Davis. But if you turn out to-morrow night you will hear much more from me, even as I have spoken to you before. So that I have to thank you for coming out to-night and for the support you have given Dr. Gibson in bringing up this branch to where it is. If you will have confidence in the Black Star Line you will not only see the "Yarmouth" in port, but in the next two months we will have a regular service running between Boston, the West Indies, Central America and Africa. (Great and prolonged cheers.)

The Black Star Line is only nine months old and we have now three ships.[12] (Cheers.) As I just said in the next two months we will have a regular service in Boston, and we are going to take good care that some of the Boston folks who have bought stock in the Black Star Line will reap some of the benefits of being employed in the Black Star Line. (Hear, hear.) At the present time the Black Star Line in carrying out of its great commercial campaign all over the world has fully 500 employes. We have strong branch offices in Cuba, in British Guiana, in Haiti, in Jamaica, Bocas del Toro, in Port Limon, Costa Rica, Lagos, West Africa, in Sierra Leone, in Monrovia, Liberia, and we have branch offices in fifteen States of the Union. So we are ripe and ready for business—big business. (Cheers.) We have now 500 employes to take care of this business, and in the next twelve months we feel sure we will have in our employ at least three or five thousand Negroes (Cheers.)

These employes will not be porters and spittoon cleaners, but they will be presidents, secretaries, vice-presidents and treasurers and clerks and clerical assistants in the office of the Black Star Line. (Cheers.) If you good folks want to see something save some money and come to the convention in New York in August, and when you get there visit the offices of the Black Star Line, 54 and 56 West 135th street, and you will see one hundred or more Negro men and women in the offices there. (Applause.) You will find over sixty or seventy girls as typists and stenographers. You will find over fifty men working there as clerical assistants, just as you will see in the offices of the United Fruit Company going down State street in Boston. (Applause.)

It is our purpose in the U.N.I.A. to make the Negro a commercial and industrial factor in this country, as well as in every other country. The white man has built himself up as a great commercial and industrial force. You see his great office buildings, you see his great factories in Boston. It is our intention that in the next five years at least you will see many factories operated and controlled and owned by Negroes in these United States of America. (Cheers.)

Whilst we have three ships already for the Black Star Line[;] whilst we have three buildings for the U.N.I.A., we also will start to-morrow the first factory of the Negro Factories Corporation (applause) situated at 141st street and Lenox avenue, New York City. When you get to the convention you will also have the privilege of visiting our factory.

Thus you will realize that the movement you are supporting is not a sentimental movement; is not a movement that merely talks for the sake of talking; but it is a movement that is doing things. It is a movement that will be bringing later on bread and butter to thousands of us. I suppose some of you have read the attacks on the association by the Emancipator (a paper subsidized by the white Socialists). To-night I am not in good form to speak. Now if you want to hear me speak and speak as I have often spoken before thousands in New York and other parts, come out to-morrow night. (Cheers.)

Printed in *NW*, 8 May 1920. Original headlines omitted.

   1. Paraphrase of Prov. 13:12.

   2. In the nineteenth century, Boston was a major center for abolitionist activity and antislavery sentiment. UNIA officials often emphasized Boston's historical significance to blacks in their recruitment efforts. William Ferris, in a report on his 1922 tour of various

Massachusetts UNIA divisions, asserted: "For thirty-five years, from 1866 to 1900, Boston was the Black Man's Paradise. In those days I. H. Lewis was her leading tailor and Joseph Lees one of her leading caterers. . . . In those days and shortly afterwards, M. H. Lewis, William Matthews [Garvey's attorney] and other colored men won athletic laurels at Harvard. . . . In those days Boston was a mecca for representatives of colored schools, poor students and mendicant colored teachers, preachers, lecturers and politicians . . . " (*NW*, 13 February 1922).

3. Cleveland Augustus Jacques, brother of Amy Jacques.

4. Possibly Revela Hughes, a 1920s jazz pianist who recorded with the famous orchestra leader Fletcher Henderson (*Esquire World of Jazz* [New York: Esquire, 1962], p. 40).

5. Cyril A. Crichlow, coowner of a shorthand and stenographic service in Harlem, was a member of the high executive council of the UNIA in 1921. He was sent as resident secretary of the UNIA commission to Liberia in February 1921; the commission was charged with starting the UNIA's building and farming program in that nation. Crichlow was "responsible for all our records and all data and reports pertaining to the interests of the [UNIA] in Liberia" (Marcus Garvey to Gabriel Johnson, 1 February 1921, DNA, RG 84; *Crisis* 20, no. 2 [June 1920]: 104).

6. William Clarence Matthews (1877–1928), an Alabama-born lawyer, completed his early education at Tuskegee Institute in 1897. He later attended Phillips Andover Academy, Andover, Mass., and Harvard University, graduating in 1905. As a student at Andover and Harvard, Matthews won wide acclaim as a football and baseball player; for a brief period he played semiprofessional baseball in Vermont. In 1907, after earning a law degree from Boston University, Matthews opened a law practice in Boston with William H. Lewis (1869–1949), a supporter of Booker T. Washington, and he subsequently served as one of the political lieutenants of the Tuskegee machine. These connections enabled him to obtain a patronage position as a special assistant to the United States district attorney for Boston. Matthews served in France during World War I. Although he became a supporter of Garvey and the UNIA, throughout the rest of the 1920s, he resumed his involvement in Republican machine politics; he was appointed special assistant to the attorney general of the United States as a reward for his role in the successful 1924 campaign of President Calvin Coolidge (*WWCR*; Phillips Andover Academy Archives, vertical file; Harvard College, class of 1905, *Report*).

7. The *Yarmouth* arrived on 12 May 1920.

8. Joseph D. Gibson (1880?–1963), Barbados-born physician, banker, and political organizer, was surgeon general of the UNIA (1920–22). Gibson, who immigrated to the United States in 1909, graduated from the Boston College of Physicians and Surgeons in 1915. Gibson was later impeached by the third annual UNIA convention in 1922 for alleged disloyalty (*NW*, 12 August 1922). Arrested and released on charges of mail fraud at the same time as was Garvey, he subsequently moved to Logan, W.Va., and worked for some time as a physician for the United Mine Workers. In 1933 he became the first black to run for Congress in Logan. He was active in the 1940 and 1952 Republican election campaigns (*NYT*, 16 November 1963).

9. The U.S. Shipping Board commandeered millions of tons of American ships at the beginning of the American involvement in World War I. When the war ended, however, escalating competition between American and British shippers led American shippers to demand that the seized vessels be released. The scarcity of vessels for American shippers worsened when the government used American merchant vessels to repatriate soldiers and to provide food relief. Moreover, ships borrowed by the government from the British had to be returned, as did the neutral vessels used in the United States war trade in South America. When the shipping board finally released commandeered vessels to private control, it triggered a rush for overseas trade in the United States that temporarily outdistanced the capacity of available ships. Shortly afterward, however, a glut of ships produced a depression in the shipping business (Jeffrey J. Safford, *Wilsonian Maritime Policy, 1913–1921* [New Brunswick, N.J.: Rutgers University Press, 1978], pp. 141–253).

10. The report of the Department of Justice's examination of the books of the Black Star Line indicates that during the fiscal year ending 30 June 1920, the *Yarmouth* incurred over $138,000 in expenses while earning slightly less than $45,000 from freight and passengers. The following fiscal year, the *Yarmouth* amassed over $54,000 in expenses but could manage an income of only $13,340. By January 1922 operating losses amounted to over $136,000 (DJ-FBI, Thomas P. Merrilees, "Summary Report of Investigation of the Books and Records of the Black Star Line, Inc., and the Universal Negro Improvement Association").

11. Portions of Smith-Green's speech have been omitted.

12. The Black Star Line Board of Directors voted to approve the contract for the purchase of the *Yarmouth* for $165,000 on 20 September 1919. The board of directors voted to purchase *Shadyside* for $35,000 on 22 March 1920. Negotiations for the purchase of the *Kanawha* were approved at the 23 April 1920 meeting of the board of directors. The board later approved a purchase price of $60,000 (Thomas P. Merrilees, "Summary Report").

Editorial Letter by Marcus Garvey

[[Philadelphia, Pa., May 3, 1920]]

THE DRIVE TO LAUNCH THE THIRD SHIP OF THE BLACK STAR LINE

Fellowmen of the Negro Race, Greeting:

It is with great joy and gladness that I write to you, after a successful visit to Philadelphia, Brooklyn and Boston.

In Philadelphia last Monday we addressed a gathering that filled the spacious Academy of Music on a rainy night. In Brooklyn last Thursday night we were greeted by an audience that nearly filled the Academy of Music. And on Friday night we addressed a large gathering in the People's Temple, Boston. Thus we have been fortunate in having an opportunity to reawaken interest in the Black Star Line in the three great States of the East.

For the past quarter of a century the darker races of the world have felt the heavy hand of the Caucasian oppressor. In the Southern section of the United States of America the Negro has been robbed of his citizenship. In Africa the natives have been robbed of their land and subjugated in the bargain. In the past the black men have either weeped and wailed or shaken their fist at and cursed their Caucasian oppressor.

But the New Negro has realized that something else than mere protest and demands must be made. He realizes the full significance of Darwin's phrases, "Struggle for Existence" and "The Survival of the Fittest." He realizes that if he becomes economically self-sustaining and becomes a factor in the commercial and industrial life of the world, he will not only gain some of the good things of this world, but will also gain prestige and standing. For these reasons we have not asked other races to help us, but have endeavored to help ourselves by starting the Black Star Line and the Negro Factories Corporation. Already we have purchased the "Yarmouth" and the "Shadyside," and in a few days we will take over the "S. S. Antonio Maceo." At the same time we are taking over a steam laundry and starting a millinery and hat factory. In a word, the Universal Negro Improvement Association, the Black Star Line and the Negro Factories Corporation are enabling the Negro to successfully stand the struggle for existence and to become fit to survive industrially.

At the same time the Universal Negro Improvement Association is planning to have a great convention of Negroes from different sections of the world meet in Liberty Hall, New York, from the 1st to the 31st of August to outline a constructive plan and program for the uplifting of the Negro and the redemption of Africa.

You have generously backed the Black Star Line and have rallied to the Negro Factories Corporation, and I am now asking you to perfect the work which was so magnificently begun. You can best do so by buying five, ten, twenty, thirty, forty, fifty and one hundred or two hundred shares in the Black Star Line by writing or calling at the office of the Bl[ack] [Star] Line Steamship Corporation, 54–56 West 135th [Street, New] York, N. Y., U.S.A.

The drive is on to launch the third ship on the 9th of May. Let us go over the top again, as we have heretofore. Fortune favors the brave.[1] With very best wishes for your success, Yours fraternally,

MARCUS GARVEY

Printed in *NW*, 8 May 1920. Original headlines abbreviated.

1. From Vergil's *Aeneid*, Bk. 10, line 284.

Passengers on the S.S. *Yarmouth* Arriving from Cristobal[1]

Philadelphia, May 6th 1920

NAME IN FULL.		AGE.		CALLING OR OCCUPATION.	NATIONALITY.	RACE.	LAST PERMANENT RESIDENCE.	PLACE OF BIRTH.	
Family name.	*Given name.*	*Yrs.*	*Mos.*					*Country.*	*City or town.*
Hamlett	[Ros]]/etta/	24	2	Dom.	British	West Indies/Afr/	Panama City	Domini[ca]	Rose[a]u
Dottin	Ophelia	19	3	Dom.	British	West Indies/Afr/	Panama City Panama	Barbados	St. Mich[a]els
Fraser	Anita	31		Dom.	British	West Indian/Afr/	Ancon, Canal Zone	Grenada	St. Patrick
Chambers /Jeffreys/	James /A./	41		Clerk	British	West Indian/Afr/	Panama City	Jamaica	FALMOUTH
	Emandus	29		CLERK	BRIT-ISH	WEST INDIAN/ Afr/	Panama (Panama City)	Grenada	St. Patrick
Shepherd	Fred	30	6	Sign PAINTER	British	West Indian/Afr/	Panama City (Panama)	Barbado[s]	St. Michael
Proud-homme	Thomas	28	6	/Stone/ Mason	British	West Indian	Panama City	Grenada	ST. JOHNS
Proud-homme	Zila /E./	33	0	Dom.	British	West Indian/Afr/	Panama City	JAMAICA	KINGSTON
Burke	Fred /Austin/	29	0	Sten.	British	West Indian/Afr/	Panama City	Jamaica	Linstead
DeCoteau	Ruby	24	0	/Dress-maker/	British	West Indian/Afr/	Panama City	Grenada	Gouyave
Brath-waite	Eunice	37	0	Dom.	British	West Indian/Afr/	Panama City	Barbados	Christchurch

Surname	Given	Age		Occupation			Birthplace	Origin	
Goban	Katherine	36	6	Dom.	British	West Indian	Panama City	Barbados	STANNS
Goban	Victor	8	6	School	PAN-AMA	West INDIAN	Panama City	Panama	P. City
Goban	Reginald	[7?]	3	School	Panama	West INDIAN	Panama City	Panama	City
Goban	Lucille	5	6	School	Panama	West INDIAN	Panama City	Panama	City
Francis	Benjamin	26	9	Carpenter	British	West Indian	Panama Colon	Barbados	CHRIST-CHURCH
Hynds	Rebecca	36	0	Dom.	British	West Indian	Panama City	Jamaica	LUCEA
Hynds	Esau	6	0	——	Canal Zone	West Indian	Panama City	Canal Zone	Bas Obispo
Beard	Emma	30	0	Dom.	British	West Indian	Panama City	BARBADOS	ST. ANDREW
Henry[2]	Cyril	33	0	Chemist Agr'l	British	West Indian	/New York/	Jamaica	Spanish Town
Brath-waite	James /(R.P.)/	34	0	A.B.	BRIT-ISH	West Indian	Panama [C]ity	BARBADOS	ST. PHILLIPS
Fletcher	Arnold	29	8	Welder	British	West Indian	Panama City	GRENADA	GRANVILLE
Aquart	Cyril	30	3	Clerk	British	West Indian	Panama City	GRENADA	ST. JOHNS
Hinds	Lester	16	7	Clerk	British	West Indian	Panama Colon	JAMAICA	OLD HARBOR
Layne	Aubrey	25	2	Mechanic	British	West Indian	Panama Colon	Barbados	CHRIST-CHURCH
MacIntosh	Percival	30	0	Fitter	British	West Indian	Panama City	Jamaica	Falmouth

Passengers on the S.S. *Yarmouth* Arriving from Cristobal (Continued)

Philadelphia, May 6th 1920

NAME IN FULL		AGE.		CALLING OR OCCUPA-TION.	NATION-ALITY.	RACE.	LAST PERMANENT RESIDENCE.	PLACE OF BIRTH.	
Family name.	*Given name.*	*Yrs.*	*Mos.*					*Country.*	*City or town.*
Clarke	Ethel	26	0	Domestic /Wife/	British	West Indian/Afr/	Panama City	Barbados	St[.] Johns/
Clarke	Fitz Allen	35	0	Painter	British	West Indian/Afr/	Panama City	Barbados	Christch/urch/
Phillips	James	49	0	Sten.	British	West Indian/Afr/	Panama City	Grenada	Granville
Brown	Jonathan	32	0	Laborer	British	West Indian/Afr/	Panama Colon	Jamaica	St. James
Trotman	Richard	29	1	/Laborer/	British	West Indian/Afr/	Panama City	Barbados	Christ/church/
Heuton	Michael	30	4	Chauff[eu]r	British	West Indian/Afr/	Panama City	GRENADA	/St. Patrick/
Spence	Daniel /R./	28	0	/Account-ant/	British	West Indian/Afr/	Panama Colon	Jamaica	West./more-land/
Gittens	Caroline	30	0	Dom.	British	West Indian	Panama City	Barbados	St[.] Phillips
Earl	Levinia	33	0	Dom[.]	BRIT-ISH	West Indian	Panama City	Barbados	St[.] Thomas
Earl	Clarence	6	6	School	PAN-AMA	West Indian	Panama City	Panama	City
Earl	Evelyn	4	6	School	PAN-AMA	West Indian	Panama City	Panama	City
Brown	Leopold	29	8	Mechanic Black-smith	British	West Indian/Afr/	Panama City	Jamaica	Kingston

Robinson	Cedric	21	0	Printer	British	West Indian/Afr/	Panama City	/Grenada/	St. Johns
Trotman	John /E./	48	0	Carpenter	British	West Indian/Afr/	Panama City	Barbados	ST. THOMAS
/Jeffreys/	Amos	28	0	Painter	British	West Indian/Afr/	Panama City	Grenada	St[.] Patricks
Elcock	Miriam	32		Dom.	British	West Indian/Afr/	Panama City	Barbados	ST. GEORGES
Elcock	Kirkham	7		———	Panama	West Indian	Panama City	Panama	City
Elcock	Wellesley	3	7	———	Panama	West Indian	Panama City	Panama	City
Bryan	Ida	30		Dom. /seam-stress/	Panama	West Indian	Panama City	Barbados	Christchurch
S[p]ringer	Thomas	39	3	Artisan	British	West Indian	Panama City	Barbados	ST. ANDREW

DNA, RG 85, file T-715. Printed form with typewritten and handwritten insertions.

1. The *Yarmouth* sailed from Cristobal, Panama Canal Zone, on 4 April 1920.

2. Cyril Henry was returning from his Central American tour on behalf of the BSL.

Frank Burke to C. B. Welsh,[1] Acting Chief, Passport Division, Department of State

[*Washington, D.C.*] May 7, 1920

Dear Sir:

Reference is made to your verbal request to Mr. Ruch, for further information concerning the activities of HUBERT HARRISON and DR. W. H. EASON.

Both of these subjects, for the past month, have been making every possible effort to leave this country for the purpose of making necessary arrangement with the Liberian Government in Africa, to establish headquarters of the "UNIVERSAL NEGRO IMPROVEMENT ASSOCIATION".

They are being sent to Africa, for this purpose, by Marcus Garvy, president of the Universal Negro Improvement Association, New York City, whose activities have been observed by this Bureau for sometime, and it appears that this individual is the cause of the greater portion of the negro agitation in this country.

Rev. Eason is the pastor of the "Peoples Church" in Philadelphia, and appears to be the nucleus of the negro activities in that city.

Hubert Harrison is the assistant editor of Garvy's publication "The Negro World".

It is the understanding of the Bureau, that Eason gave as his reason for going to Africa, that he was to act as a missionary. This of course is known to be untrue, for his real purpose is as stated above.

It is the opinion of the Bureau that it would be simply furthering the operations of this organization should these passports be granted, and it is therefore requested that same be declined.

Kindly regard this information as strictly confidential, as it was obtained from a very confidential source. Very truly yours,

[FRANK BURKE]
Assistant Director and Chief

DNA, RG 65, file OG 185161. TL, carbon copy.

1. Charles Brelsford Welsh (b. 1880) was first employed by the Department of State in 1900; he was made chief of the passport bureau in December 1917 (U.S. Department of State, *Register*, 1916–1917 [Washington, D.C.: GPO, 1916–17], p. 148).

UNIA Chaplain General's Weekly Message

[*Negro World*, 8 May 1920]

Chaplain General's message to the chaplains of all divisions and through them to the members of the U.N.I.A. and A.C.L. throughout the world: "Select Jesus Christ as your standard bearer."

J. W. [H]. EASON

Printed in *NW*, 8 May 1920.

THE
NEGRO FACTORIES
CORPORATION

Build Factories!   Operate Factories! And Control Your Own Destiny.

NOW IS THE TIME FOR EVERY MEMBER OF THE RACE TO INVEST AND MAKE MONEY

The Negro Factories Corporation

Capitalized at $1,000,000 under the laws of the State of Delaware, offers 200,000 shares of common stock to the Negro Race at par value of $5.00 per share.

This Corporation is to build and operate Factories in the big industrial centers of the United States, Central America, the West Indies and Africa to manufacture every marketable commodity.

FACTORIES MUST GO UP IF THE RACE IS TO SUCCEED

BUY YOUR SHARES NOW AND HELP TO MAKE THE FUTURE

THE NEGRO FACTORIES CORPORATION is backed by 3,000,000 members of the Universal Negro Improvement Association of the World.

BUY YOUR SHARES TODAY AND NOT TO MORROW IN

The Negro Factories Corporation

CUT THIS OUT AND MAIL IT
SUBSCRIPTION BLANK

NEGROES FACTORIES CORPORATION
56 West 135th Street, New York City

Date.............................

Gentlemen:

I hereby subscribe for .... shares of stock at $5.00 per share and forward herewith as full payment $ .... on same.

Name..

Street...

City..

State...

(*Source: NW*, 8 May 1920)

LET US GUIDE OUR OWN DESTINY

BY FINANCING OUR OWN COMMERCIAL VENTURES.
HELP US TO HELP YOU HELP YOURSELF AND THE NEGRO RACE IN GENERAL
YOU CAN DO THIS BY PLAYING A MAN OR WOMAN'S PART IN THE WORLD OF COMMERCE:
DO YOUR FULL SHARE IN HELPING TO PROVIDE
A DIRECT LINE OF STEAMSHIPS OWNED, CONTROLLED AND MANNED BY NEGROES TO
REACH THE NEGRO PEOPLES OF THE WORLD
AMERICA, CANADA, SOUTH AND CENTRAL AMERICA, AFRICA AND THE WEST INDIES

There should be no trouble about making up your mind to help your race to rise to a position in the maritime world that will challenge the attention and command the admiration of the world. "Men like nations fail in nothing they boldly attempt when sustained by virtuous purpose and firm resolution."
Money awaiting an advantageous investment should go to purchasing shares in the Black Star Line and reap the reward that is bound to follow.

DO A MAN'S PART RIGHT NOW

Send In and Buy Your Shares Today

"THE BLACK STAR LINE," Inc.

Capitalized at $10,000,000 Under the Laws of the State of Delaware

2,000,000 shares of common stock now on sale at par value of $5.00 each for a limited time only at the office of the corporation, 56 West 135th Street, New York City. Phone Harlem 2877.
The Black Star Line, Inc., is the result of a Herculean effort on the part of Hon. Marcus Garvey, world-famed Negro orator, who in July, 1914, founded a society known as the Universal Negro Improvement Association and African Communities League, of which he is now President-General.
The Association now has a membership of over three million persons, with branches all over the United States, Canada, South and Central America, the West Indies and Africa.

THE BLACK STAR LINE, Inc.

is backed today in its operations by the full strength of its organization—to say the least, of millions of other Negro men and women in all parts of the world.

BUY SHARES TODAY AND NOT TOMORROW

- -

CUT THIS OUT AND MAIL IT

SUBSCRIPTION BLANK

"THE BLACK STAR LINE, Inc."
56 West 135th Street, New York City

Date...........

Gentlemen:

I hereby subscribe for........shares of stock at $5.00 per share and forward herewith as full payment
$.........on same.

Name ....
Street ....
City ....
State ....

(Source: NW, 8 May 1920)

338

Bureau of Investigation Reports

Cleveland, Ohio May 14, 1920

MARCUS GARVEY[,] Negro Radical

Agent in Charge Morton was called on long distance telephone, by Mr. Grimms, Bureau office, Washington, D. C. Mr. Grimms stated that subject left New York City, at eight P.M. May 4th, and was due to reach Cleveland some time during the morning of May 5th, and suggested that subject's activities be watched while in this city. Agent following instructions of Agent in Charge Morton to meet Train No. 23 due in Cleveland at 11:47 A.M. over the N. Y. C. and to follow subject, in order to ascertain where he was going to make his headquarters in this city, proceeded to Union Depot in automobile. Agent was present when the train, No. 23, arrived in Cleveland, and saw subject accompanied by two other colored men, and three colored women get out of the pullman. At the Depot they hired a touring car, Ohio License No. 100014. The touring car with subject and companions, left the Depot, and was followed by Agent in Agent's automobile to Lakeside Ave., to East 9th St., to Woodland Ave., going east on Woodland to East 40th St., and north on East 40th, and stopping at 2380, where the women of the party got out of the machine. The three men proceeded in the machine to 3505 Cedar Ave., where their suitcases and other baggage was taken into the upper apartment over an empty store by subject, and two companions, after which subject dismissed automobile. Agent returned to Bureau office, and informed Agent in Charge Morton where subject was making his headquarters. Agent later received information that subject was scheduled to speak at the Cory African Methodist Church on the evenings of May 5th and 6th. Agent made preparation to have meetings covered.

Agent received report of Meeting at Cory M. E. Church, May 5th, from confidential informant, which is as follows:—

There were present about four hundred or more negroes at the meeting at the Cory M. E. Church, 35th St., and Scoville Ave., at which Marcus Garvey was the principal speaker.

The first speaker of the evening was a man named Fuller[.] Fuller had the audience sing a psalm and then offered a prayer. The Rev. Gleason [*Eason?*] from New York City was then introduced and if ever a man tried his utmost to put hatred against the white race into the hearts of the negroes, it was Gleason. He constantly tried to impress on the minds of the negroes that they are just as good as the white folks and any negro who took his hat off to a white person ought to be put to death. He also pictured the Universal Negro Improvement Association and the African Communists' [*Communities?*] League as a garden of Eden, in which the negroes will become millionaires after they are members and contribute 35¢ a month, and buy shares at $5.00 each in the Black Star Line.

After two colored ladies offered a few songs, Marcus Garvey was introduced as the savior of the negro race. Garvey was very hoarse and it was hard to catch his words, but he opened his speech by calling the negroes of America a bunch of fools for wanting to work for white folks, when the 4[0]0,000,000 negroes could after being organized solidly, demand the freedom and independence of Africa, the same as the Irish are fighting for Ireland and the Hindu for India. He praised Germany for its superior leadership which will shortly again put Germany in the front ranks of world powers, but he condemned the U. S. Constitution for refusing to let a negro become President of the United States.

Garvey, the same as Gleason, tried his best to poison the minds of those present against the white race and urged the negroes to organize to fight for liberty and freedom and then demand Africa as their free and independent Republic. He also told of his plans to build negro factories which will be owned by the negroes only, worked by negroes only and manufacture for negroes only, and about the Black Star Line Steamship Co., which already owns three ships which are manned by negroes only, and which will send ships throughout the world demanding a free African Republic for the negro race. He told of the ship "Yarmouth" transporting five million dollars worth of whiskey from New York to Cuba and of the large profits his enterprises will make for all those who will buy stock from [*him*] or his agents, at $5.00 per share—one person to own not more than 200 shares. About two thirds of those present joined Garvey's organization, paying 25¢ each initiation fee and about 200 bought from one to ten shares at $5.00 each. A separate collection was also made, which netted Garvey about $150.00. It is really a crime to let Garvey fool the poor negroes of Cleveland with his schemes.

Agent received report of meeting at Cory M. E. Church, May 6th, from confidential informant, which is as follows:—

Marcus Garvey has apparently made a hit with the Cleveland negroes. Central Avenue was all excited today over the promises made by Garvey. About fifteen of Garvey's agents canvassed the black region of Cleveland, and they were very successful in securing members and share holders for Garvey's various enterprises.

Fuller, the official Cleveland representative of Marcus Garvey, is an outspoken radical, but very shrewd and well schooled in the art of camouflage. Prior to December 1919, he was a member of the I.W.W. recruiting Union in New York City, but since January has not paid his dues into the I.W.W. on the advice of Garvey, who wants to build up a labor movement of negroes alone. Garvey has a newspaper of his own, called "The Negro World", which has nearly a million readers in the U.S. and South and Central America, and over two hundred agents are now working in various parts of Africa to preach the Garvey Gospel and Slogan—"A Free and Independent Republic of Africa for the Negroes of the World."

Garvey is a wonderful orator, an efficient organizer and possesses plenty of nerve. His most valuable asset is his art of camouflaging his real aim and purpose. He looks to Ludwig Martens[1] as a true friend and supporter.

The following is a report of a colored man, who at the request of this Agent covered Meeting held at Cory M. E. Church, May 5th and 6th:—

Garvey in his talk told about the plans for the advancement of the negro, saying that they should organize themselves into a body, as all the other races of the country had done for their advancement, so that they could have means for promoting various industries. He said that he had traveled all over this country and Europe, and his intention was to organize the colored people into such a body. After speaking along this line for quite a while then his talk was about his promoting the Black Star Line, and he also stated that the District Attorney at New York had called him into his office ten different times trying to get something on him, and at one time when he called him into his office, after he heard that he was going to start this Boat under the corporation name of the Black Star Line, he said to him that you will not have the Black Star Line[.] Garvey in reply to this said, he would have the Black Star Line, or swim in blood, and on the 31st of October 1918, [*1919*] the first ship of the Black Star Line was placed in the water, for which they paid $180,000.00, and this ship was operated by black men from the top to the bottom.

The balance of this talk was telling that he was there to sell stock, and they could purchase any amount from one to two hundred shares.

According to informant Garvey left Cleveland at midnight, May 6th, for New York City.

Investigation concluded.

J. [F.] SAWKEN

[*Endorsements*] NOTED W.W.G. Noted F.D.W.

DNA, RG 65, file OG 329359. TD. Copies of this report were furnished to the bureau's Washington D.C. (three copies) and New York (one copy) offices, as well as to the United States attorney (two copies). Stamped endorsements. See also DNA, RG 165, file 10015-95.

1. Ludwig Martens was the self-styled ambassador from the Soviet Union.

Wash., D.C. May 22, 1920

MARCUS GARVEY, RADICAL LECTURER TO NEGROES

Agent visited the office of "THE WASHINGTON EAGLE,"[1] a colored newspaper, having learned that in case subject would appear in Washington to speak[,] this office would no doubt have acknowledge of the fact as this office has covered all of his lectures in the past.

Agent purchased a copy of this paper but could not find any advertising or anything in the paper to indicate that subject would be here on the evening of May 20th or 21st.

Agent also visited the office of MURRA[Y] BROS., Colored printers, 1731 7th St. NW., where he was informed that subject is a radical and editor of a radical New York paper; that he had no following in Washington, and to the best of their knowledge, he would not speak here.

At the same place Agent interviewed MR. JOHNSON, manager of the HOWARD THEATRE,[2] who looks after the booking of speakers and entertainers, and who claims that he would know if subject was to appear in Washington. Informa[nt] stated that he had not heard that subject was to speak here on May 20th, or May 21st; that there hadn't been any advertising or any literature of any description announcing that he would be here.

Agent visited quite a number of colored business places in the northwest section but failed to find any one that knew of subject's appearance here.

Agent called up the HOWARD UNIVERSITY[3] on the telephone and was informed by the woman in the secretary's office that they had not heard that subject would be here to make a speech but in case he did, the only place they knew of as likely to be[,] would be before [the] . . . [*word mutilated*] Congress with headquarters at the Washington [ho]tel.

Agent [foun]d [ou]t at the Washington hotel that speeches were to be made at Continental Hall on the evening of the 20th and 21st. Agent visited Continental Hall on the night of the 20th, but failed [to find] subject's name on the programs. Several colored persons were in the audience. Subject did not appear before this Congress.

INVESTIGATION CONTINUED.

AGENT HORN

[*Handwritten endorsement*] J See Wash. Star for May 18 or 19 (Amusement page) W.G.
[*Stamped endorsements*] NOTED W.W.G.
FILE G.F.R. Noted F.D.W.

DNA, RG 65, file OG 329359. TD.

1. The *Washington Eagle* was edited by J. Finley Wilson (b. 1881), who established the paper with T. Thomas Fortune as the *Sun* in 1913. Born in Nashville, Wilson was educated in the city's public schools and at Fisk University, Nashville. After a colorful career as a cowboy, miner, and journalist in the Canadian and American West, Wilson became a reporter for the *New York Age*. He later reorganized the *Norfolk Journal and Guide* and established newspapers in Baltimore and Harrisburg, Pa. (*WWCA*).

2. Howard Theatre was not connected with Howard University but was a white-owned commercial concern. A check through its booking records and the *Washington Bee* of this period did not reveal any speaking engagement by Garvey during this time in May (Michael R. Winston to Robert A. Hill, 25 March 1982).

3. Howard University, founded in 1867 and located in Washington, D.C., was already the largest and most prestigious black university in the United States by 1920. Howard University students reportedly established a university branch of the UNIA (*NW*, 2 February 1924; Emory J. Tolbert, interview with Rev. De Witt Turpeau, February 1971).

Article in the *Baltimore Observer*

[May 1920]

MARCUS DECLARES HIMSELF.

At Bethel Church on the nights of May the eighteenth and nineteenth, the Hon. Marcus Garvey, president of the Universal Negro Improvement Association, president of the Negro Factories' Corporation, president of the African Communities' Association and president-general of the Black Star Line Steamship Corporation, addressed two large gatherings. After a snappy program, the Hon. Marc took the rost[r]um and explained in detail the different organizations, their accomplishments up to date and his program for the future. Now the Hon. Marc is some speaker and at different times he worked the audience up to such a pitch you could almost see a Black Empire, and whereas he has really accomplished something in the past of course it was not necessary to take the proverbial grain of salt along with his utterances.

We have been for some time cognizant of the fact the Black Star Line is no myth but a reality. We know that they have three ships and intend to launch two ocean-going vessels every two months, but we did not know anything about the battle cruisers which are to be built, but Mr. Garvey says so and we have to take his word because he brought us the three merchant vessels according to schedule. Now [o]n that day some fool will ask—what are we going to do with battle cruisers and whom are we going to fight? To this question the Hon. Marc would answer, when the World War starts up again (the nations are only resting on their arms) the black man will take his place in the strife and fight his own battles. Some battles are fought on the high seas or under the high seas so it is absolutely essential that we have battle cruisers. To which we answer—if we are going to have battle cruisers also let us have some submarines, battleships, airships and aeroplanes. You can't tell what circumstances might cause the fight to be staged anywhere. Then too, a battle cruiser is known to have great speed for making its get away and surely we would not run, we want to stand our ground and get beat or beat some one else. At any rate we are going to have them and in due course of time we shall build a wonderful fleet and will be able to hold our own with anyone. As to whom we shall fight—why we will fight anybody who wants to fight. Further on in his speech he told of the Black Empire which is to be formed. We didn't know that either, but now that we do know, we think it is a swell idea. Anything to get away from this "Safe for Democracy" stuff. Just look at our condition now. We are safe for democracy and can't buy a drink. Sugar is so high it's in the class with Terrapin and Canvas Back Ducks. One new potato has a greater purchasing value than a dime and clothing has reached the stage where a man has to join a building association to get a new suit. The price of a pair of shoes with the war tax is enough to buy a new refrigerator. A straw hat which is guaranteed to turn either brown or yellow within three weeks, will make you think you are paying off a plumber for an eight-hour day's work, and two hours overtime at double time. We wouldn't mention the landlord for nobody wants to hear such disagreeable talk, we prefer to talk about chicken at from sixty-five to eighty cents a pound or a railroad ticket to New York at six dollars and three cents, with a proposed raise of thirty-three per cent. coming. Which goes to show that when you are safe for democracy you are in a devil of a fix. Now Marcus is going to stop all this by forming a Black Empire. There will be no prohibition, no high prices, nothing to take the joy out of life and you can do anything you like but get in the Royal Family.

This all looks very strange and sounds very good, but Marcus gathered quite a few "kopecks" during his two days' stay and received into the Universal Negro Improvement Association many new members. He also sold stock for the Black Star Line and the Factories' Corporation. Ordinarily some people might not take him seriously, but we might mention that the maritime interest in New York and London don't feel so good about The Black Star Line. Then, too, Marcus has three million negroes in his organization, which to our mind is a great achievement when we think of how hard it is for any one to keep three negroes together. As a matter of fact we don't know of any one up to date who has kept that many working in peace and harmony except Marcus, and any man who can keep three million negroes together is capable of any accomplishment.

For his support he is depending on the only class of colored people who support anything. Individually their contributions are very meagre, but so constant, and when the contribution is multiplied by three million the stack of crumbs grows very large. This gang has financed many movements successfully, and so far have never failed to put their projects on a firm foundation. For reference they can give you the Baptist, A. M. E., A. M. E. Z. and C. M. E. churches, all Negro insurance companies, county and city schools all over the South which they have kept open when the different States only supplied from two to three months' terms, college graduates from all big universities, banks, secret orders and many other things too numerous to mention. Their money came by the sweat of the brow, and in numerous cases they gave up when they had nothing for themselves. Patriots of the first water, whose backing is as strong and as sure as the sun is hot, make up Chief Garvey's following. Cooks, porters, hodcarriers, wash women, skullions, day laborers and many other kinds of toilers are on the roll of honor, and we can't see how they can miss, according to past performances. Marcus should have on the official seal of the empire, a washtub, a frying pan, a bail hook and a mop. As long as he sticks to them and does not pay any attention to the smart fellows, he is bound to go ahead, whether he builds the battle cruisers and establishes the Black Empire or not.

Printed in the *Baltimore Observer*, May 1920.

J. Edgar Hoover to George F. Ruch

WASHINGTON, D.C. June 8, 1920

MEMORANDUM FOR MR. RUCH.

I am in receipt of your memorandum of the 3rd instant advising me of the result of the investigation of Informant No. 800, to the effect that there is a possible violation of the MANN White Slave Act on the part of MARCUS GARVEY.

I believe that we should continue our investigation into this matter but that no definite action should be taken toward the prosecution of Garvey at this time until all evidence is collected. It might be advisable for 800 to submit [as] much evidence as he has in his possession upon this matter. Respectfully,

J. E. H[OOVER]

[*Typewritten reference*] JEH-GPO
[*Handwritten endorsements*] File RHR
[*Stamped endorsement*] NOTED F.D.W.

DNA, RG 65, file OG 329359. TLS, recipient's copy.

Elie Garcia to President C. D. B. King

Monrovia, Liberia, June 8th, 1920

Honorable President:

The U.N.I.A. and African Communities' League, Inc., is an organization with a membership of three millions scattered in the United States of America, South and Central America, the West Indies, Great Britain and Africa.

This organization was founded for the following purposes:

To establish a universal confraternity among the races; to promote the spirit of pride and love; to administrate to and assist the needy; to assist in civilizing the backward tribes of Africa; to assist in the development of Independent Negro Nations and Communities; to establish Commissionaries for the representation and protection of all Negroes irrespective of nationality; to promote a conscientious spiritual worship among the natives of Africa, to establish universities, colleges, and academies for the racial education and culture of the people; to conduct world-wide commercial and industrial intercourse for the good of the people; to work for better conditions in all Negro communities.

The U.N.I.A. controls the Black Star Line Steamship Corporation, capitalized at 10 million dollars in the United States of America, as also the Negro Factories Corporation, capitalized at one million dollars under the laws of the United States.

For the successful accomplishment of the program, above outlined, the U.N.I.A. is extremely desirous to transfer its headquarters to the City of Monrovia or any other convenient township of Liberia.

Owing to rumors prevalent in the United States with respect to the unfriendly attitude of the people of Liberia to persons of other Negro communities, the statement which my organization had great reason to doubt, it was thought best to broach the Government of Liberia on the subject of lands before settling our future program.

Therefore, as Commissioner of the said organization, I beg on its behalf to [make the] following [re]quest: "That in case the objects as stated above are approved by the Liberian Government, which would mean a written assurance that it will afford us every facility for procuring lands for business, agricultural or industrial purposes and that the Government will do everything in its power to facilitate the work of the Association along these lines.["]

In return, it is the intention of the organization with its membership of three million members to lend financial and moral assistance in building and subsidizing institutions for the highest education of Liberia, for improving generally the international prestige of the country by organizing outside of the country, developing corporations backed by the entire membership of the U.N.I.A.

The U.N.I.A. would be prepared to do anything possible to help the Government of Liberia out of its economic plights and to raise subscriptions all over the world to help the country to liquidate its debts to foreign governments.

It is the intention of the U.N.I.A. to establish a trade route between America, the West Indies and Liberia through a line of steamships of the Black Star Line Steamship Corporation.

All these things will be unselfishly done in the interest of the people of Liberia and those who may seek future citizenship under her flag.

It is the intention of the U.N.I.A. to encourage immigration by Negroes from the United States of America, South and Central America and the West Indies to develop Liberia.

It is the intention also of the U.N.I.A. that the transfer of its headquarters to Liberia to bring with it a well-equipped medical and scientific unit for the development of higher science in Liberia, to build hospitals, sanitariums and other institutions for the benefit of the people of Liberia.

Trusting that Your Excellency will give due consideration to my request. I am, Your Excellency, Your most obedient servant,

U.N.I.A. & A.C.L. Inc.,
ELIE GARCIA,
Commissioner

[*Address*] To His Excellency, The Pres. of the Rep. of Liberia, Executive Mansion, Monrovia.

DJ-FBI, 61–826. TL (transcript).

Edwin Barclay to Elie Garcia

Department of State, Monrovia, Liberia
14th June, 1920

Sir:

The President directs me to say in reply to your letter of June 8th, setting forth the objects and purposes of the U.N.I.A., that the Government of Liberia, appreciating as they do the aims of your organization as outlined by you, have no hesitancy in assuring you that they will afford the Association every facility legally possible in effectuating in Liberia, industry, agriculture and business projects.

I have the honor to be, Sir, Your obedient servant,

EDWIN BARCLAY,[1]
Secretary of State

[*Address*] Elie Garcia, Esqr., Monrovia.

DJ-FBI, 61–826. TL (transcript).

1. Edwin James Barclay (1882–1955) was the nephew of former President Arthur Barclay. From 1916 to 1920, he was attorney general of Liberia; he later became the secretary of state and was president of Liberia from 1930 until 1944 (*The Times*, 9 November 1955).

Editorial Letter by Marcus Garvey

[[*New York*, June 15th, 1920]]

Fellowmen of the Negro Race and All Negro Organizations of the World. Greeting:

This is to extend to you an open invitation to attend the great world convention of Negroes to be held at Liberty Hall, New York City, from the 1st to the 31st of August of the present year. This invitation goes out to you without reservation. All friendly, fraternal, social, religious, political, industrial and commercial Negro Organizations are requested to send accredited delegates to attend this convention. The convention is to be held under the auspices of the Universal Negro Improvement Association and African Communities League of the World. It is to be the first convention of its kind. At this convention all the American citizens who will send representatives from their lodges, churches and other organizations will elect for themselves a leader of American Negro thought. This leader to be elected at the convention, will be the accredited spokesman of the fifteen millions of American Negroes residing in the United States of America. At this convention, also, the Universal Negro Improvement Association will elect His Highness, the Potentate, [wh]o will be the accredited head of the Universal Negro Improvement Association movement all over the world; he will occupy [th]e place of world leader of all Negroes. At the same time other [lea]ders will be elected, who will exercise control over their respec[tiv]e fields of operation. The Universal Negro Improvement Associa[tio]n is composed of three million active members scattered all over the world—in Africa, the West Indies, South and Central America, [an]d the forty-eight States of the United States of America. The co[nve]ntion will be representative of the feelings, sentiments and aspir[atio]ns of the four hundred million Negroes of the world. There ca[n] [b]e no excuse for any Negro not attending this convention in tha[t] [a]n open invitation is given to each and everyone.

For thirty-one d[ays] the delegates at the great convention will discuss the problems [th]at confront the Race universally, during which time the Mag[na] Charta of Negro rights and liberty will be enacted. Now is [the] time for all Negroes in all parts of the world to become active in helping the Universal Negro Improvement Association to make this convention the success it ought to be. All delegates coming to the convention shall first receive from their lodges, churches or fraternal organizations or the institutions they represent, credentials, so that these credentials can be recorded and verified by the Recorder of the Convention. All branches of the Universal Negro Improvement Association must now elect and send their delegates to the convention. All branches not yet informed through the office of the Secretary-General of the number of delegates they are to send, may use their discretion, according to the constitutional limit of delegates.

The cry of the 31st of July must be: "On to Liberty Hall!" All roads will lead to Liberty Hall on the morning of the 1st of August. A great celebration will take place in New York City to mark the opening of the convention on the 1st of August; therefore, all delegates are requested to be in New York not later than the evening of the 31st of July so as to witness and take part in the great celebration on the morning of the 1st of August. Let the one purpose of your thought, from today, be the great convention of August, 1920.

In the matter of the Black Star Line, I am now asking all the members of the Association and members of the Race to send in and buy as many shares as possible, so that by August we may not only have the three ships we now own, but six ships, flying the colors of the Red, the Black and the Green. The shares of the Black Star Line are still going at Five Dollars each, and you may buy from one to two hundred shares. My advice is to write in today and buy more shares. Address the Black Star Line Steamship Corporation, 56 West 135th Street, New York City, U.S.A.

All those who desire to know more about the convention are requested to write the Secretary-General, Universal Negro Improvement Association, 56 West 135th Street, New York City, U.S.A.

With very best wishes for your success, Yours fraternally,

MARCUS GARVEY

Printed in *NW*, 19 June 1920. Original headlines omitted.

Report on *Black Star Line* v. *The Chicago Defender*

[*Negro World*, 19 June 1920]

BLACK STAR LINE VINDICATED BY WHITE AMERICAN JURY

WINS FIRST CASE AGAINST CHICAGO DEFENDER THAT PUBLISHED LIBEL

CORPORATION WILL PUNISH ALL ITS ENEMIES TO VINDICATE HONOR OF THE RACE

The first of the suits of the Black Star Line against the Chicago Defender for libel came up for hearing last week in the United States District Court before Judge John R. Knox[1] and a jury. Considerable interest centered around this hearing—it being an issue of vast importance to the Negro race the world over, as to whether or not the U.N.I.A., through the crystallization of whose sentiment has been evolved the Black Star Line Steamship

Corporation and its allied organizations, can be held up to contempt and ridicule with impunity and thus be hampered in the fight it is making for Negro uplift and betterment. Today the U.N.I.A. and the Black Star Line stand vindicated in the eyes of the world as bei[n]g, in law and in fact, legitimate and going concerns, and not the air-castle propositions, the cheats and frauds, on a par with Chief Sam's schemes, that the Chicago Defender and other green-eyed publications among Negroes have said they were. A jury of twelve men, whose prejudices were played upon to the limit in an attempt to warp their judgment, sat through the case for three days' hearing, sifting and weighing the evidence presented by both sides. They decided that Garvey and the Black Star Line were all right and their verdict was confirmed and made of record in the United States District Court in New York City. The Chicago Defender said the Black Star Line was a fake. Garvey said it isn't and never was. The Chicago Defender said it was a cheat and a fraud. Garvey said it never was and it isn't now. The case was decided solely on its merits and Garvey was vindicated. The Chicago Defender lied. Garvey told the truth.

LIBELLOUS ARTICLE.

The libel arose out of an article which appeared in the issue of the Chicago Defender dated September 20th, 1919, concerning the Black Star Line and Mr. Garvey. This article was published conspicuously on the first page of the paper entitled (in large black-faced t[yp]e): "Attorney Bares New York Editor's Plot. Marcus Garvey Found Guilty of Criminal Libel—Recalls [O]ther Schemes." The article purported to be a dispatch from New York dated Sept. 19, 19[19], and commenced with the statement that "Marcus Garvey, editor of the Negro World, a tiny weekly publication issued in the city and state of New York, was found guilty of criminal libel by Magistrate Simpson in Jefferson Market Court, and that the comp[l]ainant against him was Assistant District Attorney Edwin R. Kilroe." Following this statement the paper also published another statement which Mr. Garvey claimed was malicious, false, slanderous and defamatory.

These statements being untrue, the Black Star Line brought suit against the Chicago Defender for libel. The Black Star Line's attorneys were Messrs. Rosenheim and Jas. Watson, while French and French conducted the defence for the Chicago Defender.

Mr. Rosenheim in opening the case in behalf of the Black Star Line explained to the jury that it was a corporation for the purpose of operating a line of vessels and boats and acting as a common carrier of passengers and freight from the United States to various ports. It was exclusively a colored organization. It was organized by Negroes; its officers were Negroes and it expects to do most of its business with respect to passengers among Negroes. The President of the Black Star Line is Marcus Garvey, who is colored. He was born in Jamaica, West Indies, and came to New York a short time ago;

and immediately assumed a position of leadership among Negroes through-out the world.

The plaintiff was prepared to show by evidence that every statement in the article complained of was absolutely untrue; that the plaintiff had suffered damage in reputation and credit and therefore asked for a verdict, with substantial damages.

EVIDENCE OF MARCUS GARVEY.

The first witness, in behalf of the plaintiff (the Black Star Line) was Mr. Marcus Garvey, President of the corporation, who, on being sworn, gave the following evidence:

DIRECT EXAMINATION BY MR. ROSENHEIM.

Q.—Where do you reside, Mr. Garvey? I now reside at 133 West 129th street, New York City.

Q.—Where were you born? I was born in the Parish of St. John,[2] Island of Jamaica, B.W.I.

Q.—When did you reach this country? About 3 1/2 or 4 years ago.

Q.—Before you reached this country had you been interested in public affairs in your own country? I had been interested in public affairs for a number of years.

Q.—How did you manifest that interest? By being editor of a news-paper and by taking part in the politics of the country.

Q.—What newspaper were you editor of? I was editor of the "[Garvey's?] Watchman."

Q.—Was that a weekly or a daily publication? Weekly.

[Q.]—About how much circulation did it have? About three thousand copies.

Q.—How long did you publish that newspaper? Between 12 and 15 months.

Q.—Were you connected with any other newspaper? I was also con-nected with the "Catholic Opinion" of Kingston, Jamaica; the official organ of the Catholic diocese. I was also owner and managing editor of a daily paper in Costa Rica by the name of "La Nacion" and editor of a tri-weekly paper in Colon.

Q.—What education did you have? I have an elementary education and a high school education; and I spent 18 months at a public college in London.

Q.—Was that college a part of the University of London? Yes.

Q.—What part did you take in politics in your own country before you came here? I took the part of supporting various candidates for the Legisla-ture of the country.

Q.—How did you manifest that support? By speaking for them and by writing for them and supporting them in my paper.

Q.—Are you connected with the Universal Negro Improvement Association? I am acting President General of that organization.

Q.—What is the membership of that organization? The present membership is about three million people.

Q.—Where was this Association first organized? It was first formed in the Island of Jamaica in 1914.

Q.—When you came to New York how large a membership did it have? About 600 members in Jamaica.

Q.—Any members in the United States? No; I organized it in the United States after I came here.

Q.—How many members has it in the United States now? It has approximately one million members in the United States.

Q.—Is that a New York corporation? Yes.

Q.—Who caused it to be incorporated[?] I did.

Q.—About when? In 1918, I believe.

Q.—Is it a stock corporation? It is a membership corporation.

Q.—Who owns the "Negro World"? The African Community League owns the Negro World.

Q.—And what is the relation of the Universal Negro Improvement Association to the African Community League? The stock in the African Community League is owned by the Universal Negro Improvement Association.

Q.—What is the African Community League? It is a business corporation incorporated in the State of New York.

Q.—Is it a co-operative scheme for the benefit of the Negro? Yes.

Q.—And it publishes the Negro World? Yes.

Q.—Who is the editor of the Negro World? I am the managing editor of the Negro World, and Prof. W. H. Ferris is the literary editor.

Q.—Do you still contribute articles to it? I write the front page articles in the paper.

Q.—Were you the editor of the Negro World on September 20, 1919? I do not think so; I was not active editor.

Q.—What is the Negro World? It is a weekly paper.

Q.—What is its circulation? Its present circulation is 50,000 copies. At the time that the libel was published its circulation was about 10,000 or 15,000.

Q.—Do you know the Chicago Defender? I am acquainted with the publication.

Q.—Who is the publisher of the Chicago Defender? I understand that the Robert S. Abbott[3] Publishing Co. publishes that paper.

Q.—Do you know the circulation of the Chicago Defender? According to their published statements filed with the Postmaster General, it is 250,000 copies weekly.

The Black Star Line Ships.

Q.—When was the Black Star Line incorporated? On the 27th of June, 1919.

Q.—Is it a Delaware corporation? Yes.

Q.—Who caused it to be incorporated[?] I did.

Q.—Are most of the members of the Black Star Line members of the U.N.I.A.? A large number of the stockholders of the Black Star Line are also members of the U.N.I.A.

Q.—Where does the Negro World circulate? It circulates throughout the United States of America and in foreign countries, namely: the West Indies, Central and South America and Africa.

Q.—Where does the Chicago Defender circulate? Principally throughout the United States of America and the American colonies.

Q.—Does the Negro World circulate in the City of New York? Yes; they have a large circulation here.

Q.—Have they an office for the transaction of business in New York? Yes.

Q.—Does the Negro World compete with the Chicago Defender? We do not compete with any other paper; in that the Negro World is the official organ of the U.N.I.A., and it is published to maintain the policy of the organization.

Q.—Are the readers of the Negro World about the same as the readers of the Chicago Defender? I believe so.

Q.—And you seek subscri[p]tions from the same people from whom the Chicago Defender seeks subscriptions? We seek the support of all Negroes.

Q.—Does the Chicago Defender do likewise? Yes, I understand so.

Q.—In what manner were the funds of the Black Star Line raised? By the sale of stock.

Q.—Who sells that stock? The officers of the corporation.

Q.—And you have various agents selling the stock as well? Yes.

Q.—Are these agents spread throughout the United States? Yes[,] and in different parts of the world.

Q.—Please state the places where these agents are scattered. In the United States, we have agents in Philadelphia, Boston, Chicago, Newport News, Va., Norfolk, Va., Portsmouth, Va., and a few other places. In foreign countries, we have agents in Costa Rica, Colon, Panama, Panama City, Kingston, Jamaica, Montreal, Canada and other places.

Q.—Are those places you have mentioned principal centers of Negroes? Yes.

Q.—Does the Chicago Defender circulate at all those places? Yes.

Q.—Does the Negro World circulate in Chicago? Yes; [it] has a very small circulation.

Q.—Does the Chicago Defender circulate in Chicago? It has a very large circulation in its own city.

The certificate of incorporation of the Black Star Line was here offered in evidence but was objected to by defendant's counsel on the ground that there was no evidence to show that the person whose name appeared on the certificate as the Secretary of State of Delaware was the bonafide Secretary of State.

The Court overruled the objection and the certificate was admitted in evidence.

Another certificate filed in the office of the Secretary of State on February 9, 1920, increasing the capital stock of the Black Star Line was also offered in evidence and admitted; as also the certificate of incorporation of the U.N.I.A. and the African Communities League, together with a copy of the Chicago Defender containing the alleged libellous article.

Q.—Mr. Garvey, what is the present value of the assets of the Black Star Line? $297,378.49.

Q.—In a general way, what do these assets consist of? They consist of an equity in three ships.

Q.—What are the names of the three ships? The Yarmouth, the Shadyside and the Kanawha.

Q.—What is the amount of the equity of the Black Star Line in the steamer Yarmouth? $180,000.

Q.—What amount was paid on account of the purchase of that ship? $120,000.[4]

Q.—Since it was purchased what amount has been expended on repairs? $60,000.

Q.—Does the Black Star Line own that boat? Yes.

Q.—Did it own it on September [20?], 1919? Yes.

Q.—What is the equity of the Black Star Line in the steamer "Shadyside"? $14,000.

Q.—Is that the amount actually expended on account of the purchase of the boat? Yes; with repairs.

Q.—How much do the repairs amount to? $5,000.

Q.—Did the Black Star Line own that boat on September 20, 1919? No.

Q.—Had it made a contract for the purchase of that boat? No.

Q.—About the Kanawha—what did the Company pay for that boat? $15,000.

Q.—Have any repairs been made to the Kanawha? Yes; to the amount of $12,000.

Q.—Does the Black Star Line own that boat? Yes.

Q.—Did it own it on September 20, 1919? No.

Q.—Are there any libels filed against the Yarmouth? Yes.

Moneys on Deposit.

Q.—Has the Black Star Line deposited monies to bond these libels? Yes; $10,500.

Q.—Does the Black Star Line own any buildings? Yes; Nos. 54 and 56 West 135th Street, New York.

Q.—How much did it pay for each of these buildings? For No. 56, $15,000 and for No. 54, $11,000.

Q.—How much equity has the Company in these two buildings? Seven or eight thousand dollars.

Q.—Does the Black Star Line own any auto trucks? Two.

Q.—What did it pay for these trucks? $4,000 for one and $1,500 for the other.

Q.—Has the Black Star Line any money on deposit in the Bank? Yes.

Q.—Please state the amounts in the various banks deposited to the credit of the Black Star Line. In the Chelsea Exchange Bank, $16,000; in the International Bank of Colon, $500; in the Crown Savings Bank, Newport News, Va., $300; in Brown & Stevens Bank, Philadelphia, [$]200; with the Tremont Trust Co., Boston, Mass., $3,200. There are also deposits in the Royal Bank of Canada in the island of Cuba; the Bank of Liberia, West Africa, and in the Bank of Lagos Nigeria, Africa; all amounting to $279,378.

Q.—That is the total valuation of the assets of the Black Star Line? Yes.

Q.—How many stockholders has the Black Star Line today? About 15,000 or 17,000.

Q.—How many did it have on September 20, 1919? About 9,000.

Q.—What was the paid up capital of the Black Star Line on September 20, 1919? $45,000.

Q.—And what is the paid up capital today? $383,000.

Q.—When you say paid up capital you mean the amount of capital stock actually issued? Yes.

Q.—That is—sold on the partial payment plan? Yes; inclusive.

Q.—What is the number of shares of stock that has been issued? 76,798.

Q.—In this article which the plaintiff complains of, Mr. Garvey, it is said that you were found guilty of criminal libel by Magistrate Simpson in the Jefferson Market Court. Were you ever found guilty of criminal libel by Magistrate Simpson or any one else? No.

Q.—Did District Attorney Kilroe ever torpedo the Black Star Line? No.

Q.—Has the Black Star Line continuously done business since its formation? Yes.

Q.—Was there ever a time that it ceased to do business? No.

Q.—Was it ever ordered to cease to do business by District Attorney Kilroe or any one else? No.

Q.—Has there ever been an order by the U.S. Court or any other department to discontinue operation? No.

Q.—Has it continued operations steadily since its formation? Yes.

Q.—Is it the aim of the Black Star Line to operate Jim Crow steamship lines between Africa, South America and the West Indies? No.

Q.—Between what ports does the Yarmouth operate? Because of the lies published in the Chicago Defender, we were forced to send the ship to far-off ports where there were prospective purchasers of stock in the Black Star Line who had become doubtful of the existence of the corporation. We sent her to Panama, Costa Rica, Bocas del Toro, and now she is on her way to Kingston, Jamaica.[5]

Q.—The latter is the regular route of the boat, is it not? Yes.

Q.—Was the purpose of the trip of the Yarmouth to those other ports you mentioned, to show people that the Black Star Line did actually own a boat? Yes; for that purpose.

Q.—Was there any other purpose? No.

Q.—What was the cost of sending the boat to those ports which were not on the regular route of the boat? We had to expend between $30,000 and $40,000 to send the boat there.

Q.—What did the Yarmouth carry on those trips? Cargo and passengers.

No Jim Crow on Black Star Line

Q.—Does it discriminate between whites and blacks? We have taken white passengers on both trips.

Q.—Have you any rule against taking white passengers? No; the present captain is a white man.[6]

Q.—Have you carried freight for white firms? Yes; nearly all the freight has been from white firms.

Q.—She is a common carrier indiscriminately of whites or blacks? Yes.

Q.—What is her tonnage? 1,400 tons.

Q.—Tell us about the Shadyside. Where does she operate? She operates on the Hudson River as an excursion boat.

Q.—Is there any discrimination between whites and blacks on that boat? No; the captain is a white man[7] and the chief engineer is a white man.

Q.—Has it ever been announced by the Black Star Line that only black passengers will be carried on the Shadyside? No.

Q.—Has she ever carried white passengers? She has carried white passengers up the Hudson.

Q.—Does the Shadyside carry freight? She is simply an excursion boat.

Q.—What is the Kanawha? It is a steamer we have bought for the purpose of putting her on the intercolonial trade.

Q.—What do you mean by intercolonial trade? To trade between the islands of Cuba, Hayti and Santo Domingo and Jamaica.

Q.—Does the Black Star Line discrim[i]nate in respect to that boat between whites and blacks? No; the present captain who is supervising the repairs to the boat is a white man.[8]

Q.—Do you carry freight on that boat? We intend to; she has not sailed yet.

(The contracts and agreements by which the Black Star Line became the owner of the Yarmouth, Shadyside and Kanawha were offered in evidence and ad[mi]tted[.)]

No Similarity Between Chief Sam Movement and Black Star Line

Q.—Are you familiar with the scheme of Chief Sam? No; I read something about it in England in 1912 or 1913.

Q.—Is the purpose of the Black Star Line anything like that? Absolutely not.

Q.—Is the purpose of the Black Star Line to charter a dilapidated ship and set out on an ocean voyage to reach the shores of Africa? No.

Q.—Is the purpose of the Black Star Line to establish a colony in Africa? No.

Q.—Is the purpose of the Black Star Line to help the American white man to get rid of the Negro? No.

Q.—This article in the Chicago Defender says that Assistant District Attorney Kilroe declared the Black Star Line a fraud. Is that true? No.

Q.—Is it true that the District Attorney ordered you to discontinue the sale of stock in the Black Star Line? No.

Q.—Is it true that prominent citizens wrote the District Attorney asking him to investigate the Black Star Line? No.

Q.—Did the District Attorney investigate the Black Star Line? Yes; he did.

Q.—When was that? Some time in August, I believe, 1919.

Q.—Did the District Attorney call for and receive the books of the Black Star Line? Yes; he did.

Q.—Were those books delivered to him for examination? Yes.

Q.—Did you have a personal talk with Mr. Kilroe? We had several combats in his office.

Q.—After that examination were the books of the company returned to the company? Yes.

Q.—Did Mr. Kilroe tell you what he found with reference to the company? No.

Q.—Did he order you to discontinue operations? No.

Q.—Did you ever cease to sell stock in the company? No.

Q.—Are you still engaged in the sale of stock of the company? Yes.

OFFSETTING "THE DEFENDER'S" LIBEL

Q.—Have you ever been arrested or indicted for selling stock in the Black Star Line? In Chicago in October, 1919, I was arrested for violating the Blue Sky Law.

Q.—That was because the Black Star Line had not obtained a license to do business in Illinois? I was instructed by my attorney at that time that it was not necessary to hold a license to sell stock in Chicago.

Q.—Outside of that, did you have any other trouble with regard to selling stock? No.

Q.—After this article was published concerning the Black Star Line what did the Black Star Line do in order to counteract it? We had to send speakers all over the country and to foreign countries where we had prospective subscribers.

Q.—Who paid these speakers? The Black Star Line.

Q.—What was the amount paid to these speakers for their services? Approximately $25,000.

Q.—Was that done with the idea of selling stock and for the purpose of counteracting the article? It was done to counteract the impression created by the article and convince the people that we were a legitimate concern; and at the same time to sell stock.

Q.—What other things did the Black Star Line do in an effort to counteract the article? We had to practically use two-thirds of the space of the Negro World publication, so as to counteract the libel of the Chicago Defender.

Q.—How did you use the Negro World? By paying for the space.

Q.—Did the Black Star Line pay the Negro World by check? Yes. (The checks were offered in evidence for the purpose of identification, but were ruled out by the Court on the ground that the measure of damages could not be determined by the amount of money spent on advertising.)

Q.—Without specifying the amount paid to the Negro World, state what else was done in an effort to counteract the libel besides advertising and employing speakers? We had to print thousands and thousands of circulars which we distributed all over the country and abroad.

Q.—Would you have published those circulars except for this libel? Not in the quantities we did.

Q.—What was the nature of the circulars?

Defendant's attorney objected to question and the Court sustained the objection.

Q.—After these circulars we[r]e published did you receive reports from the various selling agents throughout the country as to the effect of this libel? We received reports that a great deal of confidence had been manifested in the Black Star Line as a result of our speaking campaign and the circulars.

Q.—Did you receive reports as to the impression that the libel had created on the minds of prospective investors? Yes.

Q.—It was because of those reports that you did these various things? Yes.

Q.—What reports did you receive? We received reports that at some of the branch offices of the Black Star Line stockholders had demanded the return of their money, stating that they had seen it published in the Chicago Defender that the Black Star Line was a fraud and a cheat and not bona fide. That there was a continuous rush of people at the offices inquiring into the integrity of the Black Star Line; so we had to do some[t]hing to counteract the impression.

Q.—What did you find with respect to those who were prospective purchasers and with whom you had been negotiating for the sale of stock? Some of them refused to purchase stock.

Q.—Tell us the names of those people from whom you received reports you have referred to, who are present in the Court. Mr. Toote, the representative of the Black Star Line in Philadelphia;[9] Mr. Potter, representative in Montreal, Canada; Dr. Gibson, the representative in Boston; and we received reports from foreign agents.

Q.—Is Miss Davis in Court? Yes; we had to send her to foreign fields to counteract the influence made by the Chicago Defender.

Q.—Where does Miss Davis make her headquarters? In New York.

Q.—Did you send her abroad? Yes, to Cuba, Jamaica, Panama, and Costa Rica.

Q.—What did you find with respect to the circulation of the Negro World after the article was published in the Chicago Defender? There was an immediate falling off of the support of the Negro World; and we had to make special effort to get additional agents to handle the paper.

Q.—Did the Chicago Defender commence to print articles about the Black Star Line immediately after the organization of the Black Star Line? Yes.

Q.—Did those articles appear regularly from time to time? Every week something was published about the Black Star Line detrimental to its interest.

Q.—Do they still appear? Not since the beginning of this suit.

Q.—I show you an issue of the Chicago Defender dated September 6, two weeks before and ask you whether or not the article appearing on page 4 relates to the Black Star Line.

The defense objected, but the plaintiff's a[t]torney argued that he was endeavoring to show actual malice.

After a brief argument on both sides the Court overruled the objection and the paper was admitted in evidence, together with another issue of the Chicago Defender dated August 23, 1919, containing an article in criticism of the Black Star Line.

Q.—I show you an issue of the Chicago Defender, dated October 4, 1919, and ask you whether or not this article (handing paper to witness) relates to the Black Star Line? Yes; that was published while I was in Chicago.

Q.—What were you doing in Chicago on that occasion? I was sent there by the Black Star Line to offset the libellous impression created upon the minds of the people by the Chicago Defender.

Q.—How did you endeavor to accomplish that? By speaking at several meetings in the city.

Q.—While you w[ere] [t]here, were you questioned about [the] [art]icle that appeared in the Chic[ago] Defender on September 20? Not in the immediate meeting, but afterwards individuals came forward and questioned me about what was published in the Chicago Defender.

Q.—What did they ask you? If it was true that we were an air-castle concern and were selling stock on pretence; and other questions of that kind.

Q.—Did any of them express their opposition towards the purchase of stock, based upon this libel? They said they would have bought stock if it had not been for the libel published in the Chicago Defender.

Q.—In the issue of the Chicago Defender of October 4 there is a big headline, "Brundage Sinks Black Star Line"—who is Brundage?

The defence objected, but the Court overruled the objection.

Answer:—I believe he is the State Attorney of Illinois.

Q.—Did he ever sink the Black Star Line or order it to discontinue operations? No it was never sunk.

Q.—Was it ever ordered to cease business in Illinois? In the Court I was instructed by the Magistrate not to continue to sell stock in Chicago until I had registered the stock.

Q.—That is in accordance with the provisions of the Blue Sky Law, is it not? Yes.

Q.—Can you give the names of some of the people [for] whom the Yarmouth has carried freight? We carried cargo for Marcelius Garcia of Sagua La Grande, Cuba; for Franklin Baker & Co., of 90 Wall St., on the first voyage; on the second trip from New York to the West Indies we carried a cargo of whiskey for some distilling concern—I don't rememb[e]r the name.

Q.—How large a cargo was it? Approximately $5,000,000.

Q.—The Government finally permitted that cargo to sail, did it not? Yes.

Q.—Are there any more firms for whom you took cargo? Oakes Mfg. Co., Pan Union Steamship Co., G. S. Alexander Co., L. Schepp & Co., Fromm & Co.

CROSS-EXAMINATION BY DEFENCE

Q.—You are a native of Kingston? Yes; St. Anns Bay, Jamaica, W.I.

Q.—You were born there and went to school there? Yes.

Q.—To what school? Public school and high school.

Q.—In your going to school there, did you study the government of this country in United States history? I studied the history of all countries.

Q.—Did you study the history of this country? Yes; I did.

Q.—Do you know the form of government we have here? Sure, I do.

Q.—Do you concur in the form of government here? Yes.

Q.—You are satisfied with it? Perfectly satisfied.

Q.—You propose[d] to form the colored people into one mass—is that [true]? Not in mass.

[*Four lines mutilated*].

THE CONVENTION THE PEOPLE'S OWN IDEA.

Q.—You will have a convention in August—is that so? Yes.

Q.—In that convention your purpose is to elect a High Potentate for the Negro race? Yes.

Q.—And you are getting people from all over the country to come here? All over the world.

Q.—And you are collecting large sums for that? The Universal Negro Improvement Association is collecting a fund of $2,000,000 to capitalize the convention.

Q.—You are the moving spirit in that, aren't you? I am the acting President General of the U.N.I.A.

Q.—Are you the moving spirit? No more than the other officers of the organization.

Q.—Who conceived the idea? All the people.

Q.—Have you communicated the idea to all the organization to which you belong? The U.N.I.A. has branches all over the world, and in their constitution it is determined that we are to hold a convention annually; and in August we are holding our first annual convention.

Q.—You say you are going to take colored people from all over the world and form them into a government in Africa? I am not going to do it.

Q.—Well you are starting out with that purpose. I am only one of two million.

Q.—Is not that your purpose? It is my purpose in common with others.

Q.—Are you at present forming colonies in Africa? No[.]

Q.—When you get over there you propose to have the same kind of government as here—that is[,] are you going to elect a High Potentate? I cannot say relative to that question.

Q.—Are you going to elect a High Potentate? I am not going to do it.

Q.—Well your organization is going to do it? They are going to do that in August.

Q.—The Potentate is to rule over all the people in Africa? No.

Q.—Have you not so stated in your circulars and papers?

(Objection was made to this question and the Court sustained it.)

Q.—You say that your paper circulates in various parts of the world which you have named; and you also stated that the Chicago Defender circulates in these same countries? In several of those countries to my knowledge. Several copies have been sent to me from agents of the Black Star Line in Panama, Jamaica and other places.

Q.—From what source did you get the information that the Chicago Defender circulates in different parts of the world? From individuals who have knowledge of it.

Q.—What is the circulation of your paper? 50,000.

Q.—Last August what was the circulation? About 7,000 or 10,000.

Q.—And what was the circulation in September? I believe the same.

Q.—And what was the circulation in October? I cannot tell you.

Q.—Do you recall the circulation in November? I do not.

Q.—In December[?] I do not.

Q.—In January? 50,000.

Q.—When did it come to your notice that the paper had increased from 7,000 to 50,000? The increase was between September and January.

Q.—In other words, the circulation increased from the time that the alleged libellous article appeared in the Chicago Defender? [*No answer given*].

Q.—You say you bought how many ships? We have three ships.

Q.—When did you buy the first ship of the Black Star Line? Between August and September.

Q.—When you made contracts for this ship did you pay for the ship at that time? We made a large payment on the ship.

THE 3 SHIPS PAID FOR

Q.—Did you ever state at any time during the month of October, November or December that you had paid for your ship? No.

Q.—And have you now paid for that ship? We have paid the major portion.

Q.—How old is that ship? I believe 32 years old.

Q.—And you also bought the Kanawha? Yes.

Q.—What is the tonnage of the Kanawha? I believe 400 or 500 tons.

Q.—Is it in commission now, plying to and fro? She has not sailed yet.

Q.—How many trips has the Yarmouth made? She is at sea now on her third voyage.

Q.—Did you say in direct examination that the Yarmouth had made a number of voyages—some 7 or 8? I never said that.

Q.—When you bought that ship your purpose was to have her ply between the different ports? According to the license given to us, she was only a coasting steamer.

Q.—Did you intend to have her go as far as Jamaica? That is on the coast.

Q.—When you bought that ship it was your purpose to keep her sailing as much as possible, is not that so? Yes.

Q.—When you sent her out on these voyages you had cargo for that ship[,] did you not? We had no cargo when we sent her to Panama to counteract the libel of the Chicago Defender.

Q.—Did you have cargo on the ship when she sailed from this port? From here to Sagua La Grande, Cuba.

Q.—How long a time elapsed between the first and second sailing from the port of New York? About 5 or 6 weeks.

Q.—She made the round trip in that time? Yes.

Q.—What is the tonnage of the Yarmouth? 1,400 tons.

Q.—What is the tonnage of the Kanawha? 400 or 500 tons.

Q.—Is the Shadyside constantly sailing, carrying passengers and freight? She carries passengers only.

Q.—Does she sail daily? Not daily; two or three times a week.

Q.—She has been sailing two or three times a week since you bought her? Yes.

Q.—On the first trip of the Yarmouth how many tons of cargo did you carry[?] I cannot remember; the secretary of the corporation handles that.

Q.—Did you have her loaded fully when she left here? Yes.

The Court: General cargo? Yes, sir.

Defendant's attorney: Did you carry passengers when she left out of port the first time? Yes.

Q.—Has the ship lost money? We lost money on the trips we had to make to central America to counteract the libel of the Chicago Defender.

Q.—Did you have this ship before the article appeared in the Chicago Defender? Yes; she was under our control.

Q.—Was she in port before this article appeared? I don't remember.

Q.—When did she come into port? I don't remember.

Q.—How long did you have it under control before you sent her out of port? A month or so.

Q.—Did she sail at the time you had advertised her to sail? Yes.

Q.—On the very day? Yes.

Q.—Do you recall the second voyage that ship made? Yes; it was an historic voyage.

Q.—At that time what cargo did she take? She carried a cargo of whiskey.

Q.—Where was that cargo consigned to?

Objection was taken [to] this question as irrelevant to the matter before the Court, and the objection was sustained.

On further cross-examination, facts were re-stated relative to the expenditure on the Yar[m]outh and the Shadyside, and the status of the Black Star with reference to the sale of stock after the publication of the article in the Chicago Defender.

Q.—Prior to the publication of the article of which you complain, had any statements appeared in the Chicago Defender relative to you and the Black Star Line? Yes.

Q.—Had you published anything against the Chicago Defender in your paper? Not to my knowledge.

Q.—You have never said anything against the Chicago Defender in your paper or in your speeches? Not that I remember.

Q.—Were you in Chicago in October or September? Yes.

Q.—In your speech on October 7th in Chicago, did you not make a statement that you were going to put the Chicago Defender out of business?

Objection to this question was sustained by the Court.

Q.—You say you were born in the West Indies? Yes.

Q.—Are you still a subject of Great Brit[ai]n? Yes.

Q.—Your purpose, you say, is to unify the colored people of the world—is that true? Yes.

Q.—You propose in your unification to have rulers elected—are you going to have a monarchial or a republican form of government? I do not know.

Q.—The principal purpose of the Black Star Line you said, was to run a line of steamships between various countries where colored people prevail and carry on commerce with them? Yes.

Q.—When you were in the West Indies—in Kingston—you were employed with various concerns? For a time.

Q.—In what capacity other than running a paper? I was manager of the P. A. Benjamin manufacturing plant for 4 or 5 years.

FORMER ACTIVITIES OF MR. GARVEY.

Q.—When you went to London you fell in with one Duse Mahommed? Yes; I did.

Q.—Were you employed by him? Yes; I was a writer on his paper.

Q.—Were you ever employed to do various things other than writing for his paper? I was employed as contributor to the African Times and Orient Review.

Q.—You never did any menial work around that place? I never did any menial work.

Q.—Did you ever work as a printer? Yes; but that is not menial labor.

Q.—Did you ever have a project to build an institution sim[i]lar to that of Booker T. Washington in this country? In Jamaica, yes; for the Universal Negro Improvement Association.

Q.—Did you collect monies over there for it? Not for that institution but for the U.N.I.A.

Q.—Did you ever collect money in this country for the Tuskegee Institute in Jamaica? No.

Q.—Did you ever collect money for a school in Jamaica on the model of the Tuskegee Institute in this country? I did; about $50 or $60.

Q.—How did you go about that? By speaking, giving concerts and lectures and writing letters to friends.

Q.—Did you collect money in any of the public halls?

Objection was raised to this evidence as being immaterial, and the Court sustained the objection.

Q.—Have you ever been convicted of crime? Never.

Q.—Did you at any time during the month of August appear in criminal proceedings in Jefferson Market Court where you were the defendant charged with criminal libel? Yes.

Q.—You were held by the Magistrate of that Court, weren't you? Yes; in $3,000 bond.

Q.—And that case is still pending? Yes.

Q.—Have you appeared in the Criminal Court since in relation to that same case? Yes.

Q.—Did they ask you whether you were guilty or not guilty? Yes; I pleaded not guilty.

Q.—On or about October 19, did you appear in a criminal proceeding in the City of Chicago in the Criminal Court? I did.

The defence here produced the record of proceedings before the Criminal Court in Chicago showing a conviction a[ga]inst the witness for selling stock without a license.

Q.—When you say you were never convicted of crime you are wrong? I was not under the impression that that was a conviction for crime.

RE-DIRECT EXAMINATION BY PLAINTIFF'S COUNSEL.

Q.—How much were you fined on that occasion? About $20 for violation of the Blue Sky Law.

Q.—Before you entered Chicago to sell stock did you consult your counsel as to the legality of selling stock there? I was told by my attorney that I could sell stock in Chicago. Because of that I spoke at a meeting where stock was sold and I was held responsible. At that meeting I understand the Chicago Defender had detectives to be present at the hall.

Q.—You were asked whether or not the circulation of the Negro World had increased from 7,000 to 50,000 between September and the present time—do you remember this? Yes.

Q.—Will you explain wh[at] was done after this libel which res[ul]ted in the increase of the circulation of the Negro World? We printed [ext]ensive advertisements in the Neg[ro] World and placed large numbers of [co]pies of the paper in all places where the Chicago Defender had circulated [s]o as to get the people there to read [it] in order to counteract the statemen[t] which the Chicago Defender had [pu]blished.

Q.—Did that increase the circulation? Yes.

RE-CROSS EXAMINATION [B]Y DEFENCE.

Q.—Do you know [by] your own knowledge whether the Chicago Defender circulates exten[si]vely in Panama, Bocas del Toro, Jamaica, and other places where you sent your paper? I know the paper is circulated there.

Q.—What is the source of your information? Reports from those countries.

Q.—You are the head of the Black Star Line? I am the President.

Q.—And you are President-General of the U.N.I.A.? Yes.

Q.—And the officers in one are the officers in the other? Not all the officers are the same.

Q.—But most of them are? Several of them are.

EVIDENCE OF MR. ALLEN HOBBS.

The next witness called was Mr. Allen Hobbs,[10] an agent of the Black Star Line in Norfolk, Va., who testified that he saw the Chicago Defender of September 20, containing the article complained of, on sale in Norfolk, and several persons brought copies of the paper to the meetings of the U.N.I.A. held in that city. In conversation with several people the[r]e they called his attention to what the Chicago Defender had published about the Black Star Line and accused the Black Star Line and Mr. Garvey of making false reports regarding the ownership of ships whe[n] they had none. On several occasions he was met on the street and asked whether or no[t] the reports were true and he denied them, saying that he had had word from the headquarters in New York to that effect. Because of the reports made in the Chicago Defender a large number of persons who had subscribed to stock in the Black Star Line demanded their money back and prospective investors refused to purchase stock. Upwards of one thousand persons, the witness said, had called his attention to the statement published in the Chicago Defender and wanted to get an explanation as to the truth or untruth of the statements.

On cross-examination by the defence, the witness stated that prior to the appearance of the article he had sold stock to about 150 persons, and since then up to the present time he has sold stock to about 300 or 400 persons altogether.

MISS DAVIS' EVIDENCE

Miss Henrietta Vinton Davis, Second Vice-President of the Black Star Line, was the next witness, who testified that she was sent abroad in November, 1919, in the interests of the Black Star Line and the U.N.I.A. to sell stock and organize branches of the U.N.I.A. She stayed abroad during December, January, March and April and visited Panama, Bocas del Toro, Port Limon, Costa Rica and Jamaica. During the months of December and January she saw several copies of the Chicago Defender of September 20, in the hands of various people. Upwards of 100 persons in Panama had called on her with copies of the Chicago Defender and directed her attention to the article which it contained with reference to the Black Star Line. They expressed their belief that the Black Star Line had been torpedoed, basing that belief on what they had seen in the Chicago Defender. Mme. Patti Brown, a native of Chicago, approached her one day and said she (Miss Davis) was selling stock for a fake corporation and that she intended writing to the Chicago Defender informing them of that fact. Because of the article published in the Chicago Defender, she (Miss Davis) had a good deal of trouble convincing the people that the Black Star Line was a legitimate going concern, and were it not for the presence of the ship the faith of the people would not have been restored in the corporation. She spoke to thousands of people at different times in public meetings and had personally sold stock to about 200 people. She testified that the Chicago Defender was sold in large numbers in Colon, Panama.

DR. GIBSON'S EVIDENCE

Dr. Joseph D. Gibson, D.D.S., President of the Boston Division of the U.N.I.A., and agent for the Black Star Line S.S. Corporation, in that city, was the next witness to take the stand. He testified that he bought a copy of the Chicago Defender on Sept. 20 in Boston and a large number of stock-holders there also brought copies of the paper to his office at various times. His office was literally stormed, the witness said, with excited persons demanding to know something about the Black Star Line, and pointing to the article in the Chicago Daily Defender said[,] "Look at the fake stuff you are trying to sell us." He did his best to pacify them and showed them letters from the headquarters denying the reports given out by the Chicago Defender. Approximately about 65 persons who had previously promised to buy stock refused to do so after the article appeared in the Chicago Defender.

In cross-examination, this witness said he could not sell any stock in September after the article appeared nor in early October.

CIRCULATED FALSE REPORTS.

Mr. Alfred Potter, the stock representative of the Black Star Line in Montreal, Canada, testified as to the circulation of the Chicago Defender in Montreal. The Negro population in his section is about two or three thousand and at various times 25 or 30 people had approached him with copies of the Chicago Defender calling his attention to the article. They refused to buy more shares stating as their reason that the Chicago Defender had said Garvey was a fake and was imposing another Chief Sam scheme on them. He spoke at several meetings and on several occasions inquiries were made in open meeting regarding the status of the Black Star Line as a result of what the Chicago Defender had published.

In answer to the Court, the witness said he received a commission of 3 per cent on the sale of stock, but no salary.

Mr. Frederick Toote, a selling agent of the Black Star Line in Philadelphia, testified that he first saw a copy of the Chicago Defender of Sept. 20th, at a meeting of the U.N.I.A. held in that City. On that occasion about 900 persons were present and he saw at least 500 copies in the hands of people there—almost everybody had a paper. They stampeded and demanded their money back; things got so hot for him that he had to leave through a back door. There was a man standing on the outside selling the Chicago Defender and shouting the headlines regarding the Black Star Line.

On cross-examination, the witness stated that he received a commission of 2 1/2 per cent for selling the stock of the Black Star Line.

MR. GARVEY RECALLED.

Mr. Garvey was recalled and upon examination stated that the highest commission paid to stock salesmen was 3 per cent. Questioned as to the membership of the U.N.I.A. in New York, he said the Association had 35,000 members in New York City.

On cross-examination he testified that his salary was $100 per week from the Black Star Line and $25 per week from the U.N.I.A.

Mr. W. F. Green, selling agent of the Black Star Line in Portsmouth, V[a]., testified that prior to the appearance of the article in the Chicago Defender he had sold 94 shares of stock, since its appearance he had only sold eight shares. He was a member of the U.N.I.A. and got no salary or commission for the sale of stock.

A GREAT BOON FOR THE RACE.

His idea in selling stock for the concern was that it would be a great boon and benefit to the race in the future, and therefore he did it as a racial duty with no money consideration. Prior to the publication of the article his division of the U.N.I.A. had about 600 members, but it had since dropped to about [1]50. He first saw the article in the Chicago Defender about ten days after it had appeared. It was mentioned to him by a member of his Church, who said the Black Star Line was no good, and that he relied on the Chicago Defender for his information. He further said that Marcus Garvey was [*taking money*?] from them and putting it [*into a*?] fake proposition.

DR. EASON TESTIFIES.

Rev. Dr. J. W. H. Eason, Chaplain-General of the U.N.I.A., testified that the article of the Chicago Defender was first called to his attention in Philadelphia while he was attending a Methodist Conference on September 21st or [2]2d. The Secretary of the Conference condemned him for speaking for and being identified with what he termed a "fake" corporation, adding that he had got his information from a reliable publication, namely, the Chicago Defender, to which he had been subscribing since 19[1]6. About 120 ministers were present at the meeting and they represented about 60,000 Church members. Outside of the Church there was a man selling papers and saying: "Read what the Chicago Defender says about the Black Star Line."

He (the witness) had had a hard time disabusing the minds of people of the impression made by the article in the Chicago Defender. He had spoken at public meetings to 75,000 people in various cities and he found that the Chicago Defender had reached all of them.

This closed the plaintiff's case and the defence moved the dismissal of the complainant on the ground that the plaintiff had not shown that what the defendant published was untrue; that he had failed to prove malice in fact, and had therefore failed to make out a case.

The motion was denied by the Court and the defence then proceeded to present its evidence.

THE CASE FOR THE DEFENCE.

Assistant District Attorney Kilroe was called by the defence to testify and upon re-direct examination by Mr. Rosenheim admitted that he had never been able to find any evidence of fraud or misappropriation of funds on the part of Mr. Garvey. In the several investigations undertaken by his office of the Black Star Line, the only objectionble thing he had been able to discover was a full page advertisement in the "Negro World" purporting that the Black Star Line had ships owned, manned and operated by the corporation at a time when the corporation did not own any ships at all just when it started.

Mr. Garvey was called in rebuttal and it was brought out from testimony that this advertisement was written during his absence in the South by the very men who went to Mr. Kilroe's office to get him to investigate the Black Star Line. It was brought out further that Mr. Garvey was indicted by the Grand Jury but not convicted, the case against him not having yet been tried, and the Court took pains to make it clear in the minds of the jury that indictment was not conviction, and that this circumstance therefore should not be allowed to prejudice the case. It was brought out further that Mr. Garvey had preferred charges against the men alleging misappropriation of funds, and as showing his animus that Mr. Kilroe refused to prosecute them, but proceeded in the investigation of Mr. Garvey on the strength of their testimony; that he would not accept any evidence against the men until the termination of the criminal proceedings; that this was the cause of the article of criticism against him by Mr. Garvey for which he had him indicted. Among the thousands of stockholders in the Black Star Line Corporation, Mr. Kilroe admitted that there had been only one complaint, and when pressed to tell who the complainant was, said it was an anonymous communication, on the strength of which he had charged Mr. Garvey with criminality. Mr. Kilroe had one witness alone upon whom he depended to prove his case against Mr. Garvey and when pressed to tell who that was had to admit that it was the man who shot Mr. Garvey and shortly thereafter committed suicide in jail from self-[re]morse.

MR. ABBOTT TESTIFIES.

Mr. Robert S. Abbott, owner and editor of the Chicago Defender, the defendant in the action, was asked on re-direct examination by Mr. Rosenheim whether it is true that, as his paper published, it reaches all corners of the globe, and had to admit that it does not; that it really has but a limited circulation outside of the United States. This was the first spike put in the guns of the defense that everything that the Chicago Defender says is not the truth. When asked if he was in sympathy with the scheme of Mr. Garvey to unify the Negro peoples of the world, Mr. Abbot[t] replied, "Well, I am in sympathy with anything for uplift, as far as I know." He was then asked if he regarded the unification of Negroes as uplifting and whether, as a matter of fact, he was not opposed to Mr. Garvey's plan to unify the Negroes. Mr. Abbott replied: "I have no feeling one way or the other." When asked if the Chicago Defender is a broad, influential sheet, he replied that he did not know how influential. When asked how it is regarded among the people, he replied that he could not say. When asked if he didn't know from experience that people who read the Chicago Defender generally believed to be true what they read, Mr. Abbott said, "Yes"; but later modified his answer by saying he did not mean to array one race against another. "I am purely an American," he said; "I believe in American institutions; I have always stood for American institutions; I know nothing else; I believe in fighting side by side with every American to unify the races of the common weal right here in America." Asked on cross-examination whether he was opposed to the scheme for taking American Negroes to Africa to nationalize them, he said he was not opposed to the scheme unless it affected this country.

NO SIMILARITY IN MOVEMENTS.

Editor Anderson of the Amsterdam News[11] and Dr. D. W. Onley were called to testify as to the similarity of the Chief Sam movement to the Black Star Line corporation but failed to establish any kinship between the two movements. Chief Sam, they admitted had disappeared, but Garvey was still on the scene. In answer to a question whether Mr. Garvey was the recognized leader of Negroes in Harlem or elsewhere, Mr. Anderson said Mr. Garvey was well thought of by a very large number of people; but as a leader he did not know that he was.

BLACK STAR LINE VINDICATED.

The jury after hearing the arguments and the summing up of the Court brough[t] in a verdict for the plaintiff (The Black Star Line) allowing nominal damages in the sum of 6 cents and thus vindicated the name of the Black Star Line.[12] There are ten other cases against the Chicago Defender by the Black Star Line. The case of Mr. Garvey against the Chicago Defender will come up shortly.

Printed in *NW*, 19 June 1920.

1. John Clark Knox (1881–1966) was appointed federal judge in the United States District Court, Southern District of New York, in 1918 and remained on the bench until 1965 (*NYT*, 24 August 1966).

2. A misstatement, since Garvey was born in the parish of St. Ann.

3. Robert Sengstacke Abbott (1870–1940), founder and editor of the *Chicago Defender*, was responsible for much of the publicity that led thousands of southern blacks to migrate to northern cities in the years immediately before and after the First World War. Born to slave parents in Simmons Island, Ga., Abbott was strongly influenced in childhood by his stepfather, Henry Sengstacke, a clergyman and teacher. In 1896 Abbott graduated from Hampton Institute, Hampton, Va., and later he attended Kent College of Law in Chicago, graduating with an LL.B. degree in 1899. Advised against practicing law in Chicago because of his color, Abbott worked as a printer for several years. Profoundly affected by the Atlanta riot, the high incidence of lynching, and the generally worsening situation of southern blacks, Abbott launched a four-page handbill, the *Chicago Defender*, in May 1905. Calling his paper the "world's greatest weekly," Abbott soon edited a thriving publication that in 1917 reached a circulation of 230,000 (Metz T. P. Lockhard, "Robert S. Abbott—Race Leader," *Phylon*, 1947, pp. 124–28; *WWCA*).

4. On 31 October 1919 Garvey paid $50,000 to Harriss, Magill & Co. toward the purchase of the *Yarmouth*. On 24 November an additional $23,000 was paid, and by May of 1920 the Black Star Line had paid a total of $122,000 in cash and another $49,500 by notes (Thomas P. Merrilees, "Summary Report of Investigation of Books and Records of the Black Star Line, Inc., and the Universal Negro Improvement Association," p. 31).

5. The *Yarmouth*'s tour of the Caribbean took it to Cuba, Jamaica, Panama, and Costa Rica. The ship carried a consignment of four hundred tons of logwood and had a full list of passengers when it returned to New York on 8 January 1920.

6. Captain Dickenson.

7. Capt. Jacob Wise.

8. Capt. Leon R. Swift.

9. Frederick Augustus Toote (1895–1951?) was president of the Philadelphia division of the UNIA (Division No. 47) and a member of the board of directors of the Black Star Line. Born in Nassau, Bahamas, Toote was the son of Thaddeus Toote, a member of the Bahamian House of Assembly and a well-known merchant. He was educated at Boys' Central School in Nassau and, after immigrating to the United States, he became a student at the City College of New York. He reportedly completed a master's degree at Oskaloosa College as well as a theological course at the Philadelphia Divinity School prior to his ordination into the priesthood of the African Orthodox church in April 1923. He was elected speaker of the 1920 UNIA convention, during which the *Negro World* praised him as "next to President Garvey in energy." At the time, the membership of the Philadelphia UNIA was estimated at 9,500, making it one of the largest divisions (*NW*, 21 August 1920). During 1921 Toote became an associate member of the Bahamas Rejuvenation League (*Crusader* 4 [March 1921]: 10). After he was ordained by George Alexander McGuire, founder of the African Orthodox church, he immediately became the associate editor of the church's organ, *The Negro Churchman*. He was also appointed dean of the Bishop Holly Theological School but was stripped of both posts by the September 1924 synod. Toote reemerged as an influential UNIA leader shortly after Garvey's imprisonment in February 1925, spearheading the revival of the Philadelphia division after a precipitous drop in membership. In March 1926 Toote was elected first assistant president general (*The Negro Churchman* 1, no. 5 [May 1923]: 3, and 1, no. 9–10 [September–October 1923]: 9–11 [reprint ed., Millwood, N.Y.: KTO, 1977]; *NW*, 7 March 1925).

10. Allen Hobbs was later president of the Norfolk UNIA (*NW*, 19 February 1921).

11. James Henry Anderson (1867?–1931), born in Columbia, S.C., was the founder and managing editor of the New York *Amsterdam News*, one of the most influential black newspapers. Anderson arrived penniless in New York City in 1883 and began publishing the paper in December 1909 with an initial investment of ten dollars. In 1913 he ran as a Republican candidate for the post of New York alderman, but was defeated (*WWCR*; [New York] *Amsterdam News*, magazine supplement, 22 December 1934).

12. For the *Chicago Defender*'s version of the case, see "Six Pennies End Damage Suit" in its 26 June 1920 issue.

Advertisement

[*Negro World*, 19 June 1920]

LAUNDRY SERVICE

INCOMPARABLE

WET WASH OR FINISHED WORK

By Negro Experts in a Modern Sanitary Steam Laundry

EVERY CUSTOMER GETS INDIVIDUAL SERVICE

Orders Called For and Delivered

WE RETURN EVERYTHING EXCEPT THE DIRT

Address UNIVERSAL LAUNDRY, 62 West 142nd St.

Owned and Operated by

The Negro Factories Corporation

54–56 West 135th Street

MARCUS GARVEY, President

Printed in *NW*, 19 June 1920.

Let's Go... "OVER THE TOP" Some More

--FOR WHAT?

A Direct Line of Steamships Owned, Controlled and Manned by Negroes, to Reach the Negro Peoples of the World
America, Canada, South and Central America, Africa and the West Indies

A great victory was gained for the race when the first ship, S.S. Yarmouth, to be rechristened the S.S. Frederick Douglass, was launched on Friday Oct. 31. This ship will trade between New York, the West Indies and Panama, carrying freight and passengers. We want your help to launch a ship every two months, until the Negro becomes a power in the maritime world. Help yourself to make money and become prosperous. Untold profits will be gathered from the various Negro countries of the world for those who invest now.

SEND IN AND BUY YOUR SHARES TODAY

"The Black Star Line," Inc.

Capitalized at $10,000,000 Under the Laws of the State of Delaware

2,000,000 shares of common stock now on sale at par value of $5.00 each for a limited time only at the office of the corporation. 56 West 135th Street, New York City. Phone Harlem 2877.

The Black Star Line, Inc., is the result of a Herculean effort on the part of Hon. Marcus Garvey, world-famed Negro orator, who in July, 1914, founded a society known as the Universal Negro Improvement Association and African Communities League, of which he is now President-General.

The Association now has a membership of over two million persons, with branches all over the United States, Canada, South and Central America, the West Indies and Africa.

THE BLACK STAR LINE, Inc.

Is backed today in its operations by the full strength of its organization—to say the least, of millions of other Negro men and women in all parts of the world.

BUY YOUR SHARES TODAY AND NOT TOMORROW

— CUT THIS OUT AND MAIL IT —
SUBSCRIPTION BLANK

"THE BLACK STAR LINE, Inc."
56 West 135th Street, New York City,   Date ....

Gentlemen:
I hereby subscribe for .... shares of stock at $5.00 per share and forward herewith as full payment,
$ .... on same.

Name ....
City ....
Street ....
State ....

(*Source: NW*, 19 June 1920).

373

Convention Fund

[*Negro World*, 19 June 1920]

$2,000,000 CONVENTION FUND FOR GREAT RACE MOVEMENT

HOW MUCH WILL YOU GIVE TO HELP REDEEM AFRICA AND THEREBY YOUR OWN FUTURE?—SEND IN A DONATION TODAY

The time has come for every true and loyal patriot of the Negro race to do his bit or her duty in helping to restore to the world the ancient glories of Ethiopia. The hour has struck for universal emancipation. The Negro race, like all other races, must now find a place in the sun, and the Universal Negro Improvement Association and African Communities League of the [W]orld is now calling upon the four hundred million members of the race to do their duty in helping to build up a mighty nation for the race. On the 1st of August the greatest convention ever held by any race will assemble at Liberty Hall in New York, and will be in session for thirty-one days. Negroes from all parts of the world will be sent to this convention as delegates, to there discuss the future government of the four hundred million Negroes who are now domiciled in all parts of the world. All great races have their leaders, their kings, their emperors, and their presidents. We think the time has come for the Negro to find a universal leader, whose leadership the four hundred millions will follow. If Germany is to follow the Kaiser,[1] if England is to follow George V, if Italy is to follow Emanuel,[2] if France is to follow its President,[3] and Ireland is to follow De Valera,[4] then the time has come for four hundred million Negroes to follow a Negro elected by themselves. At this convention fifteen millions of American Negroes will elect a leader for themselves in America who will not be hand picked by any other race, but truly elected by themselves. The West Indians will elect their own leader, and the American[,] West Indian, South and Central American and African Negroes, four hundred million strong will elect a Universal Leader, who will forever guide the destiny of the race. We are now raising a fund of two million dollars ($2,000,000) to capitalize this, the greatest of all conventions.

After the convention adjourns on the 31st of August, the headquarters of the great movement, known as the Universal Negro Improvement Association, will be transferred to Monrovia, Liberia, West Coast of Africa. New buildings are to be erected, administration buildings are to be built, colleges and universities are to be constructed; therefore there will be a great demand for finances to carry out the work. So each and every member of the race is hereby requested to contribute as much as he or she can to help this convention fund. If you can give $100, give it, or $50, $30, $25, $10, $5 or $1—give as much as you can to help this world cause. Wherever you be, whether it be in the United States of America, the West Indies, South and Central America, or Africa, as you read this appeal send in your donations, addressed to the

Chancellor of the Universal Negro Improvement Association, 56 West 135th Street, New York City, U.S.A. Your donation will be acknowledged in the columns of The Negro World and published in book form to be circulated at the convention, so that a proper record will be kept of those who helped to save the day for glorious Ethiopia.

Be sure to send in your donations today to the Chancellor.

CONVENTION FUND LIST, JUNE 14TH, 1920.

Carried forward	$4,675.28	Reginald Rymer	.05
Friend	.05	Maxi Christopher	.05
W. Manning	.50	Salvadore DaCosta	.12
Friend	1.00	Wm. Penn	.16
Friend	1.00	Wm. Jones	.25
Friend	.50	Wm. Vanderpool	.50
Friend	.50	James Nichols	.05
Mrs. Mary Hall	1.00	Albert Elliott	.10
Mr. Nelly	2.00	Samuel Newton	.10
Mr. Shell	1.50	Christian Thomas	.50
Mr. A. E. Warner	1.00	Clemencia Thomas	.25
Alfrida Yard	1.00	Sophia Calender	.25
Louis Jeffery	[1].00	Alexander James	.05
Mr. and Mrs. Jemott	3.00	James Lake	.05
Mr. and Mrs. Yard	2.00	Amos	.05
Samuel Agard	1.00	Edward Hodge	.25
R. Morrison	1.00	H. E. Norman	.25
Mrs. Sarah Brown	1.00	Paul Penn	.10
P. Holder	1.00	Saml. Joseph	.10
A. M. Clagar	.25	Dudley Wiltshire	1.00
Mrs. Brown	1.00	Edward Robinson	1.00
Friend	1.00	A. Gasher	1.00
J. S. Phillips	1.00	Jas. Malcome	1.00
W. S. James	1.00	Samuel Bertha	1.00
Mrs. Sally Francis	1.00	Mrs. M. L. Fauntleroy	1.00
F. Welsh	1.00	B. B. Snyder	1.00
M. Brown	1.00	J. H. Pierre	2.00
R. Austin	1.00	I. Reddie	2.00
D. Plummer	1.00	W. O. Norville	1.50
Miss Elmar	1.00	S. E. King	1.00
Mr. Peter Francis	1.00	O. M. Morville	1.00
Mr. and Mrs. E. Gatewood	1.00	J. M. Dougl[as]	1.00
J. S. Phillips	1.25	V. P[......]	1.00
Verlenicia Cregine	1.00	J. M[......]	1.00
Rosa Barnett	.10	P. Dan[iel]	1.00
James Bausell	.10	J. Daniel	1.00
Joseph Daniel	.05	G. Edwards	1.00

J. Brown	1.00	James George	1.00
S. Proctor	1.00	I. Pinn	1.00
C. Gibson	1.00	Phillip Roberts	1.75
B. G. Richardson	1.00	T. H. Johnson	1.00
Alex. Inniss	1.00	Joseph E. Peterson	1.00
J. Henry	1.00	Hendrick Brown	1.00
E. Bishop	1.00	Friend	.25
A. Prince	1.00	Friend	.25
F. Alexander	1.00	Robert E. Slie	1.00
L. Garnett	1.00	Rev. Abraham Atkins	2.00
W. Reid	1.00	Thomas H. Semley	.25
J. Callender	1.00	Frank Wright	.50
J. Baptiste	1.00	Chas. H. Mills	1.00
G. Boddie	1.00	Daniel Eldrige	.50
T. Adolph	1.00	Denis Daniel	.10
H. Gouston	1.00	E. Jones	.10
O. Edmunds	1.00	Isaiah Cormise	.25
G. Waghorn	1.00	Abraham Ford	.50
Mrs. Knights	1.00	Victoria Buckman	1.00
M. Alexis	.75	John Carey	.25
McD. Reid	.50	George Spray	1.00
H. Cobham	.50	William Virtue	1.00
F. Estwick	.50	Mrs. Peter Black	.10
G. R. Lampkin	.48	James Young	.25
J. Daytes	.48	Edward Scott	1.00
S. Moise	.48	Hester Coleman	.50
J. Mason	.48	Lea Hardy	.50
A. Marshall	.48	Mrs. E. Edwards	.50
C. York	.48	Prince E. Allent	1.00
E. Grant	.48	Charles Walker	.50
T. Girard	.24	R. Jenkins	.50
D. Pitcairn	.24	Columbus Cheery	1.00
E. Murray	.12	Walter Morton	.50
W. Buriss	.12	L. M. Day	1.00
Valent St. Omer	.12	Ernest Anderson	1.00
L. Nathan	.06	Alexander Overley	.50
M. Richards	.06	James E. Hackett	1.00
Lilia Richards	.06	Harold Williams	.50
Leo Richards	.02	W. B. Dowell	1.00
Leona Clarke	.02	John Powell	2.00
Fredk. Desir	1.00	Manuel Lopez	1.00
A. Francois	.24	William Parker	.50
Mary Wickham	.10	Henry Sopps	.50
Mary Davis	.06	Wesley Howell	1.00
L. Payne	.06	Alexander Young	1.00

Henry Smith	.50	Chas. Moodie	1.50
Sam Dixson	.50	Leonard Brown	1.00
Edgar Simms	1.00	Selvin Hibbert	1.00
Peter Leal	.50	A. T. Robins	1.00
William Hester & Family	7.00	Cyril N. Ellis	1.00
Mr. & Mrs. Skinner	10.00	Arnold S. Cumming	1.50
Brooks Sims	.50	Rev. E. Blackwell's List	4.40
Mrs. Robson	.50	L. H. Campher	1.50
George Hicks	.25	J. H. Pilgrim	1.00
Mrs. Cymthias	.50	T. Brown	1.00
Isaac Anderson	.50	G. S. Davis	2.00
Walter Jackson	.50	Mrs. E. E. Burrows	1.00
B. J. Jackson	1.00	Miss A. M. Rose	1.00
George Scott	1.00	E. A. Kerr	1.00
J. T. Leary	.75	Mrs. Adams	1.00
Mrs. Laura Taylor	.50	Miss Louise Wilson	1.00
Mr. & Mrs. Carter	1.00	Herbert A. Morris	1.00
Clementina Dunkley	1.00	Thomas Barrett	1.00
Jacob W. Murray	1.00	Ernest B. Hill	1.00
Caleb Wilson	1.00	Clement C. Hackett	1.25
Cecil A. Willis	1.00	D. Corson	.25
Uriah Henry	1.00	T. W. Buckley	.25
Charles Green	2.00	James Rock	1.00
Marcus Simons	1.00	C. M. Greenidge	1.00
Harold Mallett	1.00		

Printed in *NW*, 19 June 1920.

1. The kaiser (William II) had abdicated on 28 November 1918.
2. Victor Emmanuel III (1869–1947) was king of Italy from 1900 to 1946 and an active participant in the negotiations after World War I (*WBD*).
3. Paul Deschanel (1856–1922).
4. Eamon de Valera (1882–1975) was an American-born Irish political leader who participated in the Irish nationalist uprising in 1916. He was president of Sinn Féin (1917–1926) and leader of the Irish Free State in 1932 (The Earl of Longford and Thomas P. O'Neill, *Eamon de Valera* [Dublin: Gill and Macmillan in association with Hutchinson of London, 1970]).

Marcus Garvey to Capt. Joshua Cockburn

[*New York*] June 19th, 1920

Dear Capt. Cockburn:

This is to inform you that at the regular meeting of the Board of Directors of the Black Star Line, the matter of your claim was brought up for discussion. The Directors have advised me to write to you conveying the following:

In view of the fact that the Corporation has been unable to gather in its complete report of transactions for the last two voyages of the "Yarmouth" from the agencies and to have their accounts properly adjusted in accordance with business routine, they are asking you to allow your claim to remain in the office for another thirty days at which time we hope to get sufficient data from the agents in Havana, Jamaica, and Panama to straighten out our mutual obligations. This is done because the Directors do not desire to be unfair to you in any of its transactions. Neither do they desire you to be unfair to them. It is desired that we have an amicable settlement in our business relationship. The Directors also feel that you can be of great service to them whilst you are ashore until the Corporation secures another ship to place on an African route as per conversation with me, at which time we shall be pleased to call you into active service. The Corporation instructs me therefore to pay you two weeks' salary at $50 per week for services you have rendered the Corporation since you have been ashore and that as soon as the Corporation arranges its itinerary of tour, that your services be retained at $50 per week. You will find herein enclosed the check of $100 to cover the two weeks' salary. You will be informed by my office at what time we shall be ready to call you into service under the new arrangements. With very best wishes. Yours faithfully,

BLACK STAR LINE, Inc.
MARCUS GARVEY

Printed in *Garvey* v. *United States*, no. 8317, Ct. App., 2d Cir. 2 February 1925, government exhibit no. 32.

Announcement of Rev. H. M. Mickens, UNIA Secretary-General

[[New York, June 19, 1920]]

To the Officers[,] Members and Friends of the U.N.I.A.:

As our convention approaches, we are making one supreme effort to have every division properly represented and the many thousands of our people in the territories hereinafter outlined in my campaign tour reached and brought into our association.

I am hereby asking that you plan mammoth mass meetings on the dates which I have set for each place.

H. M. MICKENS,
(Signed) Secretary-General.

LIST OF APPOINTMENTS.

June.
21st—Freeport, L.I.
22nd—Brooklyn, N.Y.
23d—Albany, N.Y.
24th—Binghamton, N.Y.
25th—Newark, N.J.
27th—Flushing, L.I.
28th—Stamford, Conn.
29th—New Haven, Conn.
30th—Norwich, Conn.

July.
1st—Hartford, Conn.
2d—Providence, R.I.
3d—New Bedford, Mass.
4th—Boston, Mass.
5th—Wilmington, Del.
6th—Richmond, Va.
7th—Petersburg, Va.
8th—Suffolk.
9th—Franklin.
10th—Capron.
11th—Grafton, W. Va.
12th—Cape Charles.
13th—Smithfield.
14th—Backwater.
15th—Oyster Point.
16th—Mundon Point.
17th—Tidewater.
18th—Newport News, Va. [3] p.m.
1[9]th—Norfolk, Va.
20th—New York City (office).
22d. 23d. 24th—Montreal.

Printed in *NW*, 26 June 1920.

Report of UNIA Meeting

[[*New York*, June 20, 1920]]

Tonight's meeting brought together the thousands of followers of the U.N.I.A., hailing from all parts of New York City and suburbs, who have come to look upon Liberty Hall as the forum of Negro thought and intellect, and the fountain of inspiration which has its reaction in the ever-increasing race consciousness that is pervading Negroes the world over.

Among the many encouraging messages delivered from the platform was the announcement that the delegation which was sent from Liberty Hall some time ago to Africa as a forerunner to the great convention to be held in August, has reached Liberia and reported back by cable that Africa was all for the U.N.I.A. The cable, Mr. Garvey stated, said that the delegation was received as if it was royalty and had received everything for which they asked.

The speakers of the evening were Prof. Ferris, Dr. Eason, Dr. Lewis, President of the Montreal Division; Mrs. Kinch,[1] a returned missionary from Africa; Rev. Dr. J. D. Brooks[2] and Hon. Marcus Garvey. Because of certain rumors which were current during the past week several members of . . . [*line mutilated*] but after listening to the fervid appeals of the various speakers for support to the President-General, and the latter's outspoken declaration of principles, they departed, after the meeting, re-dedicated to the cause and with the utmost faith and confidence in the leader (Hon. Marcus Garvey).

HON. MARCUS GARVEY SPEAKS.

The Hon. Marcus Garvey, President-General of the U.N.I.A., in opening the meeting said:

"Once more it is our good fortune and privilege to find ourselves in Liberty Hall. These Sunday night meetings have become regular features in the life of the U.N.I.A. and in the career of each and every member. Thousands of people are attracted to Liberty Hall during the week nights, and more so are they attracted because it is a center of learning on all questions of vital interest to the race. Whenever you happen to miss anyone who is anybody on a Sunday night, you can find such a one in Liberty Hall. If I can use the expression, the best people come to Liberty Hall, because the sentiments and the best of human knowledge and information radiate from Liberty Hall. When you want to keep up with the times, when you want to know what is happening in the Negro world, you come to Liberty Hall. If you cannot get all the information you want at Liberty Hall, then you are not really seeking that knowledge that is worth while, because we have here men and women who know everything about the Negro and can tell all that is worth while telling about him—his past, his present and his future. I am therefore really pleased to see you crowding this celebrated hall in such large numbers night after night. It makes the heart of those who are leading the movement feel good to realize that their work is not in vain.

AUGUST CONVENTION.

"We are now looking towards a glorious day in our history as a people. We are looking toward the first of August, 1920, which will go down in the pages of human history as a red letter day for Negroes, because on that day, and from that day, the Negro peoples of the world will write their own charter of liberty—a charter that they who write it and succeeding generations of Negroes who will li[v]e after that charter is written, will pledge their life-blood to uphold. It is a charter that will mean freedom and liberty to untold millions of colored men, women and children born to this age and to succeeding ages. Every country has a constitution of its own. Every nation has a code of government; and for that constitution and for that code of government those countries will go to war and sacrifice the last drop of the blood of the nation in defense of that code and constitution. The constitution and the code that we will give out to the world from the first of August will be a constitution and a code that every Negro in the world will risk his last drop of blood to defend and to uphold.["]

PROF. FERRIS SPEAKS.

Prof. Wm. H. Ferris, M. A. literary editor of the Negro World, was next introduced and said:

I was interested in what the Hon. Marcus Garvey said about the convention and about our Magna Charta. The Magna Charta which the English nobles wrested from King John has gone down in history just as the Declaration of Independence which was signed in Philadelphia on July 4, 1776. Why have these two documents played such a great part in history? It is because they gave the English people and the American people an ideal. What is an ideal? An ideal is an idea which enters into our mind and is capable of giving us inspiration and nerving us. I remember when I was a boy they told us that if we walked nine miles to Mount Carmel where there was a great hill 400 feet high with the shape of a giant's head, and would climb to the top of that hill we could see not only New Haven but on a clear day could look across Long Island Sound to Long Island City, making a view of fifty miles altogether—thirty miles in one direction and twenty in another. I remember well how we trudged up that hill in order to get the view. It was the ideal—the idea that was before us that nerved us onward, tired and trembling though we were, in seeking the prospect and the view which we expected to find. Well, this has been the secret of the motive force—the power behind the U.N.I.A. and the Black Star Line. It is that which has given the Negro race the ideal of economic independence, the ideal of

381

manliness and the ideal of the redemption and regeneration of Africa. It is that which has given the Negro race something to hope for in the future.

THE NEGRO'S MAN.

This afternoon we had a wonderful Sunday meeting. My friend Mr. Adrian Johnson[3] packed a tremendous amount of history in fifteen minutes, and Dr. Brooks philosophized about the Anglo-Saxon and his propaganda, and Dr. Lewis also g[a]ve us words of inspiration. I have taught and preached in North Carolina and Florida, and have travelled in other sections of the South. I have studied the psychology of the Southern type of Anglo-Saxon whose propaganda is reflected in his Jim Crow and Segregation Laws and disfranchisement clauses. What is the purpose of all these? They are intended to do one thing—to break down the Negro's morale and to convince him that he is inferior to the rest of mankind. As we study the history of the slavery debate in this country we find that for one hundred years that has always been the philosophy and the program of the South—to convince the Negro that he is inferior to the rest of mankind and to convince the world likewise that he is inferior to the rest of mankind. But the new Negro refuses to believe that he is inferior to the rest of mankind, but holds his head up and strikes out for himself, struggling along and aspiring to the highest things in American civilization.

The wisest words uttered by Ralph Waldo Emerson were these: "If you wish men, black or white is insignificant." What does he mean by that? By men he means those intellectual, those moral, those esthetical and those spiritual qualities which differentiate a man from the lower animals, and in proportion as a man has brain power, in proportion as a man has thought power, in proportion as a man has will power, in proportion as a man has self-possession and self-control, in that proportion will he be the master of his own fate and the architect of his own destiny.

As I have studied the careers of eminent Negroes and have looked at the status of the Negro race all over the world and have seen the Negro disfranchised in the South and have seen how he was robbed of his labor and exploited in Africa, I wondered why it is that those millions of black men in Africa, that those millions of brown men in India have allowed a few thousands of Anglo-Saxons to dominate and boss them. It is because they have been asleep. The consciousness that they are men of the same powers and possibilities, that they can have the same careers and destiny has not yet entered their souls. And I believe that this is one thing that the U.N.I.A. and the Black Star Line has done to the Negro aside from any thought of pecuniary prospect—it has taught the Negro to feel that he is a man. It has taught him to come to his senses and to realize that in this hostile world men get the prize of life, not by whining, not by crying out, not by begging, but by striving and struggling for the things which give power and decision. And for that reason I saw last August that there was something about this movement which was far different from any other movement of protest and agitation that I have been connected with. This movement started on the conviction that before a man can do the big things of the world he must have a secure economic foundation; he must have commercial strength. Otherwise his liberty will be determined by the powers that be in the dominant races. But if the Negro can obtain and possess within himself the means for his subsistence then he will get that economic independence by which he can strike blow after blow for his civil and political rights.

In the long run the world only estimates a man by the estimate he puts on himself. Why was it that Toussaint l'Ouverture was able to rise from slavery and Frederick Douglas could start out as slave and yet write their names indelibly upon the pages of human history? Why is it that the Hon. Marcus Garvey in two years and a half could perform miracle after miracle? It is because of the spirit that has dominated them. It is because they believed in God and in their own possibilities, and [*God*?] has given the Negro race faith in itself, courage and ability to do and dare, and strive and achieve. This U.N.I.A. has preached a new gospel to them and has in it the potency of a new religion.

THE STRUGGLE FOR BREAD.

Rev. Dr. J. W. H. Eason, Chaplain-General of the U.N.I.A. delivered a discourse on the subject, "The Struggle for Bread." "There are signs," he said, "which portend an economic pressure all over the world at some future time. So severe will that economic pressure be that unless men—white men and black men—have prepared themselves for that day they will be hard pressed. Unless black peoples organize themselves to shun the impending calamity, they will wake up one day to find themselves completely shut out of the economic struggle—that other peoples were so far in advance of them that fate would consign them to be hewers of wood and drawers of water. In the struggle for bread it is possible for us to struggle sensibly and intelligently—struggle together as one, so that when the time of economic pressure dawns upon us, and other races shall attempt to cast the fetters of slavery around us, we will be able to break them asunder and rise to freedom because we are prepared for it. Prepare now," he exhorted, "and get ready for the great pressure which will beset the world economically, by organizing ourselves all over the world and by buying shares in the Black Star Line, and the Negro Factories Corporation, so that we may be fraternally and economically independent. Since we are strong now numerically, and since it is possible for us to be strong financially, why should not we band ourselves together into one solid whole and make preparation for the struggling times that are to come, preparing for our own daily bread and for the daily bread of our children and our children's children? We have a land that is rich in natural resources. The natural resources of our motherland have hardly been touched; and while it takes money, education and sacrifice to take possession of that which belongs to us, it is worth while. Negroes are not going to do very much until they learn to die for their liberty and for their honor. The

U.N.I.A., led by Hon. Marcus Garvey, was blazing the way to liberty and honor, and Negroes the world over must be prepared to dedicate themselves and their lives if necessary, to the end that its lofty aims and purposes may be achieved."

DR. BROOKS SPEAKS.

Dr. J. D. Brooks was the next speaker, and said among other things: "I am glad to have this opportunity to give my testimony. It is a sort of testimony for me to tell you how I came to join the church (speaking metaphorically of the U.N.I.A.). I was converted on the preaching of Dr. Mickens at New Haven; the President-General received me into the church the other day; Dr. Eason gave me the hand of fellowship and Prof. Ferris read my credentials. I feel now that I am a full-fledged minister of the African gospel.

DOING THE IMPOSSIBLE.

"The white people of this country," Dr. Brooks said, "revere the names of Christopher Columbus, the Pilgrim Fathers, George Washington, Patrick Henry, Abraham Lincoln, and Theodore Roosevelt. There must never come a time in the history of Negroes here or elsewhere when we forget to honor Marcus Garvey. I am not one who is given to being a hero worshiper, but I lift my hat to this man, who has succeeded in doing that which no Negro anywhere has ever done. (Cheers) Where did you ever see Methodists, and Baptists, and Episcopalians, and atheists, and infidels all touching and agreeing on one thing? Never before in the history of the world have Negroes rung true to one thing. It is due to the genius and foresight and power and courage of this man—Marcus Garvey. Do not forget that he brought something out of nothing; he did the impossible thing. Negroes have been trying to do it for years. Every movement that has ever attempted to gather together colored folks all over the world has failed until Mr. Garvey appeared on the scene.

"Some poeple say they are not going back to Africa because they have lost nothing there. They have lost everything they ever had—manhood, virtue and everything else. The question now is are we ready to take back that which we have lost. There is but one way to get ready for this African movement. You cannot do it by yourselves. You have got to unite with influence and forces, and this movement is the movement that tends towards retaking our motherland. You say some of us have got to die. You have got to die anyhow, so what difference does it make if smallpox or pneumonia kills you. It is just as well to die in Africa as anywhere else. I care not whether British, French, Belgians or anybody else is there, that is my fatherland; I would rather die there, and by the eternal God if I ever get a chance I will dispute every inch of land there that I set my foot upon.

IS THIS THE TIME?

"Is this the time? Negroes have been talking about time so much. They say it is not time yet. When I was a boy they were talking that. 'Wait a little while,['] they said, 'and God in his own time will bring everything all right.' The Republican party told me, 'Wait a little while; we will fix everything for you.' I have waited and got nothing. The Democratic party, 'Wait a little while'; I waited and got nothing. Negroes have been saying[,] 'Wait a while.' I believe this is God's time, I believe that I am working in harmony with God's plans and purposes. I believe the iron is hot and the time to strike is now. Whe[n] in the history [of] the world have Ne[g]roes . . .[*words mutilated*] owned three ships? Never [be]fore. When in the history of [the] world have Negroes come together with one common purpose as they have come here tonight? When in the history of the world have we had a leader selected by ourselves whom we accept as our leaders? There was never a time before when we have united with one purpose and one aim as we are united now. Let the folks who do not believe the time has come, go to heaven (?) as soon as they can go, and let the rest of us who believe in the advancement of the race—who believe the time has come—who believe this is the hour and believe we can make it if God helps—who have our faces towards the rising sun and who are determined to march on now and give the African a chance to reclaim his native land—go forward with the work that we have started.

["]There is something about Africa that appeals to me. It has not been my pleasure to put my foot on Africa's soil. I have never seen the shores of Africa; but it is my native land because my kin folks are there. Talk about my mother, and though she is ugly and has wrinkles in her face, and stumbles and leans on a cane, she is to me the sweetest, prettiest and best woman in the entire world. So with Africa. Talk about the white man being there and the climate being so that I cannot live there. To me it is the sweetest, prettiest and best place in the entire world, and some day I would like to put my foot on Africa's shores. I don't want to die until I have reached that place so that my confidence in God may be renewed. I want to be there to play my part in the redemption of Africa; then if I die, I die with faith in God, hope in my race and a martyr to my conviction["]. (Cheers)

MRS. KINCH SPEAKS.

Mrs. Emily Christmas Kinch, a returned missionary from Africa of the A.M.E. Church, was next introduced and said in part:—

"I am sure you know I am very happy to be here to-night, for whenever Africa is discussed it is my great fortune and pleasure to be present. And yet I never felt happier in all my life than I do tonight, for it is one of my great ambitions, especially since returning [f]rom Africa, to meet a group of people who have an idealism similar to my [o]wn, and that is—Back to Africa. And somehow, in my travels throughout the United States I feared the peop[l]e had lost the vision of their opportunity—of going back to

Africa and possessing the land. Is it time? Is the time ripe? Yes, it is time. It is quite time. This is the noon hour of our opportunity. First of all, because Africa [n]ever was in a more susceptible, recept[iv]e mood for the U.N.I.A. than today. Before the world-wide war practically every door was closed to the Negroes of America. But God has mysteriously moved on the heart of the world, and everywhere there is unres[t]; and because of conditions brought about through the Belgians and Germans and other nations who had a strong and powerful grip on Africa today that grip has been gradually loosened, and everywhere the African wants to know why we in America do not come home.

"BACK TO AFRICA."

"I have never had very much use for the man or woman who said they have lost nothing in Africa. It has been a great pleasure for me to tell them they found nothing here. (Cheers) If lynching and burning and disfranchise-ment and Jim Crow law has given you a disposition to remain there, then remain. But there is a land that flows with milk and honey. There is a land that would receive you gladly—a land that you have turned your back on, a land to which men have gone over and come back bring[ing] the joyful tidings that we are fully able to go and possess the land. Let us go forward in His name and take it.

"Now if there are men of vision and men of brains and men of character and men who will gladly die for this cause, then I want you to know that there are women also who will join you and will gladly die with you that Africa might be redeemed. (Cheers.) I want you men to remember that while you are the stronger part of the great whole that the larger numbers in this great group are the women, and the African womanhood is the one object of pity that stands out preeminently in all these deplorable conditions. The missionaries, for instance, have been gathering the boys and the men for many years around them, and this womanhood that has been crushed has been the object of the unscrupulous practices of the white man. They look today to the American Negro and to the men and women of this particular organiza[tion] for redemption. I was speaking to a friend of mine [who was] recently . . . [*line mutilated*] told me that in Sierra Leone every other man was changing his name to Marcus Garvey. (Applause.) She told me that two weeks ago in the city of New York. And if the men of Africa have been so enthused and have caught the spirit of this man whom they have never seen, what about the men and women who are privileged with contact with this man of vision? 'Where there is no vision the people perish,'[4] and who knows but what we are come to the kingdom for such a time as this?[5]

LIBERIA RECEIVES OUR DELEGATES

"Talk about the resources of Africa, I want to tell you just this one thing: There is enough mahogany [b]urned in Liberia alone to furnish eve[ry] family in the United States with thr[e]e pieces of furniture. They do not need chimneys. All they need is just a little fire to cook, and they burn mahogany to cook with. Now then, if you want to grind out your life over the washtub, if you wish to spend the rest of your days upon the cooking table, if you are satisfied with these conditions, why, you can do nothing better than to remain here. But those of you who believe, who know that what I have said is the truth—Africa wants you. How I should have liked to be in Monrovia when the delegation arrived there, and seen the welcome which they received. The Africans waited long and patiently for the delegation that would come from the descendants of the men and women who were slaves, and they have often said to us: 'Why have you stayed so long? What has civilization and freedom meant to you if not to come back and give your life more . . . [*line mutilated*] mountains, bridged the rivers, thrown up skyscrapers for America, and yet you cannot go into a first-class hotel because you are black. You cannot ride in the Pullmans if you are tired, but must sit up or do the next best thing. Why not come back to Africa and make this a great country for ourselves, our children and our children's children?'

"This friend of mine told me that the young men of Sierra Leone are giving up first-class jobs and waiting for the Black Star Line to touch the shores. This friend is a woman of integrity, and I believe every word she has said, and she says that the day a ship comes into the harbor of Sierra Leone there would not be an English army large enough to keep back the Sierra Leonians, for they are determined that having gone to the trenches of Europe to die for the white man, if needs be they will die that Africa might be redeemed."

In concluding her remarks, Mrs. Kinch said:

"You think it is a wonderful thing to be in Harlem, but you have never enjoyed you[r] manhood until you have walked in Liberia and have come in contact with the black President of that country and received invitations to come to the banquet that is prepared in the State House. You surely cannot go to Washington to one. And so, after all, I would rather be in Liberia to-night, all things being equal, without her trolley cars, without her subways, without her elevated system, and to feel and know that I am a woman for all of that. Black skins or short hair, money or no money, you are a man and have the opportunity of being the greatest person in that republic; for the only requirement of Liberia is that you are black. Let us therefore join hands and back up the man who is leading us out of this wilderness into the Promised Land." (Applause.)

Printed in *NW*, 26 June 1920. Original headlines omitted.

1. Emily Christmas Kinch (d. 1932) was a missionary in West Africa from 1908 to 1910, serving in Sierra Leone and in Liberia, where she founded the Eliza Turner Primary School. Born in Orange, N.J., she was the daughter of a prominent AME minister, Rev. Jordan C. H. Christmas. She became the first president of the AME New Jersey conference's Sunday School Institute and was also the author of a pamphlet, *West Africa: An Open Door*, written shortly after she returned from Liberia. She was a well-known recruiter of black missionaries for Africa (Randall K. Burkett, *Black Redemption: Churchmen Speak for the Garvey Movement* [Philadel-

phia: Temple University Press, 1978], pp. 43–46; Richard Robert Wright, *Encyclopedia of African Methodism* [Philadelphia: AME Book Concern, 1944], p. 589).

2. James David Brooks became UNIA secretary-general at the August 1920 convention. Before assuming his post, he was foreign mission secretary of the National Baptist Convention and a prominent Afro-American clergyman. As secretary-general, Brooks conducted successful speaking tours in Oklahoma and North Carolina. In May 1922 Brooks sued Garvey for $7,000 in unpaid wages and for an unpaid loan of $1,000, but he lost both cases (*NW*, 19 June and 5 August 1920; *Philosophy and Opinions*, 2:283).

3. Adrian Fitzroy Johnson resided in New York and was a colonel in the African Legion. Johnson was raised in Panama though he probably had Jamaican parentage. The third annual UNIA convention impeached him in August 1922 on charges of being "an unfinancial member" and part of "a conspiracy to disrupt the convention and damage the interests of the association" (*NW*, 19 August 1922). In 1951 Johnson was the secretary general of the UNIA, Inc. (Lionel Francis to Amy Ashwood, 6 August 1951, Amy Ashwood Papers, Lionel Yard, Private Collection, New York; DNA, RG 65, file BS 202600-22-46x).

4. Prov. 29:18.

5. Esther 4:14.

Marcus Garvey to Chicago District Attorney

[*New York*] 21 June 1920

. . . As per report of morning papers it is apparent that one Grover C. Redding[1] is operating in Chicago under the guise of an Abyssinian and representative of colored people. Has often used the name of the Black Star Line Steamship Corporation in representing himself to the people. This man has been operating all over the United States and is a fraud. We have had cause to denounce him in many cities, recently in the City of Boston. He is a fraud and ought to be apprehended.

. . . R. D. Jonas the man implicated in Chicago riot[2] is an impostor who uses the name of the Black Star Line and the Universal Negro Improvement As'n to extract money from negroes. He has no connection with these corporations. He and Redding are frauds. Deal with them according to law. They are unworthy of sympathy.

Black Star Line, Inc.,

MARCUS GARVEY, PRESIDENT

DNA, RG 65, file BS 202600-805. TD. Garvey's letter was transcribed as part of the bureau's report. Copies of this report were furnished to the bureau's Washington, D.C., and Chicago offices.

1. Grover Cleveland Redding (d. 1921) was denounced in the *Negro World* after his arrest in Chicago for murder. A subsequent advertisement warning UNIA members and the general public read: "One man (Grover Redding) for several months lied to the people all over the country that he was a representative of the UNIVERSAL NEGRO IMPROVEMENT ASSOCIATION and took thousands of dollars from the poor people, claiming that he was to send them to Abyssinia. God being not asleep, this man, who exploited the poor of our race, has just been SENTENCED TO BE HANGED IN CHICAGO" (*NW*, 19 February 1921). Redding, also known as George Brown, Grover Reading, and George Reading, was born in Baldwin County, Georgia, and had been a member of the UNIA in Chicago before helping to organize what he called the Star Order of Ethiopia and the Ethiopian Mission to Abyssinia. According to testimony given at his trial, Redding told his followers that he was an Abyssinian prince and a direct descendant

of King Menelik and the Queen of Sheba. He claimed that the Abyssinian government had appropriated a large sum of money to facilitate his efforts to gather blacks in the South and transport them to Abyssinia. Reports that Redding's group planned to sail on Black Star Line ships led to vigorous denials by UNIA officials (*CD*, 15 January 1921).

2. Redding's friend and adviser had been R. D. Jonas, a white minister who also was an informant for British intelligence and the Bureau of Investigation. Jonas helped to revitalize the Ethiopian movement and later posed as the American ambassador to Ethiopia. Through this ruse, Jonas supported Redding's claims to Ethiopian royalty. On 20 June 1920 a procession of members of the Star Order of Ethiopia led by Redding gathered in front of a café in South Chicago and burned an America flag. A black policeman who attempted to stop the destruction of a second American flag was shot and wounded, and a white sailor who also intervened was killed. A restaurant employee was later killed when the "Abyssinians" fired into the café. The commission that investigated the Chicago riot of 1919 also commented on the Abyssinian Riot, noting that timely work on the part of the police and black business leaders prevented a recurrence of full-scale rioting. Redding was convicted of murder and hanged in Chicago in June 1921 (Chicago Commission on Race Relations, *The Negro in Chicago* [Chicago: University of Chicago Press, 1922], pp. 59–64; DNA, RG 65, file OG 44062).

Frank Burke to Bureau Agent Pierce, Philadelphia

[*Washington, D.C.*] June 22, 1920

MARCUS GARVEY Negro agitator and his secretary arrived in Philadelphia yesterday afternoon stop Locate and cover movements very closely securing address while in Philadelphia stop   Very important Stop five

BURKE, Chief

[*Typewritten reference*] GFR-HMP

DNA, RG 65, file OG 329359. TL (telegram), carbon copy.

Marcus Garvey to Leo Healy

New York, U.S.A. June 22nd, 1920

My dear Mr. Healy:

I am sending to you Mr. Thompson, our accountant,[1] with check to cover two months' notes on the S. S. "Yarmouth" for the 17th of June and 17th of July. I am asking you to bring the matter before Mr. Harris again and ask him to help us in the matter.

As I have explained to you, we have been a little tied up with some of our cash and we have had to make so many repairs recently to our ship that we are a little set back, and we are asking that Mr. Harris be good enough to hold our check over until the 17th of July, when he will cash same to cover both loans.

If he helps us in this matter, we shall be pleased to redeem the other notes even earlier than they become due.

With very best wishes and thanking you for the kind help given us in the past, We are   Very truly yours,

BLACK STAR LINE, INC.
MARCUS GARVEY,
Per President

Printed in *Garvey* v. *United States*, no. 8317, Ct. App., 2d Cir., 2 February 1925, government exhibit no. 15.

1. Orlando Montrose Thompson (b. 1879) was born in Barbados and immigrated to the United States in 1907. Thompson succeeded Jeremiah Certain as vice-president of the Black Star Line after the August 1920 convention and was placed in charge of negotiations for the purchase of additional ships. Thompson had been an accountant before assuming his duties, and his major task was to locate and purchase a suitable ship to sail between ports in the Western Hemisphere and Africa. Thompson saw the finances of the Black Star Line steadily decline, confiding at one point that the corporation's future was "just a little doubtful" (Orlando Thompson to Louis La Mothe, 1 October 1920, in *Garvey* v. *United States*, no. 8317, Ct. App., 2d Cir., 2 February 1925). When Thompson was unable to complete negotiations on the *Orion*, the ship chosen for the Black Star Line's first transatlantic run, UNIA critics seized the opportunity to increase their accusations of fraud. In February 1922 Thompson was indicted along with Garvey, Elie Garcia, and George Tobias on charges of mail fraud. Thompson was later acquitted (Orlando Montrose Thompson, declaration of intention, U.S. Department of Labor, Naturalization Service, no. 85077, 5 March 1920).

Editorial Letter by Marcus Garvey

[[*New York*, June 22, 1920]]

Fellowmen of the Negro Race[,] Greeting:—

And now the world is in an upstir! The Universal Negro Improvement Association has succeeded in arousing the sleeping consciousness of millions of Negroes! And that which was thought impossible has now happened. No one thought up to recently that the Negro was capable of striking out of the barriers of racial entanglement to free himself on the great ocean of Truth. This is the age in which truth has a hearing; when men oppressed and men abused are determined that their cause should be heard at the bar of public opinion, and that justice be meted out to them. Among those who are demanding justice at this time are the four . . . [*several lines mutilated*] membership of three million black souls. The world is now in an upstir because this association is about to hold its great convention in New York City, from the 1st to the 31st of August. At this convention the Magna Charta of Negro rights will be written. A constitution will be given to the world by which the present and future generations of Negroes shall be governed. The constitution to be written in the month of August is one that will be so s[acre]d to the Negro as to cause him to pledge his very life, his very [la]st drop of blood in its defense. As men of other races and na[tion]s regard their constitutions with a holy sense of respect, so will [*all*?] Negroes of the world, after the 31st of August, regard the new constitution of the Negro Race as a sacred epistle to be protected by their very life blood.

For thousands of years and within modern times, for hundreds of [ye]ars, the Negro has been the outcast of the world. He has been [th]e one lone and helpless wanderer who has never found a haven [*to*?] rest, but today he forms a part of the new world's reorganiz[atio]n. He is determined that he shall play his part in the reorgan[izati]on of world affairs. He numbers four hundred millions. He realizes that by unity of purpose and of action great good can be accomplished, but with division of interest the race will continue to be at the mercy of the organized races and nations of the world. This is indeed the hour for concentrated action on the part of all of our race, and that is why the Universal Negro Improvement Association calls this great convention to assemble in New York from the 1st to 31st of August. All Negroes who are interested in themselves, in their race, and in future generations will wend their way to New York City to form a part of this great convention assembled. Let no influence outdo your determination to be a part of this great convention. Let no business prevent you from being in line with the thousands who will assemble at the great metropolitan city of the United States of America . . . [*several lines mutilated*] races of the world, and the Negroes who are now living and who form a part of the Universal Negro Improvement Association are the ones who will write their names across the pages of this new history. Let us all be a part of this movement; let us all perform our duty to ourselves and to our race; let us all forget that there has ever been a superior race and let us all realize that God created, of one blood, all nations of men to dwell upon the face of the earth.[1] Fellowmen, I beseech you to do what you possibly can at this time to help the Universal Negro Improvement Association in carrying the cause of the Negro to victory. Each and every one of us can help morally and financially. You can help by lending your presence to this great convention as well as by sending in your contributions to the convention fund of two million dollars which is to be raised for the purpose of establishing the headquarters of the movement on the west coast of Africa. The problems that will be discussed at the convention will be of interest to one and all and every member of the race should embrace the opportunity of hearing these serious and grave problems discussed. Let it be understood that all roads will lead to Liberty Hall, 114–138 West 138th street, New York City, U.S.A., on the morning of the 1st of August, 1920. And now let me say a word for the Black Star Line Steamship Corporation.

Now, more than ever, this corporation needs the loyal support of all Negroes. The slogan of this corporation is "Ships and still more ships." We have three ships at the present time of small tonnage, but the corporation needs larger ships; ships capable of being placed on trans-Atlantic routes; ships that will sail the seven seas and lend honor and glory to the race that owns them. You can help the Black Star Line to own and control these larger ships by buying more shares in the corporation. The shares are still going at five dollars each. You may buy from one to two hundred and thus help to build up a merchant marine second to none. Write immediately to the Black Star Line Steamship Corporation, 56 West 135th street, New York City, U.S.A., and buy your shares which will mean so much profit to you in the near future. Write also to the Chancellor of the Universal Negro Improvement Association, 54–56 West 135th street, New York City, and send in your donation to the great convention fund.

Trusting each and every one of you will do your duty by your race and by yourselves, with very best wishes, Yours fraternally,

MARCUS GARVEY

Printed in *NW*, 26 June 1920. Original headlines omitted.

1. Acts 17:26.

Bureau of Investigation Report

PHILADELPHIA, PA. June 24, 1920

MARCUS GARVEY   RADICAL ACTIVITIES   BLACK STAR LINE

Regarding Bureau telegram, above referred to, notifying us that the above Negro Agitator, and his secretary had arrived in Philadelphia on the afternoon of June 21st, which directed that we locate and cover their movements very closely, securing their address while in Philidalphia; I have to report that I immediately began an investigation, and found that GARVEY was here on the 21st, 22nd and 23rd of this month; that, while here, he lectured at the PEOPLE'S CHURCH, at the North-east Corner of 15th and Christian Streets, where a colored man by the name of J. W. H. EASON, of 1635 Christian Street, is the pastor. It developed upon further investigation that EASON is no longer connected with that church, and that he no longer resides at the Christian Street Address, but is living at 1825 Bainbridge Street, and that he is in the employ of MARCUS GARVEY, and that there is considerable difference of opinion among the colored people here in Philadelphia, as to whether or not GARVEY and his crowd are to their minds strictly on the level. They held meetings of THE BLACK STAR LINE people in the basement of the church at 15th and Christian Streets, and, on account of these differences of opinion, the matter was taken up recently at a conference of ministers, and GARVEY's activities met, it appears, with very little support, outside of what support was given him by a colored minister name[d] DOCTOR [A]. E. ROBINSON, pastor of the Shiloh Church at 11th and Lombard Streets, whose home is at 1639 Christian Street. I was unable to interview DOCTOR ROBINSON, because he was out of town. It is said that ROBINSON told the conference that GARVEY was all right, [because he] had an investigation made of his activities. This support of ROBINSON has been given out to the colored people, which, of course, has helped GARVEY's cause somewhat, but it is the opinion of the better classes of the colored people that GARVEY's supporters are of the less intelligent type of colored people and the type which could be very easily led. Inquiries at 1825 Bainbridge street, which were made by me, on a suitable pretext, developed that EASON and GARVEY had both left Philadelphia last night for either New York, which is GARVEY's home, or Portsmouth, Virginia. EASON's wife is at the Bainbridge Street address, and I have made arrangements to meet her tomorrow, and I feel that I will have very little trouble in finding out where her husband is located, as I have learned that EASON has given up his church work and is travelling with GARVEY. Whether or not MRS. EASON gives me the information, I have opened up an avenue which will give us the movements of EASON himself, and will therefore, probably be able to keep a line on the movements of GARVEY.

The line of information that I understand is very much desired in Washington is GARVEY's relations with the person, who it is said, is his secretary. Without my making any leads whatever that would attract suspicion, information was handed to me at the Bainbridge Street house by the colored woman, who runs the house, that GARVEY never remains in Philadelphia over night when he comes to Philadelphia, but always returns to New York. This bit of information came from the woman in a manner that made me feel as though she had been put wise not to say anything that might later work against GARVEY.

The Bainbridge Street home is located in a very respectable part of the colored section of the City. The house is clean, and the woman, herself, appears to be a very respectable colored woman.

JOSEPH F. McDEVITT
Special Agent

[*Handwritten endorsement*] J
[*Stamped endorsements*] FILE G.F.R. NOTED W.W.G.
Noted F.D.W.

DNA, RG 65, file OG 329359. TD. Copies of this report were furnished to the bureau's Washington, D.C., and Philadelphia offices.

O. M. Thompson to Messrs. Harris, Irby and Vose, Attorneys

New York, U.S.A. June 24th, 1920

Gentlemen:

Attention Mr. Healey.

Herewith enclosed please find check to your order, post-dated July 17th, as explained before. We have changed the figures on our book to read— balance due $49,500.00 instead of $45,000.00, and would kindly ask you to see whether your notes read 4500, or 4950. If they are incorrect, kindly return and we shall be very glad to send you corrected notes.

With thanks for your courtesy in the matter, we beg to remain, Yours faithfully,

BLACK STAR LINE,
O. M. THOMPSON,
Dept. of Accts.

[*Address*] Messrs. Harris, Irby & Vose,
35 South William Street, N.Y.C.

Printed in *Garvey* v. *United States*, no. 8317, Ct. App., 2d Cir., 2 February 1925, government exhibit no. 16.

Notices

[*Negro World*, 26 June 1920]

NOTICE EXTRAORDINARY

To the Presidents and Officers of the U.N.I.A. Throughout the World:

This comes to inform you that the world-wide convention of the U.N.I.A. will meet at New York City, Liberty Hall, August 1, next, and that you are hereby directed to call your association together and elect your delegates. In that this is the first convention, you are hereby authorized to elect as many delegates as you can support during the convention period, August 1 to 31.

Send the names of the delegates to the office of the secretary general immediately following the election.

By direction of the president general.

H. M. MICKENS

[*Negro World*, 26 June 1920]

NOTICE TO UNIVERSAL LEGION!

TO THE OFFICERS OF THE UNIVERSAL AFRICAN LEGION:
UNIFORM RANK OF U.N.I.A.:

Kindly report at once standing of your regiments and prepare to take part in parade August 1st, and August 2d, at 8 p.m.

D. D. SHIRLEY, Brig. Gen.
J. W. JONES, Adj. Gen.
56 West 135th Street, New York.

Printed in *NW*, 26 June 1920.

Report of UNIA Meetings

[[Liberty Hall, New York, June 27, 1920]]

Universal Negro Improvement Association Triumphs in the Mid-West

An excellent program, consisting of speeches, recitations and vocal and instrumental selections, was delivered last Sunday night, June 27, 1920, at Liberty Hall in the presence of thousands of members and friends of the U.N.I.A., who turned out in mass, despite the hot weather, to welcome the President General and his staff on their return from a successful and triumphant tour of the Middle West, including Philadelphia and Pittsburg[h], Pa. The Hon. Marcus Garvey presided, and selections were rendered by the Black Star Line Band under the leadership of Prof. William Isles, the U.N.I.A. choir, directed by Prof. Arnold Ford;[1] the Acme Quartet, a violin duet by the juvenile members of the association, and solos by Mrs. Francis Lee and Miss Ethel Clark.

Following the public meeting a membership meeting was held for the election of delegates representing the New York division of the U.N.I.A. to the August convention: The following were elected: The Hon. Marcus Garvey, Mr. John E. Bruce, Attorney Vernal Williams,[2] Mr. Adrian Johnson, Prof. Arnold Ford, Miss Sara Branch, Miss L. V. Johnson, Madame Barrier-Houston, Mrs. Janie Jenkins, and Mr. Rudolph Smith.

Speeches were delivered by Attorney Vernal Williams, Miss Sara Branch, Mr. Adrian Johnson, Mr. Rudolph Smith and Miss Henrietta Vinton Davis.

Black Men Must Come Forward.

Mr. Vernal Williams, who accompanied the President General on the trip to Philadelphia and Pittsburg[h] in the interest of the U.N.I.A., voiced his impression of the enthusiastic interest displayed by the people of those cities toward the U.N.I.A. and its allied corporations. To his mind the people of New York would soon be compelled to give precedence to Pittsburg[h] and Philadelphia in their activities and sincerity in the cause of the U.N.I.A. "We spent three nights in Philadelphia," he said, "and there was not a night on which the Liberty Hall of Philadelphia was not packed to the doors. Philadelphia came out in all its strength and power to show that they stood solidly behind our President and behind this movement. Pittsburg[h] was another impressive center. Even on Saturday night," he said, "I saw in Pittsburg[h] a crowd that I had never beheld on any Saturday night in our own Liberty Hall. Black men and women outside of New York have undoubtedly caught the spirit of the day. They have caught the spirit which says that now or never the black race must be free forever. (Cheers.) They have caught the spirit that says for now and for all times black men must come forward and protect their lives, their honor, the sacredness of their woman-hood and their home against external aggression, even at the cost of their very life blood. They have caught the spirit that we are engaged in a serious business, and as such there must be no looking back, because the hour has struck when all the oppressed peoples of the world must declare themselves free to determine their own self-existence.["]

THE NEED FOR SELF-RELIANCE.

Mr. Adrian S. Johnson, of the Field Corps of the U.N.I.A., said: The march of mankind from the very cradle day of man's existence has been impulsed by a cause. We, as a struggling people have had a cause—that of unity in the U.N.I.A. and the Black Star Line. Our unity desires force to effect what we desire; and that which we desire is liberty.

We have heard quite a lot from time to time from all kinds of white people. We have tested their magnanimity; we have tested their hypocrisy. They have shown us a civilization camouflaged with all kinds of policies and religious pretenses, and in the very heart of their civilization we have seen the charred bodies of our brethren hanging from the tree tops in the Southern cities. We have seen our people mobbed, our children gathered up and thrown into the flames kindled by the beastly mobs; we have seen Mr. Jonas, who for some time was attached to this association and pretended to be the greatest friend toward the Negro, eventually tell the American authorities that he was acting as a spy against us for the British people.[3] It behooves us members of the U.N.I.A. therefore, if we desire to achieve our goal, to throw all clannishness aside; denounce all forms of pretenses of alliances from any people alien to ourselves, and unite ourselves in one common army to fight against the injustice and ignominy that has been heaped upon us for 543 years.[4]

It is high time that we unite our efforts to achieve our object. It has been said that the Negro is quite contented to be the slave of other races; but the spirit of the new Negro has manifested itself in the U.N.I.A. and the Black Star Line. No longer does the Negro intend to be a slave for any other races alien to himself. We desire to be free. We have fought for white people; we have bled on various battlefields, and the same courage that had pushed us on the battlefields of white people will push us on more and more to achieve our victory that we desire to achieve. (Cheers.) So do not falter; even though amongst you there be lots of bickerings; in many a white institution or organization there are bickerings. Remember that during the world war it was quite a long time before the British populace made up their minds to fight, and after they made up their minds to fight, then and only then did Germany feel that her end was coming. And if we continue to be bickering amongst ourselves and be deceived by this and that person by a kindly pat on the back—not remembering what Judas did to our Lord and Savior—you will never achieve what we have set out to achieve. Our way through this life has been very stormy, and we must take this as our slogan: "Bind up your wounds; put sandals on your feet. The way is long and dark, but the end is sweet." (Cheers.)

BACK TO AFRICA?

Mr. Rudolph Smith, in an eloquent speech filled with zeal and burning with enthusiasm for the work of the U.N.I.A., flouted the idea of failure of the movement. With the nearly four million followers from all parts of the world, he said, who had dedicated themselves to the cause of the U.N.I.A. and a free Africa for the Africans, failure was impossible. It remained for us in conjunction with all the Negroes of the world to cooperate and support the movement and buy shares in the Black Star Line, so that the task which we have set for ourselves may be accomplished. The people of Africa are waiting for us to send our first ship over, and when the Phyllis Wheatley is launched and sets sail for the shores of Africa it will mark the day when the Negroes of Africa and the Negroes of the Western Hemisphere joined hands together for the purpose of restoring themselves to that native land which was divinely theirs.

HON. MARCUS GARVEY SPEAKS.

The Hon. Marcus Garvey, President General of the U.N.I.A., was the last speaker, and said in part:

Once more it is my good privilege to be able to speak to you in Liberty Hall. The past week has been one of triumphant success for the U.N.I.A. in other parts of this country. I left here last Monday to speak in Philadelphia for three nights, and from there to Pittsburgh to speak three nights. The three nights I spent in Philadelphia were nights of open, unreserved manifestation of the loyalty of the 9,000 members of that division. They turned out and packed the Liberty Hall of Philadelphia every night, even though they had to pay 50 cents a night for admission. They packed the hall every night and hundreds and thousands were unable to get in. They bought shares in the Black Star Line as never they did before. We have proved that Philadelphia is not to be found wanting in any way or in any respect in her loyalty to this great universal cause of ours.

PITTSBURGH'S GREAT ENTHUSIASM.

From Philadelphia we journeyed to the great steel center of this country—the city of Pittsburgh. There we found a branch which had been organized but two months anxiously awaiting us. When we arrived at the Union Station there was a delegation of ladies and gentlemen. They brought flowers, and some of the ladies were so enthusiastic that they held on to me (laughter); but anyhow, I got away. We arrived in Pittsburgh just half an hour before the meeting was scheduled to start, and we went immediately from our lodgings to the meeting place. And for enthusiasm I have not yet seen in any section of the U.N.I.A. anything to beat the enthusiasm of Pittsburgh. (Applause.) The people turned out by the hundreds and thousands to listen to the doctrines of the U.N.I.A., in spite of the whole city of preachers, who spoke against the U.N.I.A. All the members from all the churches came to worship at the shrine of the U.N.I.A., and Friday night it went so bad with the preachers that they just had to come, too. And the people bought stocks not in fives or tens, but one and two hundred dollars. (Cheers.) The members of the churches bought stock for spite, in so much that the preachers had to start buying stock, too. That is the success we had in Pittsburgh. They did not want us to leave last night, but we were compelled to do so in order to be in Liberty Hall tonight. Wherever I go throughout this country I always turn my thoughts and attention toward Liberty Hall, and on Sunday nights especially, because this is the center of this great world movement of ours, and because now more than ever our enemies are busy and very much on the alert to do all they can to prevent this movement from achieving success.

Printed in *NW*, 3 July 1920. Original headlines abbreviated.

1. Arnold Josiah Ford (1877–1935) was a Barbados-born composer, musician, linguist, and theologian. He was a member of the musical corps of the British Royal Navy during World War I; after the war he moved to Harlem, where he joined a black Hebrew sect. Through his tireless study of the Torah, the Talmud, and the Hebrew language, he was elevated to the position of rabbi. Out of his concern for the destiny of Africa, a concern that was common among black Hebrews, Ford and many others of his sect joined the UNIA. Ford tried to prevail upon Garvey to adopt Judaism as the official religion of the UNIA, and although Garvey rejected the idea, Ford agreed to serve as the musical director of Liberty Hall. He wrote music and lyrics for many UNIA songs, including the "Universal Ethiopian Anthem"; he also published *The Universal Ethiopian Hymnal*. When the UNIA declined, Ford devoted himself full-time to strengthening his synagogue, Beth B'nai Abraham, on 135th Street in Harlem; he also became increasingly preoccupied with repatriating blacks to Ethiopia. After a chance meeting in 1929 with the Ethiopian Falasha scholar Tamrat Emanuel and a discussion in 1930 with Gabrou Desta, an Ethiopian diplomat, Ford migrated to Ethiopia along with three other members of his group. He undertook the journey at the behest of his own synagogue as well as of another group, the Commandment Keepers Congregation, and two of its affiliated organizations. Ford's mission was to consider a site for a black settlement in Ethiopia and to attend the coronation of Haile Selassie. When the Ethiopian monarch granted eight hundred acres of land for the establishment of a black colony, Ford encouraged members of his sect to emigrate, and within the next two years, more than fifty black Hebrews responded. Internal problems and difficulties with the Ethiopian government as well as hostility from whites within Ethiopia combined to wreck the small community by 1934, when over half of the settlers had returned to the United States. Ford died in Addis Ababa a year later (K. J. King, "Some Notes on Arnold J. Ford and New World Black Attitudes to Ethiopia," *Journal of Ethiopian Studies* 10, no. 1 [January 1972]: 81–87; Arnold J. Ford, *The Universal Ethiopian Hymnal* [New York: n.p., ca. 1922]; *WWCA*; William R. Scott, "Rabbi Arnold Ford's Back-to-Ethiopia Movement: A Study of Black Emigration, 1930–1935," *Pan African Journal* 7 [Summer 1975]: 191–202).

2. Vernal J. Williams (1896–1952) was born in Jamaica and came to the United States at the age of nine. He obtained his law degree from New York University and served as attorney for Garvey and the UNIA. In the 1930s Williams took part in the campaign to protect tenants from unfair eviction by writing several articles on this problem and forming the Consolidated Tenants League. He was also active in the Jamaica Progressive League (*NYT*, 9 February 1952).

3. R. D. Jonas was employed by British intelligence between January and April 1920.

4. This would refer to the year 1377.

Louis La Mothe to the Secretary, United States Shipping Board

NEW YORK. U.S.A. 28 June 1920

The Steam yacht S/S Kanawha now o/w/ned by the Black St[ar] Line Corp. and formerly in the service of the Navy, is undergoing repairs that will enable her to be classed as a passenger Steamer.

We are desirous of having the S/S Kanawha changed from American Registry, to British Registry, as she is now owned by the Black Star Line of Canada, and not the Black Star Line of United States of America.

The following d[i]mensions are hereby given:—

Length O.A. .... 227 Ft. 8 Ins.

Length W.L. .... 192 Ft.

Beam .... 24 Ft.

Draft .... 1[0] Ft.

Depth .... 14 Ft. 6 Ins.

Hull .... 90 Ft.

Ton/n/age .... 475 Tons Gross.

Hoping that we will obtain the order for the transfer of this registry. I am Sirs, Yours with respect.

LOUIS LA MOTHE

[*Handwritten endorsements*] To Mr. Hunt:
Law rept for action JBJ 6/30/20
[*In the margin*] How??

DNA, RG 32, USSB, file 1091-3520. TLS, recipient's copy.

Bureau of Investigation Reports

Pittsburgh, Pa. 6/28/20

In Re: MARCUS GARVEY, Universal Negro Improvement Association of the World—Meeting in Pittsburgh, Pa.

Upon information telephoned by M[r.] [G.] F. Ruch and pursuant to instructions from Acting Agent in Charge J. C. Rider to cover a meeting scheduled to be held at the John Wesley A.M.E. Church, Agent arranged to have three men cover the meeting and report to this office.

Here follows copy of the reports received:—

"Pittsburgh, Pa., June 25, 1920

There was a meeting held to-night at John Wesley African Methodist Episc[o]pal Church, pastored by Rev. Gaines, located at No. 44 Arthur Street, Pittsburgh, Pa., for the purpose of introducing the Honorable Marcus Garvey, President General of the Black Star Steamship Line, and also The Universal Negro Improvement Association, which is alleged to be incorporated, with headquarters in New York City.

The ultimate object of the meeting, seemed to be to get stock subscriptions, in both of the above named corporations. Stock per share, in the latter, is being sold for $.[2]5, and in the former, it was not quoted at the meeting.

Rev. Gaines, the pastor of the church, made the opening remarks, in which, among other things, he stated, that he had been advised by certain other colored ministers, having churches in Pittsburgh, not to allow Garvey to speak, claiming, that he was too radical. Gaines stated, however, that if radicalism meant telling the truth, he was glad to have Garvey with him. This statement was met with much enthusiasm by the crowd.

It was an overflow meeting, there being, conservatively five hundred people present, (all colored), both men and women about evenly distributed. The aisles of the church were crowded, as well as the entrance, there even being people in the street who were unable to get in.

Scattered along, on various telegraph poles on Arthur Street, between Wylie and Center Avenues, were posters, bearing the inscription, "Black Star Line, I am sailing for Africa. Come out and hear Hon. Marcus Garvey, the greatest leader to-day. Be on time, June 24, thru 26, 1920 at 8 P.M. John Wesley A.M.E. Zion Church. Admission Free."

The first speaker of the evening, after the opening remarks of Rev. Gaines, was an attorney by the name of Williams, a colored man, who is supposed to have offices in New York City, but who has given up his practice and taken up Garvey's cause. The gist of his remarks, was to the effect, that the colored man has borne the yoke of oppression of his white brother long enough, and it is now time, to take some action, toward the accomplishment of tangible results in favor of the Negro, financially, spiritually, and otherwise. Williams, I am informed, is natively, a West Indian. He stated, that an attempt is being made, through the medium of The Universal Negro Improvement Association, to organize four hundred million Negroes, through out the entire world, in this Association, though just what is expected to be accomplished by this organization, is still a matter of conjecture, as it was not mentioned in his remarks. Williams, in his remarks, did not suggest, or urge any violent action, but addressing a crowd, of practically uneducated people, continued statements of the kind, would undoubtedly eventually cause trouble. The audience was quite enthusiastic about his address.

Garvey, in making his address, spoke of the origin of The Black Star Steamship Line, stating that there are over three million Negro[e]s at the present time, who have subscribed for stock in the corporation. Further, he stated, that it is his notion to colonize as many Negro[e]s in Africa as possible. He states, that it is his intention to take as many Negro[e]s from America to Africa as he can, and each one, he expects to give one acre of ground, this to adults as well as children. The remarks of the man Garvey, were not nearly so radical as those of Williams.

It seems that in traveling around to different cities, Garvey carries his own orators with him, as well as two or three women who sing, thereby making out some sort of a programme where ever they are given an audience.

While in Pittsburgh, a temporary headquarters was maintained at No. 52 Arthur Street, two or three doors below the church, at which place, subscriptions for stock were solicited.

This man Garvey, is an educated man, having attended college at Oxford, England, being born in the West Indies[.] He has traveled extensively throughout the entire world, and is a very fluent speaker, capable of moving his audiences at will. He seemed to exert a sort of magnetic influence at the meeting to-night, bringing forth applause almost at will.

The Black Star Steamship Line, of which he is the President General, has already purchased three ocean liners, all of which have their habitat in New York City, and make frequent sailings, though they have no set route.

Garvey, is also the editor of a periodical called "The Negro World", which is supposed to be published weekly, but as a matter of fact, comes out every now and then. This paper, is nothing more than a speaking organ for his steamship company, and is published in New York City.

It is the writer's opinion and belief, that practically all of the people present at the meeting to-night were either members of the church, or friends of theirs who had been notified about it, as there was absolutely no notoriety of Garvey's coming through the medium of either of Pittsburgh's colored weeklies, "The Pittsb[ur]gh Courier",[1] and "The Pittsburgh American",[2] which ordinarily, for[e]tell the coming of any colored speakers of note.

Whereas there was nothing un-American said at this meeting, still, if he secures the cooperation of all of the people with whom he comes in contact, and addresses, there will eventually be trouble, not so much from what he says, but what the people will think about themselves as a result of his talks. Incidentally, Garvey spoke somewhat at length about a convention, which is going to be held in New York City, throughout the entire month of August of the current year, furthering his cause.["]

Signed—G.H.W.

"Pittsburgh, Pa., June 26th, 1920.

Following is a report as given by Ptl. Charles Pryor in regards to a meeting which was supposed to have been held at 44 Arthur Street and instead was held at #42 Arthur Street in the A.M.E. Church of which Rev. G. W. Gaines is Pastor, it was held for the Universal Negro Improvement Association and also for the Black Star Steamship Line with Home Offices in New York City, N.Y. The Hon. Marcus Garvey, colored, a native of West India, is President of the Association for which he was soliciting members at the rate of 25 cents per member, and the Black Star Steamship Company was selling shares at the rate of $5.00 per share.

Mr. Garvey's speech was mostly confined to the Treatment the Negroes receive from the white people, and he said that these conditions would exist until such time, till the Negro would be able to make War on the white race and that time would come when Africa would be returned to the Negro Race. Mr[.] Garvey spoke against Radicalism and Repudiated those men that have been going through the country causing trouble between the white and the Negro Race.

Enclosed is a pamphlet of their literature.[3]

(signed) T. J. CAVANAUGH, Police Clerk."

"Pittsburgh, Pa., June 26th, 1920.

Following is a report as given by Ptl. James Hughes, in regards to a meeting held at #42 Arthur St. June 25th, 1920 in the John Wesley A.M.E. Church.

The meeting held under the auspices of the John Wesley Church in the name of the Black Star Line Inc. with offices at 56 West 135th Street, New York City, N.Y. This Black Star Line is known as a Steamship Company incorporated at ten million dollars and selling stock at $5.00 per share, also known as the Negro Improvement Association and to become a member of the Association (Universal) is necessary to Pay a Fee of 25 cents as dues per month and is known as a Ben[e]ficial Branch of this corporation and supposed to pay Sick Benefits. The office for this city is at #44 Arthur Street in that Hall[.] [T]here will be another meeting at the John Wesley Church on the night of June 26th, 1920.

You will find on the enclosed pamphlet[4] the President of the Organization and the main speaker, who is a West Indian, who is well versed and has traveled all over the country, in the name of Marcus Garvey, he is supposed to leave this City for Chicago, Ill., Saturday, June 26th, 1920.

His talk was mostly of the bible and of Ancient History, and urging negroes to organize in order to have some claim on Africa, as the whites claim all other countries, the negro should have one as they are four hundred million population, Mr. Garvey urges organized representation as a race and protection to the race and goes on to say that there should be four hundred million to be a[s] one in case of necessity. Mr. Marcus does not talk or believe in radicalism or in Race Rioting, he urges organizing as a race and as a stock selling body.

(signed) T. J. C[AV]ANAUGH, Police Clerk"

Copy of advertising matter secured, attached to this report[5] for Washington.

Agent requested the Police Department to cover the meeting this Saturday night, and also to obtain copies of any literature that might be distributed.

Agent Rider wired Chicago Office that MARCUS GARVEY was expected to leave for that City to-night.

This case is open.

HENRY J. LENON, Special Agent

[*Handwritten endorsement*] J
[*Stamped endorsement*] NOTED W.W.G.
Noted F.D.W. FILE G.F.R.

DNA, RG 65, file OG 329359. TD. Copies of this report were furnished to the bureau's Louisville, Ky., Chicago, and New York offices.

1. The *Pittsburgh Courier* was established in January 1910 by Edwin Nathaniel Harleston, a black guard at a local food-packing plant. A few months later, Robert L. Vann (1879–1940), a young black lawyer who was an early backer of the newspaper, took over as editor, and by 1920 the *Courier* was an influential black weekly. In the 10 December 1921 *Negro World*, Robert Vann was reported to have joined the Liberty Division of the UNIA in Pittsburgh. Beginning in the early 1920s, Vann's career in politics accelerated, and the *Courier* eventually became the nation's most widely read black newspaper (Andrew Buni, *Robert L. Vann of the Pittsburgh Courier: Politics and Black Journalism* [Pittsburgh: University of Pittsburgh Press, 1974]).

2. The *Pittsburgh American*, owned by R. F. Douglass and William P. Young, was founded in 1918 (Andrew Buni, *Robert L. Vann of the Pittsburgh Courier*, pp. 120, 126).

3. Not found.
4. Not found.
5. Not found.

Chicago, Ill. June 29, 1920

MARCUS GARVEY, PRESIDENT, BLACK STAR LINE and UNIVERSAL NEGRO IMPROVEMENT & DEVELOPMENT [ASS'N]

Investigation made in keeping with the following telegram from Acting Special Agent in Charge RIDER, Pittsburg[h], Pa. office:

Dated June 27, 1920.

"MARCUS GARVEY Colored representing Black Star Line leaving Pittsburgh for Chicago today expecting address colored element tonight and tomorrow stop Consider it important his activities be covered."

Employe who previously covered the activities [of] MARCUS GARVEY in the city of Chicago several months ago, [at] which time he organized the UNIVERSAL NEGRO IMPROVEMENT AND DEVELOPMENT association branch in this city and sold shares of the BLACK STAR LINE, etc., immediately interviewed R. L. ABBOTT, owner and editor of the CHICAGO DEFENDER, who has had difficulties with GARVEY, and who has been ever ready to co-operate with this office on all investigations pertaining to Negro radical activities, Sheridan A. Bruseaux, (also colored) principal of the KEYSTONE NATIONAL DETECTIVE AGENCY, who has previously and is at present watching the activities of GARVEY, REV. A. STEWART, who is opposed to the activities of GARVEY and who has rendered able assistance to this office on previous occasions, stated that to the best of their knowledge, and diligent investigation, GARVEY was not now nor was he expected in Chicago, although it had been remarked among some of the negroes in the "Black Belt" that GARVEY would visit Chicago shortly. Careful investigation establishes that no hand-bills or newspaper advertisements in negro publications announced meetings or lectures by GARVEY. Inquiry was also made among confidential informants, negroes, but all had no knowledge of GARVEY's arrival in Chicago. Employe with a view of positively establishing whether or not GARVEY was in Chicago, called on CHARLES H. DICKERSON, (negro), of 3600 South Wabash Ave., who is the commissioned representative of the BLACK STAR LINE, and one of the officers of the above mentioned association, in Chicago, and with whom Employe is acquainted, stated that to the best of his knowledge GARVEY was not in Chicago, and that if GARVEY had been in Chicago he would have been the first person to know of it on account of representing GARVEY's organizations. DICKERSON also remarked that he was prepared to send GARVEY a night telegram (Sunday June 27, 1920) concerning a matter of the BLACK STAR LINE, and that if GARVEY was in Chicago he would not have to do it. The telegram DICKERSON referred to was on his desk, and it was noticed that the addressee was MARCUS GARVEY, Pres., Black Star Line Co., New York. DICKERSON stated that the telegram was strictly Black Star Line business, and therefore did not care to divulge its contents.

DICKERSON further remarked that it was his impression that the State's Attorney of Cook County, Illinois, held an indictment against "GARVEY" said to be brought about through some seditious remarks he is alleged to have made when on his last visit to Chicago while addressing a meeting under the auspices of UNIVERSAL NEGRO IMPROVEMENT AND DEVELOPMENT ASS'N, and therefore as he understood it GARVEY did not care to come here to be arrested.

Employe on June 28, 1920 talked to the State's Attorney office, and information was given that an indictment is pending against GARVEY, No. 19378, January 30, 1920, for violation of the State Criminal Syndicalist Law.

In the event of receipt of information of GARVEY's presence in Chicago, his activities will be covered and report will follow.

Investigation closed.

JAS. O. PEYRONNIN

[*Endorsements*] H.W.G. NOTED
Noted F.D.W. NOTED W.W.G.

DNA, RG 65, file OG 329359. TD. Copies of this report were furnished to the bureau's Washington, D.C. (two copies), Pittsburgh (one copy), and Chicago (one copy) offices. Stamped endorsements.

MARCUS GARVEY—Colored Activities—BLACK STAR LINE.

Refer to my report of June [24]th entitled as above. As stated in that report I had an appointment with MRS. EASON. I called at her home and had quite a lengthy interview with her on a suitable pretext. She is a very good looking young colored woman about 24 years old with brown [hair]. When talking with her regarding any information she might care to give me about GARVEY she said she would be willing to tell me anything she could but that I could get more information at the office of the NEGRO IMPROVEMENT ASSOCIATION at the S.W. Corner of 17th & South Sts., which is the headquarters of the Philadelphia Division of the BLACK STAR LINE which also has /its general/ headquarters in New York. MRS. EASON claimed that her husband was still the pastor of the PEOPLES' CHURCH which is contrary to the information that I received from other apparently reliable sources the other day. MRS. EASON said that her husband J.W.[H.] EASON is very close to GARVEY and travels with him a good deal of the time, but at present he is in Virginia while GARVEY is in New York.—I then in a very discreet manner and I feel without attracting any suspicion on the part of MRS. EASON that I was a Government officer, received the following information:

"GARVEY is a married man. He married MISS AMY ASHWOOD a native of the West Indies Islands. They live together in New York but just where they live I do not know, and it seems that no one else knows. MR. GARVEY himself can be seen at any time at the headquarters of the BLACK STAR LINE in New York. He is about 32 years of age with a little mustache, short and stout; the Ashwood woman is the General Secretary of the Ladies' Division of the entire UNITED NEGRO IMPROVEMENT ASSOCIATION she and GARVEY were married at Liberty Hall on 138th Street between Lenox and 7th Avenue on Christmas Night 1919. I attended their wedding. MR. TOOTE is the President of the PHILADELPHIA BRANCH OF THE UNITED NEGRO IMPROVEMENT ASSOCIATION."—

Case to be continued from time to time.—

JOSEPH F. McDEVITT
Special Agent

[*Endorsements*] NOTED W.W.G. H.W.G. NOTED

DNA, RG 65, file OG 329359. TD. Copies of this report were furnished to the bureau's Washington, D.C. (three copies), Philadelphia (one copy), and New York (one copy) offices. Stamped endorsements.

Edward D. Smith-Green to the Secretary of State, Delaware

111 West 143rd Street, New York City,
[*ca. June 1920*]¹

KINDLY SEND REPLY IF ANY TO MY HOME ADDRESS

Sir,

I am now taking this opportunity as one of the responsible officers of the above Corporation which was granted its Charter under the State Laws of Delaware, to place myself on record as protesting officially, having already done so several times to the other Directors, severally and collectively, against the methods adopted for the management of the Black Star Line, Inc.

Before going further, allow me to make it quite plain that, this is not intended for any other purpose but an "OFFICIAL PROTEST", so that, in the event of anything occuring in the future whereby an investigation by the STATE is deemed necessary, I shall not be held responsible for neglect or to be numbered among those who may have contributed to the u[l]timate ruin of the Corporation by negligence and mismanagement.

It is now nearly a year since I have been elected as Secretary of the aforementioned Corporation and one of its Directors and, I have never been given the scope to exercise my authority as such, nor have I been allowed to have a voice in the management of the affairs of the Corporation such as my position should warrant as its Secretary.

It is not my intention to go into a lengthy or detailed discussion of the affairs of the Black Star Line, Inc. unless it was demanded of me but, I must say that the entire management of the Corporation is in the hands of its President who acts as he feels without even the consent of the "BOARD OF DIRECTORS", which BOARD is, as a matter of fact but a dummy, its members merely at all times bowing to the dictates and domination of the President. For instance, when one of the ships was negotiated for, the President, without first consulting the members of the Board, personally inspected the ship and, without procuring expert knowledge so as to benefit by the experience such an individual might have had, actually paid the sum of $5,000.00 and clinched the deal. After this was accomplished, he then went before the Board of Directors to obtain their consent for what he had already done. The result of that is, that, the ship is now lying in the harbor and will not be granted a licence to ply as a commercial trader because of the fact that she has been previously used as a pleasure yacht.² Before such licence will be granted, the United States Steamboat Inspectors have demanded that reconstruction to the amount of $10,000.00 be done.

You will at once see what a hardship such a transaction has worked upon the Corporation and, all through the fact that one man attempted to do, without the opinion and advice of his fellow officers, that which he had no previous experience in.

Through gross mismanagement, however, there is the possibility, unless more businesslike methods are immediately adopted, of this promising business enterprise going to the wall and, as its Secretary and a responsible officer to the State as well as to the public, I do not intend to resign my position without being first placed on record as having attempted to protect the rights of the Stockholders as well as securing myself against being held responsible along with the others for the possible failure of this Corporation. I have etc. Sir, Very truly yours

EDWARD D. SMITH-GREEN
Secretary

De-SS. TLS on Black Star Line letterhead, recipient's copy.

1. Smith-Green was a prominent speaker at UNIA meetings during May. His break with Garvey came sometime in early July, as evidenced by Garvey's warning to the public against Smith-Green printed in the *Negro World* of 31 July 1920. Moreover, since Smith-Green was elected to the Black Star Line directorate in July 1919, his reference to "nearly a year since I have been elected Secretary" places the composition of this letter sometime in June 1920.

2. The *Kanawha* had been the private yacht of Henry Huddleston Rogers (1840–1909), a vice president of the Standard Oil Company and a leading mining and railroad magnate. Rogers was also a philanthropist who contributed to Booker T. Washington's Tuskegee Institute (Lewis Leary, ed., *Mark Twain's Correspondence With Henry Huddleston Rogers* [Berkeley: University of California Press, 1969], pp. 2–4, Harlan and Smock, eds., *BTW Papers*, 8:177).

C. H. Hunt, Attorney, United States Shipping Board, to the Black Star Line

[*Washington, D. C.*] July 1, 1920

Gentlemen:

Your letter of June 28, 1920, making application for permission to transfer the SS KANAWHA from American to British registry, has been referred to me.

The information furnished in your letter is not sufficient to warrant consideration of this application by the Board, and I am therefore enclosing herewith application blanks which should be filled out in duplicate and returned to this office. In addition to the information contained in these blanks you should also state fully in a letter accompanying the application full reasons for desiring this vessel transferred from American to British registry, and why it is more convenient for your company to operate under British than under American registry. I do not understand your statement to the effect that the vessel is now [own]ed by the Black Star Line of Canada and is under American registry. Was it purchased from the Navy by the Black Star

Line of the United States, or by the Black Star Line of Canada, which company placed it under American registry? If the vessel was purchased by the Black Star Line of the United States was it sold by the Black Star Line of Canada, without the approval of the Board[?]

Kindly give this matter prompt attention, answering in full the inquiries, and upon receipt of such reply and the application blank properly filled out, the matter will be brought to the attention of the Board for prompt consideration. Very truly yours,

C. H. HUNT
Attorney

DNA, RG 32, USSB, file 1091–3520. TL, carbon copy.

Gloster Armstrong, British Consul General, to the British Foreign Secretary

NEW YORK, N.Y. July 2nd, 1920

My Lord:

I have the honour to report for your Lordship's information, that I have had an application for a British passport from a Mrs. Amy Ashmond Garvey, of 552 Lenox Ave., New York City. This woman is a native of Jamaica, B.W.I., and the wife of Marcus Mosiah Garvey, also a native of Jamaica. He is a well known negro agitator.

Mrs. Garvey has asked for a passport to travel to England and subsequently to Liberia, on business connected with the "Health Sanitarium" 34a Peel Street, Montreal, Canada.[1]

She states that she has separated from her husband[2] and is not in communication with him.

I have issued to her an Emergency Certificate, to travel to England only, and reported the matter to the Passport Control Officer here, who is reporting fully to the Foreign Office, asking the Passport Control Authorities, who are in full possession of the facts to take what steps they consider desirable when Mrs. Garvey applies for a further passport to Liberia.

I have the honour to be with the greatest respect My Lord, Your Lordship's most Humble Obedient Servant,

GLOSTER ARMSTRONG[3]
H. M.'s Consul General

PRO, FO 372/1475. TLS, recipient's copy.

1. The sanitarium was actually located on 134-A Peel Street, Montreal. Dr. D. D. Lewis, surgeon general of the UNIA, practiced there (*NW*, 7 May 1921).

2. In his complaint against Amy Ashwood Garvey, Marcus Garvey stated that "on the 6th day of March, 1920, the plaintiff [Garvey] left the defendant and has not since cohabited with her." Garvey's complaint, which was brought before the Supreme Court of New York County

on 15 July 1920, sought an annulment of their marriage (*Marcus Garvey* v. *Amy Ashwood Garvey*, no. 24028, NNHR, 15 July 1920).

3. Sir Harry Gloster Armstrong (1861–1938) was the British consul general for Connecticut, New Jersey, and New York from 1920 to 1931 (*WWW*, 1929–1940).

Report of UNIA Meeting

[[LIBERTY HALL, July 11, 1920]]

THOUSANDS PACK LIBERTY HALL TO HEAR MESSAGES OF INSPIRATION AND HOPE

As the convention approaches interest in the U.N.I.A. is quickened and manifests itself in the increased attendance at Liberty Hall night after night. Sunday night thousands packed the hall and overflowed to the outside to receive the messages of inspiration and hope that emanate from the spokesman of the U.N.I.A., and which send them forth to their respective homes and callings with renewed hope and confidence in themselves and in their race.

Speeches were delivered by Hon. Marcus Garvey (who presided over the meeting), Prof. William H. Ferris, Miss Henrietta Vinton Davis and Mr. Vernal Williams. The choir, under the tutelage of Mme. Houston, rendered a splendid program of sacred songs and selections, while the Black Star Line Band, under the leadership of Prof. Wm. Isles, dispensed music that cheered even the most sordid soul.

HON. MARCUS GARVEY SPEAKS

The Hon. Marcus Garvey, President General of the U.N.I.A., in opening the meeting said:

Once more it is my privilege to bid you welcome to Liberty Hall. Tonight, it seems to me that as I look into the faces of this mighty throng, I see the manifestation of an eagerness for something. To my interpretation, that something is our forthcoming convention. I feel that that is what preys on your mind at this time, because from the four corners of the globe there comes a wild enthusiasm over this forthcoming convention of ours. Men and women in all parts of the world are now preparing to wend their way to New York to see and to take part in this great convention for which we are preparing. We are drawing nearer the time when we will, as members of this organization realize a part of our great dream—the part of seeing assembled under one roof the legal representatives of all the Negro peoples of the world gathered together for one purpose and for one common object.

It has been said that the Negro has never yet found cause to engage himself in anything in common with his brother—that he has always had a single and an individual purpose; that when he leaves off his own personal interests, he sees nothing further than the interests of his own environment, his own natal environment (and apparently that has been the way we have been living in this Western World under Western civilization for 300 odd years). But the dawn of a new day is now upon us and we see things differently. We see now, not as individuals, but we see as a collective whole having one common interest. (Applause.) It is that common interest that will draw us here on the first of August to remain in convention for thirty-one days, during which time we will have worked wonders to ourselves and wonders to the world. (Great applause.)

The loyalty and the devotion of 25,000 members of the U.N.I.A. in New York stretching over a period of two and one half years; the loyalty and devotion, moral and financial, of 3,000,000 colored men, women and children claiming allegiance to the U.N.I.A., has not been made manifest for naught. It was for a glorious purpose. It meant something. And we are now about to realize what it really meant. In our assembling here as a mighty race on the first of August, we will have taken steps to demonstrate to the world the earnestness of our Convention—the earnestness of our desire for liberty and fuller democracy. (Applause.) We have not spent our monies in vain. We have not spent our monies for fun or p[l]easure in coming to Liberty Hall, New York, and the various Liberty Halls all over the world where the members of the U.N.I.A. assemble themselves. Whenever a man or woman joins the U.N.I.A., it is for the specific purpose of paving the way for a brighter day for Africa and for this race of ours. (Applause.)

This organization does not encourage people to join it because of any idle sentiment. It does not encourage you to come here for anyone to appeal to your emotions. Those who speak from the platform of Liberty Hall are fully conscious of the aims of this organization and speak to you, not for the purpose of appealing to any frivolous or idle sentiment that you may have, nor for the purpose of stirring up your emotions; we speak to you because we ourselves have a firm conviction that the time is come, the hour is here, when Africa and the children of Africa—those at home and abroad—should make one desperate effort to free themselves now and forever. (Enthusiastic applause.) Caring not what other men may say, caring not what criticism they may level at us, it is our firm conviction by that higher intelligence which God Almighty has endowed us with that the hour is here for Africa to strike the blow for liberty. (Applause.) We would be untrue to our race, we would be untrue to this age and to posterity, if we allowed this century to roll by, this age to roll by, this decade to roll by, this very year to roll by, without striking a blow for our liberty and our freedom as all other peoples are doing. I do not care what the preacher in his criticism may say. I do not care what the politician in his criticism may say. I do not care what the journalist in his criticism may say. There is one conviction I have and that is that the Negro in this age is entitled to as much liberty as any other race on the face of the globe. (Applause.) I care not, therefore, how loud or long they preach.

I care not how long their editorials are written. I say, what is good for the Irish in this age; what is good for the Jew in this age; what is good for the French, the British and the white American in this age—is also good for the black man. (Applause.) And, therefore, no power whether it lies between heaven and hell will stop the onward rush of Negro sentiment to have that liberty and democracy delivered to them. (Applause.) We have suffered for 300 years and we think it is long enough. Therefore, no one need think that we are still the servile, bending, cringing people that we were up to 50 odd years ago in this country. We are a new people, born out of a new day and a new circumstance. We are born out of the bloody wa[r] of 1914–18. A new spirit, a new courage, has come to us simultaneously as it came to the other peoples of the world. It came to us at the same time it came to the Jew. When the Jew said, "We shall have Palestine!" the same sentiment came to us when we said, "We shall have Africa!" Therefore, that is the purpose that reveals why we have rallied around the colors of the U.N.I.A. all over the world until we are three and a half million strong, and on the first of August the representatives of the three and one-half millions and the representatives of the 400,000,000 of the race will assemble themselves at Liberty Hall to write the Magna Charta of our liberty and our rights. (Wild and enthusiastic cheers.)

THE GLORY OF A VISION.

I am slated to speak tonight on the subject of "The Glory of a Vision." This is a time when all peoples have a vision of their own. We, like the rest, have a vision also—the vision of liberty, the vision of freedom, the vision to see ourselves a great and mighty people. We are too large and great in numbers not to be a great people, a great race and a great nation. In scanning world events I cannot recall one single race of people as strong numerically as we are who have remained so long under the tutelage of other races. I cannot recall one instance in history. We have remained under the domination of other races too long and the time has come now when we must seek our place in the sun.

Tonight I have before me a great vision, and I would rejoice to know that every man and woman in this edifice has a similar vision. The vision before me is that of a great country, a country inhabited by 400,000,000 people, a country from east to west, from north to south, controlled and dominated by the race that inhabits its great cities, its great powerful states, all forming themselves into one mighty nation, one great empire. That is the vision I have before me. The people I place within that vision are the 400,000,000 Negroes of the world. (Cheers.) The country that I see as this great vision, this great empire, is the great country of Africa. (Cheers.) That is the vision I have before me, and that is the vision I would like for each and every one of you to have.

Men, it is a dream now; it is a vision now; but do you not know that you can make this dream, this vision, a reality? As a proof that you can make it so I will take your memories back to a couple of centuries ago in this country now called the United States of America. Some hundreds of years ago some people came to this country who were called the Pilgrim Fathers. They came to this country because they were dissatisfied with that part of the world in which they lived before they came here. When they came here they saw a great forest country, a country of wilderness, a vast wilderness. They saw uncivilized and untutored men, unlettered men. They had before them the vision—they had the dream—that one day through their labor, through their sufferings, through their sacrifices, they would be able to build up a mighty nation for their protection and for the protection of their posterity. The other people in the country from whence they came regarded them as madmen and mad adventurers, and they said all manner of disrespectful things about them. They never gave them any encouragement. Nevertheless, those men, with this vision of a great country before them, with a vision of freedom set out to build and to construct. They felled the trees and settled in little hamlets and villages. They built and they built until the hamlets and the villages became towns, and those townships became larger ones, which developed afterward into great cities, and the cities multiplied and multiplied. And then they divided up the country into colonies and the years rolled by. Still they worked and suffered; they sacrificed and they died.

One generation passed away and another generation came and continued the work. And as the years rolled by, the little cities became larger, the colonies became more prosperous and more powerful, and more progressive. Then the men who lived in that generation, in the progress of the then thirteen colonies met 144 years ago in a place called Independence Hall, in Philadelphia, and they said to themselves: "We as men ought to be free men, we as inhabitants of this country ought to be free and unfettered in the government of the country, in the administering of the affairs of the country. Because we feel as men, we desire a lar[g]er liberty; we desire to make of these thirteen colonies a great nation—one great country, one republic." With this spirit and with this sentiment, 144 years ago, those men wrote a thing called the Declaration of Independence. Out of that Declaration of Independence came America's freedom—came this light in which we now live and move and have our being, the light of freedom and democracy. That was the vision of the Pilgrim Fathers, who came to this country hundreds of years ago.

THE VISION OF AFRICA.

It is a similar vision that I am trying to bring to you to-night—the vision not of America, but of a greater country, the vision of Africa, the greatest country in the world; the country wherein the black man first saw the light of day; the country where it is destined that the black man shall meet his judgment in common with other men when Gabriel blows his horn. (Great applause.) To-night, I am endeavoring to portray to you, to picture to you, the vision of Africa in her imperial or republic greatness. Can we make it, men? Can we make it[,] women? Can we not imitate the Pilgrim Fathers of America? Were the Pilgrim Fathers divine? (Cries of no, no!) Were the Pilgrim Fathers super-human? (Cries of no, no!) No, the Pilgrim Fathers were human—men and women like us to-night. But they had a purpose; they had a vision—it was the purpose of freedom, it was the vision of liberty. Let us also catch hold of that vision, because in it lies our destiny, our hope. Let our faith and confidence be firm. Let us believe that what other men have done for themselves, let us believe that what we have done for other men to make them great, we can by applying ourselves to our own industries do to make ourselves also great. If we as 400,000,000 people will just make up our minds for the next five years that we shall apply ourselves to the building up of Africa, irrespective of where we may be, whether we are in America, the West Indies, South and Central America, or wherever we are—in five years Africa would be free and the greatest country in the world. That is just what we are asking you to do—just to think about Africa for five years. Will you not try for five years and see the results?

Men, I want you to realize that this is a fast and progressive age. To-night I see out there two acres of waste land. It has been there for fifty years. To-morrow morning, one hundred men go out there and say, "We will construct a magnificent building on these two acres of land. We will do it." And they go out to do it. You pass along there in the next six months and you see no more waste land; you see a magnificent building there according to the design of those men. Bring back the picture. To-night you see Africa a great forest country, a great wilderness, and 400,000,000 people saying: "It shall be a wilderness, it shall be a forest, no longer. Where there are forests, we will build cities. Where the wilderness is, we will build great townships. Where there is no place of human abode, we will make great settlements. Where there is not even the semblance of government, we will make a great nation." And as those one hundred men, six months ago, turned that two acres of land into a great magnificent building, so can 400,000,000 Negroes in five years make Africa the most magnificent and the greatest country in the world. (Cheers.)

But, first of all, you must have the vision of greatness. You must first believe that you are able to do, that you are capable of doing. How many of us believe that we are capable of doing? How many of us believe that the white man in his own physical self can do more than we can do in ours? (Cries of Nobody!) Well, go out and do what the white man has done. The white man has taken the forest country and made a great nation of it. If you believe in your firmest convictions from the depths of your soul that you are as good as the white man, your chance has come now. Go out and make barren Africa a great nation, as great a country as America is through the sacrifice of the blood of the Pilgrim Fathers and the early settlers who came here. Now is your chance.

The Race of Life.

I never would believe myself to be as good as any white man if I did not believe in myself that I could do anything a white man under similar circumstances and environment could do. If I a man of thirty-three met another white man of like age who passed through the same schooling like myself, and that white fellow was able to rise into national greatness by becoming a great statesman or diplomat simply through the education he had, and I, having had the same training and education, was not able to rise to the same position, given the same opportunity, then I would feel myself less than that white man. I can recall having read and studied in the same class room with white boys, but up to now none of them has made a better success in life than I have on their own initiative. Hence, I come to the conclusion that I am as good as any white man. Now I want you to feel the same way.

There is a counterpart to every man. Black as you are, you have your counterpart as a white man. Make up in your mind that your counterpart will not outdo you in the great race of life. The white boy who was born along with you in your township, who possibly had the same schooling as you— make up in your mind that that boy shall not and will not beat you in the great race of life. If by circumstances, if by better opportunities, within the nation in which you live as fellow citizens in common, he has a better chance to show his ability, because they will make of him and give him a chance to be the President of the country where in you both are born and will not give you the chance, don't lose heart. Find a country of your own and look for a chance to be the President of that country. Find your chance and find your purpose. If you cannot live alongside the white man in peace, if you cannot get the same chance and opportunity alongside the white man, even though you are his fellow citizen; if he claims that you are not entitled to this chance or opportunity because the country is his by force of numbers, then find a country of your own and rise to the highest position within that country.

And you are not without a country. God Almighty gave you a country— the richest and the most prolific among all the continents. He gave you the great continent of Africa. It is for you to repossess yourselves of it. Remember, men, the African is in each and every one of us colored men. We cannot get away from it if we tried. One sixteenth of the bloo[d] makes you an African and we cannot get away from it. Therefore, do not play the fool and talk about your not being an African. All of us are Africans. But the only difference is: some are Africans at home and others are Africans abroad. We are the Africans abroad, unfortunately. Why, I am so sorry I was born abroad! I wish I was born at home; there would be some trouble there today. I was born in an alien country, and when I was a boy at home they asked me to sing, to dance and play in a foreign country; and I gave them the answer that that ancient people did when they were asked in Biblical history to sing and dance: "How can I sing and dance in a strange country, in a strange land?" They have asked us to laugh, and they have tickled us and said: "Dance, coon!" "Will you sing for me, Sambo?" Now we have sung for three hundred years. How can we sing and play in a foreign land? Let us stop laughing for the white man. Let us stop mimicking for the white man. Let us be serious for ourselves. Let us be in death seriousness. Even the white man has been so to win his liberty.

I cannot understand the idle talk of some of the preachers—and I have to talk about some of the preachers, and I am sorry that I have to do it; because the ministry represents the highest social ideal among men. If it were not for religion, the world would be peopled with barbarians and savages. Religion has been the greatest civilizing and socializing force known to man all through the ages since Jesus of Nazareth came to this world. But religion is very much abused today, especially by the Negro preacher. The Negro preacher who comes forward and tells you: "Why, you are too radical. You shouldn't talk about the white people like that. You should not be so outspoken, because we do not want to offend the good white people"—now, just imagine! A man who has kept me in slavery for 250 years; a man who has robbed me for fifty years—I must not offend him! Why, I have all in the world to do with that fellow. He owes me 250 years' worth of slavery. You mean to tell me that you would work for a man for two weeks and you ask him to pay you and he will not do it, and somebody should come and tell you: "Don't talk to that man; you must not offend him!" What would you think of such a man to give you such advice? The first thing you would do would be to get out a summons for him, if kind words will not do, and get the courts to force him to pay you your two weeks' salary. Now, there is no court that will compel the white man to pay our salary for 250 years, because he is judge and jury. It is like appealing to Caesar. Now, if the preachers think that civilization means nothing to the Negro in this age, they make a big mistake. Civilization means to the Negro just what it means to the white man or any other man. It means liberty. It means freedom and it means death to get that freedom if necessary. Tell me about compromising with the man who has my property! Here is a man who has 12,000,000 square miles of my land and your land and our children's land. He has it from east to west, from north to south, and these jack-leg preachers (laughter) tell us: "You must go easy!" Suppose the Allies had gone easy with Germany—what would have happened? Why, the Kaiser would be cutting up in Buckingham Palace tonight! But they did not go easy, because they had a cause which they believed was righteous.

The Negro has a cause coming down the ages five hundred years. It is righteous and more than righteous. And we want it understood that we are not compromising anything; we are not begging anything. We young men of the Negro race are not begging anything. The old men begged, but I believe there is a moral in one of the school books I read that said there were some boys who used to go and pick the old man's apples, and the old man used to go to the apple tree and beg them to come down. "Boys," he said, "do not pick my apples." And the boys laughed at him and continued to pick the apples. He threw straws at them and said: "Boys, do not pick my apples;

come down," but they only laughed the more. And then he said: "Well, if kind words cannot do, if straws cannot do, I will try what virtue there is in stones," and picked up some large stones and threw at them, and they all cried out and ran away. Now our fathers have begged by petitions and mass meetings and so forth, and no virtue has ever come out of begging. Now, we young men are going to try what virtues there are in the materials they gave us to use in France, Flanders and Mesopotamia. (Cheers.) The life I could give in France and Flanders and Mesopotamia I can give on the battle plains of Africa to raise the colors of the red, the black and the green forevermore. (Cheers.) So I say to you young men, be steadfast in your purpose. I say to you women, be true to your men; be as true to your men in this crisis as the white women have been to their men through all their difficulties. When the Allies and America called the men of the nation the women of the nation responded simultaneously in the Red Cross units and went to the battle-fields, and there in those units and the Salvation Army succored the men on the battle plains. Women, there is a higher purpose for you, and methinks I can see you performing the work of a Florence Nightingale—this time, not on the Crimean battle plain but on an African battlefield. Women, the hour has come when princes shall come out of Ethiopia, and princesses, too. Let me thank you again for the splendid support you have given to the U.N.I.A. It is a support that you will feel glad you gave in the days to come, and methinks the days are not very far off.

THE AUGUST CONVENTION.

This great convention to assemble here in August will be the turning point in the history of the present day Negro. In the month of August we will do things with serious meanings behind them that will register us for all time as a great international power and a great international force. After August no man will dare, no nation will dare treat with the Negro singly or individually; but whenever any race or nation desires to treat with the Negro they will have to come to the accredited representatives of the Negro race. After August there will be no more "divide and conquer"—divide the people and conquer the people. There is but one Negro today, and he is 400,000,000 strong. I feel sure that lynchings and burnings will be an expensive institution after August 31, because if they continue it anywhere it is going to react somewhere. React it must. React it surely shall. Do you think that we have spent nearly a million dollars for two and a half years to call this convention for fun when Negroes are so poor and when Negroes have to work so hard for a [d]ime? Do you think we have spent all this money and have come to Liberty Hall every night for so long for fun? Somebody must be dreaming to think thus. Men, make up your minds that your liberty, your freedom is near—nearer than you probably anticipate. Methinks I can see the war clouds of Europe—I give them ten years from now. Oh, I believe in time. I am not one of those men who tell you we are going to win the world tomorrow. I am not so crazy. I believe in time, and I give them ten years to send up that war cloud and that war smoke again. We are waiting for it. We are just waiting for it. Men, get ready. Women, get ready. Get ready in mind; get ready in thought. Get ready for action everywhere, because the hour is at hand to free Africa once and for all.

The other day in Pittsburgh I took up an African newspaper that was sent to me. It came from South Africa—from the Cape—and I was reading the speech of one of the parliamentarians—one of the members of the South African Parliament, a white man, where he said that we must keep the natives in compounds; we must not allow them to encroach upon the city limits, because they will become a disgrace to our civilization; we cannot allow them to enjoy these beautiful privileges and opportunities we have created for our children. And in the newspaper there were big advertisements. The newspaper was as big as any of the New York papers. They had advertisements of all kinds—big department stores, big business and big banks, and big mansions were advertised for sale, for rent and for lease, and I laughed and said: "Oh, how good is God, in that we worked in America for 250 years for the white man and built up such beautiful homes for him and farms for him in the Southland, and look how he in turn has built up beautiful homes for the black man!" Yes, Miss Davis says it is the law of compensation. Surely it is. We work for them, and brotherly-like they are working for us.

Men, if you do not make them work for you you will be unworthy of the breath of life. Because you have worked for them they are driving you out of the South. They are driving you out of all those parts where you helped to make for them a home. The time has come when you must drive them out of every inch of land you possess by right divine. We are not making any fun. What does it cost to get the alien out of Africa? It costs the manhood and the blood of a race. What did it cost to weld the scattered Prussian states into one great German empire? It cost the blood and manhood of the Germanic race—the Teutonic race. As of theirs, so it will be of ours. What was good for them, blood and sacrifice,[1] to bring liberty is also good for us. Therefore we shall not shrink from the task or the duty. We did not shrink in the Revolutionary War of America. We did not shrink in the Civil War of America. We did not shrink from our duty when Great Britain called us to fight in the Ashanti [wars] or to fight the native tribes of Africa.[2] We did not falter when France called us forth a million and a half strong in this last war. We did not falter for an alien race—why should we falter when our own race calls? So tonight I bid you be firm in your resolutions. I bid you continue your devotion to the cause, because a brighter day is in store.

PROF. FERRIS SPEAKS.

Prof. William H. Ferris said: Two years ago the "flu" epidemic swept over the world and struck the white, yellow, black, red and brown races. It showed that all men were physically akin; and the spirit of liberty swept over the world and struck the white, yellow, black, red and brown alike, which showed that all men are spiritually akin. Just as the Negro's physical organism responded to the "flu" and contracted it, so his intellectual spirit has responded to the spirit of liberty which has been sweeping over the world like a whirlwind.

I heard Dr. Eason yesterday afternoon give a very short but effective answer to a critic and objector. We were standing on Seventh Avenue and three preachers of various denominations were attracted by us. One of them gave us a philosophic dissertation of the inadvisability of ant[a]gonising the Anglo-Saxon and the possibility of the foreign born Negroes and Africans catching the spirit of the laws and customs of this country. Dr. Eason said to him: "Brother, I have just finished a good meal and have got to make money for another meal. You don't know a d—— thing about what you are speaking so good-bye." That terse and trenchant answer silenced all the philosophical dissertations and disquisitions.

Yesterday afternoon two of the most distinguished men of our race visited our office as I was informed. One was Dr. Vass[,][3] an intellectual giant of the Baptist denomination, and the other was Dr. William S. Scarborough, former president of Wilberforce University, and the greatest Greek scholar our race has produced. When Calhoun[4] doubted the ability of the Negro to master Greek syntax, the world was startled when Prof. Scarborough wrote his Greek text book; and he startled the world further by writing a disquisition on "The Thematic Vowel in the Greek Verb" and "The Birds of Aristophanes." Then he startled a gathering of scholars when he expounded the Greek verb "Luo" as written by Thuc[y]d[i]des. The fact of these men representing the acme and the climax of Negro intellectual development visiting our office shows that the U.N.I.A. and the Black Star Line are magnets. When we were schoolboys we used to take a magnet (that is shaped like a horseshoe) and put it near a needle to see whether it would draw it. A weak magnet would only draw a needle from a distance of half inch; but a strong magnet would draw from a distance of two inches or more. We placed a piece of wood beside a needle and the wood would not draw at all. What was the difference? The magnet had the power that reached beyond itself and drew other bodies towards it. This earth is magnetic. What do we mean by the power of gravitation? When an apple is separated from the limb, why does it fall to the earth? It is the power of the earth that draws the apple down towards it. Were it not for the force of gravitation we would fly off in space. Just as this earth has gravitation which radiates all over, so the U.N.I.A. has a spirit of gravitation that encircles the globe; and you will see it in August when you behold men coming from the different quarters of the globe to attend our convention.

What is the spiritual power of the U.N.I.A. to draw men and individuals into its fold? I was interested to-day while riding on the subway to find that sometimes I was up in the air, sometimes I was on the surface of the ground and sometimes I was under the ground. What was the secret? It showed the power of man to conquer nature and transform a hostile environment. The secret of the supremacy of man that differentiates him from the lower animals is that the lower animals have no power to overcome environment. When it gets warm the birds fly to the North and when it gets cold they fly back to the South. The only way they can escape the extremes of warmth and cold is to go from one portion of the globe to the other. But man can stand in one place and by building a fire around him and generating heat, defy the cold; in the summer time when it gets warm, with his electric fans and lemonade and cold drinks he can defy heat.

It is this power in man to overcome hostile environment that makes man king of all creation. But in the moral and the spiritual world we have wiles of men to overcome. And what makes a man great is not only power to overcome nature but to overcome the wiles of other men. From time immemorial races which have been up have tried to keep others under them. When Egypt was powerful she oppressed the children of Israel; when Babylon and Assyria and Persia were powerful, they held the Children of Israel and other races as slaves; when Rome was powerful she held the whole world under her power—from Britain to Parthia, from Germany to the Sahara Desert. When Alexander the Great was supreme in Greece he conquered the ancient and eastern world. It seems to [be] the law of human nature that when a man gets up he tries to keep others under his feet.

It is because of the pride and conceit in man that he desires to dominate and to master all others of his kind. So when we see races oppressed by the Anglo-Saxon, they are only doing what other Caucasian races have been doing for 4,000 years. How can we overcome this oppressive power? One reason why the superior or dominant race can keep others in subjection is because of the p[s]ychical force as well as physical force that it uses. Rome with her majesty inculcated the idea that to be a Roman was to be superior to the other races of mankind; and that is why the brawny Africans, the brawny Britons, the brawny Gauls, and the brawny Germans wanted to become Roman citizens and march under the Roman army and under the Roman eagle.

The Anglo-Saxon south of [the] Mason-Dixon line and the Englishman in Africa retain their control over the darker races by spreading the doctrine and gospel of the superiority of the Anglo-Saxon and the inferiority of the Negro; so that the darker races have sat at the feet of the Anglo-Saxon and have blindly swallowed everything that he said. It has been difficult for the A.M.E. Church to spread its missionary propaganda in Africa because some English statesman said of the A.M.E. Bishops that they were inculcating ideas in the African by which he would aspire to a higher state than his intellect was capable of reaching. That is what they said 25 years ago when industrial education swept over this country like a wave of lunacy, taking the wings of the morning and going forward. We were urged not to strive for the unattainable; and Booker T. Washington and his supporters preached the doctrine that the Negro ought to be satisfied with tilling the soil, and that the high intellectual and political things transcended the range of his skill. But black boys and black girls going to the universities of the land and wresting honors disproved that assertion.

And so we must counteract the propaganda of the Englishman by inculcating and instilling into the mind of the Negro youth the idea that all that other men have achieved and accomplished he can achieve and accomplish. We must inculcate into him the idea that he was designed by the Almighty not to be a hewer of wood and a drawer of water for other races—not to be the servant of other races, but that he was intended to carve a career and a destiny himself. It was intended by the Almighty that he should unfold his mental, his moral and spiritual faculties, that he should be lord and king of creation as well as his fair-skinned brothers.

In the last two centuries we have had an aristocracy of color. In the ancient times it was an aristocracy of wealth or an aristocracy of military prestige. But the Anglo-Saxon has endeavored to build up an aristocracy of color. He has endeavored to base his ascendancy not upon the fact of his great intellectual achievement, but simply because his skin was nearer that of the color of snow than the darker brother. And because of that dogma he has tried to prove the Negro inferior. In ancient times Ethiopians, despite their dark skin and frizzly hair, were men of a higher state. Does not Homer refer to Eurybates,[5] that Ethiopian warrior who, with sable skin and frizzly hair, was a hero in the Trojan war? Why is it then that when they began to enslave us they called us Negroes and stigmatized us as an inferior race? They wanted to divorce us from our historic past; they wanted to teach us by calling us Negroes that we were not allied with those men who on the banks of the Nile and by the waters of Euphrates laid the foundation of the world's civilization.

I trust that out of this Convention not only resolutions—not only skilled oratory will evolve, but an educational propaganda that will encircle the globe and teach the Negro who he is, what his past has been and what his future will be. (Applause.) Two words come down from history which epitomize all that Greece had to teach the world. Over the doors of the Greek temple at [D]elphi were these two words: "Know thyself!" It is because Marcus Garvey has taught the Negro to "know himself" that the Negro has lifted up his head and is not only talking but is building and creating and erecting his factories and launching his steamship lines. When a man knows himself—when he realizes his powers and possibilities, then the thought comes to him that "I am too big—too great and have too much of a future for me to be ever a slave again."

What the African needs is to "know himself"; with his vitality—with his genius for philosophy and religion—with his courage and enthusiasm, he needs to have his mind awakened; he needs to awake from the hypnotic sleep of centuries and realize that his country with its undreamt of wealth and unheard of possibilities belongs to him; and when this self-consciousness arises and awakens in the African he will enjoy the fruits of his native land

and will speak of empires and republics which will dazzle the admiration of the world. (Applause.)

MR. VERNAL WILLIAMS SPEAKS.

Mr. Vernal Williams was the next speaker introduced by the President General, who took opportunity to eulogize the relentless energy this brilliant young member of the legal profession was putting into the work of the U.N.I.A. Mr. Williams delivered an eloquent and impassioned speech which moved the sentiments of the audience and evoked frequent applause. "Liberty Hall," he said, "in spite of its tremendous capacity cannot hold the multitude of men and women who flock here evening after evening. Why are you here?" he asked. "Certainly you have not come here to be entertained because there is entertainment outside of the walls of Liberty Hall; certainly you have not come to hear the speeches, because men are speaking from other platforms. It is the new spirit for which the world is clamoring—the spirit of self-determination that has brought you here together tonight and that has manifested itself here. At this period of the history of this movement—the pre-convention crisis—we are faced by foes—black and white; but the indomitable force that is within the membership of this organization can never be defeated; and tonight Liberty Hall stands as the Mecca of the spirit of freedom that is permeating the Negro peoples of the world. (Applause.) The day is coming when black men and women of Harlem, of New York, of America, of the entire world, will turn their backs on the hypocritical construction placed upon the white man's religion by political intrigue and they will come to the Liberty Halls of New York and America and the Liberty Halls all over the world and worship at the shrine of true religion—the religion of their own freedom, their own self-existence and their own liberty. Let us, therefore, bury criticisms in the forgotten past and let us push out along the paths we have hewn for ourselves; let us set aside the besetting sins and obstacles and push on with hope and confidence looking toward the great Creator who is the finisher of our faith. Liberty Hall will radiate its spirit over the entire land and tell the white man that now and for all time black men and women must either be free or they will create for themselves their own free existence. (Cheers.) The day will come when the red, the black and the green will be seen on every water and every ocean; will float over the administrative, executive and judicial buildings of Africa; will, like the emblem of England, never be touched by the rays of the setting sun. The day will come when the U.N.I.A. shall be the great organization that shall be the mentor of Negro thought—will be the medium through which the ideas, thoughts and aspirations of the entire Negro race will be known. (Cheers.) But this cannot be achieved unless the movement is backed up by the 400,000,000 of black men and women the world over. If you are going to create for yourself a new existence—a new modicum of life—it means that you must begin to think, and think now, not only to create that existence, but how to maintain that existence after it has been created. This is not the first time that black men have sought their liberty. Black men once had their liberty, but it was lost because in the days when our forefathers held sway in ancient Egypt they had forgotten to get down and think how to maintain their liberty. You must not only achieve liberty but you must maintain it by the independent institutions we are going to set up through the U.N.I.A. We must not only maintain the Black Star Line in its initial stages, but we have got to send it down the ages and make it stronger and stronger from time to time, backed up by our moral, financial and physical force.

Miss Henrietta Vinton Davis Speaks.

Miss Henrietta Vinton Davis, International Organizer of the U.N.I.A., was the next speaker introduced, and said:

Hon. President General, officers and members and friends of the U.N.I.A. and A.C.L.: In thinking of our great responsibility concerning the convention that will soon meet in Liberty Hall, where will be gathered the best brains of the race from all parts of the world, I was thinking what an important occasion it is—a most important occasion to us as a race that means that we shall either go forward or backward. There is no such thing as standing still. We must go forward or go backward. It is the wish in every Negro's heart that we should go forward, and in going forward we must enlist in the ranks of the U.N.I.A., because it means the great forward movement of the 400,000,000 Negroes of the world. Those who have not yet joined are bound to join. They won't be able to stay out of it, because as the Hon. Frederick Douglass once said about the Republican Party, that the Republican Party was the ship and all else was the sea, so the U.N.I.A. is the ship—the ship of safety—and all outside of that ship is the sea. (Applause.) It behooves every Negro to get on board this ship, not alone on board the ships of the Black Star Line, but on board the ship of the U.N.I.A. and A.C.L., expressing as it does the hopes, the aspirations of a whole race of people. "United we stand and divided we fall," and the time has come when the Negro feels it in his heart that this is the time when he should become a united people, regardless of color, regardless of sex, regardless of creed. We are Negroes, once, forever and shall always be. I am speaking to-night that you support, as our friend (Mr. Vernal Williams) so eloquently said, all the branches of the U.N.I.A. It is all right to start a thing, but it means something to support that thing. There is no use in starting a thing if you cannot finish it. And so, you must stand by the Black Star Line, the Negro Factories Corporation and all the other propositions and branches that have grown out of the U.N.I.A. and A.C.L.

As I think of our people, I feel that that great law of nature, the law that runs throughout all nature and is irrevocable, the law of compensation, we have to pay. The white man has forgotten that great law of compensation. When he committed his dastardly deed[s], he thought that he would not have to pay for them. But he has had to pay for them with his blood. That is what has been demanded by God, and so he will have to pay the price more and more. He will have to pay for the 300 years of slavery that he put upon the Negro people. He will have to pay for all the money that he failed to give them in compensation for their labor. He will have to pay for the dragging and the wrenching from the Negro mother's breasts of her little babe. He will have to pay for the stripes he helped to put upon the back of the Negro by way of punishment, as he said. And this accumulated debt of hundreds of years, the Anglo-Saxon is beginning to pay for and he will have to pay to the very last penny. He has only commenced to pay the compensation that that great law of nature requires of all of us. We must all pay our debts; and the white man's debts to the world, his debts to the darker races and the people of the world, have only just commenced to be paid. (Cheers.)

Printed in *NW*, 17 July 1920. Original headlines abbreviated.

1. *Eisen und blut* ("blood and iron") was one of von Bismarck's well-known sayings (*BFQ*).
2. The West India Regiment served in West Africa beginning in the early nineteenth century. West Indian troops served in Sierra Leone, Gambia, Gold Coast, Nigeria, and other areas, playing an important role in the maintenance of British authority. In the Second Ashanti War of 1873–74, British military officers recommended that British troops be brought in to replace the West Indians. The plan was abandoned, however, because there was not a sufficient number of British troops to maintain British control and hardly enough to battle the Ashanti alone. The regiment also fought in the Third Ashanti War of 1893–94, in which British forces were finally able to defeat the Ashanti and set up a protectorate. In 1926 the regiment was disbanded (S. C. Ukpabi, "West Indian Troops and the Defence of the British in the Nineteenth Century," *African Studies Review* 17, no. 1 [April 1974]: 133–50; *Gleaner*, 23 December 1923, 17 December and 20 December 1926).
3. Samuel N. Vass (b. 1866), religious lecturer and author, was born in Raleigh, N.C., and received his B.A., M.A., and D.D. degrees from Shaw University, Raleigh. He was a professor at Shaw from 1885 to 1893 and gained prominence in the Baptist church for his role in promoting Sunday school missionary work (*WWCR*).
4. John C. Calhoun (1782–1850), U.S. senator, vice-president (1825–33), and apologist for the Southern cause (*WBD*).
5. Eurybates, the herald of Odysseus, was described by Homer as an Ethiopian in appearance (Frank M. Snowden, Jr., *Blacks in Antiquity* [Cambridge: Harvard University Press, 1971], pp. 19, 102).

Black Star Line to the United States Shipping Board

New York NY July 12, 1920

We respectfully request that you wire permission to collector of customs New York allowing bills of sale for steamer SHADY SIDE and steam yacht KANAWHA to be registered by Black Star Line Inc of Delaware first and second vice president American citizens also five of nine directors interest in two boats 90% American Please wire today to facilitate sailing of boats.

BLACK STAR LINE INC
56 West 135th St NY

DNA, RG 32, USSB, file 1091–3520. TL (telegram), recipient's copy.

C. H. Hunt to the Black Star Line

[*Washington, D.C.*] July 12, 1920

Your telegram today reference steamer SHADY-SIDE AND yacht KANAWHA stop see Section thirty-eight Merchant Marine Act which defines citizen of the United States and which required that in order to constitute a corporation citizen of the United States its president and managing directors must be citizens as well as majority of stock owned by citizens stop you state in telegram that five of nine directors are citizens also see Section three page fifteen Navigation laws stop Board cannot waive requirement of law stop take matter up with Commerce Department.

[C. H.] HUNT
Shipping Board

DNA, RG 32, USSB, file 1091–3520. TL (telegram), carbon copy.

Reports by Special Agent 800

New York City July 14, 1920

Sir:[1]

In registering the letters to-day I came across a letter from a man in Wareham, Mass., who says he is a white man but is very much interested in negroes, and advises Garvey to write to both of the Presidential nominees[2] and ask them their views on the race question. He said he was going to write to them and try and get them to express their views and he wanted Garvey to do likewise. He said in his letter he believed in greater independence for the negroes, and fair play. From the tone of his letter, he is a radical. He signed his name D. Warren [*illegible*]—Box 2[38], [Wareham,] Mass. I had this letter in my possession but upon second thought, thought it best to let it go in Garvey's files. Will keep a look out for further communications from this man.

I also saw a letter from a man in Chicago who signs himself Rev. L. D. Horton—3315 Forest Ave., Chicago, Ill., complaining about Dickerson. He goes on to tell Garv[e]y in the letter that they were getting on nicely until Garvey made Dickerson President of the Chicago Division, then, he says, the trouble started. He says that Dickerson began to let the white people come around and all they brought was trouble. I think he is referring to Jonas although he doesn't say so. He goes on to say that the whole body does not want Dickerson as their President. I thought it best to let this letter go through also.

If I can only hold this job of registering the letters I expect sometime to get some real good information. The hardest thing I have to do now is keeping my name off some kind of a committee. I was notified to-day that I had been put on the publicity committee, whatever that is. I am trying to keep as much out of the lime-light as possible, because I know there are going to be people here from Washington for this convention.

There seems to be an unlimited amount of money coming in for shares in the Black Star Line. I registered letters to-day for over four thousand dollars, most of it from the West Indies and the central part of the U.S. One old woman down in Virginia wrote she was old and poor but she was sending twenty-five dollars towards the "cause", because she wanted to go home to Africa. Respectfully

800

[*Handwritten endorsement*] Negro Act
[*Stamped endorsements*] Noted F.D.W.

DNA, RG 65, file OG 258421. TD.
  1. Agent 800 addressed his reports to George F. Ruch.
  2. The presidential nominees for the Democratic and Republican parties were Ohio's Gov. James Middleton Cox (1870–1957) and Sen. Warren Gamaliel Harding (1865–1923).

New York City July 16, 1920

Sir:
Received my check, many thanks.

I am mailing you under separate cover the mailing list of the Negro World agents and subscribers. Most of these people are more or less radical and I thought it would be best to have their names and addresses in case anything may happen in their towns or cities.

I saw a letter to-day from Phila. to Garvey warning him that last Sunday night four men, two white and two negroes, drove up to the hall where Garvey speaks when in Phila., and the two negroes got out of the cab and came into the hall, and said they came to take Garvey to the station. Garvey was not in Phila., but the letter went on to tell Garvey to be careful in the future and not to ride in any cab with strangers as these men appeared to be. Garvey was in Phila. last night but returned to New York this morning.

Do you wish me to notify you by wire whenever Garvey leaves town? Respectfully

800

[*Endorsements*] NOTED J.E.H. NOTED W.W.G.
Noted F.D.W.

DNA, RG 65, file OG 185161. TD. Stamped endorsements.

Marcus Garvey to W. E. B. Du Bois

NEW YORK, U.S.A. July 16th, 1920

Dear Dr. Dubois:

At the International Convention of Negroes to be held in New York during the month of August, the Negro people of America will elect a leader by the popular vote of the delegates from the forty-eight States of the Union. This leader as elected, will be the accredited spokesman of the American Negro people. You are hereby asked to be good enough to allow us to place your name in nomination for the post.

Hoping to hear from you immediately, and with best wishes, Yours very truly,

> PARENT BODY—
> UNIVERSAL NEGRO IMPROVEMENT ASSO.
> MARCUS GARVEY/PER FWE
> President General

MU, WEBDB. TLS, recipient's copy. Reprinted in Herbert Aptheker, ed., *The Correspondence of W. E. B. Du Bois*, vol. 1 (Amherst: University of Massachusetts Press, 1973). Used by permission.

CONVENTION OF THE UNIVERSAL NEGRO IMPROVEMENT ASS'N
August 1st to 31st, 1920.

ADMIT TO CONVENTION HALL

MR. DR. W. E. DUBOIS.

of NEW YORK CITY.

representing

Delegate to Convention
120 West 138th Street

Negro World Advertisement

[*Negro World*, 17 July 1920]

SHADYSIDE IS TO MAKE DAILY TRIPS UP THE HUDSON RIVER

"Hot, isn't it?" You hear this expression daily. New Yorkers have been sweltering for the past few weeks in the grip of the hottest weather experienced here in some years. The roofs and parks afford very little relief and the poor tired working man comes home evenings to suffer from the excessive heat with his family. He takes his kiddies on the roof or to the park, but finds it just as hot there and just as uncomfortable. Now, however, he need not worry about the heat. He may take his family for a most delightful sail up the Hudson River on the Shadyside, the excursion steamer of the Black Star Line, and enjoy the cool summer breezes. The Shadyside will make these trips daily and there will be no excuse for anyone complaining of the excessive heat when they can find much needed relief from the congested tenement districts by taking these trips up the Hudson. The most beautiful scenery on both sides of the Hudson is presented to the gaze from the decks of the Shadyside. A fellow and his girl find it more enjoyable to take one of these trips than to go to some crowded resort where he and she are continually jostled by a seething mass of humanity. Then it costs a good deal of money to show your girl a good time at Coney Island or one of the other resorts. It costs a small fortune for the poor workingman to take his family there. The price of these trips up the Hudson are placed within the reach of every one. With the music furnished by the Black Star Line Band on all these trips, the beautiful scenery and the cool breezes from the Hudson, the decks of the Shadyside will prove to be the greatest recreation center during these hot days.

Printed in *NW*, 17 July 1920.

James Coker to the *Negro World*

[17 July 1920]

Editor Negro World:

We, the victims of the Fort Sam Houston court-martial,[1] respectfully solicit your aid in securing the Negro World, magazines and other up-to-date literature published by colored people. Our object is to be kept informed in regards to passing events as portrayed by colored authors, writers, etc. Those among us having the necessary funds to subscribe for the above-mentioned literature are few, and the papers, etc., subscribed for by them are eagerly sought after and before going the rounds are completely worn out.

No greater opportunity than this to educate our race men confined in prison here along the proper lines, we believe, has ever presented itself. Sir, we wrote the Chicago Defender and several other publishing companies the tenor of this letter some weeks ago, and only the Boston Guardian and the Cleveland Gazette responded to our appeal. Hoping you will use your powerful influence in our behalf, I remain Sincerely yours,

JAMES COKER[2]
Box 7, Leavenworth, Kan.

Printed in *NW*, 17 July 1920. Original headlines omitted.

1. On 23 August 1917 an armed band of black soldiers left a military camp near Houston, Tex., after the arrest and pistol-whipping of a black military policeman by white police officers. Fifteen whites died and twelve were assaulted during the ensuing riot. Over a hundred black soldiers were subsequently arrested and court-martialed in three groups. The first case, called the Nesbit case, involved sixty-three soldiers; forty-one were sentenced to life imprisonment, and thirteen were hanged. The second case, the Washington case, involved fifteen soldiers, with five sentenced to death. The third case, the Tillman case, involved forty soldiers, with twelve given life sentences and eleven sentenced to death. On Secretary of War Newton Baker's advice, President Wilson commuted ten of the death sentences to life in prison in "recognition of the fidelity of the race to which these men belong . . ." (Newton Baker to Woodrow Wilson, 22 August 1918, DLC, Wilson Papers, no. 84224; Robert V. Haynes, *A Night of Violence: The Houston Riot of 1917* [Baton Rouge: Louisiana State University Press, 1976]).

2. James Coker enlisted with the all-black Twenty-fourth Infantry Regiment on 19 February 1915 and was transferred with his regiment to Houston in 1917. He was one of over one hundred black soldiers court-martialed for participation in the Houston riot. Coker was found guilty of mutiny, murder, and assault and sentenced to hard labor for life. The black press condemned the execution and imprisonment of the soldiers, sending petitions to the president and publicizing their fate. The last imprisoned soldier was released in 1938 (Herbert Aptheker, ed., *A Documentary History of the Negro People in the United States, 1910–1932* [Secaucus, N.J.: Citadel Press, 1973], pp. 184–85; DNA, General Archives Division, general court martial, order no. 1299, file no. 109045).

William H. Ferris to Roy Pensius

[*Negro World*, 17 July 1920]

Prof. Wm. H. Ferris has received letters from Mr. Pensius, of the Canal Zone, and a score of other persons, asking where his work, "The African Abroad," and other books and pamphlets by Negro authors could be procured. He gave a list of eight books, and, thinking that perhaps hundreds of other readers of The Negro World might desire the same information, he takes pleasure in reprinting his letter:

Mr. Roy Pensius, Drawer "J," Cristobal, Canal Zone.
Dear Mr. Pensius:
Here is the list of Negro books:

1. "The African Abroad," by Wm. H. Ferris, published by Tuttle, Morehouse & Taylor Co., New Haven, Conn., U.S.A., in two volumes.

2. "Alexander Crummell, an Apostle of Negro Culture," published by Wm. H. Ferris, Universal Building, 56 West 135th street, New York city.

3. "Racial Integrity," published by A. A. Schomburg, 105 Kosciusko street, Brooklyn, N.Y., U.S.A.

4. "The Negro," by Dr. Du Bois, published by Henry Holt & Co., New York city, U.S.A.

5. "The Negro in American History," by Prof. J. W. Cromwell,[1] 1439 Swann street, N.W., Washington, D.C., U.S.A.

6. "Missing Parts [of] American History," by [Miss F. E. Wilkes,][2] 1404 Franklin street, Washington, D.C.

7. "Frederick Douglass," by Miss F. E. Wilkes, 1404 Franklin street, Washington, D.C.

8. "Phyllis Wheatley's Life and Poems," by A. A. Schomburg, 105 Kosciusko street, Brooklyn, N.Y.

These books will give you a great deal of information about the Negro. I remain, Very sincerely yours,

WM. H. FERRIS

Printed in *NW*, 17 July 1920. Original headline omitted.

1. John Wesley Cromwell (1840–1927) was a founder of the American Negro Academy and briefly its president. Born in Portsmouth, Va., Cromwell received his law degree from Howard University and was admitted to the Washington, D.C., bar in 1874. Between 1908 and 1921 he was principal of the Crummell School in Washington, D.C. (*WWCA*; Alfred E. Moss, *The American Negro Academy* [Baton Rouge: Louisiana State University Press, 1981], pp. 216–21).

2. Actually Laura E. Wilkes (1871–1922), teacher in the Washington, D.C., public school system and the author of various textbooks on black history (*NW*, 28 January 1922).

Report by Special Agent 800

New York City   July 21, 1920

Sir:

... Now, Mr. Ruch, getting back to my work here; to-day a Dr. [Rosc]oe Brown,[1] a colored man of the Public Health Service, came into my office. I have known this man for several years and he knows who and what I am, and when he went out of the office he said to a Mr. Thompson, the head book-keeper, "What is [he] doing here? He was a government detective at one time." Now, Mr. Ruch, this man works for the Government and he must have known that I was here on business. I met this same man in Richmond several months ago and told him to keep his mouth shut as to who I was. Aft[er] he had gone, Thompson came into my office and remained there for several minutes just looking me over. Just what the result will be I do not know as Garvey is in Phila[.], but will return in the morning. Brown told me he was leaving town but if I ever see him again the next time he sees me he will have sense enough to keep his tongue between his teeth. Just what else he said to Thompson I don't know as they walked off down the street together.

I am enclosing a circular that Garvey had printed for the convention. Now Mr. Ruch, the phrase in there "A President for Africa" is a joke for any sensible man but when you take into consideration the fact that 95% of Garvey's followers are ignorant, it is a different matter. Most of these people haven't any idea of the geographical location of Africa or under what conditions Africa i[s] governed by the several European countries. Some of these people really believe that after this convention they will have elected a president for Africa and all they will have to do is to go over there and set up their government.

The Mayor of Monrovia Liberia is here as a delegate [to the] convention.[2] Garvey has given him a desk in the office next [to] mine while he is here.

Some of the letters that come through my hands, especiall[y] from the southern part of the U.S., the writers speak of going back home to Africa. One woman wrote to-day as soon as she cou[ld] sell her cow she was going to send the money to the great convention. A woman was in the office to-day from Oklahoma, said sh[e] had just heard about this great convention and she came all the way up here to find out about this convention so she could go back to Okla. and tell the people about it.

They are preparing for a great parade on the 2nd of August but I think, Mr. Ruch, that the city authorities should not issue a permit. I don't look for a repetition of the Chicago affair[3] but you can never tell what may happen. I simply make this as a suggestion, sir. They are making great preparation for this parade. Will report any new developments. Respectfully

800

[Handwritten endorsement] Negro Activities New York City
[Stamped endorsement] Noted F.D.W.

DNA, RG 65, file OG 258421. TD.

1. Roscoe Conklin Brown (b. 1884), dentist, was born in Washington, D.C.; he graduated from M Street High School in 1903 and received his D.D.S. degree from Howard University dental school in 1906. He established his dental practice in Richmond, Va., from 1907 to 1915. Brown served in the office of the surgeon general of the U.S. Army in 1918–19 and in the U.S. Public Health Service until 1923. Brown also held positions in the National Medical Association and the North Carolina Mutual Life Insurance Co. of Durham, and he lectured and wrote extensively on public health problems (WWCA; WWCR).

2. Gabriel Moore Johnson (b. 1871) was a member of a politically powerful and socially prominent Americo-Liberian family who became potentate of the UNIA at the August 1920 convention. He was a building contractor by profession and helped to operate his family's commercial house. His grandfather, Elijah Johnson, a black freeman, recruited other black Americans for colonization in Liberia in the nineteenth century and is considered by some to be the father of Liberia. Gabriel Johnson's father, Hilary R. W. Johnson, was an associate of

Edward Wilmot Blyden at Liberia College; he defeated Blyden in the Liberian presidential contest of 1884. Gabriel Johnson's brother, F. E. R. Johnson, Liberian attorney general and member of the Supreme Court Justice of Liberia, was a delegate to the 1900 Pan-African Conference held in London.

Gabriel Johnson attended Liberia College but left in his sophomore year to become apprenticed to an architect. In 1887 he entered the Liberian army (later called the Liberian Frontier Force) and eventually rose to the rank of brigadier general. According to his own testimony, a group of Liberians interested in learning about the UNIA paid Johnson's passage to the 1920 convention. His contact with the UNIA was preceded by that of his son, who appeared at Liberty Hall in November 1919 and "expressed the hope that all might have an opportunity to visit Liberia" (DNA, RG 165, file 10218-364-167).

Gabriel Johnson claimed that Liberia's president, C. D. B. King, approved of his mission, primarily to find out what role the UNIA could take in salvaging the insolvent Liberian state and in reviving its stagnant economy. Indeed, Johnson's mission closely followed the meeting in New York in September 1919 between President-elect King and a group of UNIA supporters, among them Rev. F. Wilcom Ellegor and John E. Bruce, at which King discussed the needs and aspirations of the Liberian government in obtaining $5 million in credit from the United States.

Gabriel Johnson, however, was a representative of the faction within the Americo-Liberian ruling elite that was opposed to the idea of a loan from the American government, which had also become the receiver of Liberian customs as a result of earlier foreign loans. It appears that Johnson's faction sought the assistance of the UNIA as an alternative to the U.S. loan option. Johnson would have objected to the provision in the proposed loan agreement that called for Americans to be appointed as the "native" commissioners in order to ensure reform in Liberia's "native" policy. Such a provision challenged Johnson's considerable involvement in the recruitment of Liberian labor for contract work in Fernando Po and other places in Africa. The Liberian Frontier Force was the primary coercive weapon in the system of forced labor recruitment and also the proposed target of a U.S. reorganization plan.

After Johnson lost his bid for reelection as mayor of Monrovia in December 1921, President King made him consul general to Fernando Po, a lucrative post because of the active role that the consul general customarily played in supplying Liberian contract laborers to Fernando Po. Garvey claimed that Johnson was influenced to accept this position so that he would relinquish his office as potentate of the UNIA. Johnson remained politically anti-American, a posture that he reaffirmed by financing the publication of a speech attacking American imperialism given in Monrovia by C. L. Simpson in 1930 (DNA, RG 84, file 10465; *NW*, 8 August 1921; DNA, RG 59, file 880-L-2, 20 July 1921 and 4 August 1921 reports; Thomas Shick, *Behold the Promised Land* [Baltimore: Johns Hopkins University Press, 1980]).

3. A reference to the Abyssinian Riot of 23 June 1920.

W. E. B. Du Bois to Marcus Garvey

[*New York*] July 22, 1920
Personal

Dear Sir:

Answering your letter of July 16, I beg to say that I thank you for the suggestion but under no circumstances can I allow my name to be presented.

However, I desire to publish in THE CRISIS some account of you and your movement.

For some time THE CRISIS has been in receipt of inquiries concerning you and your organization. To these we have simply answered that we had no reliable information at hand.

It seems, however, increasingly important as your movement grows that we should present to our readers a critical estimate of it.

We wish, however, to be sure to have all the essential facts in hand and I therefore write to ask the following questions. I expect, of course, only such answers as you are willing to divulge and to have the public know.

I trust I may have as early a reply as your convenience permits. Very sincerely yours,

W. E. B. Du Bois

WEBD/PF

P.S. Will you please also send a recent photograph and an account of your life?

Questions

NAME OF THE ORGANIZATION? and of all subsidiary companies, if any.

HISTORY: When and where founded, when and where incorporated; address of principal office.

OFFICERS: Names and duties of officers and directors.

FINANCES: Source and amount of income; chief items of expenditure, amount of capital stock authorized and amount issued, classes of stock and par value of shares, salaries of officers, balance sheet for last fiscal year. Are the books audited annually and by whom?

MEMBERS: Number and conditions of membership, distribution.

PROPERTY: Kind and location, and liens, if any, on same.

ACTIVITIES AND ACCOMPLISHMENTS

PUBLICATIONS: (Sample copies of such as you distribute free and price list of others). Such further general information as you may care to give.

MU, WEBDB. TL, carbon copy. Reprinted in Herbert Aptheker, ed., *The Correspondence of W. E. B. Du Bois*, vol. 1 (Amherst: University of Massachusetts Press, 1973). Used by permission.

A. J. Tyrer, Acting Commissioner of Navigation, to United States Customs, New York City

[*Washington, D.C.*] July 22, 1920

Wire any reasons why steamer KANAWHA should not be documented foreign trade by Black Star Line Inc[.]

A. J. TYRER
Acting Commissioner

[*Endorsements*] Memo. N.Y. telephoned
knew nothing about case. Matter taken up
with Shipping Board—See 8/B order will
issue

DNA, RG 41, file 116430-N. TL (telegram), carbon copy. Handwritten endorsements.

C. H. Hunt to the United States Shipping Board

[*Washington, D.C.*] July 23, 1920

MEMORANDUM FOR THE BOARD:

Application by Black Star Line, Inc., New York City, a corporation 90%
of which is controlled by Americans for the approval of the Board to
purchase the steam yacht KANAWHA, official number 161123, from J. M.
Briggs, Brooklyn, N.Y. and to document the said vessel under their name.

DESCRIPTION: The KANAWHA, official number 161123, is a steel steam
yacht with a gross tonnage of 475 and a [net] tonnage of 323. She is 227 feet in
length, 24 feet in breadth and 14 feet deep and was built in 1899 at New York.

REASONS FOR TRANSFER: The applicant states that this vessel is to be
used in passenger service, also that the President of this company is interested in negro colonization.

RECOMMENDATION: In view of the foregoing it is recommended that
this application be approved.

C. H. HUNT
Attorney
Approved _____
General Counsel

DNA, RG 32, USSB, file 1091-3520. TL, carbon copy.

Leon R. Swift to the United States Shipping Board

NEW YORK, July 24, 1920

Attention Mr. Nottingham

Dear Sir;—

It has been rather a disa[p]pointment that the Collector Hamilton, U.S.
Cu[s]tom House has not received the order from you authorizing the enrollment of the "Kanawha" to the Black Star Line, Inc. This steamer is ready and
has perishable goods on board. I would greatly appreciate it if you would

wire this authority at my expense providing it is impossible to get this matter fully closed to-day, should you have to let it lay over till Monday.

Again thanking you for the courtesy you have shown me while I was in Washington. Very truly yours,

LEON R. SWIFT

DNA, RG 32, USSB, file 1091-3520. TLS, recipient's copy.

Frank Burke to Patrick J. Ahern[1]

Washington. July 24, 1920

Dear Sir:

I am advised by a confidential source that Marcus Garvey and his secretary, left New York last night for Washington.

As you will recall, Garvey is president of the Negro Improvement Society, and has been active in negro agitation for some time.

Kindly make immediate effort to locate this individual and cover his activities very closely while in Washington. Very truly yours,

FRANK BURKE
Assistant Director and Chief

[*Typewritten reference*] GFR:MMP
[*Address*] P. J. Ahern, Esq.,
1330 F Street, N.W., Washington, D. C.

DNA, RG 65, file OG 329359. TL, carbon copy.

1. Patrick J. Ahern (1863–1940), born in County Cork, Ireland, was employed by the secret service from 1902 to 1929. He was assigned on various occasions to protect President Wilson and President Harding (*NYT*, 5 September 1940).

Truman K. Gibson to W. E. B. Du Bois

COLUMBUS, OHIO July 24 1920

My dear Doctor Du Bois:

I have made diligent inquiry into the matter of the activities of Garvey here and I find that there is nothing being done here, at least actively.

Several months ago a woman, Estelle Henderson, who claimed to be a lawyer, tho she had not been admitted, wrote letters to several persons, among them Peyton Allen and J C Ross, soliciting their interest in the Black Star Line. Both of these men have lost the letters and Allen states that so far as he knew no one in this city "bit". The woman is not here now.

I shall continue investigation and if I find anything important I shall notify you.

Three weeks ago while I was in Cleveland Ohio one of my agents there was speaking of the activities of Garvey in that city. I was told that he had spoken there once and was to return but one of his coworkers fell out with him over some question of interest and was preparing to enter legal proceedings of some kind, whereupon the second meeting was called off. It may be that I could secure some information from Cleveland if you so desire. I had no particular interest at that time in Garvey, knowing all along that he was engaged in a questionable enterprise.

I am sorry that I can give you no more definite information at this time, but I shall be on the alert for something in the future. Sincerely,

T. K. GIBSON[1]

MU, WEBDB, reel 8, frame 1292. TLS, on Supreme Life and Casualty Co. stationery, recipient's copy.

1. Truman Kella Gibson (b. 1882) was president of the Supreme Life and Casualty Co. of Columbus, Ohio, and one of that city's leading black citizens. Gibson was born in Macon, Ga., and educated at Atlanta University and Harvard University, receiving his A.B. degree in 1906 (*WWCA*).

W. E. B. Du Bois to H. L. Stone

[*New York*] July 24, 1920

My dear Mr. *Stone*[:]

I want to trouble you with two matters in which I think you could help me. First, you remember that some time ago you spoke to me concerning Marcus Garvey and the Black Star Line. I have got to write something on the subject for THE CRISIS and I am afraid that Garvey is financially more or less a fraud. I want, therefore, to follow up his operations very carefully. I want to find out if he bought the steamship Yarmouth or any other ships and if he still owns them and in case he does whether there are any liens or mortgages on them. How shall I go to work to get hold of this information. . . . Very sincerely yours,

[W. E. B. Du Bois]

[*Address*] Mr. H. L. Stone 239 Fourth Ave.,
N. Y. City c/o Outing Magazine.

MU, WEBDB, reel 9, frame 237. TL, carbon copy. Inside address is handwritten.

Report of UNIA Meeting

[[NEW YORK, July 25, 1920]]

NEAR APPROACH OF GREAT CONVENTION DRAWS RECORD CROWD AT LIBERTY HALL

With but one Sunday left before the opening of the greatest convention held by Negroes anywhere in the world and with the new extension to the building that is in course of construction almost completed, Liberty Hall was again packed to overflowing at the meeting held tonight. The outstanding feature, in contrast with former meetings, was an increased enthusiasm on the part of the people in the merits of the cause they have espoused under the leadership of the Hon. Marcus Garvey and an unbounded, unshakable confidence in the efficacy of the means by which its leaders are carrying to fruition the great work they have undertaken.

The weather, after several nights of continued rain, was cool and refreshing, and everyone seemed in a happy mood. People began assembling in the hall as early as six o'clock in order to secure seats. Long before the band played the opening piece the amphitheatre was crowded to its utmost capacity.

Promptly at 8:15 o'clock President Garvey, accompanied by his official family, entered the building amid the plaudits of the people, everyone rising to their feet, waving hats and clapping hands at his approach. It was indeed an inspiring scene, for it meant that the Negroes of the world not only want a leader and intend having a leader but that they have, in fact, already chosen their leader, and love, honor and respect him as no leader of any other race has ever been loved, honored and respected. It was a fine tribute to the man, and a still finer tribute to the greatness of the cause he has founded and represents.

An appropriate, interesting preliminary program was render[ed] in which the Universal Negro Improvement Association quartet and the band took the leading part, inter[s]persed with solo and chorus singing, everyone present joining in the latter with a will.

This part of the program over, President Garvey, who occupied the chair, delivered one of the most stirring addresses that has yet been heard in Liberty Hall. It seemed as the man spoke that he was suddenly inspired anew and caught as never before a prophetic vision of the future great possibilities of the race, coupled with a strengthened, redoubled determination with God's help to go on with the glorious work he has inaugurated, despite whatever obstacles there may be in the way and regardless of how long it may take to attain the ultimate object in view. His hearers soon caught the wonderful magic of his words as they listened with unwonted silence and interest, and the thrill of admiration and approval of the speaker seemed to communicate itself from one to another throughout the audience like the passing of an electric current, sweeping them again and again off their feet and causing them involuntarily to applaud and shout approval of his eloquent periods as he outlined what had been done in the comparatively short history of the Universal Negro Improvement Association and what would still be done by it for the emancipation of the Negroes of the world from discrimination, injustice and oppression to which they are now subjected the world over. Other addresses were made by Rev. Dr. Ferris, Rev. Dr. Brooks and Rev. Dr. Eason[,] all of which were ably delivered and listened to with expressions of approval. But as for President Garvey, like a magician with his wand, he was able at will to move his hearers and sway them first this way and then that as he told in clear, concise, forceful and majestic language what was in his mind and on his heart for the salvation of his race from all the untoward influences of hatred, malice and injustice of the white race and the attempt of those whose deliberate purpose it is to keep the Negro in degradation and prevent him from marching on with the progress of the world in these greatest of all times in the world's history.

In their order the addresses of the evening are as follows:

HON. MARCUS GARVEY SPEAKS.

Mr. Garvey in welcoming the gathering said:—

"We are pleased to welcome the members and friends of the association once more to Liberty Hall. We are here tonight for the purpose of doing our duty to the movement which claims us all as members. There is a universal activity just at this time and it leads to the anxiety of the thousands of members and delegates who are looking toward the great convention for which we have been preparing ourselves for the last two years. This forthcoming convention of the Universal Negro Improvement Association has sent a thrill throughout the civilized world in so much so that in every community there is a spontaneous outburst of enthusiasm over the outcome of this great convention that is to take place in the month of August.

"I have just returned from Baltimore, Washington and Delaware, where I had the pleasure of speaking to the various branches scattered in those parts. The enthusiasm of the branches is more than I can explain to you tonight. Suffice it to say, it is warm; it is wholehearted and it is looking toward Liberty Hall. I feel sure that Liberty Hall, with the annex completed, will not be able to seat the thousands and thousands who will be coming to Liberty Hall for this month of August that we have before us. People are coming from all parts and they are coming because they are impressed with the seriousness of the time in which we live. And after the outcome of this convention—after we will have written our names across the pages of human history—after we will have given to the world a constitution and a charter of our liberty and our rights, we who form the membership of the New York Division will have to compliment ourselves on the great work we have done—for the great victory achieved in the name of Liberty. (Applause.)

"It shall go down to the everlasting credit of the Negroes of New York that they sponsored the great movement of the U.N.I.A. and made liberty possible for the Negro in the twentieth century. I say 'liberty possible,' because there is absolutely no doubt about it that liberty will be a possibility for the Negro in this twentieth century. We are not speculating about it; we are not hoping about it; we are positive about it. (Cheers.)

"This morning as I was about to board the train in Washington for Wilmington, Del., I got hold of a 'New York World' and in turning its pages I saw where they lynched a black man in France because he was a black man.[1] They wanted one black man and they saw another black man, and as I have often said to you, as far as a white man is concerned with us Negroes now 'Any Chinaman is a Chinaman'; because as far as we are concerned 'Any Negro is a Negro.' They wanted a certain Negro for a certain alleged crime; they could not find him; so the first Negro they saw they lynched him under the old established custom of 'Any Negro is a Negro.'

"It proves our contention—the contention of the U.N.I.A.—and the positive declarations I have made from the platform of Liberty Hall and the various platforms from which I have spoken for the last two and a half years, namely, that the Frenchman is no different from the cracker in Georgia; that the Englishman is no different from the cracker in Alabama; neither is the German different from the cracker in Mississippi. They are all the same. Hence this lynching and burning, and disrespect of Negroes is not confined to any one country. It is spreading all over the world; and it means that if we in this present age do not go out and do something to stop lynching, every inch of ground in the world will become unsafe for the Negro in the next twenty years. Th[e]refore the time is now—before the world is thoroughly reorganized and reconstructed, in that we fought for the reorganization and reconstruction of the world—because before 1913 it was a despotic world— for us to do our duty and take part in the reorganization of the world. If we refuse to do so, we are doomed for the next 500 years.

["]That is why we are not speculating about this convention. We are positive that between now and the 31st of August we shall give a declaration to the world which shall mean, "Give us liberty or give us death." After the French took a million and a half black men from Northern Africa and other parts of Africa and her colonial possessions, brought them into the war, used them as shock troops to stop the Germans at Verdun and at the battle of the Marne, their recompense is to lynch a Negro in a French city—a civilized French centre. It is a shame. It only goes to show that there is absolutely no trust to be placed in the white man's word—whether it is given by Clemenceau of France or Lloyd George of England or Orlando of Italy, we refuse now to trust the word of the white man any more. There are sufficient of us in the world to protect ourselves. If 400,000,000 people cannot protect themselves, they ought to die; and that is just the attitude of the present day Negro. We refuse to die without getting liberty; and to get liberty we are prepared to die. Therefore we must make the world understand that the Negro is no longer a cringing or a begging sycophant; but he is a man. He demonstrated his manhood during four and a half years of bloody conflict on the battlefields of France and Flanders, and as he died there, so will he die again until he gets the liberty and the democracy that he fought for. It is really heart-rending to think that there is no one part of the world the [N]egro can turn his face with the feeling that he is secure. If he lives in America, he lives in daily fear and trembling; if he lives in England he lives in daily fear and trembling; and now France has given to the world her attitude towards the Negro. And whilst they are making their countries unsafe for us—whilst they are disputing our rights to be denizens and citizens in their country they are going into our country and taking it from east to west, from north to south and telling us that that country is belonging to the white man. How long are we going to allow that state of affairs to continue? Men, Africa calls you now. The land that sent you out three hundred years ago—the God that permitted us to be held as slaves for 250 years is now calling and the land is also calling. The time has come for us to send our "Princes out of Ethiopia," and it must be done.

["]Out of this convention I say, we shall write a constitution that we shall force the world to respect. (Cheers.) We are men; we are not dogs; and if other men can write a constitution which they force every section of the world to respect and for which they will fight; and for which they will die, why cannot 400,000,000 Negroes give a constitution to the world and compel the world to respect their constitution and respect their rights. (Cheers).

["]The question is whether we are men or not; and I declare that every Negro now feels himself a man. So I ask that you prepare for this great convention. Remember we have not called this convention for fun; we have not called it for any social purpose—for the purpose of holding receptions and greeting each other and shaking hands; we have called this convention for a serious purpose—in the same way that convention was called in Philadelphia 144 years ago to write the Declaration of Independence. We are calling this convention to write a declaration of freedom and independence; and when we do and give it to the world, we will defy the world to destroy or disrupt the intelligence of that constitution. (Cheers.) We have a message to give to the world. We will give it on Monday night, the 2d of August in Madison Square Garden (Cheers). After that we will come back to Liberty Hall and talk among ourselves. We gave them a message on the 30th of October, 1919, and they scattered that message all over the world—that 400,000,000 Negroes were sharpening their swords for their protection. Now it seems likely that we may tell them on Monday night that 400,000,000 have already sharpened their swords for the next world war. (Loud cheers).

["]This is a serious age. It is serious for the Jew, for the Irishman, for the Egyptian, for the Hindoo and it is also serious for the Negro. The Negro will not play second fiddle to any race. We are too strong numerically to take second place among the races of the world. Our stand is supposed to be alongside the Chinese, who are 400,000,000; our stand is supposed to be alongside the Hindoos, who are 380,000,000. We refuse to allow 600,000,000 Anglo-Saxons to dominate us and rule us for one day longer after the 31st of August.

["]If man-power counts for anything we will test out the man-power of the Negro in the next bloody world war; and we know it is not very far off, because the Bolshevists of Russia are making it very warm for them over in Europe. President Wilson came back to us, and told us there was going to be peace. David Lloyd George went back to England, and told them there was going to be peace. Clemenceau told the French there was going to be peace. Has there been any peace? No; there is still war, and "rumors of war." Therefore, it is for the Negro to prepare to defend himself in the bloodiest war the world has ever experienced. It is coming, as surely as we are in Liberty Hall to-night. When it does come, whether in the next twenty or fifty years, we want 400,000,000 black face folks to be fighting under one banner, the banner of the Red, the Black and the Green.

["]We bid you welcome to Liberty Hall to-night; we bid you welcome to this cradle of liberty, and we ask that you continue your moral and financial support, until the convention meets.

["]It gives me great pleasure at this time to present to you, as the first speaker of the evening, Rev. Dr. Ferris.["]

PROF. FERRIS SPEAKS.

Prof. Wm. H. Ferris said: ["]I am glad to see this tremendous gathering to-night. I read in the papers last week that a million of Mohammedans around Turkey are rising in rebellion against the white world and the Russians are mobilizing their forces inside their lines. With the impending menace of the Mohammedans in Asia and Russia in Europe it looks as though the white man in the next five or six years may again have to appeal to the aid of the black man, and then I trust he will be in a position to dictate to him. Heretofore both in politics and in war we have been in no position to dictate terms. The white man said to us: "Get up and fight," and we have risen and fought. He said to us: "Get up and work," and we have risen and worked. The best thing for us to do now is to prepare to make ourselves economically, intellectually, physically and in a military and naval sense competent enough to dictate terms when we are called upon again to hold up the banner of civilization. Our position in civilization for the last three hundred years has been the same position which the Jews have occupied during the past 2,500 years. The Jews have been scattered all over the world and been suppressed by one race and then another. But the Jews have now realized that it is necessary for them to build up an empire and a republic in their native land of Palestine. In this stage of the world's history it is necessary for the Negro to build up some sort of republic and empire in Liberia so that there will be some land which he can call his own. All Liberia needs is a railway and roads running into the interior, and with mills and factories it will burst forth into a prosperity and civilization which will dazzle the eyes of this century.

["]I have faith in the Universal Negro Improvement Association because there is an aggressive spirit in it which has not been characteristic of any other organization. Students of the human mind tell us that man is divided into three parts—that man functions in three ways. He thinks, he feels and he wills. Heretofore the Negro has thought and felt; but he is now beginning to act and to will. Not until you touch the fountain of a man's personality in his will can that man accomplish anything. This movement star[t]led the world when it launched the "Yarmouth" on the 24th of last November. The world realized that the Negro's will was beginning to function; that he had stopped whining and begging and was beginning to do something. And that is why the world has taken notice of the Negro. No race can rise higher than its objective and its ideal. Just as no stream can rise higher than its source so it is with a race.

["]The Negro has three ideals; each one of them alone can inspire a race. One is the vision of a redeemed Africa; the other is the vision of himself created after the Divine image, and the other the vision of an economic independence, and I believe that in gathering around us financial strength we will have that strength on which to stand and demand all that belongs to us. In this age of reconstruction, when the world is awakened as it has never been before, when a menace to the white world is threatened, the world is looking upon the Negro to see what attitude he will take and what he will do. Heretofore he has sat down and did as he was bid by the Anglo-Saxon, but now he has reached the point and place when he has felt that under God he is a man and has a destiny in this world.

["]I was talking today with two of the most distinguished and illustrious men in the Negro race, and they said that Marcus Garvey is needed in Africa to inculcate his progressiveness and his aggressive spirit in the African. All the African needs with his millions of population, with his superb vitality, with his imagination and with his buoyant nature is the will and the energy to go forward and achieve. The Anglo-Saxon at the present day must necessarily feel superior when sixty millions of them can dominate seven hundred million brown, yellow and black men in Asia and Africa. How can we overcome that? Only by making ourselves so strong—only by mastering modern science, modern machinery and all modern and naval forces that you can dispute his claim to superiority. And when the African does that no longer will the wealth of Africa be shared among the peoples of Europe, but the African will come into possession of that prosperi[t]y which God decided that he should have.["] (Applause.)

Speech by Rev. Dr. Brooks.

["]Mr. President-General, Members of the Black Star Line, Negro Factories Corporation and Negro Improvement Association, Fellow-Sufferers, Citizens of Africa: I greet you! . . .

["]What I want to do is to interpret the spirit of Garveyism. (Applause.) To the devil with this other stuff! [*Americanism, Rooseveltism, Wilsonism*] What is Garvey[is]m? It is the spirit to help [Go]d work out the destiny of the black race. God needs some help. God wants you to help Him. The white man has been helping Him to everything that He got, and God now wants you to help Him bring Princes out of Egypt, and to let "Ethiopia stretch forth her hands" unto Him. How can you help Him? By having faith, first, in yourself, that God made you, and that you can do what any other race in the world has done. And, further, the spirit of Garveyism, as I understand it, is the spirit of independence of everybody but God. (Applause.) . . .

["]If you are going to win anything in this world, you have got to fight for it. The spirit of Garveyism is the spirit to contend for that that belongs to you, and see to it that you get it or die in the attempt of trying to get it. (Applause.)

["]Garveyism as I understand it, is the intention to hold on to everything that God gave you, until God calls you away from here to report to Him. You know, there are some Negroes in this world by accident. Some Negroes have got no more business in the Negro race that a hound has making ice cream. (Laughter and applause.) Some Negroes are praying for the day to come when they can associate themselves with white folks, and I am praying equally hard—harder than they are—praying that the day will come when all these "time-servers" and "white folks Negroes" will get out to themselves, so that the race can march on to God and to victory. (Applause.) Let me tell you, if they don't get out pretty soon—if they don't move out, I'm going to find a way to get at least one out, and after the 400,000,000 Negroes have found a way to get them out, none will be left to tell the story.

["]Garveyism is the spirit of self-reliance; (and I have followed him around this thing a little bit, and know whereof I speak); the spirit of self-reliance depending upon the power that God has given you, not the power of somebody else; not the power somebody else may have, but the power that God gave you, depending upon that to find the way. I like that spirit, too.

["]The spirit of Garveyism, further, is the self-denial, self-sacrificing spirit for the Negroes everywhere that we may accomplish that unto which we have set our hands.

"Garveyism, further, is for the freedom of Africa. Everywhere we have been—and I have heard this splendid man speak—folks have stopped smiling about Africa, indeed. Negroes have grown serious. Negroes have begun to love their homeland. Negroes are getting it into their heads that that country belongs to them and that God set it apart that they may have it for their own heritage. They have stopped smiling. They have a grim, determined look on their faces now; the look that two millions of Negroes I heard about went with over to Europe to fight for Democracy for somebody else. That spirit is becoming imbued in every Negro now; the spirit of freedom for Africa. How is it going to be done? It is going to be done by such men as the Hon. Marcus Garvey, and folks who will stand by him till the death—men who will give their energies, their might, their strength, financial and life-blood, to the cause. I would rather be a dead dog in Africa—a black dead dog, than be discriminated again[st], ostracized, abused Negro in this or any other part of the world. (Applause.) I want to go back to my native land.

"It is said that some years ago, in England, they had a musical. They were attempting to get the spirit of the soul of Wagner,[2] and they brought musician after musician, and they played on the instrument, trying to get the soul out of the music that Wagner had composed. Man after man went up and sat at the piano and did his utmost to interpret the soul of Wagner. One huge, black, awkward-looking Negro sat far in the rear of the building. When they all had tried he went up to the master of ceremonies and said, 'Sir, won't you let me try?' They laughed at him, but when the others tried again, and couldn't get the soul of the music that Wagner had written, one of the number said it would do no harm to let the Negro try—that ugly, uncouth Negro. He went up and sat himself at the piano, and as he leaned over the keyboard the very Heavens seemed to open and Angels came down upon him, and as he struck his fingers over the keys it seemed that the Angels were touching his fingers. After a while he closed his eyes, apparently to shut out the sight and thought of everything in the world, and as he played the instrument it seemed to the hearers that they could hear the rippling streams coming down the mountain sides, the babbling brooks running through the valleys; as if they could hear the sighing of the wind and the rustling of the leaves of the trees, the birds singing in the morning in the woods, the murmuring and cooing of the doves; as if they could hear the thundering of the storm and the pit-a-pat of the rain as it came from the Heavens, after which the clouds seemed to roll away and the sun to shine all about them. And when the Negro musician had finished the plaudits of more than 2,000 persons that overflowed the building rose to bestow their unsolicited praise upon him as the true interpreter in music of the spirit and the soul of Wagner.

"And I tell you, my friends, in conclusion, what we need to get is the spirit of this man (alluding to Mr. Garvey). You have got to get the spirit of Garvey and let it touch your hearts until it becomes a part of your life. Get Garvey's interest in you until you think Garveyism, until you pray Garveyism, until at night you dream Garveyism; in short, until you get that spirit of Garveyism that will not die, that knows no Alps—no defeat or failure; that will not stop, that dares believe that God is your God. I can see before me the spirit of Garveyism, stimulating, inspiring, unifying and sweeping 400,000,000 black people of the world until they march out on the plains of Africa, under the banner of the Red, the Black and the Green; ready, if need be, to die, that the cause nearest and dearest to their hearts may live—live—that Africa may at last be free, and that Ethiopia may again stretch forth her hand to God, and become a great people." . . .[3]

Printed in *NW*, 31 July 1920. Original headlines abbreviated.

1. Possibly a mistaken reference to a lynching in Paris, *Texas*, on 7 July 1920. Two black men,

I. Arthur and H. Arthur, were charged with killing two white men and were subsequently burned at the stake by a white mob (*NYT*, 8 July and 9 July 1920).

2. Wilhelm Richard Wagner (1813–1883), German composer.

3. The speech of Rev. J. W. H. Eason is omitted.

John J. Flaherty, Secretary, United States Shipping Board, to C. H. Hunt

WASHINGTON July 26, 1920

MEMORANDUM FOR MR. HUNT:

Referring to your memorandum dated July 23, 1920, relative to application by Black Star Line, Inc., New York City, a corporation 90% of which is controlled by Americans, for the approval of the Board to purchase the steam yacht KANAWHA, official number 161123, from J. M. Briggs, Brooklyn, N.Y., and document said vessel under their name, at a meeting of the Shipping Board today this application was approved and the permission requested was granted.

JOHN J. FLAHERTY
Secretary

JJF:CI
Copy to Mr. Nottingham

DNA, RG 32, USSB, file 1091-3520. TLS, recipient's copy.

C. H. Hunt to Capt. Leon R. Swift

[*Washington, D.C.*] July 26, 1920

BOARD AUTHORIZES PURCHASE BY BLACK STAR LINE INC YACHT KANAWHA ALSO DOCUMENT SAID VESSEL UNDER THEIR NAME STOP ORDER FOLLOWS

C. H. HUNT
Shipping Board

COLLECT

[*Address*] Capt. Leon R. Swift,
68 Broad Street, New York City.

DNA, RG 32, USSB, file 1091-3520. TL (telegram), carbon copy.

Woolsey W. Hall to S. F. Goggins, Bureau of Investigation

1406 Swann St., N.W., WASHINGTON,
July 26, 1920

MEMORANDUM FOR MR. S. F. GOGGINS.

It would be well to have a man like Mr. Paul Jones attend the meeting Wednesday night and join the Washington Division and on his own responsibility attend the convention as a representative of this Division. Garvey and his party put up at The Whitelaw. He has a Mr. and *Miss* Jacques acting as secretaries. I talked with them over the phone. They speak with a West Indian accent and are very crafty. I think the entire control of this venture must be in the hands of West Indians.

WOOLSEY W. HALL

Woolsey W. Hall,
Division of Printing and Stationery,
Treasury Department, Br. 38—Chief's phone.

DNA, RG 65, file OG 329359. TMS, recipient's copy.

Bureau of Investigation Report

Washington, D.C. 7/26/20

MARCUS GARVEY, (COLORED) and HIS SECRETARY, (NEGRO RADICAL MATTER.)

Agent got in touch with "The Washington Eagle", a Colored newspaper, by phone, to ascertain whether MARCUS GARVEY and his secretary were going to speak in this city. Agent received information from this newspaper office that they were in the city and were going to speak at the Mt. Carmel Church, 3rd and I Sts., at 8 P.M. Saturday, July 24.

Agent then got in touch with Officer PAUL JONES, (Colored), of #8 Precinct, to get his assistance in getting a Colored stenographer to attend this meeting. Through the courtesy of the Police Department, they placed Officer Jones in civilian clothes to assist agent.

Officer Jones and agent made several attempts to secure the services of a Colored stenographer, but were unsuccessful until 7:45 P.M., when agent got in touch with WOOLSEY W. HALL, Colored, of 1406 Swan[n] St., NW. MR. HALL stated that he would assist the Government without hesitation. Agent then placed Officer Jones and WOOLSEY [W.] HALL in said meeting, the latter to make stenographic notes of what transpired. Attached to this report is typewritten copy of notes taken by WOOLSEY W. HALL at said meeting. Also, there are attached several copies of circulars distributed at this meeting.[1]

There is to be a meeting at the Mt. Carmel Church on Wednesday evening, July 28th, to elect a delegate to attend a convention that is to be held in New York City from August 1st to 31st.

Investigation continued.

S. F. GOGGINS

[*Handwritten endorsements*] Mr. and Miss Jacques
[*Stamped endorsement*] Noted F.D.W.

DNA, RG 65, file OG 329359. TD. Copies of this report were furnished to Hoover and to the bureau's New York office.

1. Not found.

Enclosure

MOUNT CARMEL BAPTIST CHURCH
WASHINGTON, D.C. July 24, 1920
9:15 P.M.

(Presiding Officer: Mr. Uzziah Minor.)
(Following brief invocation by The Reverend Nicholson)

THE PRESIDING OFFICER. We are indeed delighted to see you present here tonight to hear our distinguished visitors who are to entertain you this evening and who are to sell shares in the Black Star Line. I might take advantage of this opportunity to announce that I have just made arrangements with the trustees of this church for the use of this church Wednesday night for a called meeting of the organization, at which time we shall endeavor to *elect* a delegate or *delegates* to the great convention that is to be held in New York City from the 1st to the 31st of August. I shall not take up much time in preliminaries, as I am sure you are anxious to hear from those who are on the platform who are better acquainted with this organization than myself. I shall, before introducing the distinguished speaker who entertained us so well last night with his logic and with his beautiful flow of oratory—I refer to Reverend (J. G.) [*J. D.*] Brooks (of New York City)—before introducing him I wish to present a gentlemen who is president of the Baltimore Branch of the U.N.I.A., in the person of The Reverend Cranston,[1] who will give us a few words of encouragement.

THE REVEREND MR. CRANSTON. Mr. President-General, Officers and Members of the Washington Division of the U.N.I.A., I can assure you it gives me the greatest of pleasure to be here at this hour. Nothing could have filled me with greater joy than the fact that we are coming together as a people, as a race, in order that we may have ultimate recognition by and from all races. Organizations heretofore have been formed, but they have been all wrong, they have had narrow scopes, and this is the only association, The Universal Negro Improvement Association, that takes in its scope every Negro throughout the entire world. I say that this is a God-given movement because it has been but three years ago since this great organization through the instrumentality of the President-General was formed in New York City, but in three years time its membership has increased to three and a half million. This proves that it is God's plan, that He is leading. Every age has its leader. The Israelites in their oppression—when they cried unto God for deliverence, Moses was raised as their leader. And when this country, as many other countries, were under the bondage of slavery, when our people were under the bondage of slavery, they cried to God and God gave the indomitable Frederic[k] Douglass the foresight, the vision, to lead them. He was then the man of the hour. But notwithstanding this happy fact that through his instrumentality, with the stroke of the [pen] Abraham Lincoln signed that document which brought an end to slavery—yet our race is still downtrodden in various parts. We are not industrially and commercially safe, and in this age it called for another man, it called for a man with a higher vision, it called for a man who is interested in every one of his race, wheresoever he is living and wherever he is found. And I am proud of this organization because it does not confine itself to America, it does not confine itself to the shores of the West Indies, it does not confine itself to the shores of Central or South America, but it stretches from pole to pole, north to south, east to west, to the four hundred million people of the Negro race scattered all over the world. It was but two months ago that the Baltimore Division of the Association was organized, if I may say, reorganized, by Hon. Marcus Garvey, and I am pleased this evening to bring to you from the Baltimore Division the heartiest greetings. We ask you to persevere despite the difficulties that may confront you. No success is worth having without striving for. It is the one who toils, the one who climbs that finally reaches the top. Perseverance is the thing that counts. On the night when our Baltimore Division was organized we had 130 members enrolled. You will be pleased, I am sure, to know that at present we now have over 300 members. (Applause.) And I can assure you, with God as our guide, and with determination in our hearts, we mean that in the next month or two we shall have not less than half a thousand members in Baltimore. We believe in the cause because we realize that it is a just and an honest cause. We realize that the land of Africa, our motherland which has been robbed from us and which has been painted in very dark pictures so that heretofore many of us even hated to hear about Africa, not to think of the possibility of returning to our motherland, but we find out strangely that, as we are told these things, why is it that other nations of the world are holding on to it, that they won't take their hands off? It is because Africa is the richest spot on God's earth, and that is why every nation goes there and tries to hold on and get more and more day by day. But we as a race must remember this fact, that it does not matter where we are now, the land of our forefathers is our country. (Applause) And today you will find that every nation is struggling for its independence. The Irish are struggling for Irish independence. Egypt is crying [ou]t to England against the atrocities and is proclaiming its independence. The islands here and there are clamoring for their independence, and I say this, that this is the day and time when as other nations are clamoring for their independence, as other nations are being loyal to their countries, this is the day when we as a race, four hundred million strong, should combine ourselves together as one and don't rest our cause until we shall have our motherland redeemed. (Applause.) . . . Let me advise you, fear not difficulty, fear not hardships, but let difficulties be stepping stones to your success, and when you look back you may be able to say, ["]O what a rugged road I have come, and I have reached the summit at last.["] Let the thought of the difficulties, even of our motherland, inspire us to press on[w]ard, and I trust that the next time I have the honor to come here and visit Washington it may be that these seats may not be enough to accommodate those who shall congregate themselves here, filled with enthusiasm for the uplift of the world, and the glorious days may come when as a race we shall be absolutely united and when other nations shall look down upon us and shall be able to say, "well, they have reached the standard. We never thought that they could have attained to such great heights. We used to think that they were less than men, but we find that they are." In conclusion, let me say, let us press onward and upward, and fear not, and at last the victory is at hand. (Prolonged applause.)

THE PRESIDING OFFICER. Last night at Doctor Callis's church in Southwest Washington (H. J. Callis, Met. A.M.E. Zion Church)[2] we were thrilled, we were encouraged, we were filled with hope and with race pride while listening to the matchless eloquence, the irresistible logic, and the convincing argument of the next speaker, who is an orator of unusual ability and power. I therefore take great pleasure in introducing to you the Rev. Dr. J. G. Brooks, of New York City, the next speaker of the evening.

THE REVEREND J. G. BROOKS. Mr. President-General, members of this Division, members of the U.N.I.A. and African Communities League, shareholders in the Black Star Line, fellow sufferers in this great world, kinsmen, countrymen, black men all: I am mighty proud to have this opportunity to speak to you, and I want to forewarn you that you will not interrupt me by buying shares while I am attempting to speak. In fact it will rather encourage me. I get a deal of encouragement by your buying shares. It is an amen to me when I see you buy a share, that is an amen. It makes me know you are in sympathy with the statements I am making. It is Saturday night and the most of you have left other things to be here at this meeting, and since you are here you have let some things go that you might attend this meeting. I want you to take advantage of this splendid, quiet opportunity and buy shares in the Black Star Line. It is an investment that will pay you, aside from the fact that it will pay dividends[,] it will pay you in race pride. It will pay your children's children. Your children's children will pass by your tomb and call you blessed if you make the way possible for them now, but if you don't do it, but if you don't make it possible for your children to have ships, for your children's children to become captains and officers, that they may go to their native lands and elsewhere, they will pass by your tomb and curse you. You are living in an age of opportunity; make the most of it. You are getting large wages and many of you are in business, and it is up to you to see to it that your children's children get a square deal and fair opportunity in this world. If you do not do it, better you had not lived. If the Negro of today does not hew down trees, if he does not mark out and cut out a path for the generations that are coming on behind him, he had better not have lived. Better that he had been born dead than not to have taken advantage of the opportunity to fix for his children's children.

I want to call your attention to an article that has been going the rounds of the Associated Press that refers to color and justice. A number of broad-visioned white newspaper editors—it is a syndicated article—have taken advantage of this editorial and broadcasted it throughout the land, that their white [r]eaders might get a different attitude and viewpoint as regards lynching, that their colored readers might take heart and know that some men believe in justice. It is cut out of the Washington Eagle. It is a copy, and I simply want to call attention to just this part of it as a part of the speech I am going to deliver to you: "There are twice as many colored folk in the world as there are white. They are increasing more rapidly. Read Lothrop Stoddard's new book on 'The Rising Tide of Color.'[3] While the white race has been soaking Europe with its best blood, Japan has been tightening her grip upon the hordes of Asia. Japan is a yellow nation. But the yellow, the brown, the red, the black have something in common against the white. What one colored people has done, another may do. In India, in Egypt, in Africa, there is growing bitterness against the white man, bitterness based upon injustice, and such bitterness is deep. There is no cure for color, but there is a cure for injustice. That cure is justice." I pass on from this article, written by a white man and syndicated, without comment. It speaks for itself. And then I call attention to another thing in this Washington Eagle. This is from the Associated Negro Press: "There is another mighty exodus of the Negroes from the South.[4] The chief cause this time is not economic, although practically all who come are able to get work, but the movement is due to intimidation and lynching. Since the first of July there has been an astounding epidemic of murder and lynching in several sections of the South."[5] The Negro, so this article states, is leaving the South to the tune of a thousand per day, going North, East, and West, anywhere, any direction, to get away. Any way, any direction, so long as he gets away from the South, because of this tidal wave of lynching, and of unfairness, and injustice on the part of those who have charge of the States, the counties, the cities in which they live. The fact of it is that the Negro is not getting tired—you know there is such a thing as reaching the point that you are getting tired, if you have worked any. I remember working on the railroad one day and the sun was shining very hot, and about 11 o'clock my shoulders began to get sore, muscles began to get tired. I found myself growing tired, but when the whistle blew I was fully tired. The whistle has blown for the new Negro in this country and he is no[w] getting tired, he is tired of being oppressed, of being abused, of being lynched, of being discriminated against. Don't let anybody fool you. Anybody who tells you the Negro isn't tired is somebody who is trying to softsoap somebody for a position. Don't mind the Negro's smiling, he is fooling you, because he is tired. Don't mind his grinning. That is a sham. He is putting that on to save his life, but he is tired. As to just what steps he is going to take to remedy those things remain to be seen, but the fact remains that he is tired of the injustices that are practiced against him everywhere, not only in this country, but wherever he is[,] he has been treated wrong. And then, I found this thing out too. I have found out—I don't know whether I said this to you last night or no—that crying babies are the babies that get attention. The good, quiet baby gets no attention. The mother of that baby calls him a good child. She says, "I have got the best baby in Washington. He never cries." Pins may stick in him, he may be hungry, the sun may be shining on him, it may be that his clothing should be changed, but he gets no attention because he does not cry, but a squalling baby gets attention. (Laughter and applause.) As far as I am concerned, I am a crying baby, and the new Negro is a crying baby, and he wants the world to know that he is tired of being imposed on and he wants the world to know that he is not being treated right, and he is going to keep on crying until somebody gives him some milk or takes the pin out that is hurting him. And if nobody takes the pin out, we are going to take the pin out ourselves and get some comfort. The fact remains that all nations that are getting anything today are nations who are crying. When Italy was refused a certain concession she kept on crying until she got it.[6] Ireland is a crying baby. She is crying and she won't be quiet, and the governments of the world—especially England—can't make her be quiet, and she won't hush, until she gets home rule and gets freedom. And I am for home rule and for Ireland, and the same thing is what Africa is crying [for], we want freedom too, and if freedom comes to Africa, we want Africa too.

What means the coming of these thousands from the South? What means their moving north? Does it mean that there is a new heaven opened up for the Negro? No, sir. Does it mean that larger avenues are being opened? No, sir. Does it mean that the folks North, East, and West are more gracious to us because we are Negroes[?] No, sir. It does not mean that, it is almost like jumping out of the frying pan into the fire. It does mean that the Negro has found out that they are punishing him so terribly in the South that he is trying to move away where they won't punish him so much. But it isn't North, it isn't South, it isn't West. I need not call attention to the things that have gone on. I simply make this significant statement, that there are no houses to rent when they go North, East, and West. There is no place for them to stay. They are piled up in houses, wherever they are in houses, four or five in a room, and the large territory East, West, and North can not be purchased. They can not buy property that they may have homes. What does it mean? What means the [b]oast of the New York World that the immigrants are coming back into this country? It simply means that there will not be as many jobs for Negroes now as there were before the immigrants started back this way. I see the hand of God in all. I believe it is God's way of fixing it so that we will go back to our native land and rebuild that land. (Applause.) And why should anybody be disturbed because a fellow starts home? Nobody gets mad because an Italian packs up his $500 and his bed and starts for home. I see even women riding in the smoking car coming on to New York to go back home. Anybody said anything about it? They felt that the Russians and the Polish folks had a right to go back home. Frenchmen were going home, Chinamen going home, nobody raised any confusion over the fact that the Jews in large cities in America have raised thousands and millions of dollars and [are] sending the money back to Palestine. Nobody said anything about it. Nobody has to go to jail about that. In fact, they are asking that they grant a Jewish mayor to that seat in Palestine. Nobody is saying anything about it. They say it is all right for the Jew to go back home, and I wonder why anybody should feel disturbed when the feeling of home comes over me, the place my feet have never touched, the only land God ever did give to me. I recognize the fact that God has given the white man certain lands, the yellow man certain territory, and, as truly as I stand here, I believe that God gave Africa to the black man (applause) and there will be no peace, there can be no peace, there can not be a righteous peace until men get that that rightfully belongs to them, and so if we get the home thought in our minds and start back to our home I think it is the solution of the whole problem. All of you are not going, but I would like to create interest, create love in your breast for the native land, just as the Irishman born in this country loves Ireland as he loves no other place, and I would like to have the Negro love Africa just as other folks love their home. This is no dream now. We have three ships. God gave us a man of power and of vision, and of prophecy—and the Negroes lack vision. They had praying, singing, and shouting. They had splendid things that led up to one thing, but we had no vision that would make us see ships sailing from Boston, New York, and Baltimore, manned and controlled by Negroes, because our spirits had been broken. The spirit of the American Negro had been broken. It took the folks from Central America and South America, and from the Islands, whose spirits have not been crushed, to rekindle the spirit of manhood in the American Negro. I have wondered—you never heard a man scream, burning, have you? The last thing that was done to break the spirit of the American Negro was to burn him, chained to a piece of railroad iron, chained to a tree, because he had protected his wife, or protected his home, or his own life. I pay no attention to the "usual crime." The usual crime has gone from rape to stepping on a man's foot. Now, they lynch and burn men for debt, or for a claim, or because a man won't work for a certain man—it is for anything where a white man gets mad with a Negro in the South, or any other place, and has sufficient [num]bers to do him to death. They must always have a big crowd. They do it, and you had just as well face these facts just as they are, and to hear a man scream the agonizing tortured screams of a soul going to his God was enough to break the spirit of anybody. A fellow don't mind dying so much, but to be tortured to death breaks the spirit. Then there were two or three other things that I haven't the time to talk to you about that served to break the spirit of the American Negro so that we scarcely dared lift our heads. And then the protectionless Negro women. God knows that when a Negro woman is good in America, when she is good in America, she is the best woman in the world, for she has the bad Negro after [her] on one side and the bad white man after her on the other side. If she is good she is the best woman in the world. If a white man insults her in the South and if she tells her husband about it and he goes to see the man about it, she knows that he will either have to leave that community or be shot to death. We need a little bit of backbone. We have been getting ready to die for 50 years. We have millions of dollars tied up to bury us when we die. But we had to learn that death was the portion of every man. We learned it in the trenches, in the trenches fighting the Germans, and we woke up when we got back home and made up our minds that we would be ready to die for ourselves. And if a fellow has got to die anyhow, just as well die fighting for himself. Better to die fighting for himself than to die fighting for somebody else. (Applause.) And so the spirit of the American Negro now has developed so that he turns his face toward his motherland. We did not know anything about ships until there c[a]me on the scene, I believe, a God-given man. I believe that God led him to such a time as this. He said, "if you gather your moneys together, if you get your forces together, you will be able to put some ships out on the ocean that will command the respect of all the nations of the world," and that man is the Honorable Marcus Garvey, who gave us ships. And he has made good. He bought three ships, *The Shady Side, The Maceo,*[7] and *The Frederick Douglass.* And God will have it so that the Frederick Douglass carried the last liquor out of America, so that the folks, whether they wanted to or not had to write that the Black Star Line carried the liquor out of America. I want you to hear Mr. Garvey. Those who are going to contribute will please put it on the table. I didn't get many "amen's." Perhaps you are going to say "halleluiah" when Mr. Garvey starts. (Applause and laughter.)

THE PRESIDING OFFICER. Ladies and gentlemen, members of the local branch of the Universal Negro Improvement Association and African Communities League, and visiting friends: I have the honor at this time to present—I started to say I have the honor to present to you the Theodore Roosevelt of the Negro race. (Applause.) In many respects he reminds me of Colonel Theodore Roosevelt. For standing up for that which he thought was right and advocating it, Col. Theodore Roosevelt was shot down. He refused to die. For standing up for that which he believed was right and doing what he could for the interests of his race, the next speaker of the occasion was also shot down not long ago, but like Theodore Roosevelt he, too, refused to die and is with us tonight carrying on the good work. For being maliciously and grossly misrepresented in a newspaper article out in Michigan Colonel Theodore Roosevelt sued the editor of a certain paper for libel and won his case. For being grossly and maliciously misrepresented in the columns of the Chicago Defender, the Hon. Marcus Garvey of New York sued the Chicago Defender, and, like Roosevelt, he, too, won his case and is with us tonight still carrying on his great work. (Applause.) We twelve million Negroes of America need more than anything else a real race leader[.] (Applause.) Not a leader who is all the time bowing and scraping and grin[n]ing in the face of a white man in order to get a few political jobs. What we want is a leader who is fearless. Such a leader is the Hon. Marcus Garvey of New York. (Applause.) Twelve million Negroes of the United States want a leader who has backbone, who is uncompromising, who is not afraid to look a white man in the face and tell him what he wants. Such a leader is the Hon. Marcus Garvey of New York City. What we want as a race in this country is a leader with vision, a leader who has ability to do great things. Such a leader is the next speaker of the occasion. I therefore take great pleasure in introducing to you a great man from a great city, in the person of the Hon. Marcus Garvey, President-General of the Negro Improvement Association and the African Communities League, chief promoter of the Black Star Line Steamship Corporation, who will speak to you at this time.

HON. MARCUS GARVEY. Mr. President, it is a very long time since I have met so many people (there were about 75 people present). (Laughter and applause.) But I am always at home in a crowd, so I am quite at home tonight.

On this, the eve of my departure from your beautiful city, I want to leave a few words with you to think over. Just at this time the world in which we live is reconstructing itself, readjusting itself, reorganizing itself. It has been a mixed-up world heretofore, a one-sided world wherein one class of men of a certain race of men swayed the rest of the world, dominated the rest of the world, and practically destroyed the rights and privileges of the other peoples of the world. We, too, like the many oppressed races of people who suffer from this unrest that I speak of, are about to take an active part in this reconstruction, in this reorganization of world affairs. We have just realized that we are four hundred million people, that we stand out as one of the strongest groups in the great human family. Outside of the Chinese with their four hundred millions, there is absolutely no race as strong numerically as the Negro. We have been sold for hundreds of years, for centuries. The strongest race of people numerically in the world—in our physical, racial strength—we are allowing an insignificant race, numerically, to rule, to dominate us, to deprive us of our rights, of our privileges, simply because we never realized our st[re]ngth and our ability before a bloody war was fought. It was fought for four and a half years. We were told that it was being waged for the purpose of establishing a reign of democracy throughout the universe, for the purpose of freeing the weaker races and nations of the world. From our large-heartedness we answered the call of the respective nations who desired us to fight in the bloody conflict. Great Britain called out hundreds of thousands of Negroes—her colonial troops from the West Indies and from Africa. France called out a million and a half of her colonial troops from Northern Africa and East Africa. America called out thousands of her Negro soldiers, and all of us, two millions of Negroes, fought in the bloody war believing that we were fighting for democracy, for the reign of justice and equity among men. The war was won, was won by the side on which we fought. We were sent back to our native habitats. The African was sent back to Africa, the American was sent back to America, the West Indian was sent back to the West Indies, and what did we find in our respective homes? We found that Africa was the same uncomfortable place after the war as it was before the war, as made for us by the white man. We came back to America and found the Southland as unsafe for the Negro after the war as it was before the war. We went back to the West Indies and found out that the economic condition after the war was as bad and worse than before the war, and in the general summary we found out that the idea of democracy pertaining to the Negro was only a farce and a lie. In America we are confronted /today/ with the same barbarians and the same sophistries as were inflicted upon me in 1913 and the early part of 1914. We are confronted with that now. Men are lynched, women are lynched, and children are burned at the stake. In Africa they are still suffering from peonage practiced by the white colonists who are exploiting the natives of Africa. We have come together through the Universal Negro Improvement Association, four hundred million strong, and say that the time has come for us to take our liberty into our own hands. (Prolonged applause.) We have been depending on the white man for 500 years to lead us into light, and he has led us into darkness. We are not prepared to trust our future, our destiny, to any other race, any other time, but to ourselves. In the past they said that we were uncivilized people, that we were not Christians, that we were pagans and savages and therefore unable to take care of ourselves. Can they say that of us now? They might have said that three hundred years ago, they might have said that 60 years ago in America, they might have said that 85 years ago in the West Indies, but can they say that now? They can not say that now, because in a civilized age like this it does not take savage men, barbarians and pagans to win a war fighting against civilized men. It takes civilized men to win a bloody conflict fighting against civilized man, and two million of us proved our higher civilization when we, by our prowess, won the war for the white man, when he was unable to win it for himself. (applause.) Take this and give it to the white man every time: If it were not for the Negro, those white folks would have been fighting in France, and Flanders, and Belgium still. It took the Negro, two million strong, to be the shock troops, to be the dividing line between the white man and the white man. It took the Negro in his great physical and military prowess to stop the Germans when the other whites ran away from the Germans. Let them know, *as we are going to make them know on the* second of August in Madison Square Garden, that it took the Negro to win the war and stop the Germans, and that we are going to do it again, we are going to do it for African independence and African freedom. We will make them know in New York, from the platform of Madison Square Garden on the second of August when the great convention assembles there, we will make them know that the Negro who fought—two million strong, in France and Flanders, and Mesopotamia—still lives. What do they think, that they are going to exterminate four hundred millions of blacks as they have exterminated the millions of North American Indians that they found in this Northwestern Hemisphere? Do they think that they are going to exterminate four hundred millions of blacks as they have exterminated the aborigines of [*New Zealand*?] and Australia? God Almighty brought the Negro out of slavery for a purpose, and that purpose is now. (Applause.) Men, as I said to you last night, all that is necessary is for you to know yourselves. Know that God Almighty created you, that he made you, he fashioned you after His own image, and for a purpose. I say for a purpose, and that purpose keep in view. The purpose of the Universal Negro Improvement Association is to /make of/ ourselves a greater, powerful people, a greater, powerful nation. We are tired of being slaves, we are tired of being [peons], we are tired of being serfs, we are now determined to be freemen. I have never yet met a white man in all my travels throughout the United States of America, in all my travels throughout Europe, who ever had the belief that the Negro ought to occupy in the world a similar position to that of the white man. He has always had some compromising suggestion to make about the Negro. He is always—when he is charitable, he is always willing to advance the idea that the Negro is not fairly treated, but he is never willing to advance the Negro to his stature, to his height. I have never met him yet, and we will never meet him between now and the judgment until we compel him to realize it. If you think that the white man is going to share a part of what he has and give it to you, you make a big mistake. You have enjoyed a portion of what the white man has because the white man was unable to keep it away from you, because he wanted more, and in order to get that more he had to get help to get it, but the time will come when he will have all the help he wants, and that is why this sudden immigration has started to the United States of America at the rate of 15,000 a day—alien white men coming back to the United States of America at the rate of 15,000 a day.[8] Do you know what that means? It means this: That in the next three or four years one-third of the Negro population of the United States of America will be in a [sim]ilar condition or position as we were in 1913 before the war. We will be out of jobs, we will be starving, we will be living next door to starving and starvation except you start out to do something for yourselves. We have been a dependent race of people for too long. If we continue to de[pend] upon somebody else we are going to depend upon our coffins and our tombstones. Almighty God gave you physical strength. He gave you health to do things for yourself. If you refuse to do it for your[self] the fault will be yours, as far as results go. There are Negroes [all] over this country, all over the world for that matter, who feel . . . [*word missing*] to be in the white man's employ. Now, the time will come whe[n] [white] men will have to decide between you and another white man. [The time will] come when the white man will have to decide between employ[ing] [*a Negro?*] on the one hand, or employing two white men on the other [hand,] why? Because in the next 100 years this population of white people in America, 90 millions of them, will have multiplied into a population of four hundred millions, and where you have one white man today in the next 100 years you will have four white men. Do you think the white man will give the black man bread when you have three white men over there starving? Too long we have said[:] "I am not interested in tomorrow," and that is why we are what we are. The white man has always been interested in the tomorrows as far as his life is concerned. He has always been interested in the next century, and that is why he is so powerful, so great today. If the white man had lived for his day and for his time, there would not be any America for us to be in tonight. If the Pilgrim Fathers had thought only of their day, there would not have been any church edifice on this spot tonight. They thought of their children of the future. They suffered, they bled, and they died to make a future, and where is the future they died for? It is being enjoyed by ninety millions of their children. Can you wonder why Woodrow Wilson is President of the United States and not a black man? Because his forefathers suffered and died to place him in the White House. Negroes, what are you doing to place your son or grandson as president of some country? Absolutely nothing, believing that one day you will get the vote and you will be able to become President of the United States. Well, wait until that day; you will wait until the judgment. You have absolutely no guarantee that tomorrow there will not be a terrible bloodshed for all Negroes in the United States of America. Have you any guarantee? Absolutely none. Can you tell me positively now that tomorrow morning we may not take up one of the papers in Washington and read that 10,000 Negroes had been lynched in Mississippi, or Georgia, or Alabama? You can not tell me positively. Why, because you have no guarant[ee] of protection. Why? [B]ecause you are not an organized people, you are not an organized race, you are not an organized nation. Any race of people not organized is a race of people to be abused, to be taken advantage of, and that is why you have been abused for over three hundred years in this Western Hemisphere, because we have refused to become organized. Do you know why the Universal Negro Improvement Association is feared so much now? We have a National Association for the Advancement of Colored People, we have a National Equal Rights League, we have many organizations in this country. Do you hear the Government saying anything about them? Not a word, but the Universal Negro Improvement Association does. You have white men poking their noses in to find out just a glimpse of what is going on. They send secret service men all over the country to hear the utterances of the men who are speaking all over the United States. You will find volumes and volumes of documents coming from England, [f]rom France, and from . . . [*word missing*] treasuring all the information possible about the Negro Improvement Association. Do you know why? Because the Negro Improvement Association is after them as they have been after the Negro for three hundred years. We are after them because we say every alien man must clear out of Africa that God Almighty gave us as our right and our heritage. We have said that to them and they are afraid. They want to know what time we are coming. The State Department won't know what time we are ready. No one will know until the great Napoleon of the Negro race sounds the /bugle/ call to arms, and four hundred million Negroes all over the world will answer on the great battle plains of Africa. Tell me that I could have died in France and Flanders fighting for an alien race, and I could not die in Africa fighting for my own country, when God Almighty saved us in this age or in this crisis for the purpose, and I do hope that I am looking in the faces of some of you men here tonight who will be probably the future presidents of Africa, and future generals of the great African army which will fight for our liberation, for our independence. (Applause.) God Almighty has a plan and a purpose for every race, and we have suffered long enough now to realise our purpose and enter into our plans. (Applause.) They tell us that God is white. That is a lie. They tell us that all of His angels are white, too. To my mind, everything that is wicked, everything that is devilish, is white. ("Yes, sir," and applause.) They told me that the devil was a black man. There isn't a greater devil in the world than the white man. I believe that if God has any color, God is black and the devil is white, but God has no color, God is a spirit, he is omnipotent, a mighty being that respects neither the color nor race, nor creed of men. He doles out to man just what he is entitled to, and I believe that—and I believe the time has come that some one has got to reckon with his God. Men, have absolutely no fear. We want you to have all the courage possible in this world. A race of cowards never conquered yet, a race of cowards never won their liberties yet. Don't be a cringing sycophant today as you were yesterday. You will always bow to the footstools of a superior master, but the moment you realize your ability, that very hour will see you a free man among men. There is a great purpose for us, and that purpose is being opened to us. We are preparing for this great convention to assemble in New York City for 31 days. During those days we will write a charter of liberty for four hundred million people. As the Constitution of the United States is to the white people, as the constitution of Great Britain is to the English, as the constitution of France is to the French, so will the constitution of the Universal /Negro/ Improvement Association be to every Negro after the 31st of August—the thing for which they will die, the thing for which we will shed the last drop of our blood. So I say to you in Washington, prepare for the greater day is in store. President Wilson came back from the Peace

Conference of Versailles. He told us "there is to be peace." He brought the draft of the League of Nations and told us that this thing will settle the peace of the world forever. Haven't you read of the great and bloody conflict now in Eastern Europe[?]⁹ The war is still on, and will continue until every race will get its rights. Caring not what Woodrow Wilson, Clemenceau, and Lloyd George says, there will be no peace as long as the strong oppresses the weak. And at the present moment, the Anglo-Saxons of Europe, the Italians of Europe, the Frenchmen of Europe are oppressing three hundred million men in Africa, and there can be no peace until those Africans, those at home and those who are abroad, are free and enjoy the benefits of democracy for which they fought for four and a half years of this bloody world war. So we are asking you tonight to fall in behind the colors of the Universal Negro Improvement Association, the red, the black, the green. We have written a great national anthem. I do hope that you will be in New York to hear, on the night of the second, 25,000 Negroes sing the new national anthem of Africa. We will sing to the knowledge of New York a national anthem on the second of August. It will not be the national anthem of England, it will not be the national anthem of France, but it will be the national anthem of Africa, and 25,000 of us will sing as led by the Black Star Line Band of 200 pieces and a choir of 200 pieces. Because in those days of the convention we will impress ourselves to the world, because we will assemble there as serious men and women. Our delegates are coming, as I said last night—they are coming from all parts of the world. The Mayor of Mo[n]rovia, Liberia, is in New York. The delegates have come from all parts of Africa, from South Africa, from West Africa, from North Africa, from Central Africa. Every state in Africa has sent delegates to this convention. Every country in South and Central America, every country in the West Indies, and delegates are coming from the 48 States of the Union, and I hope Washington will be represented.

We have started the Black Star Line for the purpose of bettering the industrial and economic condition of the race. We believe that the Negro can not succeed on sentiment or emotion. We must succeed in business. You can't get business by talking about it. You must get business by going into business. Twelve months ago the shipping business was confined to the white man. Those two (?) men dominated the maritime world. Twelve months ago, we, as the Universal Negro Improvement Association, decided that we also would enter into maritime affairs, maritime competition, maritime commerce, and the white people laughed at us, and the wiseacre Negroes laughed at us also. They said, "you can't start any steamship lines," and all that sort of discouraging talk. We went on, and the Black Star Line was organized, and the people had enough confidence in themselves to believe that we could start the Black Star Line, and the supposedly big Negroes—big parasites, I mean—the biggest Negroes of this country, the biggest Negroes, are nothing but big parasites. (Laughter.) Do you know what a parasite is? A thing that sucks the blood out of something else or something living, big fellows who go to white men and beg in the name of the Negro, and that is how the white man averages [*avenges?*] the race, by these big Negroes begging the white man, begging Marse Charles for a college, for a church, a school, and Marse George. And they say, "Joe, how are you getting on, how are your people getting along?" "Fine, Marse George," and they get $500 and slip half to the church and half to themselves and come back and tell you, "O we are big Negroes, we are diplomats and dicties," big beggars—that's all they are. I know them for what they are. I want to meet some of these big Negroes. The four hundred big Negroes rule the city of Boston. Nothing will go to Boston, no organization would go to Boston and get two members in Boston except these big dicties get around and hold a conference and say[,] "you shall come to Boston," and "shall not come to Boston." Somebody told me, you can't come here. This is a city of the four hundred. I went to Boston and in one night I tore up the four hundred and I started it to running all over the city. I spent another night there, two nights—and an organization, National Equal Rights League, has been seven years and has but 75 members—in two nights we had an organization of 3,000 members in the city of Boston. There wasn't a dicty in Boston bold enough to come out and speak for the dicties. Every one of them gave way to the Universal Negro Improvement Association, and the biggest organization now in Boston is the Universal Negro Improvement Association. I understand that you have some dicties in Washington, too. I am very sorry that I can not spend a week in Washington. I only want to get you started here with seven men, and any time I can spend sometime I will spend seven days in Washington and I tell you very few dicties will be left afterward. This isn't the age of dicties. This is the time when men must do service to their race if they want to be appreciated by that race. Men do not become dicties, do not become aristocrats, by just saying so. Men become aristocrats by working up to that position. In Washington here you are accustomed to read of some big names, names of dukes, nobilities, etc. You read of Lord Reading,[10] you read of Sir Geddes,[11] and Baron So-and-So, and So-and-So, and This and That, and Prince So-and-So. Now, how did these men become lords and dukes? According to the English way, these men, who are dukes, and barons, and peers, are raised to the nobility in their country among their own people. How did they get there? Lord Reading, before he became Lord Reading, was Rufus Isaacs. He was an eminent legist, an eminent barrister, an eminent man at law. He, because of his profound knowledge of the law, he, because of a contribution he made to the legal profession of Great Britain, was singled out as a legal mind, a legal brain, in whom the nation of Great Britain depend for salvation in a crisis. He rendered splendid services to his country in diplomacy and in all political craft which made [h]is country greater for his existence. In recognition for the services rendered to his country, they first made him Sir Rufus Isaacs. Then he rendered some more service and they made him Lord Reading, and he came to us in Washington as the Ambassador of Great Britain, as Lord Reading. We must have read of the Earl of Chatham. He was a man by the name of William Pitt, a hundred odd years ago in England. He was a great imperialist. He saw that the British Empire was an insignificant empire. He, through his initiative, swayed his fellow countrymen and so inspired them that he sent hundreds of them into foreign countries, like in Africa, China, Australia, there to care for the good of the Empire, and during the regime of William Pitt, who was eventually premier of Great Britain, he built up the great empire. They made him the Earl of Chatham, raised him from the common people and made him a noble because of the services he rendered to his country and to his race. These big dicties we have, have never rendered any services but go to the white man and beg some money. After getting the money they say, "we are the big dicties of the race, we are the aristocrats.["] The one who goes out and begs for money and the one who accomplished something for his race, who is the greater man, the man who goes out and begs or the man who [g]oes out and does service for his country? There is room for every Negro to be a noble man, there is room for every Negro to be an aristocrat, but it must be done through service. So, I say to these supposedly big Negroes of America, that we are going to prove your bigness in this very age, and when we are through with the convention in New York by the 31st, we will then tell who are the big Negroes of this United States of America. (Applause.) So that I am asking your support for the Universal Negro Improvement Association, because we have a big proposition before us. I am asking your support for the Black Star Line. The Black Star Line will open up new possibilities for us in the very near future. We have already linked up the West Indies and Central America. We [are] sailing out every week taking freight and passengers to the West Indies, taking passengers and freight to the West Indies. If you wish to leave Washington, you can sail the ship of the Black Star Line. If you desire to go from here to Panama or Costa Rica, to any of the Islands of the West Indies, you need not be jim-crowed on the white man's ship, you can buy a first-class passage on the ship of the Black Star Line. We have two boats now running between New York and Central America and the West Indies. Between now and next September we will have a big ocean liner running regularly between New York and Monrovia, Liberia. (Applause.) We have bought three ships already. We are not speculating. We are not asking you to experiment. We have bought the ships already. We have bought three ships already. It isn't a matter of whether we can run ships or not, we have run them for twelve months successfully. (Applause.) We have run them through storms, and when the storms raged and the white man's ship went down the black man's ship of the Black Star Line braved the storm and came back to port. Therefore you will realize that we can run ships. So tonight I am asking you in Washington to get behind the Black Star Line and make it a power commercially. Men, we can do it. There are four hundred million Negroes in the world, and if each and every one of us will make up our minds to buy a share it means that in the next twelve months we will have 1200 ships. Do you know what it means for all the Negroes to say "we are going to have one great and mighty Black Star Line"? It means that we will have that Black Star Line. It will be some line, and that is what we are endeavoring to do, men, if each and every one will do your part. There isn't a man or a woman in this building who can not buy. It costs only $5 a share, and in buying shares in the Black Star Line you are not doing it for charity. It isn't that we are begging you for anything. You are investing your money to make profit, the profit we make in carrying cargoes, the profit comes back to you by way of dividends. You put your money in the bank and it is there for twelve months. You get three per cent for the use of a hundred dollars for a year. In some banks you get $4 for the use of $100 for one year. What does the banker do with your money? You put a hundred dollars in the bank tomorrow morning and two hours after that the banker has invested your hundred dollars. He has loaned it out. He has bought several things, and at the end of a year that $100 you put in the bank yesterday or today for one year, that [banker] makes probably $500 on your $100 by turning it over every day of the year, and at the close of the year he will have made probably $400 or $500 from your $100, and how much he pays you? Three dollars for the use of it. (Laughter.) What has he done with that money? He invests it in stock or he loans it to certain corporations and he makes his money. Now, we say to you /that/ if you can use your money yourself and make 400 to 500 per cent every year, and that is what the Black Star Line is asking you to do. The moment you buy a share of the Black Star Line you become part owner of the Black Star Line. Therefore, whatever the Black Star Line makes for the whole year, you make for your own investment. Every shareholder is a partner /part owner/ of the Black Star Line. If you buy a share for $5 and you see a ship of the Black Star Line, you are part owner of that ship. And so it is if you have $100 or $500 invested. Your $500 or $1,000 are all scattered, just as all that $5 is scattered in all the properties of the Black Star Line; so you are part owner when you become an investor in shares. I hope that you will invest tonight to help yourselves and help your race to build up a great maritime fleet, a great marine fleet that will one day surprise and startle the world and bring respect to us as a race. The white man measures you by your success. We can make success of this age because it is the age of reorganization, of reconstruction. So—I am about to close now—but /before/ I do so I am asking all of you who have not bought any shares to do so tonight. Let me see how many share-holders are in here. Thank you. Please, those who are going to buy shares tonight who have not bought yet, come forward and buy at once, whether one share or two shares or twenty shares. Is there anyone? Hold your hand up—have you all bought your shares already? Come forward, remembering what I said to you; we are not asking you for a collection, we are not asking you for charity, we are asking you to buy shares in a corporation that will bring profit to you at the close of the financial year. Your money invested in the Black Star Line is safer than in a bank, because it is invested in ships. You will say, "well, if the ship goes down in the ocean?" If a ship of the Black Star Line goes down anywhere it is covered by [25] per cent more than its original cost and insurance. That is to say, we bought the *Frederick Douglass* for $168,000 and she is covered with $200,000 in insurance. If she goes down tomorrow or tonight, we make money and have lost nothing. Therefore you have absolutely nothing to lose and those of you who have not bought shares yet, I am asking you to buy shares tonight.

I hope that you will, Mr. President, send your delegate to the convention, so that you will be able to see for yourself a crowd here at New York, a crowd here of men and women who will be sent to this great convention which will assemble for 31 days. I hope in the near future to come back to Washington to speak to you. I am very much interested in you, because there are so many in Washington. When I read about your riots I saw you were not organized. There are no race riots in New York because we are organized. If any man is foolish enough to start anything in New York he knows he has seen his last day. In Washington, if you want to live in peace, get organized. When men know you are organized, they are not going to disturb you. When they know you are disorganized, any child will take advantage of you. Do you know why they don't [t]rouble Japan? Because Japan is organized. Do you know why they don't trouble the great empire nations of Europe? Do you know why they brutalize the Hindoo, because they know they are not organized. Do you know why they lynch and burn Negroes all over the world? Because they are not organized. We have some new stunt to put off all over the world, because if you lynch one Negro you will have to lynch four hundred million Negroes. That is the new stunt we are going to put off and that is why you want to send your delegate[s] to New York for this great convention. Now, we will close this meeting and I trust that you men and you ladies who have not joined the Black Star Line will do so. It would be a crime for any man or any woman to leave this building without doing something for this glorious cause, realizing that you are not helping any person but yourself and your children, realizing that if you keep back this advantage you could give in common with others, you are keeping back yourselves and your cause. There isn't one of us in here that God Almighty hasn't blessed sufficiently in the last five years to help us earn our daily bread. We have enjoyed those opportunities now. To what advantage are we using the benefits that we got out of the war? It is for you tonight to invest in the Black Star Line and to join the Universal Negro Improvement Association. We will now stand and sing "Onward Christian Soldiers."

Benediction by The Rev. J. G. Brooks.

STENOGRAPHIC NOTES ACCOMPANY THIS TRANSCRIPT.

DNA, RG 65, file OG 329359. TD.

1. Rev. Joseph Josiah Cranston was president of the Baltimore UNIA and a minister of the Universal Ethiopian church. Cranston, ordained presbyter in the Church of God by Dr. George Alexander McGuire in April 1921, resigned from the Baltimore division to work for the UNIA and ACL in Pittsburgh (*NW*, 19 June 1920, 7 May 1921).

2. Henry J. Callis (1858–1955) was born a slave on a plantation in Matthews County, Virginia. Freed during the Civil War, he graduated from Hampton Institute, Hampton, Va., in 1879. In 1892 he became pastor of the AMEZ Church in Ithaca, New York, later serving as

pastor of the Metropolitan AMEZ Church in Washington, D.C. (1916–24), and the Lomax AMEZ Church in Arlington, Va. (1933–46). Callis, who also worked in Boston for one of the first branches of the NAACP, earned a reputation as an outstanding orator and preacher. In 1950 he was one of the founders of the National Council of Churches (*Washington Post*, 13 March 1955; *Washington Star*, 13 March 1955).

3. A book written by Theodore Lothrop Stoddard (1883–1950), *The Rising Tide of Color Against White World-Supremacy*, was first published in April 1920 and quickly elevated its author to a prominent position among racist theorists. Stoddard's Ph.D. thesis at Harvard had examined the Haitian revolution and the black government that it brought to power. He eventually came to believe that "the key-note of twentieth century world politics would be the relations between the primary races of mankind" (p. v) contending that the "inferior" races would soon inundate the "Nordics" because of their higher birthrate. Garveyites apparently read his book with interest. Many of them, while disagreeing with Stoddard's assessment of blacks, were heartened by his prediction of an end to white supremacy (Stoddard, *The Rising Tide of Color Against White World-Supremacy* [New York: Charles Scribner's Sons, 1920]; Emory J. Tolbert, "Outpost Garveyism and the UNIA Rank and File," *Journal of Black Studies* 5, no. 3 [March 1975]: pp. 240–41).

4. The out-migration of blacks from the South increased during the twenties, so that the total number of blacks moving to the North from 1920 to 1930 exceeded that of the previous decade. This second wave of blacks was driven to the North by news of higher wages and an economic boom in the North and by the simultaneous increase in lynchings in the South (Eric Walrond, "The Negro Exodus from the South," *Current History* 18 [September 1923]: 23–29).

5. Brooks's speech was delivered while the NAACP was conducting a crusade for passage of the Dyer anti-lynching bill. Lynchings in Oklahoma, Texas, and West Virginia received nationwide coverage during July 1920, prompting Calvin Coolidge, the Republican vice-presidential candidate, and Warren G. Harding, the presidential candidate, to urge federal laws against lynching (*NYT*, 23 July and 28 July 1920). Rumors that blacks were being lynched for voting Republican may have motivated the candidates. Ultimately, however, neither political party was willing to make lynching a campaign issue in 1920.

6. Italy had been promised recognition of her territorial claims in Europe, a share of the Turkish Empire, and an extension of her African colonies in exchange for entering World War I on the side of the Entente. At the war's end, however, Italy received only nine thousand square miles of territory and none of the former German colonies in Africa as a mandate. Italy's complaints about her large expenditure in money and lives but comparatively small reward were soon followed by the seizure of Fiume (also known as Rijeka) by Italian nationalists led by Gabriele D'Annunzio in September 1919. At the time of Brooks's speech, negotiations between Yugoslavia and Italy over Fiume and other territories were under way. However, under the completed treaty, Italy gained little, and Fiume was declared an independent state until, after a period of disorders, Italian Fascists seized the city in March 1922.

7. Antonio Maceo (1848–1896) was a Cuban general of African descent who led the fight for national independence, defeating the Spanish at the battles of Jobito and Sao del Indio in 1895. Garvey chose to rechristen the *Kanawha* in Antonio Maceo's honor after its purchase by the Black Star Line on 26 July 1920.

8. Immigrants from southern, central, and eastern Europe continued to arrive in the United States in great numbers. Nearly four million came in the period from 1910 to 1919, while census figures reveal that 1,114,730 immigrants came from 1920 to 1924 (Stanley Lieberson, *A Piece of the Pie: Blacks and White Immigrants Since 1880* [Berkeley, Los Angeles, London: University of California Press, 1980], pp. 20–24).

9. A reference to the Hungarian uprising of 1919.

10. Lord Reading served as a special envoy with ambassadorial rank to the United States from February 1918 to 1919.

11. Lord Auckland Campbell Geddes (1880–1954) was the British ambassador to the United States from 1920 to 1924. Born in Scotland, Lord Geddes was for a time professor of anatomy at McGill University in Montreal. After a brief stint in the army during World War I, he became director of military recruiting and later held the positions of minister of national service and president of the Board of Trade. Known as "the scientist with the empire mind," Geddes was one of the leading figures at the Washington Disarmament Conference of 1921–22 (*NYT*, 9 January 1954).

Black Star Line Annual Report

[*New York*] July 26, 1920

It was a record crowd which marked the attendance at the first annual meeting of the stockholders of the Black Star Line, Inc., which was held at Liberty Hall, 120 West 138th street.

The spacious hall was packed to its fullest capacity, and many were forced to remain outside.

All of the officers of the corporation were present with the exception of the secretary (E. D. Smith-Green), assistant secretary (Fred Powell) and D. D. Shirley.

The most intense interest was manifested during the entire proceedings. The president, Mr. Garvey, gave a stirring address, in which he stated that the directors are the servants and trustees of the stockholders, and if they (the stockholders) were satisfied with the reports of the year's work when presented it was for them to sustain the directors. If dissatisfied they can select a new Board of Directors.

Continuing, the president said: "We are here principally as members of the U.N.I.A., which incorporated the Black Star Line to achieve the objects it set itself out to accomplish. We entered as a people with but little experience in the running of steamships. The policy of the U.N.I.A. is to control this corporation so as to help the parent association in achieving its objects." Alluding to the subscribed stock of the corporation he said that $500,000 is but a drop in the bucket in order to purchase steamships, "but," said Mr. Garvey, "because we desire to show to the world that we can achieve, we were satisfied to purchase small boats so as to show that we can run them. We have much to be thankful for, in that no unfortunate accident has befallen us. As a matter of fact, the work of the past year is of great benefit to us, for it has brought recognition to us as a race—it has elevated our men. (Cheers.) We have encountered many drawbacks, but you must bear in mind that the directors alone cannot run ships. However, our experiences of the past will help us to run things better in the future. We have tried to do our best, and because of our determination we have been able to bring the corporation to this point as solvent and as intact as any corporation can be." (Loud applause.)

The balance sheet was then presented and showed as follows:

Assets.

Invested Assets—
Real estate, 54–56 West
    135th st., Schedule 2 .... $26,000.00
Delivery equipment,
    Schedule 3 .... 4,620.27

Furniture and Fixtures 8,354.74
S.S. Yarmouth, Schedule 4 .... 178,156.36
S.S. Kana[wh]a, Schedule 4 .... 75,359.01
S.S. Shadyside, Schedule 4 .... 35,000.00

    Total invested assets $328,190.38

    Deferred Charges—
Prepaid insurance on steamships,
    property, etc. 5,729.00
Due from subscription to capital stock 118,153.28
    Current Assets—
Cash in bank $1,933.48
Deposit (security) 5,500.00
Loans, receivable, Schedule 1 .... 14,551.73
    Total current assets 21,985.21

Organization expense 289,066.27

                                    $763,124.14

Liabilities.

    Capital—
Capital stock issued $442,625.00
Subscription in capital stock 168,235.00
    Total capital $610,860.00

    Fixed Liabilities—
Mortgages payable, Schedule 6 .... 21,500.00
    Current and Other Liabilities—
Accounts payable, Schedule 5 .... $12,148.02
Accrued salaries and wages 1,539.30
Notes payable, Schedule 7 .... 117,076.82

    Total current and other liabilities $130,764.14

                                      $763,124.14

Respectfully submitted,

                      GEORGE TOBIAS, Treas.

The following were elected as the Board of Directors for the ensuing year:

    Marcus Garvey, O. M. Thompson, C. B. Curley,[1] George Tobias, Henrietta Vinton Davis, Cyril Henry, William H. Ferris, Fred Toote, El[ie] Garcia, J. M. Certain, Jennie Jenkins.

Printed in NW, 14 August 1920. Original headlines omitted.

1. Clarence Benjamin Curley (b. 1889) was born in Memphis, Tenn.; he graduated from Howard University in 1911 and earned his law degree there in 1914. When World War I started, Curley helped lead the movement to establish the black officers' training camp at Des Moines, Iowa, and became a first lieutenant in the 368th Infantry. After the war, he attended New York University, where he received his M.B.A. degree in 1922. He served in many administrative and business-related positions: general accountant and secretary for the Black Star Line; vice-principal of Manassas Industrial School in Virginia; business instructor at Dunbar High School in Washington, D.C.; assistant supervisor for the Department of Public Markets in New York City; inspector for the Alabama Life Insurance Co.; and comptroller of the North Carolina Life Insurance Co. in Durham. In 1928 Curley also founded and served as secretary of the National Negro Fraternal Association (*WWCA*, vol. 2).

Editorial Letter by Marcus Garvey

[[NEW YORK, July 27, 1920]]

FELLOW MEN OF THE NEGRO RACE, Greeting:—

This is to inform you that on Sunday, August 1, the Universal Negro Improvement Association and African Communities' League of the World will call its great convention to order at 10 A.M. in Liberty Hall.

Millions of people have been looking towards this great event for the last two and a half years. The hour [ha]s come at last for the Negro, in the risen strength of his manhood, to demonstrate to the world the seriousness of his intention towards world conditions. It was thought impossible a couple of years ago for the Negro to organize for any definite purpose, but it is an acknowledged fact today that the Universal Negro Improvement Association has done the impossible in the space of two and a half years. We have been able to organize three and a half million men and women of our race with a definite plan; the plan of a redeemed Africa; the plan of a free race. This Convention, which will assemble for the first time on Sunday morning at 10 o'clock in Liberty Hall, will go down on the pages of history as the greatest assemblage of Negroes for the last fifteen hundred years. I now send out a last call to all the Negro peoples of the world to be represented at this Convention. It must be remembered that all the problems confronting the race will be discussed during the thirty-one days of August; that no phase of the Negro question will be shelved. Every complaint will be listened to and steps taken to remedy existing wrongs. When the Convention adjourns on August 31 it will be with the purpose of having four hundred million Negroes all over the world standing behind the great and glorious constitution to be written, and to defend it with the last drop of their blood. The cry of the Negro is for "LIBERTY," is for "JUSTICE," is for "EQUAL OPPORTUNITIES." He has cried for these things for hundreds of years. He is determined now to demand them. The Negro no longer thinks he is a weakling. He refuses to admit that he is a cringing sycophant. He disbelieves the idea that he is not a man. He realizes that he is a man bearing likeness to his Creator. As a man the new Negro shall go forward and demand from the world all those things to which he is entitled. The glorious Continent of Africa stands to be redeemed. A mighty nation must be built in Africa. Within the next fifty years the Imperial Parliament of Africa must stand out among the great Parliaments of the world and our statesmen shall, within the wa[ll]s of our Parliament, legislate for the good of the four hundred million members of our race. The black man refuses to be dictated to by foreign Parliaments and alien statesmen. This is the time when all races feel it incumbent upon them to protect their own interests, and if sixty million Anglo-Saxons can be dominant in Europe, and a few million French and Italians and Germans, we do not see why we should allow ourselves to be dominated and abused by alien power. The Convention of the Universal Negro Improvement Association shall give new life and new spirit to the Negro peoples of the world; hence, I ask that every Negro lend his moral and financial aid to this great cause. The first meeting of the Convention will be at 10 o'clock on Sunday morning, August 1; the second meeting at 3 o'clock in the afternoon, and the third at 8 o'clock in the night. On the morning of the 2nd the Convention will assemble at 10 o'clock, to adjourn for a parade at 2 o'clock and to assemble at 8 o'clock sharp in Madison Square Garden in a great public demonstration. Twenty-five thousand delegates will be in line to march in the great processional of the Convention. All members of the Association in New York and surrounding States are asked to report in New York not later than 8 A.M. on Sunday, August 1. Everybody should report in time to be properly seated in the Convention and to take part in the parade. Madison Square Garden on Monday night will be the Mecca of the Negro peoples of New York. It can be said without fear that there will not be a seat vacant in Madison Square Garden at 8:30 Monday night. All roads will lead to this world-famed building. Churches, lodges, fraternal organizations, clubs and educational institutions that are sending delegates to the Convention are requested to have their delegates report to the Registrar's office at 56 West 135th Street, New York City, before they attend at Liberty Hall, so that proper credentials can be given by the Registrar for admission to the Convention. Let your thoughts for the entire month of August be centered around the great Convention being held at Liberty Hall. Pray for the success of this Convention, so that out of the thirty-one days of deliberation will come a new people, a new purpose, and a new nation realized.

Immediately after the convention the Black Star Line contemplates opening up direct routes between America and Africa and South America. More ships must be bought, and bigger ships. The Directors, therefore, ask that every Negro make now a desp[e]rate effort to buy more shares in the Corporation. The more ships the Black Star Line has the better accommodations we will be able to give to the race. Liberia must be built. Men must be transported. Skilled mechanics and craftsmen are wanted. We cannot transport them in balloons, in air ships; we can only transport them in the ships of the Black Star Line. First of all, we must buy ships to make transportation possible. Hundreds of miles of railroads must be laid down in Liberia. Docks must be built; educational institutions must be built; industrial enterprises must be constructed, and all will mean the transportation of skilled men from this Western Hemisphere, so we ask that every Negro who can afford it to buy more shares in the Black Star Line. You may buy from one to two hundred at Five Dollars each. My advice to you is that you buy now, so that by the close of the Convention the Directors will be able to give a statement to the world of the acquisition of more ships for the Black Star Line, which will make it possible for us to transport at our will. Write the office of the Black Star Line, 56 West 135th Street, New York City, N.Y., U.S.A., for your shares.

And let me say to you adieu for a while until we meet at the Convention on Sunday morning at 10 o'clock in Liberty Hall. Yours fraternally,

MARCUS GARVEY

Printed in *NW*, 31 July 1920. Original headlines omitted.

Frank Burke to Patrick J. Ahern

Washington July 31, 1920

Dear Sir:

Reference is made to report of Agent S. F. Goggins, for July 24–25, in re: MARCUS GARVEY.

It is desired that you advise this office immediately as to the names and addresses of the individuals with whom Garvey connected during his stay in Washington. Very truly yours,

FRANK BURKE
Assistant Director and Chief

[*Typewritten reference*] G[FR]-MMP

DNA, RG 65, file OG 329359. TL, carbon copy.

GREAT WORLD CONVENTION OF NEGROES

Members of the Race From All Parts of the World to Assemble at Liberty Hall, New York, Sunday, August 1, at 10 A. M.—Biggest and Most Representative Assemblage in History of the Race

CONSTITUTION OF NEGRO LIBERTY IS TO BE WRITTEN

HON. MARCUS GARVEY, WORLD FAMED ORATOR

WILL SPEAK FOR THE "BLACK STAR LINE" AT HUGE CONVENTION AT

LIBERTY HALL

120 WEST 138th STREET
Bet. 7th and Lenox Aves., New York

SUBJECT: "OUR CONVENTION"

SUNDAY, AUGUST 1, 3:30 AND 7:30 P. M.

(*Source: NW*, 31 July 1920).

469

Negro World Notices

[31 July 1920]

To the Negro People of the World and Stockholders in the Black Star Line

You are hereby warned that Edward D. Smith-Green and Joshua Cockburn are no longer connected with the Black Star Line for reasons that will be explained by public announcement.

Edward D. Smith-Green, having failed to satisfy the President and Directors of the Black Star Line of his honest integrity as an officer of the corporation, was held under suspicion for some time to investigate his accounts, and before such accounts could be thoroughly investigated he sent his resignation to the Board of Directors and is now making capital, by publication, that he is no longer connected with the Black Star Line.

All stockholders are, therefore, advised accordingly. It is understood that this man Smith-Green is now associated with a steamship company under the name of the African Saw Mill Steamship Company which has been incorporated since March, 1919, and which has not yet purchased any ships, and that he has been publishing and making statements detrimental to the interests of the Black Star Line in the interest of the said African Saw Mill Steamship Company.

The public is asked to investigate before placing credence in what is being said by this man Edward D. Smith-Green.

Any information as to the true name of Edward Smith-Green, whether his name is Green or Smith-Green, will be highly appreciated by Marcus Garvey, the President of the Black Star Line, 56 West 135th Street, New York City.

Printed in *NW*, 31 July 1920.

[31 July 1920]

Panama Gentleman Brings up $50 in Gold for Convention Fund

Mr. F. S. Ricketts,[1] a prominent business man of Colon, Panama, arrived in New York last week for the August Convention. He brought $50 in gold for the Convention Fund.

Visitors are crowding New York for the convention. Mrs. Mary Jones, of Oklahoma City, is one of the enthusiastic arrivals.

Prof. O. Z. Parris, of Newport News, Va., a talented musician, speaker and writer, visited the Negro World office on Friday of last week and was entertained at dinner with General Johnson, Mayor of Monrovia, Liberia, by Rev. Wm. H. Ferris, Literary Editor of the Negro World.

Printed in *NW*, 31 July 1920.

1. F. S. Ricketts was president of the Colon Independent Mutual Benefit Cooperative Society.

Article by William H. Ferris

[*Favorite Magazine*,[1] July 1920]

GARVEY AND THE BLACK STAR LINE

Two years ago last winter, Marcus Garvey, a native of Jamaica, British West Indies gathered together thirteen colored people in a little room and formed a local division of the Universal Negro Improvement Association. From these thirteen people, results have been achieved which are unparalleled in Negro history. These thirteen people have now developed into an organization in Harlem which numbers thousands of people. They have bought Liberty Hall and two adjoining office buildings on West 135th street. They operate a laundry and a millinery store, and publish the Negro World, which in less than two years has a bona fide c[i]rculation of 50,000 and have launched the Black Star [L]ine which now has two boats, the "Yarmouth" and the "Antonio Mac[e]o," sailing between New York and the West Indies, and an excursion steamer, "The Shady-Side," which makes almost daily excursion up the Hudson. All these allied corporations and organizations have on their weekly pay roll upwards to 800 people so that if you were to visit the offices at 54 and 56 West 13[5]th street, you would find scores of young colored men and women employed as managers, accountants, cashiers, stenographers and clerks, etc[.]

The most spectacular sight is Liberty Hall. It is now summer time, were you to visit any of the big [c]hurches on a Sunday night you would find some empty seats but go to Liberty Hall and you would find nearly 2,000 people packed and jammed in the building from the platform to the outer doors and outside the church an equally large number of people will be found clustered around the building, crowding the sidewalk and streets and the adjoining lots, endeavoring to listen from the open doors and windows. And on week nights, Liberty Hall is comfortably filled every night and sometimes packed and jammed.

The band plays every night. The choir sings three nights a week, and soloists like Mrs. Marie Barrier Houston, Mrs. Frazier Robinson, Miss Revella Hughes and Miss Ethel Clark regale the audience with delightful music. Nowhere in the country will you find the Negro gathering that you find in Liberty Hall. Never in the history of Negro journalism has any paper attained a circulation which the Negro World has in 21 months. Never in the history of Negro organizations has any organization assumed the colossal proportion in two years and a half which the Universal Negro Improvement Association has. Never in the history of Negro Corporations has any corporation sold the amount of stock which the B.S.L. has in a short space of one year.

During the past eleven months which I have served as literary editor of the Negro World and acting chancellor of the parent body of the U.N.I.A., I have seen the Negro World grow from a circulation of 17,000 to 50,000. I have seen the steam laundry and millinery factory started and I have seen three ships, three buildings, one lot and two auto trucks purchased. The U.N.I.A. has also grown to an enormous proportion.

MARCUS GARVEY THE MAN.

This sounds more like the Aladdin's Lamp or a Tale of the Arabian Nights. What has been the secret of the miraculous changes which Marcus Garvey has brought about[?] He was a man of the hour who appeared at the psychological moment. Marcus Garvey was born in Jamaica some 33 or 34 years ago. He quit school when he was 16 and entered a printing shop; he worked in the printing shop until he was 20. From 20 to 24 he was foreman in a printing shop. Then he went to England and remained three years studying in a London university and serving on the editorial staff of the "African Times" and "Orient Review," which was edited by Duse Mohammed. Then he returned to Jamaica and edited a paper in Jamaica and in Panama. About six years ago Mr. Garvey started the first branch of the U.N.I.A. in Jamaica. He came to America about four years ago. We first met him in January, 1917, when we published one of his articles in Champion Magazine. For nearly two years, Marcus Garvey toured this country as a lecturer with an observing eye but he did not create any stir until he set down his stakes in New York. At first he addressed the Liberty League, which was founded by Mr. Hubert H. Harrison,[2] former editor of the "Voice" and now associate editor of the Negro World. Then Mr. Garvey with other Negro radicals and the Socialist orators spoke from a soap box on Lenox avenue. Some of them like Messrs[.] Randolph and Owens, the editors of the "Messenger," were more trained in sociology and history than Mr. Garvey and were more polished speakers. But none of these soap box orators achieved the big things that Mr. Garvey did. "Why?"

When the United States declared war against Germany in the spring of 1917 and President Woodrow Wilson announced that America was waging war "To make the world safe for democracy," the Negroes went into hysterics through joy. They thought the millennium had come. But after the war was over they found out that they were disfranchised, Jim Crowed, segregated and lynched as in the days of yore. Then the Negro orators began to cry out from the housetops, "We want democracy, we want liberty, we

want freedom, we want self-determination and we want our rights.["]
Marcus Garvey cried out for the same things, but he did something more. He
was a magnetic speaker but he also possessed business insight.

He saw that the Negro could not consistently defy the white man one
day and beg him for a job the next day. He saw that only when the Negro
attained commercial strength and economic independence, and built a real
republic or empire in Africa, would he command the respect and challenge
the admiration of a hostile world. He saw that in the long run that the
Negro's destiny and salvation rested in his own hands. He preached with
telling force and earnestness Emerson's gospel of self-reliance. And because
he had something else than hot air, because he did something more than
"shoot the bull," because he had a definite program and propaganda, the
Negroes hailed him as a new Moses and dove down in their pockets and
produced what is called the "mazuma." Then again Mr. Garvey was keen in
observing whether a man or woman possessed literary, musical, oratorial and
business ab[i]lity, and he was quick to press into service Miss Henrietta
Vinton Davis, Mr. John E. Bruce, Dr. J. W. H. Eason, Rev. Dr. Brooks and
Hudson [C.] Pryce.[3]

Inasmuch as nearly all of the other big Negro Stock Companies have
failed, the question is being asked, "Will the Black Star [L]ine really succeed
as a dividend-paying enterprise[?]" The chances are very roseate at present,
but we cannot forecast the future. A good deal depends upon the prudence of
the men in charge. Something depends upon the weather, something depends upon the good will of the Anglo-Saxon, and something depends upon
the presence or absence of strikes among longshoremen, etc. In any business
investment, the investor more or less takes a chance. All he can judge is the
probability and not the certainty of success. As we are not gifted with divine
omniscience and have not the all-seeing eye of the Almighty, we can only say
that at present the probability of success is on the side of the Black Star
[L]ine.

Just now, New York is at a fever heat of excitement over the convention,
which will be held in Liberty Hall from August 1 to 31 of the present year.
Delegates will assemble from all over the world to discuss the Negro status in
the two Americas, in the West Indies and in Africa, and to formulate
constructive and practical plans for the elevation of the Negro and the
redemption of Africa. Sky-Pilot oratory and aerial [f]lights of the imagination may be indulged in, but when the delegates leave for their respective
homes, they will have discovered that they have had a serious grapple with
modern, social, economic and racial problems. And they will realize that
deeds and not words will in the last analysis determine the Negro's status and
destiny on this terrestrial ball.

Printed in *Favorite Magazine*, vol. 4 (July 1920). Copy found in DNA, RG 65,
file OG 374877.

1. *Favorite Magazine* was edited by Fenton Johnson.

2. Hubert H. Harrison became associate editor of the *Negro World* in January 1920.

3. Hudson C. Pryce served as the business manager for the *Negro World* during 1921–22 (*NW*, 18 March 1922).

Editorials in the *Crusader*

[July 1920]

GARVEY'S "JOKER"

Marcus Garvey, writing in the *Negro World* for June 19 in behalf of the Universal Negro Improvement Association and African Communities League, has at last issued a belated invitation to Negro organizations outside of the U.N.I.A. to attend "the convention of Negroes of the world" to be held in New York August 1 to 31 under the conception and auspices of the U.N.I.A.

Belated as is this invitation, and apparently issued only as a result of THE CRUSADER'S fight to make the convention in reality a convention of, by and for the Negroes of the world, THE CRUSADER would gladly and generously commend Mr. Garvey for the same were it not for the "joker" contained in Mr. Garvey's "open invitation" to the great mass of the Race outside of the organization of the U.N.I.A., a "joker" that leaves the situation practically as before. Our fight for genuine race representation at the convention was based wholly and solely upon the announcement by the U.N.I.A., that the convention was for the purpose of electing "His Supreme Highness the Potentate, His Highness the Supreme Deputy and other high officials *who will preside over the destinies of the Negro peoples of the world until an African Empire is founded.*["] Were the U.N.I.A. merely engaged in electing officials for its own control and guidance those of us not connected with the organization could have no interest in making the elections an open affair. But it is because of the terrible importance for which the convention is called and the dangers involved to race unity that we have insisted that the Race should have genuine representation in the same. And yet Mr. Garvey, after extending his "open invitation" to all Negro organizations to send delegates, qualifies this invitation and confines the participation of other delegates than those of the U.N.I.A. to the balloting for the election of a leader for Negro America:

["]At this convention all the American citizens who will send representatives from their lodges, churches and other organizations will elect for themselves a leader of American Negro thought. This leader, to be elected at the convention, will be the accredited spokesman of the 15,000,000 of American Negroes residing in the United States of America.["]

Mr. Garvey then proceeds in the following ominous words to insert his "joker" and make null and void his self-styled "open invitation":

["]At this convention, also, the Universal Negro Improvement Association will elect His Highness, the Potentate, who will be the accredited head of the Universal movement all over the world; *he will occupy the place of world leader of all Negroes.*["]

And the election of this individual who is "*to occupy the place of world leader of all Negroes,*" and as such would occupy a paramount position to the leaders of the American and other groups, is to be the exclusive privilege of the U.N.I.A., and as we remarked last month, "without our consent and without the co-operation of the vast body of Negroes outside the membership of the U.N.I.A., and in comparison with whose numbers those of the U.N.I.A. are small indeed."

Thus does a noble concept suffer from selfishness and smallness of mind, and a convention that should be the greatest event in modern Negro history is made to approach the proportions of a gigantic farce.

Printed in the *Crusader*, July 1920.

[July 1920]

THOSE RESPONSIBLE

Already there is a tendency on the part of the unthinking to saddle upon one group of our people all the blame for the alleged mistakes made by officials of the Black Star Line Corporation. Nothing could be more unjust.

In its incipiency and for many months of its development the Black Star Line Corporation may quite possibly have been the result of the efforts and energies of a certain group of our people, but latterly the project has been as much supported and controlled by one group as another. For its mistakes, as for its successes, one group is as much responsible as the other.

Marcus Garvey may be held responsible for much of the success, as well as the mistakes, made prior to the time when certain facts as to the management and real ownership of the "Yarmouth" were made public by THE CRUSADER and *The Emancipator*. After the publication of those neither Mr. Garvey nor any special group can be held solely responsible for events that are in the future; the blame and praise must be shared jointly by every shareholder in the corporation. That Mr. Garvey has yet to issue a public statement on the affairs of the Black Star Line (moneys taken in, how spent, etc.) is as much the result of the rabid, unbusiness-like attitude of the shareholders who meet at "Liberty Hall" as of the negligence of Mr. Garvey and other officials. And all groups of our people have been represented at the "Liberty Hall" meetings. Success or disaster must be shared equally by all!

Printed in the *Crusader*, July 1920.

Opening of UNIA Convention

[[Liberty Hall, New York, *1 August 1920*]]

INTERNATIONAL CONVENTION OF NEGROES OPENS IN BLAZE OF GLORY

IMPRESSIVE GATHERING REPRESENTING ALL CLASSES OF NEGROES TAX THE CAPACITY OF LIBERTY HALL.

Under threatening skies, which continued throughout the day, interspersed with rain every now and then, the long-heralded and much talked of International Convention of Negroes, under the auspices of the Universal Negro Improvement Association, was formally opened this morning, in the presence of a gathering of more than 10,000 Negroes, representing every class of the race from all over the United States, Africa, Central and South America and the West Indies.

The building, recently enlarged to three times its former size, occupying a floor space of 17,000 square feet, and having a seating capacity of 12,000, presented a striking appearance, and was filled to overflowing during the three sessions of the day. It was tastefully decorated with bunting, American flags intertwined with the flags of the Universal Negro Improvement Association (Red, Black and Green). The hall is amply provided with windows and exits, and is fully lighted. The speakers' platform, a d[ai]s accommodating 200 persons, was draped with the American flag; flowers of variegated kinds were [. . .] on the speakers' desk, while on either side of the platform stood beautiful palms.

MORNING SESSION

Long before the opening of the morning session a seething mass of humanity could be seen wending its way to the hall. Promptly at ten o'clock, the combined bands of the U.N.I.A. and the Black Star Line, under the direction of Professors Arnold Ford and William Isles, played the Star Spangled Banner. This concluded, a procession took place, while the hymn, "Onward, Christian Soldiers" was sung by the audience, with the accompaniment of the two bands. The procession comprised a choir of 200 female singers, all robed alike in white dresses, with black mortar board hats, led by two special officers of the association also in uniform. The officials of the tripartite organization, garbed in their multi-colored silken robes of office, brought up [*illegible*] the rear. Among the distinguished persons who occupied seats on the platform were: Hon. Marcus Garvey, Hon. Gabriel Johnson, mayor of Monrovia, Liberia; Rev. Dr. W. H. Ferris, chancellor; Miss Henrietta Vinton Davis, international organizer; Rev. Dr. J. D. Brooks, general secretary; Mr. Vernal Williams; Rev. Dr. E[a]son, chaplain-general; Rev. Dr. P. E. Paul;[1] Rev. E. F. Wilcolm Elligor; Rev. J. W. Selk[r]idge;[2]

Miss Sarah Branch; Mr. Watkins;[3] Mr. Adrian Johnson; D. D. Lewis, M.D., president Montreal Division, and with him, Miss O'Brien, lady president of the Montreal Division; Mr. Rudolph Smith, of the Field Corps.

The delegates were seated directly in front of the rostrum, with standards representing the respective divisions. Among the standards in evidence, were those from Jamaica, Nevis[,] B.W.I.; from New York and other States in which branches of the organization have been established. The delegates wore buttons of the association, and bands on the arm, in the association's colors.

The ushers handled the immense crowd with credit to themselves and those in charge of the arrangements. Printed programs with the order of services for the three sessions (including Monday's session) were distributed among the audience.

Revs. Paul and Dr. Ferris assisted in the opening ceremonies of the morning services. The Hon. Marcus Garvey, President-General, occupied the chair and delivered the address of welcome to the delegates. This was followed by the invocation and an eloquent, forceful sermon by the Rev. Dr. E[a]son, Chaplain-General. Prior to the opening address a solo, entitled "The Lord Is My Light and Salvation," was rendered by Mr. Edward Steele. Mr. Steele has a tenor voice of remarkable quality and range.

PRESIDENT-GENERAL WELCOMES DELEGATES.

The Honorable Marcus Garvey delivered the opening address as follows:

Fellow Members of the Universal Negro Improvement Association, Delegates to the Convention, Friends and Fellow Negroes: At this hour it is my honor to inform you that the Universal Negro Improvement Association of the World declares its first annual convention open. For two and a half years we have been scattering the doctrines of the U.N.I.A. to the four corners of the world, and because of the success of our work, we found it necessary to call together, at this time in Liberty Hall, the delegates of the 400,000,000 Negroes of the world, and they are here assembled in this hall this Sunday morning. They are here for the purpose of discussing the great problems that confront the Negro; they are here for the purpose of framing a bill of rights for the [N]egro peoples of the world; they are here for the purpose of laying plans for the redemption of the great continent of Africa. We assemble ourselves together because we believe this is the age in which the Negro, like all the other oppressed peoples of the world, should strike out for his own redemption. From the four corners of the world come delegates who are imbued with the spirit of liberty.

For over 300 years we who are citizens and denizens of this Western Hemisphere have been held in slavery. For that period of time we have been separated from our brothers and our sisters in the great continent of Africa, but this Sunday morning brings native Africans, Negroes of this Western

Hemisphere, and Negroes from every country together, because we suffer in common.

Wheresoever we turn our eyes unto the four corners of the world we find the Negro suffering from the abuse of other races. Because of the perpetration of these injustices we find it necessary at this time to so unite our forces morally, financially, and physically to tear asunder the bonds that held us in slavery for 300 years. So we are here this morning, not for the purpose of compromising the cause of the Negro with any race or with any nation; we are here this morning as a free people, claiming equal rights with the rest of mankind in this creation that God Almighty gave to us all. We are here, as I said awhile ago, to frame a bill of rights, to write a new constitution that 400,000,000 black men, women and children shall support with their life blood if necessary. We are here because this is the age when all peoples are striking out for freedom, for liberty, and for democracy. We have entered this age of struggle for liberty at the same time with the people of Ireland, the people of Egypt, of India, and the people of the Eastern states of Europe.

We are here, the representatives of 400,000,000 of Negroes, determined to carve a way for ourselves in this world that God placed us in. We are here because we recognize ourselves as men, and we desire to be free men.

INTRODUCES DISTINGUISHED DELEGATE.

The delegates assembled here this morning come from all parts of the world. We have on the platform at this time one of the most respected and distinguished citizens of the great Republic of Liberia, the future headquarters of this U.N.I.A., after the convention ends on the 31st of August. I take great pleasure in introducing to you at this time the Hon. Gabriel Johnson, mayor of the city of Monrovia, Liberia, and general of the Liberian army. (The audience here stood as a token of respect to Mr. Johnson, and the band played the national anthem.)

Continuing, Mr. Garvey said: Considering all the circumstances and environments that surround the Negro in Western civilization, we of the U.N.I.A. believe that the best thing for the Negro to do is to consolidate his racial force in building his own motherland, Africa. We believe that any progress, any advancement made by the Negro in Western alien civilization is a progress, is an advancement that is insecure, because at any time the alien forces desire to destroy the progress and development of the Negro—the advancement of the Negro—they can do so.

For the security of our racial strength, economically[,] commercially, educationally, and in every way, we have decided to concentrate on the building of the great Republic of Liberia, and to make Liberia one of the great powers of the world. We believe that the Negro is entitled to national protection. Whether we be citizens or denizens of America, we suffer from the abuse of an alien race. Whether we be citizens or denizens of Great Britain, we suffer in a similar manner, and so, too, all through the nations and the countries where alien races hold sway. We therefore believe that the time has come when the 400,000,000 of us—the millions of America, the millions of the West Indies, of South and Central America, and of Africa—should unite our physical, moral and financial strength for the building up of a great government, a great nation that will protect us, whether we be in the United States of America, in Great Britain, or under any other alien government.

PROPAGANDA CIRCLES GLOBE

For the last two years we have spent over a million dollars to scatter our propaganda to the four corners of the world, and we who spent the money, and the members of the association who subscribed the money have absolutely no regret for so doing. We are satisfied that our sacrifice of two and a half years has brought together this great convention of Negroes from all parts of the world and we feel sure that within the 31 days of this month the Negroes who come to this convention will not depart without writing history for their own race—a history that we ourselves will be proud of and our posterity cherish.

Today as you assemble in Liberty Hall you present to me the noblest company and most brilliant array of Negroes in the world at this time. I feel sure that outside of the scattered branches of the U.N.I.A. there is no group of Negroes thinking as we are in terms of freedom, not fettered freedom, but absolute freedom.

We are the only set of Negroes who believe that if it is right for the white man to rule and dominate, if it is right for the yellow man to rule and dominate, it is also right for 400,000,000 black people to rule and dominate and shape their own destiny. That is the reason why we meet in Liberty Hall, not as cringing sycophants, but as men and women standing erect and demanding our rights from all quarters.

Let me bid the delegates welcome to Liberty Hall, the cradle of Negro liberty. Let me compliment the members of the United [*Universal*] Negro Improvement Association for the splendid work they have done in the last two and a half years because the burden of this work fell on us here in New York. For two and a half years we have had to sacrifice thousands and thousands of dollars, indeed, hundreds of thousands of dollars. We have had to sacrifice our time day in and day out, in order to spread this propaganda. When men of our own race despised and discouraged us, when men of other races spurned us and did everything to prevent us from organizing, we got together and floated the banner of the red, the black and the green until today we have over 700 branches of this association in every nation of the world. We have an active membership of three and a half million and after this convention we feel that in the space of twelve months we will not only have three and a half but at least one hundred million members in the U.N.I.A.

We are hoping in another decade that the Negro will be organized universally so as to be able to take care of his own liberty, of his own freedom, and establis[h] his own democracy. And let me say to you that we will do this not because we are all powerful among ourselves, but because we will hold Jesus Christ as our standard bearer, and wheresoever He leads, we will follow in like manner as we followed Him up the heights of Calvary. When the white man despised and spurned Him, a member of the black race, Simon the Cyrenian, took up the cross and bore it with Jesus. And as we bore it then and followed Him up the heights of Calvary, so are we following Him now.

The delegates who came to New York have absolutely nothing to fear. There is no race or nation in the world that can intimidate the present day Negro. The New Negroes' cry is that we must have liberty or death. We are men. We were sent to France and Flanders and Mesopotamia by the white man to fight for democracy. That democracy we have not yet won, and we will continue to fight for it until we have completely won it for ourselves. We refuse to beg or cringe any longer; we demand our rightful place in the sun. So let me bid you again welcome to Liberty Hall—welcome to the first convention of the U.N.I.A. I trust our deliberations for the 31 days of August will be brimful of great results. I feel they will be. Therefore I ask the support of every Negro in this State, morally and financially, to help this convention achieve the success which it rightly deserves.

SILENT PARADE.

Following the morning session a silent parade took place, in which over 5,000 members and delegates to the convention participated. The pageant extended in length from 130th to 140th streets. The line of march was from Liberty Hall on West 138th street to Lenox avenue, thence to 140th street and Seventh avenue, down Seventh avenue to 130th street, thence east to Lenox avenue, up Lenox avenue and back to Liberty Hall. The parade was headed by Hon. Marcus Garvey and other high dignitaries. In automobiles were the Mayor of Monrovia and others, followed by officials and representatives of the association, all in their robes of office. The bands of the U.N.I.A. and Black Star Line were in line and also members of the Black Cross Nurses, with the insignia of the black cross on their caps. What drew particular attention (and the sidewalks of the streets along the entire course of the parade were thronged with people watching the pageant as it passed) were the placards and banners carried by the marchers with the inscriptions, "Africa for the Africans," "The Negro Wants Liberty," "Negroes Helped Win the War."

The parade created a profound impression, being conducted in an orderly manner and reflecting creditably not only upon the association, but upon the race as well as an earnest of their desire to unite their forces for mutual benefit.

AFTERNOON SESSION.

The afternoon session was even more largely attended than the morning session. The services were of a religious character. Addresses were delivered by the Rev. Dr. J. D. Brooks, Secretary-General, and by Dr. D. D. Lewis, president of the Montreal Division, Canada. The President-General occupied the chair. Dr. Brooks made a stirring, eloquent appeal to individualism among the Negroes as a race—to originality of thought and independence of action. Dr. Lewis is a prominent physician in Montreal. He spoke forcefully, and, like Dr. Brooks, struck a responsive chord in the hearts of his auditors.

The Hon. Marcus Garvey in welcoming the delegates, said: Fellow members of the Universal Negro Improvement Association, delegates to the convention, once more it is my good fortune to welcome you to Liberty Hall. We are assembled here this afternoon for the second meeting of the opening of our great international convention, the purpose of which is known to all of us. For two and a half years the Universal Negro Improvement Association has been teaching the doctrine of unity among the Negro peoples of the world. Through the success of the teaching of this doctrine we are able to bring together in New York at this time Negroes from every known part of the world. We are here to celebrate the greatest event in the history of the Negro for the last five hundred years. We are here because we are a suffering public. We are here because we are tired of being a suffering people. We are here because we desire our liberty. We believe that all those human rights that are common to the rest of mankind should also be enjoyed by us and for that purpose we assemble ourselves in this great international convention to discuss the ways and means through which we will get that liberty that we have been deprived of for the last five hundred years. We are here not for the purpose of apologizing for our race, our color, or anything pertaining to us as a people. We are here because we regard and respect ourselves as men, and as four hundred millions of a race we desire our place in the sun. That place has been denied us; that place we are determined to take for ourselves (applause).

So we are assembled for the second time in this cradle of liberty— Liberty Hall is indeed the cradle of liberty. It is the Mecca at which all men who desire freedom assemble for the purpose of giving expression to their thoughts and we no less than the rest of mankind shall continue to give expression to our thoughts until we achieve the things we have set for ourselves. There is a glorious destiny for the Negro and before the Negro, but that destiny is to the Negroes' own making and we of the Universal Negro Improvement Association are determined to carve a way to a brighter and more glorious destiny. So I once more bid you welcome to Liberty Hall. I once more say to you delegates: Be of good cheer. I once more say to the members of the Universal Negro Improvement Association: Be without fear. There is but one fear that we know and that is the fear that Roosevelt talked about, namely: Fear God and know no other fear. (Applause.)

As men we live; as free men we shall die. This is an age that is causing all men to feel that they are entitled to liberty and to freedom. We are not selfish in our desire for freedom. We know that there are many other peoples that are suffering just as we are suffering. We are in sympathy with the great Irish people who have been overrun for the last 700 years by the tyrants of Great Britain; we are in sympathy with the people of India, with a population of 380,000,000, who are also dominated by Great Britain. We are in sympathy with the Chinese, with the Egyptians but one and all we are in sympathy with ourselves, and we shall so unite our forces that within the next decade we shall find ourselves a free people and a great people, too. Therefore, let me again welcome you to Liberty Hall. We will not prolong the service this afternoon, because we are to prepare for the greater service tonight. There will be two principal speakers. I will now introduce the first one to you, one whom you know well, a man of great eloquence, of great ability, a man of great foresight, who has linked himself with the Universal Negro Improvement Association because he believes it is the only way, the only one and true way for the Negro to seek his salvation. It gives me great pleasure to now present to you the Special Secretary General of the Universal Negro Improvement Association, Dr. Brooks.

DR. BROOKS SPEAKS.

Rev. Dr. J. D. Brooks said: ["]Mr. President General, Members, Fellow Sufferers, Pilgrims Far From Home, Seeking Their Way Back to Their Father's House—I greet you this afternoon. This is one of the many times in my life that I am too happy to even think of speaking. This convention is a distinct triumph for Garveyism. If ever a man triumphed over all his foes this splendid man triumphed in that parade held this afternoon. (Applause.) There has been nothing like it among Negroes since God said 'Let there be light.' And I was happy because I could see a burden being lifted from his heart and shoulders and see that slow smile that so seldom comes over its face, because of the burdens that he has to bear. And each moment, each second of that parade this afternoon, my heart went out as I read the banners, the words and the inscriptions on the banners. I have been thinking for a day or two of some of the lasting statements of our Lord, some of the statements that come into our lives, that affect us as human beings. Some statements that should be treasured by all folks everywhere, and this statement has been clinging to me for the last several days. Our Master uttered it in speaking to a crowd of discouraged, disheartened, persecuted, abused Jews who had lost their liberty, who were even then suffering at the hands of the oppressor and nation that governed them. They were tired; their souls were weary; they were burdened; they had looked long, and with expectant eyes. Their hopes had been raised. Men of their mind had come to them and bid them have hope and said that the Lord would lead them on and on, and that the blessing of heaven promised them would be theirs. They had grown weary and discouraged, so many men had come to them; a leader had arisen here and one there, and the crowd had followed after each leader, but at no time had a leader come who was able to gather them together because of the message that he brought and because of the force and personality that he had. But this Man of Galilee, standing in the crowd, knowing they were discouraged and disheartened, said this thing to them. The Jews wanted liberty, they wanted freedom. The Jews were tired of being oppressed, tired of the burden they had to bear. Their very souls were growing tired and were crying out for liberty, and the Master said to them: 'If the Son shall make you free, you shall be free indeed.'[4] That message went into the hearts of those Jews. It touched the keynote, it revived their spirits, for I tell you that there is no freedom save that freedom that gives freedom to soul as well as to body. If you are going to be actually free, then you must be untrammeled entirely.["] . . .[5]

EVENING SESSION.

The evening session was the climax for the day of the convention. So great was the attendance that all available space in the vast auditorium was occupied, equally as many persons being on the outside eager to gain admittance. The services were of the same character as in the morning. Those officiating were Rev. Paul, Rev. S[e]lkridge and Rev. Ferris, with the President General occupying the chair. A solo was rendered by Mr. Edward Steele, a duet by Mesdames Houston and Robinson and a solo by Miss Ethel Clark. The Rev. Dr. Ferris, Miss Henrietta Vinton Davis, Rev. Dr. Brooks and Rev. Dr. E[a]son delivered stirring addresses.

Despite the somewhat inclement weather the first day's session of the greatest Negro convention ever held in this or any other country was a distinct success. The presence of so many self-conscious, determined people, all members of the Negro race, was an inspiration in itself to all who witnessed the ceremonies. . . .[6]

DR. LEWIS SPEAKS

Dr. D. D. Lewis rose and said: His Majesty (addressing the chair), I must say that never in the history of my life was I called upon that words so completely failed me to express how much I appreciate the fact of having a man who has toiled as you have until you have brought to reality one of the greatest gatherings of Africans in the history of North America. And sir, when I say "His Majesty" it means far more than when the king is approached, because of the great difficulties under which you have labored. Sir, we honor you beyond what words can express (cheers), and if it were not for the fact that you are such a young man and are just beginning your career, I think I speak the sentiments of every African—and I am not forgetting the Afro-Americans or what not—we are all Africans today—when I say we would put you down in some great big cosy place and say: "Rest, my lord, you have worked hard and you are worthy of all that we can do for you" (cheers).

But inasmuch as in two and a half years you have come to a city—the biggest in North America—the hardest city in North America, to bring people together and to do such wonderful work in such a short time, we feel that we will have to continue to keep you in harness until you are [at] least about 80 years old and then we will sit you down (Cheers).

We know, sir, what you have undergone. We watched you closely even before I gave a snap for what you were doing. I heard a great deal about the movement, and I began to watch critically, and I began to watch suspiciously, and when you made good I decid[ed] I would lock arms with you and [fol]low you to the end.

My friends, pardon me whe[n] [I] say that, to save me, I do not know what to say; but I want with all my heart and with all my might to congratulate you for the great work you have done. When I remember that just a little more than a month ago I was in your city and found just half of this building—they were just beginning to dig a little—I talked with this great man (pointing to the chairman) and he said: "Yes, we will have it ready; we are having difficulties, but we are going to have it ready." I said to myself, "This man is dreaming night dreams; he is hoping for the impossible." I went back to Montreal and although I wanted the thing to come to pass so badly, I just had to say they were busy as could be in New York getting ready for the convention; but down in my heart I said to myself: "My God, what is going to happen when [the] people find out the building is [not] going to be ready?" (Laughter.) The first thing yesterday morning when I arrived in this city, Mr. Garvey took me in a taxi and we drove by here, and when I saw the building completed, I said: "Well, this man is going to do anything in this world but turn white." (Cheers and laughter.)

My friends, whatever you have suffered—whatever disappointments you have gone through—whatever toil you have undergone, today you are paid thousandfold for your labor. When you are able to make the demonstration you have made under the terrible conditions in which we live now, it means that you undoubtedly have got God on your side; and if it is the devil on your side who has enabled you to succeed as you have, let God go and follow the devil. But God is undoubtedly with you, and I am proud beyond measure.

I am glad today that I am among Africans, American-Africans, German-Africans, Canadian-Africans, Japanese-Africans, Chinese-Africans, white Africans and all kinds of Africans that there are other nations. That is true, and because of that you ought not to be surprised that we are a wonderful race[,] you ought not to be surprised that we are able in thirty days' time to do what we have done, when you realize that the brains of the whole world are all concentrated in one race—this race of ours. We have got some of the other [fe]llow in us and we have got a [lot] of ourselves. So we are compelled to do wonders; we are compelled [to]make the world open their [eyes]. But my friends, let us remember—let us not forget that this is only the commencement.

Twelve years ago last month, when I was finishing school to begin my life's work, Dr. Watts said to me: "Young man, do not lose your head, you have not finished anything; I am going to give you a diploma tomorrow, but it is only the beginning of your life's work." Now that you have gone ahead and made it possible for these delegates from all over the world to meet here because of the propaganda you have started, it means that you have created a great interest and you are just beginning to do your life's work. And now more than ever you have reasons to concentrate your mind, your heart, your soul, on doing something real, tangible and worth while. You have done something now to make the world [open] their eyes; to let them know [th]at you mean business, and that you are in earnest. You have shown to the world that you can do things, and now you want to be able to measure arms.

I never will think that the other fellow did me any harm when he brought me here. The greatest blessing that ever happened to me was when I was taken from my home in Africa, and I do not give a snap what the man looks like who brought me from there, for color does not appeal to me. What a man is capable of doing is the only thing that interests me. Had he not brought me over I presume I would have been paddling around Lagos, wandering, and thinking nothing. But coming into contact with civilization, coming in contact with something different to what I was used to, put into me the determination to cope with other men. We need something to bring out the best that there is in us. The troubles through which we have gone are only the result of what you see today.

When we as medical men go into a sick room we always think of cause and effect. The cause that has brought about this effect has meant to you and me a great awakening; has brought to you and me the idea that we are sleeping on our [*word mutilated*]—that we have been crying [and] pleading for somebody to do [som]ething for us which we can do [for] ourselves. Every man must take care of his own house. I do not expect a man to take care of my wife unless he enjoys the comforts that I should enjoy, and inasmuch as I would not like that, I am going to keep on the job and work day and night to take care of my own wife. So, my friends, if you expect the other fellow to do something for us, he is going to do it to his own advantage, and he is going to enjoy what we ourselves enjoy.

So this great man Marcus Garvey woke up over there and he saw that things were not going right, and whether he knew how to pray or not, he realized that he had a mouth with which he could speak with a voice of thunder, and as soon as he had gone through school he began to speak; he spoke in spite of criticism, and here is the result of his speaking. (Applause.) We [hon]or him, and we must now give [sup]port to carry this work on. He has said: "I have carried it by mys[elf] as far as I can, but it is a big job, and I have called you together to help me to form some kind of constitution which will be creditable to bring before the world and say: 'Here is our platform, what are you going to do about it? Are you going to regard us as one, one like all other races, or have we got to fight for it,' and the other fellow is going to look us over and scratch his head and say: 'Well, boys, you seem to mean business, I am going to settle with you fifty-fifty.'["] But if you go scattered and unorganized, one bunch saying I want this, and the other bunch saying I don't want anything, I have a place to sleep and something to eat, I can rent a car once in a while and tour the streets, I can buy a second-hand suit on the installment plan, and therefore I am quite satisfied— you will get no recognition from the other fellow. But when you go showing that you have an organization, that you mean business, that you have got money, ships, factories, etc., he will say: "Boys, we kept you back as long as we could, but we are going to work hand in hand, and we are going to make this a great world for all mankind." I do not feel that I am free and that the world is free until we are able to go wherever we please if we can pay our way. I feel like the devil if I go somewhere and I cannot have comforts when I am able to pay for them. If I am ragged, di[rty], uncouth, and do not know how to meet people, then I am willing to take a back seat, but if I [can] act as decently and speak as in[telli]gently as the other fellow, the color of my skin has nothing to do with it. (Cheers.)

And so, the other fellow is waiting until we can measure arms with him; he is only waiting until we can do as much as he can do; then he will have to come across, and if not it will be an awful day. They say we are 400,000,000 Negroes. I do not think anybody in the world but God knows how many Negroes there are; and, inasmuch as we are so many, and we do not know how many there are, let us get organized, and the other fellow, since he does not know how many we are, will say: "Boys, it's all right; we are going to do business; we are going to exchange commerce; we are going to enjoy prosperity in common; we are all men, and according to the Constitution we are all born equal." Thus we will be [able] to understand one another and [we] will have here a perfect heaven on earth. I am not concerned about [that] heaven over yonder. What I want is a heaven here. Although the preachers tell us about a heaven over there they do not seem willing to leave here very quickly, and inasmuch as they want to stick around, so do I.

I am proud to see here my own countryman, the Lord Mayor of Monrovia, the Hon. Mr. Johnson. I am proud for you to see that he is a real man. I know that you have often wondered when you saw a native African, how he was made a little different from what you have been told. I am also proud that we have here a prince from my own home—Lagos. You will see that we understand one another, and nobody is afraid. Through this great organization, and through the instrumentality of this great man (meaning Mr. Garvey) we are able to come together, and we are going to do some real business. We may have little spats, but that is natural. Men differ so far as their opinions are concerned, but we will settle our differences and shake hands afterward. To my mind the most daring men I have ever seen, read or heard of are Teddy Roosevelt and Marcus Garvey. (Loud cheers.) . . . [7]

Printed in *NWCB*, 2 August 1920. Original headlines abbreviated.

1. Rev. P. E. Paul was the chaplain of the New York local of the UNIA (*NW*, 31 December 1921).

2. Actually John Frederick Selkridge, a bishop of the United Christian church who served as a special adviser to Garvey. Selkridge later became a "field worker" for the UNIA. His main responsibility was selling notes for the Liberian Construction Loan and selling stock in the Black Star Line. While traveling in Pennsylvania, Selkridge reported the loss of his suitcase and all of its contents, which included stock certificates and loan notes. He was dismissed in February 1921 for carelessness in performing his duties. He later joined the African Orthodox church, and in May 1926 he was ordained into the AOC ministry, serving at Christ Church in Brooklyn (*NW*, 26 February and 10 September 1921; *The Negro Churchman* 4, no. 4 [April 1926]: 8).

3. Actually Harry R. Watkis, who worked at the BSL office and later served as a witness on Garvey's behalf in his legal actions against Amy Ashwood Garvey (*Marcus Garvey* v. *Amy Garvey*, NNHR, case no. 24028).

4. Probably a paraphrase of John 8:32, "The truth shall make you free."

5. Portions of Brooks's speech have been omitted.

6. The speeches of William Ferris and Henrietta Vinton Davis have been omitted.

7. J. W. H. Eason's address has been omitted.

PROGRAMME

SUNDAY, AUGUST 1ST.

1. Divine Service in Liberty Hall, 10 A. M. All High Officers of the Executive Council in Robes of Office

2. Silent Parade of All Members and Delegates at 1 o'clock P. M., Starting from Office of the Association, 54-56 W. 135th Street.

3. Divine Service in Liberty Hall at 3 o'clock P. M. Officers in Robes of Office.

4. Divine Service in Liberty Hall at 8 o'clock P. M. Officers in Robes of Office.

MONDAY, AUGUST 2ND.

1. Opening of Convention at 10 A. M. at Liberty Hall. All Delegates Presenting their Credentials.

2. Mass Parade of All Delegates and Members, Starting from 54-56 W. 135th Street, at 2 o'clock P. M.

3. Big Public Mass Meeting in Madison Square Garden. 26th Street and Madison Avenue, at 8 o'clock sharp

2

PROGRAMME

OF

FIRST TWO DAYS

INTERNATIONAL
CONVENTION

OF

Universal Negro Improvement Association
AND
African Communities League

SUNDAY, AUGUST 1st
AND
MONDAY, AUGUST 2nd

1920

NEW YORK CITY

(*Source:* NN-Sc).

Presentation by the Brooklyn Division

[*Negro World Convention Bulletin*, 2 August 1920]

A striking feature of Sunday's program was the presentation of a specially upholstered chair, the gift of the Brooklyn Division to the Hon. Marcus Garvey. Dr. Paul, who made the presentation address, said in part:

"Hon. President-General—It is the sincere wish of the Brooklyn Division of the U.N.I.A. that I should at this time honor you for the faithful and indefatigable services which you have rendered, not only to the people of America, but to the people of the world—honor you for the splendid leadership you have rendered to us. They have asked me at this time to present to you the chair which stands behind you now, that you shall use it as long as you are president of this association; and if it please the association and God Almighty to send you to Africa, that you shall take that chair to Africa with you. I take great pleasure, then, in presenting that chair for your use and comfort."

MR. GARVEY RESPONDS.

"It is with a heart full of gladness that I accept from the Brooklyn Division of the Universal Negro Improvement Association for the people of Barbados[1] this chair. I shall make use of the chair, as you so stated, and I shall endeavor to occupy the chair and to perform the duties incumbent upon me even as I have done in the past. No token of appreciation, caring not how small it is, that comes from the members of this association, goes by without my grateful thanks. I thank you for this token. And I repeat that I shall continue to do for this association my very, very best; and as Barbados has shown so splendidly in the getting together of the various groups—I believe they are at the head of the list financially—it seems to me that Barbados has great inspiration behind it as a country and that that inspiration follows the citizens of that country wheresoever they go; and if, in sitting in that chair, I can get some of the inspiration of Barbados, I shall be satisfied. I thank you, sirs, in the name of the Universal Negro Improvement Association for the splendid gift."

Printed in *NWCB*, 2 August 1920. Original headline omitted.

1. The Brooklyn Division may have been composed of many recent Barbadian immigrants.

Report of UNIA Convention

[[New York, August 2, 1920]]

The morning session convened precisely at 10:30 o'clock. There was a large number of delegates present from the various States and branches throughout . . . [*words mutilated*] and South America, Central America, the West Indies and Africa.

Hon. Marcus Garvey, President-General of the Association, arrived promptly at the appointed hour and, addressing the gathering, said: I have to announce to the delegates and visitors that this morning's session is only for the registering of delegates by the registrar, and the visitors and delegates can make use of the hall until the parade starts from the offices of the Association, 54–56 West 135th street. I repeat it is only for the purpose of registering the delegates, so that we can know the people who have come to be represented at the convention. So, the delegates will please form in line and get their credentials verified, so that there will be no confusion.

The convention opens up in real business form tomorrow morning (Tuesday), when delegates will present their cards at the door to show that they were duly elected or sent as delegates to this convention. I would like it to be clearly understood that delegates will occupy front seats and participate in the deliberations of the convention, while members who are not assigned as delegates will have to occupy rear seats and act merely as listeners. They will not be allowed to take part in the debates. I reiterate that you can make use of the hall till one o'clock and then adjourn to the Association office, from whence the parade starts. . . .

Printed in *NWCB*, 3 August 1920.

Report of UNIA Parade

[[New York, 3 August 1920]]

. . . They said he couldn't do it. He did. He kept his word. That, in brief, is the story of yesterday's [*2 August*] parade, led by the one man who, by his vision and backbone, is putting the Negro on the map of real achievement—Marcus Garvey. Hitherto the name has been a household word among those who said he couldn't. It remains a household word among those same people, who now say he did. From one to another, like an electric current, the expression passed, "You've got to give it to Garvey!" Men who before hated, and denounced him were forced to admire him to-day; they still may not like him, but the man has conducted himself so nobly, on a plane so lofty and irreproachable, that his rankest and most persistent enemies are compelled to doff their hats out of sheer admiration and respect for the man's ability and achievement.

Put all the minuses of his mistakes and omissions against all the pluses of his successes, and by every known test, algebraically and otherwise, Marcus Garvey is great. To-day's parade has added one more feather to his already numerously feathered cap—one more chapter to the history of the New Negro in his strivings for self-determination and freedom; one more achievement to the credit of the race.

The day was ideal for the parade; not a cloud flecked the sky; no untoward incident arose to mar the propitiousness of the event. All Harlem was bedecked with streamers and bunting and flowers, the predominant colors being those of the U.N.I.A.—the red, the green and the black. The flags of the U.N.I.A., intertwined with the Stars and Stripes, were like unto a benediction, in the peaceful effect and calm it brought to the soul: the one emblematic of its peculiar liberal institutions that made possible such a demonstration as to-day's parade, the other no less significant of the much larger and greater freedom that will come to every Negro in his own UNITED STATES OF AFRICA. Truly, it was a scene that would have given the fathers untold satisfaction to behold. The aged, like Simeon, may now exclaim: "Now may thy servant depart in peace!"[1]

THE CRY OF LIBERTY.

The insistent note of the parade was Liberty; and so insistent, indeed, was this appeal that white women were seen to cry as in imagination they beheld the Negro achieving that measure of success that they themselves, under similar distressing conditions, in other parts of the world, are fighting to achieve for themselves.[2] One emotional Irishwoman, as the parade wended its way on 125th street, with tears upon her cheeks, in the anguish of despair, in the gloom of hopelessness, cried: "And, to think the Negroes will get their liberty before the Irish!" It was, indeed, pathetic.

One could observe, moreover, a visible change in the attitude of the Irish towards the Negro as manifested in to-day's parade. Hundreds of the police reserves (mostly Irishmen) were on duty for the parade, and their behavior was exemplary; so notably different from their customary conduct that it was almost astonishing. What was the reason for this remarkable change? It was largely sympathetic, and it takes a fellow-feeling to make us wondrously kind to each other. So were these Irish cops. May they and their fellow kinsmen never forget the day of their sufferings and tribulations should fortune favor them in their struggle for independence and freedom!

BIGGEST PARADE EVER STAGED

To-day's parade was the greatest ever staged anywhere in the world by Negroes. It was a parade expressive, as it was intended to be, of the Negro's serious, his unswerving and unswervable determination to solve his own problems by a larger reliance on his own resources and powers, physically, economically, religiously and otherwise, than heretofore. From now on the

Negro means to strike out for himself, or die in the attempt. For him it is a case of "root hog or die,"[3] and he means to do oodles of rooting before he dies. He doesn't intend to say "die" either until he is dead, when he can't say it at all. So, there! That is the New Negro's perspective in a nut-shell.

The procession lasted nearly three hours, and comprised not only the thousands of members of the New York Division of the Association, but the members of the numerous branches scattered throughout the Union, as well as members from the established branches in the West Indies, South and Central America, and Africa. These members all came to the city as delegates to the great convention to be held here during the entire month of August for the purpose of framing a constitution—a bill of rights—for the Negro peoples of the world.

THE LINE OF MARCH.

The parade started promptly at 2 o'clock from the offices of the Universal Negro Improvement Association, 54–56 West 135th street, marching up Lenox avenue to 145th street, down Seventh avenue to 125th street, and returning on Lenox avenue to point of departure. As the procession wended its way through the streets of Harlem it presented a thrilling, spectacular scene that was dazzling to the eyes of the most imaginative (this time imagination having been outguessed, as every onlooker must admit), and the great crowds that gathered along the route of march displayed their enthusiasm by cheering wildly as first one branch and then another of the association passed by.

The parade was headed by four mounted policemen, followed by Mr. Jeremiah Certain, first vice-president of the Black Star Line Steamship Corporation, and Mr. "Socrates,"[4] secretary of the Negro Factories Corporation, both of whom were mounted. Immediately following in an automobile were the Hon. Marcus Garvey, president-general of the association, and the Hon. Gabriel Johnson, Mayor of Monrovia, the capital city of Liberia. Mr. Garvey, attired in resplendent robes of office, was vociferously acclaimed by the people all along the line. Following the president-general were other high officials of the association, also in automobiles and wearing their regalia. Conspicuous among these were the Rev. Dr. Eason, chaplain-general; Prof. Wm. H. Ferris, M.A. (Harvard and Yale), chancellor; Rev. Dr. [J]. D. Brooks, secretary-general; Miss Henrietta Vinton Davis, international organizer; Mr. Vernal Williams, counsellor at law, and Mme. Barrier Houston, sweet singer and popular soloist of the association. The remainder of the procession was made up as follows:

ORDER OF MARCH.

Black Star Line Choir, on foot; the Philadelphia Legion, marching, nearly 200 strong; the Philadelphia U.N.I.A. Band; the Philadelphia contingent with banners showing they represent the 9,500 members of that division

of the association; the Norfolk, Va., Band; the Black Cross nurses of Philadelphia, who with their fellow sisters of the New York division, made a truly
inspiring spectacle. Clad in their white costumes, with their flowing white
caps and their black crosses, these beautiful women of a sorrowed and
bleeding but determined race, thrilled us men with pride and devotion to the
cause that eventually will send us the call to make the supreme sacrifice on the
battle plains of our beloved Africa, where their banner inscription, "We
Mean to Aid Our Boys," will be realized in faithful and loving ministrations.
Following were the U.N.I.A. Band of New York city; contingents from
Jamaica, Virgin Islands, Panama, St. Lucia, St. Eustatius, New York, North
Carolina, South Carolina, Georgia, Illinois, Ohio, Bermuda, Nigeria (West
Africa), Grenada. Then came the New York Fifteenth Band, who whooped it
for themselves as is their wont. Next were contingents from Trinidad, St.
Kitts, the Bahama Islands, Barbados, Nevis, East Orange (N. J.), British
Guiana, Washington (D. C.), Montreal (Canada) and about 500 automobiles
bringing up the rear, and behind these for the finale two mounted policemen.

SLOGANS GALORE.

The various branches all carried banners bearing such appropriate
inscriptions as: "Africa for the Africans"; "Advance to Victory"; "One God,
One Aim, One Destiny"; "Down With Lynching"; "Liberty or Death"; the
Black Cross nurses of New York carried the slogan[:] "We Stand Ready to
Aid our Boys"; "Africa Must Be Free"; "The Negro Fought in Europe; He
Can Fight in Africa"; "The Negro Is the Greatest Fighter"; "Freedom for
All"; "Long Live America"; "We Live for a Purpose"; "What Will France Do
in Africa?"; "The Negro Gave Civilization to the World"; "United We Stand
for African Liberty"; "We Trace History and Our Claims"; "Under This Sign
We Conquer" (the sign of joined hands signifying Negroes united); "What
of the New African Army?"; "What Will England Do in Africa?"; "Will They
Make the Negro Fight in Africa?"; "Honor to the Stars and Stripes";
"Garvey the Negro Moses—Long May He Live"; "All Men Were Created
Equal"; "The New Negro Wants Liberty, 400,000,000 Black Men Shall be
Free"; "What Will Italy Do in Africa?"; "Africa First, Last and All the
Time"; "Freedom for All"; "We Believe in the Liberal Institutions of
America"; "Africa a Nation One and Indivisible"; "Toussaint L'Ouverture
Was an Abler Soldier Than Napoleon"; "Garvey, the Man of the Day"; "The
New Negro Has No Fear," etc.

NEGROES OF THE WORLD.

The parade was truly a getting together of Negroes of the World, for
nearly all America and the West Indies were represented nor was Canada,
Panama nor Africa omitted. Each group was identified under the banner of
its respective country, state or island. Among them were New York, Georgia,
Virginia, North and South Carolina, New Jersey, Ohio, Illinois, District of

Columbia, Massachusetts, Pennsylvania, Panama, Nigeria (West Africa), Jamaica, Barbados, Trinidad, St. Kitts, Nevis, Virgin Islands, the Bahamas, etc.

The Black Star Line, the U.N.I.A. and the Fifteenth (New York Regiment) bands were in attendance, with nine additional bands from other divisions of the association. The crowd went wild with applause as the Fifteenth Band swung along up Lenox avenue and down Seventh avenue, playing marches, interspersed with popular, jazzy music.

The parade on the whole was carried out without a hitch and proved a great success. It demonstrated more than anything else the popularity of the great movement organized by the Hon. Marcus Garvey two and one-half years ago, which now embraces Negroes from every known part of the world.

Printed in *NWCB*, 3 August 1920.

1. Luke 2:29.
2. A reference to the British suffrage movement, led by Sylvia and Cristabel Pankhurst.
3. Southern folk expression, meaning to struggle to escape a lethal enemy.
4. Socrates was the nickname given to Arden Bryan by Garvey.

Report of a Meeting at Liberty Hall

[*Negro World Convention Bulletin*, 3 August 1920]

The parade ended at Liberty Hall, where for about half an hour the assemblage listened to speeches delivered by President General Garvey and representatives of delegations from various parts of the United States and from abroad, all of whom expressed themselves in terms of highest enthusiasm at the magnificent demonstration which had been witnessed and extended the greetings of the respective branches which they represented.

President General Marcus Garvey said: "Fellow members of the Universal Negro Improvement Association, Delegates to the Convention—Today [*2 August*] marks the formal opening of the first annual convention of the Universal Negro Improvement Association and African Communities League. As you view this assemblage you will find it composed of men and women delegates who have been sent from different parts of the world to attend this, our first annual convention. We are assembled for the purpose of discussing the great problems that confront us as a race and as a people. We are assembled for the purpose of framing a constitution that will govern the Negro peoples of the world. We are assembled as delegates to this convention for the purpose of framing the Bill of Rights of the Negro peoples of the world. We are here because, as a suffering people, we desire freedom. We are here because we are tired of being abused by the other powers and races of the world. We are here because we desire to make Africa a great power and the greatest power in the world. (Cheers.) We are here out of 82 years of slavery—those of you from the West Indies. We are here out of 50 odd years of slavery in America—those of us who are Americans. All of us, whether West Indians or Americans, being Negroes, have been separated from Africa for the last 300 years, and we are now united into one solid body under the colors of the red, the black and the green to declare the freedom of Africa. (Tumultuous applause.)

THANKS NEW YORK LOCAL.

["]Let me compliment you for this splendid parade in which you marched today. You have at least impressed this great city of New York—and this city will flash the news to the other cities and countries of the world—that we are a serious and determined people. (Cheers.)

"The parade of yesterday and the parade of today has at least driven home to the hearts and souls and minds of those who looked on that the New Negro is not to be trifled with, but that the New Negro must be taken seriously in his desire for liberty and for freedom and for a fuller democracy. (Cheers.) Again it gives me great pleasure to welcome to the shrine of liberty—Liberty Hall—all the delegates of the U.N.I.A. from all over the world. Let me say a few words of compliment to the representatives of the New York Local that has done so much to enable the delegates to find seats in Liberty Hall. We of New York have done the best we possibly could to make Liberty Hall sufficiently large to accommodate and seat all the delegates who have come to us. New York has done splendid work in two and a half years. It is through New York that the world became afire for the U.N.I.A., and it is my bounden duty to give second place in this great World Convention to the great division of Philadelphia. (Cheers.) Philadelphia has rung true to the colors of the red, the black and the green; but there is no city that can vie with New York with its 25,000 members." (Cheers.)

DELEGATES OFFER CONGRATULATIONS.

Prof. W. H. Ferris, Miss Henrietta Vinton Davis and Dr. J. W. H. Eason, in a few well-chosen words, congratulated the members of the Association on the grand showing made in the parade.

Rev. Dr. J. D. Brooks: "All honor to God and Hon. Marcus Garvey, who has made a new page in the history of the world, and who by the parade of yesterday and today has served notice on all of the folks everywhere that the Negroes hereafter must be reckoned with." (Loud cheers.)

Miss Sara Branch: "I am glad to see such a great demonstration and I hope to meet you all in Africa soon." (Vociferous cheers.)

Rev. Tobin,[1] delegate from Bermuda, said: "Over there in mid-ocean lies 365 islands which are coupled together and called 'The Land of the Lilies and the Roses.' It is Bermuda. She is but a three-months-old daughter, but by making rapid strides she numbers 600 members. I bring the greetings of Bermuda and want to let you know that we stand side by side with you, and that we hope that within the near future the banner of the U.N.I.A. and

A.[C].L. will float not only over here in New York, but over in Liberia and the other portions of Africa, so that indeed Africa which gave civilization to the world, and Ethiopia may yet stretch out her hands unto God, not only in the attitude of pleading, but in bestowing upon mankind once more those blessings she gave to the world when it was yet unborn." (Cheers.)

Rev. Cransom,[2] delegate from Baltimore: "I bring with me greetings from nearly half a thousand members in the city of Baltimore. As I viewed the great procession today my only regret was that the entire population of the city of Baltimore is not present here to witness it. But as I shall return and tender to them the news, I am sure that they shall get the enthusiasm and the vigor that shall cause them to unite with us not only numerically, but in every phase of membership. I hope that as we marched along in this great procession today, the time will not be far distant when we shall congregate ourselves as a mighty army marching to the conquest of our motherland, Africa." (Loud and prolonged cheers.)

Mr. Fred Toote, delegate from Philadelphia: "I bring greetings from the City of Brotherly Love. I want to say to you that we, the members of the Philadelphia division, are 9,500 strong (cheers), and our word to you is this: That the sword has been withdrawn from the scabbard and it will not return again till yon continent of Africa be in the hands of the men of color." (Loud cheers.)

Dr. J. D. Gibson, delegate from Boston, Mass.: "I bring to you greetings from the conservative city of Boston, Mass. Today we represent 2,300 strong who have enlisted under the banner of the U.N.I.A. and the colors of the red, black and the green, marching on with one cause to the goal—our Fatherland, Africa."

Mr. Napoleon Francis,[3] delegate from the Republic of Hayti: "I represent the division from the land of Toussaint l'Ouverture. We have heard your voice in America and have sent a delegate to bring you greetings and to say to you that when the time shall arrive to blow your bugle and cross the ocean to Africa we shall send you every available officer of the Haitian army." (Cheers.)

Printed in *NWCB*, 3 August 1920. Original headline omitted.

1. Actually Rev. Richard Hilton Tobitt (b. 1873), an Antigua-born minister, educator, and writer. He resided in Antigua throughout his childhood and pursued a career as a schoolmaster until his departure for Canada and the United States in 1910 for further education. Tobitt eventually graduated from Mico College in Jamaica, where he established an outstanding record as an athlete. In 1912 Tobitt went to Bermuda to become principal of St. George's High School, and he later became pastor of St. David's AME Church in Hamilton. Tobitt's career as an AME minister received a serious setback when he accepted a leadership position in the Garvey movement. His prominent role at the UNIA convention and his signing of the convention's "Declaration of Independence" resulted in an investigation by the Bermudian colonial government that led to a forced resignation from his position as pastor. While Garvey was on his West Indian tour in June 1921, Tobitt visited British Guiana (Guyana) on behalf of the UNIA. The local authorities discussed the possibility of expelling him, but could not find a legal basis on which to act. Tobitt received the support of the British Guiana Labor Union and enjoyed their approval during his campaign to form new UNIA divisions and sell shares in the Black Star Line. The government of Trinidad, Tobitt's next destination, prevented him from

landing at Port of Spain on 4 June 1921. After resigning from his pastorate in Bermuda, Tobitt left there and became pastor of an AME church in New York City. His position as chaplain of the Pioneer Negroes of the World, a Garveyite group based in New York City in the 1940s, is evidence of a continuing affiliation with Garveyism long after the movement declined (*NW*, 20 October 1923; Richard H. Tobitt to Winston S. Churchill, 15 August 1921, PRO, CO 318/364; Nellie E. Musson, *Mind the Onion Seed* [Hamilton, Bermuda: Musson, 1979], p. 138).

2. Actually Rev. Joseph Josiah Cranston.

3. Napoleon J. Francis was a UNIA organizer and representative of the Black Star Line in Port-au-Prince, Haiti. Francis also served as president of the UNIA branch in Haiti in 1921 (*L'Essor*, 25 November 1919; *NW*, 8 September 1921).

Report of a Madison Square Garden Meeting

[*Negro World Convention Bulletin*,
3 August 1920]

Never before in the history of the Negro has there been a gathering of the magnitude, splendor and enthusiasm of that held at Madison Square Garden last night under the auspices of the Universal Negro Improvement Association.

Following upon the heels of the unique parade that took place in the afternoon the [*illegible*] throng hurried to the Garden in order to secure seats early.

The seating capacity of the Garden, including the arena, is estimated at 25,000. Every available seat was occupied, not only the boxes and tiers of the four galleries were crowded, but the vast floor space of the building as well. On the north side was erected the speakers' platform, which was covered with the American flag and the flag of the U.N.I.A. These flags, similarly intertwined, hung in other parts of the hall, which together with the banners of the various branches and divisions of the association throughout its jurisdiction, presented a patriotic and pleasing appearance to the eye.

MR. GARVEY ACCLAIMED

Promptly at 8:45 o'clock the Hon. Marcus Garvey, President-General, entered the building from the west side, accompanied by other high officials of the association, distinguished guests and delegates to the convention, all regaled in their magnificent multi-colored robes of office. As the procession wended its way toward the speakers' stand, the audience rose en masse, saluted and cheered, the huzzas and applause that greeted the new leader of the Negro race created a deafening sound that reverberated throughout the great building. In the procession, and at its head, were the various bands of the association, as the Black Star Line Band, the U.N.I.A. Band, and the Fifteenth Regiment Band. The bands played "Onward, Christian Soldiers," as they marched into the hall, countermarching while Mr. Garvey and his official family took their places. Pandemonium reigned, so thunderous was the applause, the shouts and plaudits of the people as they gazed on the spectacle. Men and women cheered, waved handkerchiefs, threw their hats up into the air, and did everything else they possibly could to give vocal expression to their feelings of delight and admiration. If any one ever doubted that the Negroes of the world can be united, and are now actually uniting, such doubts, were any such persons present, must at once have been dispelled forever.

Marcus Garvey was acclaimed as no black man ever was acclaimed by black people before in this or any other country. And the vociferous acclaim given him was spontaneous and genuine, the enthusiasm manifested knowing no bounds. He bore the plaudits and cheers with becoming grace and dignity, bowing to right and left as the procession proceeded, in evident grateful acknowledgment of the extraordinary honors that were bestowed upon him.

DR. McGUIRE DELIVERS INVOCATION

Miss Henrietta Vinton Davis, International Organizer of the Association, presided and introduced the Rev. Dr. McGuire[1] who delivered the invocation. This was followed by a musical program, in which Mesdames Houston and Robinson, also Miss Clarke, took part. Mr. Edward Steele, the noted tenor, also sang. The Acme Quartet rendered several numbers. This part of the program was greatly enjoyed by the audience and gave a breathing spell, as it were, after their exertions in the great welcome accorded Mr. Garvey. Especial mention must be made of the solos rendered by Mesdames Houston, Robinson and Clarke, which were of the highest order and elicited encore after encore. The Acme Quartet did itself proud by singing original selections composed especially for the occasion.

Mr. Garvey, who was in evident splendid form and voice, delivered a most stirring and masterful address. It was a superb, eloquent statement of the purposes and objects of the Universal Negro Improvement Association. He was frequently interrupted by applause. Ther[e] could be no doubt, judged in the light of his address, the thoughts it expressed, and the spontaneous expressions of approval it evoked that Mr. Garvey is the man of the hour—the hero and recognized leader of the Negro race.

Other addresses were delivered, principal of which was the address of the Chaplain-General, Rev. Dr. J. W. Eason.

The meeting adjourned at 11 o'clock, thus closing a most memorable chapter in the race's history, the scenes attending which, and the addresses that were heard, being such in character as doubtless will ever remain vivid in the recollection of those who were present. It has carried the race one step higher in its march onward to higher things, and is further proof that the black people of the world have before them a great destiny to achieve which is now in course of realization.

PAYS MR. GARVEY GLOWING TRIBUTE

Miss Henrietta Vinton Davis, in introducing the President-General, said: I esteem it a very great honor to have the pleasure of introducing to you the man of the hour. (Cheers.) The man who has stood upon the Olympian heights, who has caught the vision of the gods for his people, whose clarion voice has been echoed from mountain top to mountain top until it has circled the globe, calling his brothers to arms. That man is the undaunted, the unconquerable, the incomparable Marcus Garvey. (Loud applause.)

Hon. Marcus Garvey rose and said: I have in my hand two telegrams, one received and one to be sent. The one received is from Louis Michael,[2] a Jew from Los Angeles, California. It reads as follows: "Los Angeles, Cal., August 1, 1920. Delegates of the Universal Negro Improvement Association: As a Jew, a Zionist and a Socialist I join heartily and unflinchingly in your historical movement for the reclamation of Africa. (Applause.) There is no justice and no peace in this world until the Jew and the Negro both control side by side Palestine and Africa. Louis Michael." (Loud applause.)

I hold also in my hand a telegram to be sent to the Hon. Edmund De Valeria, President of the Irish Republic: "25,000 Negro delegates assembled in Madison Squar[e] Garden in mass convention, representing 400,000,000 Negroes of the world, send you greetings as President of the Irish Republic. Please accept sympathy of Negroes of the world for your cause. We believe Ireland should be free even as Africa shall be free for the Negroes of the world. (Loud applause.) K[eep] up the fight for a free Ireland. Marcus Garvey, President-General of the Universal Negro Improvement Association." (Applause.)[3]

Members of the Universal Negro Improvement Association, Delegates to the great convention, Ladies and Gentlemen: We are met in this historic building tonight for the purpose of enlightening the world respecting the attitude of the new Negro. We are assembled here tonight as the descendants of a suffering people and we are also assembled as a people who are determined to suffer no longer. (Applause.) For three hundred years our forefathers and even ourselves suffered in this Western Hemisphere. For over five hundred years our forefathers on the great continent of Africa suffered from the abuse of an alien race. It was claimed that we were a backward people, not knowing the higher calling of civilization. That might have been true eighty-five years ago or eighty-three years ago. But when we remember that eighty-two years ago in the British West Indies—eighty-two years up to yesterday—millions of Negroes were set free from the bondage of slavery; when we remember that fifty odd years ago, in America, Negroes were set free from a bondage of slavery, and when we realize now that the Negroes of America and the West Indies claim a civilization co-equal with that of the white man, we declare, therefore, that what is good for the white man in this age is also good for the Negro. (Loud applause.)

The white race claim freedom, liberty and democracy. For that freedom; for that liberty; for that democracy they drenched Europe in blood for nearly four and a half years. In that bloody war, fought to maintain the standard of civilization and freedom of democracy they called out two million black men from Africa, the West Indies and America to fight that the world might enjoy the benefits of civilization. We fought as men; we fought nobly; we fought gloriously; but after the battle was won we were deprived of our liberties; our democracy, the glorious privileges for which we fought. And as we did not get those things out of the war, we shall organize four hundred million strong to float the banner of democracy on the great continent of Africa. (Loud applause.)

We have absolutely no apologies nor compromises to make where Negro rights and liberties are concerned. Just at this time, as we can see the world is reorganizing, the world is reconstructing itself, and in this reconstruction Ireland is striking out for freedom; Egypt is striking out for freedom; India is striking out for freedom; and the Negroes of the world shall do no less than strike out also for freedom. (Applause.) Freedom is the common heritage of mankind, and as God Almighty created us four hundred millions strong, we shall ask the reason why, and dispute every inch of ground with any other race, to find out why we also can not enjoy the benefits of liberty. (Applause.) We as a people do not desire what belongs to others. We have never yet desired what belonged to others. But others have always sought to deprive us of those things which belong to us. Our fathers might have been satisfied to have been deprived of their rights, but we new Negroes—we young men who were called out in this war; we young men who have returned from this war shall dispute every inch of right with every other race of the world until we win what belongs to us. (Applause.)

This convention of the U.N.I.A. is called for the purpose of framing a Bill of Rights for the Negro Race. We shall write a constitution within this month of August that shall guide and govern the destiny of four hundred million Negroes of the world. (Applause.) You know and understand what a constitution means to a people, to a government and to a nation. The Constitution of the United States of America, the greatest democracy of the world, means that a white American shall shed the last drop of his red blood in the defense of the Constitution. The Constitution of Great Britain means that every Anglo-Saxon shall shed the last drop of his blood to maintain the integrity of Great Britain. The constitution that we shall write within this month will mean that four hundred million black men, women and children shall shed the last drop of their blood to maintain this constitution. (Loud applause.) Wheresoever I go, whether it is in England, or in France, Germany, Spain or Italy; whether in Canada or in Australia, I am told, "This is a white man's country." Wheresoever I travel throughout the United States of America I am made to understand that I am "a nigger." If the Englishman claims England as his native habitat, and if the Frenchman claims France as his native habitat, and if the Canadian claims Canada as his native habitat, then the time has come for four hundred million Negroes to claim Africa as their native land. (Loud applause.)

If Europe is for the white man, if Canada is for the white man, then, in the name of God, Africa shall be for the black peoples of the world. We say, and we mean it[,] that we pledge our life's blood, our sacred blood to the battle-fields of Africa, to plant there the flag of Liberty, of Freedom and Democracy (applause). The most glorious death a man can die, is that which is given in self-defense, and to maintain the integrity of his race. We have been dying for the last five hundred years—and for whom? For an alien race. The time has come for the Negro to die for himself. (Great applause.)

The great President of this country, President Wilson, returned from Europe, and tells us that there is to be peace. David Lloyd George returned to England, and tells his fellow-countrymen that there is to be peace. Clemenceau returned to the cabinet of France, and gives out the statement that there is to be peace. Orlando and Sononi[4] of Italy went back to their government, and told their people that there is to be peace. But the hand-writing on the wall shows that the bloodiest and greatest war of all times is yet to come—the war when Asia shall match her strength against Europe for "the survival of the fittest," for the dominance of Oriental or Occidental civilization, one or the other.

STRIKE FOR AFRICAN REDEMPTION

Men, let me tell you this: That the hour has come for the Negro to mobilize his forces, 400,000,000 strong, for that bloody war, that bloody conflict, when Asia shall array herself against Europe. The time has arrived and is now opportune for the Negro to strike for African redemption (applause).

It is apparent that it is left to the Negro to teach the principles of mercy and justice. Shakespeare says:

"The quality of mercy is not strained;
It droppeth as the gentle rain from Heaven upon the place beneath;
It blesseth him that gives, and him that takes."

It is a glorious principle. The Negro has carried that principle with him for thousands of years; but the time has come for us to call a halt. And why? We realize that the other races of the world are living in a material and practical age of the world. They do not regard glorious and noble principles; they regard only those things that will make them happy and comfortable. Whilst the white man, for ages, taught us to despise Africa, told us how hideous a place Africa was, inhabited by savages, by cannibals, and by pagans, trying to persuade Negroes not to take any interest in Africa, they have gone to South Africa, and taken up all of South Africa. They have gone to North Africa, and taken up all of North Africa. So with East Africa, and so with West Africa; and so much so that there is very little of Africa left. But the hour has come when North and South and East and West Africa and Central Africa shall be the domain of the black peoples of the world. (Applause.) We shall not seek to ask England, "Why are you here?" We shall not seek to ask France, "Why are you here?" We shall not seek to ask Italy, "Why are you here?" We shall not seek to ask Portugal, "Why are you here?" The only thing that we will ask—the only command we will give, will be: "Get out of here!" (Thunderous applause.) We mean that. (Cries of "Yes!") And because we mean that, we believe in the principles of Justice and of Equity. That is why we are in sympathy with Ireland. That is why we are in sympathy with the Zionist movement. That is why we are in sympathy with the Nationalist movement of Egypt, and of India. We believe all men should be free. (Great applause.)

WANT A PLACE IN THE SUN

We have no animus against the white man. All that we have, as a race, desired is a place in the sun. Four million people are too numerous not to have a place in the sun. (Applause and cries of "Hear, hear!") If 60,000,000 Anglo-Saxons can have a place in the sun, if 80,000,000 Germans can have a place in the sun, if 60,000,000 Japanese can have a place in the sun, if 7,000,000 Belgians (groans and hisses) can have a place in the sun, I cannot see why, under the same principles, 400,000,000 black folks cannot have a place—a big spot in the sun also. (Great applause.) If you believe that the Negro should have a place in the sun; if you believe that Africa should be one vast empire, controlled by the Negro, then arise, and sing the National Anthem of the Universal Negro Improvement Association.

At this juncture, the entire audience stood up and sang the anthem suggested by the speaker.

On concluding his speech, President-General Garvey took over the chairmanship of the meeting, and said: It now gives me great pleasure to present to you the Rev. Dr. J. W. E[a]son, chaplain-general of the Universal Negro Improvement Association and African Communities League. (Great applause.)

DECLARATION OF AIMS

By Rev. Dr. Eason: Mr. President-General, Officers, Members of the Race, Ladies and Gentlemen here assembled: I would be strangely constituted and regarded as devoid of emotions as a human being were I to arise at this hour to address you, unmoved. Assembled as we are, in this, the largest assembly-room of its kind in the world, under such circumstances as we are, to listen to a declaration of our aims and objects now, henceforth and forever, and to renew our determination to continually organize, to continually agitate, continually to get together, until the 400,000,000 black folks of the world shall have one God, one aim, one destiny (applause) and shall realize the fondest desires of their hearts. And the most reasonable thing to ask, expect and demand of the world, is a free and a redeemed Africa. (Loud applause.)

We are mindful of the fact, distinguished delegates from all parts of the world, ladies and gentlemen, that the Negro has suffered well and long, for more than five hundred years. He has been the tool, the serf, the slave and the peon of [*deletion in original*][.]

For three hundred years in this country he suffered, he bled and he died. For hundreds of years in the islands of the sea and in some parts of Asia and of Europe and Australia and in all parts of the world he has been regarded as less than a man. But during those years, and especially since the coming into existence of the U.N.I.A. and A.C.L., under the inspired leadership and the indomitable courage of Marcus Garvey, he has determined that he shall suffer no longer. (Applause.) Suffering seems, therefore, to have fitted the Negro peoples of the world to come together with an idea of teaching the world the fatherhood of God and the brotherhood of man. (Applause.) For 1920 years the world has heard the mighty voice of the man of Galilee saying unto humanity everywhere, "Do unto all men as you would that they should do unto you." (Applause.) And up until August the second at ten o'clock, 1920, nearly all the dominant nations of the world have failed to heed the command of the man of Galilee. And so tonight we, the representatives of the New Negro; we, the people made out of the same dust as other people by the same Creator, formed and fashioned by His hand, and endowed with the same chance and opportunity, though we differ somewhat in form and feature—yet we, being children of the same God, have decided that on the account of our numerical strength, on account of our religious nature, on account of the sufferings that we have gone through, we are now able to teach the world "to do unto all men as you would have them do unto you." (Great applause.) I believe, my friends, that the All-powerful Spirit has breathed inspiration through His divinely-called leader—through him to the Negroes of the world, calling them to come out in the open and let the world know that their sufferings have been long and intense; let the world know that they have been mistreated, and let the world know that they do not want to be mistreated any longer, and then let the world know that we will not be mistreated any longer. (Vociferous applause.)

NEGRO HAS PLAYED A MAN'S PART.

I realize, my friends, that the Negro has played well his part in all the countries where he has lived. Though taken from his native land as a slave and as a servant, and though he has been partially set free everywhere with few exceptions, yet he has always been better to the foreigners in a foreign land than they were to him a long way from home. Under the English Government he was even brought to this country and sold as a slave; under the French Government he has been partially recognized as a man, and only partially so in his native land; under the German flag he has been a beast of burden, a hewer of wood and drawer of water; under the Belgian flag (hisses from all parts of the hall) he was deprived of his life; under the other flags of Asia and of Europe he has suffered long and patiently, and they called him to the battlefields by the millions to "make the world safe for democracy," and to beat the Germans back across the Rhine, and he did it (tremendous cheers), but with little results to himself. My friends, I was born in the United States of America, under the sunny skies and beneath the waving palms of North Carolina (cheers); I know that during the days of slavery our people suffered in this country, and I know that in different sections of this country now we are called upon to undergo terrible hardships. It is not because of our form of government, but because of the radical folks who are not fit to be under the Stars and Stripes. The preamble to the Constitution of the United States of America says:

"We hold these truths to be self-evident, that all men are created free and equal, that they are endowed by their Creator with certain inalienable rights, that among these are life, liberty and the pursuit of happiness." (Applause.)

THE NEGRO'S WAR RECORD.

It is not the Negro's fault that he does not enjoy these things. Neither is it the republican form of government; but it is the fault of rebels North, South, East and West, who do not hold up the Constitution of the United States. (Loud and continued applause.) Ah, we have the right to boast of our loyalty, because when Old Glory was being formed and fashioned, preparing to be floated in the breeze, when it was thundered from the halls of Legislatures and from the Continental Congress that America could not exist under the English heel; on the Commons of Boston; while white men argued and paused and faltered by the way, black men under the leadership of Crispus Attucks fired the first gun. (Vociferous applause.) Though we were still slaves and still suffering, we loved the cause of liberty so greatly that we were willing to give our lives that other men might be free, hoping that after a while we would get to enjoy the same freedom. (Cheers.)

Time will not permit me to speak of our loyalty during the Civil War period. Time will not permit me to tell how we climbed San Juan Hill that Old Glory might not trail in the dust. (A voice: [']Tell about the 15th, too.[']) Time will not permit me to tell how we fought, bled and died on the battle plains of France and Flanders that the world might be "made safe for democracy." But permit me to say this one word, that when the Kaiser held the world at bay and when German militarism threatened the progress of the civilized peoples all over the world, Uncle Sam sent the black boys of New York over and the war stopped. (Thunderous applause.)

SELECTED OWN LEADER.

So much for our sufferings in the past. Let us for a moment glance at the present condition of our peoples throughout the world, and I can better call your attention to that by letting you know why we are here, who is responsible for us being here, and what we intend to do as a result of being gathered here. (Cheers.) I want it to be distinctly understood by everybody here present that all of us black folks here assembled have selected our own black man to be our leader. (Cheers.) When we selected him we did not have millions of dollars at our backs to tell him to go ahead and fight our battles for us and we will back you with money already in hand; we were not organized throughout the world to follow where he led; but, like the leaders of old—like Moses, like Christ, like Abraham Lincoln—he had to shed his own blood to bring us where we are tonight. (Applause.)

You may judge somewhat of our present standing—I mean the Negroes of the world; we are talking from a world standpoint now; we are not narrow any more; we do not represent the English Negro or the French Negro or the German Negro or the American Negro or the African Negro; we represent all Negroes. (Enthusiastic applause.) Time will not permit me to tell of our present progress from a world viewpoint. You may read the "Negro Year Book," whose editor is in the building tonight. (The speaker here referred to Mr. Monroe N. Work, director, Department of Records and Research, Tuskegee Institute, Ala.)[5] You may need to read the Negro papers—the Negro World especially—to find out for yourselves how we stand in the world of commerce, of industry, of education and in the world of religion. I am speaking about generalities tonight. So they come from Europe representing the Negroes there; they come from all the Americas, and all the States in the union representing the Negroes there; they come from far off Australia, and they come from where every prospect ends (and man is not so vile in Africa)—they come representing the Negroes of the world assembled here—the progressive Negroes—the New Negroes—the Negroes who believe that what is good for anybody is good for him and he is going to have it (cheers); Negroes who do not believe in doing harm to anybody, and who will not allow anybody to do harm to them (cheers). I am glad to be living in such an age as this.

So much for our past. Let us take a little look into the future. I am not a prophet nor the son of a prophet. In my ministerial career I have been a seer of visions and dreamer of dreams, and tonight as I stand before you in the presence of royalty; as I stand before you in the largest city of the world and in the best country of the world—until we have redeemed Africa (tumultuous applause) I will take a little look into the future. Do you know that the war has not been officially ended as yet so far as the Congress of the United States is concerned? We are hoping that a Republican Congress and a Republican President will declare the war over immediately after the election in November (laughter) but, however, while the Stars and Stripes are still over there, technically protecting the foreign lands, we are going to ask Old Glory to do a large thing for us when it comes back; and I believe that on account of what we have done for Old Glory the folks who are in charge are going to give us what we ask for. (Cheers.) We are going to ask them if they cannot help us—diplomatically—to just stand off and look at us go across. (Loud and prolonged cheering.) And so, Old Glory, when you come back, won't you remember that we have shed our blood that you might be the proudest banner in the world? Old Glory, when you come back won't you protect my brother and my father in the South as you do other folks? Old Glory, when you come back won't you cry aloud and recognize Palestine for the Jews officially, Ireland for the Irish officially, and Africa for the African officially? (Tumultuous applause.)

LAUDS MR. GARVEY

All honor and all glory to the man who has brought this mighty movement to pass, where all the Negroes of the world can come together and legislate and form plans by which the great African Empire shall be established on the African continent and turned over into the hands of the Negro. (Cheers.) And so they may fix it that every Negro everywhere shall be protected. (Cheers.) Some folks get the idea that all the Negroes who join the Universal Negro Improvement Association and all the Negroes over whom the U.N.I.A. have charge—and it is going to have charge over all of them pretty soon—that they all must go back to Africa. But friends, you have got the wrong idea. Some of the Negroes are not fit to be here and we would not have them in Africa. (Cheers and laughter.)

EXPECT TO DEFEND THE COLORS.

What it does mean is, that as the Englishman wraps the Union Jack around him and says: "Fire, if you dare, and a million men will march tomorrow morning to defend it!" It means that as the Tricolor of France is floating in the breeze and the Frenchman wraps it around him and says: "Fire, if you dare; and a million men will go out and fight for France!" It means that if an African citizen is anywhere in the world he wraps the red, the black and the green around him and 400,000,000 black folks will say: "Fire, if you dare!" (Vociferous cheers.)

But let me stop. (Voices, "Go ahead.") Let me thank the President and the officers and members of the U.N.I.A. for calling me into existence and giving me the opportunity to speak to you tonight as Chaplain-General of this organization representing the spiritual interests of the Negroes throughout the world. I am a man of peace, but I further understand that my God is a God of war. I see into the future men marshalled around a plain—east, west, north, south—not to fight an aggressive warfare, but a defensive warfare. I see a black emperor, or a black president, or a black whatever you might call him—potentate, if you please—at the head of the black folks of the world with headquarters in Africa. (Cheers.) I see black generals, black colonels, black captains, black corporals, black privates, all standing with drawn swords ready. (Cheers.) I see black physicians, black dentists, black hospital attendants and Black Cross nurses (cheers) on the African battlefields. My head may be gray; my shoulders may be bowed with age; my steps may be feeble and slow; my voice may be cracked and broken. Some day in the dim distant future I hope to be able to creep out in my old age, if necessary and in my inf[i]rmity, and raise my hands to heaven, and call down God Almighty's benediction upon the black soldiers of Africa as they go forth to make the world safe for everybody. (Loud cheers.) Lest we forget the depth from which we have come; lest we forget the sufferings through which we have passed; lest we forget the good things that have been done for us here, and lest we forget to ask for greater things; lest we forget each other; lest we forget our leader; lest we forget his supporters, let us ask the Lord God of Hosts to be with us here, lest we forget, lest we forget.[6] (Loud and prolonged applause.)

DISTINGUISHED VISITORS INTRODUCED

Some of the distinguished visitors who occupied seats on the platform were introduced. Conspicuous among these was the Hon. Gabriel Johnson, Mayor of the city of Monrovia, Liberia, who was received with great enthusiasm. The presidents of the various branches and divisions in this country, British West Indies, South and Central America, were also introduced.

Hon. Marcus Garvey then said: I want to invite everybody to Liberty Hall, where a convention will be held during the 31 days of this month. Tomorrow night will be the opening proper of this convention, when the mayor of Monrovia will be the speaker of the evening. It gives me great pleasure to now present to you one of the most brilliant scholars of the Negro race. Dr. William H. Ferris, literary editor of The Negro World. Dr. Ferris is a graduate of Harvard and Yale Universities, and is known throughout the length and breadth of this country as the author of "The African Abroad." Dr. Ferris will speak to you for five minutes.

PROF. FERRIS SPEAKS

Professor Ferris said: Mr. President-General, Ladies and Gentlemen: This is the largest Negro gathering I have ever witnessed. What does it mean? It means that the Hon. Marcus Garvey is a human dynamo, and that the Negro has now begun to do for himself. The old Negro believed in prayer; but the new Negro believes in deed. The old Negro believed in taking any place which the white man wanted him to have; but the new Negro believes in blazing a path for himself, in Africa, if necessary.

The Negro is the acid test for American Democracy and American Civilization. There are some who desire to wait until the American white man becomes Christianized; but there are others who are trying to build up a civilization for themselves.

I have faith in the Universal Negro Improvement Association, because I believe in the possibilities of the Negroes. A race that can stand slavery for two hundred and fifty years and emerge with physical vitality and with faith in God; a race that is segregated, disfranchised, jimcrowed and that can pile up two billion dollars' worth of property and accumulate one billion dollars in the banks; a race that can marshal the forces from the four corners of the world as has this Negro convention, such a race I believe has great possibilities for the future. (Applause.)

Rev. Dr. J. D. Brooks was next introduced and said: "Mr. President-General, Members of the Universal Negro Improvement Association, Ladies and Gentlemen: There are but two great things in my life now; two large letters; two capital letters; two Gs; Garvey and God. (Applause.) God represents to me all that is spiritual, and since I have been following Garvey I have learned that God made me just as He made other things. I had some doubts in my mind as to the God the folks told me about being my God; but since I have followed Garveyism I have changed my mind and believe that God is my God. Garveyism to me represents Independence of thought; Freedom of action; Independence of everything, everybody, but God.

The Negro has depended on other folks too long instead of depending upon God and himself. No race in the world has been foolish enough to depend upon other races to help them get what belongs to them but Negroes. Other races have gone out and demanded what rightfully belongs to them and either got it or died trying to get it. Negroes have been waiting on God to give them their rights. And God has never been on the side of a coward. God always has been on the side of those who are brave. God selected the Jews because the Jews would fight for what they wanted to have. No Negroes anywhere nor any other race of people for that matter, are going to get their rights unless they are willing to fight and if necessary die for their rights. (Applause.) Until the Negro stops talking about dying and gets ready to die, he is not going to have anything. If he died for other peoples he can also die for himself. (Applause.)

The meeting was then adjourned till ten-thirty o'clock tomorrow morning (Tuesday), when the convention meets at Liberty Hall.

Printed in *NWCB*, 3 August 1920.

1. George Alexander McGuire (1866–1934) was elected chaplain general at the 1920 UNIA convention. He was born in Antigua, BWI, and educated at Mico College and the Nisky Theological Seminary of St. Thomas, Virgin Islands. After immigrating to the United States in 1894, McGuire was ordained a priest in the Protestant Episcopal church and undertook several missionary assignments in the Caribbean and the United States. He was invited to Philadelphia in 1901 to become rector of the historic Afro-American Church of St. Thomas, founded in 1794 by Absalom Jones. In 1905 he became the first black to be appointed archdeacon when he was placed in charge of the "colored work" in the diocese of Arkansas. Later, during a stay in Massachusetts, McGuire attended Jefferson Medical College in Boston, and in 1913 he returned to Antigua to work for the Church of England and practice medicine. McGuire's departure from the Episcopal church and his subsequent work for the Church of England was prompted by his disappointment over racism within the white Episcopal church in Boston and his inability to secure greater independence from the national body for his growing black congregation at St. Bartholomew's Church in that city. McGuire's strong belief that black clergy should be elected to higher positions within the Episcopal church also contributed to his decision. This conviction led as well to another major decision in 1919. Later in his career he reminisced: "Then came 1919! Down into the Valley of Decision I went with my race . . . and

when I emerged from the Valley after six months, I brought with me the embryo of what is now the African Orthodox Church" (*Voice of the Patriarch* 1, no. 1: 1). McGuire returned to the United States in 1919 and joined the Garvey movement. He began to promote the idea of an independent black Episcopal church among UNIA members, and in the first half of 1921 he drafted the UNIA's Universal Negro Ritual and Universal Negro Catechism. While in Cuba during July 1921, McGuire was elected bishop of the Independent Episcopal churches by a group of blacks who convened at St. Saviour's Church in Brooklyn. McGuire soon began recruiting members by using his influence as UNIA chaplain general and gathering names from lists of UNIA members and contributors. Seeking to make his sect the official religious body of the UNIA, McGuire launched his most determined effort during the early part of 1921, when Garvey was absent from UNIA headquarters. McGuire's bid to establish a footing for his group led to his dispute with Garvey, who forced McGuire to resign as chaplain general, opening the way for McGuire to organize the African Orthodox church in September 1921 (*NYT*, 12 November 1934; *NW*, 6 November 1920, 6 August and 8 October 1921; William Newton Hartshorn, *An Era of Progress and Promise* [Boston: Priscilla Publishing Co., 1910], p. 477; Gavin White, "Patriarch McGuire and the Episcopal Church," *Historical Magazine of the Protestant Episcopal Church*, 38 [1969]: 109–141; Richard Newman, "The Origins of the African Orthodox Church," pp. iii–xxii, introductory essay to the reprint edition of *The Negro Churchman* [Millwood, N.Y.: Kraus Reprint Co., 1977]; Randall K. Burkett, *Black Redemption: Churchmen Speak for the Garvey Movement* [Philadelphia: Temple University Press, 1978], pp. 157–180).

2. According to Bureau of Investigation reports monitoring radical activities in southern California in 1921, Louis Michel was a Russian Jew and socialist who had become a naturalized American citizen. During the campaign to deny Asians the legal right to own land in California, Michel addressed black audiences in opposition to the proposed legislation. In September 1919 Michel spoke before a large black audience in Los Angeles on the topic "Why I am a Friend of the Negro," and in December 1919 he wrote a lengthy poem, "Sail on for Brotherhood and Light," praising Garvey and the Black Star Line. Later, in 1921, Michel spoke in Los Angeles on "The Second Emancipation of the Negro." A Bureau of Investigation agent reported that in his speech he "advocated Socialism, glorified [Eugene V.] Debs, and advocated the return of the Negro to Africa and the Jew to Palestine to escape the present American system of Government and prejudice and persecution encountered here" (DNA, RG 65, files BS 202600-5-33X and BS 202600-5-32X; Louis Michel, "The Black Man," *California Eagle*, 13 September, 27 September, and 13 December 1919).

3. Garvey's telegram to de Valera came after the Irish republican cause had suffered disappointments at the conventions of the two major American political parties. At the Republican National Convention in June 1920, de Valera and the Irish-American judge who had presided over the Third Irish Race Convention in 1919, Daniel Cohalan, took opposing positions on the question of Republican party recognition of an Irish republic. Cohalan's plank calling on the party to advocate self-determination in Ireland narrowly passed the party resolutions committee, while de Valera's plank calling for the outright recognition of an Irish republic failed. When de Valera openly condemned the Cohalan plank, the Republicans quietly erased the Irish question from their platform. When the Democrats met in July, they passed a mild resolution expressing sympathy for Irish aspirations without any reference to the legitimacy of a republic (Donal McCartney, "De Valera's Mission to the United States," in Art Cosgrove and Donal McCartney, eds., *Studies in Irish History* [Dublin: University College, Belfield, 1979], pp. 304–23; Alan J. Ward, *Ireland and Anglo-American Relations 1899–1921* [Toronto: University of Toronto Press, 1969], pp. 220–24).

4. Baron Sidney Sonnino (1847–1921), Italian statesman and representative at the Paris Peace Conference (*WBD*).

5. Monroe Nathan Work (1866–1945) became head of the Tuskegee Institute's Division of Records and Research in 1908. He was born in Iredell County, North Carolina, and educated at the Chicago Theological Seminary and the University of Chicago. He became editor of the *Negro Year Book* in 1912 and later edited the *Bibliography of the Negro* (*WWCR*).

6. From the poem "Recessional" by Rudyard Kipling (1865–1936).

Reports of the Convention

[*New York*, August 3, 1920]

Following the monster public meeting at Madison Square Garden, at which nearly 25,000 persons were present, the Internation[al] Convention of Negroes entered its third day's session in Liberty Hall, on Tuesday, August 3. The session opened with a full attendance of delegates. President-General Marcus Garvey occupying the chair.

DELEGATES REPORT CONDITIONS

The first part of the convention was given over to the hearing of complaints from delegates. The complaints they brought from their respective countries and States. "We want this convention to clearly understand the universal Negro situation," said Mr. Garvey. "We can only understand it when the representatives from Georgia tells of the real conditions in Georgia; when the representative from Mississippi tells of the real conditions in Mississippi; when the representative from Basutoland or any other part of Africa tells of the real conditions in Africa. And so with the various islands of the West Indies, and South and Central America. We want to understand the universal situation of the Negro so that we can have conditions so arranged as to meet the demands of 400,000,000 people who are being represented at this convention.

"So the first five or six days of the convention will be devoted to reports of every delegate. Every delegate will be given a chance to lay the grievances of the community he or she represents before this Conference of Negroes. We do not want it said after this convention is over that Georgia did not get a hearing to explain the conditions in Georgia; Canada did not get a hearing to explain the conditions in Canada; Africa did not get a hearing to explain the conditions in Africa, or the British West Indies did not get a hearing to explain the conditions in those islands." Continuing, he said[,] "When the convention adjourns on the 31st of August, we want to feel that every Negro understands the universal situation of the Race; so that when anything is to be done, whether in the British West Indies or Canada, Africa, South and Central America, or in any of the forty-eight States of America. You as delegates elected by your respective peoples will be able to enlighten the convention as to the exact situation in that State, or island or country."

SIX DAYS TO BE DEVOTED TO DISCUSSION OF CONDITIONS.

Five or six days will be devoted to a discussion of the conditions obtaining in the communities represented by the delegates.

"I offer the suggestion," said the chairman, "that fifteen minutes should be the maximum time allowed any delegate to lay the conditions of his State or country before the convention and that the time should range from five to fifteen minutes. This suggestion is now the property of the house."

Mr. James Williams, of Montclair, N.J., put the suggestion in the form of a motion.

ADOPT FIFTEEN MINUTE RULE.

Mr. Phillip Van Putten, of Haiti, made an amendment to the motion to the effect that if in the discretion of the chairman a delegate's cause is of such great importance to the convention, as to consume more time than fifteen minutes, additional time be extended to the delegate. The motion, with the amendment, was carried.

"We are assembled here for a serious purpose," declared the President-General. "Some of the delegates have come from thousands of miles away. They have left their homes and families to attend this convention. I hope you will bear these facts [in] mind and try to expedite matters as much as possible."

RULES OF ORDER ADOPTED.

Mr. H. W. Kirby[1] (Washington, D.C.), offered the suggestion that a parliamentarian be called to expedite time upon discussion of questions and that rules of order be adopted for guidance.

President General: "The gentleman has brought up a question that might as well be settled now so as to prevent trouble as to whose rules of order we should follow. I want to say this, that we have been held up pretty often by parliamentary rules, but we are endeavoring to get away from them. I myself am not concerned much about parliamentary rules if we can get where we want to get. But, at the same time, there must be some order in every well constituted assembly, and it is for you to adopt Rules of Order to guide the deliberations."

Acting upon this suggestion, motion was made and adopted that Robert's Rules of Order be the parliamentary guide of the convention.

COMMITTEES APPOINTED.

Mr. Green, of Virginia, arose to offer the suggestion that the time of the convention be not wasted in interminable discussion from the floor, but that time would be saved to designate committees to whom certain question[s] could be referred accordingly for their more deliberate consideration and recommendation to the house.

EDUCATION IN BRITISH HONDURAS

Mr. Lee Bennett, delegate from British Honduras, speaking on conditions obtaining in that country stated that the conditions affecting Negroes in British Honduras are not what they ought to be. "We who have started this organization down there are looked upon with suspicion by the government. We are treated as people trying to stir up sedition, so that we have had to go very carefully.

"There are any number of things that we might complain about," he said, "but principally, we would like to complain about educational conditions that are keeping us down. Our children are not being educated as they ought to be; and while we cannot say that there is color discrimination as existing in other places, yet there is educational discrimination. That, in brief, is the condition of affairs in British Honduras. That is what we desire to lay stress on—our need and desire for educational improvement.["]

E. H. Ware[2] (Cincinnati, O.), representing a welfare association in that city, stated that he is a staunch member of the U.N.I.A. After the demonstration Sunday and Monday he was willing to surrender his banner from Cincin[n]ati and unite with the Negroes of New York. "I would like to have one of the speakers from New York to come to Cincin[n]ati and organize a branch there," he said, "it would mean a new birth to the Negroes of Cincinnati—to the Negroes in that section of Ohio.["]

THE DELEGATE FROM COLON.

Mr. F. S. Ric[kett]s (Colon, Panama), speaking on conditions in Colon, Republic of Panama, said:

"When the U.N.I.A. was started in 1918 we were scoffed and jeered at by the white man. We got together and we did our best. There are a number of little grievances which I hope will be taken up here later on but I will not venture now to speak of them, because the time is not opportune. I want to tell you that the people in Panama, especially in Colon—10,000 Negroes there and between 7,000 and 8,000 in Panama—a body of fully 22,000 there, for the most part coming from the various islands in the West Indies—have been accorded the worst treatment at the hands of the white man.["] [He] went on to show the United [Brot]herhood called a strike to get more pay for the work they performed.[3] When the strike was called, 17,000 Negroes stepped out. Describing conditions during the strike he said: "Drawn bayonets were fixed and the workers were practically ousted from the Panama Canal by military forces. They took possession of the houses and the workers had to rent houses from the Panama Canal authorities so that they were compelled to work for them. Women and children were ejected from their homes at the point of the bayonet, and many a man has been forced to commit suicide from the time that work ceased on the Panama Canal for them.

WON'T SELL THEM PASSAGE.

"You cannot get a boat to leave there. If you go to the United Fruit Co. and ask for passage on one of [their] boats in order to leave Colon, they say, 'No, we have no passage for you; wait for the Black Star Line.'

["]That strike is the first strike in history where men have had to go back to work for less than they were getting. Men who had gotten $75 a month had to return for $50, and had to accept it because their wives and children were there. All our belongings were dashed to pieces. In Panama and Colon men are out of positions they formerly held, and the offices that were formerly held by colored men for years—fourteen and fifteen years—are now being held by white men and women. The man who formerly had an avocation now has to push a truck. But the U.N.I.A. is still doing its utmost to relieve the situation, and when the time comes I shall present the resolution that my society has forwarded by me."

DELEGATE FROM NEW HAVEN.

Mr. William Hester (New Haven, Conn.) said in part: "Connecticut is indeed one of the tightest States in the Union; but I believe I can say we have broken the ice, and more than 500 people throughout the State are clamoring for a demonstration. New Haven, as you know, is a college bred town; but some of the most ignorant people in the State of Connecticut are to be found in that town, and they are about as ignorant as any people to be found anywhere else in the United States. A college town it is, but some of the [bigg]est fools throughout the entire country are to be found there. We had the hardest time getting a [bran]ch of the U.N.I.A. established in New Haven. We fought; we mobilized; we went from one little church to another; we met in different houses until we finally were able to get together. Only one minister in that big town would give us his support, but I am glad I can tell you this morning that we are pretty nearly 300 strong.["]

NIGERIA REPRESENTED.

Prince Madarikan[4] (Lagos, West Africa), representing conditions in Nigeria and West Africa, said: "I received a report day before yesterday from one of the natives in Nigeria who came here two weeks ago, and he told me that in Nigeria you have sold over one thousand shares in the native land. It proves to you that the U.N.I.A. is going to redeem Africa." (Hear, hear.)

"I want you to bear in mind that [you] are not doing things for any [one] place in Africa; you are doing [it] to redeem the whole continent of Africa (applause); because what is good for the goose is good for the gander. (Applause.) I have made up my mind that if it takes my life to build up my country, I will die for my country. (Cheers.)

AFRICANS SEEING THE LIGHT.

"The conditions in my part of Africa [are] somewhat peculiar. The people in my country are coming up little by little. We are not monkeys, we are not wild, as some would have you think, we are New Negroes, who are trying to learn something, and we are going to learn something. My people are well to do, some of them. I know four men in my country, if I take myself back home and say, 'I want so-and-so,' who would say they are ready. I saw lots of Africans here, and they came to me, one from Liberia, the others elsewhere, and they wanted to know, 'Are they doing this for Liberia, or Nigeria, for the Zulu country, or for the Kaffir country.['] And I said, 'Boys, they are doing this just to help us out of darkness, so you can see the light yourselves. They are doing it all for Africa.' We have different tribes in my country, that speak different tongues and do not understand one another; but in the meantime we boys here are going back there to organize the chiefs and kings together and make them understand, so that when you come to us, our chiefs and our kings will open their doors and help you to build up Africa.["] (Great applause.)

NEW YORK DELEGATE.

Mr. Rudolph Smith, a member of the New York delegation, said:

"Many members of my race who have settled here from all parts of the world have been subjected to the environments and unfair conditions of the Caucasian race. Here positions are only offered to a few members of the race commensurate with their abilities, and these, for the most part, are obtained through politics.["]

CONDITIONS IN PITTSBURGH.

Mr. James Young (Pittsburgh, Pa.), speaking on conditions in that city, remarked:

"The conditions in Pittsburgh at this particular time, as one of our delegates says, are that the preachers in Pittsburgh are our biggest hold-back.["]

CONDITIONS IN GUATEMALA.

Mr. Clifford Bourne,[5] (Guatemala, Central America)—"I have brought a special message from the members of the Universal Negro Improvement Association in Puerto Barrios, Guatemala. On the 17th of February, last, we established there a branch of your Association with just about eleven members. I am glad to tell you that through proper organization and systematic handling, we stand today at 250. That community there is especially a Spanish community, and among us there are about 2,000 colored men. When we started our association, the United Fruit Company, a company that has tried to down everything done by the Negro, and especially, the Black Star Line, tried to get the President of the Republic, Manuel Estraba Cabrera, to forbid us from having our meetings. But your humble servant came out and told him he could not stop us. I told him: "You may stop us temporarily, but we are going to be conquerors in the end."

["]The United Fruit Company only paid the laborers $1.50 per day. After we established our Association we got together and succeeded in establishing a union; we then demanded of the United Fruit Company that it raise the laborers['] salary 100 per cent. (Cheers). Our Association said: "If you do not raise them, we will support them." We established a charitable fund and everybody held up work for about fifteen days and they came to us and we supported them. When the white m[a]n saw that we were determined not to be led by him, the manager of the company gave the men 100 per cent raise. All of that was accomplished through the Universal Negro Improvement Association. (Cheers).

GOT MERCHANT INTERESTED.

["]There is a noted colored merchant by the name of Mr. George C. Reneau in the city of Puerto Barrio[s] who came to me and told me that nothing at all that has been tried by Negroes has been a success. I told him this movement is to be a success. So I lectured to this gentleman. A few days after he came to my office and said to me: "Mr. Bourne, here is my check for $1,000, send it to the President-General, for 200 shares in the Black Star Line." I had converted him, and that is the kind of work we are doing over there. "If we are going into anything, we must exercise system; and system can only be exercised through co-operation. Let us turn our minds toward the same object, and whatever we do, let us do it systematically, and when the day shall come and the automatic button shall ring, we shall be one for Africa.["] (Cheers).

MIDDLETOWN DELEGATE.

Rev. P. E. Batson,[6] (Middletown, N.Y.)—"Let me tell you about the temperament of the people and the conditions in Middletown," said Rev. Batson. "There are not many Southerners there; they are mostly Easterners and they seem to stick in this rut of being dissatisfied with the white man, but do nothing to remove conditions. I succeeded in getting a little over twenty of them to unite for their own good, and we got twenty-six members from February to the 26th of last month. We have got our charter and we are now existing as an organization. There is nothing succeeds like success; and that is because we put our minds to it.["]

CONDITIONS IN BOSTON.

Dr. Joseph Deighton Gibson, (Boston, Mass.), in describing some of the conditions there, said: "In Boston we did not meet with many discriminations as in some other places. Since we have organized the U.N.I.A. there, we have got a zealous field of workers who have the spirit of determination to go back to our country knowing that we are living in an alien country. Some years ago, we had played in our city, a photoplay, the "Birth of A Nation,"[7] which you no doubt, have read of. It showed us a picture that I cannot express; it caused, during those weeks and weeks after, a hatred to exist with the white man and the black people of Massachusetts. We appealed to the

Mayor whose name was James Curley, and he promised to do everything to prevent the picture being shown in Boston. But he did nothing.

["]In Boston we organized a branch of the U.N.I.A. last October. The preachers were our biggest enemies. Why? Because they are weak-kneed. The majority—95 per cent of them cannot stand the acid test; the final analysis they cannot stand. They refused to support us and when we asked them to permit us to hold our meetings in their church, we had to pay them big prices, and then they would go ahead and knock us. But today we stand on solid ground that cannot be broken. It will never die. You and I may go, but let us plant this seed, and let us get to business knowing that 400,000,000 Negro men and women will redeem their Fatherland, Africa. (Cheers). This is the sort of determination that Massachusetts has. I have organized Boston, proper; I have organized Lynn, proper; I have organized Brockton, proper; I have organized Everett, proper. I am doing my part. Get busy when you go home and do your part. I am living up to my contract and you must live up to yours.["]

BOCAS DEL TORO.

Mr. A. N. Willis,[8] (Bocas del Toro, Republic of Panama)—"Our town is situated on the borders of the Division—that is, on the province of Bocas del Toro and on the Costa Rica Division—just the Sixola Bridge divides us. The Division I represent takes in thirty-six miles on the Costa Rica side and about thirty-seven miles on the Panama[n]ian territory," said Mr. Willis. "When Mr. Samuda, the former President, and Mme. Duchatillier,[9] the lady president, came to us about ten months ago, we were organized. Since then we have been to the best of our ability, working in the interests of this Association. There have been many difficulties in the way, brought about by the influence of the United Fruit Company. They have done everything in this world to prevent our organizing along the various sections of the line. The place is so situated that they own entire territories of land and houses. The people living in this section are foreigners, and in very few instances do you see natives there. The United Fruit Company has sent their diplomatic agents all along the lines to prevent us from organizing. I do not like to say anything uncomplimentary about the ministers, but I cannot help telling you, my friends, that they have been the greatest enemies to this movement. The ministers along the lines, controlling the various churches, get in contact with the people and tell them they must not allow any meetings to be held in the churches owned by the United Fruit Company. They get a small salary of $75 per month from the United Fruit Company and they are allowed to ride on the train on a pass. Knowing the United Fruit Company is opposed to the movement and have done everything in the world to prevent us from organizing along the lines, and knowing that the United Fruit Company can take away their passes and cut off their $75 a month, which forms a great part of their support, they have not stood by the people; and hence we had to take it upon ourselves and we went into this section and forced a way to success.

CHANGED CONDITIONS.

["]Conditions have changed since we have organized the association in the Republic of Panama. Two years ago we had a strike in Bocas del Toro and the white men drew swords and killed two or three of the strikers; when we appealed to Jamaica for some representation they gave us none.

["]The Division I represent is in good standing with the government and you will be privileged to see one of the biggest officials. He is here with us—Mr. Ogilvie.[10] He is treasurer of Bocas del Toro. Conditions to-day are very satisfactory for the association. We are all organized with but little exception and those not yet in are waiting to see what can be done.["]

WANTS TO BE CALLED AFRICAN.

Mrs. Sarah Branch, of the New York delegation, expressed the hope that the convention will modify the name Negro and let the white man have his pet name back[.] "We are tired of being called Negroes," she said, "we are not Negroes, we are Africans. (Applause.) And we want to be called Africans. God gave us the name Ethiopians and we want to be called Ethiopians or Africans. Negro is simply a pet name that the white man, when he went to Africa and stole our foreparents, gave us.

"Let us all in this convention, with one voice, cry out 'we will not be called Negroes any longer, but Africans.' "

TUESDAY AFTERNOON'S SESSION.

The Black Star Line Band was in attendance, and played lively music at intervals.

PORTO RICO.

The first speaker at the afternoon session was Mr. James Benjamin, a delegate from Porto Rico. He said: "I believe I am one of the few Spanish speaking delegates in this hall. I am not speaking my native language, my native language is Spanish. With my knowledge of English, however, I shall try my best to inform you of conditions in my home. I would like to he[re] say that the fact of Spanish speaking Negroes joining hands with English speaking Negroes means that language makes no difference with us as long as we are Negroes. My country is a small island 36 by 130 miles, with a population of 1,500,000 inhabitants. It is one of the most thickly populated islands in the West Indies. Ninety per cent of the inhabitants of this island are Negroes. Conditions confronting Negroes in Porto Rico are the same conditions that confront Negroes all over the world. I can see no difference in the conditions of Negroes no matter where they reside. We Negroes are the same all over the world. We are beasts of burden and servants of the white man.

"A few months ago representatives of the Universal Negro Improvement Association came to my home and I lost no time in joining the association. I saw right away that this association would eventually be productive of much good.

"Many other persons would have joined also, but the Universal Negro Improvement Association labored under a great disadvantage in that their propaganda was disseminated throughout the country in English, whereas the majority of my countrymen cannot understand English. I would advise them the next time they send a delegation to my home to send persons who can both read and write Spanish, and who can deliver addresses in the Spanish language. I tried to help the association out, however, by condensing their speeches, translating them into Spanish and publishing them in some of the local newspapers. By so doing I was instrumental in getting several persons to join the association.

DENIED SUITABLE EMPLOYMENT.

["]The San Juan people are greatly enthusiastic over this idea, and I hope Ponce will be the city of Porto Rico that will hold the banner for the U.N.I.A. I do not want to take your time talking about conditions among the Negroes of Porto Rico, for they are the same everywhere the Negro lives. Negroes are educated in Porto Rico. That is all right. But what happens after that? A father works twelve or fifteen years to educate his son; he finds when his son leaves college that he cannot find suitable work in keeping with his attainments because he is a Negro. He is intelligent, but the white man will not permit him to get into an office. That happens in Porto Rico, and it is the same thing that is happening all around the world. So the only thing I have to say is that Porto Rico is getting the feelings and the sentiment that the Hon. Marcus Garvey is spreading all around the world. I see in this convention any number of English-speaking Negroes represented; and we want all Negroes to be represented; we want all Negroes organized under this flag of ours. (Applause.) I believe that we have a great work to do in those islands where English is not spoken. I want our leader to send some representative to our island who knows the language of the island to explain what this association means. We don't want any Negro to be neglected; we want every Negro in every land to be informed of the U.N.I.A. and its principles. I am sure that our banner—the red, green and black—will wave in triumph all around the world and at last claim the independence of Africa.["] (Applause.)

NORFOLK, VA.

W. H. Johnson (Norfolk, Va.): ["]Among the difficulties we have in Norfolk is that the preachers preach against the organization to their people telling them it is nothing that is worth while. I have come here to learn and get everything I can to help this organization along. There are only two ways, and the preachers are leading us one way or another; so if the preachers say it is wrong, the congregation goes wrong, and if the preacher says right, or goes right, the congregation goes right. I am a preacher myself, so you see I know what I am talking about.

["]The people in Norfolk are going ahead, however; there is no doubt about it; we are gaining ground.

["]I want to say this for some of the white people in Norfolk. If they are against us, they manage to hold their peace; they do not have anything to say against it. They commended us in their papers when the Black Star Line boat came to Hampton Roads, stating that it was one of the grandest events that ever happened in the Negro race.["]

CHICAGO'S DELEGATE.

Mr. W. A. Walters[11] (Chicago, Ill.): "Having resided in the city of Chicago for the last twenty-eight years, I believe that I am somewhat in a position to describe conditions existing there. We find that the prevailing conditions are to a large extent the same as those portrayed as existing in other parts of the country. There are 160,000 of our people in the city of Chicago. We have within those realms the possibilities that within a few months after we shall have returned and given our report to that community of the work that has been done of bringing into our midst from five to six thousand members at least.["]

BERMUDA'S DELEGATE.

Rev. R. H. Tobitt, (Bermuda)—["]First of all, I want to lay before this convention conditions in the Island of Bermuda, respecting the Government.["] Mr. Tobitt said, "As you know, Bermuda is a British possession that has representative government. It has what Ireland is craving for today, small as it is. It is only about twenty-five or twenty-seven square miles but I want to say its population consists of 75 per cent of Negroes or people of Negro blood; yet for all that, in the House of Parliament there are at present only two colored representatives; and one of these is dubbed by the natives as "the white man's tool." Consequently, you see the disadvantages to which these people are subjected. That is due to the fact that the people have not been far-sighted enough to own property so as to be able to be entitled to the franchise. The powers that be have put up the franchise at such a rate that only men who own property of great value can be set up to be members of the House of Parliament. In the 'Courts of Justice' the people who are condemned by the law are subject not only to fine, but after being imprisoned for a certain number of years, during that time to be flogged, as they do in some parts of Africa. For stealing a bicycle an offender was given about two years imprisonment and during that time flogged. A colored boy and a white boy got to scrambling in the streets. Both were hailed before the Court of Justice, and I saw the white boy allowed to ride on his bicycle to the Court while the colored boy was dragged before the Court of Justice—and by a colored policeman. These are some of the things that stand out prominently in that country.

URGES MERCHANT MARINE.

["]Bermuda is an agricultural country. Though small in square miles, its soil is very productive—very rich. You will get from one lot of land as great a return as you will get from an acre in some other places, simply because the soil is naturally rich. I have told you before that 75 per cent of the inhabitants are Negroes and the majority of these are farmers; and many a time during the crop season on account of the fact that all the shipping is in the hands of the white men, and he also is engaged in farming on a large scale, when the market prices are high in New York City, the white man with his own ships sends his produce to New York City and other parts and catches the high prices, but the colored farmer's produce remains in the Customs House or on the wharf, and then when shipping is available, his produce is hardly of any value. The colored man owns but very little land and he has got to pay high rent for his land; then he has to bide the time for his crop to be sent abroad. There is the necessity, therefore, of our owning ships by taking shares in the steamship company operated by the Association, so that the people who [are] looking for shipping may be [able] to avail themselves of their [own] shipping facilities. The shipping trade is monopolized by the white man because he has got the means.

ALL PRIVATE SCHOOLS.

["]The next point I want to bring before you is the educational conditions. Would it astonish you to know that in the Islands of Bermuda, there is not a single school that is owned and controlled by the Government[?] They are all private schools. The rule says that the Government or the Education Board will give a grant in aid to assist teachers to carry on the work of education. Instead of the country educating its citizens, they leave it into the hands of the teachers and give them a small grant in aid.

["]And, therefore, the work of educating the natives in Bermuda has fallen largely in the hands of the [scho]ol teachers who are doing it [as a] sacrifice to themselves. It is only within recent years, through the instrumentality of your humble servant, that we have formed what is called a Teachers Union, which is working for a better condition. Another thing is that in the schools the books are not suited to the natives. They heap upon us books that have been written by white men and books that give inspiration to the white boy because some white hero is held up before him. The colored boy reads about what white men have done and then he thinks that honor is only for the white boys. But for all these years your humble servant has been taking into his own hands to inculcate into our children that there are black heroes as well as white heroes.

FREE TO TEACH SELF RESPECT.

"My school is a private school and is aided by the Government, but I made it clear to the Education Board that I was free to teach what I liked, and so I give essays on such great men like Toussa[i]nt L'Ouverture, Frederick Douglass and Crispus Attucks and such great men belonging to our race, so that the colored child can aspire to some of their own race. (Cheers.)

["]Now on the industrial side. We find that our young men have measured up very well indeed. That is due to the fact that the dockyard is owned and controlled by the British Government. Young men are given a chance. They are [allow]ed to take a trade as the white boy does. I must say that the greatest difficulty is experienced not with the Englishmen so much, [but] the native white Bermudians who are very much prejudiced against the colored people. You will find there that the colored boy has the opportunity to learn different trades at the dockyard, consequently you can find some competent tradesmen there. I hope to recommend some to the Black Star Line later. You can find engineers, fitters, plumbers of all descriptions— Negroes who are capable. We have licensed pilots who hold first, second and third class licen[s]es, many of them members of the association; and I may tell you this much: that among our pilots we have some of the most skillful in the world and there is not one white man among them. They have told us to tell our President General that they are willing at any time to give their services to the Black Star Line. You now have one of our Bermudian boys on [your] boat—Mr. Henry Tucker.

WANT SHIP OF THEIR OWN.

["]These are the main facts I want to lay before you; and we hope that in this convention some means may be arrived at to bring results. The people there have asked me to ask our illustrious leader to pay a visit to Bermuda. I want to say before you, and I declare it, that the day he touches the shores of Bermuda, he will capture all the communities of Bermuda wholesale. (Cheers.)

["]The beautiful onions and potatoes which Bermuda is celebrated for are grown chiefly by the native people—the Negroes—and they are quite willing to ship them here if they have a ship of their own, and to have the trade controlled by the members of the association in New York City. (Cheers.) We have had a visitor there from Boston in the person of Dr. Gibson, and he said Montreal [*Boston?*] is quite willing to deal with the native people of Bermuda in the shipping line. And so we look forward hopefully and we feel the day is not far distant when through the instrumentality of the Black Star Line Steamship Company that Bermuda may be the means of helping to build up this association. She has got the goods if we can find the means to deliver them.["]

NEWARK DELEGATE.

Rev. J. W. Locke (Newark, N.J.): ["]It would be wisdom and righteousness to try to unite instead of divide,["] declared Rev. Locke. ["]We have presented the claims of this association to the Ministers' Conference in Newark, New Jersey, and to the leading ministers of this city, and they have expressed their willingness to unite us and to co-operate with the movement.

["]I want to report on discrimination in New Jersey. New Jersey, as you know is north of the Mason Dixon line, but the wind that blows [is] from the fields of Jimcrowism, and segregation finds its way into the field of New Jersey. So that we are not free from those evils even because we are on this side of the Mason Dixon line.

["]Discriminations in factories against which our very souls and sense of justice cry out obtains in Newark. In a factory, in the town of Bloomfield, in the suburbs of Newark, where we had a number of colored men working, many of them had to pass through the residential sections, and hundreds of the white residents wrote a protest to the Safe Pin Factory, that they must either remove their factory or prevent the employment of colored women in that section. First they said that when persons of their race came along colored women would be on the other side of the factory and the white women could not b[ear] their presence in the streets, they declared that colored women would go into the parks and would sit on the benches where there were probably white nurses and other persons to get a little rest, and that the white ladies from the high class residential sections could not enjoy the pleasures of the parks in the presence of colored women.

RESTAURANTS DISCRIMINATE.

["]There are many places where they refuse to serve you in the great City of Newark, and they will turn you away from the door with the money in your hand, perfectly good money bearing the image of the old eagle on it, that is prized so highly in these United States, and with the motto on one side: In God we trust; but they won't even trust the man that is carrying this money. There are many cases I could tell you of, but I shall not do it here.

HOUSING CONDITIONS BAD.

["]The worst housing conditions obtain in Newark. Something must be done on our side in order that conditions might be remedied. True, the houses may be buil[t] by others, but we feel that since we are part and parcel of the community we have a right to enjoy those rights and privileges that all other races enjoy.

["]There is one thing that makes me feel so bitterly—this discrimination.

["]I had the pleasure and the sorrow of spending two years in the military service of the United States, for twelve months right in the battle zones of Europe, and for sixty days right on the front lines. White men came to me and begged for a drink of water from my canteen. Now that I have come back to Newark I find that some of those men do not want to serve me, even though they drank out of my canteen when they were in hell.["]

Mr. Philip Hemmings (Philadelphia, Pa.): ["]The greatest trouble we have is among our own people, and those people, as usual, are preachers and politicians. When our branch of this organization was in its infancy—when all the preachers turned us down—there was one preacher who stood by us—Rev. Dr. Eason. He in conjunction with our bulldog president, Mr. Toot, made the Philadelphia branch of the organization a great success.["]

MR. NOBLE OF NORFOLK.

R. C. Noble (Norfolk, Va.) made some observations on the conditions in Norfolk and endorsed what was said by another delegate, that ministers have tried to do this association a great deal of harm. There are, however, many members of the ministry of Norfolk who, through their preaching, have done this association immeasurable good and have been the means of adding to the association's already long list, he said.

Conditions in Norfolk as far as they affect Negroes are fairly good, he continued. They are much better than in other cities in the South.

MONTREAL'S DELEGATE.

Dr. [D.] D. Lewis (Montreal, Canada): "I come to state briefly the conditions as they exist in Canada for our people, and especially in the Province of Quebec, which is controlled solely by the French. The laws there are very loose. The Frenchman by nature is a sportsman, and thus he sees to it that things are left loose, so that he may have all the freedom he wants. These conditions tend to make colored people lazy and indolent, and live what is generally termed a 'happy-go-lucky life.' Indeed, it is hard to find a colored men employed unless he happens to be a railroad man. But these statements refer to just one class of colored people. The other classes lead entirely different lives; but they are scattered all over the city and it is difficult to get them together. The result was that when this movement was first introduced in Quebec it was only the toiling class—the railroad men—who took kindly to it.

"We are all getting away from the old saying of 'Give me Jesus and you can have the world.' We are determined now in Quebec to have some of this world, and, what is more, the best part of the world, and we will take a chance on having Jesus. (Applause.) We believe the people in this world, no matter whether they be white or black, who have not enough sense to get a living, and a profitable living, have not sense enough to get to heaven. Therefore, the only heaven we are thinking about now is the making of a heaven in this world; and as much as the other fellow has toiled and shed his blood to make this country his heaven, we can only look over yonder where conditions are such that he is afraid to launch out too far to get our heaven.["]

Printed in *NWCB*, 7 August 1920. Original headlines omitted.

1. Harry W. Kirby was later elected president of the Washington, D.C., branch of the UNIA, in 1921 (*NW*, 4 June 1921).

2. A reference to William Ware (b. 1872), who was born in Lexington, Ky., and who organized the Welfare Association for Colored People in Cincinnati in 1917 and served as president until 1920. He attended the UNIA's annual meeting in New York in August 1920 and returned to Cincinnati to convert his organization into a branch of the UNIA. As president of the local chapter of the UNIA, Ware reportedly established a membership of eight thousand. Faithful in attending the subsequent annual meetings of the UNIA, he was knighted at the August 1924 convention and became known to his associates as Sir William Ware (*WWCA*, vol. 2; Wendell P. Dabney, *Cincinnati's Colored Citizens* [Cincinnati: Dabney Publishing, 1926], pp. 213–14).

3. On 24 February 1920 the United Brotherhood of Maintenance of Way Employees and Railroad Shop Laborers, led by William Preston Stoute (d. 1923), called a strike in the Panama Canal Zone. According to American military intelligence, "Seventy-five percent of the total force walked out or 12,750 of a total force of 17,000 employees of the Panama Canal and Panama Railroad" (DNA, RG 165, file 10634-672). Virtually all of the black employees, with the exception of hospital attendants and those in the military, stayed out on the first day. MID estimated that 38 percent of the blacks in the military honored the strike on the first day only. Although the canal and the railroad continued to operate, practically all of the utilities were shut down. The Panamanian government initially refused to interfere, and the Panamanian Labor Union, while refusing to strike in sympathy with the United Brotherhood, nevertheless aided the strikers by blocking the use of Panamanian workers as strikebreakers. Stoute's objectives included an increase in wages, a schedule of periodic promotions for employees, equal pay for male and female employees performing similar work, salary increases for workers promoted to positions normally paying a higher wage, and parity for black employees given "acting" positions that would normally go to higher-paid whites. American military intelligence noted that local UNIA organizers sided with the strikers and cabled Garvey for help. Stoute met with the British minister in Panama City (most of the black workers were British subjects) and with Harding, the American governor of the Panama Canal Zone, but they reached no compromises, and Harding agreed only to grant the strikers an additional two days to return to work. Before the allotted time expired, however, the Panama Canal Zone police began to arrest and evict the strikers and their families. On the first day of evictions, fifteen hundred employees were forced from their homes. The prospects for the strike's success deteriorated further when the president of Panama banned public meetings on 2 March. In addition, the American Federation of Labor suspended the United Brotherhood, so that any moral or financial support that might have come from the AFL was lost. With the leadership jailed or deported and the strike broken, Governor Harding announced that all returning strikers would be reinstated but that they would be treated as new employees, therefore receiving a lower wage and a possible loss of company housing ("Negro Labor Agitation," DNA, RG 165, file 10634-672).

4. Prince Madarikan Deniyi emerged as one of Garvey's critics during the 1920 convention. Deniyi's conflict with Garvey at the convention led to a long and bitter round of charges and countercharges. According to the *Negro World*, Deniyi had spoken before UNIA meetings in New York, Brooklyn, Jersey City, N. J., and Philadelphia appealing for funds to secure passage back to Nigeria. Describing him as a "tramp preacher," the *Negro World* accused him of trying to "dominate the convention" (*NW*, 9 July 1921). The *Chicago Defender*, a longtime rival of the *Negro World*, printed many of Deniyi's criticisms of Garvey ("Native Brands Back to Africa Movement a Farce," *CD*, 14 May 1921). Garvey in turn warned his adherents and branded Deniyi a fraud (*NW*, 14 April 1921; advertisement in *NW*, 6 August 1921). While biographical information on Deniyi is scarce, he claimed to have been a druggist and embalmer from Lagos, Nigeria (*CD*, 14 May 1921; [New York] *Amsterdam News*, 25 May 1921).

5. Clifford Stanley Bourne (b. 1880?) was born in Barbados and educated at St. Steven's Grammar School and Combermore High School. He worked in England for two large commercial houses, and from 1906 to 1913 he worked in Guatemala as an accountant for a wholesale firm. He later opened his own business as a commission merchant. Bourne won a reputation in Guatemala as a protector of West Indian immigrants, often interceding with the governor on their behalf, and in 1920, after meeting with visiting UNIA officials, he became president of the Guatemalan branch of the UNIA. In September 1921 he was appointed commissioner for Guatemala with authority to supervise divisions of the UNIA in that nation. In 1923 Garvey selected Bourne as one of a trio of high chancellors to run the UNIA during his incarceration. When Garvey split with the New York faction of the UNIA in 1929, Bourne remained with the American-based group; beginning in 1931 he served for one year as its president general (*NW*, 28 August 1920, 29 September 1923).

6. In 1921 Rev. Peter Edward Batson became pastor of a new church, Community AME Church in New York (*NW*, 25 June 1921).

7. D. W. Griffith's controversial film about the Civil War and Reconstruction, *The Birth of a Nation* (1915), was based on Thomas Dixon's novel *The Clansman*. Griffith's stereotypical portrayal of the film's black characters (white actors in blackface, in most instances) caused the NAACP to condemn the film as racist when it appeared in New York, Boston, and Chicago (Donald Bogle, *Toms, Coons, Mulattoes, Mammies, and Bucks* [New York: Viking Press, 1973], pp. 10–18; John Hope Franklin, " 'Birth of a Nation'—Propaganda as History," *Massachusetts Review*, 20 [1979]: 417–434).

8. Rev. Andrew N. Willis was president of the Guabito, Panama, branch of the UNIA (*NW*, 17 July 1920).

9. Marie Duchatellier (spelled also Duchaterlier) was a well-known Panamanian lecturer on Africa and an advocate of black nationalism when she joined the UNIA. Addressed as Lady Duchatellier, she delivered lectures during the 1890s on such topics as "The Race Must Keep Pace or Disappear" and "The Negro Must Have a Nation" (*Voice of the Negro*, May and July 1897). In 1911 Duchatellier was a corresponding member of the Negro Society for Historical Research. By January 1920 she was an active organizer for the Garvey movement, touring Panama on behalf of the Black Star Line (Tony Martin, *Race First* [Westport, Conn.: Greenwood Press, 1976], pp. 82, 100, 182).

10. Henry Ogilvie.

11. Actually William A. Wallace, president of the UNIA chapter in Chicago and also delegate to the 1921 convention (*NW*, 3 September 1921; DNA, RG 165, file 10110-2211/1).

[[*New York*, 3 August 1920]]

. . . Evening Session.

A large attendance of the public was in evidence at the evening session. After the customary opening a musical program was rendered. Mesdames Lulu Robinson and Barrier Houston each sang a solo, and were followed by the Acme Quartette of male voices.

The President-General presided, while the other leading officials of the association occupied seats on the platform. In presenting the Rev. Dr. Ferris to the audience, Mr. Garvey took occasion to make an allusion to Professor Du Bois. Dr. Ferris, he said, had spoken to him last night, at Madison Square Garden, of the fact that Dr. Du Bois was present, to which he (Mr. Garvey) replied that Dr. Du Bois was no more to him than anyone else; that "we only think of those Negroes who feel that the hour has come for Negroes to stick by Negroes." We believe Negroes are big, not by the size of their pocketbook, not by the alien company they keep but by their being for their race. You cannot advocate "close ranks" today and talk "dark water" tomorrow; you must be a hundred per cent Negro. This reference to Professor Du Bois drew forth loud applause, and everyone seemed to relish Mr. Garvey's thrust at the noted editor of the "Crisis."

Dr. Ferris, in his address, said that, being a slow thinker, he would take up the subject regarding Dr. Du Bois at some future time, as he would have to brood over it, as it were, nurse it, turn it inside out, before he could come to a conclusion and make an appropriate reply to Mr. Garvey's reference to that eminent gentleman from the University of Atlanta.

The rest of Dr. Ferris' remarks were very scholarly and entertaining. Among other things he said that the Negro made a big mistake in this country in 1895, when Booker T. Washington told the world that we began at the Senate, instead of at the plow. Booker T. Washington had good economic philosophy, but in placing the Negro a little lower in the category of mankind he did the race much harm. The U.N.I.A., however, is here to correct the mistake and other similar mistakes made by former so-called leaders of the race which believes in deeds, and in achievements; that "faith without works is dead."

The Hon. Gabriel Johnson, Mayor of Monrovia, Liberia, was next introduced, and the chair in presenting him said that the distinguished visitor appeared at the convention and would address them merely as a citizen of Liberia, not in an official capacity. . . .

Printed in *NW*, 14 August 1920.

Address by Gabriel Johnson, Mayor of Monrovia, Liberia

[[*New York*, 3 August 1920]]

MAYOR OF MONROVIA, LIBERIA, TELLS OF POSSIBILITIES IN THE NEGRO REPUBLIC

. . . Mr. Garvey, who presided at Tuesday night's meeting, announced:—

THE LONE STAR.

"We have among the delegates some celebrated characters, some able men, and it is but right that we should give you the opportunity of hearing them. Among the many we have with us is the Mayor of the City of Monrovia, Liberia. He is also president of the Monrovia division of the

U.N.I.A. He has not yet spoken in convention, but he will say a few words tonight, giving us an outline of the great country founded several decades ago on the West Coast of Africa by American Negroes. Liberia is the stronghold of the Negroes in Africa. Whilst the greater portion of Africa is now controlled and dominated by alien races, we are glad that the Divine Architect and Creator has seen fit in His great wisdom to preserve at least one spot on the West Coast for the Negro.

HON. GABRIEL JOHNSON

"I have to say that we must first congratulate ourselves and this organization on having been blessed by God by the appointment of the man (turning to and addressing Mr. Garvey) who occupies the position of President-General," his honor began.

"I am very pleased that he has mentioned to you that, although I occupy an official position in Monrovia I am here solely as a delegate from the local division of the Universal Negro Improvement Association in Monrovia. Therefore, I am not able to give you any guarantee of the Republic of Liberia in an official capacity, or from the government officials there. I am [able] to give you an outline of the possibilities of Liberia.

["]I may say that the idea of the U.N.I.A. when first presented in Liberia was no more favorably accepted there, than it was in many of your States here in America. Of course, the people there live under different conditions from those you live under here; the environment is different; the troubles and perplexities they have are different, and we have our troubles and our differences, just the same as you have yours. But, I may say to you that after a few weeks we succeeded in forming an organization in Monrovia, the capital city of Liberia, as well as two or three smaller divisions further in the interior.

TO MAINTAIN INTEGRITY.

["]To tell you that the possibilities of Liberia are great would be putting it in a very mild form. Of course, Liberia is yet an undeveloped country for several reasons. I remember a gentleman asking a very important official of the government why it is that Liberia does not develop more rapidly and did not receive more capital from foreign investors and carry on the country better than it is. The reply was that it was better to try to preserve intact what we desired for future generations and the integrity and autonomy of Liberia than to have an open hand to those who would be willing at any moment to swallow her in consequence of their might and their capital. (Cheers.) Being left alone, almost, Liberia has had inducement of all kinds. We have had them coming to us and saying, "If you will only grant us this, we would support you." "If you would only grant us that, we would protect you." "If you would only grant us that, we would finance you." But all these proposals have been refused one by one to maintain the integrity of the republic.

RICH IN PRODUCTS.

["]Liberia abounds with palm kernels, which come from the palm tree; with piassava, with rubber and coffee. As you know, palm kernels are taken from the palm tree; piassava grows wild and does not have to be cultivated. The palm tree gives several benefits to man. The natives use the leaf for thatching their houses. That thatch also is fibered and used to make fishing nets. The tree produces several bunches of nuts, and on the outside of that nut is a pulp that they use to make sauce for eating, and out of that sauce comes an oil which they use for food also. It is gotten in large quantities and shipped abroad to Europe and to other parts. After this pulp is taken off the outside of the palm there is a hard shell that covers the kernel. That shell is used in their homes in place of coal, as we have not discovered any coal yet. The blacksmith uses this shell in his furnace; it produces great heat and is very easily got. Inside of that shell is the kernel, and that is the palm kernel that is shipped by the ton to Europe and America whenever possible. The palm tree brings a large number of comforts to civilization. Not only have the oils been in great demand during the war, but since, and today there is a great demand for Liberia's palm kernels and palm oil, and the price has gained to such an extent as never before in the history of the country.

OTHER VALUABLE PRODUCTS.

["]Next comes the bamboo tree which resembles the palm tree. It is slightly different. The leaf of the bamboo tree is much better for thatching but it grows no nuts or anything that can be eaten. It produces though, a very hard nut kernel that is termed "Vegetable Ivory" which is of commercial value; although it is not in large quantities at present and has never been shipped very largely, yet there is a great deal of them growing. Piassava is taken from the stock of the tree. It is a very coarse fibre which is used mainly in England and other parts for making heavy brooms and brushes. We are also told that this piassava was used during the war for making all the white powder. Whether this is true or not I am unable to say. The bamboo tree or the piassava tree also produces, when it is very old, a wood which is very beautiful and which is polished and made into different pieces of furniture; but is very small and can only make any small parts.

LIBERIAN COFFEE.

["]The real Liberian coffee is indigenous to the soil of Liberia. It did not grow in any other country until about two years ago when explorers went into Liberia and brought away plants as well as the seed of the Liberian coffee and transplanted it into some parts of South America. Having facilities there, they were able to disturb the Liberians in their coffee manufacture; and before the European war the prices of the Liberian coffee went down so very low that the farmers there had almost given up hope of ever recovering their plantations again. At the close of the war the Liberian coffee took a jump and where the price was never over sixteen cents, coffee now went up to twenty-two cents a pound. It had fallen as low as four cents during the war.

["]Therefore, you see we have in the natural products of Liberia something worth the while of any farmer or commercial man if he desires to go there.

["]I bring you greetings from Liberia and we hope that this organization will take on the right spirit and with concerted action on your part [*and*] with our assistance—[t]hat Liberia some day may grow and prosper and be what we all desire it to be—a great Republic.["] (Cheers.)

Printed in *NWCB*, 7 August 1920. Original headlines omitted.

Reports of the Convention

[[Liberty Hall, New York, Aug. 4, 1920]]

The sessions of the great International Convention during Wednesday and Thursday were taken up with the hearing of reports of delegates respecting conditions in their own countries or [local]ities.

ROTTEN CONDITIONS IN ANTIGUA.

[Dr.] Geo. Alexander McGuire, of Antigua, spoke of conditions in the Island of Antigua, Leeward Island Colony, B.W.I. His report, one of the most interesting, was a revelation in itself. Conditions existing in that section of the British possessions, he said, are abominable and deplorable; not only politically, but industrially and religiously as well. In graphic language Dr. McGuire gave a picture of the situation in that part of the world as affecting colored people, and is a strong appeal to the American Negro to give the subjects of the British West Indies a helping hand to ameliorate conditions there prevalent.

The crown colony system of government keeps Antigua, as well as most islands of the British West Indies, under the thraldom of crown officialdom, he said. The Governor is sent out from the British Colonial Office. His Legislative Council consists of the heads of all Departments of Public Service, known as "official members," and an equal number, also appointed by the Governor, known as non-official members.

The taxpayers and people have absolutely no say in their choice for representatives in the Legislative Council, but the Governor is "graciously pleased," to use the bombastic phraseology of the petty government, to appoint one "colored" man—[not] Negro, not black, but "colored" [i]f you please, to give "color" to his Legislative Council and such gentleman knows that he is merely a c[ipher?], to fill out space. These ten persons and the Governor make all laws, levy all taxes, and railroad through the most important legislation in an hour, and the people, the masses of the people, over 90 per cent. being Negroes, have no part in making laws or in protesting against unjust legislation. Crown colony government is the great incubus which inhibits the progress of Antigua.

THE CONTRACT LAW.

The Contract Labor Law, an iniquitous and heinous and archaic piece of legislation, about 80 years old, introduced soon after emancipation and amended at various times, holds the black laborers in veritable peonage. These people are not free to move from one sugar estate to another, or from one estate to village, not free to stop one day from labor if their proprietor demands their services, not free to sever their connection on the weekly pay day if they desire, but must give from 30 to 90 days' notice. The proprietors and managers of estates thus hold an unfair and unjust advantage over the laborers who are dragged into the magistrates' courts, fined or imprisoned and sent back to work on the same estates. "Plantocracy," or domination by the planters is the second great affliction of Negroes in Antigua.

OPPRESSIVE TAXATION.

Taxation is out of all proportion with the limited resources of the people. For the benefit of the salaries of a top-heavy and unnecessary official force, there are high rates of taxation, both internal and external. Everything is taxe[d], even the uncultivated and non-arable rocks and sands when it was threatened by the people that if the cocoanut trees in their backyards which served to cool their thirst on sultry days were taxed they would cut them down, and if their chickens which served to supply the community with eggs were taxed, they would kill and eat them, the Governor and his council refrained from taxing these.

POOR WAGES.

Unremunerative wages. Men in agricultural toil received about 50 to 60 cents for 10 hours under a tropical sun, and they do not always get even five days' work in a week. Women laborers get from 16 to 18 cents per day. Is it any wonder that they are underfed, that their physical vitality is low, that their powers of resistance against disease are diminished and that tuberculosis, skin diseases, hookworms, malnutrition and similar conditions take their heavy toll? Is it any wonder that men and women go about in tattered rags and boys about the age of 12 to 14 can be seen playing in the villages clad only in Nature's garb—in other words absolutely nude?

ABSENTEE LANDLORDS.

Absentee proprietorship is a bane on Antigua. The owners of most of the estates live in England. Their money is invested in sugar cultivation and production, and they do nothing for the economic betterment of the laboring people, whose sweat and whose brawn till the soil and reap the harvests. They stay in England and suck the island dry, while the islanders get the husks.

RIGOROUS CENSORSHIP.

Press Regulation and Censorship. In the island of Antigua there is one newspaper—so-called. It is run by a Barbados Negro. Its motto is, "I shine for all." Its name is the "Antigua Sun." But the "Sun" does not dare shine for all. The government won't let it. There are articles from my own pen in the editor's pigeon-holes that he states are "untimely." He cannot offend the government, or the planters, or the merchants. The government requires a bond of $100 from any man who publishes a paper, and that means some one must go his security, and he is tied hands and feet. He has to submit for censorship his forms every day before printing them next day. Attempts were made to suppress the Negro World and other so-called seditious literature, but up to date the Legislative Council has not committed this unpardonable sin.[1]

CUBA.

Mr. Richard Marks, of Preston, Cuba, in his report, covered only part of Cuba, in referring to discriminations in various forms in evidence there against Negroes.

NORTH CAROLINA.

Rev. C. W. Cheek, of Nashua County, N.C., told of the injustices and other troubles of our people in his section of the country, chief of which, he said, is complete submission and subserviency to the white man in all things and his unjust, cruel and harsh domination over them.

HAITI.

Mr. Napoleon J. Francis, of Port a[u] Prince, Haiti, spoke of the revolutions instigated in that country by white men either from the United States or other foreign countries, their object being to divide the natives and oppress them and take advantage of their helplessness. The Republic of Haiti, he said, needs help from every Negro in the United States of America. Actual independence they do not have, but they hoped to possess it and complete freedom in the not distant future, with God's help and the aid of black people from this country and other parts of the world.

DOMINICAN REPUBLIC.

Delegate Philip Van Puton, of the Dominican Republic, Santo Domingo, said he spoke for 75,000 Negroes in that country. A system is there in practice whereby the white Spanish and white Americans conspire to exclude further immigration of Negroes into the Republic. Conditions there, he said, are terrible. The Negroes there, however, who come chiefly from the West Indian Islands, are now uniting for their own salvation. They no longer are possessed with Anglomania, but are determined to obtain and maintain their rights at all hazards, and [are] preparing themselves, silently, yet surely, for the time when their services will be needed for the reclamation and redemption of Africa for the Africans. No place is more productive and fruitful, he continued, than this Island. Millions of dollars are being made by the white people, but nothing by the Negro.

WHITES DOMINATE.

Everything there is controlled by foreigners. Laborers get only a dollar a day. In the northern part the Negroes (who emigrated there from America 75 years ago) raise an abundance of bananas and cocoa, but have no facilities for transporting it.

PHILADELPHIA.

Mr. Fred A. [T]oote, of Philadelphia, spoke of the troubles with the Irish element in that city. He mentioned also, with regret, the existence there of a caste system among colored people. This, he said, is an undoubted obstacle to the progress of the race, since unity of action is absolutely essential for its advancement and welfare. Efforts, too, he said are being made by the churches there to hold back the success of the U.N.I.A. This opposition is also shown by the secret societies in Philadelphia, of which there are many. Little or nothing is being done by the Negroes there to improve their industrial conditions; yet the opportunities are ripe and preg-[n]ant with big results, the population among the Negroes being 150,000. There is not a factory there owned and operated by Negroes—in fact, nothing to indicate any substantial progress since his emancipation. Employment conditions, also, are bad for colored men and women.

BERMUDA.

Mr. Benjamin Diet, of Bermuda, outlined conditions existing in his country. He mentioned the discrimination against the race in the matter of government positions, and said that in the factories men and women are given work only of the lowest and most menial character.

AFTERNOON SESSION.

On the reconvening of the convention for the afternoon session, Mr. William Musgrave Le Motte, of Brooklyn, N.Y., spoke of the deplorable housing conditions in that city among colored people. More stores owned and conducted by them are needed there. Unlike New York, where Negroes are practically all in one section, the people there are scattered throughout the city, so that they cannot co-operate with one another as in New York. He further mentioned the discrimination in Brooklyn against colored people, in ice-cream parlors and other places.

PHILADELPHIA.

Miss Louis[e] Crofutt, of Philadelphia, also addressed the convention, saying there are some places in the Quaker City where a Negro man or woman cannot walk in the streets without being molested.

NEWARK.

Miss Louise Wilson, of Newark, N.J., said that the colored people there seem not to care to take upon themselves responsibilities. Three classes exist there, she said: the low, the middle, and the very high class. The first are so low in character and training that to interest them in work, would be doing a wonderful thing. The second class are satisfied with conditions, content so long as they have a job and a suit of clothes or a dress to wear in which to make a showing. The third class live exclusively among themselves, disdaining to associate among the others, and taking no interest in affairs affecting the race. Upon returning home, however, at the close of the convention, she would put forth especial efforts to arouse some of the good people to activity.

PITTSBURGH.

Miss Nettie Clayton of Pittsburgh, Pa., related conditions in her city. Referring particularly to housing matters, she said that much discrimination is in evidence against colored people there, only the most dingy and dilapidated houses being rented to them.

DISCRIMINATION.

Rev. A. J. Mann, of Newark, N.J., said that conditions in the North are practically the same as in the South, as far as discrimination against the colored people is concerned. He expressed the hope that the U.N.I.A. would be able to do something to help improve things in this respect.

PRAISES THE JEW.

Mr. S. Williams, [2] of Cleveland, O., spoke favorably of conditions there, saying there had never been any race riots in Cleveland; that a good feeling exists between the whites and the blacks in his city. This is due chiefly to the Jews, he believed, who practically control everything there. The Jews lend the colored people in Cleveland support and encouragement, and freely give them employment. Housing conditions there, are bad, however.

SEATTLE.

Rev. F. H. Simms, Seattle, Wash., spoke of conditions among colored people in the Far West, and said they are very much enthused in their support of the U.N.I.A. When asked by a brother delegate about actual conditions there, he said: "The white men won't leave our women alone and our men look on white trash."

OHIO.

Mr. J. A. Hudson, of Hamilton, O., said that there are plenty of empty houses in that city, but that notwithstanding this, the colored people there cannot obtain sufficient housing accommodations, because of discrimination against them.

Rev. B. F. Smith, Philadelphia, said that the United States of America is hell for the colored man to live in. He expanded his remarks on this belief, by relating his personal experience from contact with white people in various parts of the country.

BALTIMORE.

Rev. J. J. Cranston, of Baltimore, Md., made a splendid report describing conditions as they exist in that city.

Other delegates spoke, representing Yorktown, N.Y., Boston and Miss James of the Impelling and Industrial Enterprise Association.

THURSDAY'S SESSION.

Mr. Allen Hubbe,[3] (Norfolk, Va.)—Colored people in his city, he said, are Jim-crowed, segregated, ostracized and given everything but a square deal.

NEW HAVEN.

Mr. Enos A. Harsford,[4] of New Haven, Conn., followed, and said that the hospitals there treat colored patients with indifference and injustice. They are informed that if they do not like the treatment accorded them, they should build hospitals of their own. There is mistreatment of colored people, also, in the street cars in New Haven. Though colored women have a chance to fill positions[,] they are greatly underpaid. There is need there for trade schools for our colored boys and girls, most of whom are without a knowledge of any of the trades.

Mr. Thomas E. Bagby, of Stamford, Conn., continued the story of conditions in the Nutmeg State. His home town, he said, is a very unsanitary place for colored people; the houses they live in are not properly taken care of. Plenty of work can be had, but it is of the menial kind only. As among themselves, there is sadly noticeable a lack of self-respect, which makes it impossible for others to respect them. Nor is there any banding together of the people.

Mr. Walter Green, of Portsmouth, Va., said that the chances for better conditions in that city are good, but there is no pulling together on the part of the people. Even the Government, in the giving out of employment in the Navy Yard[,] discriminates against the colored men, giving preference in almost every instance to white men; not only that, but colored mechanics and workmen receive less pay from the Government than whites receive.

Mr. William C. Matthews, counsellor-at-law, Boston, stated that in the Bay State there are about 50,000 to 75,000 colored people, distributed in the principal cities, and in quite a few of the smaller towns. The great trouble there, he said, is not discrimination and the like; it is rather the tendency of the Negro himself not to unite together. Since November last, 1,800 persons in Massachusetts have joined the U.N.I.A. This, in view of the coldness and indifference of the people there to the movement, is a wonderful feat. Opportunities for obtaining an education and availing oneself of the many public institutions there are good.

Dr. Louis.

Dr. Louis, of Montreal, Canada, said that for years the Negro has been crying about the unfavorable conditions by which he is surrounded. Now that we know what the trouble is, we should get busy and start at once to take action to remedy the conditions. A discussion thereupon ensued as to the wisdom of ceasing the hearing of further reports from delegates, that the convention may begin to take definite action on the matters before it. It was finally decided, in accordance with the original plan, to let the hearings go on until the end of the fifth day—six days in all.

Nova Scotia.

Mr. George D. Cre[e]se,[5] representing Nova Scotia and Eastern Canada, stated that about 2,500 black people are resident there, and that conditions affecting them are far from satisfactory. The majority work in the iron and steel industries and receive wages of from $4.50 to $6 per day, in many instances receiving the same pay as the whites. We have many skilled mechanics, printers, carpenters, masons, photographers, engineers, riveters, but they cannot get employment at their trades. Hence they have to seek work in the steel plants as laborers, as bricklayers, and as firemen. There is no open discrimination. A system exists there of collecting a poll tax, everyone being required to pay $10 for police protection, good streets, etc. If the tax is not paid, the police call at the house and take the individual to jail. This practice applies only to the colored people. There are no colored lawyers there to represent the colored people in the courts. Housing conditions, too, are deplorable in Eastern Canada and in Nova Scotia. Rents are excessively high.

THE INFLUENCE OF THE CHURCH.

Mr. Daniel Ford, of New York City, said he had made a special study of conditions here, and spoke at length, taking up in detail questions relating to the church, the theatre, moving pictures, dance halls, economics, trades unions, hospitals, education, the social atmosphere, etc. He said that the churches exert no influence among our people in the matter of bringing them together as a race. Thousands of dollars are wasted by them in attending these places, out of which they get not one cent of real or lasting benefit. While there are many hospitals in New York, none is owned by colored people, nor is there any in which colored physicians are permitted to practice. There are ample educational facilities here, he said, such as libraries, schools and colleges, but the people do not take full advantage of them, as they should.

MONTREAL.

Mrs. Thomas O'Brien, Montreal, Canada, stated there is no interference on the part of the whites with the blacks[;] the colored people are allowed to do almost as they pleased. There is no segregation there at all. But they spend their money too freely.

ST. LUCIA'S DELEGATE.

Randolph Felix (St. Lucia, B.W.I.): After speaking on the progress of the organization in St. Lucia, Mr. Felix said: "I am sorry to say that conditions otherwise are not to my satisfaction. We have not as much privilege as explained by the last speaker from Bocas del Toro. The preferences that have been given us are the little cultivation of cane manufactures [*manufacturers?*]; and how much do they earn? The poor workers have very little money to spend out of the two shillings a day for ten or twelve hours' work. Then again, a little cocoa is cultivated in various parts of the island, and when it is brought to town they get seven or ten cents a pound for it. Another means of existence is as a coal carrier. Some of the people—and especially women—are compelled to carry coal for their living. They get from one to three cents for this work; so you can see that their suffering is very intense.

NO STEAMSHIP ACCOMMODATIONS.

"We have had people booked for the last two or three years for different parts of the world, and up to the present time they cannot receive passage on any of the boats. My own case is an example of this. I was booked three months in anticipation of getting passage to come to this country to attend this convention, but I could not get it, and I was three months coming from St. Lucia to New York. So you see that we are surely in need of a boat in that part of the world. We need not only a boat, but we need the help of every individual Negro of the world. The movement started by Mr. Garvey has brought the West Indies around, and to-day it has reached the hearts of the people of St. Lucia. To-day we have a following, a membership, of thirty-one hundred; and, mind you, that was three months ago, when I left. They are praying for the day to come when he will be able to surprise them with a boat."

SEGREGATED IN NEWPORT NEWS.

Miss Nellie G. Whiting (Newport News, Va.): "We are segregated in the Eastern section of the city," said Miss Whiting, delegate from Newport News. "All of our people are huddled together over in one section, yet white men are allowed to come over there in our section and set up their stores and sell to colored people. We are not allowed to go over in their section. We have a shipyard there. Our men and our boys work in the shipyard; they are segregated there. The white man goes to one window for his pay and the colored man goes to another. Our men there are building ships. When we ride on the ships we are put in one corner; the white people can walk anywhere they want to go.

"And as to the schools, the white man lets the white children study books in order to keep going upwards, and they deny us the use of the same books in order to keep us down, but give us books instead to study that will lead us to worship the white man and keep ourselves down.

"And then we have men in our town who believe in segregating themselves. We have barber shops in the white sections that shave the white man but not the colored man. And then we have the preachers. Why, during October last year, when we staged a meeting in one of the churches in behalf of the launching of the 'Frederick Douglas,' the next night we could not meet there. We went to some of the other churches, and the minister of one church caused the deacon to go over to the Town Hall to ask the mayor for assistance in suppressing us, and the mayor asked him whether he was a member of the organization, and he said, 'No.' The deacon had told him that those colored folks over there had come to take all the money from the town, so he replied, 'Well, I can't do anything; I can't stop them; the thing for you to do is to go and join them, too.' (Laughter and applause.)

TROUBLESOME PREACHER.

"Then there is a certain minister in that town who, after we had advertised that we would stage a meeting for Thursday night, canceled the engagement at his church and gave us very short notice to that effect. He said we could not have our meeting there. It was during the drive for the 'Frederick Douglas,' and for some reason that church caught fire and burned up. (Cheers.)

"And as to the moral condition of our people, they are very bad in our city. We are segregated; we are not allowed to mingle with the white people; yet white people won't leave our girls alone."

Printed in *NWCB*, 7 August 1920. Original headlines omitted.

1. Antigua's Seditious Publications Ordinance of 1920 was passed in February and was intended to "prevent the publication and importation of seditious newspapers, books and documents" (PRO, CO 137/369). The ordinance was based on the earlier Seditious Publications Ordinance of 1915 and included an additional feature removing the option of a jury trial for those accused of violations.

2. Shedrick Williams served as president of the UNIA branch in Cleveland in 1921 (*NW*, 19 February 1921).

3. Actually Allen Hobbs.

4. A reference to Innis Abel Horsford, president of the New Haven branch of the UNIA during 1920 and 1921 (*NW*, 3 December and 31 December 1921).

5. George D. Creese, an active member of the UNIA branch in Sydney–New Aberdeen, Nova Scotia, was chosen commissioner to Canada at the 1921 convention (*NW*, 16 July and 10 September 1921).

[[*New York*, 4 August 1920]]

. . . EVENING SESSION.

The evening session of the convention began at half-past nine o'clock. President-General Marcus Garvey occupied the chair and the Rev. Dr. [W]. H. Ferris delivered the invocation. A short musical program followed.

Mr. Garvey delivered the principal address which dealt with the editorial comments on the part of the metropolitan white press upon the U.N.I.A. and the mass meeting held Monday night in Madison Square Garden. He said the purpose of the white man in Africa is the same as the purpose of the white man in America, which caused the extermination of the Indian, but that four [*hundred*] million black people are too strong to be exterminated at this stage of the world's history. His reference to England evoked greatest applause. He said that though England had ruled Ireland now for seven hundred years that has nothing to do with the fact that Ireland belongs to the Irish. Similarly, though Africa has been occupied for centuries by alien races that does not alter the fact that Africa belongs to the Africans, and that by Divine right. Said he: "We have simply been on a long vacation from Africa, and it is now time to think about closing our vacation. Therefore we are sending notice to the continent to expect our coming. We are serving notice, and will continue to serve notice to the alien races now in possession of the country there, that we are coming, and this we will continue to do for another fifty years if need be; but when the time comes to take possession it will not be a question of 'Why?' It will simply be a question of 'We are here.' "

Mr. Garvey also said that the Negro here is too weak and impotent to retaliate in any way in the United States, but is too strong in Africa not to do so. His address was most interesting and was punctuated with loud applause frequently throughout.

Rev. Dr. Ferris and Rev. Dr. Brooks also spoke, after which the meeting adjourned.

Printed in *NW*, 14 August 1920.

L. Lanier Winslow to William L. Hurley[1]

London, August 4, 1920

Important. 1169, August 4, 3 p.m.
 . . . Confidential. I should be glad to receive full report regarding negro convention in New York[2] and activities of Marcus Garvey.

[L. LANIER WINSLOW]

DuL.

[*Endorsements*] Hold Awaiting information from Ruch of D.J. Tel London 8-7-20
WLH/LAW

DNA, RG 59, file 811.108 G 191/26. TL (telegram), recipient's copy. Handwritten endorsements.
 1. William Lee Hurley (b. 1880) was a career employee of the State Department. Hurley was later a vice-consul at Warsaw in 1923 (U.S. Department of State, *Register*, 1924 [Washington, D.C.: GPO, 1924], p. 144).
 2. Hurley requested and received photostatic copies of the *Negro World* convention bulletins (nos. 1 and 2) from the special assistant to the attorney general; on 11 August he passed these on to Winslow (special assistant to the attorney general to William L. Hurley, 6 August 1920, DNA, RG 65, file OG 185161; DNA, RG 59, file 000–612).

Report by Special Agent P-138

New York City Aug. 5, 1920

In Re: Negro Activities
 I visited Garvey's convention at Liberty Hall this evening [*5 August*] and listened to the reports of the delegates. Garvey, himself, at the opening said that to-night he would [give] way to the out-of-town speakers as to-morrow would be the last day dev[o]ted to the hearing of reports from the delegates.

Radical Delegates
 Among the most radical speakers of the evening was a man whom Garvey introduced as the Reverend Dr. Harton,[1] pastor of a church in Boston, Mass. and a delegate from some churches in Mass. and Rhode Island. Reverend Harton told the crowd that he was President of the New England Baptist Association and that he had always been appointed delegate to all of the conventions, religious, fraternal, etc. He was also a member and officer in "The Equal Rights League", organized by Monroe Trotter of Boston, but now, after finding out Marcus Garvey's movement to be the best of them all, he has decided to join with him heart and soul.
 He claims to be well acquainted with Governor Cooldridge of Mass.[2] and criticized him for not appointing a Negro Judge.

Anti-White Speech

Harton flayed the white people in Boston for not extending social equality to the negroes. He told the audience that during the war he labored in the camps, and our men fought in France for the white man, but if another war should be declared he would refuse to fight, as the only way he would fight is to fight the white man in the south. He told them that the negroes have been bearing on and having to[o] much patience with the white man, being kicked about and ill-treated, so he would advise them to move things, and not to ask them to move anymore. He told them that he believed in fighting for things and for his rights, of course he said we might be called upon to fight them, but his advice to them is "Keep your guns loaded and your powder dry". The crowd went wild with cheers accompanied by the bass drum of the band.

He said that there were a lot of cowardly negroes who refuse to fight for their rights, so he advised the crowd to shoot and kill all those cowardly and cringing negroes. This was followed by cheers, loud and long. He emphasized his advi[c]e not to fight the white man's wars, except a war against the white man.

This Rev. Harton is a powerful, gymnastic preacher of the old Baptist style of negro minister, who speaks in a fighting manner and emphasizes his words with gestures. He is a native born American negro and he is well acquainted with the Boston politician[s]. He would be a very good instrument to spread the Garvey type of "Race Hatred", owing to his connection with the churches, coupled with his impressionable manner of speaking.

Body-Guard for Marcus Garvey

So as to make sure just how much truth there is about Garvey's keeping a body-guard, or his so-called Secret Service Squad, I spent a few hours investigating with the following results: I watched Garvey, after the close of the evening session, until he entered his home. While in Liberty Hall I observed five men standing around him, and they followed him wherever he moved in the Hall—among them was a light complexioned fellow whom I mentioned in one o[f] my previous reports. On leaving the hall, Garvey was accompanied by his girl, known as his Secretary, without whom he never walks. He walked on Lenox Ave[.], from 138th to 129th Street, and I observed that these five guards were around him, walking as follows:—Garvey and his girl in the center, two of the guards some distance in front of him, one a little nearer to him in front, forming a triangle, the other two men came behind about thirty feet apart. I noticed that when anyone passed near to Garvey these rear men closed ranks, drawing near to Garvey until everything was O.K. They followed Garvey to his home, a large apartment house at 133–135 West 129th Street, and after Garvey and his girl took the elevator they left him and walked in a group, talking, until they reached 134th Street and Lenox Ave.

I now have definite proof that these Garvey guards are armed. While the Garvey guards were standing talking at the S.W. corner of 134th Street and Lenox Ave., one of the fellows put his hands behind his back, clasping them to-gether thereby lifting his coat tail, exposing the shining butt of a revolver, in his left hand back pants pocket. He was standing near the light so I could easily observe it. It is doubtful whether these men have a permit for a gun, but at any rate, with the Red speeches and the Anti-White talks that they are listening to daily, I would not be at all surprised if some day these teachings would be put to practise, as these men are not of the intelligent type.

So far as one can judge from the daily talks etc.[,] Liberty Hall is to-day the greatest hot-bed for the teaching of race antagonism, race hatred, and class hatred, and Garvey is the head of the stress. It is therefore impossible to expect anything from it which would in any shape or form help to make the races here and abroad live in peace and harmony[.] To-night Garvey spent a lot of time begging the people for six thousand dollars to pay for the hall etc.

P-138[3]

[*Endorsements*] NOTED W.W.G. Noted F.D.W.

DNA, RG 65, file OG 329359. TD. Stamped endorsements.

1. Probably a reference to Rev. T. S. Harten, who was born in York, S.C., and moved to Cambridge, Mass., to become minister of a church there. He was the pastor of Holy Trinity Baptist Church in Brooklyn from 1922 to ca. 1930 (*WWCA*, vol. 2).

2. Actually John Calvin Coolidge (1872–1933), governor of Massachusetts in 1919–20 and president of the United States from 1923 to 1929 (*WBD*).

3. Available evidence strongly suggests that P-138 was Herbert S. Boulin, the Jamaican-born president of the Berry and Ross Toy and Doll Manufacturing Co., which was located in Harlem. Boulin was one of fourteen Jamaicans living in the United States who signed a letter denouncing Garvey in 1916 (*Jamaica Times*, 7 October 1916). Moreover, the letterhead of the West Indian Protective Society, an anti-Garvey group, listed Boulin as one of its field agents in 1920. His later friendship with Garvey gave him frequent and easy access to Garvey, in both his home and his office (DNA, RG 65, file BS 198940-249, 30 August 1921). In 1921 Boulin was also president of the Gold Coast Import and Export Corp., with headquarters at the same address as the Berry and Ross Co. and with an identical slate of officers (*NW*, 4 June 1921). In an advertisement for Boulin's National Detective Agency in December 1921, Boulin revealed that he was "formerly with the Department of Justice." Bureau of Investigation Special Agent 800 reported, in connection with the appearance of the advertisement, that this was "the same Boulin that was being used by the Department here in New York." He also made it known that "Garvey called my attention to this advertisement and said, 'this only proves my suspicion I have had of this fellow all along.' He went on to say that these things were only helps to him, that is to trust no one." In September 1922 the UNIA purchased the Berry and Ross Co., and the following month the *Negro World* began advertising "Negro dolls" for sale by the "UNIA doll factory." Boulin remained active in New York's West Indian community for years to come. In the early 1940s, he founded the American West Indian Association on Caribbean Affairs, an organization formed to urge the governments of the United States and Britain to appoint West Indian representatives to the Anglo-American Caribbean Commission. During factional disputes within his association, Boulin earned a reputation as a vocal opponent of left-wing influence in American West Indian organizations. In 1942, Boulin described himself as a former member of the Department of Justice "radical squad" while testifying against the leaders of the Ethiopian Pacific Movement, a group of West Indians accused of sedition. He had infiltrated the group on behalf of the Federal Bureau of Investigation (*NYT*, 17 December 1942; DJ-FBI, file 61-826-X10, 6 December 1921; *NW*, 16 September and 22 October 1922).

Frank Burke to George F. Lamb

[*Washington, D.C.*] August 5, 1920

Dear Sir:

Confirming conversation with Mr. Matthews, on this instant, it is
desired that you forward promptly report of the informant covering the
convention of the Universal Negro Improvement Union. Very truly yours,

[FRANK BURKE]
Acting Chief

[*Typewritten reference*] GFR:MAS

DNA, RG 65, file OG 185161. TL, carbon copy.

Report of the Convention

[[*New York*, 5–6 August 1920]]

... THURSDAY, AUG. 5, 1920.

That the meetings of the International Convention of Negroes now
being held here are attracting widespread interest and eliciting considerable
comment, both adverse and favorable, is most apparent. In particular the
metropolitan white press have given much space in their columns not only to
reporting the news of the convention but in commenting editorially upon
the great movement as a whole. The white journalists seem nonplussed by its
unusual character and far-reaching objects, and view it more as being a wild
dream, referring to the redemption of Africa for the black peoples of the
world and the establishment there of a Negro Republic. But in the most
aggressive, clear-cut speech yet delivered in Liberty Hall since the opening of
the convention, the Hon. Marcus Garvey, President-General, last night took
his critics to task and pointed out that nothing is impossible of achievement
which 400,000,000 black people make up their minds to do.

The verbatim reports of the speeches delivered at the sessions of the
convention, and the detailed narrative account of its doings, as recorded in
the Daily Bulletin issued by the Universal Negro Improvement Association
and in the weekly edition of the Negro World are a unique feature and have
set the town ablaze with gossip; so much so that the manifestation of interest
in the convention's proceedings is constantly augmenting. It has created two
hostile camps:—one that favors and espouses the cause of the U.N.I.A., and
the other which, like doubting Thomas, looks on with incredulity and with a
manifest spirit of jealousy and ill-will. The latter indulge in unfair criticism.

Unable themselves to offer a feasible solution of their own, or a better plan for the salvation of the Negro and his emancipation from the injustices, oppression, segregation, discrimination and what-not to which he is subject the world over, they stand aloof, and attempt to scoff at, even to ridicule, the new movement. Such an attitude, to say the least, is discreditable to them and an unworthy reflection upon the race.

The further the meetings of the convention go on the more the U.N.I.A. is succeeding in confounding its enemies and putting them to flight, and the more adherents are being recruited to its ranks; so that it is now confidently believed, despite the stand which many colored people are taking, unfavorable as it may be, toward the movement, that those opposed to the principles of the association will be in such a hopeless and humiliating minority when the convention at the end of its thirty-one days' sessions, shall have adjourned, as to be unwilling to stand up and be counted.

That it is the most historic and notable convention of colored people ever held cannot be gainsaid, and people everywhere are beginning to realize, more and more, the undoubted great good that ultimately will inure to Negroes in both hemispheres as the result of the deliberations and the steps which this representative assemblage will take, not only in respect of ameliorating conditions under which black men now live, and in removing the cruel and unfair practices indulged in against him in all countries, but as well in obtaining and holding forever secure for him, wherever he may be, his just rights and an equal opportunity in the pursuit and enjoyment of happiness, based upon his status as a man, the equal of all other men; the final restoration of Africa to Africans, as their native homeland, and the founding there of a Black Republic, a Black Nation, which the world will and must respect.

Thus far the weather has been ideal for the holding of the meetings of the convention, causing great numbers of people to flock to Liberty Hall. Many are attracted thither, prompted only by morbid curiosity, as if the convention were a circus, instead (as it is) of a parliament of Negroes, the largest ever witnessed, whose delegates are from all parts of the globe, assembled for the serious, deliberate consideration of matters vitally affecting their welfare as an oppressed people. But all such curiosity seekers, upon attending and listening to the proceedings, soon find their curiosity changed, subconsciously, to a feeling and spirit of enthusiasm by what they see and hear, only to be converted, before leaving the auditorium, to a belief in the worthiness and greatness of the cause, and the efficacy of the movement, under the unmatchable leadership of Marcus Garvey, as a potent agency in promoting untold good for the Negro in general. And even though one may prefer to be neutral in the matter of the principles of the Universal Negro Improvement Association, or inclined to stand aloof from it, it is a treat and a pleasure to attend the sessions, particularly those held in the evening, when a fine musical program is given (free of charge), followed by eloquent, soul-inspiring addresses by the new, stalwart, fearless leaders of the race.

Friday, August 6, 1920.

With a slight falling off in attendance on the part of the public (owing to inclement weather), but with the full presence of the delegates who have thus far arrived to participate in its deliberations, the International Convention of Negroes being held here, the sixth day's proceedings opened this morning, with the President-General presiding. Oral reports (in the form of addresses), submitted by delegates, as to conditions among Negroes in all parts of the world, continued throughout the day.

Such is the character of these reports, so full and comprehensive are they, though none are prepared or written in advance by the speakers, and so much valuable information do they contain as to actual conditions, that the interest taken therein on the part of the convention as a whole, has thus far, been sustained unintermitt[ent]ly. This is unusual, since the submission of reports, if long drawn out, at conventions soon becomes tiresome and uninteresting.

So, too, unlike conventions hitherto held by Negroes, there is perfect order throughout the sessions. The delegates act with becoming decorum and with proper respect toward the chair and to each other. A complete absence of those features bordering on the ludicrous and the grotesque, and exhibiting not only lack of mutual respect on the part of those attending as delegates, but scenes as well that make impossible an orderly and systematic dispatch of the business on hand, that in the past have almost invariably characterized large Negro assemblages, as the conventions of secret societies, churches, etc., is pleasingly conspicuous; there is no effort made to play to the galleries, no attempt on the part of anyone to ride rough-shod over anybody else, no indulgence in personalities or acrimonious debate; in short, instead of presenting the semblance of the traditional Lime Kiln Club that has manifested itself from time immemorable at other gatherings of this kind among colored people, the sessions of this convention are marked by orderly, business-like procedure, and a soberness and seriousness in deliberation that is highly commendable and in keeping with the grave, momentous problems of the Race which the convention is endeavoring to grapple with and solve. This is due in no small measure to the genius of the President-General, who has shown himself a master-parliamentarian as well as an able leader of men. His adroitness, tact and skill in handling every situation that arises and in untangling knotty questions that come up and will ever arise in all public assemblages, his thorough grasp of all that goes on and his quickness to allay any feeling of dissatisfaction among the delegates, while at the same time seeing that each is given a fair hearing, is admirable. Moreover, his rulings are sensible and fair, and meet the approbation of the delegates as a whole. Presiding officers of the high type of the Hon. Marcus Garvey are rare, and he may well serve, in this respect, as a worthy model to the presiding officers of many of our other big conventions, as the B[*iennial*] M[*ovable*] C[*onference*]. An illustration of the man in this respect may be seen in the following extract from his remarks toward the close of the morning session: "It is time that we now, as a race, get down to business. Amendments to amendments, amendments to motions, and points of order, we will forget for the good that we have before us. If we find out that it is the intention of anyone to thwart this movement, we serve notice on that individual now that we will use the iron hand and put him out. We have no time to indulge in foolishness, needless talk or discussions not directly pertinent to the great cause that is dearest to our hearts, and for the accomplishment of which we are here assembled."

For its own protection, the convention has engaged a number of secret service men instructed to see to it that no suspicious persons are allowed to enter the auditorium, and that any attempt to frustrate the meetings or interfere with its work in any way by creating disorder or stirring up dissension, is promptly checked and all offenders vigorously dealt with. Like all great movements of this kind, the U.N.I.A. undoubtedly has many enemies, the result of ignorant jealousy of some individuals, and the ill-will of others, who, lacking the brains to enable them to succeed in their own narrow spheres, look with disfavor upon the Association because of the marvelous strides and success it has made. All trouble-makers, therefore, should take warning, and let themselves be neither seen nor heard anywhere within or near the convention hall.

RESULTS OF FIRST WEEK'S SITTINGS.

The first week's proceedings of the convention have been extraordinary, far beyond the expectations of all, and have opened a new epoch in the history of the Negro. Judged by the enthusiasm, in[t]erest and sympathy it has evoked on the part of the masses, and viewed in the light of actual work done toward accomplishing the immediate objects of holding the convention, the sessions, thus far, have been a distinct success, creditable to all who have shared in the labor of arranging for it, and those who have participated in its proceedings. No untoward events have occurred; everything has been done and conducted according to schedule, and the original programme, mapped out, closely followed. Save for the never-ceasing references to the oppressions and needs of the Negro, and the complexion of the faces of those taking part and in attendance, there is nothing to distinguish the convention from that of any other assemblage of its kind held by the members of the Caucasian Race, so orderly have been its proceedings, and all else in connection therewith been done without a hitch, including even the never-to-be-forgotten and memorable mass-meeting held in Madison Square Garden last Monday night.

Printed in *NW*, 14 August 1920.

Report by Special Agent P-138

New York City 8/6/20

IN RE: NEGRO ACTIVITIES (MARCUS GARVEY)

Today [4 *August*] I visited Garvey's afternoon and evening sessions of the Convention now being held in Liberty Hall, which were well attended. The afternoon session was given over to hearing the reports of delegates. Two delegates of note spoke. One was from Hayti and the other from San Domingo. They expressed themselves as in hearty accord with the movement and think Garvey will be the Saviour of their country. They further pledged moral and financial support to carrying on and spreading of Garvey's anti-white propaganda. On the whole all the delegates['] reports played to the tune of "Down with the White Man".

So as to learn all that is possible regarding any Japanese activity among the Garvey followers, I succeeded today in getting in touch with Garvey's associate Editor of the "Negro World" who works in the office and very near to Garvey. This fellow's name is Hudson Price. During a lengthy conversation with him on the street this eve, commenting on the Madison Square Meeting, Sunday and Monday parades, etc., by a series of "drawing out" questions I learned from Price that there were two Japanese whom were very much in sympathy with Garvey's movement and he said that means a great deal to them as the Japs were smart people.

Price had a long talk with one of them especially who visited him at the office, told him to put a Japanese paper on the mailing list which he claims to represent in Tokio, Japan. But Price told me that this said Jap is a "big man" and was only using that as a farce. Price said that the name of this Jap was Kataran or Ketarama.[1] He also stated that six weeks ago Katarama visited the office, 56 W. 135th St. Black Star Line Office, and handed him, Price, a news item which appeared in the Negro World. Of course, I expressed my sympathy with entire movement and affairs and asked Price to secure that particular [*issue*] of the paper for me which he promised to do.

Tonight Garvey spoke on the race question at length. He worked his followers up to a height of frenzied enthusiasm when he told them that for years the white man told them that everything which is black was bad or evil and everything which was white is good. That God was white. The devil was black, but now the negro must turn it the other way about that God is black and the Devil was white. The Negroes will therefore in future worship a Black God and not a White One.

I simply cite the foregoing to give an idea of the plans and method which Garvey used in playing on the crude minds and undeveloped faculties of his followers. Another favorite story of his is that it was the White man who killed Jesus and it was the Black man who helped Jesus to bear the cross up the hill of Calvary, hence God will always help the black man now. The foregoing Biblical story naturally touches the Religious Chord of his hearers.

The con[s]ensus of opinion which one can draw from the reports of the various delegates is that the greatest opposition which they encounter in their respective territory is from the Preachers and all the intelligent Negro Business and Professional men whose attitude is either right out hostility or a Hands Off policy. So far as I can see the movement has ceased to be simply a nationalist movement but among the followers it is like a religion. The majority of them are hard working poor men and women who absolutely refuse to think and reason for themselves. Of course men such as Rev. Easton and Brooks, Ferris, etc., are simply paid employees who must talk as Garvey wants them to or else lose their jobs.

After mixing in among the officers and followers of this movement I spoke with Garvey himself. Two days ago I met him in the street, shook his hands and congratulated him on the wonderful hit he made at Madison Square Garden. I am fully convinced that Garvey's teaching is without doubt a purely anti-white campaign and the Negro World is the instrument employed to spread the propaganda. That the various branches of the movement are only nucleus for further spreading of same. That he gives the leaders of these different branches high titles so as to let them feel important and carry on the work. That he is flirting with the leaders of the Irish, Egyptian, Indian and Japanese only so far as to further his aims. That Garvey is becoming bolder everyday, having been fed along with the hand clapping and cheers of his worshippers. That his followers are under the impression owing to Garvey's statement from the platform, that he has defied state and Government, outwitted the State District Attorney[,] hence he is looked upon as a black Moses. That the convention and movement is only stirring up race hatred and widening the gap between the Races which the other intelligent leaders took years to build up.

P-138

[*Endorsement*] Noted w.w.G.

DNA, RG 65, file OG 258421. TD. Stamped endorsement.

1. A reference to Sen Katayama (1859–1933), director of the International Bureau of Red Syndicates, a contributor to the leftist journal the *Revolutionary Age*, and a leading Socialist and Communist organizer in the United States, Mexico, Canada, and Japan. Born in Hadeki, Japan, Katayama first came to the United States in 1884, working as a houseboy, cook, and farm laborer in San Francisco while he studied English. After twelve years he returned to Japan to organize that nation's first labor union. In 1903 he conducted an extensive speaking tour in the United States on behalf of the Socialist party of America. In 1914 persistent government pressure in Japan caused Katayama to return once again to the United States, where he continued his organizing efforts, especially among Japanese-Americans. By 1919 Katayama was an active worker for the Communist party, drawing the attention of the Bureau of Investigation with his speaking and organizing activities in the United States and Mexico. In 1921 he traveled to the Soviet Union, where he received a hero's welcome. He was eventually elected to the presidium of the Communist International Congress and, at the 1928 Comintern, he helped to frame the official position on the "U.S. Negro question," which included "the right of Negroes to self-determination in the Southern states." When he died, 150,000 mourners attended his funeral in Moscow (Karl G. Yoneda, "The Heritage of Sen Katayama," *Political Affairs* 14, no. 3 [March 1975]: 38–57; DNA, RG 65, files BS 202600-58-11, 7B 136944, and OG

17969; Sen Katayama, "The Socialist Movement in Japan," *New York Call*, 11 November 1917; Hyman Kublin, *Asian Revolutionary: The Life of Sen Katayama* [Princeton: Princeton University Press, 1964]).

Charles E. Ashburner to J. Edgar Hoover

NORFOLK, VIRGINIA August 7, 1920
Attention of Mr. Hoover:

My Dear Sir:

The bearer of this letter is Inspector W. L. Stephens,[1] head of our plain clothes department. He has some information that he is anxious to present to you for your consideration.

Mr. Stephens can be absolutely trusted with any confidential matters that you may see fit to discuss with him.

With the kindest personal regards, I remain, Very truly yours,
CHARLES E. ASHBURNER[2]
City Manager

[*Address*] Radical Division, U.S. Secret
Service, Washington, D.C.
[*Endorsement*] NOTED J.E.H.

DNA, RG 65, file OG 185161. TLS, recipient's copy. Stamped endorsement.

1. William Leroy Stephens (1874–1935), a Norfolk policeman, was appointed inspector of detectives on 15 August 1919 (*Norfolk Ledger-Dispatch*, 25 February 1935).
2. Charles Edward Ashburner (1870–1932) in 1908 became the first city manager in the United States. The son of a British army officer, he immigrated in 1899, working as a building and railroad contractor before accepting the newly created position of city manager of Staunton, Va. He was later city manager of Springfield, Ohio (1914–18), Norfolk, Va. (1918–23), and Stockton, Calif. (1923–28) (*Virginia Cavalcade* 1, no. 4 [Spring 1952]; *Virginia Pilot*, 26 October 1932).

L. Lanier Winslow to William L. Hurley

London, August 7, 1920

No. 449.
Dear Bill:

You may be interested in what the DAILY TELEGRAPH has to say about the convention recently held at Madison Square Garden of the General African Communities League of America. As always,

L. L. W.

DNA, RG 59, file 000–1386. TLI, carbon copy.

Enclosure

[*Daily Telegraph* (London), 4 August 1920]

Ethiopia for the Ethiopians.

"Logic is logic; that's what I say." So wrote Oliver Wendell Holmes in "The Tale of the Wonderful One-horse Shay."[1] It is what the General African Communities League of America has also been saying. Twenty thousand members of the G.A.C.L. have held a meeting in Madison-square Garden to explain their views. These are quite modest. They will be satisfied if all the white nations with colonial possessions in Africa will kindly clear out of that continent and leave it to the black races to whom it rightfully belongs. Let Great Britain, France, Italy, Spain, and the others haul down their flags and sail away from Africa's torrid shore. Then "a Black Democracy for Ethiopia" will take charge, and, in the language of the country of which many of these Ethiopian gentlemen are citizens, will proceed to make things hum. This demand, as we have admitted, is based on logic, and rests on the great principle of national and racial determination. The blacks outnumber the whites in Africa by some forty millions or more; they are the children of the soil; they have as much right, it is urged, over the land as the Poles have over Poland or the Czecho-Slovaks over Czecho-Slovakia. The G.A.C.L. feels it like that, and at Madison-square Garden it informed an already somewhat pre-occupied world that the black race was determined to suffer no longer. It has hoisted the flag—the Black Flag, we presume—and if all "Ethiopia" is not presently made over to the blameless Ethiopians, the G.A.C.L. will want to know the reason why. Its members are[,] in fact, holding a thirty days' Convention to decide what they are going to do about it. The logic of history does not always lead to the same conclusion as the logic of the class-room. History has never been able to find a time when the negro and negroid races were the real masters of Africa, unless it was in the paleolithic age. Civilisation has always come in from without, and power has been wielded by the brown, or white, or mixed peoples, who have imposed it on the black population. Almost the oldest of human cultures was developed on the banks and in the delta of the Nile; but the ancient Egyptians were not negroes any more than are their modern descendants. Hamitic, Semitic, and "Mediterranean" peoples ruled and civilised Northern Africa and held it till they were in turn subjugated by Aryans or Turanian conquerors. So the tale has gone on through the centuries. WINWOOD READE called the story of Africa "The Martyrdom of Man,"[2] which is one way of looking at it. Taking it from another angle, one may say that the negro race, with its many amiable qualities and fine physique, has never proved capable of self-dependence and self-government, except in the primitive tribal form. Beyond that stage it has been "bossed" or trained by peoples, often less agreeable and less kindly, but with higher political aptitudes—Persians, Phoenicians, Romans, Arabs,

Turks, French, English, Portuguese, and others. There is not, and we think there never has been, a great African city which was not planted and colonized from abroad, as Carthage was from Tyre and Alexandria from Greece. Even the mixed races, which have a dash of Semitic or "dark-white" blood, have risen above the negroes, like the Bantu of the East and the Fulani in the West. It is to these aggressive stocks that the negro populations would speedily succumb if European protection and tutelage were withdrawn. We hope that in course of time a "black democracy" may rule over wide territories of "Ethiopia," in addition to that which already exists in Liberia; and it is the declared policy of the Western Powers and the League of Nations to prepare the natives for this consummation. But the training must go on through many generations yet to come, and we hardly think that the youngest of the Madison-[sq]uare Garden orators will live to see it [com]pleted.

Printed in the *Daily Telegraph* (London), 4 August 1920.

1. The correct title of this poem is "The Deacon's Masterpiece, or, the Wonderful One-Hoss Shay," by Oliver Wendell Holmes (1809–1894) (*WBD*).

2. William Winwood Reade (1838–1875), British author and explorer of Sierra Leone, Senegal, and Gambia (*DNB*).

Bainbridge Colby, Secretary of State, to
L. Lanier Winslow

Washington, August 7, 1920

Forwarding photostat copies of official Bulletin of quote The Negro World unquote. Will endeavor keep you fully informed.

COLBY[1]

DNA, RG 59, file 811.108G 191/26. TLS (telegram), recipient's copy.

1. Bainbridge Colby (1869–1950), appointed secretary of state in the Wilson administration on 22 March 1920, was a founder of the Progressive party and a supporter of Theodore Roosevelt in the 1912 presidential election. He left the Progressive party for the Democrats shortly after Roosevelt's refusal to contest the Republican party presidential nomination in 1916 (Association of the Bar of the City of New York, *Memorial Book*, 1950, pp. 23–26).

Reports of the Convention

[[*New York, 8 August 1920*]]

DETAILED REPORT OF SUNDAY'S MEETING AT LIBERTY HALL

MORNING SESSION.

The President-General spoke as follows:

There will be a special service at three o'clock this afternoon in honor of the members of the New York local who helped to secure the new Liberty Hall. All members of the association are requested to attend, as well as all friends and delegates. The members of the New York local will occupy the front seats and the services will be dedicated to their honor. The usual night convention will be held at 8 o'clock, at which time all the high officers of the association will be present to take part.

Tomorrow opens the second week of the convention and all delegates are requested to be in attendance. We are expecting this week, starting from tomorrow, to formulate the bill of rights. We will come to the conclusion of this bill of rights through the reports we heard last week as coming to us from different parts of this country and different parts of the world. The convention, which meets for the month, is of such great interest that it is attracting attention of the entire civilized world, and whilst we as citizens of New York have the opportunity to see and hear the things written and said about us, we have proof and assurance that thousands and thousands of miles away, across the Atlantic, the people are very much concerned about our deliberations in this convention. The importance of this convention seems to be more realized by others outside our race than our race itself. The very keen attention paid by other races reveals the fact that they regard us at this time as being in a very serious mood and we who are members of the race should be more than concerned because whatsoever we say or do during this month will concern us especially and will mean that we will as a race four hundred million strong have to stand by just what we have decided to do. So I think we should not allow people of other races to be more interested in this convention that we are. That some of us are deeply interested goes without saying, because we have people who come from four thousand miles away to be present at this convention and to take part in the deliberations. I trust that all the delegates and members of this organization will remain during the entire month except unforeseen circumstances call you away, so that you can well understand and grasp the meaning of this coming together of representatives of the Negro peoples of the world.

Dr. Brooks will preach the sermon for today. Dr. Eason gave us an eloquent discourse last week at the opening of the convention. He has been called away to Philadelphia in the interest of the Philadelphia branch of this association. He will be here this afternoon and tonight. We are hoping to have Rev. Dr. Gordon of California[1] as one of the speakers for tonight, along with Dr. Eason and others. I will now give way to Dr. Brooks, who will speak to you.

The Afternoon Session.

The afternoon session opened with the Hon. Marcus Garvey, President-General of the U.N.I.A. and A.C.L., in the chair. There were the usual preliminaries, consisting of instrumental and vocal selections, among which was the "Pilgrim Chorus From Tan[n]hauser" by the Black Star Line Band, under the efficient direction of Prof. William Isles, and a piano recital by Madame Frazer Robinson, which were well received by the audience.

Mr. Garvey began the speaking by saying:

Hon. Marcus Garvey Speaks.

This service this afternoon is for the special purpose of doing honor to the members of the New York local who helped our organization to secure this new building. There was a time in the history of this association when the support it received was very meager and poor, because the people had not then caught the great vision, had not seen the great ideal the founders of it had in view. Those were the pioneer days. Although the organization is about a little over two and a half years old in New York City, it has had nearly 16 or 18 months of hard, difficult struggles when we passed through our Gethsemane. During those days we had critics who could not see with us, and we had very few members within who were able to carry on the movement by their support, but with the determination of a few we were able to continue the work we started and with their sacrifice, with their devotion, with their loyalty to the cause we were able to convert others to the vision and to the ideal. Out of this conversion we were able to enroll hundreds of followers. As the new followers came they gave their earnest support. That support helped us to expand the work and to make better accommodations for the increasing membership.

This was not our first building. The first building the U.N.I.A. occupied in New York was situated at 131st street and 7th avenue—one of the lodge rooms of the Lafayette Building where we used to meet once a week every Sunday afternoon at this hour. From there we moved into the Odd Fellows building on Fifth avenue, and from there we moved into our own rented or leased building—the Crescent building on 135th street. Then we removed from there and took over an independent building which we called the Universal Building, where the offices of the Black Star Line and the U.N.I.A. are now situated at Nos. 54 and 56. While we were holding our meetings in the Universal Building, the membership multiplied to such large numbers that we decided to hold Sunday night convention meetings in the Palace Casino, and those meetings were very successful. Thousands of people attended those meetings and we made members by the hundreds every Sunday. Then, suddenly, those who never wished the movement any good, started to undermine our business association with the owners of the Palace Casino; and while I was away on a lecture tour in the South—in Virginia, the other representatives of the Association had advertised to hold the usual Sunday night meeting in the Palace Casino; but at the very last moment, when they had everything arranged, and were about to go to the Palace Casino, they were told that they could not have the use of the building and they were shut out of the building that Sunday night. I came back to town the Monday or Tuesday following and the circumstance was related to me, and I made desperate efforts to get in touch with the Pastor of the old Metropolitan Baptist Church which was then vacant, in that the church had removed somewhere else in the city; and I asked him to rent us the building. He said that someone occupied the building and they were prepared to sell and not to rent, but that the one in charge had a lease running for two months longer and that he could not sell until the two months had expired, but that during which time he could give me some concession. We immediately got hold of the building with the understanding that we could get it in two months after purchasing and contract was entered into and the papers properly signed; and I believe that it was just ten or eleven months ago we signed the papers and bought the building.

Our members then began to grow to such large numbers that on Sunday nights especially we were unable to accommodate the large crowds. There were as many inside as there were outside at these Sunday night meetings. We decided, therefore, to purchase the vacant space of land—this land here which was then adjacent to the old building. (The speaker referred to the site on which the new extension is now erected), at a cost of $35,000 and have paid $45,000 for the old building and the land; and just about that time we had to prepare for our convention which is now in session, it was decided that the old building was too small to seat the convention and acco[m]modate the membership and the people, and we were instructed to erect this building on the new land we had bought for the $35,000. We sought estimates on the new building and the cheapest estimate we had was one for $35,000 for the putting up of this new building. We had calculated raising that money by celebrating a Rose Day in the city of New York, but we were held up in this calculation through the action of one of the Al[de]rmen, although all the others had voted for it. This holding up of the permit[2] came as a surprise to us and at the last moment we were unable to do anything else, but to raise the money in the quickest possible way. We, therefore, decided that we would raise the money needed for the erection of the building through our membership by loans, and in the space of two weeks the membership that sits in this roped-off part of the building gave the money amounting to $28,000.

This service is called this afternoon to do honor to them. They remind me of the builders of a race and a nation. In all history, we had read of the desires of people and of the upward growth of peoples; and the closest parallel in history that I can draw to your attention is the history of these United States of America. There were many people living in these United States for hundreds of years and the vision of a great country, the vision of a great nation, never appealed to them. There were others, on the other hand, who had the vision of greatness and who desired to be great. Those who taught the vision of greatness desired help to bring about the greatness. They taught among the people the doctrine of freedom; and that after freedom we must work and build up the nation, but there are a few who were willing to fight for freedom and there were very few who were willing to fight and work for the building of the nation. Yet the nation concerned all—each and every one. Through the work and the sacrifice of those who were prepared to do something immediately for freedom and for the building of the nation, we now see a great America partitioned into forty-eight great states and each state as great as any country in the world. We now see in America the greatest republic in the world—the greatest nation in the world. And why? [B]ecause a few out of the many who inhabited America a couple of hundred years ago were satisfied to work and to sacrifice in order that the nation might be built up and become great. There were others—their next door neighbors—who lived in the same country with them, enjoying the same environment, who, while the workers worked, were satisfied just to enjoy the blessing of that environment, thinking the nation would be able to take care of itself.

And so, as in the growth of America, in this organization, there are thousands of us who are members who believe that the thing we aim at is a great and glorious thing. All of us believe that there should be a free and redeemed Africa; but when it comes down to the realization of it, you will find that we are divided into groups.

NOTHING COMES BY CHANCE.

Some belong to the working group, and others belong to the lounging group, who believe that everything comes by chance. I want to say that the age of chance and miracles has passed. There was once upon a time when good men would pray and the Lord would build a temple over night, but those days are gone. We are living in a practical material age now when the Lord does not manifest himself in feeding people and making clothes for people and finding a place to shelter people. He says that you must go out and do for yourselves and I will bless you spiritually and physically so as to do that much for yourselves. Now, if you were living in the time of miracles all that we would have done would be to assemble here and pray to the Lord: "Please build us a building," and then we would have come here and seen a large Liberty Hall to hold our convention. But in that[,] those days of miracles have passed and we have to do things ourselves. We were unable to transform the land—the barren waste land—into a Liberty Hall except through the work and sacrifice of the membership, and out of that membership these ladies and gentlemen who sit in the front seats where the rope encircles them are those who have worked the miracles. They have taken the place of our Lord in saying that the building must go up, but it can only go up by our contributions to the common fund; so that since the Lord is not here to work miracles for us, we will work miracles for ourselves. (Cheers.) Hence we are able to come in here this afternoon and sit in this large and commodious building. We are prevented from going to the door of the white man and knocking and asking for a chance to be let in just for one afternoon to hold our meeting. If we had not done this thing and wanted to hold a convention such as this we would have to go to the white man at the Palace Casino in this neighborhood and say: "You turned us out last year, but we have to come back to you and say let us meet here for a couple of hours this afternoon." And if he were of the same attitude as last year, he would say: "No you cannot come in." But we are here in our own Liberty Hall, the doors of which are open at all times for every member of the association. You can come at any time and make yourselves at home in Liberty Hall so long as you behave yourselves and do not try to take anything out of Liberty Hall. You can come always into Liberty Hall; if it goes so bad that your landlord locks you out and you cannot find a bed, you can come right to Liberty Hall; and if you become so hungry by being out of employment later on we will have a soup kitchen right here; so that when anything goes wrong you can always come to Liberty Hall so long as you are a financial member of the U.N.I.A. and we will take care of you. (Cheers.)

So that this meeting is held in honor of those good and noble souls who have helped us along. It is all well to talk, but sometimes we have got to do something after talking. My pleading and the pleadings of those who have helped in this movement would have been in vain if some practical real work were not done, and the appreciation that we have received this week from the white newspapers I think should be enough to encourage us to go on some more. (Cheers.) You notice there is not so much ridicule. And why? Because we said we are going to fight. (Cheers.) If we had opened some prayer meeting up here—if we had opened some revival meeting up here—why, all the publications last week would have been ridicule. They would have said:—Half a dozen jack-leg preachers up in a Billy Sunday[3] tent in 135th street between Seventh and Lenox avenues are appealing to the emotions of the Negroes, who are jumping out of their seats and crying "Yea, Lord!"

That is what they would have published. But we are [not] holding a prayer meeting; we are holding a preparatory meeting for a great battle on the great continent of Africa (Cheers), and that preparatory meeting they take seriously, and they write about us in a serious vein. We have given them at least a new opinion of the Negro—that he has some blood and fighting blood.

There are some men who are so cowardly that they are afraid to talk out even in their own defense. But we impressed those reporters who came here during the week that we are not afraid of anybody or anything. They carried back our message all right. They got us mixed up sometimes, but that is all right. They made someone say what I said and they made me say what someone else said, but it was said anyhow—whosoever said it, it was said.

We are here this afternoon to pay our respects and to give our thanks to those noble members of the organization. There are a few thousand dollars still to be raised on the completion of the building. The loans up to date are $28,000 and we have to raise $35,000, making a balance of $7,000. The building is still incomplete; it will be completed some time this week and we hope by the time it is completed and the contractors are ready to turn over everything to us, we shall have raised the entire amount. The building must also pass the inspector. We are now here on a temporary permit; as soon as the ceilings and all the woodwork, etc., are complete, the inspectors from the Building Department will come here, and then, if the building passes inspection, we will have to pay the balance of the money, $7,000; and I am appealing to the members who have not done their duty yet to fall in line and loan this $7,000. We are borrowing this $7,000 under these conditions: For six months the money is borrowed, bearing interest of 6 per cent. During those six months if any member by force of circumstances, through sickness or through some unfortunate demand, needs the money loaned to the Association, the Association stands ready to redeem the bond immediately with interest up to date. So that you need fear nothing; because within six months you get back your money ordinarily if you do not desire it before six months. Some of the members have loaned us from $10 to $700. There is one member who has loaned $700; some have loaned $600, some $500, some $400, some $300 and all the way down to $10, just as they could afford it. I think this balance of $7,000 could be raised in one day if the rest of us will only make up our minds so to do. So that I trust by next Sunday my report will be complete in being able to say that all the money has been subscribed on the new building.

I will ask Rev. Dr. Brooks to give a special prayer and offer a special blessing for those loyal and true members of the Association who have done their duty by the organization and have answered the call.

SUNDAY NIGHT MEETING.

There was again an over flowing house at Sunday night's meeting. Hon. Marcus Garvey, President-General, presided, supported by Mrs. Henrietta Vinton Davis, international organizer. Among others on the platform were, Rev. Dr. [E]ason, Chaplain-General; Prof. W. H. Ferris, Chancellor, and Rev. Dr. J. D. Brooks, Secretary-General.

The proceedings began with a selection by the Choir. Miss Ida Ash rendered a solo which was highly applauded. Madam [M]. B. Houston thrilled the house with one of her excellent renditions. Hon. Marcus Garvey said:

Marcus Garvey Speaks.

We are pleased to welcome you once more to Liberty Hall. We are here tonight to celebrate the opening of the second week of our convention. Last week the convention occupied its time in listening to reports from the different delegates from the different parts of the world and from the different States of this country. This week the convention will give itself over to the framing of the Bill of Rights. (Applause.)

On last Sunday we met in divine service and gave thanks to Almighty God for bringing us through to this part of the journey, and our prayers were answered, it seemed, in that He blessed us wonderfully in the past week. And we are assembled tonight to invoke His blessing through our prayers that He might bless our deliberations over the constitution that will govern this race of ours four hundred million strong. This will be a serious week for us, because through the sufferings of three hundred years we will find language out of which we will write this constitution of liberty. To me the language cannot be too strong—(applause)—in which to encouch the Negroes' declaration of liberty. We must make the language so strong that men cannot mistake its interpretation, that nations and governments will not mistake the interpretation. We want ourselves clearly understood. The new Negro wants no mistake made about him, because he is man enough to stand up and defend whatsoever he says and to defend whatsoever he writes. And in defence of this bill of rights and of this constitution we will write we intend to count on four hundred million black men to see that the integrity is maintained and respected. So we are assembled here tonight in prayer to ask God's blessing on the second week of this convention of ours. I can well understand that we are making great sacrifices to be here in this very cool weather—(laughter)—when we can find ourselves assembled so many thousands at such a time shows clearly that we have put all other things aside and are looking forward to the seriousness of this movement to produce the things that we want, the things that we have longed for and yearned for for over three hundred years. The newspapers have been speculating. Hearst a few days ago told us that Jack Johnson,[4] being a Negro, was only a few degrees removed from the gorilla, and that the Negro as a race was nearer to the ape kind. Well, that was before he heard of the program of the [U.]N.I.A., but when he found out that these apes were thinking about government he wrote another editorial and said that the things were impossible. First, he said that Jack Johnson was but a few degrees removed from the lower animal, that he was a beast, practically speaking. He argued that way because Jack Johnson's race probably had no civilization to show and satisfy him. The moment we endeavor to show him that we are to march into a civilization entirely our own he said the thing is too big, it is impossible. It only proves that these people have absolutely no respect and no regard for us as a race of people. So long as we were satisfied to be their servants, their slaves and their peons they will regard us as lower animals to be taken care of.

We have allowed them to do that for three hundred years, but we are going to prove to them now that we are higher animals who can take care of ourselves. (Applause.) And those things that they say are impossible for the Negro we are determined to make possible out of this convention. So before the thirty-first of August goes by when we give them our Bill of Rights we will surprise them a little more. Apes never wrote any books. Apes never wrote any bill of rights. But we are going to surprise them now and show them that these modern apes can write a bill of rights and write them so plainly as not [to] be misunderstood even by those who claim to be the masters and lords of this creation. (Applause.) These big fellows who sit down in their security, believing that they are almighty, will be very much surprised one of these days if they continue to believe that the Negro is an ape. Let them continue that the Negro is a monkey. These monkey Negroes will yet surprise them and surprise the world if they have not better sense to know that monkeys could not have done what Needha[m] Roberts and Johnson[5] did in France. And we think this[,] that the time has come for us irrespective of the world, irrespective of how strong other races and nations are, that the time has come for us to strike out independently for our rights and for our liberty. And that is just what we are about to do in this month of August. After we listened to all the complaints as they came to us last week from all parts of the world and from the forty-eight States of this Union, we have come to the conclusion that there is but one thing to be done, and that is to mobilize the strength of the Negro all over the world, because wherever the Negro suffers his complaint is one. Whe[ther] in far off Trinidad, whe[ther] in far off Zululand, whether he is in Georgia, or whether he is in Barbados or in Jamaica or in Texas, his cry and his complaint is the same. The delegate from Zululand told us of the brutal treatment received in Zululand by the natives from the white race.

The delegate from Trinidad told us of the system of peonage and serfdom, under which the Negro population of Trinidad had to work to satisfy the white Colonial. The people from Georgia and Alabama and Texas have told us of the disadvantages they had to suffer from, and when we summ[a]rize the complaints as they come to us, we find out that the Negro is suffering universally. Hence the hour has struck for the Negro to organize, not locally, not parochially, but universally. One newspaper—I believe either the Herald or the Telegram—wrote this week and said that "we like our Negroes, and we are going to make things comfortable for them and we believe that the time will come when they will be satisfied." It took them a very long time to write that. (Laughter). They should have written that fifty years ago at least. They should have written that all the time. But it is the white man's strategy. Whenever he finds out that the opposite class, or the opposite nation, or the opposite race, is making an attempt to liberate itself from their thraldom, it is always his subterfuge and his camouflage to present just at the time that the agitation is going on, the most rosy and encouraging opportunities so as to distract the people's attention from their complaints and make them perpetually slaves and let them believe that it is not necessary to free themselves because they are going to enjoy all those things just now. All that is but a lie and a camouflage, and if you delegates who have come here and who live here, allow the white man to fool you in this age, you ought to die, so help me God. (Loud and prolonged applause). Do you think that a man can love me today, when that same man three hundred years ago, when I was free, when I never disturbed or troubled anyone, when that man came where I was, shackled me, took me away from my father and mother and from my country and brought me three or four thousand miles and shackled me again for two hundred and fifty years[?] He worked me, he murdered me, he did everything to me for two hundred and fifty years. Something happened, and perforce, he had to free me from that slavery, and he brought me into another one.

DEVELOPING AFRICA.

The doctrines of going "Back to Africa" must be clearly understood. We are not preaching any doctrines to ask all the Negroes of Harlem and of the United States to pack up their trunks and to leave for Africa. We are not crazy, because we have to wait until we get a Lenox Avenue and a Seventh Avenue before we could get the Negroes of Harlem to leave for Africa. We have to put up those big apartment houses and get the bell boys to say "Going Up" before you get Negroes to leave Harlem. But we are asking you to get this Organization to do the pioneering work. The majority of us may remain here, but we must send our scientists, our mechanics, and our artisans and let them build railroads, let them build the great Educational and other institutions necessary and when they are constructed, the time will come for the command to be given, "Come home" to Lenox Avenue, to Seventh Avenue. Not until then. So whilst the white man is trying to camouflage us, that now everything is all right, let them believe that we are satisfied everything is all right. We are going to live for a higher purpose, the purpose of a free and redeemed Africa, because no security, no success can come to the Black man, so long as he is outnumbered in the particular community where his race may become industrially and commercially strong. We may control all the business places in Harlem, all the department stores, we may succeed in Harlem, but as long as there are six million white people in New York, there is always danger. If there is a great economic [de]pression there are thousands of white people in New York belonging to the old and unreasonable elements. Do you think the poor white people, poor white trash as they are called down South, do you think that they would allow the Negroes to succeed in Harlem and they remain starving? Do you know what they will do? They will march up one day and run every Negro out of Harlem. This [is] not an idea, it is a fact, because it is demonstrated every day in the South. The successful Negro, the thrifty Negro, will work there for years. He will build up a splendid business and a home for himself and family, and then the poor white people in the neighborhood, seeing the successful man having his automobile and fine house will get together and say, "That Negro is a little too uppish, he has no right to succeed, while we cannot; that Negro has too much money in the bank; so let us run him out." And over night they serve notice to him, "Negro, we give you twenty-four hours to get out!" This is the demonstration of the white man's love for us, therefore, you have absolutely no assurance that the white people will protect you, so long as we are only ten millions. Therefore, it is your duty to protect yo[u]rself and to build yourself, where you cannot be deprived of your belonging[s]. Hence, we are asking you to help us this week to formulate this Bill of Rights in order to build up a Free and Independent Africa.

DR. GORDON SPEAKS.

The chairman then announced that the speaker of the evening will be the Rev. Dr. Gordon, of California.

Dr. Gordon said in part: "It is exceedingly embarrassing that the Chairman should call upon me after listening to that most eloquent flaming documentally oratori[ca]l dissertation of the highest manhood truth. It is embarrassing, but while the Dr. was talking about the treatment that we have received at the hand of the white man I could not help wondering why so many of you were not at your churches to-night. I concluded that you had been embarrassed by his religion and in fact I concluded long ago that the Negroes ought to call an ecclesiastical convention and indict the white man for his conduct to his fellow brother. (Laughter.) I think the white man ought to be given a chance to answer in the judgment and then I think that if he does not immediately show signs of quick and complete repent[a]nce he should be excluded from the kingdom of civilized Christianity. There is absolutely no harmony between the message of Christ and the practice of American civilization. I think what we ought to do is to indict and then declare outside the pale of Christianity and let the Negro claim that proper relationship of Jesus that they so stoutly claim. If you were to do this then there are white folks all over the world, whose minds would wake up to the wrong and to the evils, and when a man is convinced he is wrong he is no longer protected, you pull down the bulwarks, you exposed him to his own conscience when you make him realize that he is wronging his fellow brother. We ought to indict him and convict him and exclude him from the religion of Jesus Christ. I would do that because some of you all are so angry now I am afraid that you will fall out with Christianity and think that Christ and Christianity is one. But you are all mistaken. Jesus who washed your sins away is different. Don't go back on Jesus Christ, but the present kind of Christianity should be rejected, so I want all of us to be embued with such sentiments as we have had to-night from this Moses of our race, who is going to inspire us with true manhood through his entire exertion and help this race to go on to success. The Bill of Rights, that is what we are waiting for.

The Negroes have had variegated opinions, but now we are going to establish a Bill of Rights, a declaration of our own independence. One thing can not be done. No man can declare that you are free. You have got to declare that yourself. This will not only be our Bill of Rights, it will be a declaration of Independence, our declaration of freedom.

"I know some of you are afraid. You think you ought to ask the white folks for freedom and wait on them to give it to you. I used to think the same thing myself and would join in sending petitions to Washington; and while McKinley was riding in Georgia, they lynched a colored man in that State and he had nothing to say about it. I am not going to ask anybody for freedom any more. If the white folks want to lynch, I say let them go right on; let them go on with the lynching, it is going to be propaganda for heaven and hell. It is going to help us to frame our Bill of Rights, in which we will state to the world, not what we want, but what is ours.

"Freedom is the gift of God. You do not have to ask anybody but God for it, and you do not have to ask him about it, because he has already given it to you as part of your human rights. I am going to say this: Whenever you support the contention of liberty, you are reflecting the mentality and consciousness of that race that built the Pyramids—the Negro race; that consciousness that founded civilization. We are going to get with all of those world spirits that have gone before into eternity, and we shall get in rapport with them and you will find that things will change and reform. It is due to the fact that the church militant and the church triumphant will be co-operating in the great work of human emancipation. (Applause.) God has angels; he has all of the artillery of heaven; he has the army and the navy of the spirit world waiting to help any race that will declare itself free. If you will make the declaration, God will send his armies out to help you in a thousand ways of which you know nothing. (Applause.) I want to say to you, do not be embarrassed or afraid. You will find some Negroes just a little afraid to be free (laughter); they want the same thing we want, but they are afraid. They are the big Negroes, too, who have money, houses and land, but to whom the white folks give constant tips to keep them quiet. You all may not know that, but if you get to be a great man in the community they will tip you off in several ways. But that class of leadership can never lead the race to triumph and victory. Hear me! Who is that leader the white folks are endorsing— whoever he be, he is not leading you on to victory. You want to follow that leader that the white people oppose; he is the Moses that is going to lead you to success. Let us follow our present leader; let us go on with him to the end; let us live with him and die with him. Other races live and die with their leaders—why are we not willing to do likewise? You will never be worthy of liberty until you are willing to die. They may send all sorts of threats against you—that does not matter; threats are for cowards—what do men care about threats? Threat[s] simply put men on guard. A man does not care if all hell comes up when he knows his cause is right. (Applause.) We are denied liberty; I have been asking God Almighty to give it to me all along; but God says I have got to fight for it. God gave Canaan to the children of Israel, but they had to be men enough to fight for it. God gave us our liberty and now he says if you want it fight for it. Men and women, wake up and take your liberty; if you are not able to take it, you are not worthy of it if you get it.["]

Printed in *NW*, 14 August 1920.

1. Rev. John Dawson Gordon was elected assistant president general of the UNIA at the 1920 convention and served as Garvey's personal assistant until his resignation a year later. Born in La Grange, Ga., and raised in Atlanta, Gordon attended Morehouse College, Atlanta, and graduated valedictorian of his class. He entered the ministry at age fifteen and later became pastor of the Mt. Olive Baptist Church in Atlanta. Gordon moved to Riverside, Calif., in 1903, and in 1904 he founded the Tabernacle Baptist Church in Los Angeles. With his brother, Hugh Gordon, he also became a community activist and local black nationalist leader. He served on the committee of the National Equal Rights League, which met in Chicago in September 1918. Shortly thereafter, Gordon left Los Angeles to become a traveling evangelist, and while in New York, he became interested in UNIA activities. Following a brief return to Los Angeles in November 1919, Gordon moved to New York, and in August 1920 he accepted a position on the UNIA's executive council. After his election at the convention, Gordon became one of Garvey's most trusted lieutenants. At the 1921 convention, however, he was charged with financial mismanagement during a recent absence of Garvey's from UNIA headquarters. Gordon resigned in anger and returned to Los Angeles to become active in the UNIA faction opposing Garvey's methods, the Pacific Coast Negro Improvement Association. Nevertheless, following Garvey's tour of California in June 1922, during which he attempted to placate dissident factions, Gordon rejoined the UNIA president and remained in the association until his final resignation in November 1923 (Emory J. Tolbert, *The UNIA and Black Los Angeles* [Los Angeles: Center for Afro-American Studies, University of California, Los Angeles, 1980]; *Los Angeles Negro Directory and Who's Who, 1930–1931* [Los Angeles: California Eagle Publishing Co., 1931], p. 78).

2. The New York City superintendent of buildings, Rudolph Miller, refused to grant the UNIA a license to build an annex on the land adjacent to Liberty Hall, citing a history of building code violations by the previous owners and by the UNIA. In 1916 the unfinished structure, which the UNIA later purchased and renamed Liberty Hall, was to be fireproofed at the insistence of the superintendent of buildings. At the owner's request, however, the order was rescinded with the provision that the building was to be temporary and could be occupied for only six months. Later in 1916 the owners applied for a permit to construct a two-story fireproof building on the site. Although the permit was granted, the new building was never constructed. In March 1920 the new owners (the UNIA) filed an application for a license to extend the original structure an additional 7,840 square feet but faced the opposition of the superintendent of buildings, who insisted that a building of over 5,000 square feet must be fireproofed. The UNIA appealed the decision and was given permission to build by the board of appeals, provided the annex be removed after two years. But the superintendent intervened again, refusing to issue a permit. In response, the architect who designed the renovations for Liberty Hall, Edward R. Williams, requested that the Supreme Court of New York order the superintendent of buildings to grant the license. Williams apparently withdrew his request, however, and further out-of-court negotiations led to a permit for the UNIA (NNHR, index no. 19598).

3. Billy Sunday (1865–1932), American revivalist preacher and evangelist (*WBD*).

4. John Arthur Johnson (1878–1946), better known as Jack Johnson, was the first black heavyweight boxing champion and the subject of vicious race-baiting from the white American press following his victory over Tommy Burns in Sydney, Australia, on 26 December 1908. In July 1910 he knocked out Jim Jeffries, "the Great White Hope," who had been urged by the press to end his retirement and recapture the title. Johnson, whose career was controversial, retired from boxing after losing to Jess Willard in Havana in April 1915 (*Negro Digest*, March 1951, p. 64; Harry A. Ploski and Warren Marr, eds., *The Negro Almanac* [New York: Bellwether, 1976], p. 700; Al-Tony Gilmore, *Bad Nigger! The National Impact of Jack Johnson* [Port Washington, N.Y.: Kennikat Press, 1975]; Finis Farr, *Black Champion: The Life and Times of Jack Johnson* [London: Macmillan, 1964]).

5. Needham Roberts and Henry Johnson, black American heroes in World War I and recipients of the French croix de guerre.

[[New York, Aug. 9, 1920]]

. . . With promptness, the International Convention of Negroes, upon reconvening on the ninth day of its sittings, took up the further hearing of reports of delegates as to conditions affecting the Race in the respective countries. The President-General occupied the chair. The invocation was offered by the Rev. Dr. Luck of Newark, N.J., Mr. Arden Branch, representing Barbados, B.W.I., led off the speaking, and gave a minute account of conditions in that country, which, as in other British possessions in the West Indian Islands, are deplorable. He was followed in turn by other delegates, among whom were: Mr. Harry Ford of Rahway, N.J.; Miss Duchrateller of Bocas Delatore, Mr. James B. Yearwood[1] of Panama, Mr. John E. Ivy of Costa Rica, Mr. James Williams of Montclair, N.J.; Miss C. Ashford[2] of Atlantic City, N.J.; Rev. T. J. Jones of Newport News, Va.; Mrs. J. H. Hill of Petersburg, Va.; Mr. John Montgomery of Grand Basse, Africa. All told practically the same tale—the same heartrending story of cruelties, injustice, oppression, discrimination, etc., now commonly practiced against the Negro everywhere.

The afternoon session was a continuation of the morning session, among those who spoke being Mr. C. L. Holum of Baxley, Ga., whose account of conditions in the State of Georgia was graphically told.

At this juncture the chair announced that the Bill of Rights was before the house for discussion. He said some outside influence, it appeared, is endeavoring to control the sentiment of the convention by approaching delegates and asking them to block the passage of certain measures that would come up before the Convention and to place obstacles in the way of other things. He brought to their attention that they (the delegates) represented their constituents, those who had sent them to the Convention, and expressed the hope that none would allow himself to be thus influenced by the sinister efforts of the enemies of the Association, who are seeking to destroy it if possible, but that they should all act according to a proper sense of their responsibilities.

A discussion then arose as to whether the public should be excluded from the room during the discussion of the Bill of Rights. A motion was accordingly made to that effect and seconded and carried. But the President-General hesitated putting it into execution, being reluctant to do so. This precipitated further discussion. Finally a motion was made to reconsider the action thus taken, but the second motion was defeated. The chair thereupon announced that he must request all visitors to leave the hall in order that the question of the Bill of Rights might be taken up and discussed by the delegates. Still dissatisfied with this, further discussion was had upon the subject. Being obliged to leave the convention to attend to a personal matter, the President-General vacated the chair, the Acting Chaplain-General, Rev. Dr. E[a]son, acting in his stead.

Sundry talk upon matters not directly relating to the subject of the Bill of Rights was indulged in by the delegates, whereupon, at the hour of 5 o'clock, an adjournment was taken until the next morning.

The evening session was called to order at 9.30 o'clock by the President-General, who offered the Association's prayer, after which an unusually delightful musical program was rendered, in which the star singers of the Convention took part, as Mme. Frazer Robinson and Mr. Edward Steele. The band of the U.N.I.A. also played several of its choicest pieces, all adding greatly to the pleasure of the evening, as a preliminary to the speechmaking. Than those artists there are none better in the city among our people, and their talent is always highly appreciated and greatly enjoyed.

Rev. Prof. Ferris, Rev. Dr. Brooks, Rev. Dr. E[a]son and Miss Henrietta Vinton Davis were among the speakers, as also Mr. Garvey himself. Their speeches were, without exception, of the same high order of excellence as has heretofore always characterized their utterances in public, and stirred the great assemblage of people which was present despite the terrific heat to shouts of approval and unusual pitches of enthusiasm again and again. The meeting adjourned at 11.30, everybody feeling happy and benefited by what had been seen and heard.

Printed in *NW*, 14 August 1920.

1. James Benjamin Yearwood was elected assistant secretary-general at the 1920 convention. Born in Barbados, Yearwood worked as a laborer on the Panama Canal and later became a labor organizer and teacher in Panama. In 1915 Yearwood turned his part-time teaching career into a full-time pursuit by opening a school in Panama City and calling a meeting of the city's teachers to devise ways to furnish free school supplies to the city's poor. During the First World War, Yearwood organized the Universal Loyal Negro Association (ULNA) among blacks in Panama and Costa Rica, serving as secretary in 1918. This group pledged its loyalty to England, provided the British government take steps to improve conditions among black British subjects in Central America. Yearwood later encouraged local chapters of the ULNA to join with the Garvey movement. In 1920 Yearwood was a delegate from Panama to the UNIA convention, representing his own organization. He continued his association with the Garvey movement through Garvey's trial, remaining with the parent body despite the numerous resignations that shook the UNIA hierarchy in 1923 and 1924. Poor health and financial problems forced him to relinquish his post in 1925. He was awarded his bachelor's of science degree from New York University in October, 1928 (Theodore Vincent, *Black Power and the Garvey Movement* [Berkeley, Calif.: Ramparts Press, 1971], pp. 97, 119; *NW*, 1 November 1919, 5 March 1921; "Back to Africa Movement," PRO, FO 371/3705).

2. Carrie M. Ashford often presided at meetings of the Atlantic City, N.J., UNIA chapter (*NW*, 30 April 1921).

Reports by Special Agent P-138

NEGRO ACTIVITIES. MARCUS GARVEY

I visited Liberty Hall twice to-day [*8 August*]. The early services were strictly religious, but the evening service was of vital imperative importance, which was presided over by GARVEY himself with an audience of about 5000, besides an overflow around the building.

GARVEY said, that they should not trust any white man, as they were the negroes worst enemies. That it was impossible for a white man to love a negro after having ill-treated them for 300 years. He went on to paint a very horrid picture of the white race['s] brutality to negroes; then he asked them whether they can ever like or trust a white man. The audience went wild with enthusiasm, got up, waved hand[k]er[c]hiefs and shouted "NO, NO, NO". He said that the Hearst Papers and the white man called the negroes the lower animal, but now that they are organized, 400,000,000 strong, they are going to demand their rights. He succeeded in giving them another dose of race hatred, to which they responded with thunderous applause.

The audience received a very rude shock to-night, just after all the above mentioned hand-clapping. The Rev. Easton, GARVEY'S chaplain general was the next speaker. He told the audience that he had a very bad report for them to-night, that Mr. Kilroe the white District Attorney and the gang were after GARVEY and meant to persecute him, but GARVEY was innocent. After a long story about the virtues and innocency of Garvey, he suddenly turned to them and said; "Garvey will be placed on trial on Tuesday for Criminal Libel, by District Attorney Kilroe", and as they were going to secure the best legal talent in New York [or] in the United States to defend him, which will necessarily cost a lot of money, he is asking every one in the Hall to give a dollar for a defence fund. This brought a hush over the audience, which was followed by rumbling, comments, threats, etc.

Rev. Easton, told them that he wanted everyone of the members and friends to go down to the Center Street Court at the trial on Tuesday, [an]d be prepared to defend their President. They took up a collection of $680.00 for the defence to-night, and expect some more to-morrow night at another big special meeting.

I would strongly advise, that the necessary precaution be taken to prevent those thousands of fanatic[s] from at least entering the court room, as there is no earthly reason to doubt of their intentions to start trouble, so as to make Garvey a martyr.

From what I can gather, Garvey's plan is to bring down a few thousands of his followers, impress and inti[m]idate the authorities with the hope of starting something with dangerous speakers and agitators, like Rev. Easton, and obtain who keeps fanning the fire of race hatred, also it would now appear that they are making supreme effort to work up the followers for the general demonstration; one is at a loss to predict what may happen during his trial.[1]

While sitting in the audience to-night, I heard many of them already threatening to kill R. E. WARREN and Edgar M. Grey, colored, the District Attorney's two star witnesses. Hence the chief topic of to-night[']s conversation among them, is Garvey's trial, and how to defend him.

P-138

DNA, RG 65, file OG 329359. TD.

1. A report of Eason's call for a demonstration at the courthouse was sent to the New York City police commissioner "for such attention as is deemed advisable" (George F. Lamb to Richard Enright [police commissioner], 10 August 1920, DNA, RG 65, file OG 329359).

NEW YORK, 8-11-20

NEGRO ACTIVITIES.—MARCUS GARVEY.

To-day [6 August] marked the completion of report of delegates to the GARVEY RACE CONVENTION at Liberty Hall.

Delegates.

It might not be generally understood that a lot of the so-called foreign delegates to this convention, say from Africa and the West Indies, wer[e] men who were living in the United States for years. They became members of the Association and during the convention, GARVEY simply called on them to come before the audience and tell of the conditions in their respective countries; of course some of these fellows, had left their homes for years, and were living here in Harlem, ever since; hence their views do not in any shape represent present day conditions in their native land. The majority of his followers and especially the general public are under the impression that *all* these delegates had just arrived here especially for GARVEY[']s convention.

As an example of the forgoing statement, I [kn]ow and I am well acquainted with a young native African, whose name is FLANGE, his home is in Lagos, British West Africa, but he has been living in N[ew] York to my knowing for quite a long time. I met him on the street to-day going towards the Black Star Line office. He told us that Gar[ve]y had se[n]t to call him on important business, but he was sure what i[t] was, [as] for the last two months Garvey was trying to engage him to speak in the convention, to which he objected over [8?] times.

I met him on his return, and he told me that GARVEY wanted him to go over to Liberty Hall at the convention to-day, and posed as a Delegate from Lagos West Africa, but he told GARVEY that he was busy on his job down town.

To-night GARVEY didn't speak very much, but gave the opportunity to a Rev. McGuire, whom he introduced as a delegate representing Antigua B.W.I., when in truth this fellow lives and has been living at 224 West 135 Street for a long time. McGuire told the audience that whenever they get in a fight with white men, even if they are to die, they should kill at least 9 white men with them. He strongly denounced white Leadership in Politics, Church[,] Education[,] Social or any place at all; advising them to get rid of them, holding up Garvey as the one and only real leader.

He is a very powerful and eloquent speaker and a dangerous Garvey weapon to spread Anti-white feeling. The nature of his whole speech was Race Hatred, which pleased his listeners greatly, hence the education in Race Antagonism continues.

P-138

[*Endorsements*] NOTED W.W.G. FILE G.F.R.

DNA, RG 65, file OG 329359. TD. Stamped endorsements.

New York. 8-11-20

NEGRO ACTIVITIES.—MARCUS GARVEY.

To-day, [*9 August*] the so-called Bill of Rights of Garvey was taken up in the convention, but after four hours controversy, and endless disagreement among the delegates of the convention, it was moved and seconded that the whole matter be put over until to-morrow.

The contention arose over the question, as to whether the Bill of Rights should be discussed in a public [s]ession. Some claimed that owing to the fact, "the importance of subject", everyone should be excluded but delegates. Obtain clai[ms] that only those delegates who are members of GARVEY's organization, Black Star Line, Universal Negro Improvement Association, and African Coming Leagues should join in the discussion and framing of the bills. That delegates from other organizations who are not a GARVEY follower should be debar[r]ed. They claimed that these other delegates were sent there by the white man, of course this led to a fiery heated discussion, almost to a fight, after which the whole matter was put over for to-morrow.

One of the so-called African Princes, a delegate, engaged in a controversy with GARVEY got up and left the convention hall in dis[g]us[t]. After words[,] a committee was formed to wait on him, so as to ascertain just what his reasons were, for quitting. Other delegates from out of town kicked that they were l[os]ing a lot of time and money on this Bill of Right controversy.

At the night [s]ession GARVEY's trial was brought up and the members were told to stand by him, also to go down in a solid body to the trial.

To-night I learned from a colored lawyer, that he had it from the best of authority that on last Friday [a] very desperate effort was made to influence District Attorney Edwin Kilroe to drop his case against GARVEY for a consideration; that Mr. Kilroe took up the matter with Mr. Swan and he agreed, but, however, when /this/ go-between approached GARVEY, he refused to agree to the terms. That this man was expected to get $1000.00 off the deal, hence the impression created /among/ Garvey's followers in that the State is afraid of him.

A lot of time was consumed at to-night[']s meeting in urging the members to buy stocks in the Black Star Line, to which but very few responded.

P-138

[*Endorsements*] NOTED W.W.G. FILE G.F.R.

DNA, RG 65, file OG 329359. TD. Stamped endorsements.

Retraction by Marcus Garvey

New York, 11 August 1920

The defendant, Marcus Garvey, appearing in open Court on the 11th day of August, 1920, hereby publicly and openly retracts all statements heretofore made by him orally or in print, concerning Mr. Edward P. Kilroe, Mr. Edgar M. Grey and Richard E. Warner, which in any way reflects upon the integrity, honesty, or good faith of the said gentlemen or any of them, and the defendant hereby publicly apologizes for having made such statements and the defendant further stipulates and agrees that in the next issue of the "Negro World"[1] he will cause to be published a retraction in the following form, to wit:

"In the edition of the "Negro World" published under date of August 2nd, 1919, certain statements were published concerning Edwin P. Kilroe as Assistant District Attorney and Messrs. Edgar M. Grey and Richard E. Warner, in connection with the investigation of the financial affairs of the Black Star Line and the Universal Negro Improvement Association. In the course of said article, certain statements were made reflecting upon the good faith and integrity of Mr. Kilroe and Messrs. Grey and Warner and the good faith of Mr. Kilroe in connection with said investigation was questioned and reflected upon.

I am now satisfied that all of said statements in any way reflecting upon the integrity good faith and motive of the said Mr. Kilroe and Messrs. Gray and Warner were unfounded and said statements were untrue. In justice to these gentlemen, this paper cheerfully withdraws all statements contained in the said article of August 2nd, 1919, and the undersigned regrets that said statements were made, and publicly apologizes for having made them.

This apology and retraction applies not only to statements contained in the said issue of the "Negro World" of Saturday, August 2nd, 1919, but to all statements made in any preceding or subsequent issue in which any statements were made concerning the three gentlemen above-named. The undersigned likewise withdraws and hereby retracts any and all statements made by him concerning the three gentlemen above-named at public meetings and regrets having made same and hereby publicly apologizes therefor."

MARCUS GARVEY
Managing Editor Negro World

People of the State of New York v. *Marcus Garvey*, Court of General Sessions, County of New York, cal. no. 27, 759–61, ind. no. 126, 535–7. TDS. The document was notarized.

1. This retraction appeared in the 21 August 1920 issue of the *Negro World*.

Report by Special Agent P-138

NEW YORK August 12, 1920

IN RE: NEGRO ACTIVITIES (MARCUS GARVEY)

Aug. 1[0], 1920

Today I visited the Garvey Conventional Liberty Hall. The entire day probably was taken up in debating over one clause in the Bill of Right, now known as the "Declaration of Right".

The following is the clause: "That no Negro shall fight in the army of any alien, race without getting the consent of the leader of the Negro Race World, except in self defence."

Rev. McGuire and three other delegates opposed this clause on the grounds that it is against the international law, also against the laws and constitution of the Nation. Garvey ruled them out of order telling them to sit down. They then offered an amendment which reads:—"That Negroes should protest to fight in the army of any white race etc.["] Garvey after making a speech in favor of the motion which says that the Negro should refuse to fight and not only protest[,] Garvey was sustained by the majority of his fan[a]tics. After about two hours wrangling and debates a delegate from Washington and one from New York made a strong speech pointing out the great danger in adopting such a drastic clause but Garvey ruled them out of order, telling the Serge[a]nt at Arms to see that they sit down and shut up. The motion was then put to the vote after Garvey instructed them to vote in its favour. The result was 36 for and 24 against; the clause was then adopted amidst loud cheers. But, however, Rev. McGu[i]re called for a recount. Garvey of course objected [but] somehow McGu[i]re succeeded in bringing it up again. He asked Garvey this question: Mr. Pres: Suppose for instance I [as] American Citizen and a Negro, war should break out[,] say between U.S. and some other country, and I was called upon[,] drafted to fight in the meantime, I appeal to you, the Leader of the Negro People, and you say I should not fight, whom should I obey? And if you should say "No", would you be willing to do the same as Eugene Debs, Socialist Leader?[1] Garvey after trying to dodge the question said "You will and must obey the Leader of Negro People". Another troublesom[e] delegate, intelligent, from Bermuda then asked Garvey what method will be used o[r] what help should this negro who refused to fight get from this Leader. Garvey said the 400,000,000 negroes will come to his assistance and all of them would do the same thing Garvey did when war is declared. This vague answer did not seem to satisfy a few of them who kept on asking embarrassing questions and were told by Garvey to sit down, out of order. Garvey finally called them cowards and told them they must be prepared to fight or die for their rights and not fight white people's [wars] anymore. He ruled with an iron hand and reinstructed his fanatics to vote in favor of the clause which they did 35–23. The 23 refused to vote. McGu[i]re and a few other American Citizens wanted this clause to be submitted for ruling to an international Lawyer as it was dangerous. Garvey shut him up but finally agreed.

AUGUST 1[1], 1920

Owing to the fact that today was the trial of Garv[e]y's case in the Centre St., Court, he was away from the convention during the most part of the day. Hence there were no important developments. As per my report of yesterday, I learned that Garvey's case has been disposed of by some kind of a settlement hence he is set free now to continue his convention work. Tonight his followers were very jubilant and termed it a victory over the district Attorney and the law, hence he is now held in a higher esteem than eve[r] before. This instance does more to raise his prest[i]ge [and] increase his popularity among his adherents.

The only danger is that spurred on by this acquittal[,] pushed on by the plaudits of enthusi[a]sts, idolized by his followers, he may be incline[d] at anytime to use this newly acquired additional power among his followers in a wrong direction.

The night session of the convention was well attended despite the rain and the same anti white speeches were made by delegates.

P-138

[*Endorsement*] Noted F.D.W.

DNA, RG 65, file OG 329359. TD. Stamped endorsement.

1. A reference to Debs's imprisonment for his violation of the World War I Espionage Act. Debs was pardoned by President Harding in 1921 (Nick Salvatore, *Eugene V. Debs: Citizen and Socialist* [Urbana: University of Illinois Press, 1982], pp. 294–96, 327–28).

UNIA Declaration of Rights

[[New York, August 13, 1920]]

... DECLARATION OF RIGHTS OF THE NEGRO PEOPLES OF THE WORLD

PREAMBLE.

Be It Resolved, That the Negro people of the world, through their chosen representatives in convention assembled in Liberty Hall, in the City of New York and United States of America, from August 1 to August 31, in the year of Our Lord one thousand nine hundred and twenty, protest against the wrongs and injustices they are suffering at the hands of their white brethren, and state what they deem their fair and just rights, as well as the treatment they purpose [*propose?*] to demand of all men in the future.

We complain:

1. That nowhere in the world, with few exceptions, are black men accorded equal treatment with white men, although in the same situation and circumstances, but, on the contrary, are discriminated against and denied the common rights due to human beings for no other reason than their race and color.

We are not willingly accepted as guests in the public hotels and inns of the world for no other reason than our race and color.

2. In certain parts of the United States of America our race is denied the right of public trial accorded to other races when accused of crime, but are lynched and burned by mobs, and such brutal and inhuman treatment is even practiced upon our women.

3. That European nations have parcelled out among them and taken possession of nearly all of the continent of Africa, and the natives are compelled to surrender their lands to aliens and are treated in most instances like slaves.

4. In the southern portion of the United States of America, although citizens under the Federal Constitution, and in some States almost equal to the whites in population and are qualified land owners and taxpayers, we are, nevertheless, denied all voice in the making and administration of the laws and are taxed without representation by the State governments, and at the same time compelled to do military service in defense of the country.

5. On the public conveyances and common carriers in the southern portion of the United States we are jim-crowed and compelled to accept separate and inferior accommodations and made to pay the same fare charged for first-class accommodations, and our families are often humiliated and insulted by drunken white men who habitually pass through the jim-crow cars going to the smoking car.

6.   The physicians of our race are denied the right to attend their patients while in the public hospitals of the cities and States where they reside in certain parts of the United States.

Our children are forced to attend inferior separate schools for shorter terms than white children, and the public school funds are unequally divided between the white and colored schools.

7.   We are discriminated against and denied an equal chance to earn wages for the support of our families, and in many instances are refused admission into labor unions and nearly everywhere are paid smaller wages than white men.

8.   In the Civil Service and departmental offices we are everywhere discriminated against and made to feel that to be a black man in Europe, America and the West Indies is equivalent to being an outcast and a leper among the races of men, no matter what the character attainments of the black men may be.

9.   In the British and other West Indian islands and colonies Negroes are secretly and cunningly discriminated against and denied those fuller rights of government to which white citizens are appointed, nominated and elected.

10.   That our people in those parts are forced to work for lower wages than the average standard of white men and are kept in conditions repugnant to good civilized tastes and customs.

11.   That the many acts of injustices against members of our race before the courts of law in the respective islands and colonies are of such nature as to create disgust and disrespect for the white man's sense of justice.

12.   Against all such inhuman, unchristian and uncivilized treatment we here and now emphatically protest, and invoke the condemnation of all mankind.

In order to encourage our race all over the world and to stimulate it to overcome the handicaps and difficulties surrounding it, and to push forward to a higher and grander destiny, we demand and insist on the following Declaration of Rights:

1.   Be it known to all men that whereas all men are created equal and entitled to the rights of life, liberty and the pursuit of happiness, and because of this we, the duly elected representatives of the Negro peoples of the world, invoking the aid of the just and Almighty God, do declare all men, women and children of our blood throughout the world free denizens, and do claim them as free citizens of Africa, the Motherland of all Negroes.

[2.]   That we believe in the supreme authority of our race in all things racial; that all things are created and given to man as a common possession;

that there should be an equitable distribution and apportionment of all such things, and in consideration of the fact that as a race we are now deprived of those things that are morally and legally ours, we believed it right that all such things should be acquired and held by whatsoever means possible.

3. That we believe the Negro, like any other race, should be governed by the ethics of civilization, and therefore should not be deprived of any of those rights or privileges common to other human beings.

4. We declare that Negroes, wheresoever they form a community among themselves should be given the right to elect their own representatives to represent them in Legislatures, courts of law, or such institutions as may exercise control over that particular community.

5. We assert that the Negro is entitled to even-handed justice before all courts of law and equity in whatever country he may be found, and when this is denied him on account of his race or color such denial is an insult to the race as a whole and should be resented by the entire body of Negroes.

6. We declare it unfair and prejudicial to the rights of Negroes in communities where they exist in considerable numbers to be tried by a judge and jury composed entirely of an alien race, but in all such cases members of our race are entitled to representation on the jury.

7. We believe that any law or practice that tends to deprive any African of his land or the privileges of free citizenship within his country is unjust and immoral, and no native should respect any such law or practice.

8. We declare taxation without representation unjust and tyran[n]ous, and there should be no obligation on the part of the Negro to obey the levy of a tax by any law-making body from which he is excluded and denied representation on account of his race and color.

9. We believe that any law especially directed against the Negro to his detriment and singling him out because of his race or color is unfair and immoral, and should not be respected.

10. We believe all men entitled to common human respect and that our race should in no way tolerate any insults that may be interpreted to mean disrespect to our race or color.

11. We deprecate the use of the term "nigger" as applied to Negroes, and demand that the word "Negro" be written with a capital "N."

12. We believe that the Negro should adopt every means to protect himself against barbarous practices inflicted upon him because of color.

13. We believe in the freedom of Africa for the Negro people of the world, and by the principle of Europe for the Europeans and Asia for the Asiatics, we also demand Africa for the Africans at home and abroad.

14. We believe in the inherent right of the Negro to possess himself of Africa and that his possession of same shall not be regarded as an infringe-

ment on any claim or purchase made by any race or nation.

15. We strongly condemn the cupidity of those nations of the world who, by open aggression or secret schemes, have seized the territories and inexhaustible natural wealth of Africa, and we place on record our most solemn determination to reclaim the treasures and possession of the vast continent of our forefathers.

16. We believe all men should live in peace one with the other, but when races and nations provoke the ire of other races and nations by attempting to infringe upon their rights[,] war becomes inevitable, and the attempt in any way to free one's self or protect one's rights or heritage becomes justifiable.

17. Whereas the lynching, by burning, hanging or any other means, of human beings is a barbarous practice and a shame and disgrace to civilization, we therefore declare any country guilty of such atrocities outside the pale of civilization.

18. We protest against the atrocious crime of whipping, flogging and overworking of the native tribes of Africa and Negroes everywhere. These are methods that should be abolished and all means should be taken to prevent a continuance of such brutal practices.

19. We protest against the atrocious practice of shaving the heads of Africans, especially of African women or individuals of Negro blood, when placed in prison as a punishment for crime by an alien race.

20. We protest against segregated districts, separate public conveyances, industrial discrimination, lynchings and limitations of political privileges of any Negro citizen in any part of the world on account of race, color or creed, and will exert our full influence and power against all such.

21. We protest against any punishment inflicted upon a Negro with severity, as against lighter punishment inflicted upon another of an alien race for like offense, as an act of prejudice and injustice, and should be resented by the entire race.

22. We protest against the system of education in any country where Negroes are denied the same privileges and advantages as other races.

23. We declare it inhuman and unfair to boycott Negroes from industries and labor in any part of the world.

24. We believe in the doctrine of the freedom of the press, and we therefore emphatically protest against the suppression of Negro newspapers and periodicals in various parts of the world, and call upon Negroes everywhere to employ all available means to prevent such suppression.

25. We further demand free speech universally for all men.

26. We hereby protest against the publication of scandalous and inflammatory articles by an alien press tending to create racial strife and the exhibition of picture films showing the Negro as a cannibal.

27. We believe in the self-determination of all peoples.

28. We declare for the freedom of religious worship.

29. With the help of Almighty God we declare ourselves the sworn protectors of the honor and virtue of our women and children, and pledge our lives for their protection and defense everywhere and under all circumstances from wrongs and outrages.

30. We demand the right of an unlimited and unprejudiced education for ourselves and our posterity forever[.]

31. We declare that the teaching in any school by alien teachers to our boys and girls, that the alien race is superior to the Negro race, is an insult to the Negro people of the world.

32. Where Negroes form a part of the citizenry of any country, and pass the civil service examination of such country, we declare them entitled to the same consideration as other citizens as to appointments in such civil service.

33. We vigorously protest against the increasingly unfair and unjust treatment accorded Negro travelers on land and sea by the agents and employes of railroad and steamship companies, and insist that for equal fare we receive equal privileges with travelers of other races.

34. We declare it unjust for any country, State or nation to enact laws tending to hinder and obstruct the free immigration of Negroes on account of their race and color.

35. That the right of the Negro to travel unmolested throughout the world be not abridged by any person or persons, and all Negroes are called upon to give aid to a fellow Negro when thus molested.

36. We declare that all Negroes are entitled to the same right to travel over the world as other men.

37. We hereby demand that the governments of the world recognize our leader and his representatives chosen by the race to look after the welfare of our people under such governments.

38. We demand complete control of our social institutions without interference by any alien race or races.

39. That the colors, Red, Black and Green, be the colors of the Negro race.

40. Resolved, That the anthem "Ethiopia, Thou Land of Our Fathers etc.," shall be the anthem of the Negro race. (Copy anthem appended.)

THE UNIVERSAL ETHIOPIAN ANTHEM.

POEM BY BURRELL AND FORD.

I.

Ethiopia, thou land of our fathers,
Thou land where the gods loved to be,

As storm cloud at night sudden gathers
    Our armies come rushing to thee.
We must in the fight be victorious
    When swords are thrust outward to glean;
For us will the vict'ry be glorious
    When led by the red, black and green

CHORUS.

Advance, advance to victory,
Let Africa be free;
Advance to meet the foe
With the might
Of the red, the black and the green.

II.

Ethiopia, the tyrant's falling,
    Who smote thee upon thy knees
And thy children are lustily calling
    From over the distant seas.
Jehovah the Great One has heard us,
    Has noted our sighs and our tears,
With His spirit of Love he has stirred us
    To be One through the coming years.
CHORUS—Advance, advance, etc.

III.

O, Jehovah, thou God of the ages
    Grant unto our sons that lead
The wisdom Thou gave to Thy sages
    When Israel was sore in need.
Thy voice thro' the dim past has spoken,
    Ethiopia shall stretch forth her hand,
By Thee shall all fetters be broken
    And Heav'n bless our dear fatherland.
CHORUS—Advance, advance, etc.

41.   We believe that any limited liberty which deprives one of the complete rights and prerogatives of full citizenship is but a modified form of slavery.

42.   We declare it an injustice to our people and a serious impediment to the health of the race to deny to competent licensed Negro physicians the right to practice in the public hospitals of the communities in which they reside, for no other reason than their race and color.

43.   We call upon the various government[s] of the world to accept and acknowledge Negro representatives who shall be sent to the said govern-

ments to represent the general welfare of the Negro peoples of the world.

44. We deplore and protest against the practice of confining juvenile prisoners in prisons with adults, and we recommend that such youthful prisoners be taught gainful trades under human[e] supervision.

45. Be it further resolved, That we as a race of people declare the League of Nations null and void as far as the Negro is concerned, in that it seeks to deprive Negroes of their liberty.

46. We demand of all men to do unto us as we would do unto them, in the name of justice; and we cheerfully accord to all men all the rights we claim herein for ourselves.

47. We declare that no Negro shall engage himself in battle for an alien race without first obtaining the consent of the leader of the Negro people of the world, except in a matter of national self-defense.

48. We protest against the practice of drafting Negroes and sending them to war with alien forces without proper training, and demand in all cases that Negro soldiers be given the same training as the aliens.

49. We demand that instructions given Negro children in schools include the subject of "Negro History," to their benefit.

50. We demand a free and unfettered commercial intercourse with all the Negro people of the world.

51. We declare for the absolute freedom of the seas for all peoples.

52. We demand that our duly accredited representatives be given proper recognition in all leagues, conferences, conventions or courts of international arbitration wherever human rights are discussed.

53. We proclaim the 31st day of August of each year to be an international holiday to be observed by all Negroes.

54. We want all men to know that we shall maintain and contend for the freedom and equality of every man, woman and child of our race, with our lives, our fortunes and our sacred honor.

These rights we believe to be justly ours and proper for the protection of the Negro race at large, and because of this belief we, on behalf of the four hundred million Negroes of the world, do pledge herein the sacred blood of the race in defense, and we hereby subscribe our names as a guarantee of the truthfulness and faithfulness hereof, in the presence of Almighty God, on this 13th day of August, in the year of our Lord one thousand nine hundred and twenty.

SIGNATURES:

Marcus Garvey, James D. Brooks, James W. H. Eason, Henrietta Vinton Davis, Lionel Winston Greenidge, A[dr]ian Fitzroy Johnson, Rudolph Ethe[l]bert Brissaac Smith, Charles Augustus Petioni,[1] Rev. Thomas H. N. Simon, Richard Hilton Tobitt, George Alexander McGuire, Rev. Peter Edward Batson, Reynold R. Felix, Harry Walters Kirby, Sarah Branch, Mme. Marie Barrier Houston, Mrs. Georgie L. O'Brien,[2] F. O. Ogilvie,[3] Arden A. Bryan, Benjamin Dyett, Marie Duchaterlier, John Phillip Hodge, Theophilus H. Saunders, Wilford H. Smith,[4] Gabriel E. Stewart, Arnold Josiah Ford, Lee Crawford,[5] William McCartney, Adina Clem. James, William Musgrave LaMotte, John Sydney de Bourg,[6] Arnold S. Cunning,[7] Vernal J. Williams, Francis Wilcem Ellegor, J. Frederick Selkridge, Innis Abel Horsford, Cyril A. Crichlow, Rev. Samuel McIntyre, Rev. John Thomas Wilkins, Mary Thurston, John G. Befue, William Ware, Rev. J. A. Lewis, O. C. Kelly, Venture R. Hamilton, R. H. Hodge, Edward Alfred Taylor, Ellen Wilson, G. W. Wilson, Richard Edward Riley,[8] Miss Nellie Grant Whiting, G. W. Washington, Maldena Miller, Gertrude Davis,[9] James D. Williams, Emily Christmas Kinch, Dr. D. D. Lewis, Nettie Clayton, Partheria Hills,[10] Janie Jenkins, John C. Simons, Alphonso A. Jones,[11] Allen Hobbs, Re[y]nold Fitzgerald Austin,[12] James Benjamin Yearwood, Frank O. Raines,[13] Shedric[k] Williams, John Edward Ivey, Frederick Augustus Toote, Philip Hemmings, Rev. F. F. Smith, D. D., Rev. E. J. Jones, Rev. Dr. Joseph Josiah Cranston, Frederick Samuel Ricketts, Dugald Augustus Wade, E. E. Nelom, Florida Jenkins, Napoleon J. Francis, Joseph D. Gibson, J. P. Jasper, J. W. Montgomery, David Benjamin, J. Gordon, Harry E. Ford, Carrie M. Ashford, Andrew N. Willis, Lucy Sands, Louise Woodson, George D. Creese, W. A. Wallace, Thomas E. Bagley, James Young, Prince Alfred McConney, John E. Hudson, William Ines, Harry R. Watkins, C. L. Halton, J. T. Bailey, Ira Joseph Toussa[i]nt Wright, T. H. Golden, Abraham Benjamin Thomas,[14] Richard C. Noble, Walter Green, C. S. Bourne, G. F. Bennett, B. D. Levy, Mrs. Mary E. Johnson,[15] Lionel Antonio Francis,[16] Carl Roper, E. R. Donawa, Philip Van Putten, I. Brathwaite,[17] Rev. Jesse W. Luck, Oliver Kaye, J. W. Hudspeth,[18] C. B. Lovell,[19] William C. Matthews, A. Williams, Ratford E. M. Jack,[20] H. Vinton Plummer, Randolph Phillips, A. I. Bailey, duly elected representatives of the Negro people of the world.

Printed in *NW*, 11 September 1920. Original headlines abbreviated. Notarized on 15 August 1920 by John G. Bayne.

1. Charles Augustus Petioni (1885–1951) was a physician, journalist, and businessman. Born in Trinidad, Petioni immigrated to New York in 1918. After studying at the City College of New York, he attended Howard University Medical School, where he graduated in 1925. His career as a journalist included posts as associate editor of the *New Negro* in 1918 and as a reporter for the *Negro World* during his years in medical school, between 1921 and 1925. Petioni

later organized a number of associations in New York, including the Trinidad Benevolent Association and the Lupetner Finance Corp. During the 1930s and 1940s, he was extremely active as an advocate of West Indian rights, both in the United States and in the Caribbean, organizing the West India Committee in America (which later became the Caribbean Union) to support business development among Afro–West Indians and to create better relations between American-born blacks and Caribbean immigrants. After the Second World War Petioni was active in the drive to provide financial, political, and moral support for independence movements in the Caribbean (*WWCA*).

2. Mrs. Georgie O'Brien also served as the lady president of the Montreal division of the UNIA in 1921 (*NW*, 7 May 1921).

3. F. O. Ogilvie served as president of the Meron, Camagüey, Cuba division (*NW*, 15 October 1921).

4. Wilford H. Smith (b. 1863), Garvey's personal attorney, was Booker T. Washington's lawyer prior to his association with the UNIA. Smith, born in Mississippi, eventually moved to New York City in 1901, engaging in various business and legal affairs. Smith was instrumental in orchestrating some of Washington's maneuvers against his rival, William Monroe Trotter (Stephen Fox, *Guardian of Boston*, pp. 49–69; Louis Harlan and Raymond Smock, eds., *Booker T. Washington Papers: 1899–1900* [Urbana: University of Illinois Press, 1976], 5: 486–87).

5. Lee Crawford (1875–1942), born in Alabama, was active in many black fraternal and self-help organizations prior to joining the UNIA. In 1906 he was elected grand chancellor of the New York State chapter of the Knights of Pythias, a position he held until 1941. After migrating from the South to Yonkers, N.Y., Crawford eventually moved to New Rochelle, N.Y., where he became the president of the local branch of the NAACP (*NYT*, 2 May 1942; [New York] *Amsterdam News*, 9 May 1942).

6. John Sydney de Bourg was asked by Garvey to represent Trinidad at the 1920 UNIA convention, where he was elected "leader of Negroes of the West Indies, Western Province, South and Central America." Born in Grenada, de Bourg worked as a teacher there before moving to Trinidad. He became an active member of the Trinidad Workingmen's Association and was elected its secretary in July 1914. In 1919 he was a leader in the momentous strike that temporarily disrupted colonial rule on the island. His activities resulted in his deportation to Grenada in 1919, after a government investigation led to charges of sedition. In March 1921 de Bourg began a tour of the West Indies on behalf of the UNIA, beginning in Cuba, where both he and Henrietta Vinton Davis made speeches urging Cubans to purchase shares in the Black Star Line. Later he joined Garvey in Jamaica, where they continued their meetings. De Bourg resigned his office at the August 1922 convention and subsequently sued Garvey for $8,000 in unpaid salary for his twenty-two months of service to the UNIA. At Garvey's mail fraud trial in 1923, de Bourg appeared as a prosecution witness, accusing Garvey of luxurious living while touring Jamaica in 1921 and of announcing the sailing of the *Yarmouth* prematurely in order to boost stock sales ("Record of Sydney de Bourg," PRO, CO 295/527; *Garvey* v. *United States*, no. 8317, Ct. App., 2d Cir., 2 February 1925, pp. 917–53; W. F. Elkins, "Black Power in the British West Indies: The Trinidad Longshoremen's Strike of 1919," *Science and Society*, 33 [Winter 1969]: 71–75).

7. Arnold S. Cunning later served as secretary to the UNIA's chaplain general, George Alexander McGuire. In this capacity, Cunning accompanied McGuire on his 1921 tour of Cuba (*NW*, 23 April and 16 July 1921).

8. Richard E. Riley served as deputy of the African Legion for the New Aberdeen, Nova Scotia, division of the UNIA (*NW*, 4 June 1921).

9. In 1921 Gertrude Davis was the Cleveland UNIA division's lady president (*NW*, 19 March 1921).

10. Partheria E. Hills was still a UNIA member in 1926, when she petitioned for executive clemency toward Garvey after he was sentenced to prison (DNA, RG 204, file 42-793).

11. Alphonso A. Jones was director of the UNIA's trucking and delivery service (*NW*, 26 February 1921).

12. Reynold Fitzgerald Austin was president of the Brooklyn division (*NW*, 19 March 1921).

13. Frank O. Raines was a member of the Chicago chapter of the UNIA (*NW*, 25 June 1921).

14. Probably Dr. A. Ben Thomas, optometrist and leader in the Toronto UNIA (*NW*, 7 May 1921).

15. Mary E. Johnson was president of the UNIA's Hartford women's division in 1921, and she also served as executive secretary of the Women's Industrial Exhibit at the August 1921 convention (*NW*, 23 April and 16 July 1921).

16. Lionel Antonio Francis was a Trinidad-born physician practicing in London at the time he visited the United States to attend the 1920 convention. Educated at Howard University and the University of Edinburgh, Francis soon became one of Garvey's chief lieutenants and the extremely able president of the large UNIA division in Philadelphia, from 1921 until his resignation in 1924. He rejoined the UNIA in 1931 when he was elected president general of the UNIA, Inc., the New York group that split with Garvey after Garvey moved his headquarters to Jamaica. Francis led the UNIA, Inc., in its lengthy court battle with Garvey over the large Isaiah Morter estate. After the fifteen-year struggle ended in 1939, Francis went to Belize, British Honduras, to administer the estate on behalf of the victorious New York faction (*NW*, 19 March 1921, 6 May 1933; *Chicago Defender*, 18 November 1939).

17. Isaac Newton Brathwaite was coproprietor with fellow UNIA member Cyril A. Crichlow of the Crichlow-Brathwaite Shorthand School in New York (*NW*, 14 August 1920).

18. J. W. Hudspeth was later a contributor to the 1922 UNIA Convention Fund and still an active member (*NW*, 6 May 1922).

19. C. B. Lovell was also president of the Home Progressive Association, a black real estate venture, in Brooklyn (*NW*, 28 August 1920).

20. Ratford E. M. Jack was ordained a deacon by George Alexander McGuire in 1921. Jack, who had already organized several UNIA chapters in the West Indies, was to be stationed in Chaparro, Cuba (*NW*, 7 May 1921).

Under Secretary of State, British Home Office, to Under Secretary of State for Foreign Affairs

[*London*] 13th August, 1920

Sir,

With reference to your note and enclosures of the 19th ultimo relative to the issue of a passport to Mrs. [*Amy Ashwood*] Garvey, I am directed by the Secretary of State to say for the information of Earl Curzon of Kedleston that as a result of enquiries he understands that Mrs. Garvey has no connection with the anti-white activities of her husband and there appears to be no objection to the issue of a passport to her journey to Liberia when she arrives in this country. I am, Sir, Your obedient Servant,

[*signature illegible*]

PRO, FO 372/1475. TLS, recipient's copy.

DEPARTMENT OF STATE

𝔇𝔦𝔳𝔦𝔰𝔦𝔬𝔫 𝔬𝔣 ⸱ ⸱sport 𝔠𝔬𝔫𝔱𝔯𝔬𝔩

MEMORANDUM

U ✝A

Garvey is on
our refusal list
but the lady is
not.

Brist

7/27/20

(*Source:* DNA, RG 59, file 000-612).

Report by Special Agent P-138

New York City 8-14-20

IN RE: NEGRO ACTIVITIES. (MARCUS GARVEY).

GARVEY's Convention continued in session today, [*12 August*] framing the Declaration on Bill of Rights.

Anti-White. Every article introduced in this bill was anti-white, entirely void of anything constructive. The majority of these bills when read by the secretary were so ambiguous and non intelligent, that they were sent back to the framers for more and better construction.

Harrison—Socialist. Today, HUBERT HARRISON, a Socialist and pronounced Negro agitator of the rabid type, joined the convention as a delegate. He is associate editor of the Negro World, and signs his editorials "H.H." He has been keeping street meetings for years and is now holding a series of meetings at 138th St. and Lenox Ave. every night. Among one of the clauses passed by the convention today, was one forbidding Negroes to buy and use white pictures or photos in their houses. Harrison insisted that the majority of the bills were not strong and outspoken enough; that the white man must be denounced in the strongest of language in the Bill of Rights. On his suggestion, a number of them were sent back to the framers, (he offering his help), to put the necessary "kick" in them. Garvey still rules with an iron hand.

P-138

[*Endorsements*] File G.F.R. NOTED W.W.G.
Noted F.D.W.

DNA, RG 65, file OG 329359. TD. Stamped endorsements.

George F. Ruch to J. Edgar Hoover

WASHINGTON, D.C. August 14, 1920

MEMORANDUM FOR MR. HOOVER.

On the 11th instant Inspector W. L. Stephens, a detective of the Norfolk, Virginia, police force, called on me and presented the attached letter of introduction from Mr. Charles E. Ashburner, City Manager.

It appears that Mr. Stephens has a confidential informant in the Norfolk, Virginia, branch of Universal Negro Improvement Association, and desired to give the Government the benefit of the information which this informant is securing at the present time. Mr. Stephens advises that it was the idea of the City Manager to cooperate in every possible way with the Government in observing the activities of this organization. Mr. Stephens had with him several reports of his confidential informant also some literature of the Universal Negro Improvement Association. After discussing the situation to some extent with Mr. Stephens, I informed him that any information that he might secure for the Government, please communicate same to Mr. R.H. Daughton[1] at Norfolk who in turn would transmit same to this office. Respectfully,

G[EORGE] F. R[UCH]

[*Typewritten reference*] GFR:MAS
[*Endorsement*] NOTED J.E.H.

DNA, RG 65, file OG 185161. TLI, recipient's copy. Stamped endorsement.

1. Ralph Hunter Daughton (1885–1958) was born in Washington, D.C, and entered the Department of Justice in 1910. Three years later he opened the department's first bureau of Investigation office in Norfolk, Va., covering a district that included Virginia, West Virginia, North Carolina, and a portion of Maryland. He resigned in 1920 and subsequently entered politics, running successfully for the U.S. House of Representatives in 1944 (*Virginia Pilot*, 23 December 1958).

Reports of the Convention

[[*Liberty Hall, 15 August 1920*]]

THE DECLARATION OF RIGHTS READ IN LIBERTY HALL BEFORE THOUSANDS AMIDST TUMULTUOUS APPLAUSE

Inclement weather, however long continued, does not dampen the ardor and spirits of the members of the Universal Negro Improvement Association and delegates to the International Convention of Negroes, which met again this morning, for the third Sunday, [*15 August*] to hold its religious services in the spacious auditorium of Liberty Hall, where a moderate size attendance was present.

The same solemnity which has been the feature of the two preceding Sabbath day meetings of the convention marked the services of this morning, which began with a processional composed of the high officials of the association, wearing their beautiful colored robes of office, and the choir surpliced in white, headed by the world-famed sopranoists, Mesdames Houston and Robinson, under the direction of Prof. Arnold J. Ford. Madame Revella E. Hughes, was the accompanist. The Revs. J. F. Selkridge, [P.] E. Paul, P. E. Batson and W. H. Ferris and Rev. Dr. J. D. Brooks assisted in officiating at the opening service.

The scripture lessons read were Psalms 121, and Isaiah 52. Miss Henrietta Vinton Davis, international organizer of the U.N.I.A., acted as master of ceremonies and introduced the speaker of the occasion, the secretary-general,

Rev. Dr. J. W. H. Eason, who delivered the sermon, taking for his text, the Sixth Chapter of Hebrews and the Nineteenth verse.

AFTERNOON SESSON.

In the midst of a humidity and heat almost unbearable, a large, enthusiastic audience attended the afternoon sesson and listened to inspiring addresses by the president-general, the Rev. Dr. Brooks, the Rev. Dr. Gordon and Dr. Lewis. Besides the officials of the U.N.I.A., about one hundred members of the Black Cross nurses were in attendance, clothed in dresses of white, with hats to match, which bore a black cross in the front, as the insignia of their organization. These Black Cross nurses are part of an association of almost 200 members, which is an auxiliary to the U.N.I.A. Mrs. Sarah Branch is its president, while Mrs. Agnes Babbs is vice-president.

The president-general delivered an address, in the course of which he made allusion to a white newspaper in Baltimore, "The Baltimore American," which in its issue of Sunday last, contained a four-column article touching upon the U.N.I.A., which movement it regarded as a fore-runner of the "Black Peril." This, he said, showed that at last we have forced the white people of the South to sit up and take notice of the Negro as a race to be reckoned with in the not distant future. The speaker also referred to the existence of opposing propaganda that has sprung up among our own people, as well as among the whites, and urged his hearers to allow nothing to sway them from their determination to press onward in the work in which they are engaged—the ultimate redemption of Africa for the black people of the world, and the removal of the oppressions and wrongs to which the Negro is universally subjected.

Mr. Garvey made an urgent appeal to the members of the New York Division of the U.N.I.A. to help the Association pay the balance due on the cost of the construction of the new extension made to Liberty Hall. This amounts to $6,000 and he hoped the members would come forth with loans to the Association to that amount between then and Tuesday next, when final payment is to be made. These loans, he said, are to run for a period of six months and would bear interest at 6 per cent, per annum.

EVENING SESSION.
THE BILL OF RIGHTS.

A scene the like of which has never before been witnessed in any assembly of colored people took place at the meeting held to-night. It was the occasion of the reading by the President-General of the declaration of rights, or Magna Charta of the Negroes of the world. In other words, the reading of this great document created the most unprecedented demonstration of approval by the large audience, which filled the hall to its utmost. A brief musical program preceded this. As article by article of the declaration was read, the audience broke out into uproarious applause. In some instances the articles as read brought forth renewed expressions of approval, just as it was thought that the applauding was over. The cheering and shouting, even whistling, with the waving of handkerchiefs, was almost indescribable. The people were frantic with joy, and seemed unable to give sufficient vent to their feelings of approbation of all they heard touching the most sacred document any body of colored people had ever drafted. The one article which evoke[d] the greatest enthusiasm was that which declared that no Negro shall give his consent to go to war for any alien race until first having obtained the consent of the recognized leader of the Negroes of the world. There are in all 5[4] articles in the declaration. Of the document 100,000 copies will be printed and distributed in all parts of the world. Copies may be ready for distribution in ten days' time. Copies were handed out to representatives of the metropolitan press, that they may publish it in their own papers for the information of the public in general.

As the document was being read, the members of the Legion of Honor of the U.N.I.A. stood directly below and in front of the speakers' stand, while holding the flags of the various nations or countries represented by delegates to the convention. At its conclusion, the national anthem of the association was sung, entitled: "Ethiopia, Thou Land of Our Fathers." This was followed by a most fervent prayer by the Chaplain-General, the Rev. Dr. Eason.

It was, indeed, a solemn, dramatic occasion, witnessing, as it did, the declaration of the black people of the world that no longer will they suffer injustice and wrong at the hands of other races or peoples, that Africa shall be redeemed, coupled with an expression of their dependence in God, and their firm belief that He will guide and direct them and bless them with the ultimate realization of their hopes and aspirations for racial liberty, racial independence, racial unity.

Mr. Garvey, Rev. Dr. Eason, and Rev. Dr. Brooks, each spoke briefly, but eloquently, upon the adoption of the Declaration of Rights, which, the President-General said, had received the signatures of every official of the U.N.I.A. and of every accredited delegate to the convention. Every colored man, woman and child should possess a copy of it and have it in their homes.

Before the speech making began, the chair introduced to the assemblage Mr. Eli[e] Garcia,[1] chief of the Philadelphia Division of the U.N.I.A., who, he explained, had been sent abroad about three months ago as its ambassador and minister plenipotentiary to Africa, and had just returned from his mission. He went to Africa to secure certain concessions there in the interest of the U.N.I.A., and had been quite successful in his undertaking. He announced that Mr. Garcia at one of the evening meetings of the convention within the coming week would deliver an address on his observations of conditions at present existing in Africa.

It was, all in all, a memorable day for Liberty Hall, and because of its interesting, exceptional features, which should encourage and stimulate every member of the race to feel more proud than ever before of his people and to strive together as one of their mutual interests and protection, it doubtless will ever be looked back upon as one of the most unique and important events in the history of the Negro.

MARCUS GARVEY SPEAKS.

The meeting opened this afternoon in the presence of a large gathering, with the singing of the hymn, "From Greenland's Icy Mountains." Hon. Marcus Garvey, the President-General, was in the chair, and delivered the special prayer of the association, after which a song was rendered by the choir.

Hon. Marcus Garvey then spoke as follows: We are glad to welcome you to Liberty Hall this afternoon to this meeting of the New York local of the organization. As is customary we meet here every Sunday afternoon for the purpose of encouraging ourselves in the work we have started, and especially during this convention month we have so much to do and so much to say that we deem it necessary to meet as often as possible. During the days that have already passed this month we have had the pleasure of listening to some of the most eminent and eloquent men of the race—and women, too. We have been fortunate enough to have this convention held in our building, and because it is held here we have the advantage of listening to all of the able speakers who have come to attend this convention. What we are hearing from them costs other people a great deal of money and time to travel from different parts of the world in order to hear them. But because Liberty Hall is the Mecca of Negro intellectuality, whenever we come to the hall we come feeling assured that we will hear something edifying—something worth listening to. The platform of Liberty Hall has never failed its auditors yet, and as it has never done so in the past, so do I feel that the platform will not fail you this afternoon; because we have with us as brilliant intellects as have spoken to us before.

During this time I desire to make you understand that the propaganda of the U.N.I.A. looms up most prominently in the eyes of the world. It calls forth on the part of those who are in sympathy with us—a notion of support; and it calls for—on the part of those who do not agree with us—a notion of opposition and a widely scattered counter-propaganda. Some of you may be disturbed or some of you may become curious about what the counter-propagandist says. I am not. I cannot be disturbed; because all these things came to me long before I started and I calculated for them. (Cheers.)

The man, the people, the race or the nation who desires anything that is justly belonging to that race or nation or individual, who expects to get that thing from an opposite race or an opposite nation without struggling for it make a mistake before they start. You must make up your minds to encounter all kinds of oppositions and counter oppositions; and the people who fail to appreciate that these things go to make up a fight in which you are engaged for your liberty and your freedom are ignorant of the course in which human liberty has flowed for thousands of years. So that no counter propaganda at this time—no opposite view as expressed by any one—any race or nation at this time does not worry me one bit; it only convinces me of my estimate of the opponents o[r] the foes. If they have not done these things—creating counter propaganda—I would have felt somewhat embarrassed because I would feel that really the work I am engaged in and the laws that I laid down are not of so much importance as to call for opposition from those who stand on the opposite side. I would feel that I would be fighting a lone battle which would be an unnecessary battle. But they realize the worthiness of the foe; they have to be sharpening their steel, and as they are doing it we have already done it. So I cannot but say that the crowd that makes up the U.N.I.A. is the most intellectual, the most penetrating crowd I have ever met among Negroes. And why do I say that? Because you, like myself, are always ready for anything the opponent throws out; you are always willing and ready to receive, and you remain just as true, just as loyal, and even more than you were before. (Cheers.)

That has been my experience with the organization—that from within and from without the foes of our liberty have spread all kinds of counter propaganda, thinking that our support was so weak, and the intellect of those who follow the movement were so weak that they would be carried away with every counter proposition. But to the contrary, we become stronger in the U.N.I.A. when we have to encounter a counter proposition.

So that tonight I will take as my subject "The Opposition You Must Meet," and I feel sure that every member of the U.N.I.A. will rise to the occasion whenever it presents itself, otherwise we would not be true members of the U.N.I.A., or at least would not understand really the tenets of the U.N.I.A. The doctrine of the U.N.I.A. is as solid, is as firm as the doctrine of any other people who desire liberty (cheers) and we have not suffered anything as compared to others who have won their liberty and others who are still now fighting for their liberty.

Read about the political upheaval in Ireland: What are the Irish people doing? The Irish people are clamoring for the freedom of Ireland. And those of you who read your daily newspapers can recount the many skirmishes and the many battles fought in the streets of Dublin and Belfast and other towns in Ireland, where overnight people read of the massacre and the deaths of their own, and yet they continue the good work. It is fair example or illustration of the course those who desire liberty must follow. The English people have spread and scattered the universal propaganda against the Irishman, trying to impress the world that the Irishman is not fit to govern himself. In spite of that propaganda the Irish have been fighting for seven hundred years. Whatever they have done to the Irish they will do to the Negro. But to our advantage, while the Irish are only 4,000,000, we are 400,000,000. (Cheers.) And whilst the Irish have been a part of themselves, because of that of the position of England to Ireland and Ireland to England, they are all cousins if not brothers. They are all one people, and it is only a matter of national limits that caused them to be fighting one against the other. It is not a matter of injustice done because of race, because some of the men who hold their highest positions in Great Britain today are Irishmen. So we cannot say that Ireland's fight generally is just like ours. Because no where in the British Empire, nowhere in the world, for that matter, can you turn and find the Negro occupying any high positions. You will find him occupying subordinate positions, but no high positions as the Irish occupies in this country or in England or in other parts of the world where he comes in contact with other men. So that our fight is a unique one, and if they had trouble in convincing the Irish that they should be ruled by others, I think they will have greater trouble convincing us who are so far removed from the[m] that they are to rule or govern us. So that it gives me great pleasure to again welcome you to Liberty Hall and to compliment you really upon the splendid spirit you have shown; for the splendid intelligence you have manifested in supporting this cause. There are some people who cannot stand counter propaganda, or a counter idea of any kind. If you convince them of one thing and someone comes along and presents a new proposition, they start to waver, and a third party comes along and he is nowhere, he is neither belonged to one nor the other, he is nowhere; but the people who make up the Universal Negro Improvement Association in the whole are known to be people of one mind. (Cheers.)

A FREE AFRICA.

And that one mind is a free and independent Africa. (Cheers.)

Irrespective of propaganda or no propaganda, we have made up our minds on that one thing, a free and independent Africa. Some chap from Africa wrote in the papers this morning that we are talking about going back to Africa, and the chiefs are not going to receive us in Africa. He comes from Nigeria, and the white papers, the New York Times, enlarged on the matter by saying that the Africans will resent the idea of an African Republic. That is what the New York Times says.[2] It bases its argument on what this African states, that the chiefs will not welcome us to Africa. This fellow is just from Lagos, one spot in Africa, and he thinks that all Africa thinks as he thinks. But this African does not know that any African or any Negro who is paid to say certain things has absolutely no impression on us. (Cheers.) Just at this time we calculated that they would find some counter propaganda so as to distract the minds of the people, and so we know what value to place on the words of that African, one of its agencies. He claims that those who were born in this country and the West Indies have no right to Africa. As I said during one of the sessions of the convention, Africa belongs to every black men wheresoever he is found. (Cheers.) There is no logic, there is no court of law in the world to prove otherwise. No court of law, no logic, no reasoning can prove otherwise. The only country that the black man, the colored man, can claim by heritage is Africa, and whether the New York Times says nay, or any individual says nay, it may satisfy them, but it will not soothe and satisfy our logic, and our reasoning and interpretation of the law, the law of nature. The British are a cunning set of people. I had the pleasure of reading, and I will bring the paper tonight, last night, an article written in the Baltimore American, a southern newspaper, which was handed to me by a lady, a member of the association, last night. The article took up about four columns of the newspaper printed on the front page, in the first column; that is to say, as you opened the newspaper the first thing you would see to the left was this big article of four columns, and in the inside of the article was a white woman's photograph so that as one took the paper up you could see this white woman in the middle of an African article which was enough to attract you anyhow because it was said to represent one of the belles of Maryland. They had a contest there and she was voted to be the prettiest woman in Maryland; and this article was just in the front page and her photograph was reproduced in the inset of the article, so that white folks had to read it anyhow. And what did they say? The headline was worded, "The yellow peril and now the black peril," (cheers) by an ex-attache. It would appear that this man who wrote the article was attached to some government or other, may have been the American or English government, and he wrote this four-column article. And he said it was the disposition generally over the country to treat the idea of the U.N.I.A. as a joke. But now it is more serious than the ordinary man can understand and grasp, and it has attracted not only the attention of Washington, but also the friendly governments of England and France. (Cheers.) And he went on in the article to show by statements made by British administrators and colonial governors in Africa who gave their opinions of the African situation, he went on to relate what these governments said a few years ago, and among some of the things one of the governors of South Africa said after warning Great Britain was that the time is near at hand when the native tribes of Africa shall rise from coast to coast and sweep the entire continent to make one huge government, and that this Pan-African congress now meeting in New York, meaning this convention, is regarded as a serious movement of the times, and England and France are very much concerned. We told them that. We told them that we are bringing them to it, and a reaction is going to take place, and you have to prepare your minds for that reaction. You have to write to your people and inform them to prepare for that reaction. These people have started already—the British in Sierra Leone and Lagos and in other parts of Western Africa—to offer big inducements to the black people there whom they crushed just a few months ago. They have started to make overtures to them, giving them better positions and better pay as a camouflage to say that they are satisfied, and that they do not want this new thing that is now sweeping the world. The same inducements are going to be made in the West Indies and America. They are going to make overtures to you if you are not strong enough. (Laughter.) I cannot tell you not to take it. If they treat you better, thank them for it. But bear in mind Africa shall be free. (Loud cheers.)

That is just what we must expect; that is what they have done all the time, and that it is why it is so hard for Ireland to get her freedom because they get hold of a few Irishmen and give them the big jobs, put them in the House of Lords, put them in the Cabinet, send them out as Colonial Governors, and because of their positions they try to crush the idea of the free and independent Ireland. If they start out to make us Colonial Governors and even President of the United States it is all right. (Laughter.) We have absolutely no objections, but we shall not lose sight of the fact of a free and redeemed Africa. (Cheers.) And you West Indian delegates I want you to understand that this U.N.I.A. has helped you more than you can understand and appreciate because in the West Indies you outnumber the whites fifty to one. He understands from the pronouncement that we have given from Liberty Hall that we are coming, not as ten million people, not as twelve million people, not as fifteen million people, but as four hundred million. We have told them that. They know what that means. Every statement we give from Liberty Hall, every statement that we give from the Negro World on the front page, every statement we give from the public platform, we give it for a reason, and some deep reason, too. In October when we told the world that we were sharpening our swords four hundred million strong in preparation for the next war, we went back and told them from our viewpoint the greatest war is yet to come, the war between Asia and Europe, and that we would not console ourselves again as we did in the past, because we were prepared to strike the blow for our own freedom. What happened? The paper I told you a while ago of, the article which was recalled by the Baltimore American comes back to the same argument I put up. That Baltimore American printed and showed to the white world that the greatest war was yet to come. Also that it would be a war against Asia and Europe, and that their idea [*was?*] the black peoples of the world were lining up to fight with the yellow people. Therefore, white supremacy was at stake. Now they have admitted that. They have admitted openly that the white race cannot withstand the force and the s[tre]ngth of the combined yellow and black races. We never told them that we are going to fight with the yellow man. We never told them that we were going to fight with anybody else but ourselves. But now that they realize our strength they will endeavor to make us overtures. So when delegates from the West Indies return to the West Indies you may expect because of the stand we intend to take here to see overtures made to your people—probably they may consent to make Governors of the natives instead of sending our their white Colonial Governors from England. You must remember that whatsoever change takes place it can only be traced to one source, and that is the source of the U.N.I.A. (Cheers.) You delegates when you go back to the South after we have declared our Declaration of Rights you may expect better considerations; you may expect overtures to be made to you, but when you go to the bottom of it you may find all of it coming of the bold stand of the U.N.I.A. (Cheers.) And so you delegates who have come from all parts understand that they will endeavor to please and satisfy the masses now because they realize the strength and value of the masses, and they will endeavor to turn the attention of the masses from the trend of thought that is now occupying the mind of the world, a free and redeemed Africa. They will give you every consideration in the world. But I am saying to you, take every consideration that they give you, but lose not the vision of a free and redeemed Africa. (Cheers.) As for me, there is no overture in the world. They could not make me Pope of Rome, they could not make me Archbishop of Canterbury, they could not make me George the Fifth of England, they could not make me anything else but an African citizen. Tonight I will speak at length on the question after reading to you the Declaration of Rights, which were signed here last Friday at five o'clock. The white press will be represented here tonight. So tonight will be a very big night, and I want all of you who are members bring out your national anthem. We are going to sing the national anthem tonight when we are about to read the Declaration of Rights, and I want all members to be able to sing lustily this national hymn of ours because it will also tell you that the declaration is right. When you come tonight you will hear everything, and what you probably thought of you will hear, and this Declaration of Rights that we are giving out—it will not be just a matter of somebody just writing a letter and signing it—but it is [a] declaration behind which is the signature of every delegate. (Cheers.)

We are giving out a document that anybody can tell who is the author of it. We are giving out a document that tells who are the men behind it. We came here as the representatives of 400,000,000 Negroes and we signed that document as free representatives, and we have pledged the blood of 400,000,000 Negro folks. (Cheers.) So the reporters will come here and get the document and take it away. I know that by Tuesday morning the world will be in an upstir. (Cheers.) Because the Negro will have declared his freedom full and complete. But, unfortunately, the hour has not yet struck for African redemption. But George Washington and those men who signed the Declaration of Independence took several years after they had signed it to put the matter into effect. It may take us twenty years. It may take us fifty years, but we shall put it into effect. (Cheers.)

Printed in *NW*, 21 August 1920. Original headlines abbreviated.

1. Elie Garcia's role in the Philadelphia division is also discussed in "Philadelphia over the Top," *NW*, 21 August 1920.
2. Searches through the *New York Times* of 15 August 1920 have not uncovered this article.

[[*New York*, Aug. 17, 1920]]

THE GREAT CONVENTION

The first business taken up by the International Convention of Negroes of the World at the morning session of the seventeenth day of its proceedings, was the reception of the report of the committee appointed to draft a Constitution by which the three leaders throughout the jurisdiction of the

Universal Negro Improvement Association are to be governed. The President-General presided, and a full attendance of delegates, officers and members, also a goodly representation of the public, was present. The Rev. Dr. McGuire offered the prayer, and after a few other preliminaries, the reading of the committee's report began.

The report consisted of 31 articles. It was read and discussed, article by article, and was adopted as a whole, with a few slight or immaterial changes. The discussion continued throughout the day, and not having been finished, further consideration of the report will be resumed tomorrow morning.

The first article was to the effect that the leader of the Negro people of America shall be a Negro and an American citizen. His office is to be for four years. He is to be consulted on all matters pertaining to the interests and welfare of the Negro people of America. His residence and headquarters are to be in Washington, D.C.; and he is to receive a salary of $10,000 per annum, to be paid through the U.N.I.A. His home and office will be furnished to him by the association. He is not to receive any gifts or to accept any titular honors from any alien race. There are other multiform duties required of the American leader, all of which will prove interesting reading.

In discussing the residence of the American leader, some of the delegates proposed that it be New York, others that it be Boston. One delegate objected to Washington as the headquarters, lest harm might come to the leader, owing to Washington being so near the Mason and Dixon line, and the presence in the capital city of so many "crackers." But the President-General said, touching upon this phase of the subject: When this gentleman (the leader of the Negroes of America) takes up his residence in Washington, backed up by 400,000,000 Negroes all over the world, and by our big brothers in America, he will have the backing of other ambassadors and other representatives there, and his office will receive the same protection from the United States in fear of international criticism. So, there will be no danger of the "crackers" cracking his office there. He will be there where he can watch all the movements of the Federal Government, where he can meet the other ambassadors of the world and exchange ideas with them. . . . [*Several lines mutilated*] The [convention] temporarily suspended its pro[ceedin]gs, just prior to adjournment, in [order] to hear an address by the Rev. [Dr.] W. W. Brown, pastor of the Metropolitan Baptist Church of this city. Dr. Brown's presence came as a surprise to many, as his absence from the convention up to now had been taken as the absence of other prominent colored clergymen of the city, as indicating his disapproval of the movement. But Dr. Brown assured his hearers of his full, hearty sympathy with the U.N.I.A. When the convention opened, he was in Virginia, he said, but his son (also a minister) had attended the sessions quite frequently, and reported to him his observations, and he was quite pleased with the progress made and what had been done. He spoke of Mr. Garvey as the greatest Negro leader he ever saw, and added that the Rev. Clayton A. Powell, pastor of the Abyssinian Baptist Church of New York[1] (which church is holding summer tent services next door to Liberty Hall) had called him up on the telephone, the other day, and said: "All the Negroes of the world should get together and honor Mr. Garvey. Any man who can influence as many folks as he has been able to do, to think along one line is a 'sure enough' leader." Everyone he meets asks him what he thinks of the Garvey movement. He replies: "The idea of Marcus Garvey is the idea that the race's salvation depends on. If the race had had somebody years, years ago to inspire them to think along the lines that Mr. Garvey has been inspiring them to think, and they had heeded his advice, they would have been vastly better off than they are today. As to the method or ways of realizing those ideals, I am not prepared to speak, but I do know that the ideals are the ideals around which the race at some time must rally."

He spoke glowingly, and let it be known that he was heart and soul for the cause, and wished it unqualified success. Dr. Brown was introduced by the president-general, who referred to him as "a leader in the Harlem community, and a leader in his church; one of the best churchmen in the Baptist connection, a master preacher, a master leader." It was Dr. Brown, he said, who offered to sell the U.N.I.A. a building when the association was looking for quarters; that the present building, now known as Liberty Hall was formerly the building occupied by Dr. Brown's church as their home.

Some persons believe that the best way of forming an opinion of anything is simply by viewing it from a distance. But sound, rational criticism is possible only under conditions of close observation of the thing criticized, and in the light of all the facts connected with or surrounding that thing, with no attendant circumstances likely to warp the judgment or bias the mind of the critic. So obvious is this, that those who disregard it as a principle when attempting to form a judgment upon concerns or movements with which they have not fully acquainted themselves by first-hand investigation, cannot complain if little or no weight is attached to their opinions by those who they would seek to influence or convince.

The bulk of the criticism which, since the opening of the International Convention of Negroes of the World that is now in session in Liberty Hall, this city, has arisen against the Universal Negro Improvement Association on the part of the Negro press is of this sort or kind. The editors of these papers delight in styling themselves conservative; a word that fitly expresses their willingness to accept the principle of standpatism on the Negro question, in the relation of the Negro to the Caucasian race—the principle of "la[i]ssez faire," which means being satisfied with conditions as they are, and letting things take their course, in the belief that everything eventually will work out satisfactory. None of them has ever been at close range to the U.N.I.A. to measure it accurately, or to observe closely its workings and understand thoroughly the principles it stands for, and the things it is striving to do and to attain. Comfortably resting back in cushioned chairs in their editorial rooms, they wait to gather inspiration from on high (more likely from below), through their prepossessions and prejudices, and then, when they think the psychological moment has come, attempt to express an opinion on what they know nothing about. This, indeed, is quite ludicrous, when it is considered that these writers have the hardihood to pose as representing the enlightened sentiment and opinio[n] of the Race, in what they say or write; whereas, in reality, they represent no one but themselves, in the narrow, cloistered views they hold.

Some of them say that the U.N.I.A. is a movement adroitly started and worked up to a point of temporary success by playing upon the emotions and sentimentalities of the people, through the adoption of high-sounding titles and names, the wearing of beautiful vari-colored robes of office, and an incessant display of meaningless rhetoric; that its purpose is Race aggrandizement, and the exploitation of those whom it can delude for the personal profit of the individuals at its head; that its leaders are trying to fool the people by leading them to believe in wild, fantastic schemes for the redemption of Africa, which schemes or ideas can never be realized in the manner and by the means proposed by the U.N.I.A., since Africa's redemption or restoration to the Black Race can only be a dream, and will so remain as long as the world exists in the present order of things.[2]

No one, however, who has attended any of the sessions of the International Convention of Negroes of the World, or any of its meetings held in the evenings, or who has made the slightest investigation of the U.N.I.A. as to its real purposes and what it has actually done and is continuing to strive to do, can see any parallel between the result of his observations or reflections thus formed, and the statements that have been made by our eminent colored editors. To the thoughtful man such extravagancies of expressions are absurd, and can only provoke a smile. They are plainly an impeachment of the intelligence of the average man and woman who knows anything at all about the U.N.I.A. As mercenary critics, these men of the pen, belonging, as they do, to the cringing class of Negroes, invariably take their cue from the white man, viewing through the white man's spectacles everything concerning the Negro, and from the white man's standpoint only; so that at a time when they should be loudest in praise and admiration of the greatest forward movement ever launched by colored people for their salvation as a race, the movement of the U.N.I.A., they are assiduously, even openly, trying to give the cause a stab in the back. But they are meeting their just reward, for already they are being thrown into the discard by the intelligent, progressive element among Negroes, and consigned to racial oblivion.

It is such men as the editors of the colored press in general who, be it said to their shame, are largely responsible for the present condition of the Negro in this country, and even in the isles of the sea, who are to blame that, until now, Negroes have been disunited, instead of united; that hitherto the Negro has remained in a state of lethargy, showing a spirit of complacence and willingness to let the white man go on in his wicked discriminations, injustice and oppression against him. They never try, they are unable, to offer any constructive plan or program of their own for the Negro's real, solid advancement, other than the nauseous preachment over and over again of threadbare, time-worn platitudes; yet when a practical movement is inaugurated in this direction by others, that has in its program the welding together of Negroes the world over, and the mobilization of their moral, intellectual, financial and material forces, they attempt to discredit it in the eyes of the public, hoping thereby to dishearten those who are upholding it, and finally to disrupt the organization. That is their conception of serving their brothers and their sisters of the race.

Indulgence in illogical reasoning, characterizing as radical those holding views opposite to theirs, denominating the leaders of the U.N.I.A.—the only practical, feasible, earnest movement ever planned and begun by Negroes—as dangerous agitators because they believe that the Negro should go forward and upward, as other races have done and are doing, shows the weakness of their position. In the conduct of a movement of the vast size and all-embracing scope as the U.N.I.A. money is required, is indispensable; otherwise it would be impossible to spread the propaganda necessary to continue its life and gain new adherents and followers. Every rightly organized and well-directed business or enterprise, every properly administered government, even every newspaper modern in type and progressive in character, has a paid force to direct and do its work, including heads of departments, managers, executive staff, and workers; and only when we have paid leaders, men whose services are actually paid for, and paid well, commensurate with the importance and dignity of the office they hold, and their ability, so that they may be able to devote all their time and their entire energies to their work, not until then can real, lasting success be achieved. It is no disgrace then to be affiliated with the U.N.I.A., because it offers to pay and does pay those engaged in its service. No one in these days of the high cost of living can afford to render services without reward or compensation—assuredly, not the critics of the U.N.I.A.—no matter what it is for, and the staff of the U.N.I.A. is no exception.

The "Is it right, boss?" type of Negro editor is no longer respected for his opinion on racial matters; he has become a relic of the past, who is fast being forgotten, or if remembered, will be remembered only because of his sycophancy—his willingness to compromise the highest interests of his race whenever discussing them, whether in private or in the public forum; for between the lines of whatever he writes can always be read that, under the plea of "good business," he has sold in advance the birthright of his race for a mess of pottage in the form of personal profit or gain.

"Unity!" is now the great call of the Negro, and he who loves his race more than all else, who wants to see his people everywhere emancipated from the horrible, insufferable conditions that now surround him in all parts of the world, the result of racial animosity against him, must see and acknowledge that the U.N.I.A., if it succeed in naught else but in effecting the union of all black people into one homogeneous whole, under responsible, wise, loyal leadership, and with an up-to-date, business-like organization, will have done more for the lasting benefit of the race than all other organizations erected among Negroes combined, have ever done or attempted to do; at least it will have accomplished the first great step that must be taken—the attainment of the complete liberation of the Negro from all those wrongs that are still done to him by alien races, and against which he has so just a grievance, and his ultimate elevation among the peoples of the world to a position of universal respect, whereby unmolested he may enjoy, as others enjoy, equal justice, equal rights, equal opportunity.

Rapid progress is now being made by the International Convention of Negroes. Already exhaustive hearings on industrial, commercial and social, as well as political, conditions among colored people in all parts of the world in their relations and contact with other races, have occupied the attention of the convention, and a formulation made, in rough outline, of the preamble and articles of a Magna Charta for the race, otherwise known as the Declaration of Rights.

A unanimity of thought runs through the convention as to the objects, as well as to the means, of attaining those objects, with respect to effecting the real emancipation of the race from the wrongs which Negroes everywhere encounter, caused by race prejudice, and an amelioration of the condition as an oppressed people. With able men and women at the helm in directing and controlling the work, there is absolutely nothing adversely to criticize as to what the convention has done and is striving to do; for, like a disinterested, sympathetic physician, the delegates feel they have a duty to perform to their race and to mankind in general: First, to make a correct diagnosis of the wrongs and grievances of an innocent, almost defenseless, people; second, to ascertain a remedy and to contrive a means by which that remedy can with safety be applied to the patient, yet with the assurance that it will ultimately produce the desired results.

More and more it is clear that the Universal Negro Improvement Association is acting for the entire Negro people of the world, and that the race will en masse rally whole-heartedly to its support. To say that it is a West Indian movement merely because the leader is a West Indian, as are also some of those associated with him at the council table, or that it is dominated by a particular class or element of Negroes, is unjust—certainly not true. For it is representative in character, embracing Negroes of every country and clime and of every complexion; in fact, its very object is the union of colored people everywhere, irrespective of the place of their birth or residence, and the intelligent pooling of their resources—intellectual and material—for the common good. Exclusiveness, based upon a caste system involving the principle of the inclusion of certain elements and the exclusion of others, is not a feature of the association, nor will it ever be. This should set at naught, once and for all, the slanderous, cowardly charge or inference, made by certain groups of people (ostensibly as an excuse or reason for withholding their support), that it is a one-man movement, or a movement in which a certain class or element has a monopoly of control. In short, the cause that brought it into being, and which the U.N.I.A. advocates, is a common cause, including and affecting all elements of the Negro race. To refuse, therefore, to affiliate with it, to spurn it, to look upon it with disdain and indifference, to carp at and unjustly to criticize it, and to persuade others to do so—this manifestly is unfair, ignorant, despicable, narrow. Whether American born or foreign born, every black man and every black woman not ashamed to acknowledge his race and proud of his color, should, and rightly so, feel it his or her duty to join this wonderful, far-reaching, historic movement, and give it their full support.

The officials of the U.N.I.A., from the President-General down, are men and women of the highest integrity, men and women of education, culture and refinement, men and women of broad experience in the world, men and women of stainless reputation. Possessing these qualifications, and animated by a holy zeal and a noble impulse and desire unselfishly to serve their race and posterity, and to establish, a new, a greater and a brighter day for their kindred people, they deserve the respect and confidence of their fellow-men and women of the same blood.

No better movement was ever instituted among colored people; nor any more systematically, ably and honestly conducted. It has attracted to it some of the most eminent men and women of the race from various walks of life. They are devoting their whole mind and energies to it, and, led and inspired by their courageous and indomitable leader, the Hon. Marcus Garvey, they are achieving results that have and will continue to electrify the world.

Printed in *NW*, 28 August 1920.

1. Adam Clayton Powell, Sr. (1865–1953), leading black clergyman and author, served as pastor of the Abyssinian Baptist Church from 1908 to 1931. Born in Franklin County, Virginia, he was ordained into the Baptist ministry in 1892, serving as a pastor in Philadelphia and New Haven, Conn., before moving to New York City. Under Powell's leadership, the Abyssinian Baptist Church grew rapidly, necessitating a move in 1923 to larger quarters on West 138th Street in Harlem (*WWCA*; *NYT*, 13 June 1953).

2. The *New York Age*, published and edited by Fred R. Moore, printed an extremely negative appraisal of the Garvey movement three days before this speech. It stated in part:

> Credit must be given to the leaders of this movement for the adroit manner in which they have played to the galleries. No detail has been omitted in the matter of high sounding titles for the officers, elaborate robes of office and the artful aids of bands of music and impassioned orators, to arouse the sentiments of racial pride and enthusiasm among their followers.
>
> But the real motive actuating the entire movement is to be found in the insistent demand for the common herd to buy stock in the various enterprises promoted by the leaders. Whether these enterprises are legitimate or not, from the standpoint of ordinary business, we have no means of telling, but the persistent appeal for subscriptions gives the whole meeting the appearance of a gigantic stock jobbing scheme, put forth under the guise of racial improvement. (*New York Age*, 14 August 1920).

Reports by Special Agent P-138

NEW YORK, N.Y. Aug. 17, 1920

NEGRO ACTIVITIES

Today [*13 August*] marks the completion of Garvey's "Bill of Rights." The conclusion of this document was marked by an impressive ceremony, praying, shouting, crying, etc. All the delegates present with one exception (Prof. Ferris) signed the document before a notary public, John Baine, at the end of the ceremony. Ferris refused to sign on the grounds that the document was too drastic and was liable to hurt him in future. The others said he was not true to his calling and the outlook is that he has been put in bad graces with Garvey, with the chances of losing his job as High Chancellor and Associate Editor of the "Negro World."[1]

Garvey gave notice that the document will be read and made public on Sunday.

Tonight's meeting was marked by the same anti-white speeches in Liberty Hall.

P-138

[*Endorsements*] NOTED W.W.G. FILE G.F.R.
Noted F.D.W.

DNA, RG 65, file OG 329359. TD. Stamped endorsements.

1. Contrary to this report, William H. Ferris remained with Garvey's organization until 1923; he was elected assistant president general at the August 1921 convention.

New York City 8/17/20

Radical Negro Activities

To-day [*14 August*] and to-night was given over to pleasure and the holding of a big picnic by the followers of Garvey's movement.

The chief topic of conversation is Garvey's divorce case.

I learned from two of the Africans attending the convention, that they had had a break with Garvey. The "African Prince" (a fellow who has been living in Chicago and New York for the last six years according to his own admission to me) told me that Garvey is an autocrat, despot and self-conceited. That he object[s] to Garvey electing himself or any other man here in America, Potentate or Ruler of all the world, as the King and Chief in Africa dont know anything about it and would be subjugated to him. On account of his objection, Garvey told him to shut up, hence he walked out of the convention.

Divorce—I learned from Attorney Pope B. Billups of 213 W. 135th St. that R.E. Warner and Edgar M. Gray will be filing a damage suit for $10,000 each against Garvey next week.

These were the men, along with District Atty. Kilroe against whom Garvey has published a lib[el], which was brought for trial last week and ended in an apology.

I also learned that Garvey's wife will be bringing a counter action for divorce, to affect [his case] against her as published in yesterdays N.Y. Journal on [front page?].

I learned that two of Garvey's ships are damaged and towed into Southern ports with $10,000 expenses to pay before release. One in Norfolk and the other in Charleston. . . .

P-138

[*Endorsements*] Noted W.W.G. FILE G.F.R.
Noted F.D.W.

DNA, RG 65, file OG 329359. TD. Stamped endorsements.

New York City 8/17/20

Radical Negro Activities

At to-night[']s [*16 August*] meeting of the convention, Garvey read his Declaration on Bill of Rights in Liberty Hall.

Each article was greeted by cheers and hand clapping but when article # 47 which says that no negro should engage in warfare for any alien race, the crowd went wild with enthusiasm, shouting etc[.]

Garvey promised to have 100,000,000 copies printed and widely distributed all over the world among negroes, to bring in their homes in place of a bible or prayer book. They should be prepared to stand by it with their lives etc.

These copies are to be ready for distribution in the next ten days. I will mail in a copy as soon as possible.

Garvey told the crowd that the white people in the[ir] newspapers said he was a dangerous [man?], but they will find it out in a few days that he (Garvey) is very dangerous indeed.

Rev. Dr. Easton spoke for fifteen minutes along the anti-white lines.

P-138

DNA, RG 65, file OG 329359. TD.

Editorial Letter by Marcus Garvey

New York, August 17, [*1920*]

Fellowmen of the Negro Race, Greeting:

It is my privilege and pleasure to inform you that during last week's sessions of our Convention the document containing our "Declaration of

Rights" was adopted and given to the world as an earnest [*sign*?] of our determination to enjoy those rights and privileges which it was intended by God and Nature that all mankind should enjoy in common.

Your delegates stood squarely for a clear and convincing Declaration—a Declaration that would leave no doubt whatever of its meaning. In consequence we have not equivocated. The Declaration is couched in language that "he who runs may read."[1]

That the world may know that this is no mere idle Declaration, no mere protest following the course of the ineffectual pleas for recognition of our rights, heretofore so often indulged and just as often ignored or laughed to scorn, we have breathed into this Declaration the spirit of the New Negro who is more than ever determined to exercise every right and privilege set forth in this our Declaration of Rights.

It is an axiom of natural philosophy that "things identical are identically in sympathy with each other." Since the sufferings of the Negro are identically the same the world over and there is not a Negro in this wide world who has not at some time felt the sting of oppression, this Declaration is the property of every Negro in every corner of the world.

Even those Negroes who think they enjoy an enviable position in their particular sphere of life are continually subjected to the insults of white men very often their intellectual inferiors, indeed inferiors in many other respects. This class of Negroes, very few in number, perhaps stifle their righteous indignation through sheer force of economic pressure. Despite this, however, it finds an outlet in private conversations. By the very virtue of their identity and in the very nature of things, they, too, are included in this manly Declaration of Our Rights.

During this week your delegates are charged with the serious responsibility of electing your leaders. It is a responsibility charged with the utmost importance. Heretofore leaders have been forced upon us, men of the type that represented the views of an alien race and submerged their manhood for paltry personal gains; men who in the very nature of the circumstances could not and did not represent our views. Within the week we shall elect our own leaders, men who will not be afraid under any and all circumstances to stand up for our rights, who will not sell our birthright for a mess of pottage; men who will not court the favor of any man or any group of men of an alien race, to the detriment of our racial aspirations.

Today the nations of the world are aware that the Negro of yesterday has disappeared from the scene of human activities and his place taken by a New Negro who stands erect, conscious of his manhood rights and fully determined to preserve them at all costs. They may not be prone to admit this, but they are aware of the fact none the less.

We are determined that our lives must be pitched higher. We must go on to a higher plane, a higher platform, where every Negro will enjoy the right to expand; where every Negro will have the right to participate in his own government without let or hindrance. Therefore we are determined to enforce the principle of "Africa for the Africans at Home and Abroad."

With this goal in view it becomes every Negro to strive for a Free and Redeemed Africa. We have made some progress in alien lands despite discrimination, lynchings and the thousand wrongs that surround us, but not until the Negro has a government of his own will he have realized that complete liberty which history indicates was the proud possession of his forbears before the ravages of slavery.

And now let me say a word for the Black Star Line. More and bigger ships are needed to meet the demands of Negroes in nearly every corner of the world for shipping accommodations.

We can float these ships with your aid.

I am asking you to buy as many shares of stock in the Black Star Line as you are able. If you have not already bought shares, buy now. If you have bought shares, buy more.

Let us put forth more strenuous efforts to bring our work so nobly begun to a splendid consummation.

The shares are $5 each and you may buy from one to two hundred.

Write the office of the Black Star Line, 54-56 West 135th Street, New York, U.S.A. Yours fraternally,

MARCUS GARVEY

Printed in *NW*, 21 August 1920; reprinted in *Garvey* v. *United States*, no. 8317, Ct. App., 2d Cir., 2 February 1925, government exhibit no. 3.

1. Hab. 2:2: "Write the vision and make it plain upon tables, that he may run that readeth it."

John E. Bruce to Marcus Garvey

[*New York*] August 17, 1920

My dear Mr. Garvey:

I have just learned that my name has been proposed by a member of the Convention now in session for the post of President of the American Sector of the League or Association, and I hasten to advise you in all courtesy, that I am not a candidate for this office, not that I do not feel it an honor to be considered worthy to occupy and serve as such officer, but that I feel that a younger and more active man than I know myself to be should be selected to fill this post. I am at one with the organization in all that it is attempting, has attempted and will attempt under your leadership to do towards the consolidation of the Negro race and for the ultimate redemption of Africa from the plunderers and buccaneers of an alien race who would barter their God for his image in gold.

I do not understand your "back to Africa" movement slogan to mean what the critics have mischievously interpreted it to mean. I think I see with tolerably clear vision that your purpose is to lay the foundation broad and deep, so that the Negroes of the coming day will know better than we, who are now blazing the pathway and preparing the race for African nationalization, how to possess and hold and develop the heritage which the Almighty has given to the black race. . . .[1]

[JOHN E. BRUCE]

NN-Sc, JEB, BL4-50. TL, carbon copy.

    1. Only this fragment of Bruce's letter has survived.

Interview with Marcus Garvey by Charles Mowbray White[1]

[*Manhattan*] August 18th 1920

Report of interview with Marcus Garvey, President of the Universal Negro Cooperative Organi/z/ation and African Communities' League. (A world movement for Negro possession of Africa by Force, if necessary) August 18th 1920 at offices of Black Star Line, 56 West 135th street, ~~Manaha~~ Manhattan.

By Charles Mowbray White.

Foreword. In my opinion the first thing that should be done in this matter is that the English government should be warned to prevent Marcus Garvey, the leader of the World Negro plan to possess Africa, from landing in Africa. He is leaving for there in several months, he told me today, to set up a Republic. [(]Without him as leader the plan will not be so formidable.)

Substantially Mr Garvey spoke as follows to me—

Mr DuBois represents the ante-bellum negro. With the war has grown up an entirely new spirit among negroes for world independence and a nation of their own. The Negro has been generally persecuted because ~~ther~~ there is no nation to stand behind them and see that they are fairly treated. For instance Japanese would receive very little courtesy or fair-play in any country if they had not a nation of their own to back them up in case of persecution. The negro desires to have a nation of his own for the identical reasons.

T/h/is Universal movement is only two and one half years old but already has over 3,500,000 members throughout the world. A weekly fee of one dollar is paid by every member to cover expenses and toward a fund to purchase steamships for trade between Africa and all seaports of the world.

The name of our association is the Universal Negro Coop[e]ration Organization and African Communities' League. Every corner of the g/l/obe where negroes reside is represented in this organization.

We believe in the U[.]S[.] Constitution for the Americans, but we stand for the idea of Africa for the /A/fricans. It is not our intention or purpose to send all negroes back to Africa.

The War has made the negro better economically, but worse politically. He has been given no right of way to work for control of his own affairs.

In the League of /N/ations' covenant Art. 10 concessions are made to small racial groups, including even the Jews, but not one concession or reference is made as to the freedom of the Negroes. Africa is covered by a mandate from foreign countries, but the natives numbering about 280 millions are refused an opportunity for self-government.

The West Indian negroes are kept subjected by poverty so as to prevent them from economic betterment and independence.

More than One and One half millions of Africans fought in the great War for the democracy of the World.

Mr DuBois is against this new movement, principally because he is not footloose, and secondly because he is not the leader. He has obligated hi[m]self to the White folks, and is in no sense or way free to break with them now. Many negroes wrote him about this great worldwide movement and the es[ta]blishment of the Black Star Steams[h]ip line, and he advised them /n/ot to invest i/n/ it. Of course he knows that negroes can establish their own steamship lines between Africa and all world seaports and thus put the shipping of the White people out of business, as far as trade with Africa i[s] concerned.

Lynching of negroes was confined to the United States until the past few [m]onths. Recently however a negro was lynched in England and another in France. This but further tends to show that the War has but /injured/ the negro politically.

In French Africa the negroes are treated the best of any place on earth. But of cou[r]se they have no political freedom even there.

Those negroes who leave this country to /settle/ perm[an]ently in Africa will be the pioneers—the Pilgrim Fathers—of thi[s] new Nation.

It is the decision of the negro to make Africa a nation, to which the negroes of the world can look for help and support, moral and physical, when illtreated or abused for being negroes.

[deletion illegible]

(Note—Mr Garvey handed me the following manuscript which contains in detail the program of the Work of the Universal Negro organization.[)] Please mark the "colors" adopted by the Universal Organization of World Negroes is [are] Re/d,/ Black and Green. Mr Garvey told explained that the Red showed their sympathy with the "Reds" of the world, and the Green their sympathy for the Irish in their fight for freedom, and the Black—the negro.

Mr Garvey was asked by me how he had liked and what he thought of the article herewith that appeared in the Evening Post of Friday, August 13th, and he replied that it was absolutely correct and interpreted his thoughts /on/ the negro question absolutely correctly. [S]ee also clippings from The Tribune and The World. Garvey told me his own weekly paper— "The New World Negro" has a circulation of 50,000.

A complete copy of the Negro Dec[lara]tion of Rights will be found following this report.

NN, NCF. "The Negro," box 152. TD, draft copy with handwritten corrections and portions underlined for emphasis.

1. Charles Mowbray White was a lecturer on socialism and radicalism with close ties to the antiradical National Civic Federation. In the spring of 1920 White interviewed four American church leaders, in preparation for a series of lectures on bolshevism he was to deliver before New York City's West Side YMCA. He turned the text of his interviews over to the National Civic Federation, claiming that the four leaders were "utterly unfitted for their work because of their close sympathy and affiliation with the ultra-radical forces" (*NYT*, 15 July 1920). In August 1920 White interviewed five black leaders on the events at the UNIA convention and the general prospects for Garveyism, claiming once again to be preparing for a YMCA lecture. Besides Garvey himself, White interviewed Du Bois, Fred R. Moore, Chandler Owen, and A. Philip Randolph, sending transcripts of the inverviews to the federation (Marguerite Green, *The National Civic Federation and the American Labor Movement, 1900–1925* [Washington, D.C.: Catholic University of America Press, 1956], pp. 402–9; NN, NCF, "The Negro," box 152).

Maj. E. J. Ely, Acting Chief, Negative Branch, Military Intelligence Division, to Assistant Chief of Staff for Intelligence, Eastern Department

[*Washington, D.C.*] August 18, 1920

SUBJECT: Negro Universal Improvement Society.

1. In reference to our conversation over the telephone today concerning the negro convention in New York, the following are ten questions that we want especially covered:

    (a) The organization of this Negro Universal Improvement Society

        (1) Theoretical organization.

        (2) Actual organization.

    (b) Aims of the society.

        (1) The public announced aims.

        (2) The actual secret aims.

    (c) The program of accomplishment whereby they hope to obtain their aims.

(1) The announced open program.

(2) The actual under-cover program.

(d)   Where is the permanent headquarters of the society to be? Has it yet been established? Who are to be in charge of it? What authority is it to have?

(e)   Who are the actual leaders?

(f)   What are the motives of these leaders?

(g)   How are these leaders organized into a controlling group and what is the thing which holds this controlling group together?

(h)   Who controls the controlling group?

(i)   What foreign influences are at work in and through the society?

(1) Influences of foreign individuals.

(2) Influences of foreign governments.

(j)   What is the nature and strength of the foreign influence?

2.   In addition to the foregoing, it is desired that you apply the Strategic Index in all four factors to this movement with a view to providing us as soon as practicable with a complete basic monograph of this movement, which we look upon as being one containing grave possibilities to the United States through the opportunity that it may afford our future enemies to strike us in our weakest point.

For the acting Director of Military Intelligence:

C. H. MASON,
Major, General Staff Corps,
Situation Officer
By: E. J. ELY,
Major, Cavalry,
Acting Chief, Negative Branch

[*Endorsements*] Mailed 8/19/20 B. C.

DNA, RG 165, file 10218-2101-53-501. TL, carbon copy. Handwritten endorsements.

Report by Special Agent P-138

NEW YORK. 8-18-20

NEGRO ACTIVITIES.

The sessions of GARVEY'S CONVENTION were devoted to making nominating speeches and nominating officers and leaders for the various countries.

GARVEY's vice president, a member of the Board of Director[s] and J. Certain is now at odds, owing to the drastic nature of the Bill of Rights. It is expected that he will resign in a few days. Certain told me that he was an American Citizen and could never think of signing such a Bill, which would cause him or any other citizen to disobey the laws of the U.S.A. There seems to be dissatisfaction among the non-intelligent elements over the same point, but in spite of all that GARVEY continues to rule with an iron hand.

The African Prince delegate who left the convention in disguise a few days ago, wrote a caustic article against GARVEY in last Sunday[']s New York Times.

He also said, he had sent a cable to his people in Africa, warning them against GARVEY's theories, and also against himself.

P-138

DNA, RG 65, file OG 329359. TD.

M. C. Dodd to W. E. B. Du Bois

33 Olivier Place, Kingston [Jamaica],
19th Aug '20

My Dear Doctor DuBois,

I regret that owing to sickness in my family I was retarded in gleaning the information solicited in respect to Mr. Marcus Garvey in yours of the 21st ult.[1]

I must say that Mr. Garvey is no leader of men so far as Jamaica is concerned; nor do we think for a moment that his scheme of colonisation in Africa attracts any number of people here.

Miss Vinton Davis with whom I am on speaking terms could not sustain in the mind of the general public of Jamaica, despite her eloquence and grandiloquent speeches the veneration & adoration for Mr. Garvey which she herself evinced.

I have enclosed[2] all that I can gather relative to the party in question and trust that it may be of service.

Kindest regards Yours truly

M. C. DODD

MU, WEBDB, reel 8, frame 1253. ALS, recipient's copy.
1. The copy of Du Bois's letter has not been found.
2. Enclosure not found.

Reports by Special Agent P-138

New York City 8/19/20

Negro Activities—Radical Matters

I visited the convention at Liberty Hall to-day [*17 August*] which was engaged chiefly in the framing of laws [that] govern the various officers who will be elected as leaders of the Negroes of the different countries of the world. Of course [G]arv[ey] [makes sure?] that only laws which he approves of, are passed.

The convention also took up the [ques]tion of voting a salary for these leaders. The delegates voted a salary of $10,000.00 per year exclusive of living expenses for the leader of the Negroes of America. The salary of the other leaders will be voted to-morrow.

Garvey pointed out to them at the opening that the salaries must be at least five figures so as to make it possible for the leaders to live at ease and be able to move in the best society, as these leaders will rank and be on the same basis as the Ambassadors of Great Britain, France and Italy. His headquarters must be in Washington, D.C. where he must be recognized by the U.S.A. and other countries. In other words, he told them that this movement was equal to a government.

During the afternoon session, Garvey read an article from the New York Globe, front page of the early three star edition, about "Black Policemen Strike" in Jamaica, British West Indies refusing to be ruled by white officers, and also the striking of railroad workers on that Island.[1] Garvey told the convention that he was glad to hear this good news which he attributed to the result of his propaganda and the s[i]tting of his convention, sa/y/ing that this is only the beginning and to look out for more. He moved that the convention send a cable to the strike leader in Jamaica, assuring him and his movement of support. The cable was sent at once amid wild cheers.[2]

Later in the afternoon I met Garvey on Lenox Ave. on his way home from the afternoon session. He told me of his action relative to the Jamaica matter. Of course I warmly congratulated him and praised his work, telling him how wonderful a man he is etc. This gives me an opening to speak further with him.

P-138

DNA, RG 65, file OG 329359. TD.

1. On 16 August 1920 the second-class constables of Kingston and Half Way Tree went on strike under the leadership of the local Federation of Labor branch. Later, second-class constables at Spanish Town, Morant Bay, and Montego Bay also struck. The issue in all cases was a demand for higher wages, since constables' wages did not reflect the general increases enjoyed by Jamaican laborers. Newspaper reports that a 25-percent grant-in-aid for police would be awarded also raised expectations but proved untrue. Government authorities responded to the strike by calling in special constables, the Kingston Infantry Volunteers, and

government troops. On the fourth day (19 August) the strike ended, with 217 constables and recruits receiving jail terms, fines, or dismissal by the inspector of general police (PRO, CO 137/742/3012).

2. The cable read: "EXTEND TO STRIKING POLICEMEN AND RAILROAD EMPLOYEES SYM-PATHY AND SUPPORT OF FIRST INTERNATIONAL CONVENTION OF NEGROES NOW IN SESSION IN NEW YORK" (PRO, CO 137/742/3012). Michael de Cordova, manager of the *Gleaner*, sent a copy of the cable to the Jamaican attorney general, who in turn sent it to the colonial secretary in Kingston. In an exchange of handwritten notes, the attorney general, the inspector of general police in Kingston, and the colonial secretary speculated on Garvey's role in the strike. Upon receiving a copy of the cable, the colonial secretary remarked: "Here we appear to have proof of the direct connection between the Negro Association presided over by Marcus Garvey and the president of the local Federation of Labor [Bain Alves]." Alves sent a cable thanking Garvey for his message and indicating that the brief strike had ended. The American consul in Kingston also sent a message to the secretary of state noting Garvey's cable (Charles Latham to Bainbridge Colby, DNA, RG 59, file 811.108 G 191/11).

New York City 8/19/20

I visited Garvey's convention to-day [*18 August*] where rules were being formed for the leaders of the various countries in which Negroes live. The question of who should be elected as an African president caused a very heated discussion [almost?] b[or]dering on blows between Garvey and the other delegates.

Garvey insisted that a native born African should not be elected as President of Africa, as in his opinion, such a man would be under very grave suspicion by England, France and other European countries who own terri-tory there. Also that he would be gotten out of the way in a short time owing to the fact that his duty was chiefly that of founding a Republic in Africa and spreading propaganda for that purpose, thereby incurring the displeasure of all European /powers/.

Garvey also made a ruling that only men from their own countries could vote on legislature affecting the[ir] own country. This also caused a leng[th]y debate which Garvey carried with an iron hand.

The ruling that native born Africans were not eligible to the office of president of that country, met the [una]lterable resentment of an African delegate. The African delegate insisted that they as Africans can better understand the nature of African chiefs, kings etc. who would resent an outsider. But Garvey ruled him out of order, told him to shut up, sit down and be quiet, thereby carrying out his own ruling.

Garvey exercises perfect control over the so called delegates who vote just as he wants them to, and those who differ are clapped down and called traitors of the race by the audience, hence a delegate is utterly afraid to vote against Garvey's will.

I am keeping a close watch for Japanese and other aliens.

P-138

[*Endorsements*] FILE G.F.R. Noted W.W.G.

DNA, RG 65, file OG 329359. TD. Stamped endorsements.

Interview with Chandler Owen and A. Philip Randolph by Charles Mowbray White

Manhattan, August 20th 1920

Report of Interview with Chandler Owens and A. Philip Randolph editors and publishers of The Messenger (Negro) and leaders of the Negro Socialist Party of the Bronx and Harlem. Mr Owens did most of the talking but the sentiments expressed were concurred in by Mr Randolph. Interview held on Friday August 20th in the office of The Messenger, Seventh avenue and 135th street, Manhattan.

By Charles Mowbray White.

Mr Owens spoke substant[i]ally as follows—

Garvey is either a fool or a rogue. He is of course an uneducated man—an ignoramus, and is appealing to the negroes through their emotional nature. He is a dem[a]gogue and a weak character without the scientific type of mind necessary to lead a big movement. It is possible he is working in conjunction with the depa[r]tment of Justice, to destroy negro solidarity. He has no strong men around him. He prefers to be looked up to as a hero, and hence has a cabinet of advisers so called, who are all more ignorant than himself and dense as a stone wall. Whatever he says to them is law.

The New Negro will not be gulled into action by emotionalism nor [b]y Utopian dreams. That day is past when a man can carry the negroes through their emotions. The leader with the scientific mind—the philosophic mind— alone will be able to get the mass of the negroes to follow him. It would be too bad if such a fool /as Garvey/ were a success, as thus he would set back ten ye[a]rs at least the Socialist movement we are leading among the blacks. They are giving Garvey money in stacks with which he is purchasing huge hulks of ships at huge figures and which are unseaworthy or incapable of doing any real work. For instance one of the tubs for which Garvey paid $35,000 was wrecked on its first trip and sold for $4,000.[1] Two others are tied up in Southern ports and are unseaworthy. How long his followers will continue to fill his /the/ coffers of the Universal Negro Improvement Association to bac[k] such rotten business deals is a question. Meantime one thing is certain as long as he is successful in getting these mon/ey/s so long will the right movements for the real improvement of the negro's condition be neglected /retarded/. He is also killing the subscription and contribution market of the negroes. As long as he gets the vast sums he does, no other /negro/ movement will succeed /can prosper./

He claims his association has 3,500,000 members paying 35 cents per month dues. As a matter of fact if he has 100,000 [m]embers he is doing well.

He discredits his entire Utopian program by his tall lying. His statements regarding the number of his followers, and the number of stockholders in the Black Star Line and that his mo/v/ement is equally represe[n]ted in all countries of the world, are lies pure and simple.

His talk of force to bring about the rights of the Negro will result in race riots all over this country the coming winter.

Our Socialist movement among the negroes of America is for equality in all things with the whites, even intermarriage. We believe the negro the equal of the white socially, and with education he will be the equal of the white from every standpoint. Therefore we do not think it will be necessary for the negro alone to fight this war for his freedom. If he joins with the Socialists of the world he will share equally with the /W/hite in all things when Socialism becomes the order of the day.

We don't believe in the cry of the Garvey gang—"Africa for the Africans," no more than we accept the cry of America for the Americans. We are not nationalists but internationalists. And when the worl/d/ is Socialized the negro and white will be equal in all countries under the sun. To nationalize the negro would have only one effect—that of crystalizing more strongly against him the /white/ world's feeling of inequality.

Garvey's plan is Utopian and impractical, and is offsetting our scientific plan to equalize the rights of the negro throughout the world. When countries shall be internationalized there will be no nations no patriotism and no ha/t/red for any race. It is the scientific way of settling the black question.

If force will be needed to produce this change that force will be supplied when the time is ripe, but not by the negroes alone. It will come from a combination of the various white classes who favor a world change with the assistance of the negroes. But, remember, we educated scienti/f/ic-minded and higher minded negroes do not want a negro nation. It would for/ev/er kill our dream of world equality.

To prove this let me point out that the Japanese have a nation but they are persecuted like negroes all over the w[h]ite world, and especially in this country.

The treatment accorded the negro soldiers by American white soldiers in Fran/c/e, the lynchings throughout the United States and the inequalities and insults under which the negro /e/verywhere lives, have resulted in creating the New /N/egro, and his world movement from his independence. I shall repeat this can be best brought about by the negroes joining the Socialist movement and helping the radical whites, than by any Utopian dream and "bubble" like that visioned by Garvey and his satellites.

Our editorial in the next issue of The Mess[e]nger (Sept 15) will deal in a len[g]thy and scientifi[c] manner with the Gar[ve]y movement and will clearly state what we think of him and it.[2]

The circulation of the Messenger is c/lo/se /to/ 34,000. Twelve thousand of these subscribers are white folks.

Garvey is a British negro and knows little of the conditions of the negro in America. His mo/v/ement is purely West Indian. It is understood he has the support and is working hand and glove with the Bolshevists and the Sinn Feiners and all other revolutio[n]ists throughout the world, but I fail to see how this is possible, since he has made no effort to study the Socialist movement headed by us.

There are four groups or factions of negroes with headquarters in this city who are working for the emancipation of the negro and who are at variance on certain points. They should be interviewed by you before you attempt to lecture before the YMCA or any other body on the negro situation. These factio[n]s are—

1. The National Urban League, E K Jones,[3] ~~president~~/secretary/, 200 Fifth avenue, who represents Wall street[,] or the right wing of the negro betterment fight. (Roger Baldwin and his Aunt, Elizabeth Walton[4] are its chief supporters[.])

2. The National A[ss]n for the Advancement of Colored People, 70 Fifth avenue, Dr W E B DuBois, which represents the Liberals, and is supported by capitalists. It is known as the "Anti-White" organization.

3. The Messenger, a So[c]ialist monthly, supported by radicals and labor, Socialists etc.

4. The Universal Negro Improvement Association, headed by Marcus F. Garvey. A "Back to Africa" movement based upon extreme reaction of the negro to the whiteman's per[s]ecution. This is bound to fail. We give this move/m/ent three more months of life.

Garvey has pu/b/licly stated that before his movement can hope to be a final and assured success all the mulattoes (Half white-blacks) in the world [m]ust be killed. . . .[5]

NN, NCF, "The Negro," box 152. TD, draft copy. Corrections are handwritten, and portions are underlined for emphasis.

1. At the time of this interview, none of the ships of the BSL were either wrecked or sold.

2. The *Messenger* published an editorial entitled "The Garvey Movement: A Promise or a Menace to Negroes?" in its October 1920 issue, which went on sale 15 September (*Messenger* 2 [October 1920]: 114–15).

3. Eugene Kinckle Jones (1885–1954) was executive secretary of the National Urban League from 1917 to 1941. He was born in Richmond, Va., and educated at Virginia Union University, Richmond, and Cornell University. He joined the Urban League in 1911 after a period of teaching in Kentucky. He focused at first on the black community in New York City, preparing a report on its status. In 1913 he arranged the first meeting of black leaders with Samuel Gompers and the American Federation of Labor. During his long career Jones served as a member of President Franklin Roosevelt's special advisory group, often called "the black cabinet." When he retired in 1950, Jones had guided the Urban League to a position of prominence among civil rights organizations (*NYT*, 12 January 1954; Guichard Parris and Lester Brooks, *Blacks in the City* [Boston: Little, Brown and Co., 1971]; *WWCR*).

4. Elizabeth Walton was the daughter of James Walton, an officer in the Civil War, and Mary Walton, the founder of the Walton Free Kindergarten for black children in New York.

When Mary Walton died, Elizabeth Walton took her place on a number of boards representing her mother's interests, including that of the Sojourner Truth House. She served as the first chairperson of the New York Urban League (clipping from *The Urban League Bulletin*, National Urban League Papers [n.d.], p. 7).

5. No statement to this effect has been found in Garvey's extant speeches, written statements, or correspondence.

Reports by Special Agent P-138

NEW YORK, N.Y. AUG. 21, 1920

IN RE:—NEGRO ACTIVITIES.

To-day [*19 August*] I had a talk with a number of the Garvey followers whom I saw standing around his office in the early part of the day. The chief subject on their minds was the election of the various leaders of the various countries, whom were nominated a few days ago. They still have absolute confidence in Garvey as the man whom God sent to save them from the white race and redeem Africa. . . . *Opinion of Business Men*. The chief object of my visit to the Philadelphia Business League was chiefly to mix in with them, join their league, talk with them in order to sound them out on this Garvey movement, which I found was in very great disfavor among them. Their minds are fixed on doing real honest work and improving negro business instead of agitating. No one took Garvey seriously or took time to investigate his African fad.

P-138

[*Endorsement*] FILE G.F.R.

DNA, RG 65, file 329359. TD. Stamped endorsement.

NEW YORK, N.Y. AUG. 21, 1920

Garvey was elected President of Africa at a salary of $12,000 per year plus expenses. Rev. East[on] was elected President of the negroes of America at a salary of $10,000. Two other West Indian negroes were elected President of West Indies and South America at $6,000 per year.

These men are to devote their entire life in the spreading of anti-white propaganda and the "back to Africa movement." Rev. Mc[G]uire said that he told the people last night to pray and fight, which was reported in the New York World this morning, and he was repeating it again to-night [*20 August*].

Garvey Absent. To-night at the Liberty Hall I did not see Garvey, but saw two of his bodyguards, whom I asked for him. They told me that he was off to-night. The Hall was not well attended and the most of the evening was taken up by Rev. Mc[G]uire boosting and praising Garvey, telling the people [*they*] must follow him wherever he leads them as he is their saviour.

Collections. There seems to be a deficit in Garvey's treasury owing to the persistent begging for money and collections to-night by Dr. Easton. He tried to sell shares in the Black Star Line but the crowd was not responsive. I learned that the Association is very much short of funds and that Garvey tried to borrow $5,000 from a Loan Company, two days ago, but was refused. . . .[1]

P-138

[*Stamped endorsements*] FILE G.F.R. Noted
F.D.W.

DNA, RG 65, file OG 329359. TD.
   1. The omitted material dealt with the activities of Domingo, Randolph, and Owen.

William L. Hurley to L. Lanier Winslow

[Washington, D.C. August 21, 1920]

Dear Lanier:

In view of your solicitude for the colored race in general and friend Marcus Garvey in particular, I enclose herewith photostat copy of the NEGRO WORLD issued August 14, 1920, from which you will see that the new spirit of the negro has asserted itself in a great world convention.[1]

You will note that Marcus ~~believes~~ /places/ the welfare of the Black Star Steamship Line on ~~paredy~~ /parity/ with the welfare of his race. For your information, I understand that the one and only vessel of this line recently left Norfolk for [L]iberia, but through some fortuitous circumstance, it was compelled to put back into port. Some inquisitive officer, in making a casual inspection of the boat, discovered that it had as a part of its cargo a large amount of the prohibited stuff of an alcoholic content greatly in excess of 3-1/2 per cent. This is somewhat aside from the question involved, but I am sure that incidents of this nature can not but have your interest. Sincerely yours,

[WILLIAM L. HURLEY]

Enclosure: Copy of NEGRO WORLD.

EY/BMD-SS
U-H

DNA, RG 59, file 800.9-71. TL, carbon copy. Handwritten corrections.

   1. Hurley received this copy of the *Negro World* from J. Edgar Hoover (J. Edgar Hoover to William L. Hurley, 18 August 1920, DNA, RG 59, file 800.9-71).

Report of the Convention

[[Liberty Hall, 22 August 1920]]

MARCUS GARVEY, REV. DR. EASON, REV. DR. SMITH, REV. DR. CRANSTON, AND DR. LEWIS AGAIN ELECTRIFY THOUSANDS IN LIBERTY HALL

The fourth Sunday of the International Convention of Negroes of the World assembled again under the most favorable weather conditions. The sun shone beautifully, and not a cloud marred the cerulean blue sky. A good attendance was present at the morning service which, on Sundays, is the same as is conducted in any Episcopalian Church, with a slight variance here and there.

The services began at 11.30 o'clock with the singing by the choir and congregation of the hymn, "Come, Thou Almighty God and All Ye Faithful," the Rev. Dr. W. H. Ferris presiding. Prayer was offered by the Rev. Dr. Tobi[t]t, of Bermuda. The Scripture lesson, taken from Psalms, 126th and 132d chapters, was read by Rev. G. E. Stewart, of Jamaica. Bishop Selkridge also assisted in the opening.

Rev. Dr. J. H. Eason, chaplain-general, delivered the sermon, taking as his text that passage in the Bible reading: "If God be for us, who can be against us?"[1] It was a sermon filled with beautiful and appropriate Bible illustrations and embellished with many figures of speech and in language filled with imagery of thought and expression, characteristic of Dr. Eason's well-known style of preaching. The burden of the sermon was that i[f] the black peoples of the world, in their longed-for freedom and emancipation from their present wrongs have God on their side, if they will take Him as their true leader, success will be theirs, no matter who may be against them, or what obstacles may present themselves. Few ministers have the power of imagination which is Dr. Eason's peculiar gift, a gift that enables him to electrify his hearers and touch their hearts and sway them into ecstasies of spiritual delight, like the gentle wind as it passes over the wheat field and moves first this way and then that way[,] the golden tassels that hold up their heads as if in praise and glory to God.

The sermon was followed by prayer by Rev. Batson, after which Dr. D. D. Lewis was introduced and made a short address, saying, in part, that he had just received a telegram from his wife in Montreal, his home, to the effect that she was very ill and that he should return home immediately. He said he hoped to return to the convention before its close, so that he could help pass some effective resolutions for the good of the U.N.I.A., but that if he was prevented in this, he asked the prayers of everyone present, and expressed the great pleasure and benefit it had been to him to attend the convention thus far.

Bishop Selkridge delivered the closing prayer. The collection that was taken up amounted to $105.25.

At the afternoon platform meeting a large crowd gathered and listened to several interesting addresses. The president-general delivered the principal speech. He, however, said he did not feel well. Mr. Edward Steele, the tenor, sang a solo, entitled "The Lord Is My Strength," which was well received. . . .[2]

MARCUS GARVEY SPEAKS.

The chairman then spoke as follows: "We are assembled once more to give our moral and other support to the great cause of the Universal Negro Improvement Association. During this convention time it is mete that we speak from the ful[l]ness of our hearts to those who have not yet caught the great spirit—the great vision of this great movement. While we are gathered together in this convention there are hundreds and thousands who come to us accidentally—who follow the crowd—and it is our duty to explain to one and all the meaning of this coming together of the Negro people of the world.

["]We have met in convention for a month for the purpose of laying plans for the drawing together or bringing together into one united whole all the 400,000,000 Negroes of the world. This, as you have often heard me say—those of you who are members of the association—is an age of reorganization in human affairs—in material temporal things. This great reorganization of the world calls for an extra amount of activity and energy on the part of all peoples if they desire to be a part of the new world to be reconstructed out of this, the old. In the process of reconstruction we who lead the U.N.I.A. see and realize that very little is being made and very little has been made by the other races, and especially those who have led us as a race, to make us be a part of the reconstruction and reorganization and to enjoy the benefits thereof. Because we who are leading the movement have discovered that we are to be left out according to the plans of those who have led the world, we have come together from our highest intelligence and have said we also shall form a part of the reconstruction; but we shall not be led by others but by ourselves. (Applause.) Hence this getting together under the banner of our own race. It seems strange that Negroes could have met in such large numbers for nearly twenty-two days and kept together and have succeeded in doing so many wonderful things without one white face appearing on the platform to speak or to advise us or to lead us. (Applause.) It seems miraculous, yet it is true. Who here today could say that they have ever seen one white face or one alien face on this platform telling us what to do for the twenty-two days we have been here? None can say that and none will say that for the thirty-one days of our convention. (Cheers.) At first we thought of inviting some of the big white folks to see us in convention, and to invite them to the platform, but a second thought came to us that they and others might have misinterpreted our intention and that we brought them to give their advice and to get their inspiration. So we invited them, it is true, to the public meetings, and they sat among the people and we told them what to do and they did not tell us what to do. (Applause.)

["]So that this convention for the month will be truly a convention of Negroes, the results of which will be the outcome of the higher intelligence of the Negro himself. Whatsoever is to be said will be said from Negro minds and [Negro] intellect, so that we may be [able] by our works to prove to the [whites] that we are capable of doing things that are necessary in this age of reconstruction. In the reconstruction—in the reorganization of the world, I feel perfectly sure that the Negro shall find his place, shall keep his place, shall maintain his place. (Applause.) And his place shall be a large part in the sun of men. All the other races have found their spot in the sun. Though late—it is better late than never—we are now making the effort to find our spot and hold our spot—a spot of 12,000,000 square miles of African territory. (Cheers.)

THE SPIRIT OF MANLINESS.

["]I hope the delegates who are attending this convention will get the real spirit of this movement. Understand it well, fellow delegates; it is not a spirit of cowardi[c]e, it is not a spirit of cringing, it is a spirit of manliness which we believe must first exert itself if this race is to be free. History teaches us no race, no people, no nation has ever been freed through cowardice, through cringing, through bowing and scraping, but all that has been achieved to the glory of mankind, to the glory and honor of races and nations was through the manly determination and effort of those who lead and those that are led. Each delegate who comes to this convention is to take back the new gospel to his people, and not only to take it back, but to be a missionary—a living disciple, to go throughout the land and teach the gospel— this time not the gospel of Jesus Christ, because that is already taught, but the gospel of the new Negro (cheers), the gospel that all men are free and there is no more slavery. That is the new gospel that is to be taught, and you must go back and teach it fearlessly. We say fearlessly, because cowards in our own race are as much unwelcome to us as the foes of the other races, because we cannot do anything with cowards except to busy them, and even that takes up too much time.

["]We desire to see a spirit of bravery in every Negro in Africa, in America, in the West Indies, and throughout South and Central America, that spirit that will not down even if the forces of hell came against it—that spirit that will stand at all times and demand the rights of the Negro. We have elected men to high offices and others are still to be elected. These men we have elected because I feel sure we believe in their loyalty, in their intelligence and in their desire to serve. If they are in here, let me say, we, the Negro people in this convention, and those who support this convention, elect you as our leaders feeling sure that if you go out to represent us as we desire to be represented, we are behind you to the man. Therefore be not afraid; we want you to represent us as the leaders and representatives and ambassadors of other races have represented them. As an illustration, take a representative of the French nation going out into the four corners of the world. He goes with the courage of his conviction; he goes with the belief that his nation stands behind him; and he goes out to conquer to the honor and glory of his race. That is the kind of spirit we want our leaders and ambassadors to go out with—feeling that we are behind you four hundred million strong, and if you represent us in the proper way we will not find any honor too great to shower down on you. We will stand behind you, but you must first stand by your guns; not desert your guns at the time when things get warm, but stand as men and women believing and having confidence that your race is able to take care of you wheresoever you go to represent this race. If I felt that this race could not take care of me wheresoever I was I would die just there, because I do not want to be taken care of by any other race, or any other people. If four hundred million people cannot stand behind those whom they have sent out to represent them, then let the representative die, and let the whole race go to Hades (applause). But I feel sure . . . [*line mutilated*] where we are going to [stand?] behind our men. In the past it was a difficult thing to get a man or any representative men of the Negro race to lead. Why? Because they were afraid. Even though they meant well they said: "Well, if I go out in defense of my race I will lose my bread and butter that comes from the other fellow; he will spite me and keep me from going ahead." Why? Because there was no organization to take care of that leader when he set out in defense of his race. But, thank God, coming down the ages we have been able to make an organization as strong as any government (applause). So that as governments send out their ambassadors and representatives and stand behind them even to the last man of the nation, so we are sending out ambassadors, delegates and ministers plenipotentiary and mean to stand behind them to the last man within four hundred million. So as government representatives have no fear, we say to our leaders and delegates, have no fear; because we are behind you so long as you represent us and represent us well.

["]This movement, let met tell you has already swept the world; we are only laying plans now how to hold the world; we have swept the world already, and we have put the world in confusion (applause). Why, we have caused more of the chancelleries in Europe to be speculating now about the future than any other movement outside of the Bolshevic of Russia (cheers). When they turn their eyes from Lenine and Trotzky[,] they turn them to the U.N.I.A. (applause). It is the only thing that comes near to Lenine and Trotzky—the Soviets. But thank God, we are not Soviets, we are the Universal Negro Improvement Association and African Communities League (cheers). That we are, and that we shall be; and if they can tell what that means, it is for them to interpret. We know what it means; it means liberty, and it spells it in capital letters—no common letters in it. We spell liberty in bold capital letters, not even in old English, but in the plainest Roman so that everybody can see, even the man galloping on the horse can see written there—LIBERTY—and not make any mistake about it (cheers).

["]Therefore be assured that this movement has done what it was intended to do. We have opened the eyes of the world. Has there ever been a movement among Negroes that has yet cornered the attention of the entire globe? Do you know that since we started out on the first of August—this very month—that the news of our activity has come to every section—to every nook and corner of the civilized world. All the great newspapers all over Europe and Asia and the Western Continent are commenting on our Declaration of Rights. Do you know what that means? It means that a new estimate has been placed upon the Negro. We have received cables and messages from Negroes in far off parts—Negroes who thought they were doomed; that they had no hope. But they have gained hope from the activities of the U.N.I.A. within these recent days. So be not in any way discouraged; continue the good work you have started and if you continue to work as you are doing now for another decade at least, you and I will live to see the Promised Land (cheers). Slacken not in your efforts. Remember men, what unity is. Unity is strength. Do you think if we had kept out of the U.N.I.A. in New York, if we had faltered and gone apart, that we would have been able to call this great convention? No. Two or three or thirteen or fifteen of us could not have done this thing. It took a quarter of the population of this neighborhood here to hold together themselves and to scatter the propaganda all over the world. If one community can draw all the world to it now, when all the communities are linked up together, what will happen to the world? This is a serious proposition I am putting to you. This convention was called only through the activity of fifteen thousand Negroes in New York City; and if fifteen thousand of us in New York alone were able to draw delegates and representatives from the four corners of the world to this convention that has created so much stir in the world now, suppose it was not only New York alone but every community where Negroes live numbering all together four hundred millions. Just try to imagine the extent of the commotion you would have caused the world. If you in New York can make the world so fearful and trembling, and you are only in New York, suppose you were everywhere. Why, somebody would take up trunk and basket and everything and run away. It means, therefore, that you can see through this, the value of organization, the value of sticktoitiveness, and I am begging you delegates to go back to your respective communities and tell the people to stick together and keep together if not for more than ten years and see what will happen. I feel sure that even before ten years roll by they will see a great cloud rolling away—the cloud of abuse; the cloud of segregation and jim crowism, the cloud of slavery, and giving light to a new day—the day of liberty, the day of freedom, the day of complete independence for the great African race["] (loud and prolonged applause).

The Hon. Marcus Garvey then introduced Dr. Lewis, of Montreal, Canada, giving Mr. Lewis the first opportunity to speak because he had been called home on account of the illness of his wife.

DR. D. D. LEWIS, OF MONTREAL, SPEAKS.

["]Your Majesty, Fellow Delegates, Ladies and Gentlemen: I realize that our leader is indisposed, yet his remarks were so impressive that I was sorry to see him sit down. I want to repeat in part as I said last Sunday I think, that I hope the Black Cross Nurses, especially the president of this concern, will see to it that you find out what is best and apply the remedy to our president, to see that he keeps healthy. I hope by all means I will be able to get back to finish our lectures. If I do not get back before the convention is over I am coming anyway. I want us to look after our president, our leader. There is no subject that interests me more than that of health. It is the keynote to success. If this man of God, this man of ours, could stand up and speak to you as he has this afternoon, as physically indisposed as he is, it means that he has got behind him a mind of dynamite; that all that is necessary is to keep him as near 100 per cent. physical efficiency as possible, and we will go by leaps and bounds. I want to tell you, my friends, that I have been benefited greatly by attending this convention. I never thought of the fact of not having had some one of the opposite race to stand on this platform until he spoke of it. It has been my privilege to meet in quite a few conversations, but I always saw the other fellow; he was on the way of instruction; he always claimed to be a pioneer, and he always seemed to know what to tell us, and generally what he told us was something that was going to serve to help him solve this problem and have very little to help us serve our purpose. The greatest drunkards of the opposite race would tell us how to form societies through which we might get away from alcoholic drinks; how we may have complete prohibition, but never did he come to us and say how we might formulate plans by which to overcome the terrible and outrageous and God-cursed deeds of lynching our people. (Applause.) So his object was purely selfish, and inasmuch as we realize that it is not the alcohol that has kept us back we are not paying any special attention to that part of the question, but we are determined to have a government, a government for the black people and by the black people for the freedom of the black people. (Applause.) And inasmuch as he is concerned about his own government and has all that he can do to take care of his own affairs, we have decided we do not need him; that when God was breathing into Marcus Garvey's soul He was telling him all that was necessary to foster this race of ours. (Applause.) And all we are particularly concerned about now is to see to it that we keep him perfectly healthy; that we keep him surrounded with men that are able to help him go over the top, sending not only America but taking America to Africa and making that country the greatest country in the world. (Applause.) It is a "cinch" that we save America first. A trader would trade anywhere. If traders get to heaven then they have got to trade there. So it is not enough to just take a bunch of people and take them to Africa. We want to analyze the whole thing. We want to carry them through the task, and when we have been out there then we are. . .[3]

Printed in *NW*, 28 August 1920.

1. Rom. 8:31.
2. Speeches by Dr. Eason and Henrietta Vinton Davis have been omitted.
3. The rest of the issue is missing.

Interview with W. E. B. Du Bois by Charles Mowbray White

[*New York*] August 22d 1920

Report of Interview with Dr W E B DuBois, editor of The Crisis, organ of the National Association for the Advancement of Colored People 70 Fifth avenue. August 22d 1920.

BY CHARLES MOWBRAY WHITE.

In answer to the question of what he thought of Marcus Garvey and his Back to Africa movement, Dr DuBois spoke substantially as follows—

I do not believe that Marcus F Garvey is sincere. I think he is a demagogue, and that his movement will collapse in a short time. His movement is not represe[n]tative of the American negro. His followers are the lowest type of negroes, mostly fr/om/ the Indies. It cannot be considered an American movement in any sense of the word. Most of his following are in Jamaica and other islands of the West Indies and Ea/st/ Indies. They are allied with the Bolshe[v]iks and the Sinn Feiners[1] in their world revolution, and it is doubtful, even if success should temporarily come to them, if the negro /it/ will permanently improve /the/ condition /of the negro./

At the same time all negroes have learned to despise the white man's government more and more each day and year as lynchings continue and not a strong hand is raised by the government to stop this awful carnage.

I went to France as a reporter for "The Crisis", and the things I learned there and the facts I gat[h]ered which appear in our May edition[2] told me the reason that whereas before the war there was but one radical in a thousand negroes now there are at least 25 in every hundred. And the only reason there are not a hundred radicals in every hundred negroes is because they have not been reached with the full facts of the shameful treatment meted out to the neg[ro]es in France. The negro soldiers returned from France filled to the boiling point with hatred for the white Americans never before dreamed of.

It may be that Garvey's movement will succeed. I shan't raise a hand to stop it. Hundreds of colored people have written me asking my opinion of

Garvey and his Association, and all I have said in reply was that I /kn/ew nothing of the movement. That is, I had not sufficient information wherewith to advise anyone.

The time has come when the negro must be placed on an equal footing with the white man, socially and otherwise. If a negro wishes to marry a white woman that is his affair. There should be no distinction between peoples because of color differences. Intermarriage between negroes and whites is common in the Indies and other pa/r/ts of the world, and there is no just reason why this custo[m] should not prevail here.

"The Crisis" did not take any notice of the Garvey movement so far. But in the next issue (Sept 15) our editorial will dwell [*deal?*] with it as a West Indies matter.[3] (Advance copy of editorial herewith attached) . . .[4]

NN, NCF, "The Negro," box 152. TD, draft copy.

1. The political movement known as *Sinn Féin* ("we, ourselves") was founded in 1905 by the brilliant Irish journalist, Arthur Griffith (1871–1922). The name emphasized the movement's policy based on the ideal of national self-reliance. Griffith's newspaper *The United Irishman*, from 1898 onwards, and its successor *Sinn Féin*, which appeared in May 1906, asserted that the English Act of Union was illegal; he advocated instead a separate national assembly for Ireland to be achieved by the withdrawal of Irish members from the British parliament. Griffith also advocated setting up administrative machinery, along with an extensive program of industrialization, as the necessary bases of an independent Ireland. The constitution of Sinn Féin was changed at its convention in October 1917, held in the wake of the Easter Rising of April 1916. The constitution now called for the creation of an Irish Republic; thereafter, the term Sinn Féin became synonymous with the fighters for Irish national freedom. The movement grew to such proportions and exercised such influence that at the elections in December 1918, Sinn Féin swept the Irish nationalist party in the voting, winning 73 out of 105 seats, while the nationalist party, which formerly had held 80 seats, won only six. The elected Sinn Féin representatives came together in Dublin on 21 December 1919 as *Dáil Éireann*, proclaiming themselves as the legitimate Irish parliament and declaring a Republic. Sinn Féin courts and a system of local government were successfully set up and functioned in opposition to the British authorities in Dublin, with the result that over large areas of Ireland British rule ceased to be effective. The British suppressed *Dáil Éireann* as an "illegal assembly" on 11 September 1920, and warrants were sworn out for all the members, followed by the banning of all nationalist movements in Ireland. Griffith was arrested in November 1920 and was imprisoned until July 1921 (Donal McCartney, "The Sinn Fein Movement," pp. 31–50, in Kevin B. Nowlan, ed., *The Making of 1916: Studies in the History of the Rising* [Dublin: Stationery Office, 1969]; Karl S. Bottingheimer, *Ireland and the Irish* [New York: Columbia University Press, 1982], pp. 228–36).

2. The May issue of the *Crisis* contained documents on black soldiers in France, which Du Bois collected on an NAACP-sponsored mission to gather facts for a history of black American participation in the war. In his "Opinion" column, Du Bois criticized Scott and Moton for their insensitivity to the needs of black soldiers victimized by the U.S. Army's virulent racism and stated his belief that the League of Nations was vital to the "salvation of the Negro race." Finally, he called on the white authorities to "make way for Democracy! We saved it in France, and by the Great Jehovah, we will save it in the United States of America, or know the reason why" (*Crisis* 18, [May 1919]: 7–15).

3. The text of the editorial on Garvey for the September 1920 issue of *Crisis*, "The Rise of the West Indian," followed (*Crisis* 20, [September 1920]: 214–15).

4. The rest of the interview has been omitted.

Interview with Frederick Moore by Charles Mowbray White

[*New York*] August 23rd 1920

Interview with Mr Frederick Moore,[1] editor of the New York Age, (Negro), of 230 WEST 135th street, Harlem, and Republican leader of the district. August 23rd 1920.

BY C. MOWBRAY WHITE.

The editorial (Herewith attached) which appeared in the "New York Age" of Saturday August 14th last past covers the question of G/ar/vey and his movement from our perspective.

Absolutely we believe him to be a mountebank, a money grabber and a discredited but cunning schemer. His financial record in Jamaica, Panama, and everywh/ere/ he has been, including the United States, is bad. He dare not return to Jamaica and that is prob/ab/ly the chief reason why he wishes to go to Africa to reside permanently. If he can get several millions of good American money from the American negro, the only negro in the world who has any money, he will carry it along to Africa to operate his dream Republic. But he won't hold that money long enough after landing as the natives will pounce on him and sack his treasury so clean that he won[']t have enough to finance a meal for himself in a quic[k] lunch counter.

Garvey's movement will amount to nothing as he is ins/i/ncere, and is hoaxing a lot of good hardworking honest negroes who don[']t think for [t]h[e]mselves. He has as much effect on the average American negro as water on a duck's back.

The convention of the Universal Negro Improvement Association being held here for the past month in Liberty hall on West 138th street with Garvey at its head, is a huge joke. He claims to have representatives from all the states in our union, while as a matter of fact, few if any of the States have a representa/tive./ He paid a lot of colored men and women here in New York to get behind certain State banners and say they were from the state the banner represented. Yes he has all the states represented by banners, all right. Hi/s/ following is 95 percent foreign. At least 80 percent of his followers are from the Indies. The great majority of the attenda/n/ts at the convention are f/ro/m the Indies. Of course they are obliged to get behind different banners, such as Australia, New Zealand etc[.] But they all came here from Jamaica and neighboring countries just the s/ame./ To say th[a]t he has a representative American following is a lie. He will place a badge on any colored man who offers himself and place him behind one or other of the numerous banners which go to give the affair an international significance.

Personally I know for a fact that one gentleman (Dr Robert R Moton) was offered $10,000 to attend the convention and allow himself to be nominated as leader of the American negroes in this Universal world movement.

The Interracial Commi[s]sions now working in various states down South under the auspices of the YMCA and the Chambers of Commerce of Tennessee, Georgia, Virginia, North and South Carolina, and Mississippi, are alre/a/dy producing extrao[r]dinary results, and give more en/c/ourage-ment to the negro to hope for better days in the near future, than any such Utopian and Socialistic dreams as the Garvey m/o/vement.

Rev Dr Moton is adviser to the YMCAs in their great work for the advancement of the color/e/d man.

There are three or four groups or factions of /radical/ negroes working ostensibly for the betterment of the Blacks, and it is my humble opinion that if all of them were gotten together they would not fill Carnegie hall. The negro is loyal. He is 100 percent American. And 100 percent of the Negroes honor and love the American flag. The malcontents are a mere handful, but by much loud-mouthing and wholesale propaganda they seem more formid-able than they really are. They are in the radical field because it is a means of bringing them money. The conservative field they believe is overcrowded.

Dr W E B DuBois, was until recently[,] quite radical. His paper is certainly the most anti-White negro paper in the country, but his heart is on the right side, I believe. He means well, and I feel certain he is a loyal American. He is not for Garvey. In fact Garvey has publicly attacked him through the daily papers. But he bears a great name among the negroes and has more weight than a thousand Garveys.

Our paper, the New York Age, is probably the most conservative news-paper issued for negroes. And our contention right along is that American negroes must clean-up their own troubles within the nation, and leave worl/d/ matters alone. And they are doing it slowly but surely.

There is no need of violence or revolution. We have g/o/tten a long way from slavery days and in a few years. We are progressing fast and within a few years more brief period we shall have fully acquired equal rights with all Americans.

As for Garvey's statement of the number of his followers being 3,500,000, I don[']t believe he has more than 50,000. He has capitalized his Association for $3,000,000, but what he has to back up this amount of stock, God only knows. They have a one-story building, known as Liberty hall, in 138th street, where the convention is in session, and an old three-story house at 50 West 135th street, where the offices of the Black Star Line are located, and three or four old tubs of ships. These constitute all the assets of the Association. And not one of them is paying a cent on the investment. Why the proper authorities do not get after this organization and make him s/h/ow the reason for its existence is beyond me.

When recently asked by on/e/ of his followers to give out a financial st/a/tement, he repl[ie]d that the time was not yet ripe. When the time is fully ripe I prophesy Garvey will be in Africa.

I don[']t think the white folk need fear any national trouble as a result of the work of this demagogue. When he leaves these shores he will take along with him all his tribe, an/d/ they won[']t include any Americans[.]

note—

Attached to this report are an editorial on Garvey from "The Age" and an article on the Interracial Commi[s]sion of the South. [*deletion illegible*]

NN, NCF, "The Negro," box 152. TD, draft copy. Insertions are handwritten, and portions are underlined for emphasis.

1. Frederick Randolph Moore (1857–1943) was the publisher and editor of the *New York Age*. Although he was born in Virginia, Moore spent his childhood in Washington, D.C., where he was first employed as a messenger for the Treasury Department. He moved to New York City in 1887, working for eighteen years as a clerk for the Western National Bank and for the National Bank of Commerce. He also founded the short-lived Negro Protective League and the Afro-American Investment Building Co. before becoming an officer in the Afro-American Realty Co. in Harlem. Moore became editor of the *Colored American Magazine* in 1904, when Booker T. Washington bought the journal, and in 1907 Washington helped him to purchase the *New York Age*. In 1911 Moore was among the founders of the Urban League, and in 1927 he was elected an alderman from Harlem (*Crisis* 45, no. 3 [March 1938]: 74–92; Louis Harlan and Raymond Smock, eds., *Booker T. Washington Papers* [Urbana: University of Illinois Press, 1976], 5: 18–19).

O. M. Thompson to Louis La Mothe

[*New York*] August 23, 1920

Dear Mr. LaMothe:—

Replying to your recent letters, the S.S. "Yarmouth" put into Charleston, South Carolina, on account of shortage of coal. It is hard to understand how she could have consumed 275 tons of coal from Serrana Bank [*Nicaragua*] to New York. Of course, I could understand her running short of Provisions after being out over 10 days. However, she got over $10,000 involved, so you can readily understand the troubles of the 'Kanawha'.

The 'Kanawha' has had to undergo repairs at [N]orfolk, Va., amounting to about $6,000 so we now have to reprovision her as [*and*?] also furnish Coal amounting to about 200 tons. S[h]e will, however, clear for Cuba not later than Wednesday of this week.

Captain Swift has resigned and we are trying to get Captain Richardson[1] to take the boat out. Now Mr. LaMothe, when Capt. Richardson reaches your port, you will perhaps think the 'Kanawha' is nothing compared to the Yarmouth. In my opinion she is a better and more attractive boat than the Yarmouth, and you both must have the Cuban people inspect the boat and have everything done in a short while and also boost the sale of stocks which is very important. She will have to make this round trip in quick time, as there are many passengers who were left by the 'Yarmouth' and who are making it unpleasant for us here in the office. If everything is managed in the proper manner, the 'Kanawha' ought not to stay in Havana longer than 24 hours. There is a cargo of Onions aboard amounting to 400 crates, this will take about two hours to clear. Kindly get in touch with Arturo Armendez and tell him about what time the boat will reach Havana.

With reference to the Negro World papers, I will take the matter up with that Department and have them forward the balance of your papers.

While writing you now, the Yarmouth is supposed to be off the Quarantine Station to be docked at about 10 or 11 o'clock. Of course this makes it rather busy for me at this moment, and I cannot write to you at length to-day; but before I close I want to ask you not to get into any disputes with Captain Richardson. Let him have his 'right of way' as Captain, and you act towards him as Agent. I have requested the same of Captain Richardson, and trust you both will work together in harmony. With you both managing the affairs of the Black Star there, it is to be expected that the Corpora[tion] will be well represented and the matter pertaining to the registration will be settled without delay.

The registration papers I am getting out to-day, and will write you as soon as the Cuban Consul affixes his name to same.

With best wishes for your health, and trusting to hear from you soon, I beg to remain, Yours fraternally,

[O. M. THOMPSON]

P.S. I saw Mrs. LaMothe last night and she was anxious to know when you are coming home. I told her that after the Kana[wh]a had visited Havana and the registration papers were through, I could give her a more definite reply.

NFRC. Marcus Garvey case file of exhibits, C33-688, FRC 539–440. TL, carbon copy.

1. Capt. Adrian Richardson.

Report by Special Agent P-138

New York City Aug 23, 1920

IN RE: NEGRO ACTIVITIES. MARCUS GARVEY

. . . I met Garvey on [the street] early in the day [21 *August*] but did not engage him in any conversation, owing to the fact that at the time I was having a chat with J. CERTAIN, a member of the Board of Directors[,] an ex Vice President of the Black Star Line. Certain, who is not now on the very best of terms with Garvey, told me that Garvey is ungrateful and never rewarded or recognized him or anyone else for their service, and when he went to resign Garvey asked him to reconsider.

From close observation and minute investigation, apart from my mixing in with Garvey's followers, I find that the white daily newspapers, viz: New York World, Globe, Post, etc. are doing more to spread this anti-white propaganda by advertising and boosting Garvey, reporting his meetings, etc., than even Garvey himself.

The members buy these papers in large quantities whenever there is anything relative to Garvey, then use them as an instance of Garvey's prestige, popularity and genuineness, claiming that he must be a powerful man, a man who is right when white newspapers speak and write of him. This therefore greatly strengthens Garvey and increases the circulation of these white newspapers, thereby increasing the Negroes' confidence in Garvey, and Garvey, Easton and Rev. McGuire, use some of new material every evening to put more vim and force in their anti-white speeches, and widening the gap between the races.

P-138

[*Endorsements*] FILE G.F.R. NOTED W.W.G.

DNA, RG 65, file OG 329359. TD. Stamped endorsements.

Editorial Letter by Marcus Garvey

[[*New York*, Tuesday, August 24, 1920]]

THE RACE AND ITS TRAITORS

Fellowmen of the Negro Race, Greeting:

The Convention for which we have been preparing ourselves for nearly two and a half years is drawing to a close. This Convention in its deliberations has startled the world and given to mankind at large a true estimate of the new Negro. The Declaration of Rights that was signed at Liberty Hall on the 13th inst. is now a document that will go down in human history alongside of the Magna Charta of England and the Declaration of Independence of the United States of America. Delegates have come from the four corners of the world to attend this Convention, and every day they have sat through the discussions and debates with such keen interest as to make the leaders of the movement feel satisfied that their work was not all in vain. A new spirit has taken hold of the Negro in the United States of America, and a similar spirit is now permeating the West Indies and Africa. In very truth it can be said that the leaders of the four hundred million Negroes of the world have received their lessons and have graduated out of this great university of the Convention for the purpose of teaching the scattered millions the doctrine of Liberty and Democracy. During the Convention one or two Negroes in the pay of alien races attempted to play spy and to make statements inimical to the interests of the movement; but we have been able to satisfy the white race and the world at large of the bona fide deeds of the Universal Negro Improvement Association and African Communities

League in interpreting the sentiment of the new Negro. One Madarikan Deniyi who has been going around America for the last ten years, claiming that he is an African prince, was used by the enemies of our movement to publish a letter in the New York Times for the purpose [of] [denying?] the affiliations between the African chiefs and the people of the Universal Negro Improvement Association. This man, who represents nothing African, in that his past record has been that of going from church to church speaking for collections and telling the people that he is an African prince, has attempted to interfere with the oneness of spirit that exists between the native Africans at home and the Africans of the dispersion. But when it is considered that the accredited African representatives of the Convention have all been loyal to the cause of the Universal Negro Improvement Association, such efforts on the part of a regicide like Madarikan Deniyi will not be taken seriously. The great cry at this time is for a united Africa, and no power in the world will ever be able to stop the current of Negro thought.

This Convention has been a blessing to us as a people. It has brought out the latent qualities of some of the ablest men of the race as they come to us from the forty-eight States of the American union, the West Indies, South and Central America and the great continent of Africa. The Universal Negro Improvement Association from September 1 will start an international campaign for the linking up of the four hundred million members of the race, and each and everyone is asked to do his and her bit in helping to spread the propaganda of the organization. The 31st of August of each year is declared an international holiday for all Negroes. There will be a monster celebration o[n] the 31st of this month in observance of this holiday, and all Negroes in all parts of the world are asked to observe the day. There will be a parade in Harlem, New York City, during the day and a reception will be given by his Highness, the Potentate, at the New Star Casino, 107th street and Lexington avenue, at 8:30 p.m. At one o'clock in the afternoon the Provisional President of Africa, the Leader of the Negroes of the United States of America, the Leader of the Negroes of the West Indies (Eastern and Western Division), his Highness, the Potentate, the Supreme Deputy, the President General, and all high officers of the Universal Negro Improvement Association will be inaugurated into office at Liberty Hall. All Delegates are requested to be in attendance and all branches are requested to pray God's blessing on the inauguration.

The Black Star Line Steamship Corporation, starting from the 1st of September, will make an international drive for the purpose of securing larger ships for the line, and all members of the race are asked to send in and buy more shares from this Corporation. The shares are sold at Five Dollars [each]. . . . [*Words mutilated*] can buy from one to two hundred. Let us hope [that within?] twelve months the Black Star Line will be in a position to fly [the flag] of the red, black and green, and the black star on the seven seas. But each and every member of the race must do his and her bit by buying more shares. The shares of the Corporation can be bought at 56 West 135th street,

627

New York City, by writing to the Black Star Line, Inc.
With very best wishes for your success. Yours fraternally,

MARCUS GARVEY

Printed in *NW*, 28 August 1920.

Reports by Special Agent P-138

New York City 8-25-20

IN RE NEGRO ACTIVITIES. (MARCUS GARVEY)

Today [*23 August*] I learned from SELFRIDGE, the head of GARVEY's "Underground Squad", (who go around the streets and bring news to him), that the disgruntled Africans, headed by an African Prince, were to hold a secret meeting to discus[s] plans for the repudiating of GARVEY and his methods, among the leading African Tribes and Chiefs.

They were to make a formal protest and give a statement to the newspapers, of their disfavor on the whole African movement.

At 4 P.M. by pretense I called at the address, (178 West 135th Street), where this secret meeting was in session, and found five Africans closeted in a small room in the rear of an employment office. Their names were: "PRINCE" KPAKPA QUENTEY, (Gold Coast West Africa), WILLIAM ALFRED (Liberia), Von Dom Demison, (Accree), Rev. PRINCE BABA, (East Africa), and another African from Lagos.

Von Dom Demison keeps the employment office, hence it was natural for me to call with a pretense. They told me that the British Consul General had advised them to fight against this Garvey movement.

These Africans were greatly enraged at the fact that Garvey had elected himself President of Africa without giving the honors to them. They said it was a high-handed piece of folly to make himself, (Garvey) higher than all the African Chiefs, etc. Finally they decided to protest openly from the convention floor, besides starting a counter propaganda in Africa.

Tonight's session was devoted by Garvey in answering an attack from the pulpit of Rev. DANIEL of last night.[1] He accused Daniel of being a white man's negro, who should not be allowed to live, and turned the entire sentiment of his crowd against continuing their membership in the Rev. Daniel's church. The Rev. GORDON, from California, and MC[G]UIRE, also devoted their speeches against Daniel.

P-138

[*Endorsements*] FILE G.F.R. Noted F.D.W.
NOTED W.W.G.

DNA, RG 65, file OG 329359. TD. Stamped endorsements.

1. In an article printed in the *New York Age* and cited in a report on radical publications, Daniels stated: "White men have forced the question of color to the point of stupidity but the fanatics of our race are just as stupid. It is just as bad to think only of the black as of the white." He also complained, "At Liberty Hall I heard one speaker say: 'We are going to have democracy in this country, if we have to kill every white man in it.' Are you prepared to follow such leadership as this? Our task is to find honorable and peaceful ways of settling the differences between race and race" (DNA, RG 165, file 10218-261-58/50x).

New York City 8-26-20

I visited Liberty Hall today [*24 August*] where the Garvey Convention was in session.

The entire day was taken up in the revision of the by-laws which were passed last week, and there was nothing of interest apart from the fact that the delegates are not so very much satisfied at the despotic manner in which their objections are ruled out of order by Garvey.

I also visited the Night Session, but Garvey was not present. The speakers were Rev. GORDON and Mr. DAVIS, who spoke along the same anti-white lines, with a repeated request for more collections so as to meet urgent debts. From the appeals there seems to be a severe shortage of finances in the Garvey Treasury.

P-138

[*Endorsements*] NOTED W.W.G. FILE G.F.R.
Noted F.D.W.

DNA, RG 65, file OG 329359. TD. Stamped endorsements.

New York City 8-27-20

I visited Garvey's Convention today [*25 August*] and listened to the debates, which were confined chiefly to the revising of by-laws governing the organization.

During the night session Garvey told the audience that the entire evening would be devoted to stock selling propaganda, so as to sell enough stock to buy two more ships between now and October, which would be large enough to run to Africa. He advised them to buy shares to their limit, as the white people are bringing in white immigrants from Europe to work as laborers, who would take the place of the negro workers, which would leave the negroes without jobs, so the only thing for them them to do would be to return to Africa.

He also reassured them that after the convention, the headquarters of the association will be removed to Liberia, and his ships will run from here to Liberia, carrying back Negroes.

Tomorrow will be the election of the high officers, such as the "Potentate", High Commission[er], etc. Next Tuesday will be a general holiday, a parade, and installation of the High Officers at the Star Casino, 116th Street and Lexington Avenue, which will wind up the work of the convention.

P-138

[*Endorsements*] FILE G.F.R. NOTED W.W.G.
Noted F.D.W.

DNA, RG 65, file OG 329359. TD. Stamped endorsements.

Capt. H. A. Strauss to the Director, Military Intelligence Division

NEW YORK CITY August 27, 1920

SUBJECT: Negro Universal Improvement Society.

    1.   Reference your 10218-406, August 18, 1920.

    2.   I am enclosing herewith copy of report just as it was given to me by the man who furnished Major Loving most of his information on the Negro situation in New York.[1]

    3.   Referring to paragraph two of your letter concerning basic monograph on this movement, same is being worked on at the present time and will be forwarded to you as soon as completed.

H. A. STRAUSS
Captain, A. S.

Enc.

[*Typewritten references*] Intel. 31913 HAS/d
[*Handwritten endorsement*] Encl. # OK CW

DNA, RG 165, file 10218-261/58/50x. TLS, recipient's copy.

    1. John Lewis Waller, Jr. (d. 1981) was a civilian clerk of thirteen years' service in the Quartermaster's Department (Eastern Department, Governors Island, New York) whom Maj. Loving had recommended to the director of the Military Intelligence Division. He was the son of John Lewis Waller, the United States consul in Madagascar, 1891–94, and a former Republican party leader in Kansas during the era of the "Kansas Exodus" following Reconstruction (Woods, *A Black Odyssey*, passim). Waller was a Spanish-American War veteran who had served in Cuba and the Philippines. Maj. Loving described Waller as "intimately acquainted with the situation in Harlem" and someone whose "personal acquaintance with the leaders of the various factions [*in Harlem*] would make him an ideal man for the work involved" (Maj. W. H. Loving to director of military intelligence, New York, 21 August 1919, DNA, RG 165, file 10218-361/6 190x). Waller's home address in New York was the same as that of Maj. Loving.

Enclosure

[*New York*] August 27, 1920

I have prepared some notes and collected some literature on the Garvey movement in accordance with your request, and am sending them to you. I was not able to get a stenographer to type these notes, but presume that you can take care of that.

I have been so swamped with work lately that I could not give as much personal attention to this matter as I might have done otherwise.

I would suggest that the M.I.D. get each issue of *The Negro World*, which will enable you to keep in touch with Garvey and his movement.

The election of officers on August 30th may be of interest to you. I will bear it in mind and send you the next issue of the *Negro World*.

The organization of the Universal Negro Improvement Association and African Communities League was effected about two years ago by Marcus Garvey, a West Indian Negro.

THEORETICAL ORGANIZATION

A headquarters (to be established in Africa at a later date) with branches in all parts of the world inhabited by Negroes; each branch to have a leader in charge of some given territorial area.

ACTUAL ORGANIZATION

In the present actual organization the headquarters are in New York at 56 W. 135th Street, and the work of building up branches with a view to putting the theoretical organization into prac[t]ice is now in progress.

PUBLICLY ANNOUNCED AIMS

To redeem Africa from European rule and eventually establish on the African Continent a strong Negro Government.

ACTUAL SECRET AIMS

There is no evidence of any secret aims. If any secret aims exist they have been withheld from the rank and file of the organization and are known only to Mr. Garvey and his nearest advisors.

THE ANNOUNCED OPEN PROGRAM

To spread propaganda among all the Negroes of the world with a view to arousing a united race consciousness, with special reference to the liberation of Africa. To establish an International Negro Business Corporation to assist in the execution of this plan. A steamship line has already been started and other business enterprises, such as banks, stores, etc., are contemplated, all to be financed and controlled from the headquarters of the organization.

The Undercover Program

Same remarks as far as secret aims. No evidence of any secret plan of action.

Permanent headquarters have not yet been established. The plan is to establish such headquarters in Africa, but the probability is that the present headquarters in New York will be maintained as offering the best place for carrying out the business plans of the organization.

Leaders

The leaders are to be elected August 30, 1920. It is certain that Garvey will be elected as the Chief of the organization, but it is not known who will be elected as leaders of the various branches to be established in Africa, South America, the West Indies, etc. The election of these leaders on August 30th will terminate the convention now in session.

Foreign Influences

There is no evidence of foreign influences at work in this movement, and it seems to be purely a Negro movement, ini[ti]ated by Garvey and backed principally by West Indian Negroes.

General Observations

There are only a few American Negroes connected with this movement, and none of them are men of national repute or standing. It can be stated as a fact, however, that Garvey's success is beginning to attract many people who formerly regarded him as a joke and they are speaking more seriously of his work.

There appears to be nothing in this movement that should give the American Government concern. The whole movement is directed toward the goal of liberating Africa from European rule and all the propaganda is shaped along that line.

Publications

A reading of the following publications, which are attached hereto, will be of special interest in this matter:

1. Negro World of August 28, 1920. This is the official organ of the organization.

2. Sunday Magazine from New York World, August 22, 1920[.] (see article on page 3—"When Africa Awakes."[)]

3. "The Roots of the Universal Negro Convention".[1] This publication is selling on the newsstands in Harlem at 25 cents and is in great demand.

[JOHN L. WALLER]

DNA, RG 165, file 10218-261-57. TD.

1. *The Roots of the Universal Negro Convention* was a thirty-page pamphlet written by a twenty-five-year-old Jamaican immigrant named Ashton Sewell in collaboration with Joseph Pinckney (*WWCA*). The pamphlet offered a brief history of blacks, beginning in antiquity and ending with the UNIA convention as a crowning event in the history of those of African descent.

Report by Special Agent P-138

NEW YORK N.Y. AUG. 28th, [*1920*]

NEGRO ACTIVITIES

Today [*26 August*] Garvey convention nominated and elected the "High Potentate" in the person of Johnson, the Mayor of M[o]nrovia[,] Liberia, who is atten[ding] as a delegate. He appeared before the Public tonight but f[or] some [unk]nown reason Johnson did not show up. The others appeared on the platform and gave short addresses before a crowded house, e[ac]h pledging their loyalty.

JOHNSON CAUTIONS

One of Garvey[']s inside men told me that the reason for Johnson not showing up or not doing much speaking is because Liberia is expecting a $5,000,000 Loan from the U.S.A. and so as not to do anything to prevent same coming through, Johnson wou[ld] keep as quiet as ever for the present.

This Johnson is far from being an impressive character and would not impress one as the very least intelligent. Since attending the convention he has only spoken once. He seems to suffer from an impediment of speech.

Garvey and his followers are very much enraged at Liberia not getting her $5,000,000 loan as yet, in fact he has printed an article in this week's [N]egro World, which is causing a good deal of unfavorable comment against the U.S.A. by his followers. They claim that because Garvey will be removing his headquarters to Liberia shortly, that[']s why the U.S.A. won[']t grant the loan.[1] I am forwarding you a negro newspaper, which has started an attack on Garvey backed up by some negro ministers.[2]

P-138

[*Endorsements*] Noted F.D.W. NOTED
W.W.G. FILE G.F.R.

DNA, RG 65, file OG 329359. TD. Stamped endorsements.

1. The *Negro World* of 28 August 1920 ran an article complaining of the government's delay in granting the Liberian loan, noting that the United States had been "granting generous credits to European nations engaged on the side of the Allies." Two years had elapsed since the announcement that credit had been extended to Liberia. Yet the terms of the loan, which virtually reduced Liberia to dependency status, had proven unacceptable to the Liberian legislature, leading to the delay.

2. Enclosure not found.

Affidavit of Amy Ashwood Garvey

[*New York*] 30th day of August 1920

AMY GARVEY being duly sworn, deposes and says, that she is the defendant in this action [*Marcus Garvey* v. *Amy Ashwood Garvey*] and the lawful wife of Marcus Garvey, the plaintiff herein; that said action was brought to annul the marriage between the plaintiff and this deponent upon the grounds of alleged fraud and deception practiced on the plaintiff by the deponent and for adultery.

That the plaintiff and deponent first met at deponent's home town in the Island of Jamaica, B. W. I. in June, 1914; and that at said time the plaintiff was assiduously working to establish a world wide organization for the solidification of the members of his race; that deponent at that time had recently finished school and was very prominent in social and literary work in the community in which she lived.

That for two years thereafter this deponent was closely associated with the plaintiff and labored unceasingly in her endeavor to aid the plaintiff in the establishment of the organization of which the plaintiff is now the universal head; that deponent was the Secretary of the Association and by rea[son] of deponent's connection with said organization, deponent secured the use of her mother's domicile as the office of said Association.

That about two years after the plaintiff and deponent met as aforesaid, deponent's family moved to Colon, Isthmus of Panama. However, before leaving Jamaica, the plaintiff prepared a pledge in writing whereby said plaintiff and this deponent bound themselves firmly to each other, and each to the other vowed to be true as long as each should live and until such time as they might be married.

That after deponent's arrival in Colon, she corresponded with the plaintiff for a period of about six months, after which time deponent did not receive any reply from the plaintiff although deponent repeatedly addressed letters to said plaintiff; that upon plaintiff's [*deponent's?*] failure to receive any reply from her letters addressed to the plaintiff herein, deponent made inquiries from other persons in America and deponent was informed and verily believed that the plaintiff had become mentally deranged; therefore deponent considered the plaintiff as lost to her.

That sometime during the year of 1918, and approximately a year and a half after the plaintiff's discontinuance of correspondence with the deponent, this deponent while in Panama City, Panama, became acquainted with one Allen Cumberbatch,[1] an unmarried young man, about deponent's age, who was at that time conducting a tailoring business in Panama City and moved in the best circles of society in the community.

That during the month of September 1918, deponent left the Isthmus of Panama to come to America; that upon the day set for deponent's departure from said Isthmus of Panama, she met one Mr. Parker, who is engaged as a school teacher in the City of Colon, who informed deponent that he, said Parker, had recently received a letter from the plaintiff, who was then in New York, and that said plaintiff had inquired about deponent in said letter, that deponent made a note of plaintiff's address.

That on deponent's arrival in New York City, on or about the 6th day of October, 1918, deponent called upon the plaintiff herein, who had by that time organized and established a very large organization under the name of THE UNIVERSAL NEGRO IMPROVEMENT ASSOCIATION, INC.

That as might be expected, the deponent inquired of the plaintiff why he had failed to correspond with her as he promised; that the plaintiff in reply thereto stated that he had devoted his entire life to the founding of his organization and that he desired to sacrifice himself and his professed love for deponent until such time as he, the plaintiff had met with success and that when that time came he had planned to send for this deponent and her parents so that said plaintiff and this deponent might be married. However, plaintiff stated further that when he had finally established his organization and was sorely in need of deponent, he, plaintiff, was informed that this deponent was dead; hence he, plaintiff had not corresponded further with your deponent.

Deponent told the plaintiff about her having met the aforesaid Allen Cumberbatch and that she, deponent, had practically had a tacit understanding with the said Allen Cumberbatch that the two would be married.

That upon ascertaining this fact, the plaintiff requested the deponent's permission to write the said Allen Cumberbatch and inform him as to the said pledge heretofore mentioned between the plaintiff and your deponent; that the deponent refused to consent to this but stated that she, personally, would so inform the said Allen Cumberbatch; that accordingly, deponent corresponded with the said Allen Cumberbatch informing him of her status; that your deponent had no further correspondence [wit]h the said Allen Cumberbatch until sometime during the spring of 19[19] when your deponent and the plaintiff had a slight disagreement, a lover's quarrel and stopped speaking to each other for a period of about four months; that said disagreement was occasioned by reason of the fact that your deponent, who was at that time employed by the UNIVERSAL NEGRO IMPROVEMENT ASSOCIA-

TION and employed in the same office with the plaintiff, had intercepted a certain letter written to the plaintiff by another woman; that in order to discipline the plaintiff for his indiscretion and apparent breach of faith, your deponent again resumed correspondence with the aforesaid Allen Cumberbatch and for the purpose of arousing the jealousy of the plaintiff, your deponent would leave the letters which [s]he had received in reply to her communications addressed to the said Allen Cumberbatch as aforesaid, upon her desk, so that the plaintiff might be able to read same.

That this state of affairs continued until some time in the month of October, 1919, as well as your deponent can recall, when the plaintiff was shot by a fanatic. Your deponent on this occasion interposed her body between the plaintiff and his assailant and for this utter disregard of her own safety and the heroism shown by her, in preventing the fanatic from shooting a second time and possibly killing the plaintiff herein, your deponent was publicly presented with an African Cross of Gold, which is the emblem of the highest honor which the plaintiff's said organization can bestow; that the said presentation was made at a monster mass meeting held in Madison Square Garden in the presence of an audience estimated at ten thousand persons; that your deponent made a brief response at this presentation and after the plaintiff had recovered from the illness caused by his injuries as aforesaid, through which illness your deponent nursed the plaintiff, your deponent completely forgot and overlooked the disagreement which had existed between her and the plaintiff prior to the incident hereinbefore mentioned, and again their love stream flowed smoothly.

That your deponent had not written a single letter to or had any other form of communication with the said Allen Cumberbatch since the day upon which the plaintiff was wounded as aforesaid, except that on or about the 15th day of December, 1919, she wrote him informing him of her /coming/ marriage.

That on December 25th, 1919, the plaintiff and deponent were married, said ceremony taking place at Liberty Hall, the meeting place of the Organization headed by the plaintiff herein, which this deponent had labored so assiduously to establish. That there were approximately three thousand persons present at the ceremony, with hundreds of persons clamoring on the outside of the building for admission; that there were five hundred invited guests. Many of them coming from distant points, both within and without the United States and that five ministers of the Gospel assisted at the ceremony, and that the plaintiff and deponent received approximately three thousand five hundred dollars. ($3,500.00) worth of wedding presents.

That immediately following the wedding, which took place as aforesaid, the plaintiff and deponent left for Canada to spend their honeymoon.

That subsequent to the wedding, and in the month of March, 1920, the plaintiff carried your deponent to a furniture store where the deponent selected furniture for her new home, which the plaintiff had agreed to establish, the bill therefore amounting to upward of five thousand

($5,000.00) dollars. However, by reason of the fact that the plaintiff could not obtain a suitable apartment or private house in the locality he desired, the said furniture was stored by the dealer until a suitable dwelling might be located.

That upon information and belief the plaintiff has since the 20th day of June, 1920—caused said furniture to be removed to an apartment, until recently occupied by him and one Miss Amy Jacques at #133 West 129th Street, Borough of Manhattan. That after the plaintiff and deponent had returned from their honeymoon as aforesaid, they resided at #552 Lenox Avenue, in the Borough of Manhattan, City of New York, where deponent had, prior to her marriage, maintained an apartment which had been set up and provided for your deponent by deponent's father, that plaintiff and deponent continued to reside in said apartment from about the second week in January until on or about the 10th day of June, 1920, at which time the plaintiff abandoned your deponent.

That prior to the marriage of plaintiff and deponent, and at all times thereafter herein mentioned, the aforesaid Miss Amy Jacques also resided with the plaintiff and the deponent in their said apartment and that the said Miss Amy Jacques, was during this time, also employed as private secretary to the plaintiff.

That shortly after their return from their honeymoon, and upon intermittent occasions almost continuously thereafter, the plaintiff was wont to go for long periods of time without speaking to your deponent; although they both resided under the same roof and worked in the same office. That during such periods the plaintiff would remain away from home until late hours of the night or early morning, and of[t]times would not come home at all.

That prior to his marriage to this deponent, the plaintiff resided in a furnished room at #238 West 131st Street, Borough of Manhattan, and that throughout the whole of the times herein set forth, said plaintiff retained said room.

That ofttimes when the plaintiff failed to come home before one or two o'clock in the mornings, this deponent would go to the said room and wait there expecting plaintiff to come there, however deponent would ofttime go to sleep and morning would find her there and the plaintiff had not called at said room during the night. That deponent would then hurry back to her said apartment and find that the plaintiff had not been there during her absence. That on the following day deponent would inquire of the plaintiff where he had been on the night before; that the plaintiff would state he had remained at his room, and when deponent would tell the plaintiff that she had been in said room all night herself, then plaintiff would state he had "Slept out," but would give no further explanation nor offer deponent any assurances that such actions would not be repeated.

That during the said months of March and April, 1920, deponent had visited all the rooming houses and hotels in Harlem in search of the plaintiff when he failed to come home at nights; but at no time was deponent able to find the plaintiff.

That the first trouble between the plaintiff and deponent in their matrimonial relations occurred sometime during the latter part of February, 1920 when plaintiff discovered your deponent reading a letter. It happened that deponent had been rum[m]aging in a drawer in search of something, and came upon a letter which she had received several months prior from the said Allen Cumberbatch, and was reading the same when the plaintiff entered and demanded that she hand over the letter to him. Deponent explained that it was an old letter and refused to give it to the plaintiff. The plaintiff however, with brute strength wrenched deponent's arm causing her excruciating pain for several moments, but that in spite of the same, deponent refused to deliver the letter to the plaintiff.

This episode soon passed away as had many others when the plaintiff had refused to speak to the deponent for several days, and again they became reconciled. Shortly thereafter, during the month of March, the plaintiff and deponent purchased their home furnishings as aforesaid for their proposed new home.

The plaintiff was and is a person of many moods, whims, and idiosyncrasies and ofttimes would stop speaking to your deponent and otherwise humiliate and abuse her for the most frivolous and unreasonable cause or pretense, and ofttimes during such spells, the plaintiff would leave deponent's apartment, stating that he would never return again.

The final break between the plaintiff and the deponent came in the month of April last past, when deponent and the said Amy Jacques quarreled and the said Amy Jacques moved away from deponent's said home[.] That the plaintiff was very much incensed at the deponent thereat, and immediately packed up his personal [e]ffects and also moved away from your deponent.

That the deponent was ill at the time, and in a very delicate state, highly nervous and hysterical condition by reason of pregnancy. That accordingly this deponent looked up the said Amy Jacques and pleaded with her to return to her, your deponent's home.

That at this time your deponent felt very near and dear to the said Amy Jacques and up to that time had not had the slightest suspicion that any improper relations existed between the plaintiff and the said Amy Jacques; and that finally your deponent induced and persuaded the said Amy Jacques to return; whereupon the plaintiff within a day or so thereafter returned to the apartment aforesaid.

That the plaintiff remained in the same apartment with the deponent during the months of April, May and part of June, but occupied a separate room from the deponent as was his custom. That such action on the part of the plaintiff amounting as it did to neglect, cruel and inhuman treatment, during deponent's weak and physical condition, rendered the deponent so desperately ill that deponent's physician one Dr. Dredd, of #101 West 140th Street, New York City, summoned the plaintiff into deponent's room and told him that unless he acted differently toward deponent, that he, plaintiff would lose both the deponent and the expected child. A physician also went to the plaintiff's office to warn him of the consequences of his acts.

That the plaintiff continued to neglect, mistreat and otherwise inhumanely ignore this deponent until on or about the second week in June, when without any provocation whatever, plaintiff packed up his personal effects and unceremoniously abandoned the deponent. That upon seeing the plaintiff leave the house, your deponent sank into a state of coma and because of her extremely weakened condition, suffered a miscarriage two evenings afterwards.

That deponent remained in her said apartment for two days, at the mercy of friends, and members of the Association, when she was removed to the Community Hospital, located at No. 6 West 101st Street, New York City, where deponent underwent an operation and remained for twelve days. That during the said twelve days in which the deponent was in the hospital, the plaintiff called on her only three times; but at no time expressed any of the old love and affection which he had previously professed for this deponent. That on or about the 20th day of June, 1920, when deponent returned from the hospital, to her said apartment, by reason of the abandonment of her by the plaintiff, she remained there for a period of fourteen days only, being compelled to dispose of her furniture and remove to the home of Mr. & Mrs. J. Woodruff at #205 West 140th Street, Borough of Manhattan, City of New York.

Deponent denies unequivocally and absolutely that she drinks any alcoholic liquor to e[x]cess; that however during deponent's illness as aforesaid the several physicians who treated deponent from time to time, pres[c]ribed light wines and eggs[,] and brandy and eggs, all of which was known to the plaintiff and the plaintiff has from time to time purchased and brought to the deponent wines, for medicinal use as aforesaid, even prior to their marriage.

That from on or about the 10th day of October, 1918, deponent has been employed in the office of the Universal Negro Improvement Association, as Secretary and daily attended her duties in that capacity; and also attended nightly meetings of the organization at which thousands of members of said organization were present; and at no time has any one observed or have reason to suspect that this deponent was under the influence of liquor, nor has deponent at any time been in any way incapacitated or in the slightest degree under the influence of alcoholic beverages.

That since the said day in June, 1920, when the plaintiff abandoned this deponent, said plaintiff has not contributed towards the support of this deponent, except the sum of sixty dollars, which was paid to this deponent as follows, to wit:—thirty dollars in one lump payment, the balance in weekly instalments of five dollars each, and that the plaintiff did not even pay your deponent's hospital expenses.

That the plaintiff is the President General and undisputed dictator of the Universal Negro Improvement Association; provisional President of Africa; President of the African Community League, Negro Factory Corporation, and editor of the Negro World, as well as the dominating and controlling spirit of each of the corporations subsidiary to the Universal Improvement Negro Association; that the plaintiff receives as salary for his services in the aforementioned offices, upon information and belief, the following sums[,] to wit,—as President, Negro Factories Corporation, thirty five dollars, ($35.00) per week, as President of the Black Star Line Steamship Company, One hundred dollars, ($100.00) per week, as President general of the Universal Negro Improvement Association[,] Two hundred and fifty dollars ($250.00) per week, making a grand total of three hundred and eighty-five ($385.00) dollars per week or twenty thousand and twenty dollars, a year. This sum is exclusive of his living expenses; and that also by reason of his unique and peculiar position, influence and control, in the various Associations in which he functions, he has unlimited finance at his disposal.

That when during the month of August, 1920, the plaintiff was expecting to be called for trial, for uttering a libel against one Edward P. Kilroe, an Assistant District Attorney of New York County, the members present at a meeting of the Universal Negro Improvement Association, in response to a request from the plaintiff to raise a defense for him, immediately within the short space of twenty minutes, donated in cash the sum of seven hundred and four ($704.00) dollars.

That the plaintiff has from time to time employed the services of the most eminent counsel practicing at the Bar of the State of New York and at all times herein mentioned, the plaintiff has representing him as counsel, of some corporation, of which he is the principal figure, the following eminent attorneys, to wit:—the firm of Grossman & Vorhaus #115 Broadway, Bamberger, James S. Watson, #250 Broadway and Wilford H. Smith, who is the oldest member of his race at the Bar, and a most eminent and learned attorney.

That this deponent has no funds whatsoever and because of her weakened and feeble condition, and poor state of health, is utterly unable to earn sufficient means to sustain herself; that again by reason of being the wife of the plaintiff herein, who is the professed leader of the Negro race, deponent is bound by the conventions of society to maintain a certain standard of living which is in keeping with her position in life, as the wife of the plaintiff; that deponent is now solely dependent upon the charity of her friends for her maintenance.

That deponent's father, several months ago, purchased for the deponent a certain private dwelling which brought the deponent a net income of thirty dollars ($30.00) per month; however, since the plaintiff abandoned your deponent she has been compelled to dispose of said property by sale and devote the proceeds to the payment of her hospital bill and her own support, which it was the duty of the plaintiff to provide for.

That the plaintiff has resorted to every conceivable means and sought every opportunity to belittle, discourage and otherwise humiliate your deponent. On one occasion before an audience of nearly two thousand five hundred or three thousand people, in the aforementioned Liberty Hall the deponent being present, and acting in her capacity as Secretary of the Organization, the plaintiff stated that he had no control over his wife and any property which his wife, your deponent, had purchased or might purchase, was entirely without plaintiff's consent and contrary to his knowledge or wishes, and that he, the plaintiff would exercise every possible precaution to determine if one penny of the Association's funds had been expended for the purchase of said property by your deponent. Again, during deponent's illness, deponent submitted a claim to the said Universal Negro Improvement Association, which under its by-laws and Constitution pays a sick indemnity of ten dollars per week to its members; however when this claim came up for adjustment, the plaintiff, this deponent's husband, moved that the claim be disallowed on the ground that the deponent was unfinancial.

That on the 14th day of August, 1920, the plaintiff wrote with his own hand and caused to be delivered to the deponent, the following note:—to wit:—Miss Amy Ashwood, This is to inform you that your father is held as a stowa[wa]y on one of our boats and as soon as the boat gets here will be turned over to the Immigration Authorities, you are advised. Signed:—Marcus Garvey.

The aforesaid note was addressed to the deponent by the plaintiff as Miss Amy Ashwood, and the messenger in delivering the same asked to see Miss Amy Ashwood, said name being deponent's maiden name.

That the plaintiff in the course of his duties, as President General of the Universal Negro Improvement Association, travels extensively throughout the United States and Canada and that on each of these trips, he is accompanied by the aforementioned Miss Amy Jacques[.]

That the said Miss Amy Jacques resides in the same apartment with the plaintiff herein and appears daily on the streets locked arms with him, the two being attended always by a body guard of two or three men; that the plaintiff has and maintains a secret service organization in which he employs several persons and that on from or about the 6th day of March, 1920, up to the date hereof, deponent is constantly shadowed and watched by operatives of said plaintiff.

That deponent denies most emphatically, that she has ever had at any time since the date of her marriage, sexual intercourse with any man except the plaintiff herein.

WHEREFORE, the deponent prays that an order be made, and entered herein, directing the plaintiff to contribute toward the support of this deponent, the sum of three hundred dollars per month and that the plaintiff pay to the deponent, the sum of five thousand dollars counsel fees, in order that your deponent may be thereby enabled to procure adequate and competent counsel of the same standing as that employed by the plaintiff, so that your deponent may successfully defend this action.[2]

AMY GARVEY

Sworn to before me
this *30th* day of *August* 1920.
William C. Perry

Marcus Garvey v. *Amy Garvey*, case 24028, NNHR. TD.

1. George (Allen) Cumberbatch (1880–1948) was frequently mentioned in the annulment and divorce proceedings between Amy Ashwood and Garvey. He was a close friend of Ashwood who, according to Garvey, continued to correspond with her after her marriage. Cumberbatch was born in Barbados but was taken to Trinidad at an early age by his parents. He went to Panama in 1907 or 1909, and there he met Amy Ashwood. Cumberbatch owned a tailor shop, was married twice, and resided in Panama until his death (Robert A. Hill, interview with Elaine Lindo, August 1976).

2. A hearing on the question of whether Marcus Garvey would pay the sum of seventy-five dollars to enable Amy Ashwood Garvey to pay her counsel was set for 23 September 1920.

Report of the Convention

[[*New York*, 31 August 1920]]

BIG CONVENTION CLOSES IN GRAND TRIUMPH

INAUGURAL CEREMONIES, PARADE AND FESTIVE CELEBRATION MARK COMPLETION OF LAST DAY'S WORK—DELEGATES START FOR HOME—REVIEW OF PROCEEDINGS OF CONVENTION AND ITS INFLUENCE UPON WORLD AFFAIRS AND AFFECTING THE NEGRO.

. . . MORNING SERVICES

The inauguration ceremonies in connection with the induction into office of the men elected as leaders of the race and as officials of the U.N.I.A. were held this morning in Liberty Hall, in the presence of a vast gathering of distinguished men and women of the race, and under a heaven-favored blue sky, with cool zephyrs blowing as if all nature herself were endeavoring to contribute her share to the auspicious occasion, by lending its beauty and blessing. The hall was specially decorated for the inaugural. Bunting and flags of various countries, as England, Africa, the United States, Haiti, Panama, Central America, San Domingo, and other world empires, and nations, were tastefully arranged here and there, with the ensigns and banners of the various divisions of the U.N.I.A.

On the platform sat the elective-officers, regaled in their beautiful, bright-colored robes of office; toward the left sat the U.N.I.A. choir, dressed in immaculate surplices of white, with black mortar-board hats; while below and directly in front of the speakers' stand were seated over one hundred members of the Black Cross Nurses, they, too, dressed in white, with a black cross on their white caps as the insignia of their Society. The Black Star Line Band also gave color to the scene by their uniforms of blue and hats with gold trimming, their several instruments glistening as if specially polished up for the occasion. Stationed around the rostrum and in different parts of the great hall stood the members of the Legion of Honor. Their military uniforms, which bore in gold trim the crest of the Association, accentuated the unique setting of the final assembling of the Convention. Under their captain, they stood at attention, and looked the part, equipped with dangling, bright swords at their sides, ready on an instant's notice, to suppress any disorder, or any improper interruptions of the ceremonies that might occur.

Then there was spread out, as on a broad expanse, a great sea of human faces, the women all dressed in their Sunday best, and the men as if on parade. The spectators who composed the audience, were men and women with earnest, eager expressions on their countenances; men and women who had come, not to ridicule, nor to laugh, not to attempt to discourage, but who were there because their hearts and souls are in the cause, and because of their devotion to the work of the salvation of their race and their abiding faith in the U.N.I.A. as the only practical medium through which, under the leadership of their idol, Marcus Garvey, the Negro can hope to find ultimately his place in the sun and throw off all forms of oppression and injustice now practiced against him.

It was one of the largest attendances that had ever yet assembled in Liberty Hall; certainly the most representative and distinguished. Even some men and women who have not yet been converted, as they will in time, to the cause of the U.N.I.A., could be seen in the audience, glad to be there to witness a scene which in dignity and solemnity was fully befitting the occasion of a race that now, after centuries of injustice, was celebrating its new birth, the dawning for them of a new day, an age undreamt of by their ancestors, of racial development and racial progress, and its formal announcement to the world of a Declaration of Rights as it launches itself forth in the new work of the attainment and preservation of these rights for the benefit of themselves and of their posterity.

Promptly at 10:30 o'clock the band of thirty pieces, under the direction of Prof. I[s]les, aided by the piano, played by Miss Ravela Hughes, and the bass viol, played by Prof. Ford, struck up the hymn, "Onward Christian Soldiers," the hall having already been filled, with every seat taken. And as the strains of music of that great battle song wafted and floated upon the air and out upon the breeze, the processional of singers, members of the Legion of Honor, Black Cross Nurses, high officials-elect began marching through the south end of the hall, clear across to the centre, then around, until they reached their place on and around the rostrum.

The President-General, with his flowing robes of scarlet and turban hat with golden tassel hung down from it in the front, these being the insignia of his office, stepped forward, when immediately he was greeted with the plaudits and cheering of the audience. He bowed to the right and to the left in acknowledgment of the vociferous greeting that was extended to him. That he was the man of the hour, was obvious to everyone. The Rev. Dr. George A. McGuire, dressed in the robes of an Episcopal minister, having led the processional, with an acolyte marching before and holding a cross in his hands, was presented by Mr. Garvey as the Master of Ceremonies, whereupon he offered the invocation. The service was on the order of the Episcopal Faith. The Rev. Dr. Paul read the Scripture lesson from the Twenty-third Psalm, followed by the chanting of the Gloria in Excelsi[s]; then the Rev. Dr. Stewart read I Cor., 13th chapter. The congregation then rose and sang "Shine on, Eternal Light." This was followed by the reciting of the Apostles' Creed, after which Dr. McGuire delivered a brief, appropriate address, in which he announced the purpose of the services, and announced the names of the officials-elect of the U.N.I.A.

The Rev. Dr. J. H. Eason was the preacher of the occasion. He took for his text Isaiah 60:1, "Arise, shine, for thy light is come, and the glory of the Lord is risen upon them." Also, taken from Isaiah: "The people that sat in darkness have seen a great light."[1] Without any touch of emotionalism, but with scholarly simplicity that was edifying and convincing, Dr. Eason endeavored to show that the Negro for hundreds of years has been in a state of lethargy, a state of darkness, but now that the light has come to shine upon them, and the door of opportunity opened to them, they should arise and awake from their lethargy, their slumbers, and strive to accomplish not merely the things spiritual which God would have them do, but the things material that make for progress, success and happiness in the present world. It was a well thought out sermon, was presented in a logical way and was both timely and effective.

At the close of the sermon the national anthem of the association, "Ethiopia, Thou Land of Our Fathers," was sung. The master of ceremonies then inducted each officer-elect into office. Each officer was asked to step to the front of the platform while the following words were addressed to him with such changes in the phraseology as the particular office required: "Gabriel Johnson, you are called this day to serve the people of your race. You have been elected to the high position of Potentate of the Universal Negro Improvement Association. I trust that you fully understand the duties devolving upon you as leader of the Negro peoples of the world. I pray you to be faithful, true and honest, and may the High God bless you in your work. May Your Highness ever remember that the people's destiny rests in your hands. Take this book (presenting a Bible), your Highness, and as you kiss it, swear by the Almighty God who created you. Will you sign your name to the constitution of the U.N.I.A. after repeating in the presence of this body the following oath and vow: I, Gabriel Johnson, do solemnly declare that I shall be obedient to the constitution and by-laws of the U.N.I.A. and to the convention and executive council, and shall uphold and support the Declaration of Rights. I shall not encourage the enemies of the cause of African redemption, and shall refuse to associate with those who may have proven enemies of the cause of the organization. I shall uphold its principles everywhere, and at all times, and the cause of the organization shall come first with me in all my deliberations. Should I fail in this cause, may the Almighty Architect fail me in the purpose of life. To this cause do I pledge my life and my fortunes for a free and redeemed Africa. Being now, therefore, in possession of my senses, I subscribe my name and swear myself in the presence of this assemblage and Almighty God to serve the U.N.I.A. faithfully, so help me God."

The men sworn and inducted into office are: His Highness, the Potentate, Gabriel Johnson (salary of office, $12,000 per year); His Highness the Supreme Deputy, G. O. Marke[2] (salary, $6,000); His Excellency President General Marcus Garvey (salary $10,000); the Right Honorable Assistant President General [the Rev. Dr. J. D. Gordon] (salary $6,000); the Right Honorable Secretary General, the Rev. Dr. J. D. Brooks (salary $6,000); His Honor, Assistant Secretary General, J. B. Yearwood (salary, $4,500); His Grace, the Chaplain General, the Rev. Dr. Geo. A. McGuire (salary, $5,000); the Right Honorable International Organizer, Miss Henrietta Vinton Davis (salary, $6,000); the Right Honorable Chancellor, the Rev. Dr. Stewart [*no salary listed*]; the Right Honorable Surgeon General, Dr. D. D. Lewis (salary, $6,500); the Right Honorable Speaker in Convention, Rev. Fred Toote (salary, $3,000); the Right Honorable Commissioner General, the Rev. Dr. Ellegor [*no salary listed*]; the Right Honorable Minister of Legions, Capt. E. [L.] Gaines[3] (salary, $3,000).

The inauguration having been finished, the band played again the Negro national anthem while the audience stood. This was followed by three cheers given by the audience. This concluded the ceremonies of the morning.

THE PARADE.

The parade, the second feature of the celebration of the close of the convention and of this first international holiday of the Negroes of the world, began promptly at 2 o'clock, the line of march running from Liberty Hall thence to Lenox avenue up to 145th street, thence to Seventh avenue, down Seventh avenue to 125th street, across to Lenox avenue, up Lenox avenue to 138th street, and back again to Liberty Hall. Four mounted policemen headed the parade, which was under the direction of Bishop Selkridge, marshal, who, on a spirited charger, rode up and down during the marching, seeing that the marchers kept in line and that nothing interfered with its orderly procedure, giving orders here and there like the famous Phil Sheridan in his great ride down the Shenandoah Valley to save the day for the Union against Confederates.[4] Next followed Alonzo Banks on foot, then the Black Star Line Band in uniform, the African Legion, carrying the U.N.I.A. and American flags, open automobiles carrying the following dignitaries, Hon. Gabriel Johnson, Mayor of Monrovia, Liberia, Africa; G. O. Marke, Supreme Deputy; Hon. Marcus Garvey and Rev. Fred Toote (both of whom rode together in the same machine, their automobiles being draped with American flags); Rev. Dr. Geo. A. McGuire, Rev. Dr. Paul, Dr. Gibson, Rev. Dr. Eason, Mr. Watkins, Rev. Dr. Brooks, Secretary General; Mr. J. B. Yearwood, Assistant Secretary General; Mr. Eli Garcia and wife, Rev. Dr. Ellegor, Commissioner General; the Hon. Wilford M. Smith, Counsel General; Miss Henrietta Vinton Davis, International Organizer; Mr. Matthews, Assistant Counsel General; Rev. Tobi[t]t, leader of the West Indies; Dr. D. D. Lewis, Surgeon General, and wife, Rev. Batson and wife, U.N.I.A. choir dressed in white and on foot; representatives from the steamers Yarmouth and Shadyside and employes of the Black Star Line on foot; Black Cross nurses, 100 strong, with flowing white veils and white dresses and white caps, on foot; U.N.I.A. band, with new white uniforms; New York Division of the U.N.I.A. on foot; delegates from Antigua, Barbados, Jamaica, Gr[e]nada, British Guiana, Virginia, North Carolina, South Carolina, Georgia, Trinidad, the Fifteenth Regiment Band, delegates from St. Kitts, Nevis, Virgin Islands, Illinois, Bermuda, Marion, East Orange, N.J., Florida, the Negro Factories Corporation, the Black Star Line Corporation and numbers of automobiles conveying other representatives from Canada, Washington, D.C., etc.

As the procession wended its way through the streets, along the line of march the bands furnished lively music, playing all the latest airs and patriotic pieces. Considerable numbers of people turned out to witness the marchers, the streets being lined with spectators, white and black, from the very point of beginning until the return to Liberty Hall. The convention has stirred the people of Harlem as no other event has since colored people have come in numbers to live in this section of the city, and the feeling manifested at the first parade, of morbid curiosity and negative astonishment, has now turned to one of sympathy, respect and admiration. There was no laughing, no indulgence in mockery of the pageant as it passed by, but rather expressions of approval and hearty applause. It was an unusual, soul-stirring scene, and sent a thrill of pride through every colored man and woman who saw it, whatever his previously considered opinions or views have been regarding the efficacy of the U.N.I.A.

Transparencies with mottoes inscribed thereon were seen scattered throughout the parade. Following are some of the mottoes or sayings on these banners, which were read by the people with curious attention and evident signs of approval: "Liberty or Death." "What Will Italy Do in Africa?" "Down With Jimcrowism." "4,000,000 Black Men Shall Be Free." "The Negro Will Fight in the Next World War[.]" "United We Stand;

Divided We Fall." "Toussaint L'Ouverture Was an Abler Soldier Than Napoleon."

"N—Nothing
A—Accomplished
A—After
C—Considerable
P—Pretence."

"U—United
N—Nothing can
I—Impede your
A—Aspirations."

"The Negro Won the War." "United We Stand for Africa's Liberty." "Freedom for All." "The Negro Fought in Europe; He Can Fight in Africa." "Princes Shall Come Out of Egypt." "The Negro Has No Fear." "Down With Lynching." "What Will France Do in Africa?" "What Will England Do in Africa? "Will They Make the Negro Fight in Africa?" "Africa First, Last and All the Time." "Freedom for All." "A President for Ireland; Why Not One for Africa?" etc., etc.

The parade was half an hour in passing a given point. The parade took an hour and a half to complete its line of march, having come to an end at 4 o'clock. A slight rain came up during part of it, but the marchers stood their ground with heroic fortitude, and a few minutes later the rain ceased and the sun broke through the clouds again, the marchers feeling none the worse for the ducking they received.

It was an orderly affair, and the marchers, most of whom marched well, like real soldiers, especially the Black Cross nurses, elicited rounds of applause from the bystanders as they proceeded on. Mr. Garvey was the one person on whom all eyes were centered, this being quite natural, he being the founder of the movement and the champion of the cause. The eagerness of the people to catch a glimpse of him was as great as it would have been had it been President Wilson who was riding by instead of, as it w[as], the Provisional President of Africa and President General of the U.N.I.A., such is the fame he acquired in the brief space of two years, from a place of obscurity, unknown to the public, into the limelight of the public gaze, occupying now the highest place and rank among the progressive and intelligent body of Negroes in this and in other countries. The plaudits given him he accepted in good grace, bearing himself with commendable modesty.

The music of the three bands, in particular the "jazzy" music of the Fifteenth Band, was greatly appreciated by the populace, who applauded the players enthusiastically. The members of this famous band, under their efficient leader, Lieut. Fred W. Simpson, evidently strove to put forth their best efforts on this occasion.

The gentlemen who assisted the Chief Marshal of the parade and who deserve to share in the credit, with Bishop Selkr[i]dge for its success, are: Mr. Harold G. Salters,[5] Capt. Gain[e]s, Minister of Legions; Col. Wattley of the African Legion, Mr. Adrian Johnson, Mr. E. C. Hamilton, official traffic regulator.

Evening Reception.

The reception held in the evening at the New Star Casino, on 107th street near Lexington avenue, was a notable event. There were three principal features, and it is a tie which of them was the most enjoyable or the most popular with the people. This all depends upon one's individual taste. First was the musical program, in which Miss Lulu Robinson, Miss Ruby Fraser (Miss Robinson's sister), Mme. Houston and Mme. Ravella Hughes, also Mme. E. [O.] Clark, participated. All these were soloists and their singing was of the highest standard. Then came the speechmaking, in which the President General spoke at length, rising to unusual heights of eloquence in his plea for the cause of the redemption of Africa.

He proved himself, more than ever before, a born orator and leader of his race. There is no other man in the race today who is his equal in this respect[,] Prof. [W]. E. Du Bois and the Hon. Robert Mot[o]n, president of Tuskegee Institute, notwithstanding. More than 5,000 persons filled the hall. The speechmaking was followed by a dance, the Black Star Line Band supplying the music, and the members and friends of the U.N.I.A. danced till the "wee sma' hours of the morning." It was a diversion and a relaxation to them that they well deserved, after their strenuous exertions in behalf of their race for thirty-one consecutive days, all in all the reception being a fitting close to the most momentous event that has taken place among Negroes in recent times.

When Mr. Garvey stepped to the front of the platform and rapped with his gavel for order, it was exactly 8:45 o'clock. The Black Star Line Band, with its twenty-five musicians, played the "Star Spangled Banner" and the Negro Anthem, in which the audience joined, all standing. This was followed by a selection by the band and a rendition by the Acme Quartet, and then solos by the artist singers already alluded to.

Mr. Garvey began speaking at 9:15, and did not conclude till 10:25. It was one of the greatest oratorical efforts of his life. His speech was an impassioned utterance emanating from the very depths of his soul, and moved his hearers to the highest pitches of enthusiasm. Truly, he is the Demosthenes of the Negro Race. His allusions to David Lloyd George (in which he showed himself a master of withering sarcasm and invective), in connection with Great Britain's relinquishing her hold on Egypt and still holding fast to Ireland, brought forth ripples of laughter; while his mention of Africa and the sound, valid reasons why the Dark Continent should be returned to the black peoples to whom it rightfully belongs, stirred his hearers into a parox-

ysm of delight and approval. He read three cablegrams he said he was about
to send in behalf of the U.N.I.A., one addressed to the chairman of the
Nationalist Party in Egypt, in which he conveyed to the people of Egypt
congratulations from 400,000,000 Negroes on this their first international
holiday, and congratulations for the great success that has crowned their
efforts in securing their independence.[6] The second cablegram was
addressed, as he expressed it, to "the tyrant of Europe, David Lloyd
George." This expression evoked considerable laughter and hisses. In his
message he informed that worthy gentleman that he should let McSwiney
go, adding, "Please do not add another blot on the history of England."
McSwiney is Lord Mayor of Cork, Ireland, and was put in jail because of his
sympathy for and connection with the Sinn Feiners, and is now in a precari-
ous condition owing to his being on a hunger strike for almost 31 days.[7] The
third cablegram was to Father Dominick, confessor of the Lord Mayor of
Cork, and read as follows: "Convey to McSwiney sympathy of 400,000,000
Negroes." Again and again during the course of his address Mr. Garvey rose
to heights of eloquence of unsurpassing force and grandeur. Dressed in a
close-fitting, well-made, fine-quality frock coat, in which he looked the part
of a statesman and scholar (which he is), he spoke in thunderous tones, and
with all the energy and fire of his compact frame, and with appropriate,
natural gestures, as he told his auditors of the struggles of the race, as he
lashed with terrible fury his detractors and enemies, and as he excoriated
those leaders of the Caucasian race, as David Lloyd George, Clemenceau and
others, who would continue to hold the Negro in subjection as a peon, a serf,
a human being unfit for self-government; as he hurled defiance at the "crackers" of the South, and indulged in bitter denunciation of the so-called leaders
of the race who have been here on the ground all their life, yet who have not
done or accomplished one-thousandth as much good as Mr. Garvey has done
in the remarkably short period of two years. The speech is given in full in
another column of this paper, and should be read in full by every man and
woman of the race.

Such was the way in which the great International Convention of
Negroes that sat for thirty-one long days came to a close—a close triumphant
for the U.N.I.A. and for its great leader; a close that marks the brightest and
most encouraging chapter in Negro history; a close to which, in connection
with the many stirring days and evenings in Liberty Hall during the actual
sessions and deliberations of this body of Negro delegates from all parts of
the world, all can look back upon in the years to come with a sense of pride
and satisfaction that such a movement was begun at such an auspicious time,
and that it had for its leader one of the most courageous men of his time, the
ablest statesman of his race, and its acknowledged greatest orator—the Hon.
Marcus Garvey, Provisional President of Africa, and President-General of the
U.N.I.A.

Printed in *NW*, 11 September 1920.

649

1. Isa. 9:2, "The people that walked in darkness have seen a great light."

2. George Osborne Marke (1867–1929) held the post of supreme deputy potentate of the UNIA until 1926. He attended the UNIA convention as the official representative of the Freetown division. Marke was born in Freetown, Sierra Leone; his father, Charles Marke, who was one of the first Creole Methodist ministers in Sierra Leone, was an adherent of the racial philosophy of Edward Wilmot Blyden. The younger Marke attended Wesleyan Boys' High School in Freetown and later studied medicine, first at Aberdeen University, Scotland, from 1891 to 1893 and later at the University of Edinburgh, from 1900 to 1902, although he never received a degree. After returning to Freetown he was employed as a government clerk. In February 1921 Marke accompanied the delegation of UNIA representatives which was sent to Liberia to work out details of the UNIA's proposed settlement plan. During his sojourn in Liberia, he helped establish a newspaper in Monrovia, the *Liberian Patriot*, which brought news from the rest of Africa. Marke returned to New York in July 1922 and was appointed minister plenipotentiary of the UNIA delegation to the League of Nations, the main purpose of which was to deliver the UNIA's "Petition to the League of Nations." This petition requested that the league give back to blacks the mandates of the former German colonies in Africa. It proposed that this be done under the auspices of the UNIA, and it recommended that a black be appointed to the league's Permanent Mandates Commission.

In March 1926, at the UNIA emergency convention held in Detroit, Marke was removed from office in a power struggle within the UNIA. Garvey, who was then serving a prison sentence in Atlanta, accused Marke of collusion with William L. Sherrill, the acting president general of the UNIA and president of the Black Cross Navigation and Trading Co., whom Garvey held responsible for the auction of the S.S. *Gen. G. W. Goethals* to cover debts incurred by the company. Marke was removed from office after failing to appear at the convention. In September 1927 Sherrill, Marke, and other deposed officials of the UNIA parent body attempted unsuccessfully to establish a rival UNIA body in New York, which they claimed to be the "official UNIA."

In early 1927 Marke sued the UNIA for payment of back salary and was awarded a judgment against the New York UNIA, which had by then become insolvent. Following Garvey's deportation to Jamaica in December 1927, Marke sought an injunction from the Jamaican courts against the property of the UNIA in Jamaica. The Marke suit became the occasion of yet a further legal imbroglio for Garvey, who refused the court's order to hand over the account books of the UNIA; in July 1929 he was accordingly fined £25 for contempt. Shortly afterward, in a veiled reference to the Marke suit, Garvey called for a law to provide for impeachment and prison terms for judges who entered "into illicit agreement with lawyers and other prominent businessmen to deprive other subjects of the Realm of their rights." Garvey was brought before the court and convicted for contempt; he was sentenced to three months in jail and fined £100.

George O. Marke died in Brooklyn in October 1929. In its eulogy, the *Sierra Leone Weekly News* stated: "Sierra Leone has lost one of her thoroughly English scholars, an erudite writer and genuine patriot" (R. L. Okonkwo, "The Garvey Movement in British West Africa," *Journal of African History* 21 [1980]: 105–17; *NW*, 6 March, 20 March, 27 March, and 3 April 1926; Robert A. Hill, introduction to *The Black Man*, [New York: KTO, 1975], pp. 8–9; Archives of Foreign Affairs Ministry, Brussels, file AF 1-1, "Movements Pan-Nègres," 19 September 1922; National Archives, Paris, slotfom 88, série 3, C84[2], 13 November 1922; E. D. Cronon, *Black Moses: The Story of Marcus Garvey and the UNIA* [Madison: University of Wisconsin Press, 1964], p. 157; Amy Jacques Garvey, *Garvey and Garveyism*, pp. 193–94).

3. E. L. Gaines was a minister in Pasadena, Calif., when he joined the Garvey movement. Gaines and J. D. Gordon, the Los Angeles minister who became an assistant president general at the convention, worked as UNIA organizers in California during the months before the convention. Gaines emerged as an important spokesman for the UNIA during Garvey's four-month absence from the United States in 1921. Known to UNIA members as Daddy Gaines, he conducted extensive speaking tours in Virginia, New Jersey, and North Carolina, organizing new UNIA divisions and reorganizing divisions that had become inactive or splintered because of internal dissension. In April 1921 Gaines reported on his success before a Liberty Hall audience. Months later, in November 1921, Gaines reorganized the Los Angeles UNIA division after a series of disputes had depleted its membership (*NW*, 19 February, 9 April, and 23 April 1921; Emory J. Tolbert, *The UNIA and Black Los Angeles*, pp. 73–75).

4. Philip Henry Sheridan (1831–1888) was the commander of the Union Army of the Shenandoah in its 1864 campaign through the Shenandoah Valley during the American Civil War (*WBD*).

5. Actually George H. Saltus, an employee of the *Negro World* (*Garvey v. United States*, no. 8317, Ct. App. 2d Cir., 2 February 1925).

6. A revolutionary movement in Egypt dominated relations between that nation and England in 1919. The Egyptian prime minister, Rushdi Pasha, resigned in anger when his request to lead a delegation to London to present the views of the Egyptian cabinet before the British government was denied. This act was widely interpreted as an attempt to postpone a discussion of Egyptian independence. When the British attempted to deport four Egyptian nationalist politicians, rioting broke out in Cairo, where British troops confronted crowds of demonstrators, killing or wounding forty. As the movement spread, Bedouins joined in the protest, at one point assisting the townsfolk of Deir Mowas in an attack on British soldiers which left eight soldiers dead. Faced with a nationwide insurrection, the British special high commissioner rescinded the order to expel the four nationalist politicians, whereupon Prime Minister Pasha resumed office. He resigned again two weeks later, however, and for several weeks Egypt was without a cabinet. Finally, in November 1919, the British governor general announced a new policy, declaring that Britain would develop the autonomy of Egypt under British protection (*Chronology of World Events* [London: Longmans, 1919], s.v. "Egypt").

7. Terence MacSwiney (1879–1920) was arrested in August 1920 and convicted of possessing revolutionary documents. When he died on the seventy-fourth day of his fast, New York's governor, Al Smith, and Eamon de Valera, leader of Sinn Féin, addressed a huge memorial service at the Polo Grounds in New York City (Alan J. Ward, *Ireland and Anglo-American Relations, 1899–1921* [Toronto: University of Toronto Press, 1969] pp. 229–31; *WBD*).

Address by Marcus Garvey

[[Star Casino, August 31, 1920]]

MARCUS GARVEY INTRODUCES OFFICIALS OF U.N.I.A. TO VAST AUDIENCE IN THE STAR CASINO

The Star Casino of New York was crowded as perhaps never before in its history on the evening of Augus[t] 31st at the reception of the newly elected officials of the U.N.I.A. Every seat in the boxes and floor was occupied. Not only were people standing on the floor and galleries but the crowd over-flowed the outer halls and stairs. Seated on the platform was the Hon. Marcus Garvey, the high officials of the U.N.I.A. and distinguished guests. The Black Star Band was at its best as usual. Intense interest followed Marcus Garvey's every word as in well chosen phrases, he epitomized the careers and introduced the brilliant leaders, who will guide the destinies of the U.N.I.A., promote the welfare of the Negro race. Mr. Garvey said:

It is impossible for all the members of the High Executive Council—the Honorable Executive Council—to speak to you, each for himself or for herself; but it is my burden duty, as President-General of the Universal Negro Improvement Association, to again present these gentlemen and all the members of the Executive Council to you, in the order of merit. We elected them to serve us. They have pledged themselves faithfully to serve us and the cause of the U.N.I.A., and the cause of our race. We believe in them; and because we believe in them we shall give them all our support. We shall withhold nothing from them to help them in the great cause in whose interests they shall labor. Therefore, it gives me great pleasure in presenting to you, first, His Highness, the Hon. Gabriel Johnson, Potentate Leader of the Negro Peoples of the World and head of the U.N.I.A. (Mr. Johnson then stepped forward and bowed).

The chair has in mind, in presenting to you His Highness, the Hon. G. O. Mark[e] of Sierr[a] Leone, West Africa, Supreme Deputy of the U.N.I.A. and second World Leader of the Negro Peoples of the World. (Mr. Mark[e] stepped forward, and bowed).

Again it gives me pleasure to introduce the Hon. Rev. J. D. Gordon, of Los Angeles, Cal., Assistant President-General of the U.N.I.A. (Dr. Gordon stepped forward, and bowed).

It gives me unbounded pleasure to present to you a man who is known to each and every one of us, a man able in every sense of the word; a man on whom we have bestowed the honor of leadership; a man who has worked most assiduously for the coming together of this great Convention now assembled—the gentleman whom we have elected as Leader of the Negroes of the United States of America, His Excellency the Rev. Dr. [J.] W. H. Eason. (Dr. Eason stepped forward, and bowed.)

It gives us greater pleasure still, to present to you a worthy champion of this cause, in the person of the Right Honorable Rev. Dr. J. D. Brooks, Secretary-General of the U.N.I.A. (Dr. Brooks stepped forward, and bowed).

And still it gives me pleasure to present to you one of the ablest West Indian champions of liberty; a man who has fought his way up amidst great opposition; a man who defied the powers that be in championing the cause of his people—His Excellency Mr. Debourg, leader of the West Indies of the Western section. (Mr. Debourg stepped forward and bowed.)

There was a great Cardinal in England, one who held the power of the Nation in his hands. His name [is] known to every British student—every student of history. He made England during his time. His name was Woolsey.[1] I now take pleasure in presenting to you a Cardinal Archbishop in the person of His Grace the Honorable Chaplain General of the U.N.I.A.[,] not a Woolsey for the Anglo-Saxon race, but a Woolsey for the Negro race, in the person of His Grace [the] Hon. Rev. Geo. A. McGuire. [(Rev.] McGuire stepped forward and bo[wed.])

As the clergy played their pa[rt in] making a nation, so statesmen [have] played their part. There was s[uch a] man, a statesman in England on . . . [*word mutilated*] whom all eyes were turned duri[ng his] day. He, more than any other [man of] his time, helped rebuild the [British] Empire; his name was William Ewart Gladstone. But I am going to present to you now a man as able as William Ewart Gladstone; a statesman, a diplomat, not of the Anglo-Saxon race, but of the Negro race, in the person of the Right

Hon. Auditor General, the Hon. Eli Garcia. (Mr. Garcia stepped forward and bowed.)

Wom[e]n have also played their part in history. In French history we read of a great heroine. Her name was Joan of Arc, who is known to us as the "Maid of Orleans." There was another heroine in Spanish history by the name of the "Maid of Saragossa."[2] These women played their part in their time in the interests of their respective nations and their race. But I think history is repeating itself—not for the white race, not for the white nation, but for the Negro race, the race that we love. It gives me great pleasure in presenting to you the Right Hon. International Organizer, our modern Joan of Arc—Miss Henrietta Vinton Davis. (Miss Davis stepped forward and bowed.)

There are statesmen who were born great, and some who made themselves and who became great. We have a man from the West Indies whom we are endeavoring to make great, for during our 31 days' convention we brought out of him what was hidden in him, and we have so remade him that we are sending him back to lead his people—His Excellency the Rev. R. H. Tobitt, leader of the Eastern Division of the West Indian Negroes. (Rev. Tobitt stepped forward and bowed.)

Some men are talkative; still they are useful. Some men are quiet and silent, and even more useful. We have heard of such men. We have read of such men in history, and we have such a man here: a silent worker, a silent diplomat; a man who has proven himself worthy of the steel of any man, whether he is silent or otherwise, during these 31 days of our convention. I have reference to the Right Hon. Chancellor of the U.N.I.A.[,] the Rev. Dr. William Ellegor, whom it gives me great pleasure to introduce to you. (Mr. Elleg[o]r stepped forward and bowed.)

And we have still another—and I am glad that the men of our race who have come from the islands of the sea are gradually getting backbone, for most of these, while there in their native land, are entirely without backbone, and we have to give it to them when they arrive here. They leave the islands to come here to get that very thing—backbone. (Great laughter.) Well, we have here tonight a gentlem[a]n who came from the islands of the sea without any backbone, and we have given him a very broad backbone. We have put him so splendidly forward in the convention that we elected him, by majority vote, as High Chancellor of the U.N.I.A., so it gives me great pleasure in presenting to you the Right Hon. G. Stewart, the High Chancellor of the U.N.I.A.

Still, we must have those to tell us when we are not well and to advise us at such times (laughter). I have always been my own physician and surgeon-general. But, in the wisdom of the convention, we have elected to have a Surgeon General who is to perform all operations. (Laughter.) Well, I don't know just what I am suffering from (laughter); some people say that I am suffering from—what? "Big head." (Laughter.) Well[,] I am going to present to you the gentleman who will make that head what it ought to be—the

Right Hon. Surgeon-General of the U.N.I.A., Dr. D. D. Lewis of Montreal, Canada. (Dr. Lewis stepped forward and bowed.)

It gives me great pleasure again to present to you a small man, yet a big man—a man big in mind—the Assistant Secretary-General, the Right Hon. Mr. J. B. Yearwood.

And whilst I talk for the cause of Africa there must be someone to fight for the cause of Africa; and because of that, we have elected a Minister of Legions. It gives me great pleasure to present to you a soldier; an able man; I believe as able a soldier as any in this country or anywhere in the world, in the person of the Right Rev. Minister of Legions, Capt. E. L. Gaines. (Capt. Gaines stepped forward and in strictly military fashion saluted the President-General, which elicited rounds of applause and expressions of admiration from the audience.)

At this point the President made a very strong plea for the purchase of more shares of stock in the Black Star Line. In his appeal he entered into the particulars concerning the need of buying additional ships for the corporation in order that a gigantic ocean going traffic might be started up and carried on between the people of Africa and this country, pointing out that the building of a large merchant marine, owned and manned and supported by Negroes, was of the utmost importance and necessity in the plan of the U.N.I.A., looking forward to the ultimate redemption of Africa by the black people and for the black people of the world.

This was followed by the purchase of many shares by persons in the audience and the taking up of a substantial collection for the cause of the U.N.I.A., in behalf of which the Rev. Dr. J. H. Eason made the principal address.

Printed in *NW*, 11 September 1920. Original headlines abbreviated.

1. Thomas Wolsey (1475?–1530) was an English cardinal who exercised extraordinary political influence on Henry VII and Henry VIII of England (Jasper Ridley, *Statesman and Saint: Cardinal Wolsey, Sir Thomas More and the Politics of Henry VIII* [New York: Viking Press, 1982]).

2. A historical character from Lord Byron's epic poem *Childe Harold*.

Editorial Letter by Marcus Garvey

[[New York, August 31, 1920]]

GREAT CONVENTION OF NEGROES CLOSES AFTER MAKING HISTORY FOR THE RACE

Fellowmen of the Negro Race, Greeting:

The greatest convention in the history of the Negro race came to a close on Tuesday of this week. For thirty-one days delegates of the Negro people from all parts of the world have met in solemn conclave, discussing in the most orderly manner the questions con[fro]nting us as a race and formulating measures for their solution. [We] need hardly elaborate on the reasons for which we have been compelled to interest ourselves in our own fortunes independently of alien influence. Quite apart from the fact that we are lynched and burned in (?) civilized America with impunity (and these lynchings and burnings have followed each other with sickening rapidity), and politically, industrially and educationally lynched in other parts of the world, we can never achieve that majesty of manhood and womanhood which should be ours until we coalesce our own forces for the consummation.

The war wrought many changes in the lives of men and things, and so has the Universal Negro Improvement Association, with its branches reaching into the uttermost parts of the world. The greatest change of all was the transformation of Negroes from cringing persons, pleading for rights and privileges cruelly denied them[,] into upstanding men and women demanding those rights and privileges and determined to exercise them regardless of consequences. In the light of this transformation it is not only reassuring but refreshing to be a member of the Negro race in this day and time.

Nothing can be more encouraging to the race than the fact that it has been possible to draw Negroes from all parts of the world and keep them under one roof for thirty-one days discussing the interests of the people they represent. This achievement in itself is unparalleled in history and furnishes a lesson in optimism, showing us how a people when awakened from lethargy can become transformed into a power which ventures to challenge the tyrants of the world. The seeds of the Universal Negro Improvement Association found fertile soil. The Negro people, while scattered throughout the world, have responded nobly. We are united now upon the common bond of race, and the world must reckon with us.

The outcome of this convention has turned over to us a new arrangement for ourselves, of our own choosing, and will provide a better place in the tropical sun. Despite the ramblings of a few hirelings, whose nests are feathered by the forces opposed to Negro progress, our prosperity and happiness are so irrevocably bound with Africa that that continent is primarily the Negro's interest as an African of the dispersion.

The future opens before us, and it is for us to use the machinery of the convention to further our own interests despite the tyrants of the world.

I cannot better indicate the scope and thoroughness of the convention than by mentioning that every phase of the situation confronting us as a race has come within its scope. When your delegates return to you they will bring back a new infusion of the new spirit of the New Negro.

And now let me remind you of the cry of the Black Star Line for more and bigger ships to accommodate the needs of Negroes in Africa, Central and South America, the West Indies, and every corner of the globe.

The cry has reached us from these places for more and bigger ships. Let us join forces and answer that cry. You have responded nobly in the past by subscribing for shares. It has been said that "history repeats itself." Those who have not already bought shares send in to the office of the Black Star Line, 56 West 135th street, New York, U.S.A., and purchase them now. Those who have already bought[,] purchase more now and help the Black Star Line to give the race the greatest merchant marine in its history. You may buy from one to two hundred shares. Buy them now and contribute to the glory of the movement. With kind personal regards, Yours fraternally,

MARCUS GARVEY

Printed in *NW*, 4 September 1920. This editorial was marked "exhibit #10" as part of a file of exhibits attached to a letter of 11 May 1921 from J. Edgar Hoover to William L. Hurley (DNA, RG 59, file 000-612).

IF EVERY NEGRO WILL BUT DO HIS DUTY

In The Next Few Years The Race Would

Become A Great Commercial Power

You can do your Duty to the Race by BUYING SHARES

In the

Negro Factories Corporation

Instead of putting away all your money in the bank to be used by white men, to make themselves richer and more powerful to crush you, invest a part of it in the NEGRO FACTORIES CORPORATION and make a profit for yourself at the end of the financial year

Buy your Shares Now and make money

Call or Write

NEGRO FACTORIES CORPORATION

56 West 135th Street   New York City, U. S. A.

This Corporation is backed by 3,000,000 active members of the Universal Negro Improvement Association

When God Created the world

He made man the Lord of all things

Mr. Black Man

What are you Master of? Can you not see that the White man has full control of every living thing?

Now what are you going to do about it?

MY ADVICE TO YOU IS TO

Get busy and prove yourself a man and not a monkey

A true man always finds and makes a way for himself, and it is now up to every Negro to make a place for himself in the great

FIELD OF COMMERCE

You can make a way by buying

THE NEGRO FACTORIES CORPORATION

AT LAST THE DAY HAS COME

Negro Money, Negro Brains, and Negro Energy Must Rule The World

Mr. Black Man, what are you doing to insure a brighter future for the race? Are you investing your money wisely as to turn over profits for you and your children and posterity?

Now is the chance for you to do something real. Invest some of the money you have in the Bank, at home, or in your pocket in

The Negro Factories Corporation

This Corporation is to build factories all over the United States, Canada, West Indies, South and Central America, and Africa.

This Corporation is organized under the State Laws of Delaware, and capitalized at $1,000,000. You may buy as many shares as you desire at $5.00 each.

The Negro Factories Corporation will offer employment to thousands of Negroes. The Factories will manufacture goods of all kinds, to be sold in American Markets, and shipped by the Black Star Line Steamship to foreign countries.

Buy your shares to-day, make money and put up a factory your neighborhood to be owned and controlled by the Race.

Send in or call for your shares at. *Marcus Garvey*

THE NEGRO FACTORIES CORPORATION
56 W. 135th Street, New York, U. S. A.

Say Mr. Colored Man !

What Are You Doing Now For Yourself ?

Are you making an effort to better your condition? If not, you had better hurry up and do so. I advise you to make some desperate effort now to do something for the upbuilding of our race, because I realize from an close study and observation of the present economic situation, that the Negro in the next two years in the United States of America, the West Indies, and Central America will be up against a terrible economic plight. The race that has been the employee of the Negro within the last eighty years is now about to throw off the Negro as an industrial worker, which will mean that the Negro will be forced to fall back upon himself for his maintenance. If you do not prepare by organizing, building, and operating industrial enterprises of your own you will be forced into a state economic corner which will mean wholesale starvation. You can even see that Mr. Colored Man if you will but act now. You can act by buying shares in promising corporations like the Negro Factories Corporation, the object of which is to build factories all over these United States of America, the West Indies, South and Central America, and Africa. By so doing it will mean that the corporation will be able to find work for thousands of our own men and women to place them in positions as Clerks, Managers of Departments, Salesmen, Typists, Stenographers, and Counting House Attendants, and as skilled workers. Outside of the employment that the Corporation will offer to thousands of our people, there is profit to be gained from the movement.

When you invest Five ($5.00) or Two Hundred Dollars ($200.00) in the shares of stock it means that at the end of the financial year you will gather so much more money by way of dividends. If you want to make money, if you want to insure a better future you will invest to day and right away now in the

Negro Factories Corporation
135th Street   NEW YORK. U.S.A.

(Source: DNA, RG 65, file OG 329359).

Special Agent 800 to George F. Ruch

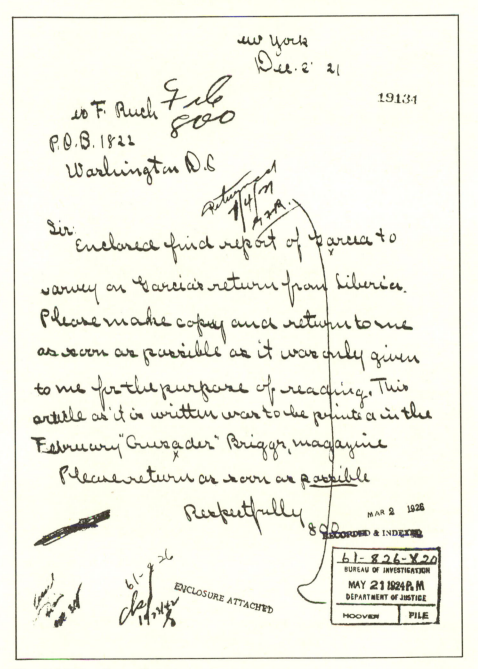

new York
Dec. 2' 21

19131

to F. Ruch File
800
P.O.B. 1822
Washington D.C

Returned
1/4/11
H.F.R.

Sir:
Enclosed find report of Garcia to
survey on Garcia's return from Liberia.
Please make copy and return to me
as soon as possible as it was only given
to me for the purpose of reading. This
article as it is written was to be printed in the
February "Crusader" Briggs magazine
Please return as soon as possible

Respectfully
800

MAR 2 1926
RECORDED & INDEXED

61-826-X20
BUREAU OF INVESTIGATION
MAY 21 1924 P.M
DEPARTMENT OF JUSTICE

HOOVER | FILE

ENCLOSURE ATTACHED

(*Source*: DJ-FBI, file 61-826-X-20).

Elie Garcia, UNIA Commissioner to Liberia, to Marcus Garvey and the UNIA

New York, August 1920

Gentlemen:

I hereby beg to submit to the U.N.I.A. and A.C.L. the following report in connection with my mission to the West Coast of Africa and Liberia.

It is respectfully requested that scrupulous attention be given to the information and suggestions therein and that they be taken into consideration—with necessary modifications—in the future establishment of the Headquarters of the Association in the Republic of Liberia.

Hoping that my feeble efforts will be appreciated by the organization, I am, Your most respectful servant,

(Signed) Elie Garcia,
Commissioner to Liberia

DJ-FBI, file 61-826-X20. TL, carbon copy. The report, according to the Bureau of Investigation, was said by the *Crusader* to have been sent to it "anonymously by an employee in the inner *sanctum sanctorum*" of Marcus Garvey. The second part of the memorandum was later reprinted in Amy Jacques Garvey, ed., *Philosophy and Opinions of Marcus Garvey*, Vol. II, pp. 399–405, with the caption: "A Confidential Report on the True Conditions in Liberia by Commissioner Garcia to Marcus Garvey: Elie Garcia's Liberian Report dated August, 1920."

[*Place unknown, post 27 June 1920*]

PART I.

I left New York Saturday, April 17th, 1920, and arrived at Liverpool on the 27th of the same month. According to my instructions, I called on the secretary of the Ethiopian Hall and made arrangements with him to hold meetings of the U.N.I.A. during my stay in Liverpool. Report in connection with these meetings having been already submitted, I will omit same in this present account.

I sailed from Liverpool May 8, 1920, and arrived at Freetown, Sierra Leone, the 22d of same month. Immediately after the clearance of the vessel, I landed at Freetown and called on Mr. S. O. Brasse, whom I found at home. After exchange of salutations, I communicated my credentials to the gentleman and the same night he took me around and introduced me to various officers and members of the U.N.I.A. branch in Freetown. I expressed to them my desire to have a meeting arranged for the next day; but, unfortunately, said being Whitmonday and also the Centenary Day in a small community near Freetown called Waterloo, the meeting could not be arranged. I was invited to go to Waterloo where I was to meet a large number of the members who went there on account of the celebrations of said Centenary. Monday at 9 A.M., accompanied by Mr. Theodore Lefevre,

Chairman of the Advisory Board, and Mr. Brasse, Organizer, I took the train for Waterloo. I indeed met a large number of the members and took opportunity to advertise the meeting for the following day. After having a splendid time at Waterloo, we returned to Freetown. Tuesday, at 7 P.M., the meeting was held with a very fair audience. Mr. Marke, the Executive Secretary and the delegate-elect of the branch, introduced me to the audience and I explained to the best of my knowledge the aims and objects of the U.N.I.A. After telling the people of the intentions of the Association in regard to Africa, I told them also of the Convention and urged them to send a delegate to represent them there. Some funds were raised immediately to this effect. I closed my remarks by asking the people to help the Black Star Line and Negro Factories Corporation by buying shares in said corporations. I outlined briefly the prospects of these concerns to the future investors. After the selling of shares and after a few words from various officers in which they pledged loyalty to the Association, the meeting was adjourned. The people of Freetown were deeply satisfied with the attention paid to Africa by the U.N.I.A. in sending a representative to visit them.

At 11 P.M., I boarded my ship and we proceeded the same night for Monrovia.

I arrived in Monrovia the 27th of May and through the custom officers I received a letter from Milton J. Marshall informing me that a delegation was awaiting for me at the wharf and requesting me to land with the Harbor Master, who himself was a member of the U.N.I.A. While I was waiting for the Harbor Master to be through with his duties on board, another delegation came on board to receive me for Mr. Turner. I noticed at once the rivalry between the two delegations, which were acting separately from each other. However, I landed in the boat of the Harbor Master, which was the first one ready to go ashore, and this to the great discontentment of the Turner delegation. (Marshall's letter, Document No. 19.)[1]

On arriving at the wharf, the situation was still more complicated, as Marshall's delegation was pulling me on one side while Turner's delegation was asking me not to have any dealing with Marshall. I managed to satisfy both parties by calling Turner and Marshall apart and telling them that I was not ready to hear any one on business matters and that I was rather anxious to share opinions with everybody as friends of the U.N.I.A., therefore giving no recognition to anyone for the while. I was then taken by both delegations to the Faulkner's Hotel, where accom[m]odations had been secured for me.

I may say at this point that I was greatly surprised to find my arrival known at Monrovia as well as the aims of my mission, as I was instructed not to disclose the objects of my visit until I had conferred with the Government. To some extent, I was greatly inconvenienced and the success of my mission imperilled by this fact.

On Monday morning, I sent to New York a cablegram informing the Association of my arrival (Document No. 7). I spent the rest of the day receiving members and officers from both branches, Marshall's and Turner's.

I spoke but very little to my visitors, giving them an opportunity to tell me all they wanted about each other. To some curious members who wanted me to declare at once whose branch I was going to recognize, I simply answered that the misunderstanding would be settled in an open meeting Wednesday night without any indication that I was in favor of any one of the parties. My intention was to invite both branches to the meeting and after asking officers of both branches to resign, to make a general election from the merged branches. But when I invited Marshall and his branch to said meeting, he stated to me that, in fact, he had not organized any branch and that he had simply secured seven persons to apply for a charter and that he and his followers were awaiting the arrival of the charter before having any meeting. On the other hand, Turner's branch was an organized body 125 strong, with regular officers and having weekly meetings. Further, I learned from Marshall himself that he was not very popular in Monrovia. It was evident after these informations that Turner's branch was the one to be recognized as being the only one, in fact, existing. But to do so without giving any further consideration to Marshall and his friends, I would have placed Turner [in?] the obligation of fighting the little gang which was surely to be a stumbling block in the way of his branch.

To adjust the matter, I had an interview with Marshall and taking advantage of his own statement of being unpopular in Monrovia, I alluded to him that I was willing to appoint him temporary Organizer for some other community if he was willing to have his friends to work along with Turner. I impressed him with the fact that the Association has splendid work for faithful and capable men. . . .[2] that by organizing other places he would deserve much more from the U.N.I.A.

He accepted the proposition and the same day I appointed him Organizer for several towns located on the St. Paul River. (See Docs. Nos. 1–6.)

At 8 P.M. that night, the meeting was held in the Hall of Representatives. The disagreement between Marshall and Turner having been settled during the day and Marshall having renounced to the organization of Monrovia, there was no use for an election. The Hall was packed and the meeting presided over by the local President, the Hon. G. M. Johnson, Mayor of the City of Monrovia. On the rostrum were seated the Hon. ex-President Arthur Barclay,[3] Treasurer of the branch, Rev. Walter Turner, Organizer and Executive Secretary, the Hon. Ladies' President, Mrs. Anna Howard, the Associate Chief Justice of Liberia and myself. After the opening address by the President, I was introduced to the audience. (Speech, Doc. No. 31.)

Some statements in my speech refer to an article published in the "Liberia Commercial News," by Mr. Butler, rather against the Association. Mr. Butler is the gentleman for whom a letter of introduction was given to me by the President General. The next day after my arrival in Monrovia, said article was submitted to me. However, I went to see [the gentleman?] and delivered the letter to him. He read it and proceeded to ask me questions concerning the objects of my visit to Liberia, and in a very incivil manner, as he kept his face turned towards his desk while addressing me. I let him know that my business was not with him and since he declared that he was asking me those questions for the benefit of his paper, I answered that I had no statement to make and I departed.

The next morning, however, to my surprise, I received a letter from him asking me to be present at a meeting for the purpose of being introduced by him to the people of Monrovia. I declined the invitation. (Docs. Nos. 26, 27, 28, 29.) I was well inspired by not going to the meeting. . . .[4] The Secretary of State who was present was compelled to take exception to some ridiculous statements made against the U.N.I.A. by declaring that any Negro who fails to see the benefits to be derived from the Association was a consummate fool. The meeting was adjourned in disorder. It is said that Mr. Butler's paper is subsidized by firms and that soon after they had learned of my coming, they started the propaganda against us, which was for a while disastrous for the selling of shares of the Black Star Line.

The first of June, I wrote a letter to the Secretary to the President, requesting an audience with His Excellency.

After exchange of correspondence (Docs. Nos. 11–13), the audience was granted.

But on the date appointed, two things occurred; first, His Excellency was informed of his aunt's death and could not receive; and also, I received a cablegram from the President General informing me that the other members of the commission were not coming. I called at once a meeting of the Executive officers of the Branch in Monrovia for the purpose of making my mission known to them. At the meeting were present Mr. G. M. Johnson, President; ex-President Barclay, Treasurer; Walter Turner, Organizer; Hilary Johnson, Executive Secretary; and Mrs. Anna Howard, Ladies' President.

After hearing me on the subject of my mission, it was decided that Mr. Johnson and the ex-President Barclay, as well as the Organizer, would accompany me to the Executive Mansion. Representations were made to the Department of State in my behalf, and on June 9th, at 12 noon, the delegation composed as above was received by the President.

Mr. Johnson, President of the Monrovia Branch, and therefore local representative, introduced me to the President. After a short speech of congratulations, I read to the President the memorandum of the U.N.I.A. (Doc. No. 18.) The said memorandum was then signed and delivered to him. Then Mr. Barclay spoke, requesting the Government, as a member of the U.N.I.A. and a leading citizen of Liberia, to welcome such a great movement. The President, the Hon. C. [D.] B. King, answered in eloquent terms and after giving high praise to the Association, condemned the articles published by Mr. Butler as being against the sentiments of the Liberians. He declared officially that the Government of Liberia itself welcomed the

U.N.I.A. to Liberia and that it will be soon when the Headquarters shall be established in Liberia, for which purpose land and other facilities will be granted. He further stated that while in the United States,[5] in a conference with the President General of the organization, he advised him to come to Liberia.[6] He closed by expressing the best wishes for the U.N.I.A., also stating that a written answer will be sent to me. Four days later the answer came through the Department of State. (Doc. No. 19.)

The negotiations [with the] Government being settled, I decided to start a campaign for the U.N.I.A., the Black Star Line and Negro Factories Corporation in Liberia. Owing to the impossibility of travelling to any long distances, whether by land or by sea, I could not visit the important cities of Cape Mount, Grand Bassa and Cape Palmas. I was compelled to limit my campaign to the communities not distant of more than 30 miles from Monrovia, which places I could reach by canoe or by walking.

According to information received from Marshall, who was appointed Organizer, I organized a party of five persons to visit with me in the interest of the U.N.I.A. the communities on the St. Paul River. All arrangements having been made by the Organizer, we started on our journey Monday the 14th of June, at 9 A.M., for Brewerville. The party consisted of Mr. Walter Turner, Organizer Monrovia, Mrs. W. L. Turner, Mrs. Anna Howard, Ladies' President Monrovia, and myself. We reached Brewerville at 5 P.M. and met the Organizer, Mr. Marshall, who was waiting for us at Brewerville's water side. The distance from the river to the town is about three miles. We started at once and after 45 minutes' walk, the first Corps of Expedition of the U.N.I.A. was entering Brewerville with five boatmen, four carriers, three boys, three or four cases of provisions and half a dozen suit cases.

We stopped at the Rev. Ellwood Davis' parsonage, Supervisor of Missions, where we were met with the most sincere hospitality. After a dinner, whose menu will long live in my memory, we proceeded to the church where the meeting was to be held.

The building was packed to standing room. I have been travelling in the interest of the U.N.I.A. for a while and it seems to me that nowhere the U.N.I.A. has ever met with more emotionable feelings. The audience was chiefly composed of the elders of the communities and [although] there were no [great] speeches, no great pomp, one could see on every face the clear indication that those poor souls who had long suffered were sincere in their welcome. The meeting as a whole was very interesting and very encouraging. The Organizer delivered the opening address and then introduced me. I spoke lengthily and was encouraged to do so by the feeling of confidence which possessed me among the people of Brewerville. Many shares were sold and after a notable citizen of the community had delivered an address of opinion which was a praise of the U.N.I.A., the meeting was adjourned. We spent the rest of the night in the town, where preparations had been made to accom[m]odate us.

The next morning at 9 A.M., we left Brewerville for Virginia, another town about five miles distant and also on the St. Paul River. A light rain was falling, but as the meeting in Virginia was scheduled for 11 A.M., we started in the rain. Unfortunately, our boat had to go up against the stream, which was very rapid. We didn't reach Virginia before 1 P.M. Immediately after our arrival, the bells were rung at 3 P.M., the meeting was called to order, attended by a goodly number of persons. We proceeded as in Brewerville, and after my speech every one in the party spoke. At Virginia, also, a notable citizen was appointed to express the sentiment of the people. The meeting was adjourned in a very good spirit.

The next town visited was Clay Ashland. We had accom[m]odations, part of us at Senator Richard's home and the ****⁷ Mr. Harris. The meeting took place at 8 P.M. at the City Hall. After the messengers of the U.N.I.A., Senator Richard and Mayor Harris delivered simple addresses in the name of the people. From Clay Ashland we crossed the river and went to Caldwell, where we met with the same success and the same enthusiasm as in the previous places. Our intention was to go to [Louisiana,] but [because of the heavy?] rain which was falling, the river was hardly navigable and not safe in a small boat, the size of ours. So on Thursday, during the day, we started back to Monrovia with the exception of /(one)/ who took by land to Louisiana to fulfil the engagement. He reported two days later that the meeting was held successfully, although the people were disappointed by not meeting me. He brought me money for several shares of the Black Star Line subscribed in the meeting. He also brought the resolutions of the various communities in favor of the U.N.I.A. (Docs. Nos. 20, 21, 22, 23).

As soon as I was back in Monrovia, I sent a letter to the Branch being formed in Grand Bassa by the Rev. Dr. Horton (Doc. No. 15) and also a cablegram to the New York Office (Doc. 9).

This cablegram was sent as there was no possibility for me to undertake any other campaign and my mission with the Government [was] settled.

On Friday June 18th, an official reception was given in my honor at the Mayor's home. All Monrovia was present.

Speeches were made by the local President, the ex-President, the Ladies' President. I was also presented with a pin from the Ladies' Division as a token of appreciation for my work in Liberia. I returned thanks for the wishes and pledges, and after bidding them God speed and success, I resumed my seat. The rest of the evening was spent in socialities, songs, music, dances and refreshments. The same day in the morning, I had called on His Excellency privately to inform him of my departure. I was cheerfully received by him and after our chat of which the U.N.I.A. took 60 minutes, I took leave. Thus was ended my mission to Liberia. I spent the two last days waiting for an answer to my cable and waiting for the boat. The answer never came, but the boat did. While the boat was in harbor, I went to the Bank of British West Africa and inquired about messages concerning me. I was then informed that a cablegram was received concerning me two days before, but being mutilated was sent back for reconstruction and would not be probably back before two more days.

I wrote them a letter asking them to transfer the money to my credit to their offices in Liverpool and using every means, I sailed for Sierra Leone the 27th of June.

In conclusion to this report, I like to say that my stay as representative of the U.N.I.A. in Liberia was made very pleasant by Liberians of all classes and that great enthusiasm and interest were shown the Association. Respectfully submitted,

ELIE GARCIA,
Commissioner to Liberia

[*New York, ca. August 1920*]

PART 2.

NOTES

To the Pres. Gen. of the U.N.I.A. (Personal)

This part of my report is for the personal information of the President General, the Hon. Marcus Garvey.

For the sake of truth, it is necessary for me to make some statements very unfavorable to the Liberians; but I am one of those who believe that the wounds have to be unwrapped in order to be cured.

I also believe that it is necessary for the U.N.I.A. to know the people with whom they are to deal.

My intention is not to instruct you or even to advise you, but simply to submit to you information which your wisdom will prompt you to use with advantage. Yours for the success of the Cause,

ELIE GARCIA,
Commissioner to Liberia

ECONOMICAL AND MORAL CONDITIONS

Liberia, although a very rich country in natural resources, is the poorest place on the face of the earth and the people are actually facing "starvation."

This condition is due to many facts. First, the strong repulsion of the Liberians for any kind of work. There is no cultivated land in the Republic and rice which is the national food is imported from England and other places and sold at a fabulous price, although it can be produced in enormous quantities there. Class distinction; this question is also a great hindrance to the development of Liberia. There are at this present time two classes of people, the Americo-Liberians, also called "Sons of the Soil," and the natives. The first class, although the educated one, constitutes *the most despicable element in Liberia*.[8]

Because of their very education, they are conceited and believe that the only honorable way for them to make a living is by having a "Government job". The men of this class having been most of them educated in England or other European places, are used to a life which the salaries paid by the Government do not suffice to maintain. Therefore, dishonesty is prevalent. To any man who can write and read, there is but one goal: a government office, *where he can graft*.

For the same reason, they are absolutely hostile to "immigration["] of American or West Indian Negroes; that is, if said Negroes show any tendency to take part in the political life of the Republic. This fact is of great importance *and I dare suggest that words must be given to any one going to Liberia in the interest of the U.N.I.A. to deny firmly any intention on our part to enter into politics in Liberia*. This attitude will remove any possible idea of opposition and will not prevent us after having a strong foothold in the country to act as we see best for their own betterment and that of the race at large.

The policy for the present must be to limit our program to commercial, industrial and agricultural developments.

The Liberian politicians understand clearly that they are degenerated and weak morally and they know that if any number of honest Negroes with brains, energy and experience come to Liberia and are prompted to take part in the ruling of the natives, they will be absorbed and ousted in a [very] short time.

Another important fact is the attitude of the Americo-Liberians towards enlightening the native tribes.

This intention of the U.N.I.A. must be kept quiet for a while. As it is, the Americo-Liberians are using the natives as slaves and human chattels still exist there.

They buy men or women to serve them and the least little insignificant Americo-Liberian has half a dozen boys at his service; for he means that he will not even carry his own umbrella in the street. Said article has to be carried by a boy and so for the smallest parcel. While in Monrovia, I went to a store and bought seven yards of khaki to have two pairs of trousers made. The merchant wrapped the khaki and gave it to me. As I was stepping out of the store, my companion (an Americo-Liberian) told me: "Why, I don't suppose you are going to carry this bundle yourself?" "Why not?" said I; "it is a very small parcel." He answered that it was not the custom in Liberia for any gentleman to carry parcels; therefore the usefulness of having slaves.

It is also deplorable to state that the highest Liberian official lives in a state of polygamy, which is highly detrimental to the improvement of morality among the natives as well as to social development among themselves.

It is unavoidable in a place where a young girl can be bought for two or three pounds and become one's possession.

To conclude, the Liberians are opposed to any element which may be instrumental in bringing to [*an*] end *their political tyranny, their habits of graft and their polygamic freedom*.

FINANCES, DEBTS AND ROADS

It is said by competent persons that the total revenues of Liberia—customs duties, taxes and others—amount to a little over four millions of dollars a year. Of this supposed amount, only a little over two millions are usually accounted for. The other two millions being divided between the high officials and some subordinate employees. This statement does not seem exaggerated, if, considering the salaries received by some officials, one would venture to investigate their expenses and ways of living. The total debts of Liberia amount to the sum of $1,700,000, the interest on which can hardly be kept up owing to the misappropriation of funds. It may be well to say that the Republic of Liberia is a concern bringing returns to a few individuals, including the three foreign receivers.[9]

There is not a mile of road in all Liberia and in Monrovia which is the capital, not a street worthy of the name. Bush grows in front and around the Executive Mansion.

Yet, with all this backwardness to his account, the average Liberian is as proud as a peacock and boasts of being a citizen of a free country. I was a silent witness to a discussion between a West Indian Negro recently arrived in Monrovia and a prominent Liberian. The West Indian was trying to show him—without malice—the tremendous work which had to be done before Liberia can be made an up-to-date place. The Liberian got vexed and in his rebuke said that he "never sang in the cornfield," alluding to the slave ancestors of the West Indian. The latter answered him that it would be impossible for him to do so as there was no cornfield to be seen in hungry Liberia. He was dismounted by the answer and departed.

I cannot help thinking that the answer was well-deserved and very appropriate.

FOREIGN RELATIONS AND FOREIGN INFLUENCES

If Liberia ever needed help, it is at this present time when the small Republic is the object of a close contest between America, England and France.

I understand that there was great hope among the Liberians that America would be their best friend and that they would be prevented from having any dealing with their two great neighbors, England and France. Representatives of both countries were making an active propaganda until my arrival against the American loan and both have made it publicly known that their governments are ready to help Liberia with any amount of money. It would seem very philanthropic from generous France and proud England if one didn't know that the statements of said help will, sooner or later, bring a loss of territory for insolvent Liberia, if not a loss of her national autonomy.[10] *** [11]when my arrival was made known in Monrovia and also what was the aim of the U.N.I.A. propaganda.[12] (Doc's. 26 & 27.)

On the contrary, the attitude of the *** [*French*] was rather friendly or apparently so. I was informed that the *** had received orders previous to my arrival not to allow the commission to sail the West Coast without visiting all of her colonies. For what purpose? I will not venture to say.

While this propaganda was going on, the Liberians were still expecting much from the United States until the famous memorandum was presented to them early in June.[13]

I have read the original document signed by the American Charge d'Affaires (Mr. Bundy),[14] and I will say that from beginning to end it is the most insulting and humiliating document ever presented to a free people for ratification.

According to the terms of this Memorandum, if Liberia wants to use the amount of five millions opened to her credit by the United States, she must first submit to the United States (Sec. or Treas.) a financial statement of all her debts and interest due on same. After said debts have been investigated by the United States and found correct and pending upon the Republic, the Secretary or Treasurer of the United States will pay them. For the rest of the amount, a Receiver General is to be appointed by the United States who will collect all revenues of the Republic of any source whatever and disburse them without the intervention of any Liberian official.

All his help, Assistant Commissioner and others, to be appointed by the President of the United States. The financial budget of the Republic, before presented to the Senate, must be submitted to the Receiver General, who shall have the power to increase or decrease some expenses for salaries or others without interference from the Government. The Receiver and whatever help he may require is to receive salaries adequate to their ranks from the revenues of the Republic. These salaries to be fixed by the President of the United States. The Receiver General shall have the power to dictate all measures necessary to the improvement of the country and such dictations to be enforced by the Government without modifications.

The Senate shall have no right to grant any concession or vote any contract without submitting same for approval of the Receiver General. The Receiver General shall also have the power to investigate the workings of all Government offices and to introduce better systems. Once a year the Receiver General will give to the Government a report of his administration— financial and otherwise.

All public works, sanitary improvements, to be directed and controlled by the Receiver General or his Deputy. The interest and principal of the Loan to be paid in *gold*.

These are only a few of the terms that I can remember from the voluminous document of 53 pages.

The adoption of this contract for 10 years, if signed by the Government, will mean the election of a white king over Liberia, and will be a great inconvenience to the U.N.I.A.

This memorandum has caused great consternation in Liberia to the great satisfaction of *** [*British and French*] who are endeavoring more than ever before to extend their influence in Liberia which is already too large.

The British Bank of West Africa and Elder Dempster Co. work night and day in Liberia and because of the presence of this only Bank, British currency is almost the legal currency of the country. Poor Liberia is hard up against three strong white nations determined to choke her. Should she have the best chance at it? This is the problem. May God help her! for, as it is, any one of the three will be harmful to her later.

The Senate has been called for an extraordinary session to deliberate about the memorandum, which it is hoped will be refused. Meanwhile, I was given a tip that the gentleman sent to the States as delegate to the Convention (Gabriel Johnson) was secretly empowered by the Government to see what help could be gotten from the U.N.I.A. My cipher cablegram was to put you wise in the case. *However, the American memorandum, though insulting as it is, proves that the United States are well informed of the unreliability of the Liberians in handling money. I make this statement to impress you, Mr. President, with the fact, that whatever finance is to be given by the U.N.I.A. to the Government, we must keep an eye open on the use made with the help so given and even manage to have a voice in the disbursements: otherwise, it will be only fattening the purses of a few individuals.*

COMMERCIAL AND AGRICULTURAL POSSIBILITIES

The possibilities along these lines are so broad that they can hardly be enumerated. Liberia is a new field, new in every sense of the word. But it is necessary to say that before any large commercial or agricultural venture can bring adequate returns, many sums of money must be spent to build roads and other means of conveying the produce to sea-ports.

The three things most urgently needed in Liberia are a little railroad, a coastwise line of steamers [and] about 100 miles of decent road. I have heard that it was the intention of the Liberians to petition the Black Star Line for the establishment of a coast line running between Cape Palmas and Freetown.

I sincerely believe that it would be of great advantage to the Company to do so, not only financially but also inasmuch as it would win the inalienable devotion of the Liberian people and of the people of the West Coast in general. There is no connection between the ports of Liberia except when it pleases the Elder Dempster Co. to despatch a boat to some of the ports. The people are entirely at the mercy of this company.

I believe that two or three little steamers from 600 to 800 tons, trading along the coast, will bring enormous profit. If any information is desired on the matter, I will furnish the Company with data and figures on the spot. At all events, I suggest that the Black Star Line will think seriously of establishing some thing of the kind at the earliest opportunity.

In what the railroad would be concerned, I have obtained from the auditor of the Sierra Leone Railroad some information on the cost of the railroad per mile.

Thirty or forty miles of railroad will be quite sufficient for the present. It costs, including surveying, clearing, grading, ties and laying of tracks, purchase and cost of rails, spikes and tools, repair shops and so forth, a little over $9000 a mile.

A corporation with $400,000 can successfully undertake the work.

IMMIGRATION BY NEGROES

Starving Liberia has no conditions[15] at the present for any large number of persons. Immigration and establishment of Negro concerns and corporations, if successfully carried out, will bring the necessary developments to induce immigration in large numbers.

While in Monrovia, [e]ight carpenters and masons came from Freetown to do some work for Elder Dempster Co. Lodging could not be found for the men, neither somebody to board them.

NOTES[16]

As shown by the memorandum which I presented to the Government of Liberia on the subject of land, I didn't—contrary to my instructions—work for immediate concession of land.

My reason for deviating from your instructions is that I found out it was [*not*] in the power of the Government to grant such concession without the approval of the Senate. If I had not changed the terms of our request, the President would simply ask us to wait for the opening of the Legislative session and to introduce our request. But I wanted, at any cost, to have from the Government a written pledge of support, *which could stir up the feelings of our members on this side towards Liberia*; therefore I asked for what could be gotten.

For the same reasons, I have managed to have written resolutions for the "Negro World" from the various communities where I have been.

The task of selecting land in Liberia is a very arduous one and I would think it necessary to have representatives looking to that end as soon as possible, so that we may be able to present our request to the next Legislature in December.

If time is insufficient for the selection, we can ask the concession of so many acres, the location of which can be determined later. Said concession has been granted in Liberia once to a white concern. When the land or a part of it is selected, the only fo[rmu]la is to register at the Department of

Interior. In this manner, if for instance 60 square miles of land are granted, 5 can be taken here, 10 there, until the amount granted is secured.

CONCLUSIONS

As a fact and a true one, the people of Liberia welcome sincerely the U.N.I.A. and expect much from it.

Liberia being in urgent need of help, it could not be otherwise. They fear only political domination from their * * * [*helpers*] blacks or whites.

The article of the Constitution dealing with the powers of the Potentate and some references in the "Negro World" in regard to the election of a ruler for all black people have been a troublesome nightmare to them.

But with diplomacy and also modesty and discretion on the part of those who will represent the U.N.I.A. in Liberia, *our work is bound to be successful along* ALL *lines*. Respectfully submitted,

ELIE GARCIA,
Commissioner to Liberia

DJ-FBI, file 61-826. TD.

1. None of the attachments mentioned in this document were printed.
2. Ellipsis in the original.
3. Arthur Barclay (1852–1938) was president of Liberia from 1904–08. Born in Barbados, Barclay was brought to Liberia at an early age. His family became prominent in Montserrado County, and he rose to political power. In 1907, Barclay negotiated a loan with England; however, his government's inability to repay its foreign debts, and its failure to control the regions in Liberia's interior, where concessions had been granted to foreigners, led to great difficulties for his administration. In his obituary, the *New York Times* noted: "After his term as President, Mr. Barclay became one of the followers of Marcus Garvey, when, in 1924, the Negro leader proposed to send 300 delegates to Africa with the intention of setting up a politically independent African republic" (*NYT*, 13 July 1938).
4. Ellipsis in the original.
5. President-elect C. D. B. King arrived in the United States in late August 1919 to confer with President Woodrow Wilson (*NYT*, 28 August 1919).
6. Evidence to confirm the meeting mentioned has not been found. However, the following exchange was officially reported to have taken place in 1919 between Garvey's representative in Paris, Éliézer Cadet, and Liberian President-elect King: "Cadet called on Secretary King and endeavored to arouse him in some sort of movement but[,] I think[,] did not receive much encouragement. Secretary King asked him, if the American Negroes were so thoroughly dissatisfied with the social and political conditions in America, why they did not go to Liberia, which is a Negro Republic founded by the United States, and become citizens there where they would have social and political equality" (DNA, RG 59, file 763.72119/5119, Henry F. Worley to William Phillips, Paris, 2 May 1919). Worley was the American receiver of customs in Liberia and an official member of the Liberian delegation to the Paris Peace Conference. (See also, C. G. Contee, "The Worley Report on the Pan-African Congress of 1919," *Journal of Negro History* 55 [April 1970]: 140–43).
7. Asterisks in the original.
8. Italics used throughout this document appear in the original.
9. In November 1912, the Liberian government secured a loan of $1,700,000 from American, British, French, and German bankers. Under the terms of the loan agreement, a general receiver appointed by the President of the United States and three assistant receivers from Britain, France, and Germany assumed responsibility for the collection of Liberian customs as a measure designed to guarantee repayment of the loan. Under the terms of the Paris peace treaty, the German receivership was eliminated, leaving the three other receivers—American, British, and French—to supervise customs collection (Nancy Kaye Kirkham Forderhase, "The

Plans That Failed: The United States and Liberia, 1920–1935," Ph.D. diss., University of Missouri, Columbia, 1971, pp. 11, 17).

10. The Americo-Liberian ruling elite held to the common belief that both Britain and France posed a threat to the territorial integrity and sovereignty of Liberia. This view was based on a series of events, during the last quarter of the 19th century and first decade of the 20th century, in which both France and Britain had occupied territory claimed by Liberia. At one point, France actually suggested that Liberia become its protectorate. Perhaps more pertinent to the observations made by Elie Garcia was the fact that the armed rebellions of the Golahs in 1918 and the Zorquelli Kpelles in 1920 created a state of unrest in the Liberian hinterland, and refugees fleeing from the areas of unrest streamed in to the neighboring colonies of Sierra Leone, French Guinea, and the Ivory Coast. In response, Britain and France warned the Liberian government in 1920 either to put an end to the "anarchical conditions" in the Liberian interior or else be prepared to face the consequence, a statement which the Liberian government interpreted as a threat of external aggression (M. B. Akpan, "Liberia and the Universal Negro Improvement Association: The Background to the Abortion of Garvey's Scheme for African Colonization," *Journal of African History* 14, 1 [1973]:113–14; Forderhase, "The Plans That Failed," pp. 4–10).

11. Asterisks throughout Part II appear in the original. When the version in *Philosophy and Opinions of Marcus Garvey* (hereafter cited as *P & O*) contains any of the words missing in this document, they have been supplied from this source and inserted in square brackets and italics.

12. In *P & O*, this sentence reads: "When my arrival was made known in Monrovia, and also what was the aim of the U.N.I.A. Br . . . propaganda did not spare the U.N.I.A." (p. 401).

13. The U.S. State Department arranged for an American vessel to deliver the financial agreement to the Liberian government. It arrived in Monrovia on 1 June 1920 with the "memorandum." (Forderhase, "The Plans That Failed," pp. 19–20).

14. Richard Carlton Bundy was appointed secretary of the U.S. legation in Monrovia in July 1919; he was subsequently detailed to the Department of State in connection with the Liberian loan negotiations, 1921–23. He had been formerly head of the mechanical department at Wilberforce University for five years prior to his first appointment as secretary to the American legation to Liberia in 1910 (U.S. Department of State, *Register*, 1924, p. 102).

15. In *P & O*, the word "accommodations" was used rather than "conditions."

16. The section entitled "Notes" was omitted from the version printed in *P & O*.

APPENDIXES

APPENDIX I

Amended Constitution of the UNIA and ACL[1]

CONSTITUTION AND BOOK OF LAWS
MADE FOR THE GOVERNMENT OF THE UNIVERSAL NEGRO IMPROVEMENT ASSOCIATION AND AFRICAN COMMUNITIES' LEAGUE

In Effect July, 1918

AMENDED IN AUGUST, 1920.
CONSTITUTION . . .

ARTICLE IV.
OFFICIALS, OFFICERS, APPOINTMENTS AND ELECTIONS.

Section 1.   The Rulers of the Universal Negro Improvement Association and African Communities' League shall be a Potentate and Supreme Commissioner, a Supreme Deputy, a President-General, an Administrator, an Assistant President-General, a Secretary-General and High Commissioner, an Assistant Secretary-General, a High Chancellor, a Counsel-General, an Assistant Counsel-General, an Auditor-General, a High Commissioner-General, a Chaplain-General, an International Organizer and High Commissioner, a Surgeon-General, a Speaker in Convention and a Minister of the Legions, all of whom shall form the High Executive Council elected at the Convention of the Universal Negro Improvement Association and African Communities['] League representing all its branches throughout the world . . . .

Election of Divisional Officers.

Sec. 3.   Divisions and subordinate organizations shall elect their officers by majority vote to be approved of by the office of the President-General.

Term of Office of Rulers.

Sec. 4.   The term of office of the Potentate and Supreme Commissioner and that of the Supreme Deputy shall be permanent. The term of all other officers shall be four years, provided that their conduct conform with the interests of the Universal Negro Improvement Association and African Communities' League at all times. . . .

ARTICLE V.

Sec. 3. . . . No one shall be received by the Potentate and his Consort who has been convicted of crime or felony, except such crime or felony was committed in the interests of the Universal Negro Improvement Association and African Communities' League or whose morality is not up to the standard of social ethics. . . .

Assistant President General.

Sec. 13. The Assistant President General shall assist the President General in the performance of such duties of his office as shall be assigned to him by the President General. He shall perform all the duties of the President General in case of absence, illness, permanent disability, resignation or death, until such time as the Convention shall have elected a new President General. . . .

The Assistant Secretary General.

Sec. 15. The Assistant Secretary General shall assist the Secretary General in the performance of such duties of his office as shall be assigned to him by the Secretary General with the approval of the Executive Council, and in the event of absence, illness, permanent disability, resignation or death, he shall perform all the duties of the Secretary General until such time as the Convention shall have elected a new Secretary General. . . .

Assistant Counsel General.

Sec. 18. The Assistant Counsel General shall assist the Counsel General in the performance of such duties of his office as shall be assigned to him by the Counsel General with the approval of the Executive Council, and in the event of absence, illness, permanent disability, resignation or death, he shall perform all the duties of the Counsel General, until such time as the Convention shall have elected a new Counsel General.

Auditor General.

Sec. 19. The Auditor General and High Commissioner, shall audit the accounts and books of the High Chancellor, and all accounts and books of other High Officers and branches twice annually, viz.: For the six months ending July 31st within twenty-one days after that date, and for the six months ending January 31st within twenty-one days after that date. He shall secure the assistance for this purpose of an expert accountant, and shall submit his report to the President General, who shall cause same to be published in the journal of the Association. . . .

Surgeon General.

Sec. 23.   The Surgeon General shall disseminate by lectures, articles and circulars information to the members of our race, with regard to hygiene, eugenics, vital statistics and necessary precautions for the maintenance of health and the increase of life expectation, and shall perform the duties of a physician and surgeon as directed by the President General. He shall publish at least once monthly in the journal of the Association a statement of the physical conditions among Negroes. He shall examine the physical fitness of the Officers and Privates of the Legions and other auxiliaries. . . .

Minister of Legions.

Sec. 25.   The Minister of the Legions shall be the Administrative Officer of the Universal African Legions of the Universal Negro Improvement Association. He shall be subjected to the commands of the Potentate, President General and Executive Council. He shall nominate the staff and Chief thereof with the approval of the President General and Potentate, who shall make the actual appointment. He shall use every means, by travel, correspondence and appeal to have a Division of the Legion formed in every City or District. He shall regulate all details as to uniforms, and shall give orders for other movements. He shall recommend Privates and Officers to the High Commissioner General for promotion. . . .

ARTICLE VIII.

Section 1. . . . That a tax of $1.00 shall be levied on every member of the U.N.I.A. each and ever year, payable on the first of January, for the purpose of defraying expenses in connection with the Leaders and High Officers of the Organization and the Negro Peoples of the World, and said one dollar collected from each member shall be forwarded to the High Chancellor through the office of the Secretary-General at Headquarters. . . .

Sec. 3. . . . That each person pay an entrance fee of twenty-five cents in joining the Association. . . .

ARTICLE X.

Section 1.   The Executive Council of the Universal Negro Improvement Association and African Communities' League shall assemble at the headquarters of the Association and shall consist of all the high officers of the Association and others elected thereto. The Potentate shall be its Chairman and the Secretary General its Secretary. It shall decide all questions arising between divisions and subordinate societies, appeals, international questions and all matters affecting the good and welfare of the organization and its members at large during the rising of convention. . . .

General Laws

ARTICLE I.
CONVENTIONS.

Section 1. . . . The Convention shall be opened on the first week of August of each year. . . .

ARTICLE III.

Sec. 20. . . . Any active member attending the meetings of the Association with motives to create disharmony among the officers and members, and disturbing the peaceful and harmonious working of the Division shall, for the first offense, be suspended for three months, and upon the second conviction for like offense by the Advisory Board, be expelled from the Association. . . .

Sec. 29. . . . And any member two months or more in arrears shall not be entitled to death benefits until thirty days after such arrears have been paid. And any member six months in arrears shall not be entitled to benefits until six months after such arrears have been paid. Any member failing to pay his annual taxation shall not be entitled to the seventy-five dollars death grant. . . .

Sec. 39a. Any member entering the meetings of any Division of the U.N.I.A. and A.C.L. under the influence of intoxicating liquors, and is noticeable by members assembled, shall be ejected from said meetings and be suspended from active membership for three months, and upon repetition of same shall be expelled.

Misappropriation of Money.

Sec. 40. No officer or member of the Universal Negro Improvement Association and African Communities' League shall retain in his possession for more than twenty-four hours, funds or moneys intended for the Universal Negro Improvement Association and African Communities' League. . . .

Sec. 42. . . . And no stock shall be invested in by any local branch, without first obtaining the sanction of the Executive Council. . . .

Sec. 54. . . . And that this journal shall be controlled and directed by the President-General. . . .

Sec. 59. The Anthem of the Association shall be played or sung at all public meetings or function[s] or whenever appropriate at the opening or closing of such meetings or both, and while it is being played all persons shall stand. The men shall stand with uncovered heads except in uniform. Uniformed men in obedience to military regulations will stand at attention or salute.

Sec. 60. The Universal Negro Improvement Association and African Communities' League Band shall be the recognized Military Band of the Universal African Legion.

Sec. 61. No member shall be permitted to take another member of the Association to any Civil Court, before placing their grievances before the Board. And if said Board fails to settle their grievances, the case will go before the President General before they be permitted to proceed to any court.

Sec. 62. That in every Division of the U.N.I.A. a juvenile branch be formed, and only teachings of Spiritual and Racial uplift be taught them.

Sec. 63. All Chaplains of the U.N.I.A. & A.C.L. must be ordained Ministers, or have their first License. . . .

THE UNIVERSAL ETHIOPIAN ANTHEM.
POEM BY BURRELL AND FORD

. . . II.

Ethiopia, the tyrant's falling,
    Who smote thee upon thy knees
And thy children are lustily calling
    From over the distant seas.
Jehovah the Great One has heard us,
    Has noted our sighs and our tears,
With His spirit of Love he has stirred us
    To be one through the coming years.
        CHORUS—Advance, advance, etc.

III.

O, Jehovah, thou God of the ages
    Grant unto our sons that lead
The wisdom Thou gave to Thy sages
    When Israel was sore in need.
Thy voice thro' the dim past has spoken,
    Ethiopia shall stretch forth her hand,
By Thee shall all fetters be broken
    And Heav'n bless our dear mother land.
        CHORUS—Advance, advance, etc.

DNA, RG 38, miscellaneous records, Military Government of Santo Domingo, 1914–20 [box 5], M201–202. Printed document.

1. The articles of the UNIA and ACL Constitution which remained the same as in the 1918 version (Volume I, pp. 256–81) have been omitted, as indicated by the use of ellipses.

APPENDIX II

Delegates to the 1920 UNIA Convention

The following is a list of some of the delegates whose names appeared in accounts of the convention printed in the *Negro World*, the *Negro World Convention Bulletin*, and in the records of the Bureau of Investigation. In some cases, spellings of the names have been standardized.

Carrie M. Ashford
Reynold Fitzgerald Austin
Agnes Babbs
Thomas E. Bagley
A. I. Bailey
J. T. Bailey
Rev. Peter Edward Batson
John G. Befue
David Benjamin
James Benjamin
G. F. Bennett
Lee Bennett
Clifford Bourne
I. Brathwaite
Sarah Branch
Rev. J. D. Brooks
Arden A. Bryan
Rev. C. W. Cheek
Miss Nettie Clayton
Rev. Joseph Josiah Cranston
Lee Crawford
George D. Creese
Cyril A. Crichlow
Mrs. Louise Crofutt
Arnold S. Cunning
Gertrude Davis
Henrietta Vinton Davis
John Sydney de Bourg
Prince Madarikan Deniyi
E. R. Donawa
Marie Duchatellier

Benjamin Dyett
Rev. J. W. H. Eason
Francis Wilcem Ellegor
Reynold R. Felix
William Ferris
Arnold Josiah Ford
Daniel Ford
Harry E. Ford
Lionel Antonio Francis
Napoleon J. Francis
Marcus Garvey
Dr. J. D. Gibson
T. H. Golden
J. D. Gordon
Walter Green
Lionel W. Greenidge
C. L. Halton
Venture R. Hamilton
Rev. Dr. T. S. Harten
Philip Hemmings
William Hester
Partheria Hills
Allen Hobbs
John Philip Hodge
R. H. Hodge
Innis Abel Horsford
Marie Barrier Houston
Mr. J. A. Hudson
John E. Hudson
J. W. Hudspeth
William Ines

Ratford E. M. Jack
Adina Clem. James
J. P. Jasper
Florida Jenkins
Janie Jenkins
Adrian Fitzroy Johnson
Gabriel Johnson
Mrs. Mary Johnson
W. H. Johnson
Alphonso A. Jones
Oliver Kaye
O. C. Kelly
Emily Christmas Kinch
Mr. H. W. Kirby
William Musgrave LaMotte
B. D. Levy
Dr. D. D. Lewis
Rev. J. A. Lewis
C. B. Lovell
Rev. Jesse W. Luck
Rev. A. J. Mann
Richard Marks
William C. Matthews
William McCartney
Prince Alfred McConney
George Alexander McGuire
Rev. Samuel McIntyre
Maldena Miller
J. W. Montgomery
E. E. Nelom
Richard C. Noble
Mrs. Georgie O'Brien
Mrs. Thomas O'Brien
F. O. Ogilvie
Rev. P. E. Paul
Charles A. Petioni
Randolph Phillips
H. Vinton Plummer
Frank O. Raines
Frederick Samuel Ricketts
Richard Edward Riley

Mrs. Frazier Robinson
Carl Roper
Lucy Sands
Theophilus H. Saunders
J. Frederick Selkridge
Rev. F. H. Simms
Rev. Thomas H. N. Simon
John C. Simons
Rev. B. F. Smith
Rev. F. F. Smith
Rudolph E. B. Smith
Wilford H. Smith
Gabriel Stewart
Edward Alfred Taylor
Abraham B. Thomas
Mary Thurston
Richard Hilton Tobitt
Fred A. Toote
Henry Tucker
Philip Van Putten
Dugald Augustus Wade
Mr. W. A. Wallace
William Ware
G. W. Washington
Harry R. Watkis
Nellie G. Whiting
Rev. John Thomas Wilkins
A. Williams
James Williams
James D. Williams
Shedrick Williams
Vernal Williams
Andrew N. Willis
Ellen Wilson
G. W. Wilson
Miss Louise Wilson
Louise Woodson
Ira Joseph T. Wright
James Benjamin Yearwood
James Young

APPENDIX III

BUREAU OF INVESTIGATION SUMMARY OF THE
MINUTES OF BLACK STAR LINE
BOARD OF DIRECTORS' MEETINGS,
14 NOVEMBER 1919–26 JULY 1920
(EXCERPT)

Increase of Capital Stock:

The increase of the capital stock and capitalization of the corporation from $500,000. to $10,000,000. was first raised at a meeting of the Board of Directors held November 14, 1919.

On December 22, 1919, the first stockholders meeting was held and the President (MARCUS GARVEY) reported purpose of meeting as being to increase capital from $500,000. to $10,000,000. and that according to the by-laws there should be an annual (stockholders) meeting, but finding it necessary and in the interest of the corporation he took the opportunity by the authority vested in him to call the meeting and as it was only by a majority vote that such action could be authorized, it was left with the stockholders assembled after considering the proposition to deal with same according to their conviction which will be manifested by the votes. A motion to increase capital stock from $500,000. to $10,000,000. was unanimously carried, the shares to be sold at $5. each par.

Control of Corporation:

At the first annual meeting of stockholders held July 26, 1920, the President (MARCUS GARVEY) stated we are here principally as members of the U.N.I.A. who incorporated the BLACK STAR LINE to achieve the objects it set itself out to do. We entered as a people of but little experience. The policy of the U.N.I.A. is to control this corporation to help the Parent Body in achieving its objects.

Stock selling plans (from Minute Book):

At a special meeting of the Board of Directors, November 20, 1919, Henrietta Vinton Davis and Cyril Henry were appointed agents of the

BLACK STAR LINE, INC., in the Republic of Panama, Canal Zone, to sell the shares of stock and issue certificates of stock for shares so sold.

At a meeting of the Board of Directors November 21, 1919, the President (MARCUS GARVEY) reported that Miss Davis, 2nd Vice President, and Cyril Henry, Assistant Treasurer, were being sent to the West Indies, Central and South America.

At a special stockholders meeting, December 22, 1919, capital stock authorized increased from $500,000. to $10,000,000.

At a meeting of the Board of Directors January 30, 1920, President (MARCUS GARVEY) authorized to appoint Agents and lawyers in the Republic of Panama and the Canal Zone to act for and on behalf of the corporation and that the authority given Henrietta Vinton Davis [and] Cyril Henry remains unrevoked.

At a meeting of the Board of Directors February 14, 1920, the sending of Secretary E. D. Smith-Green to Havana, Cuba and Jamaica, B.W.I., to represent interest of corporation approved.

At a meeting of the Board of Directors March 22, 1920, the President (MARCUS GARVEY) stated he had received report from Mr. Smith-Green that he had done business to the extent of $6,000; that he had remitted $3,000, to New York, having in hand $2,000. which he had received when going to Cuba and $3,000. balance out of the $6,000. Owing to the strike in Cristobal he (GARVEY) had instructed Capt. Cockburn to coal the ship (S.S. "YARMOUTH") in Havana and had cabled Smith-Green $3,000.

The President (MARCUS GARVEY) suggested that the S.S. Yarmouth should go to Philadelphia, Baltimore and Boston on her return so as to boom the stocks of the corporation. Carried.

At a meeting of the Board of Directors May 17, 1920, the President (MARCUS GARVEY) stated that the Secretary (Smith-Green) had been sent to Cuba in February mainly to see to the unloading of the whiskey cargo of the S.S. Yarmouth, that he had returned in April and that according to the Auditor, Mr. Thompson, the account presented by Mr. Smith-Green showed a shortage. The Secretary (Smith-Green) in reply stated he was always ready to make all explanations and had placed himself at the disposal of the accountant but that ever since his return from Cuba he was taken around the country touring with the President in the interests of the Corporation and has been given little or no chance to prepare his report. The President charged that large expenditures were shown without adequate vouchers and special mention was made of 40 shares of stock being issued without the corresponding amount being produced. Mr. Smith-Green pointed out in the special instance of the stock sale, that it was owing to lack of proper recording in the home office (in that instance and others not brought to notice of Directors) as he had accepted receipts or other evidence of parties having paid up their subscriptions on shares and issued certificates to cover, consequently no amount would be presented for such stock. Due note of such transactions was made and could be shown.

At a meeting of the Board of Directors June 3, 1920, the President (MARCUS GARVEY) remarked that complaints had come from everywhere of reckless waste. In consequence support had fallen off considerably and he attributed it to the reckless handling of the ship (S.S. Yarmouth) by Capt. Cockburn. As a result he thought it best to remove Capt. Cockburn, which he had done by making a deal with him to remain ashore for a few months and help in another strenuous campaign.

At a meeting of the Board of Directors July 22, 1920, the President (MARCUS GARVEY) said that owing to the fact that we have never received any report from Mr. Wilson (Agent, Kingston, Jamaica) relative to the sales of stock and other business of the line we were not able to say just where we stood. We did not know whether the Kingston Agency owed us money or we them. Further that Mr. Smith-Green was sent to adjust the accounts of the Kingston Agency which was not done. However, with the coming of Mr. Evans the accounts will be gone into by the accountant and proper adjustments made.

At the first annual meeting of stockholders July 26, 1920, the President (MARCUS GARVEY) alluding to subscriptions to the BLACK STAR LINE said that $500,000. as subscribed is but a drop in the bucket. But because we desire to show to the world that we can achieve, we are satisfied to purchase small boats so as to show that we can run them, etc. etc.

Taken from Thomas P. Merrilees (Bureau of Investigation, Department of Justice), "Summary Report of Investigation of Books and Records of The Black Star Line, Inc., and the Universal Negro Improvement Association, involving Marcus Garvey, Elie Garcia, George Tobias, and Orlando M. Thompson, in Violations of Sections #215 and 37 U.S.C.C., under the title 'U.S. vs. Marcus Garvey, et al,' " New York, 26 October 1922. Records of the Federal Bureau of Investigation, U.S. Department of Justice, Washington, D.C.

APPENDIX IV

FINANCES OF THE BLACK STAR LINE

The financial history of the BSL, Inc., was tangled and complicated, since the BSL never kept a reliable ledger of its finances. Ironically, the most complete financial account still in existence is the one that the government provided at Garvey's trial for mail fraud charges in 1923. The government exhibits (nos. 134, 137, 138, and 142) consisted of tables produced by a team of government accountants who made an exhaustive analysis of BSL stock ledgers, cashbooks, minute books, journals, and vouchers—a large portion of the records seized under subpoena when Garvey and his associates were indicted in 1922. The government accountants worked continuously for two months, constructing an entirely new ledger of the corporation's finances. The tables that appear below represent the portions of the original government exhibits that bear on the financial history of the BSL from its incorporation through the middle of 1921. Future volumes will include additional exhibits to cover subsequent phases of the BSL's finances.

MONTHLY SUMMARY OF SHARES OF STOCK ISSUED, CANCELED, TRANSFERRED, AND OUTSTANDING.

	Shares Issued	Shares Canceled	Shares Transferred	Shares Outstanding
1919				
July	587	4		583
August	1,401	60		1,341
September	5,530	147		5,383
October	11,182	172		11,010
November	8,090	77		8,013
December	10,352	121		10,231
	37,142	581		36,561
1920				
January	9,694	150	36	9,508
February	8,192	127	115	7,950
March	10,494	55	254	10,185
April	8,357	18	36	8,303

	Shares Issued	Shares Canceled	Shares Transferred	Shares Outstanding
May	6,856	135	82	6,639
June	5,146	58	6	5,082
	85,881	1,124	529	84,228
July	5,690	41	46	5,603
August	4,714	35	14	4,665
	96,285	1,200	589	94,496

STATEMENT OF TOTAL INCOME AND EXPENSE
JULY 1, 1919, TO JUNE 30, 1920

Operating Income:

S.S. Yarmouth	44,779.71	
Shadyside	2,882.63	
Kanawha	98.25	
Gross operating income		47,760.59

Operating Expense:

S.S. Yarmouth	138,469.55	
Shadyside	8,120.28	
Kanawha	4,060.83	
		150,650.66
Operating Loss		102,890.07
Office expense		68,329.02
Stock selling expense		63,576.82
		234,795.91
Less forfeited partial payments on stock		—
Deficit:		234,795.91

Office Expense:

Rent	550.00
Salaries	34,783.61
Books, stationery, postage, printing	9,283.54
Light and Heat	355.96
Telephone & telegraph	1,119.76

Legal & prof.	8,539.56	
Interest & discount	288.17	
Real Estate expense	3,764.71	
General	9,643.71	
		68,329.02

Stock Selling Expense:

Rent halls, etc.	6,437.47
Music	10,518.20
Traveling	10,649.26
Com. and Salaries	2,397.45
Stamps revenue	505.00
Advertising	23,369.63
Miscellaneous	16,724.13
Less Miscellaneous income	10,601.14
(a) Miscellaneous income deducted.	70,601.14[1]

1. These figures were transcribed as they appear in the government exhibit.

STATEMENT OF ASSETS AND LIABILITIES

| | *December 20, 1919* | | *June 30, 1920* | |
	Assets	Liabilities	Assets	Liabilities
Assets:				
S/S Yarmouth	108,201.95		189,361.65	
Kanawha	—		66,761.47	
Shadyside	—		35,000.00	
Phyllis Wheatley	—		—	
Real Estate	2,500.00		26,665.00	
Furniture & Fixtures	1,093.75		4,681.44	
Delivery Equipment	1,262.81		4,440.16	
Total Fixed Assets	113,058.51		326,909.72	
Cash	8,213.04		2,025.23	
Loans Receivable	1,902.64		13,742.44	
Liberian Construction Loan	—		—	

Liabilities:

Capital Stock issued		188,470.87	406,310.50
Capital Stock part paid		—	32,585.98
Capital Stock Agents returns		—	—
		188,470.87	438,896.48
Less Deficit		65,296.68	234,795.91
		123,174.19	204,100.57
Mortgages payable		—	21,500.00
Notes payable		—	117,076.82
Loans payable		—	—
Account payable		—	—
Unearned passage Liberia		—	—
TOTAL ASSETS	123,174.19		342,677.39
TOTAL LIABILITIES		123,174.19	342,677.39

Payments on Contract Prices of S/S Yarmouth, Shadyside and Kanawha, Showing Balances Due on Given Dates

Date	Yarmouth		Shadyside		Kanawha		Total	
	Paid	Due	Paid	Due	Paid	Due	Paid	Due
1919								
Sept. 15	16,500	148,500	....	....	....	....	16,500	148,500
Oct. 20	3,500	148,500	....	....	....	....	20,000	148,500
Oct. 31	50,000	98,500	....	....	....	....	70,000	98,500
Nov. 24	23,000	75,500	....	....	....	....	93,000	75,500
1920								
Jan. 10	20,000	55,500	....	....	....	....	113,000	55,500
Mar. 24	....	....	2,000	33,000	....	....	115,000	88,500
Apr. 10	....	....	8,000	25,000	....	....	123,000	80,500
Apr. 24	....	....	....	....	5,000	55,000	128,000	135,500
May 4	....	....	2,000	23,000	....	....	130,000	133,500
May 17	9,000	46,500	....	....	....	....	139,000	124,500
May 25	....	....	....	....	10,000	45,000	149,000	114,500
June 7	....	....	2,000	21,000	....	....	151,000	112,500
July 10	....	....	....	....	7,500	37,500	158,500	105,000
July 14	....	....	2,000	19,000	....	....	160,500	103,000
July 17	4,950	41,350	....	....	....	....	165,450	98,050
July 26	4,950	36,600	....	....	....	....	170,400	93,100
Aug. 6	....	....	....	....	5,000	32,500	175,400	88,100
Aug. 12	....	....	....	....	2,500	30,000	177,900	85,600
Aug. 25	....	....	2,000	17,000	....	....	179,900	83,600

INDEX

A Note on the Index

An asterisk (*) precedes annotated biographical entries found in the text. A page number followed by an *n* with a digit indicates that the entry appears in the numbered footnote cited. An entry that appears both in the text and in a footnote on the same page is indicated by the page number only, except in the case of an annotated entry. Bibliographical information can be found in the annotations that accompany the text.

When there are variant spellings of a name, the accepted spelling is used; in other instances, where there is no generally accepted usage, the spelling which seems most correct is given. Variants have not been indexed. Women are indexed under the name that first appears in the text; married names are indicated by parentheses, as, Ashwood, Amy (Garvey). Cross-references to both married and maiden names are supplied. Titled persons are indexed by title, with the family name following in parentheses, if necessary.

Government agencies are listed by name. However, cross-references to the appropriate cabinet-level department are provided, as, United States Department of Justice, *See also* Bureau of Investigation.